Cisco Secure Intrusion Detection System

Earl Carter

Cisco Press

Cisco Press
201 West 103rd Street
Indianapolis, IN 46290 USA

Cisco Secure Intrusion Detection System

Earl Carter

Copyright © 2002 Cisco Systems, Inc.

Published by:
Cisco Press
201 West 103rd Street
Indianapolis, IN 46290 USA

Printed in the United States of America 1 2 3 4 5 6 7 8 9 0

First Printing October 2001

Library of Congress Cataloging-in-Publication Number: 2001086627

ISBN: 1-58705-034-x

Warning and Disclaimer

This book is designed to provide information about Cisco Secure Intrusion Detection Systems. Every effort has been made to make this book as complete and as accurate as possible, but no warranty or fitness is implied.

The information is provided on an "as is" basis. The author, Cisco Press, and Cisco Systems, Inc. shall have neither liability nor responsibility to any person or entity with respect to any loss or damages arising from the information contained in this book or from the use of the discs or programs that may accompany it.

The opinions expressed in this book belong to the author and are not necessarily those of Cisco Systems, Inc.

Feedback Information

At Cisco Press, our goal is to create in-depth technical books of the highest quality and value. Each book is crafted with care and precision, undergoing rigorous development that involves the unique expertise of members from the professional technical community.

Readers' feedback is a natural continuation of this process. If you have any comments regarding how we can improve the quality of this book, or otherwise alter it to better suit your needs, you can contact us through e-mail at feedback@ciscopress.com. Please make sure to include the book title and ISBN in your message.

We greatly appreciate your assistance.

Trademark Acknowledgments

All terms mentioned in this book that are known to be trademarks or service marks have been appropriately capitalized. Cisco Press or Cisco Systems, Inc. cannot attest to the accuracy of this information. Use of a term in this book should not be regarded as affecting the validity of any trademark or service mark.

Publisher	John Wait
Editor-in-Chief	John Kane
Senior Acquisitions Editor	Brett Bartow
Cisco Systems Management	Michael Hakkert
	Tom Geitner
	William Warren
Production Manager	Patrick Kanouse
Development Editor	Andrew Cupp
Project Editor	San Dee Phillips
Copy Editor	Keith Cline
Course Developers	Daniel Rodriguez
	R. Eduardo Rivera
Technical Editors	Andy Balinsky
	R. Eduardo Rivera
Team Coordinator	Tammi Ross
Cover Designer	Louisa Klucznik
Composition	Octal Publishing, Inc.
Indexers	Brad Herriman
	Tim Wright

CISCO SYSTEMS

Corporate Headquarters
Cisco Systems, Inc.
170 West Tasman Drive
San Jose, CA 95134-1706
USA
http://www.cisco.com
Tel: 408 526-4000
   800 553-NETS (6387)
Fax: 408 526-4100

European Headquarters
Cisco Systems Europe
11 Rue Camille Desmoulins
92782 Issy-les-Moulineaux
Cedex 9
France
http://www-europe.cisco.com
Tel: 33 1 58 04 60 00
Fax: 33 1 58 04 61 00

Americas Headquarters
Cisco Systems, Inc.
170 West Tasman Drive
San Jose, CA 95134-1706
USA
http://www.cisco.com
Tel: 408 526-7660
Fax: 408 527-0883

Asia Pacific Headquarters
Cisco Systems Australia,
Pty., Ltd
Level 17, 99 Walker Street
North Sydney
NSW 2059 Australia
http://www.cisco.com
Tel: +61 2 8448 7100
Fax: +61 2 9957 4350

Cisco Systems has more than 200 offices in the following countries.
Addresses, phone numbers, and fax numbers are listed on the
Cisco Web site at www.cisco.com/go/offices

Argentina • Australia • Austria • Belgium • Brazil • Bulgaria • Canada • Chile • China • Colombia • Costa
Rica • Croatia • Czech Republic • Denmark • Dubai, UAE • Finland • France • Germany • Greece • Hong
Kong • Hungary • India • Indonesia • Ireland • Israel • Italy • Japan • Korea • Luxembourg • Malaysia
Mexico • The Netherlands • New Zealand • Norway • Peru • Philippines • Poland • Portugal • Puerto Rico
Romania • Russia • Saudi Arabia • Scotland • Singapore • Slovakia • Slovenia • South Africa • Spain
Sweden • Switzerland • Taiwan • Thailand • Turkey • Ukraine • United Kingdom • United States • Venezuela
Vietnam • Zimbabwe

About the Author

Earl Carter has been working in the field of computer security for six years. He started learning about computer security while working at the Air Force Information Warfare Center. Earl's primary responsibility was securing Air Force networks against cyber attacks. In 1998, he accepted a job with Cisco to research NetRanger (currently Cisco Secure IDS) and NetSonar (currently Cisco Secure Scanner). Earl spent approximately one year writing signatures for NetRanger and developing modules for NetSonar. Currently, he is a member of the Security Technologies Assessment Team (STAT). His duties involve performing security evaluations on numerous Cisco products. These products include everything from the PIX Firewall to Cisco CallManager. Presently, Earl holds a CCNA certification and is working toward earning his CCIE certification.

About the Technical Reviewers

Andy Balinsky started working with computers with a Commodore PET in 1980. He followed up on that interest by pursing a Bachelor of Arts in Computer Science from Harvard University and a Masters in Science from the University of Maryland in College Park. He was introduced to computer security at the Air Force's Information Warfare Center, where he did everything from tracking hackers to developing security software. From there, Andy moved to WheelGroup Corporation to work on the NetRanger and NetSonar security products. When Cisco acquired WheelGroup, he broadened his focus to analyzing security for the entire line of Cisco products.

R. Eduardo Rivera is an Education Specialist at Cisco Systems, Inc., where he designs, develops, and delivers network security training. He has been at Cisco for more than three years, where he has led the development of the Cisco Secure Intrusion Detection System and Cisco Secure PIX Firewall courses. During this time, he also has trained hundreds of Cisco employees, customers, and learning partners worldwide. Ed came to Cisco from the United States Air Force Information Warfare Center where he worked as a computer security engineer, performing network security assessments of USAF installations around the world. During his 11 years in the civil service, he also performed a variety of jobs, including software design and development, software engineering, and system administration. Ed holds a bachelor's degree and master's degree in Electrical Engineering from the University of Puerto Rico and the University of Dayton, respectively, and has been a part-time college computer science instructor.

Dedication

Without my loving family, I would not be where I am today. They support me in all of my endeavors. Therefore, I dedicate this book to my wife Chris, my daughter Ariel, and my son Aidan.

—Earl Carter

Acknowledgments

First, I want to say that many people have helped me during the writing of this book (too many to list here). Everyone I have dealt with has been very supportive and cooperative. There are, however, several people who I think deserve clear recognition.

I want to thank the Cisco IDS course developers, Daniel Rodriguez and Ed Rivera, whose course provided me with the foundation on which to develop this book. The technical editors, Andrew P. Balinsky and Ed Rivera, supplied me with their excellent insight and improved the accuracy and clarity of the material. I also want to especially thank Danny Rodriguez, who was always available to explore the numerous questions that arose during the writing of this book.

I want to recognize the very professional team that I worked with at Cisco Press. Without the help from Brett Bartow, Jill Batistick, Andrew Cupp, San Dee Phillips, and all the other people who worked on this project, this book would definitely not have been completed with the same quality and timeliness.

Finally, I want to thank Jesus Christ for gracing me with numerous gifts throughout my life, especially my understanding family who helped me through the many long hours (and late nights) writing this book.

Contents at a Glance

Contents

Foreword

In January, 2001, Cisco Systems, Inc. announced a new family of professional certifications called Cisco Qualified Specialist. The first CQS released was the Cisco Security Specialist 1. CSS1 is designed to certify your skills and knowledge of general network security, concentrating on intrusion detection systems, firewalls, and Virtual Private Networks. The demand for qualified network security professionals has never been greater. Each day organizations find themselves engaged in a never-ending battle to keep their networks secure from those intent on damaging systems or gaining unauthorized access. Intrusion detection is recognized as a critical skill for the network security professional responsible for detecting and preventing unauthorized access or activities from occurring within the network.

Cisco Secure Intrusion Detection System uses book format to present the knowledge contained in the lab-intensive, instructor-led course and the e-learning course of the same title. While releasing the information in book format cannot compete with the hands-on experience gained by attending Cisco authorized training delivered by a Cisco Learning Partner, it is a valuable component in meeting the worldwide demand for Cisco training. This book covers all CSIDS detection platforms including the 4200 series Sensors and the Catalyst 6000 series Intrusion Detection System Module. You will learn how to remotely manage the CSIDS Sensor, using both the Cisco Secure Policy Manager and the UNIX-based CSIDS Director. Both the CSIDS course and the Cisco Press book are dedicated to the highest standards of quality and knowledge transfer. Whether you are preparing to complete the CSS1 certification or are interested in installing, configuring, and operating CSIDS, this book will enhance your knowledge of intrusion detection systems.

This is another in a series of Cisco Press books dedicated to the transfer of knowledge and skills critical to the success of the network security professional. Additional Cisco Press books developed to support the CSS1 certification include *Managing Cisco Network Security, Cisco Secure PIX Firewalls,* and *Cisco Secure Virtual Private Networks.*

Rick Stiffler
Manager, VPN & Security Training
Cisco Systems, Inc.
September 2001

Introduction

This book explains every major aspect of Cisco Secure IDS. Previously, the main source of this information was the Cisco Secure IDS course. This book attempts to expand on the information provided by the Cisco Secure IDS course, as well as to incorporate information that is beyond the scope of the IDS course. This book serves as a useful reference on Cisco Secure IDS and serves as a standalone study guide for the Cisco Secure IDS Policy Manager exam. This exam represents one of the four major components of the Cisco Security Specialist 1 certification.

Audience

This book is intended to provide a concise reference for Cisco Secure IDS. It incorporates information on both Cisco Secure Policy Manager (CSPM) and Cisco Secure ID Director. It can be used as a standalone reference to prepare for the Cisco Secure IDS Policy Manager exam that is part of the Cisco Security Specialist 1 (CSS1) certification. It also makes an excellent reference for someone who must maintain and operate a Cisco Secure IDS. Finally, it provides a useful supplement to the Cisco Secure IDS course materials.

Before reading the book, you should have completed the CCNA certification or have equivalent level knowledge. A strong user-level experience with Windows NT operating system and a basic understanding of the UNIX operating system are important. Furthermore, having taken the Managing Cisco Network Security (MCNS) course is also beneficial.

Organization

This book is organized into eight major parts. Each of these parts explains an aspect of Cisco Secure IDS. Each part is divided into chapters as described here.

Part I: Introduction to Network Security

This section provides a good overview of network security. If you are unfamiliar with network security, this section is an excellent place to begin. It introduces the basic concepts that you need to understand as you read the other sections in the book. If you are familiar with network security, you can probably skim through this section. The chapters in this section include the following:

- Chapter 1: Need for Network Security
- Chapter 2: Cisco Security Wheel

Part II: Intrusion Detection and the CSIDS Environment

This section introduces you to the concept of intrusion detection systems (IDSs). The philosophy behind various IDSs is examined along with their strengths and weaknesses. Where Cisco Secure IDS fits into the IDS picture is also explained, along with an explanation of the major components of Cisco Secure IDS. The chapters in this section include the following:

- Chapter 3: Intrusion Detection Systems
- Chapter 4: Cisco Secure IDS Overview

Part III: CSIDS Installation

If you are installing Cisco Secure IDS on your network, this section is required reading. It explains the fundamental questions that you must analyze to determine where to place sensors on your network. It covers the installation of the appliance sensors and explains how to install the Cisco Secure Policy Manager (CSPM) Director platform. This Director platform runs on Windows NT. The chapters in this section include the following:

- Chapter 5: Cisco Secure IDS Sensor Deployment
- Chapter 6: Cisco Secure Policy Manager Installation
- Chapter 7: 4200 Series Sensor Installation Within CSPM

If you use Cisco Secure Intrusion Detection Director (CSIDD) rather than CSPM, you need to refer to Part VI for the details on how to install CSIDD.

Part IV: Alarm Management and Intrusion Detection Signatures

Signatures represent the heart of Cisco Secure IDS. Every time a signature triggers, it generates an alarm. Managing your alarms efficiently is definitely a worthy goal. Furthermore, the multitude of signatures supported by Cisco Secure IDS is explained in detail. By understanding how these signatures are constructed and what traffic causes them to trigger alarms, you can effectively manage the numerous alarms that are reported to your Director platform. The chapters in this section include the following:

- Chapter 8: Working with Cisco Secure IDS Alarms in CSPM
- Chapter 9: Understanding Cisco Secure IDS Signatures
- Chapter 10: Signature Series

Part V: CSIDS Configuration

This section explains how to configure the major features of Cisco Secure IDS, including the following:

- IP blocking
- Sensor configuration
- Catalyst 6000 IDS Module configuration
- Filtering signatures

The chapters in this section include the following:

- Chapter 11: Sensor Configuration Within CSPM
- Chapter 12: Signature and Intrusion Detection Configuration
- Chapter 13: IP Blocking Configurations
- Chapter 14: Catalyst 6000 IDS Module Configuration

Part VI: Cisco Secure Intrusion Detection Director (CSIDD)

When you deploy your Cisco Secure IDS, you have a choice of two different Director platforms. This section explains how to install and configure Cisco Secure ID Director. This platform runs on Solaris and uses HP OpenView as its graphical user interface. This section also explains how to configure the Cisco IOS Firewall IDS (a low-end router-based IDS monitoring device). The chapters in this section include the following:

- Chapter 15: Cisco Secure ID Director Installation
- Chapter 16: The Configuration Management Utility (nrConfigure)
- Chapter 17: Cisco IOS Firewall Intrusion Detection System

Part VII: Cisco Secure IDS Upcoming Releases

Cisco Secure IDS is constantly evolving. This section is devoted to explaining some of the upcoming features and changes that are being implemented and planned for Cisco Secure IDS. Many of the features will be available by the time that you read this book. The section is composed of the following chapter:

- Chapter 18: Planned Cisco Secure IDS Enhancements

Part VIII: Appendixes

This book has numerous appendixes that explain many useful concepts that do not fit easily into the main sections of the book. You probably do not need to read all of these appendixes one after the other, but they provide excellent reference material for users of Cisco Secure IDS. The appendixes include the following:

- Appendix A: Deploying Intrusion Detection: Case Studies
- Appendix B: Cisco Secure IDS Architecture
- Appendix C: Cisco Secure ID Director Basic Troubleshooting
- Appendix D: Cisco Secure IDS Log Files
- Appendix E: Advanced Tips
- Appendix F: Cisco Secure IDS Signature Structures and Implementations
- Appendix G: Cisco Secure IDS Signatures and Recommended Alarm Levels
- Appendix H: Cisco IOS Firewall IDS Signature List
- Appendix I: Cisco Secure Communications Deployment Worksheet
- Appendix J: Glossary
- Appendix K: Answers to Review Questions

Cisco Security Specialist 1

Cisco Security Specialist 1 (CSS1) replaces CCNP-Security Certification. The CSS1 designation validates skills and knowledge in four key areas of network security:

- Firewalls

- Intrusion detection systems

- Virtual Private Networks

- Managing network security

As organizations accelerate their interest in Internet business solutions, they need qualified professionals who possess the skills necessary to ensure the security of all network-based transactions and to design secure business solutions. The expertise you develop when preparing for the CSS1 designation adds to your skill set and helps you expand your professional options.

For more information on CSS1 certification, refer to http://www.cisco.com/go/securitytrng.

Cisco Secure IDS Course

The Cisco Secure IDS course (2.0) is one of the four courses on which CSS1 certification is based. This course provides an explanation of Cisco Secure IDS through classroom instruction and lab exercises. Furthermore, this course helps prepare you for the Cisco Secure IDS Policy Manager exam (one of the exams required for CSS1 designation). Being based on the Cisco Secure IDS course, this book also provides all the information necessary to prepare for this exam.

IDS Course Prerequisites

The prerequisites for the Cisco Secure IDS course (and CSS1 certification) follow:

- CCNA Certification

- Managing Cisco Network Security (MCNS) course

Conventions Used in This Book

This book is organized into eight major parts. If you are unfamiliar with Cisco Secure IDS, you will probably gain the most benefit by reading each part in order beginning with Part I, "Introduction to Network Security." If you are already familiar with Cisco Secure IDS, however, you can focus on the specific sections of interest. Furthermore, the layout of the parts enables the reader to quickly locate the needed information.

The text is sprinkled with notes and sidebars that highlight information that might be of particular importance to you. Sometimes, these notes and sidebars point out potential problems. Others clarify terms used within the text.

Each chapter also contains a set of review questions. These questions are designed to highlight the major concepts in each chapter. The purpose of these review questions is to assist you in reviewing for the Cisco Secure IDS Policy Manager exam. You can also use these questions to gauge your understanding of the material presented in each chapter. The answers to the review questions are in Appendix K.

Command Syntax Conventions

Command syntax in this book conforms to the following conventions:

- Commands, keywords, and actual values for arguments are **bold**.

- Arguments (which need to be replaced with an actual value) are *italic*.

- Optional keywords and arguments are in brackets [ ].

- Choice of mandatory keywords and arguments is in braces { }.

Note that these conventions are for syntax only. Actual configurations and examples do not follow these conventions.

Introduction to Network Security

## CHAPTER 1

Need for Network Security

Studies estimate that the current size of the Internet includes approximately 100 million hosts, with more than 350 million unique users.[1] Many companies rely heavily on electronic commerce for their livelihood. Integrating the Internet into business operations is cost effective. Home users frequently utilize cheap high-speed access to their homes through cable modems and digital subscriber lines (DSLs). The bottom line is that the Internet is carrying more traffic than ever before and still growing in size with no end in sight.

Along with this explosive growth comes an increased threat from Internet-related attacks. Historically, when someone mentions theft, you probably think of an intruder physically breaking into a facility and stealing valuable property. Traditional robberies require physical access to the target. The Internet, however, allows theft and break-ins to occur from anywhere in the world.

NOTE   The only perfectly secure computer is one that is unplugged and in a locked vault. Unfortunately, this computer is also the most useless. All computer systems and network devices must be protected in some fashion while maintaining usability. More accessibility opens up more opportunities for an attacker, but if you secure your systems effectively, this does not necessarily increase your security risk.

Implementing network security is crucial to maintaining an operational network, as well as the continued success of your business. Numerous locations within your network are especially susceptible to electronic attacks.

Understanding what these areas are is the first step toward improving your security. Understanding the types of tools that hackers use against your network is vital. Attackers utilize various tools and techniques to gain unauthorized access to your computer networks. All of these tools exploit weaknesses in your network. These attacks represent a constant

---

1. www.techweb.com, "Study Finds 100 Million Hosts," January 2001.

threat to your network and, more importantly, to your company's reputation. Security threats to your network fall into several distinct categories.

As you read through this chapter, you learn key facts in the following areas:

- Security threats
- Security concepts
- The phases of an attack
- Attack methodologies
- Network access points
- Hacking techniques

Security Threats

Businesses use the Internet to reach out to millions of potential customers. Extranets enable efficient and effective communication with business partners. Employees rely on internal networks to perform operations such as filing trip reports and making travel reservations. E-mail enables everyone to communicate quickly and efficiently with people throughout the world.

Disruption of your computer network is no longer just an inconvenience. An inoperable e-commerce Web site costs your company potentially millions of dollars a day. Employees are at a standstill when the network fails. Networks must not only be operational but also remain connected to other networks around the world in order to be useful.

This worldwide connectivity comes with a downside. Anyone with Internet connectivity represents a potential attacker. Hosts connected to the Internet are susceptible to attack. Disgruntled employees motivated by revenge frequently attack internal networks. Furthermore, geography is no longer a barrier that limits attacks against your network.

Many threats impact the operation of your computer network. Natural threats, such as flood, fire, and tornadoes, cause unexpected disruptions. Although unexpected and infrequent, most companies have well-defined procedures to handle these natural threats. Security procedures designed to combat hacker attacks, however, are usually less thought out (if they exist at all). An unsecured network will definitely be attacked. The only question is when the attack will occur.

Even if you think that your data is not interesting to an attacker, your network will be attacked. Attackers constantly search for systems that they can use as a launching platform for future attacks. By launching an attack from a compromised system, an attacker makes it difficult for anyone to identify her because the traffic is not coming from her own host.

NOTE	I installed a cable modem at my house to gain high-speed Internet access. When the cable modem installer arrived, I had not purchased the firewall that I wanted to use. Because I did not yet have a firewall, I decided to attach my computer to a hub and watch for scans against my computer. Within a day, I noticed some probing against my system. Attackers constantly search for new victims.

Attacks on your network have two attributes. The first attribute (a continuum) is the level of expertise of the hacker. The level can be low, or *unstructured*, or it can be high, or *structured*. The second attribute is the physical location from which the attack is launched. It can be launched from an *external* network or from an *internal* location.

The following sections discuss each attribute.

Unstructured Threats

Hacking tools and scripts abound on numerous Internet sites (see Chapter 2, "Cisco Security Wheel"). Intellectual curiosity drives many novice hackers to download these tools and experiment with them on local and remote networks. Others get a thrill out of breaking into computers that are otherwise off-limits.

Script Kiddies

Computer attackers range in skill from novice to highly advanced. Script kiddies fall at the bottom of this skill ladder. They have little or no programming skills, limited knowledge of what they are doing, and tend to use other people's scripts for mischief instead of learning how something works for themselves.

Most unstructured attacks against your network occur from *script kiddies* and moderately skilled attackers. Most of the time, these attacks are driven by personal gratification. A small percentage of the time, these attacks are malicious in nature. In either case, the impact on your company's image can be significant.

Although the expertise of these attackers is usually minimal, unstructured threats still disrupt your network, and represent a significant threat. Sometimes, just running a script against your network can break network functionality. For instance, running a Solaris exploit against other operating system (OS) types might have no effect or it might crash the system. A script kiddie might not realize this, so he blindly runs a new attack script against all the hosts on your network (not just the Solaris systems). His only goal is to gain access to your network, but he inadvertently crashes numerous systems on your network. Other times, a simple attempt to test someone's skill, without any malicious intent, can cause serious harm to your organization's reputation.

Suppose your network is set up as in Figure 1-1. The internal network is protected by a firewall. Your informational Web server is located on a network, separate from the Internet and your internal network. The firewall restricts traffic to both the protected network and the Web server. Externally originated traffic, however, is allowed from the Internet to your Web site but not to your internal network.

Figure 1-1 *Company X Network Layout*

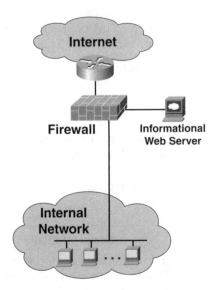

Now, assume that an attacker manages to break into your Web server and stops some processes on the Web server. Your Web page is no longer accessible from the Internet. The first result is that customers lose their ability to communicate with you. After receiving complaints, you reboot your Web server and your Web site is back up. In some situations, that is the end of the story. Other times, a news source learns of the attack and writes a news article about your attack. Other news sources might join in by writing their own articles (especially Internet news sources). Quickly, news of the attack can spread in articles that might look like the following:

An unknown attacker broke into Company X's Web site yesterday. The Web server remained inaccessible for more than five hours. The extent of the attack is unknown at this time.

Customers do not know your network topology. Their first reaction is that your network is insecure. They do not understand, or care, about the security separation between the Web site and the internal network. The incident places doubts on the security of your entire company in the eyes of your customers. Future customers might stay away for fear of having their credit card numbers compromised by an assumed lack of security.

Structured Threats

Structured threats come from adversaries that are highly motivated and technically competent. Unlike script kiddies, these attackers have the technical proficiency to understand existing tools, adapt current hacking tools, and create new custom tools. These attackers act alone or in small groups. They understand, develop, and use sophisticated hacking techniques to penetrate unsuspecting organizations.

The motivation behind structured threats is varied. Some common motivating factors include money, political activism, anger, and retribution for some hurt. Organized crime, industrial competitors, and state-sponsored groups hire technical experts to launch many structured attacks. These attacks almost always have a specific goal in mind, such as the acquisition of a competitor's source code. Major fraud and theft cases fall into the structured threat category.

Regardless of their motivation, these attackers can inflict serious damage on your network. A successful structured attack can destroy your entire business. Many times, the goal of a structured attack is to destroy a competitor.

External Threats

Attacks conducted without any privileged access to your network are known as external threats. Computer users across the world with Internet access are capable of launching external attacks against your network. This translates to a base of 350 million potential attackers with access to your network through the Internet.

You use your perimeter defenses as the first line of defense against external threats. By maintaining strong perimeter defenses, you minimize the impact of external threats against your network. Organizations usually spend most of their time protecting themselves against external threats.

NOTE   Sometimes, a network's security is labeled as having a hard shell with a chewy inside. This refers to devoting all your security resources to perimeter security. If an attacker breaks through your strong outer perimeter, he can easily compromise one machine after another inside your network. Your entire network requires securing both the perimeter and the internal networks.

Internal Threats

According to numerous reports, the largest percentage of attacks against your network will be from the internal threat category. In 1999, internal threats represented 80 percent of all computer crime.[2] With internal threats, an attacker has some initial level of access to a computer system. The initial access can be an account on a server or physical access to the network. Furthermore, this access is not available to the general public. Disgruntled ex-employees, existing employees, and contractors usually have the access necessary to conduct internal attacks.

Sometimes, a structured attack against your network is conducted with the help of an insider. In this case, the attack becomes a structured internal threat. In this situation, the attackers can inflict severe harm against the network and easily steal valuable company information. A structured internal threat represents the most severe attack that can be launched against your network.

Security Concepts

Now that you have an understanding of the basic security threats that your network faces, it is time to examine the basic security principles. Understanding these concepts is crucial to securing your network and defining a workable *security policy*. Furthermore, many attacks exploit weaknesses in one or more of these areas. Strengthening these areas of your network help to minimize the effectiveness of attacks against your network.

Security Policy

A security policy is a formal statement that outlines the rules by which access to your networks is controlled (see Chapter 2). All access to your information assets must abide by these rules. When installing security components on your network, these rules also establish a framework that defines what you need to check for and the restrictions that you need to impose on traffic in your network. An excellent reference to learn more about security policies is RFC 2196, "Site Security Handbook."

The following are key areas in which you need to direct your efforts for network security:

- **Authentication**—Authentication refers to the process of reliably determining the identity of a communicating entity. This entity can be an individual user or a software process.

- **Authorization**—Authorization refers to the rules that determine who has permission to access the different resources on your network.

---

2. "Studies and Surveys of Computer Crime" by M.E. Kabay, Ph.D., CISSP, December 12, 2000. http://www.securityportal.com/cover/coverstory20001211.printerfriendly.html.

- **Confidentiality**—Confidentiality ensures that data is protected from being divulged to unauthorized parties. Specifically, confidentiality requires that information inside a computer system (in memory or on disk) and in transit (across a network) is accessible for reading only by authorized parties.

- **Integrity**—A system protects the integrity of data if it prevents unauthorized modification of the data. Modification includes creating, writing, changing, deleting, and replaying transmitted messages.

- **Availability**—The requirement that computer system assets are available to authorized parties when needed defines availability. The purpose of a denial of service (DoS) attack is to subvert the availability of system resources, either temporarily or permanently.

The Phases of an Attack

Attacks against your network are usually divided into three distinct phases. The first phase involves defining a goal for the attack. The second phase is reconnaissance, also known as information gathering. During this phase, the attacker attempts to gather information about your network to determine prime targets on your network. After collecting information about your network, the attacker proceeds to the third phase, the attacking phase.

The following sections discuss these stages.

Setting the Goals for the Attack

Before attacking a network or system, an attacker sets her goals or objectives. When attacking your network, an attacker might have various goals:

- Data manipulation
- System access
- Elevated privileges
- Denying availability of network resources

An attacker might have a simple goal, such as looking for any systems running a specific OS to try out a new tool that she found. She might be trying to obtain well-protected trade secrets from a competitor.

Motivation also plays a significant factor. Some key motivations behind attacks include the following:

- Revenge
- Political activism
- Financial gain

Frequently, attackers attempt to disrupt your network to discredit your organization's image. Your organization's reputation is a prized asset that is difficult to build; yet it only takes potentially one DoS attack to irreparably damage that reputation.

Regardless of the complexity or motivation behind an attack, the goal dictates the methodology that the attacker needs to use against your network.

Reconnaissance Before the Attack

Collecting information is the attacker's second step in launching an attack against your network. Successful reconnaissance is also the key to a successful attack. Attackers use two main mechanisms to collect information about your network:

- Public data sources
- Scanning and probing

Public Data Sources

Sometimes, an attacker begins his knowledge search by examining public information available on your company. Although this information is freely available, it can provide the attacker with a wealth of information on your network. He can determine where your business is located, the business partners that you associate with, the value of your company's assets, and much more. He might even collect usernames or product names to use in password-guessing attacks against your network.

Scanning and Probing

Whether the attacker starts with a public data search or electronic scanning, he needs to locate vulnerable targets that he can attack. Through scanning, the attacker uses remote reconnaissance to find specific resources on your network. Remote reconnaissance or information gathering is the unauthorized mapping of systems, services, or vulnerabilities on a network.

The goal of information gathering is to pinpoint weak points on the network where an attack is likely to succeed. By pinpointing specific weaknesses on the network, the attacker can launch an attack in the future that generates minimal traffic or *noise* on the network. This greatly reduces the likelihood of detection during the actual attack.

An attacker has several avenues for remote reconnaissance. He might attempt to gather information about your network through your Internet connection. Another potential path is to look for potential dial-up lines by using a tool that dials a range of numbers looking for modem connections. He might even attempt to locate targets on one of your business partner's network, hoping to find a back door into your network.

An attacker begins his reconnaissance by choosing a specific target network. His initial data mining usually provides him with a list of networks that belong to your company. *Domain Name System (DNS)* records provide the attacker with a repository of information about networks registered to your company. Knowing that a network is registered, or belongs, to your company does not mean that the network is currently in use. Many companies have networks that are reserved for expansion and future growth. Therefore, the attacker must determine which IP addresses on the target network are associated with *live* computers.

DNS

DNS is a hierarchy of servers that provide an Internet-wide name to IP address mapping for the hosts on the Internet. This mapping enables users to enter an easy-to-remember host name to access a specific system. This host name (such as http://www.yahoo.com) is then converted, using DNS, to an actual IP address (such as 204.71.200.75) that is necessary to communicate with the host across the network.

The intruder typically *ping sweeps* the target network to determine what IP addresses are associated with actual computers. After this is accomplished, the intruder determines what services or ports are active on the live IP addresses. From this information, the intruder queries all or many ports on each system to determine which ones have active services, along with accessing their versions if possible. He also attempts to discover the type and version of operating system running on each target host. Basically, the attacker wants to learn as much information as possible about the systems on your network to increase the chances that his eventual attack will succeed.

Ping Sweep

IP provides basic control messages through the Internet Control Message Protocol (ICMP). One of these messages is an ICMP echo request, known as a *ping*. Its functionality is designed to determine whether a host can be reached electronically. When the host receives the ICMP echo request packet, it replies with an ICMP echo reply packet. Most systems include a program called ping that generates these ICMP echo request packets. An attacker sends ICMP echo request packets to all the IP addresses on the specific network. The actual hosts on the network respond with ICMP echo reply packets, indicating which IP addresses correspond to actual hosts.

Remote reconnaissance is somewhat analogous to a thief casing a neighborhood for vulnerable homes to break into. With houses, a thief looks for items such as unoccupied homes, open windows or doors, and easy-to-pick locks. The malicious hacker also looks for specific items when he cases your network. Some of these items include the following:

- Operating systems with known vulnerabilities
- Protocols with known weaknesses
- Services in use
- Network topology

By establishing a thorough picture of your network, the attacker can build a powerful toolkit. Then, at a later date, he can conduct various attacks against your network, from a surgical strike to an all-out assault. The attacks against your network fall into two broad categories:

- Gaining access
- Denial of service

The Actual Attack

After an attacker maps out your network, he researches known vulnerabilities for the systems that he detected. Sometimes, his current toolkit contains tools that already exploit vulnerabilities on your network. The attacker's goal at this stage is to gain access to resource(s) on your network. In this context, access is unauthorized data manipulation, system access, or privilege escalation.

If system access to a host is achieved, a common goal is for the attacker to attempt to elevate his privileges on the system, hoping to achieve administrator or *root* access. With privileged access, the attacker has unrestricted access to the host's services and data.

---

root

On UNIX and Linux systems, the most privileged account is named *root*. This account has virtually unlimited powers on the system. Gaining *root* privileges on a system enables an attacker to totally control the system.

Gaining access to a host is commonly referred to as compromising the host. When a host is compromised, all the data and programs on the system can no longer be trusted, because the extent of the penetration is unknown. Any trust relationships the compromised host has with other resources on the network also become a threat to your network. After compromising a host, an attacker uses those trust relationships as a stepping stone to gain access to other hosts on the network. Often the compromises follow a domino effect, until the attacker has gained control of your entire network.

After compromising hosts on your network, an attacker frequently installs back doors that he can use to access the systems in the future without being detected. He also can use these hosts to launch attacks against other networks. Tracing an attacker can be difficult if he has bounced through several hosts. Furthermore, this can pose a liability risk to your site if his attacks through your host cause damage to someone else's network.

Attack Methodologies

Regardless of the motivation or personal preferences, an attacker has several attack methodologies from which to choose:

- Ad hoc (random)
- Methodical
- Surgical strike (lightning quick)
- Patient (slow)

Ad Hoc (Random)

An ad hoc attack methodology is unstructured. An attacker using this methodology is usually disorganized and her attacks frequently fail. With this approach, it is difficult to comprehensively locate targets on the network.

Methodical

The methodical methodology provides a well-defined sequence of steps to attack a network. First, the attacker uses reconnaissance to locate targets. Next, the attacker locates exploits for known vulnerabilities on the targets that he identified during information gathering. Many times, a methodical attacker experiments with these exploits on practice systems, gaining insight into their effectiveness. Finally, when he is satisfied with his toolkit, he starts attacking systems on the target network. This attack methodology provides a high probability of success.

Surgical Strike (Lightning Quick)

Often, an attacker uses an automated script against a network. The entire attack is completed in a few seconds, before system administrators or security analysts have time to react and make any decisions. This attack methodology enables an attacker to conduct his attack efficiently and move to new targets quickly.

Patient (Slow)

Our final methodology is actually a subset methodology that can be applied to either the ad hoc or methodical methodologies. It refers to how quickly the attacker executes his attack. An attacker usually uses a patient (slow) methodology to avoid detection. Many intrusion detection systems have difficulty detecting attacks that occur over long periods of time. A ping sweep performed in hours is likely to be detected, for example, whereas the same ping sweep occurring over a month is not.

Network Attack Points

Understanding the common attack points on your network is vital to establishing a sound security policy. These attack points also represent some of the items that you need to consider when you are deploying your Cisco Secure IDS. The main attack points are as follows:

- Network resources
- Network protocols

Network Resources

Systems on a network represent a prime target for attack. Attacks against these resources generally fall into several broad categories:

- Data manipulation or access
- Account access
- Privilege escalation
- Trust relationships

Data Manipulation or Access

Many systems on your network have shared directories (either system or user created) that provide an entry point for an attacker. A common technique is for an attacker to look for shares that allow *anonymous* connections. An anonymous connection does not require authentication. Therefore, these shares provide an attacker with easy access to data.

Attackers love to take advantage of anonymous shares. Sometimes, these shares provide the attacker with the information that he needs to escalate his attack, such as account names and, potentially, passwords. At other times, an attacker uses anonymous shares to load a *Trojan horse program* onto the system. When a privileged user executes the Trojan horse program, he is unknowingly installing a back door for the attacker.

Trojan Horse Program

A Trojan horse program is a program that appears to perform some useful function. When the user runs the program, however, it also executes hidden functionality that attacks your system or opens up a back door for the attacker.

Account Access

If an attacker can gain access to a valid account on your network, she increases her chances tremendously of obtaining privileged access and eventually compromising your entire network. The first step in this process is to obtain valid account names. Account names are not hard to acquire. Many times, a person's e-mail account is equal to his logon account.

Besides obtaining account names, an attacker can also run password-guessing programs against your network. Many users choose passwords that can be easily obtained using a dictionary-based, password-guessing program. These programs repeatedly attempt to log on with an account using variations of words in their dictionary as the password. On most networks, password-guessing programs are effective at breaking weak user passwords.

Privilege Escalation

Privilege escalation attacks involve gaining elevated privileges from a nonprivileged account. These attacks are only useable if an attacker has an account on the target system.

Many nonprivileged accounts, such as anonymous access, provide widespread access to system resources. These accounts, however, can execute only a few commands and access specific files. Through privilege escalation, an attacker can convert an easily accessible account into an account with potentially unlimited capabilities.

After an attacker compromises your system, he can install back doors and other hidden software on your system. Completely removing all of these hidden programs might require you to completely rebuild the OS, which is a time-consuming task.

Trust Relationships

Trust relationships establish a privileged level of access between specific hosts on a network. This trust is usually based on an IP address or system name. An attacker can circumvent both of these mechanisms. Furthermore, if an attacker compromises one host in a trust relationship, the other members of the trust are soon to follow.

Network Protocols

Instead of attacking the resources on the network, an attacker sometimes attacks the integrity of the network protocols. The network protocols enable the resources on the network to communicate with each other. By manipulating the network protocols, an attacker hopes to achieve access to one of the resources on the network. Protocol attacks fall into two categories:

- Man-in-the-middle attacks
- Spoofing attacks

Man-in-the-Middle Attacks

A man-in-the-middle attack refers to an attack that takes over a session between two hosts that are communicating through some protocol. The attack might either completely take over the session or might act as a relay in which it alters or passes only specific data from the valid hosts. For the attack to succeed, the attacker must be located on the network that lies between the two hosts (see Figure 1-2).

Figure 1-2   *Man-in-the-Middle Attack*

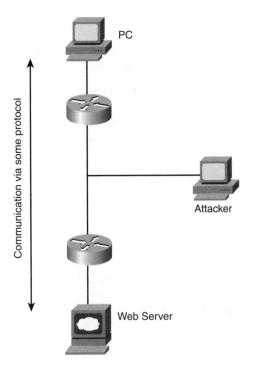

A common man-in-the-middle attack is TCP hijacking. TCP hijacking occurs when an attacker takes control of an existing TCP connection between two hosts. After taking control of the TCP session, the attacker can insert data and commands as the valid user who initiated the connection. By default, TCP provides minimal integrity checking and no confidentiality.

Spoofing Attacks

Many attacks rely on an attacker's ability to pretend to be someone he is not. Sending packets with another system's source IP address is known as *spoofing*. UDP-based protocols are especially vulnerable to this type of attack, as is the Address Resolution Protocol (ARP). Unlike TCP-based protocols that use sequence numbers, UDP-based protocols use only the source IP address for authentication. Numerous programs enable an attacker to create packets from any source IP address that he chooses.

Address Resolution Protocol

On Ethernet networks, data is sent between hosts using Ethernet frames. Hosts tend to send data based on IP addresses. Therefore, a mechanism is needed to translate IP addresses to physical Ethernet addresses. This conversion is handled by the Address Resolution Protocol (ARP). ARP provides only the address for the next hop that the packet needs to go through. An IP packet might have to go through several hops before it reaches its final destination. The final destination is determined by the destination IP address of the packet. The designers of this protocol did not even consider security during its development and it is susceptible to spoofing attacks. For more information on ARP, refer to RFC 826, "An Ethernet Address Resolution Protocol."

Hacking Tools and Techniques

Attackers and hackers use a variety of techniques in the attempt to gain access to your networks and computer resources. These techniques revolve around an initial data-collection phase, followed by an attack phase. Each of these phases requires tools. The tools and techniques used by attackers are explained in the following sections:

- Using reconnaissance tools
- Compromising weakness in your network
- Implementing denial of service techniques

Using Reconnaissance Tools

Before attacking a network, most attackers attempt to gather as much information as possible about potential targets on the network. Many tools are available to collect information about the computers on a network. Attackers use two types of tools in their reconnaissance attacks:

- Common administrative tools
- Common hacker scanning tools

Common Administrative Tools

Administrative tools enable the network administrator to debug day-to-day problems on the network. System administrators are responsible for troubleshooting problems on a computer network. To support this requirement, many troubleshooting tools are incorporated into existing operating systems. These tools include **nslookup**, **ping**, **netcat**, **telnet**, **finger**, **rpcinfo**, File Explorer, srvinfo, and dumpacl. Unfortunately, an attacker can use these same tools to scan for information on your network.

Common Hacker Scanning Tools

Most common hacker scanning tools have been specifically designed to gather network information effectively. Many tools have been designed by hackers to collect information about hosts on a network. These tools are specifically designed to gather network information quickly and efficiently.

Sometimes, collecting information without being detected by intrusion detection systems is the primary design goal for tool creation. To that end, *stealth* tools are prized for their capability to avoid detection.

Along with speed and efficiency, some of these tools are designed specifically to avoid detection. These tools include the following:

- SATAN
- NMAP
- Strobe
- Portscanner

Compromising Weaknesses in Your Network

After mapping out potential targets, the attacker attempts to gain access on the target host(s) using a variety of access techniques, including using specific exploitation tools. These tools are intended to compromise the following:

- Authentication
- Common services configured poorly
- Protocol weaknesses
- Compromised trust relationships
- Application holes
- Back doors
- Physical assets that are not secure

Authentication Compromises

Determining usernames for a network is fairly easy. Many times, e-mail accounts are the same as logon accounts on internal networks. Gaining access to a logon account requires a username-password combination. Therefore, after gaining a list of account names, the attacker will probably attempt to discover valid passwords for these accounts. Sometimes, the attacker tries a few common passwords, such as a blank password or the password equal to the username. To achieve a more comprehensive coverage of possible passwords, the attacker usually uses a *password cracker* to brute-force guess passwords.

Password Crackers

A *password cracker* is a tool that tries multiple password combinations in an attempt to find an unknown password. Some tools use a dictionary of common words and phrases. Other tools check every possible character combination, which is known as performing a brute-force attack on the entire keyspace. Dictionary password crackers can potentially crack 25–60 percent of your user's passwords when run against your network.[3]

The following are some common UNIX password crackers:

- Crack by Alec Muffett (UNIX)
- CrackerJack by Jackal (UNIX on DOS platform)
- Qcrack by the Crypt Keeper
- John the Ripper by Solar Designer

---

3. *Cisco Security Bytes*, Volume 2, Issue 5, May 2000. "Crack 5 Is Not the Only Cracker in Town" by Eric Augustus, Network Security Engineer. http://www.cisco.com/warp/pub-lic/779/largeent/issues/security/sbytes.

The following are some common Windows 95/98/2000/NT password crackers:

- L0phtCrack 2.5
- ntPassword v2.0
- PWL-Key 1.06
- Pwlhack 4.10
- PWLVIEW 1.0

In addition to using password crackers, attackers also use network sniffers to obtain passwords. Using a password cracker can be a time-consuming task. However, a password obtained using a network sniffer is usable immediately.

Authentication compromises also occur through shared directories and files on the network. Many shared directories require no authentication. If the share has write access, the attacker can place malicious executables on the system, hoping for a valid user to execute them, thus opening up the system.

Common Services Configured Poorly

Network services are located on well-known ports. The reconnaissance tools provide the attacker with a list of ports available to attack. These ports can be equated to services on well-known ports. A hacker knows these services and understands common configuration problems that can be exploited to gain access using these well-known services.

Network administrators frequently install operating systems using the basic installation from the distribution media. End users install software applications using the default configuration. Default installations are usually insecure. Some applications create default accounts with known default passwords.

Typical services configured poorly include the following:

- DNS servers
- Mail servers
- FTP servers
- Web servers

Protocol Weaknesses

Most network protocols were developed when the Internet was in its infancy. At that time, the Internet represented a small group of researchers and security was not a significant concern. Therefore, protocol developers were not concerned with security during their design process. This resulted in protocols that are not suited to withstand the security threats present in the Internet today. Attackers use weaknesses in the original protocols to gain access to systems. The following are some common protocols with security weaknesses:

- ARP
- UDP
- TCP
- ICMP
- IP

ARP and UDP are susceptible to spoofing attacks, whereas TCP is subject to hijacking and sequence number guessing attacks. Any IP-based protocol is subject to IP fragmentation attacks.

Compromised Trust Relationships

An attacker can sometimes exploit trust relationships between hosts on the network. If an attacker sends information to one host in the relationship, which appears to originate from the other trusted host, the data might be accepted as valid. Depending on the nature of the trust, this spoofed data might be enough to gain access to the system.

Attackers assault trust relationships because they are based on weak authentication mechanisms. The following are two common authentication mechanisms:

- IP-based authentication
- DNS-based authentication

IP addresses can easily be spoofed. IP protocols fail to provide an integrity mechanism to ensure that the data comes from a specific source. Therefore, IP addresses make a weak authentication token.

DNS-based authentication is a little stronger, but DNS servers are still subject to attack. One common DNS attack, called *DNS cache poisoning*, injects bad data into a DNS server's cache. Using bad DNS information results in failed DNS-based authentication.

Application Holes

Developers who write applications are driven by short timelines. Furthermore, additional user features drive new product releases. Security and protocol robustness are usually not a high development priority, unless the product is a security product, such as a firewall. When an application lacks robustness or is coded poorly, it is possible to disrupt the operation of the application by sending it malformed data.

NOTE   Sometimes, development of security products, such as firewalls, is focused on how well the product processes data through it. This can leave these devices or software open to attack against the product itself.

Back Doors

Viruses and worms provide a vehicle for an attacker to wreak havoc on your network and potentially the Internet. However, the spread of viruses and worms is much harder to determine in advance. Viruses and worms usually lack an effective targeting capability to enable them to be used for attacking specific networks.

Trojan horse programs enable an attacker to establish back doors on systems. However, Trojan horse programs require some type of transport vehicle. The transport vehicle usually performs something for the user while it installs the back door behind the scenes. A common transport vehicle is a humorous game.

Whack-a-Mole

A popular transport mechanism for Netbus (a Windows backdoor program) is a game called Whack-a-Mole. The executable WHACKAMOLE.EXE is a self-extracting WinZip file. When a user runs the program, he gets to play an entertaining game. Behind the scenes, however, the program installs a back door. Beware of gifts in the form of free games.

Physical Assets That Are Not Secure

Physical access enables an attacker to bypass many security mechanisms. An attacker might boot off of a floppy to gain access to hard drive data. An attacker might connect a laptop directly into your corporate network. Although physical security is beyond the scope of this book, it is an access mechanism that cannot be forgotten when designing your security policy.

Implementing Denial of Service Techniques

Many times, the goal of a cyber attacker is to disrupt the operation of a specific system or network. A large e-commerce corporation easily loses millions of dollars if the operation of its Web site is disrupted for a short period of time. The losses because of missed sales can usually be calculated from historical sales figures. Customer confidence, which has a more devastating impact, is much harder to quantify.

The purpose of DoS attacks is to deny legitimate access to network resources. These attacks include everything from simple one-line commands to sophisticated programs written by knowledgeable hackers. Specifically, this chapter addresses the following types of DoS attacks:

- Network resource overload
- Host resource starvation
- Out-of-bounds attacks
- Distributed attacks

Network Resource Overload (Bandwidth Consumption)

One common way to deny access to a network is by overloading a common resource necessary for network components to operate. The main common resource that can be attacked is network bandwidth. An attacker can fill the network bandwidth in several ways: generating lots of traffic, distributing the attack across numerous hosts, and using a protocol flaw that amplifies the attack by soliciting help from many different hosts on the target network.

For an attacker to fill up the network bandwidth, he must generate more traffic than the target network can handle. As home users get faster and faster home network access, these attacks become more viable against wide-area network (WAN) connections that have relatively small bandwidth.

Network resource overload attacks sometimes use a technique called amplification to increase their effectiveness. A single 10-Mb network connection can generate, at most, 10 Mb worth of DoS traffic. This will not fill up a 100-Mb network. Suppose that an attacker has launched an attack from 11 different hosts. Now he has a maximum of 110 Mb (11 hosts * 10 Mb/host). Amplification attacks produce this effect on the target network by soliciting the help of hosts on the target network. When an attacker sends a ping packet to the network address of the target, all hosts on that network receive it and most reply to it.

By sending packets that appear to originate from the target host, a target system is flooded with lots of packets. Appropriate access control list filtering can prevent external attackers from using amplification attacks against your internal networks. Common amplification attacks include the following:

- SMURF (amplification flood using ICMP ping packets)
- Fraggle (amplification flood using UDP protocol)

Figure 1-3 illustrates how an amplification attack works. The target of the attack is 172.21.12.5. The attacker sends a forged ICMP packet into the target network. This packet has a source address of 172.21.12.5 and a destination of 172.21.255.255. Because the destination address is the network address, every host on the network responds to the ICMP request. All the replies are directed to the IP source address 172.21.12.5. This single spoofed packet generated five packets against the target machine. As the size of the network grows, the impact on the target host also grows.

Figure 1-3 *Amplification DoS Attack*

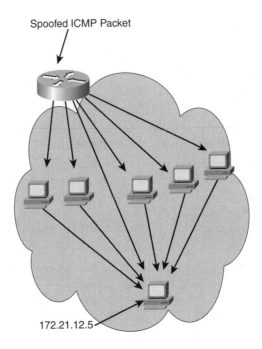

Host Resource Starvation

The resources available on a host are attack points as well. One such resource is the buffer that a host uses to track TCP connections. By filling up the buffer with invalid connection attempts, legitimate new connections are prevented. A common host resource starvation attack is SYN Flood, which sends multiple SYN packets to a host.

Disk space is another commonly attacked resource on a device. If an attacker can fill up the disk space on a network device, the device usually crashes or reboots. Shared directories and files that are weakly protected can be a prime target for this type of attack. Another technique is to attack the host's system auditing functionality. By sending a flood of traffic that generates massive numbers of log file entries, an attacker can easily fill up the disk space on the host.

Out-of-Bounds Attacks

Out-of-bounds attacks come in several different flavors. The first out-of-bounds attack category uses oversized IP packets. When a host system attempts to reconstruct the oversized packet, it overflows an allocated buffer and causes the system to crash. An oversized packet attack is Ping of Death.

The second class of out-of-bounds attacks utilizes overlapped IP fragments. When an IP packet is too large to send in one packet, it is broken down into multiple packets. Each of these packets contains an offset from the first packet. With these DoS attacks, the fragments overlap. IP fragment attacks include the following:

- Teardrop
- Newtear
- Syndrop
- Boink
- Bonk

The final class of out-of-bounds attacks involves out-of-bounds data. Sample attacks include sending packets that contain the source IP address equal to the destination IP address, such as the following:

- Land (SYN packet sent to a single port)
- Latierra (SYN packets sent to multiple ports)

Distributed Attacks

The latest trend in DoS attacks is for an attacker to compromise numerous hosts and then use all these compromised hosts to provide a massive attack against a specific target. This is known as a *distributed denial of service (DDoS)* attack. Malicious hackers have used various DDoS attacks to disrupt the Web sites for Yahoo, Inc., eBay, Inc., Amazon.com, Inc., and Buy.com, Inc.[4] Each of these companies relies exclusively on its Internet connectivity, and more specifically its Internet Web site, to conduct multimillion-dollar businesses.

Generating enough traffic from a single host to disrupt the operation of a large Web server can be difficult. However, using a large number of hosts simplifies the process greatly. Therefore, attackers have started using large numbers of compromised hosts to perform DDoS attacks. Figure 1-4 illustrates a basic DDoS attack.

All the computers, except the WWW server, represent hosts that have been compromised by the attacker. Computer 1 represents the controlling host or client. The attacker connects to the client to launch his DDoS attack. Although the figure shows only one client, there can actually be multiple clients associated with a single DDoS attack. The computers in the next tier, labeled with a 2, are known as handlers. A client can control multiple handlers. The computers at the final tier, labeled with a 3, are called agents. Each handler can control many agents. As you can see from the diagram, the agents can easily flood the WWW server with more traffic than it can handle.

---

4. www.PlanetIT.com, "Devastating DDoS Attacks Loom," September 2000.

Figure 1-4 *Distributed Denial of Service Attack*

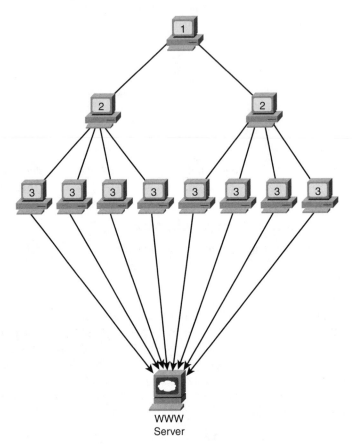

WWW
Server

Home computer users are migrating toward high-speed Internet connections such as cable modems and DSL. These connections are operational 24 hours a day. Attackers take advantage of this growing base of poorly protected hosts to establish agents for their DDoS attacks. Furthermore, it is difficult to track down the originator of the DDoS attack. Each tier obscures the path to the actual attacker who is launching the DDoS.

The targets of DDoS are multimillion-dollar, high-visibility Web sites. Recently, attackers have targeted Yahoo, Inc., eBay, Inc., Amazon.com, Inc., and Buy.com, Inc. Each of these sites maintains customer bases in the millions. The following are some DDoS tools:

- Stacheldraht
- Trinoo (or trin00)
- Tribe Flood Network

Unknown Participation in DDoS

During a distributed denial of service attack, an attacker uses numerous machines that he has already compromised. After compromising a system, the attacker installs a DDoS component (such as agents, handlers, and clients). A controlling program then launches a DDoS attack using these software components that are spread across numerous systems. The owners of these compromised machines usually do not even know that their machines have been compromised. Furthermore, when the attacker uses the compromised machines to conduct a DDoS, those owners of the machines are unwilling participants in the attack.

Summary

This chapter explained the need for network security. Your network is connected to the Internet along with 100 million other hosts. Protecting your resources is crucial to protecting your business. Attacks can be categorized as follows:

- Unstructured threats
- Structured threats
- External threats
- Internal threats

The following are key areas in which you need to direct your efforts for network security: authentication, authorization, confidentiality, integrity, and availability.

Network attacks result from a three-step process that involves defining the goals of the attack, collecting initial data, and then actually attacking the network. The attack itself can either be an attempt to gain access to your network or deny service to resources on your network. An increasingly popular DoS attack involves distributing the DoS over many machines, known as a distributed denial of service attack.

Regardless of the motivation or personal preferences, an attacker has several attack methodologies from which to choose:

- Ad hoc (random)
- Methodical
- Patient (slow)

Several points within your network are especially susceptible to attack, including the following:

- Network resources
- Network protocols

Attackers use numerous tools and techniques when attacking a network. These tools and techniques fall into the following categories:

- Reconnaissance tools
- Access tools and techniques
- Denial of service tools

The reconnaissance tools enable an attacker to collect information about your network. These tools might be generic system administrative tools or they might be highly customized scanners.

After collecting information on your network, the attacker attempts to gain access to your network using various tools and techniques. These tools focus on compromising weaknesses in your network. A prominent weakness on many networks is poor passwords. Therefore, password-cracking programs are usually effective at gaining access to your network.

Sometimes, an attacker is not interested in gaining access to your network. Instead, he wants to prevent you from using your network resources. This is when he uses his DoS tools. These tools disrupt your network resources in a variety of ways. One of the common DoS tools is a distributed attack that uses the resources on many hosts to attack a single target system.

Review Questions

The following questions test your retention of the material presented in this chapter. The answers to the Review Questions are in Appendix K, "Answers to Review Questions."

1 What are the four types of network security threats?

2 What are the three main attack types?

3 Why is network security needed?

4 What is a script kiddie?

_____

_____

_____

5 What is reconnaissance?

_____

_____

_____

6 What is a denial of service (DoS) attack?

_____

_____

_____

7 What are the five security principles that define the security on your network?

_____

_____

_____

8 What is the first step in a network attack?

_____

_____

_____

9 Attackers use what attack methodologies?

_____

_____

_____

10 What are common network attack points?

_____

_____

_____

## CHAPTER 2

Cisco Security Wheel

Completely securing your network is impossible, but even just securing your network to match your security policy can be a daunting task. Your network probably contains numerous security vulnerabilities. These security holes provide disgruntled employees and other attackers the openings necessary to gain unauthorized access to your network. Even well-secured networks require updating to address new vulnerabilities as they appear. Protecting your network is an ongoing process that involves securing, monitoring, testing, and continuous improvement.

Before you secure your network, you need to define what it means for your network to be secure. You accomplish this by establishing a thorough *security policy.* Your security policy represents the framework around which you construct all other security enhancements. It is composed of at least the following procedures:

- Login procedures
- User accounts and groups procedures
- Directory and file procedures
- Data protection procedures
- Secure transmission procedures
- Remote and mobile user procedures
- Virus control procedures
- E-mail procedures

From a high-level perspective, your security policy must address the following items:

- Identify the organization's security objectives
- Document the resources to be protected
- Identify the network infrastructure with current maps and inventories
- Identify the critical resources that need extra protection

The Cisco Security Wheel illustrates the ongoing process needed to maintain the security of your network after you have established your security policy (see Figure 2-1).

Figure 2-1 *Cisco Security Wheel*

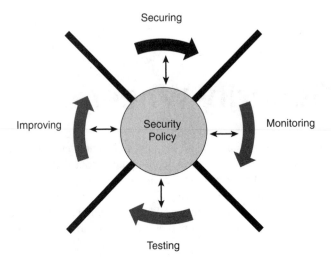

The Cisco Security Wheel breaks network security into four separate phases:

- Securing the network
- Monitoring network security
- Testing network security
- Improving network security

The phases are part of an ongoing cycle that continuously adjusts and strengthens the security of your network.

Securing the Network

To set the Cisco Security Wheel in motion on your network, you need to begin by securing your network. During this phase, you must protect the resources on the network from unauthorized access. Your security policy provides the framework outlining your security requirements, but trying to secure your entire network in one step is difficult. An easier approach is to break the task into smaller, more manageable pieces. You then can focus on hardening each of these pieces individually. Using this approach, securing your network can be broken down into the following workable categories:

- Tightening authentication
- Establishing security boundaries
- Providing confidentiality through Virtual Private Networks
- Vulnerability patching

Tightening Authentication

Attackers are constantly attempting to discover valid accounts on your network, along with their associated passwords. Therefore, limiting system access to only those users who need access is important. You can take specific steps to help facilitate stronger authentication:

- Define common privilege groups.
- Limit administrative access.
- Reduce anonymous access.
- Minimize trust relationships.
- Use one-time passwords.

Define Common Privilege Groups

Each resource on your network has access restrictions. You must give users who need access to these resources privileges. Defining the privileges needed on a per-user basis is a time-consuming task. A much more efficient method is to use common privilege groups.

Common privilege groups enable you to establish a set of privileges based on specific needs. Many times, these needs equate directly to specific jobs. Sample job categories include engineers, temporary employees, managers, and marketing personnel. Creating groups based on these categories enables you to easily define the privileges that each job requires. Instead of evaluating each new employee and determining his privileges on an individual basis (potentially having your singular decisions thwart your carefully defined authentication policies), you can instead add the employee to the correct group and he will have the privileges needed to perform his duties; that is, he will not have any privileges beyond what he needs to do his job.

Job classification makes an adequate classification scheme with respect to user functionality. You also must analyze your groups with respect to generic hierarchy based on overall network privileges. With the hierarchical approach, you begin by defining the most privileged user account all the way down to the least privileged account that has access to your system. The following list shows a sample hierarchical classification based on privileges:

- Domain Administrator(s)
- System Administrators
- Privileged Users
- Regular Users
- Anonymous and Guest Users

Using this hierarchical model, the most trusted account is the Domain Administrator. Anonymous and Guest Users receive the least amount of trust. If you apply this model correctly, the number of people in the most trusted categories (Domain and System

Administrators, for example) is minimal. The user distribution forms a pyramid, with the least privileged users filling out the base and the administrators representing a small portion of the total number of users at the top.

Limit Administrative Access

If everyone has unlimited access to your facility (keys, alarm codes, and so on), it is difficult for you to enforce security procedures. Furthermore, when a security incident happens, you cannot easily determine who was involved in the incident.

The same principles apply to your computer network. You need to minimize the number of users who have privileged access, especially administrative access. This serves two important functions. First, it reduces the number of highly privileged accounts that an attacker can potentially compromise. Second, it enables you to enforce your security policy more effectively. Security and ease of use tend to constantly compete against each other. If too many users have administrative privileges, they usually override your security policy in favor of ease of use.

Reduce Anonymous Access

You need to examine anonymous access closely. Because anonymous access does not require a password, anyone can use it to gain access to your network. Although conveniently allowing widespread access to system resources, anonymous access represents a prime initial target for attackers. Numerous attacks enable an attacker to elevate the privileges of anonymous access beyond the default allowed. Using these attacks, an attacker can quickly gain administrative privileges on your network (refer to Chapter 1, "Need for Network Security").

Minimize Trust Relationships

Trust relationships provide access to data or resources based on a host's identity, normally without further authentication. Although these trust relationships simplify usability, they also come with significant security concerns. Many trust relationships are built on weakly authenticated credentials (such as DNS names and IP addresses), allowing an attacker an excellent entry point into your network. In other situations, by compromising one host, an attacker gains access to data and resources through the defined trust relationships. It is best to minimize the number of trust relationships within your network.

Use One-Time Passwords

To ensure that only authorized users access the network systems, the use of one-time passwords is recommended. (Authorized users are those users who have been granted permission to access network resources to perform a specific task or function.) By using one-time passwords, even an attacker who has determined a user's account name and password cannot log in to the network resource because the password is used only once.

One-Time Passwords

Logging in to a network requires a username and a password. If someone discovers another person's username and password, he can log in to the network using that person's account. With one-time passwords, however, the user enters a pass phrase into a device that generates a password that is valid only once and only for a limited time. Therefore, if an attacker views the username and password, he cannot use them to gain access to the network.

Establishing Security Boundaries

Firewalls are designed to limit traffic flow on a network. Just as a physical firewall limits the spread of a fire, computer firewalls restrict network traffic flow to help enforce a predetermined security policy. Normally a company installs at least one firewall between the company's internal network and the Internet. When installing firewalls in your network, you have two tasks:

- Determine necessary traffic patterns.
- Define logical security zones.

Firewalls

A *firewall* is a security device that protects the perimeter of a network. All traffic destined for the protected network must pass through the firewall. The firewall examines each packet traveling through it against the security rules that you defined. Unauthorized traffic (for the protected network) is stopped at the firewall, and the firewall can generate security log entries to indicate security policy violations.

Determining Necessary Traffic Patterns

Your security policy needs to outline the specific network traffic that is allowed between segments in your network. Your Internet connection probably contains the most restrictions, but other segments in your network usually also have some traffic limitations. You can enforce these traffic restrictions by installing firewalls at key locations throughout your network.

You can think of these traffic restrictions like the locks on doors throughout your facility. Each employee has the ability to enter the building (but maybe only during business hours).

A limited number of people have access to development labs. Only a couple of people have access to the electrical closet. Finally, visitors must check in with the receptionist before they can enter the facility. Each of these locks restricts the flow of people throughout your facility.

Typically, you restrict traffic into your network from the Internet using a firewall. You will probably not allow any Internet hosts to directly establish connections to a host on your protected network. You might install a mail server on a partially protected network known as the DMZ because Internet hosts need to connect to your mail server to deliver e-mail to your users. The mail server then can relay mail messages to your internal network. If you are concerned about viruses entering your network, you can block e-mail traffic with attachments. Some organizations even restrict the Internet Web sites that their employees are allowed to access.

Other traffic restrictions that you need to consider involve business partners and remote access. Many times, you have business partners who require access to your network resources to do their job. This access, however, needs to be controlled and limited to the least amount of resources possible. Your employees also need to access your network from home and when they are traveling. Not allowing this access reduces productivity. Allowing it insecurely opens up your network to attack. You must examine each of these situations and establish traffic restrictions that enable your users to be productive while minimizing the risk to your network.

Defining Logical Security Zones

Firewalls establish security zones and boundaries within your network. All traffic entering a specific zone must pass through a firewall. The firewall examines all the traffic going to a protected network. It passes only the traffic that is allowed by its security rules. Furthermore, these security zones, established by your firewalls, create choke points within your network at which your security policy can easily be enforced.

Security Stance

When establishing your security policy rules, you need to adopt a basic security stance. This security stance defines how you view restrictions to traffic on your network. The two stances that you can choose from are *inclusive* and *exclusive*. With the inclusive model, you allow everything that is not explicitly denied by your security policy. The exclusive model takes the opposite stance. It denies everything that is not specifically allowed by your security policy.

With the inclusive approach, you gradually narrow the allowed traffic as you determine which traffic is harmful to your network. This approach is commonly used in university environments where many students require varied access to system resources.

The exclusive approach, however, starts by denying everything. After you determine that specific traffic is safe and needed, you add it to the allowed traffic in your security policy. This approach is typically employed in many business environments where the interest in protecting trade secrets overrides user convenience. Both approaches have their merits, and you need to carefully choose which approach best matches your organizational philosophy.

Providing Confidentiality Through Virtual Private Networks

Encryption provides confidentiality. Confidentiality and integrity are a must for sensitive traffic that needs to flow across an untrusted link, such as the Internet. You can utilize numerous approaches to incorporate confidentiality and integrity into your network traffic. One such approach is a *Virtual Private Network (VPN)*. VPNs provide an encrypted flow of traffic between two endpoints. An attacker who sniffs the network traffic between the endpoints of the VPN cannot gain significant reconnaissance because the encryption. Furthermore, the added integrity prevents an attacker from inserting bogus traffic and replaying captured traffic.

Establishing a VPN within your network is a two-step process:

- Define the untrusted link.
- Define endpoints.

Virtual Private Network

A VPN provides confidentiality and integrity for network traffic between hosts or networks using encryption. Each endpoint of the VPN encrypts traffic destined for the other endpoint. The traffic between the endpoints can traverse untrusted networks without fear of revealing information to someone who can view the data stream on the untrusted network.

Define Untrusted Links

Any sensitive information needs to be protected if it travels across an untrusted link. The most obvious untrusted link is the Internet. The flow of sensitive traffic within your network, however, also needs to be examined. Many times, multiple departments need to access a common network (such as a server network). Using VPN tunnels, you can restrict unauthorized access to sensitive traffic that must leave security zones within your network.

Define Endpoints

When it comes to defining endpoints, you can do so in one of two ways:

- Host-to-host encryption
- Site-to-site encryption

With host-to-host encryption, the network traffic is encrypted at the source host and decrypted at the destination host (see Figure 2-2). This provides the highest degree of protection because the data never appears on the network in clear text. The encryption process, however, can utilize a significant amount of CPU processing.

Figure 2-2 *Host-to-Host Encryption*

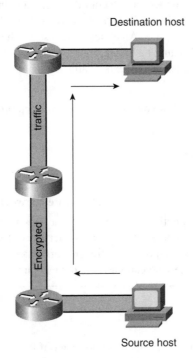

Site-to-site encryption employs VPN tunnels to encrypt all the traffic between two endpoints (see Figure 2-3). An endpoint, however, is usually a router or firewall. Individual hosts do not incur a performance penalty due to encryption. The main drawback is that the traffic is unprotected on the source and destination networks.

Figure 2-3   *Site-to-Site Encryption*

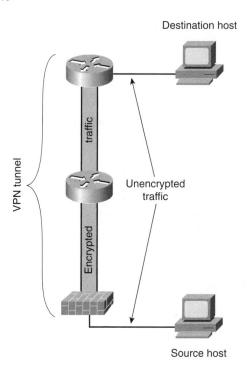

Vulnerability Patching

Vulnerability patching involves closing potential security holes that an attacker can use to gain access to systems on your network. One of the easiest ways to accomplish this task is by turning off unneeded services. Most operating systems turn on a default suite of services when they are first installed. Furthermore, these services are usually not secure, and many of these services are not even needed on every host. By removing the unused services, it is much more difficult for an attacker to find an entry point onto the system and, therefore, your network. An attacker frequently uses these unused services to execute denial of service attacks against your network. For those services that are needed, it is imperative that the latest security patches be applied to close security holes discovered with those services.

All reliable vendors maintain lists of security patches on their Web sites. You also can usually obtain security patches directly from their Web sites. Furthermore, many vendors have security mailing lists to which you can subscribe. These mailing lists send you e-mail notifications whenever a new security vulnerability is discovered. You can obtain operating system security patches from the following vendor Web sites, among others:

- Microsoft Windows at http://windowsupdate.microsoft.com
- Sun Microsystems at http://sunsolve.sun.com

- Red Hat Linux at www.redhat.com/apps/support/updates.html
- Mandrake at www.linux-mandrake.com/en/security
- Freebsd at ftp://ftp.freebsd.org/pub/freebsd
- Debian Linux at ftp://cgi.debian.org/www-master/debian.org/security
- Openbsd at http://www.openbsd.org/errata.html
- BSDI at ftp://ftp.bsdi.com/bsdi/patches
- Hewlett-Packard at http://us-support.external.hp.com

Security Vulnerabilities: The Never-Ending Battle

Patching security vulnerabilities on your network is a never-ending battle. Attackers discover new security vulnerabilities continuously. Each of these new vulnerabilities opens a hole in your previously secure network.

Monitoring Network Security

So far, you have established a security policy and secured your systems as best as possible. The next step is to monitor the network to identify violations of the security policy.

Detecting violations in your security policy involves monitoring hosts and network traffic to determine when violations occur. Your security policy defines a group of rules representing acceptable access to network resources. It also might define acceptable network protocols. You need to establish a procedure to continuously check your network to verify that your security policy is followed. Your security policy might even mandate such checking to verify that your network is not being attacked.

Usually this involves monitoring your network. Monitoring falls into two categories:

- Manual
- Automatic

Manual Monitoring

Manual monitoring is usually accomplished by utilizing the audit logging capabilities provided by the host operating system. These logs provide the system administrator with information, such as login failures, successful logins, and file access. To use these host-level audit facilities, the system administrator must first turn on the auditing. Then, he must routinely examine the logs to check for activity that violates the security policy.

Automatic Monitoring

Automatic monitoring involves watching network traffic to determine whether unauthorized activities are occurring on the network. This level of monitoring can be accomplished through the use of Cisco Secure IDS. Cisco Secure IDS can automatically monitor network traffic by providing alarms for intrusive traffic that it is designed to identify. Effective sensor deployment is crucial to enabling successful passive monitoring (see Chapter 5, "Cisco Secure IDS Sensor Deployment," for detailed sensor deployment details).

Testing Network Security

The third step in the Security Wheel involves proactively testing the network to confirm that the framework outlined in the security policy matches conditions implemented on your network. You also need to verify that known security vulnerabilities have been patched. This can be accomplished by running a network scanner against the hosts on the network to verify that all countermeasures have been installed correctly. You can test the current security posture of your network in two ways:

- Using security scanners
- Conducting professional security evaluations

Using Security Scanners

Attackers discover new security vulnerabilities daily. You need a mechanism to confirm whether specific vulnerabilities exist on your network. Manually checking each host is time-consuming and inefficient. Most system administrators use *network scanners* to facilitate checking for vulnerabilities on their networks.

Network Scanners

Tools that examine hosts on a network to locate security vulnerabilities are known as *network scanners*. They provide an efficient mechanism to check the security posture of your network on a regular basis. Attackers use similar tools to locate potential entry points into your network. By running network scanners against your network, you gain a picture of your network from the eyes of an attacker.

Some common free network scanners include the following:

- Nessus
- NMAP
- Spidermap
- SATAN (now SAINT)

Some common commercial network scanners include the following:

- Cisco Secure Scanner
- Internet Security Scanner
- Retina the Network Scanner

Conducting Professional Security Evaluations

The preceding section described how to use security-scanning tools to perform an in-house assessment of the security of your network. You can think of that step as brushing and flossing your teeth on a regular basis. Just as you go to the dentist once or twice a year, you need to obtain a professional security evaluation of your network at least once a year.

Professional security assessments involve security professionals examining your network security from the eyes of an attacker. These professionals essentially attempt to break into your network using the same tools that an attacker uses. After their evaluation, they provide you a detailed report outlining the security weaknesses that they discovered, along with ways in which to minimize those weaknesses.

You can think of professional security assessments as a reality check on your network security. You might think that your security is sound; until you confirm this through a third party, however, you might be giving yourself a false sense of security. It is much better to hear about your security holes during a professional security evaluation that you control than through an actual attack on your network.

Improving Network Security

The last step in the Security Wheel is to take the information gathered through monitoring and testing and improve the security of the network. Only by continually cycling though the Security Wheel will the security of your network remain at its peak. Remember, new vulnerabilities and risks are discovered daily. You also must keep current on the latest security events. To do so, do the following:

- Monitor security news.
- Periodically review configuration files.
- Evaluate sensor placement.
- Verify the security configuration.

Monitoring Security News

Monitoring security news on a regular basis informs you about new tools and exploits that attackers are discovering.

Attackers locate security vulnerabilities daily. Some discoveries impact a larger audience than others. Vulnerabilities in BIND (the most popular DNS program) affect an extremely large audience. Other vulnerabilities impact only a few organizations. Any vulnerability that impacts your network is significant to the security of your network. You can locate security information in numerous places. Two excellent resources are

- Security mailing lists
- Security Web sites

Security Mailing Lists

Several mailing lists provide a forum to disclose new security vulnerabilities and pose questions concerning security. By monitoring these mailing lists, you can learn about new exploits and harden you network against them. You also can learn workarounds to be used against new exploits until official patches come out. Some popular mailing lists and newsletters include the following:

- Bugtraq at `http`://www.securityfocus.com
- NTBugtraq at http://www.ntbugtraq.com/
- Security Portal's weekly newsletter at http://www.securityportal.com
- Security Focus newsletter at http://www.securityfocus.com
- Security Bytes newsletter at http://www.cisco.com/warp/public/779/largeent/ issues/security/sbytes/

Security Web Sites

Security Web sites, like security mailing lists, provide a collection point for security tools and information. Periodically reviewing these sites provides you with insight into the tools that attackers use against your network. You might want to use some of the tools to perform your own testing on your network. Some common security Web sites include the following:

- http://www.securityfocus.com
- http://www.freshmeat.net
- http://www.packetstorm.securify.com
- http://www.securityportal.com
- http://www.cisco.com/pcgi-bin/front.x/csec/csecHome.pl

Reviewing Configuration Files Periodically

The configuration files on your routers, firewalls, and other network devices enforce your security policy. Sometimes, changes are made to these configurations that break your security policy. Other times, the configuration is entered incorrectly. As long as these inadequate configurations remain in effect, your network is more vulnerable to attack. Periodic configuration file reviews enable you to locate these breaks in your policy and correct them.

Evaluating Sensor Placement

Correctly placed sensors generate a wealth of information about traffic on your network. In many instances, correctly placed sensors can help you confirm that traffic restrictions imposed by your security policy are actually enforced on your network. As your network grows, you might need to reevaluate the placement of sensors to ensure that they are positioned to provide you with best data possible. Another question that you need to consider is whether you have enough sensors deployed on your network to monitor it effectively. For a detailed analysis of Cisco Secure IDS sensor deployment, refer to Chapter 5.

Verifying the Security Configuration

Along with detecting security policy violations, it also is important to verify that the security configuration outlined in your security policy is implemented correctly.

Designing an excellent security policy does not help secure your network unless you correctly translate that policy into usable configuration files that accurately implement the policy. One way to accomplish this is to review the configuration files on the network devices, such as firewalls, to verify that the security configuration is correct. Depending on the placement of the sensors for the Cisco Secure IDS, you also can use Cisco Secure IDS to confirm that the security configuration is valid.

You can make a confirmation by placing an IDS sensor on the inside and outside of a firewall. If the security policy prohibits certain traffic from entering the network, the sensor inside the firewall can be configured to alarm if prohibited traffic is detected. Unlike periodic configuration file reviews, this technique provides immediate notification if the security configuration is invalid.

Summary

To secure your network, you must construct a security framework. This framework is defined by a security policy. Your security policy must

- Identify the organization's security objectives
- Document the resources to be protected
- Identify the network infrastructure with current maps and inventories
- Identify the critical resources that need extra protection

Using your security policy as a baseline, you need to secure your network. The Cisco Security Wheel outlines a process to continuously secure your network. The Security Wheel consists of four major phases:

- Securing your network
- Monitoring your network
- Testing your network
- Improving your network's security

First, you secure your network by addressing the following four areas of network security:

- Tightening authentication
- Establishing security boundaries
- Providing confidentiality
- Vulnerability patching

Monitoring your network is an important aspect of network security. Monitoring falls into two general categories:

- Manual
- Automatic

Testing the security of your network enables you to determine which vulnerabilities exist on your network. To locate security vulnerabilities on your network, you use a network scanner. A network scanner examines your network in much the same way that an attacker does when searching for weak points in your network. You can choose from numerous scanners, both commercial and free.

Finally, you must take the information that you learned from monitoring and testing to improve the security of your network. You also need to monitor security news sources regularly. Securing your network is not something that you can do one time and forget. It is a continuous process that keeps evolving as attackers uncover new vulnerabilities, your network topology changes, and your security requirements change. Besides staying current on the latest security news, you also must evaluate and improve your existing security configurations and components to verify that they are protecting your network at the level you want.

Review Questions

The following questions test your retention of the material presented in this chapter. The answers to the Review Questions are in Appendix K, "Answers to Review Questions."

1 What are the four steps in the Cisco Security Wheel?

2 What two types of monitoring are commonly used to detect violations in your security policy?

3 What software tool can you use to test the security of your network?

4 What are four areas that you need to examine to secure your network?

5 What is a firewall?

6 What two basic security concepts does a VPN provide?

7 Where are two places that you can monitor security news on the Web?

_____

_____

_____

Intrusion Detection and the CSIDS Environment

## CHAPTER 3

Intrusion Detection Systems

When you place a burglar alarm on the doors and windows of your home, you are installing an *intrusion detection system (IDS)* for your house. The IDSs used to protect your computer network operate in a similar fashion. An IDS is software and possibly hardware that detects attacks against your network. They detect intrusive activity that enters into your network. You can locate intrusive activity by examining network traffic, host logs, system calls, and other areas that signal an attack against your network.

Before deploying an IDS, you must understand the benefits that an IDS provides. Besides detecting attacks, most IDSs also provide some type of response to the attacks, such as resetting TCP connections.

Detecting attacks against your network (refer to Chapter 1, "Need for Network Security"), however, is primarily the goal of intrusion detection. Intrusive activity can be detected in many different ways. Therefore, people have designed various types of IDSs to solve the intrusion detection problem.

Although each type of IDS provides protection against intrusions, each approaches the problem from different perspectives. Each approach has its merits and drawbacks. By understanding how each type of IDS functions, you can make an informed decision as to which type of IDS is best suited for your business environment.

The kind of activity monitored depends on the type of IDS that you use. Each different type of IDS has its strengths and weaknesses. Nevertheless, you can evaluate every IDS by looking at the following:

- Triggers
- Monitoring locations
- Hybrid characteristics

IDS Triggers

The purpose of any IDS is to detect when an intruder attacks your network. Not every IDS, however, uses the same *triggering mechanisms* to generate intrusion alarms. Current IDSs use two major triggering mechanisms:

- Anomaly detection
- Misuse detection

Triggering Mechanisms

Triggering mechanisms refer to the action that causes the IDS to generate an alarm. The triggering mechanism for a home burglar alarm might be a window breaking. A network IDS might alarm if it sees a packet to a certain port with certain data in it. A host-based IDS might generate an alarm if a certain system call executes. Anything that can reliably signal an intrusion can be a triggering mechanism.

Anomaly Detection

Anomaly detection is also sometimes referred to as *profile-based detection*. With anomaly detection, you must build profiles for each user group on the system. Other systems might automatically build profiles for individual users. In either situation, this profile incorporates a typical user's habits, the services he normally uses, and so on. This profile defines an established baseline for the activities that a normal user routinely does to perform his job.

User Group

A *user group* represents a group of users who perform similar functions on the network. Sometimes, you can build user groups based on job classification, such as engineers, clerks, and so on. Other times, you might want to assign groups based on departments. How you assign the groups is not important, as long as the users in the group perform similar activities on the network.

Building and updating these profiles represent a significant portion of the work required to deploy an anomaly-based IDS. The quality of your profiles directly relates to how successful your IDS is at detecting attacks against your network. People have experimented with various techniques for constructing these user profiles. The most common approaches to build user profiles include the following:

- Statistical sampling
- Rule-based approach
- Neural networks

Each user-profile defines the normal pattern of activity for each user group on the system. Anytime a user deviates too far from her group's profile, the IDS generates an alarm.

Anomaly Detection with Statistical Sampling

If you use a statistical approach to profile creation, alarms are based on deviations from your defined normal state. In statistical terms, you measure deviation from normal by calculating the *standard deviation*. By varying the number of standard deviations required to generate an alarm, you can control the sensitivity of your IDS. This also can be used to roughly regulate the number of *false positives* that your IDS generates because small user deviations are less likely to generate false positives.

False Positive

An IDS generates alarms to signal when attacks are occurring on your network. When an alarm is generated because of normal user activity, the alarm is known as a *false positive*. False positives force you to waste valuable time and resources. Over time, these false positives can also desensitize your security personnel so that when a real alarm comes in, it is ignored or slowly processed. A good analogy is a home burglar alarm that goes off accidentally. Each time it goes off, the police respond. If you have too many false alarms, the police start charging you extra. Furthermore, after numerous false alarms, the police response time to your house diminishes significantly.

Standard deviation measures the deviation from the median or average of a data set. When your data is based on a well-defined distribution, each standard deviation defines a percentage of data that falls within it. For example, maybe 90 percent of all data falls within one standard deviation, 95 percent of the data falls within two standard deviations, and 98 percent of the data falls within three standard deviations. In this example, only 2 percent of the data falls outside three standard deviations from the mean. By using this process, you can define statistically how abnormal specific data is.

Anomaly Detection with the Rule-Based Approach

Instead of relying on statistical methods to define normalcy, your anomaly detection system can use rules to define normal user behavior. With these systems, you need to analyze the normal traffic for different users over a period of time and then create rules that model this behavior. Any other behavior then can be considered abnormal and generate an alarm. Creating the rules that define normal behavior can be a complicated task.

Anomaly Detection with Neural Networks

The final anomaly detection approach utilizes neural networks. Neural networks are a form of artificial intelligence in which you attempt to approximate the working of biological neurons, such as those found in the human brain. With these systems, you train them by presenting them with a large amount of data and rules about data relationships. This information is used to adjust the connection between the neurons. After the system is trained, network traffic is used as a stimulus to the neural network to determine whether the traffic is considered normal.

Issues

The user profiles form the heart of an anomaly-based IDS. Some systems use an initial training period that monitors the network for a predetermined period of time. This traffic then is used to create a user baseline. This baseline determines what normal traffic on the network looks like. The disadvantage with this approach is that if users' jobs change over time, they start generating false alarms.

Other systems keep continual statistics or constantly adjust to small deviations in user behavior. In this environment, the definition of normal continually adjusts to account for changes in user operating habits. The disadvantage with this approach is that a determined attacker can gradually train the system incrementally until his actual attack traffic appears as normal traffic on the network.

Benefits

Anomaly detection systems offer several overall advantages. First, they can easily detect many insider attacks or account theft. If a particular account belonging to an office clerk starts attempting network administration functions, for example, this probably triggers an alarm.

Another advantage is that an attacker is not quite sure what activity generates an alarm. With a signature-based IDS, an attacker can test which traffic generates alarms in a lab environment. By using this information, he can then craft tools that bypass the signature-based IDS. With the anomaly detection system, the attacker does not know the training data that has been used; therefore, he cannot assume any particular action will go undetected.

The main advantage of anomaly detection, however, is that the alarms are not based on signatures for specific, known attacks. (In this context, a signature is a set of rules that defines specific traffic that represents intrusive activity.) Instead, they are based on a profile that defines normal user activity. Therefore, an anomaly-based IDS can generate alarms for previously unpublished attacks, as long as the new attack deviates from normal user activity. Therefore, anomaly-based IDSs can detect new attacks the first time they are used.

Previously Unpublished Attacks

After attacks are published publicly, vendors can work on security patches, and signatures can be developed to detect the attack traffic by using a signature-based IDS. Before these attacks are released publicly, they are known as unknown attacks. Because anomaly detection does not look for specific traffic (just a deviation from normal), it can detect many previously unpublished attacks when they are initially used against your network.

Drawbacks

On the downside, anomaly detection has several drawbacks:

- High initial training time
- No protection of network during training
- Hard to define normal
- Must update user profiles as habits change
- False negatives if traffic appears normal
- Difficult to understand alarming
- Complicated and hard to understand

First, you must install your anomaly-based IDS and train it for a specified period of time, which can take weeks. You use this training to observe normal traffic on the network. Defining what constitutes normal traffic is not a simple task. Furthermore, during this training time, the IDS is not protecting your network.

Warning

During the initial training period, it is vital that no attacks or backdoors be present on the network. All the traffic occurring during training is establishing the patterns that represent normal user activity. If this includes intrusive activity, the intrusive activity becomes part of the defined user profile, and therefore becomes normal user activity.

Another problem is that people tend to vary their activities. They do not always follow the same exact patterns repeatedly. If the initial training period is inadequate, or your definition of normal is old and inaccurate, false positives are inevitable. When users deviate from the normal routine, the IDS generates an alarm if this activity falls too far away from normal. The IDS generates this alarm even though no intrusive activity actually takes place.

The definition of normal also changes over the life of your network. As your network changes, the traffic considered normal might also change. If this happens, you must update your user profiles to reflect those changes. For a network that changes constantly, updating user profiles can become a major challenge. Furthermore, if your user groups perform a diverse set of activities, it is extremely difficult for anything to stand out as abnormal.

A profile-based IDS can generate a *false negative* if the intrusive activity does not deviate from normal. Sometimes, intrusive activity can appear similar to normal user traffic. In these situations, it can be difficult or impossible for an anomaly-based IDS to distinguish this activity as intrusive and generate an alarm. This might be a significant problem if your user groups perform a varied set of activities.

False Negative

When an IDS fails to generate an alarm for known intrusive activity, it is called a *false negative*. False negatives represent actual attacks that the IDS missed even though it is programmed to detect the attack. Most IDS developers tend to design their systems to prevent false negatives. It is difficult, however, to totally eliminate false negatives. Furthermore, as you sensitize your system to report fewer false negatives, you tend to increase the number of false positives that get reported. It is a constant trade-off.

Unlike misused-based IDSs, anomaly-based IDSs do not have a direct correlation between alarms and potential attacks. When activity deviates from your established normal, your IDS generates an alarm. It is then up to your system administrator to determine what the alarm actually means.

The final drawback for an anomaly-based IDS is its complexity. It is not easy to explain how the system operates. With a signature-based IDS, if the system sees a specific sequence of data, it generates an alarm. With anomaly-based IDSs, however, you have complicated statistics or the information theory associated with neural networks. Users are uncomfortable when they do not understand their IDS completely. Furthermore, this lack of understanding reduces the user confidence in the IDS.

Misuse Detection

Misuse detection, also known as *signature-based detection*, looks for intrusive activity that matches specific signatures. These signatures are based on a set of rules that match typical patterns and exploits used by attackers to gain access to your network. Highly skilled network engineers research known attacks and vulnerabilities to develop the rules for each signature.

Building well-defined signatures reduces the chance of false positives while minimizing the chance of false negatives. A well-configured misuse-detection-based IDS generates minimal false positives. If a misuse-based IDS continually generates false positives, its overall effectiveness is diminished.

Benefits

Misuse detection provides numerous benefits. Some of the key benefits include the following:

- Signatures are based on known intrusive activity.
- Detected attacks are well defined.
- The system is easy to understand.
- Attacks are challenged immediately after installation.

Each misuse-based IDS detects a defined set of attack signatures. By using a misuse-based IDS, you can be confident that these defined intrusive attacks are detected. Network engineers continually develop new rules to create signatures based on new attacks. Furthermore, well-developed signatures generate minimal false positives.

With misuse-based IDSs, each attack in the signature database has a signature name and identification. A user can display all the signatures in the database and determine exactly which attacks the IDS needs to alarm on. By knowing the specific attacks in the signature database, the users have confidence in their IDS's capability to defend their networks. As new attacks come out, they also can verify that their IDS is updated to detect them.

Users understand the basic methodology behind a misuse-based IDS. Network engineers analyze real attacks and then develop signatures to detect this activity. A one-to-one correspondence exists between alarms and attacks. A user can generate attack traffic and observe a specific alarm.

Finally, a signature-based IDS starts defending a network immediately upon installation. Unlike an anomaly-based IDS, an initial training period is not required for misuse-based IDSs.

Drawbacks

Although misuse-based IDSs provide various benefits, they also have some drawbacks. The biggest disadvantages include the following:

- Maintaining state information (event horizon)
- Updating signature database
- Attacks that circumvent the IDS (false negatives)
- Inability to detect unknown attacks

To detect intrusion, a misuse-based IDS examines information and then compares it to signatures in its database. Sometimes, however, this information is spread across multiple data packets. When a signature requires multiple pieces of data, the IDS must maintain state information about a signature starting when its sees the first piece of data. This state information must be maintained for the duration of the *event horizon.*

To maintain state information, a misuse-based IDS requires storage. This storage is normally memory because of its quick retrieval speed. As the signature database grows, the amount of storage needed also increases. Furthermore, attackers might attempt to attack the IDS by filling its storage with carefully crafted attacks.

Event Horizon

To detect an attack, a signature-based IDS examines the data presented to it. Sometimes, many pieces of data are necessary to match an attack signature. The maximum amount of time over which an attack signature can be successfully detected (from initial data to the final data needed to complete the attack signature) is known as the *event horizon.* The IDS must maintain state information during this event horizon. The length of the event horizon varies. For some attacks, the event horizon is from user logon to user logoff; whereas for other attacks, such as a slow port scan, the event horizon can span weeks. The important point to understand is that your IDS cannot maintain the state information indefinitely; therefore, it uses the event horizon to limit the amount of time that it stores the state information.

Because the misuse-based IDS compares network traffic against known signatures in its database, attackers try to conceal their attacks. By making minor alterations to the attack data, they can sometimes slip the attack past the misuse-based IDS without generating an alarm, thus causing a false negative. The robustness of the signature definitions determines how successful a misuse-based IDS is at preventing false negatives.

As new attacks appear, the signature database used by the misuse-based IDS must be updated. Timely updating of the signature database is vital to a successful signature-based IDS. Currently, however, keeping signature databases updated is difficult.

The biggest drawback to a misuse-based IDS is its inability to detect previously unpublished attacks. This does not mean, however, that a signature-based IDS cannot detect any new attacks. When developers create new signatures, they try to make the signature as flexible as possible, while minimizing potential false positives. By using this technique, many signatures detect a class of attacks even though they are based on a specific exploit.

IDS Monitoring Locations

Now that you have a basic understanding of the intrusive activity that can generate alarms from your IDS, it is time to examine where an IDS watches for this intrusive traffic. IDSs typically monitor one of two locations:

- The host
- The network

Host-Based IDSs

Host-based IDSs check for intrusions by checking information at the host or operating system level. These IDSs examine many aspects of your host, such as system calls, audit logs, error messages, and so on. Figure 3-1 illustrates a typical host-based IDS deployment.

Figure 3-1   *Host-Based IDS Deployment*

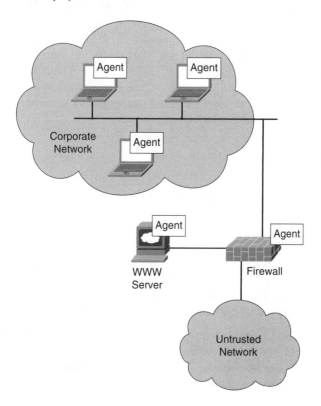

Benefits

Because a host-based IDS examines traffic after it reaches the target of the attack (assuming the host is the target), it has firsthand information on the success of the attack. With a network-based IDS, the alarms are generated on known intrusive activity, but only a host-based IDS can determine the actual success or failure of an attack.

Other items, such as fragment reassembly and *variable Time-To-Live (TTL) attacks* are difficult to detect using a network-based IDS. However, a host-based IDS can use the host's own IP stack to easily deal with these issues.

Variable Time-To-Live Attacks

All packets traveling across the network have a TTL value. Each router that handles the packet decreases the TTL value by one. If the TTL value reaches zero, the packet is discarded. An attacker can launch an attack that includes bogus packets with smaller TTL values than the packets that make up the real attack. If the network-based sensor sees all the packets, but the target host sees only the actual attack packets, the attacker has managed to distort the information that the sensor used, causing the sensor to potentially miss the attack. Figure 3-2 illustrates this attack. The fake packets start with a TTL of 3, whereas the real attack packets start with a TTL of 7. The sensor sees both sets of packets, but the target host sees only the real attack packets. Although this attack is possible, it is not easy to use in practice because it requires a detailed understanding of the network topology and location of IDS sensors.

Drawbacks

Host-based IDSs have a couple or drawbacks:

- Limited network view
- Must operate on every OS on the network

The first drawback to host-based IDSs is the limited network view with relation to attacks. Most host-based IDSs, for example, do not detect port scans against the host. Therefore, it is almost impossible for a host-based IDS to detect reconnaissance scans against your network. These scans represent a key indicator to more attacks against your network.

Another drawback to host-based IDSs is that the software must run on every host on the network. This represents a major development issue for heterogeneous networks composed of numerous OSs. Sometimes, a host-based IDS vendor might choose to support only certain OSs because of these support issues. If your host-based IDS software does not support all the OSs on your network, your network is not fully protected against intrusions.

Figure 3-2   *Variable Time-To-Live Attack*

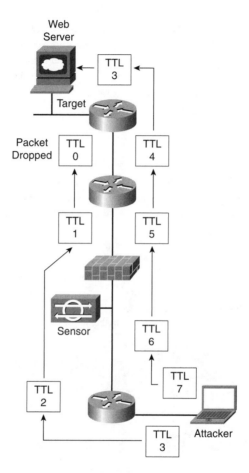

A final drawback is that when the host-based IDS detects an attack, it must communicate this information to some type of central management facility. An attack might take a host's network communication offline. This host then cannot communicate any information to the central management facility. Furthermore, the network traffic to the central management might make it the focal point of an attack.

Network-Based IDSs

A network-based IDS examines packets to locate attacks against the network. The IDS *sniffs* the network packets and compares the traffic against signatures for known intrusive activity.

Sniff

To *sniff* network packets means to examine all the packets that are traveling across the network. Normally, a host examines only packets addressed to it specifically, along with packets broadcast to all the hosts on the network. To be capable of seeing all the packets on the network, the IDS must place the network interface card (NIC) into Promiscuous mode. While in Promiscuous mode, the NIC examines all packets regardless of their destination address, including packets addressed to the network broadcast address.

Cisco Secure IDS is a network-based IDS. By using signatures, Cisco Secure IDS looks at every packet going through the network and generates alarms when intrusions are discovered. You can configure Cisco Secure IDS to exclude signatures and modify signature parameters to work optimally in your network environment. Figure 3-3 shows a typical Cisco Secure IDS deployment.

Figure 3-3   *Network-Based Cisco Secure IDS Deployment*

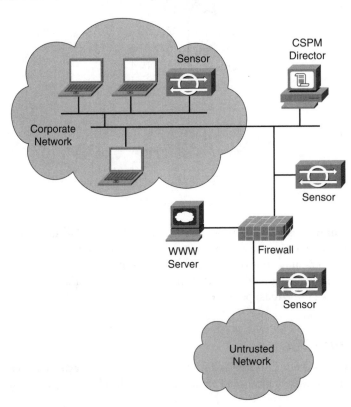

A network-based IDS, however, does not have to be signature-based. You can use anomaly detection in a network setting. The network-based label refers only to the location at which the IDS monitors the network traffic, not the triggering mechanism used to generate alarms.

Benefits

A network-based IDS has a couple of benefits:

- Overall network perspective
- Does not have to run on every OS on the network

By viewing traffic destined for multiple hosts, a sensor receives a network perspective in relation to the attacks against your network. If someone is scanning multiple hosts on your network, this information is readily apparent to the sensor.

Another advantage to a network-based IDS is that it does not need to run on every OS in the network. A network-based IDS runs on a limited number of sensors and Director platforms. These platforms can be picked to meet specific performance requirements. Besides being invisible on the network being monitored, these devices can easily be hardened to protect them from attack because they serve a specific purpose on the network. Cisco Secure IDS even supports a sensor that is a blade on the Catalyst 6000 family of switches (see Chapter 14, "Catalyst 6000 IDS Module Configuration").

Drawbacks

A network-based IDS faces a few problems, including the following:

- Bandwidth
- Fragment reassembly
- Encryption

The biggest drawback to network-based IDSs is bandwidth. As network pipes grow larger and larger, it is difficult to successfully monitor all the traffic going across the network at a single point in real time, without missing packets. Instead, you normally need to install more sensors throughout the network at locations where the sensors can handle the traffic volume.

Network packets have a maximum size. If a connection needs to send data that exceeds this maximum bound, the data must be sent in multiple packets. This is known as *fragmentation.* When the receiving host gets the fragmented packets, it must reassemble the data.

Not all hosts perform the reassembly process in the same order. Some OSs start with the last fragment and work toward the first. Others start at the first and work toward the last. The order does not matter if the fragments do not overlap. If they overlap, the results differ for each reassembly process.

To examine fragmented packets, a network sensor must also reassemble the fragments. The problem involves choosing the correct reassembly order. Attackers send attacks with overlapping fragments to try to circumvent network-based IDSs.

Another drawback to network-based IDSs comes from users attempting to protect the privacy of their data connections. As more users and networks provide encryption for user sessions, the usable information available to a network-based IDS sensor diminishes. When the network traffic is encrypted, the network sensor cannot match the encrypted data against its signature database.

Hybrid Characteristics

Hybrid systems combine the functionality from several different IDS categories to create a system that provides more functionality than a traditional IDS. Some hybrid systems might incorporate multiple triggering techniques, such as anomaly and misuse detection. Other hybrid IDSs might combine multiple monitoring locations, such as host-based and network-based monitoring. The major hurdle to constructing a hybrid IDS is getting the various components to operate in harmony, and presenting the information to the end user in a user-friendly manner.

Benefits

The benefits of a hybrid IDS depend mainly on the different IDS technologies that are combined. A combined host-based and network-based system, for example, provides the overall network visibility of a network-based IDS, as well as detailed host-level visibility. Combining anomaly detection with misuse detection can produce a signature-based IDS that can detect previously unknown attacks. Each hybrid system needs to be analyzed on its unique strengths.

Drawbacks

Normally, hybrid systems attempt to merge multiple diverse intrusion detection technologies. Combining these technologies can produce a stronger IDS. Getting these different technologies to work together in a single IDS can be difficult. Presenting the information from these multiple technologies to the end user in a coordinated fashion can also be a challenge. Again, each hybrid system needs to be examined to understand its strengths and weaknesses.

Summary

IDSs detect attacks against your network by generating alarms when they observe an intrusive activity. Although many different IDSs exist, they each support a triggering mechanism. The common triggering mechanisms are as follows:

- Anomaly detection
- Misuse detection

Anomaly detection is more complex than misuse detection, but it provides the capability to detect previously unpublished attacks. The downside is that alarms are not correlated with specific known attacks. An alarm represents a deviation from normal user activity and must be investigated by your system administrator.

Misuse detection can detect only the attacks for which it has signatures. End users know exactly which attacks trigger a signature-based IDS because the signatures are listed in the signature database. Providing updates to the signature database in response to new attacks, however, is a major challenge.

Both anomaly detection and misuse detection represent only potential ways to trigger intrusion alarms. In addition to IDS triggering, each IDS must also monitor your network at defined locations to obtain the data necessary for the triggering mechanisms to function. The two most common monitoring locations are the host and the network.

Host-based IDSs check for intrusive activity on the actual hosts on your network. This activity might be error logs, system calls, or so on. The main benefit of a host-based IDS is that it can determine the success of the attack because the IDS is on the actual host being attacked. Host-based IDSs, however, have the drawback that their software must operate on every host on the network. This can be complicated for networks with numerous different OSs.

Network-based IDSs watch for intrusive activity at specific points in the network by observing the packets on the wire. One or more sensors watch the network and generate alarms whenever they observe intrusive activity. The benefit of a network-based IDS is that it does not have to run on every host in the network. Because the IDS is examining network traffic only, the developer is free to choose the best sensor platforms.

The major drawbacks of a network-based IDS are as follows:

- Bandwidth
- Fragment reassembly
- Encryption

Sometimes, a developer combines multiple triggering mechanisms and monitoring locations into a single IDS. This new IDS is known as a hybrid. The main incentive behind developing hybrid systems is to increase the functionality of the IDS. A hybrid system might perform host-based and network-based monitoring. Another combination might combine anomaly detection with misuse detection. The hardest part of creating a successful hybrid system is to make the different functions work together in a user-friendly manner.

Review Questions

The following questions test your retention of the material presented in this chapter. The answers to the Review Questions are in Appendix K, "Answers to Review Questions."

1　What are the two major types of IDS monitoring?

_____

_____

_____

2　What are the two types of IDS triggering?

_____

_____

_____

3　What is the purpose of an IDS?

_____

_____

_____

4　What is anomaly detection?

_____

_____

_____

5　What is the major drawback to host-based IDS monitoring?

_____

_____

_____

6　What is misuse detection?

_____

_____

_____

7 What is a major benefit of anomaly detection?

_____

_____

_____

8 What are two major limitations of network-based IDSs?

_____

_____

_____

9 What is a hybrid IDS?

_____

_____

_____

10 What are some benefits to signature-based IDSs?

_____

_____

_____

11 What are the drawbacks to misuse detection?

_____

_____

_____

12 What are some drawbacks to anomaly detection?

_____

_____

_____

13 What is the difference between a false positive and a false negative?

_____

_____

_____

## CHAPTER 4

Cisco Secure IDS Overview

Cisco Secure IDS is a network-based intrusion detection system that uses a signature database to trigger intrusion alarms. The system is composed of sensors that perform the real-time monitoring of network packets and a Director platform that provides the management software used to configure, log, and display alarms generated by sensors. Cisco Secure IDS supports two Director platforms:

- Cisco Secure Policy Manager (CSPM)
- Cisco Secure IDS Director for UNIX

Cisco Secure IDS Sensors are available in two distinct platforms. The 4200 Series Sensors are network appliances that can be deployed throughout your network. (See Chapter 7, "4200 Series Sensor Installation Within CSPM.") The Intrusion Detection System Module (IDSM) for the Catalyst 6000 family of switches is a sensor that resides on a blade in your Catalyst 6000 family switch. (See Chapter 14, "Catalyst 6000 IDS Module Configuration.") A final IDS monitoring device is the Cisco IOS Firewall IDS. This platform enables you to change your router into an IDS monitoring device. (See Chapter 17, "Cisco IOS Firewall Intrusion Detection System.")

All Cisco Secure IDS Sensors have two interfaces:

- Monitoring
- Command and control

Sensors monitor network traffic for alarms in real time through the monitoring interface. All alarms are then transmitted through the command and control interface to the Director platform.

When Cisco Secure IDS analyzes network data, it looks for patterns of attacks. Patterns can be as simple as an attempt to access a specific port on a specific host, or as complex as sequences of operations directed at multiple hosts over an arbitrary period of time.

This chapter covers the following aspects of Cisco Secure IDS:

- System function and features
- Sensor platforms and modules
- Director platforms
- Cisco Secure IDS and the PostOffice protocol

System Function and Features

Cisco Secure IDS is network-based IDS that compares network traffic against known intrusive signatures to define network attacks. It is composed of two major components:

- Sensor
- Director platform

The Cisco Secure IDS communications infrastructure handles communication between these two components and represents another major aspect of Cisco Secure IDS.

The basic Cisco Secure IDS process is as follows (refer to Figure 4-1):

Step 1 A sensor captures network packets through its monitoring interface.

Step 2 Packets are reassembled, if required, and compared against a signature indicating typical intrusion activity.

Step 3 If an attack is detected, the sensor logs the attack and notifies the Director platform through the command and control interface.

Step 4 The Director platform displays the alarms, logs the data, and takes action on attacks detected by a sensor.

You can program your sensors to respond in various ways upon alarm detection. This response is configurable based on the severity of the attack discovered. The possible responses are as follows:

- TCP reset
- IP blocking
- IP logging

The TCP reset response essentially kills the current TCP connection from the attacker by sending a *TCP reset packet* (see Figure 4-2). This response is effective only for TCP-based connections. UDP traffic, for example, is unaffected by TCP reset packets.

Figure 4-1   *Basic Cisco Secure IDS Configuration*

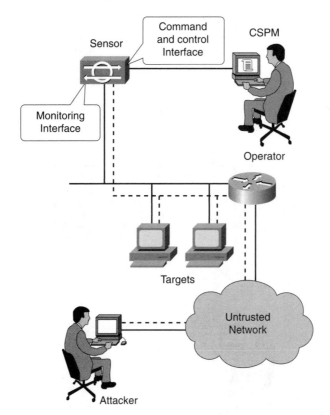

TCP Reset Packets

The Transmission Control Protocol (TCP) provides a connection-oriented communication mechanism. The connection is established through a three-way handshake. To terminate a connection, each side of the connection can send a FIN packet, signaling the end of the connection. It also is possible for one side of the connection to abruptly terminate the connection by sending a TCP reset packet (a packet with the RST flag set) to the other side. The sensor uses this approach to terminate an attacker TCP connection. For a detailed explanation of TCP/IP protocols, refer to *TCP/IP Illustrated Volume 1: The Protocols* (W. Richard Stevens, Addison-Wesley).

Figure 4-2   *TCP Reset Sensor Response*

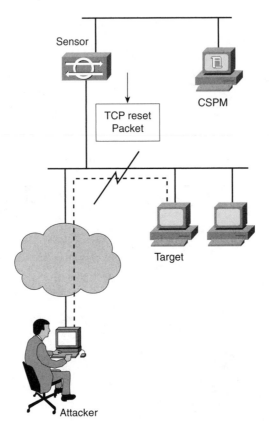

With the IP blocking option, the sensor updates the access control list (ACL) on the perimeter router to deny all traffic from the offending IP address (see Figure 4-3). This response prevents the attacker from sending any further traffic into the protected network from that specific host. (Refer to Chapter 13, "IP Blocking Configurations," for a detailed description on IP blocking.)

Note that if an attacker has multiple compromised hosts at his disposal, he can keep launching attacks from machines that have not been blocked yet. Furthermore, some attacks enable the attacker to spoof the source host from which he appears to be coming. Against this type of attack, the IP blocking option is ineffective because the attacker can always choose a new source address for his attack traffic. (Refer to Chapter 1, "Need for Network Security," for more information on different attack methods.)

Figure 4-3   *IP Blocking Response*

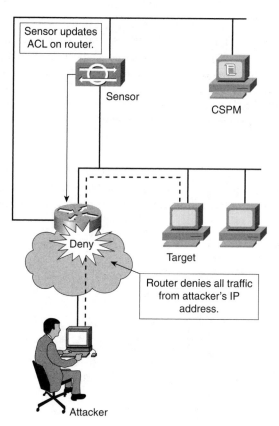

WARNING   Blocking requires careful review before it is deployed, whether as an automatic response or through operational guidelines for the operators. To implement blocking, the sensor dynamically reconfigures and reloads a Cisco IOS router's ACL. This type of automated response by the sensor needs to be configured only for attack signatures with a low probability of false-positive detection. In case of any suspicious activity that does not trigger automatic blocking, you can use the Director platform to block manually. Cisco Secure IDS can be configured to never block specific hosts or networks. This safety mechanism prevents denial of service (DoS) attacks against the Cisco Secure IDS and other infrastructure components.

Using IP Blocking as a DoS Attack Vehicle

An attacker has a couple of ways in which he can use your own IP blocking response to attack your network. First, he can launch an attack, pretending to be an important host on your network or one of your business partners' networks. When you detect the attack and invoke IP blocking, you generate a DoS against that host. If this host is critical to your network, the DoS significantly disrupts the operation of your network. Another DoS situation is when an attacker launches an attack from a multiuser machine. In this scenario, all users on that machine are blocked, not just the attacker.

The third response, IP logging, records in a session log file what the attacker is doing (see Figure 4-4). This option is passive and does not prevent the attacker from continuing his attack. The logged information provides a record of what the attacker does against the network.

Figure 4-4 *IP Logging Response*

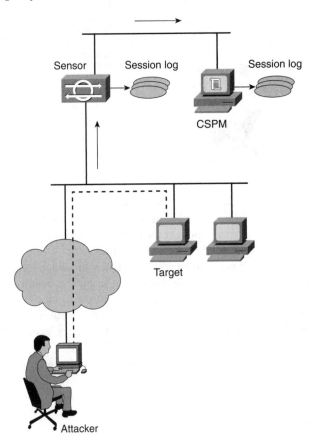

Sensor Platforms and Modules

The sensors form the workhorses of the Cisco Secure IDS. They constantly monitor network traffic looking for potential attacks. Each sensor checks network traffic looking for a match against one of the attack signatures in its signature database.

Each sensor utilizes two network interfaces. One of these two interfaces monitors network traffic; the other is a command and control interface. All communication with the Director platform occurs over the command and control interface. For further information on basic sensor configuration, refer to Chapter 11, "Sensor Configuration Within CSPM."

When network data triggers a signature, the sensor logs the event and sends an alarm notification to the Director platform. Besides notifying the Director platform, the sensor also has several response options. If the attacker is using a TCP connection, the sensor can send a TCP reset to the connection. To completely shut the attacker off from the network, the sensor can block the attacker's IP address by dynamically updating an ACL on a managed Cisco IOS router (IP blocking). The sensor also can log the IP session that triggered the signature. A final response is for an operator to manually block the host or network that generated the alarms. This manual action takes place on the Director platform.

All sensors are hardware appliances that are tuned for optimum performance. The hardware, including CPU and memory, for each appliance provides optimal IDS performance, while maintaining ease of maintenance. To protect the sensors, the appliance's host operating system must be configured securely. Known security vulnerabilities must be patched, and unneeded services removed.

This section covers the following topics:

- 4200 Series Sensors
- IDS module for the Catalyst 6000 family of switches

4200 Series Sensors

The 4200 Series Sensors come in two versions: the IDS-4230 and the IDS-4210. The IDS-4230 is the more powerful of the two sensors and is shown in Figure 4-5. Some of the features of the IDS-4230 are the following:

- **Performance:** 100 Mbps
- **Processor:** Dual Pentium III 600 MHz
- **Memory:** 512 MB
- **Monitoring NIC:** FE/SFDDI/DFDDI

Figure 4-5   *IDS-4230 Sensor*

The IDS-4210 is a more compact sensor (see Figure 4-6). With the smaller size comes a slimmed down feature set compared to the IDS-4230. The basic features of the IDS-4210 are the following:

- **Performance:** 45 Mbps
- **Processor:** Single Celeron 566 MHz
- **Memory:** 256 MB
- **Monitoring NIC:** Ethernet only

Figure 4-6   *IDS-4210 Sensor*

Table 4-1 highlights the differences between the 4200 Series Sensors.

Table 4-1   *Comparison of 4200 Series Sensors*

Sensor Characteristic	IDS-4230	IDS-4210
Performance	100 Mbps	45 Mbps
Processor	Dual Pentium III 600 MHz	Single Celeron 566 MHz
Memory	512 MB	256 MB
Monitoring network interface cards	10/100 Ethernet Single-attached FDDI Dual-attached FDDI	10/100 Ethernet
Chassis	4 U	1 U

For detailed information on installation of the 4200 Series Sensors, refer to Chapter 7.

IDS Module for the Catalyst 6000 Family of Switches

The IDS Module (IDSM) for the Catalyst 6000 family of switches is designed specifically to address switched environments by integrating IDS functionality directly into the switch. The IDSM receives traffic right off the switch backplane, thereby combining both switching and security functionality into the same chassis (see Figure 4-7).

Figure 4-7 *Catalyst 6000 IDS Module*

Similar to the 4200 Series Sensors, IDSM detects unauthorized activity on the network and sends alarms to the Director platform, detailing the event. This sensor resides directly in the switch, capturing data directly from the switch's backplane. Two methods of data capture are the following:

- Switch port analyzer (SPAN)
- Virtual LAN access control list

Using a SPAN port enables you to tell the switch to make copies of packets that are destined for certain ports on the switch. VLAN access control lists enable you to define more granular monitoring. This monitoring can be based on specific IP addresses and network services. Furthermore, the IDSM can monitor a full 100 Mbps without impacting switch performance. The monitoring is passive and inspects copies of the packets being monitored. The monitoring is not in the switch-forwarding path.

In addition, the same Director platforms that the 4200 Series Sensors use can monitor IDSM. You can deploy both the 4200 Series Sensors and IDSM on a single network to provide comprehensive coverage of critical subnets, as well as your entire enterprise network.

Some of the major features of IDSM are the following:

- Fully integrated line card
- Multi-VLAN visibility

- Full signature set
- Common configuration and monitoring
- 100 Mbps performance
- No switching performance impact

For detailed information on configuration of IDSM, refer to Chapter 14.

Director Platforms

You can deploy multiple 4200 Series Sensors and IDSMs on your network to provide complete IDS coverage. Manually monitoring the alarms on each of these sensors is inefficient. The Director platforms provide the management software necessary to configure, log, and display alarms generated by sensors efficiently. Furthermore, a single Director platform can consolidate all the alarms from multiple sensors into a single user-friendly interface.

In particular, this section examines the following:

- Director platform features
- Cisco Secure Policy Manager (CSPM) as a Director platform
- Cisco Secure Intrusion Detection Director
- Director platform feature comparison

Director Platform Features

The Director platform supplies a graphical user interface (GUI) through which you can manage your Cisco Secure IDS. The main features of the Director platform follow:

- Alarm display
- Alarm response
- Sensor configuration

Alarm Display

The GUI on the Director platform provides an excellent vehicle to view alarms generated by the various sensors throughout the network. Each alarm displays with a unique color based on the severity of the alarm. You can quickly view all the alarms that are occurring on your network at any time, as well as visually assess their potential damage.

You also can save alarm information in text log files on both the sensor and the Director platform. Logging enables you to easily archive the data, write custom scripts to extract alarm data specific to your site, and monitor attacks using command-line tools, such as the UNIX command **tail**.

UNIX tail Command

UNIX systems have a **tail** command, which enables you to display a specified number of lines at the end of a file. By adding the **–f** option to the **tail** command, you can continually watch the end of a file. This is especially useful when some program is continually adding data to a specific file. With **tail –f**, you can watch as data is added to the file. Starting with Cisco Secure IDS version 2.2.1.5, however, the log files are memory-mapped files. This prevents you from using **tail –f** to view these log files in real time.

Alarm Response

Many of the responses to alarms are configured to occur automatically upon detection of certain intrusive actions. The sensors handle these automatic responses. Sometimes, however, an operator wants to take action based on the alarms that she is viewing on the Director platform. In these situations, the operator can initiate a manual IP blocking response. This response can block a single IP address or entire network. The user initiates this manual response directly on the Director platform.

Remote Sensor Configuration

Both Director platforms enable you to centrally manage the configuration of all the remote sensors under their control. With the Cisco Secure IDS Director for UNIX, the Cisco Secure Configuration Management Utility (nrConfigure) enables you to save different remote sensor configurations and apply them as needed. The Cisco Secure Policy Manager (CSPM) supports remote sensor signature templates that can be shared between remote sensors. (Refer to Chapter 12, "Signature and Intrusion Detection Configuration," for more information on signature templates.) Furthermore, if you change a template, it is automatically applied to all remote sensors referencing it.

Cisco Secure Policy Manager as a Director Platform

Cisco Secure Policy Manager is a Windows NT 4.0-based application that provides scalable, comprehensive security policy management for the following:

- Cisco Secure PIX firewalls
- Cisco IOS routers with the IOS Firewall feature
- Cisco IOS routers with the Cisco Secure Integrated VPN software
- IDS sensors

An entire book can be written on CSPM alone. Staying within the scope of this book, however, this chapter addresses only the use of CSPM as a Director platform for Cisco Secure IDS, where it provides a centralized GUI for intrusion detection management across a distributed network.

CSPM enables you to remotely control all of your sensor configurations. You use the Add Sensor Wizard to define sensors in the *Network Topology tree (NTT)*, and you can use the panels on each sensor node to configure device-specific settings. In addition, you can define sensor signature templates and apply those templates to one or more sensors defined in the NTT. (For more information on signature templates, see Chapter 12.)

Network Topology Tree

CSPM must know the location of the objects on your network with which it must interact and communicate. The Network Topology tree is the vehicle with which you describe your physical network topology. The goal of the NTT is to define all the network objects for which you want to define a unique security policy. The extent to which you define your network topology depends on what you want CSPM to do. In your NTT, you define networks, gateways, and some hosts.

For alarm reporting, CSPM provides a GUI to view real-time alarms as the IDS sensors generate them. This real-time alarm view is accessible using the View Sensor Events option on the Tools menu of the GUI client. (For more information on alarm management, see Chapter 8, "Working with CSIDS Alarms in CSPM.")

For instructions on installing CSPM, see Chapter 6, "Cisco Secure Policy Manager Installation."

Cisco Secure Intrusion Detection Director

Cisco Secure IDS Director for UNIX is an HP OpenView application that runs on Solaris or HPUX, which, like CSPM, provides a centralized GUI for intrusion detection management across a distributed network.

It enables you to centrally manage the configuration of all the sensors reporting to it. The Cisco Secure IDS Configuration Management Utility (nrConfigure) allows different configurations to be saved and applied as needed, enabling you to maintain multiple versions of configurations for each device. You might want to establish one configuration to use during work hours and another for use after work hours. Many situations require the use of multiple configurations.

For alarm reporting, the Director for UNIX provides a GUI to view real-time alarms as they are generated by IDS sensors on an HP OpenView submap. (For instructions on installing the Director for UNIX, see Chapter 15.)

Director Platform Feature Comparison

CSPM and the Director for UNIX differ in many ways other than just the operating system on which they run. Table 4-2 shows a feature comparison of the two Director platforms.

Table 4-2   *Director Platform Feature Comparison*

Director Feature	CSPM	Director for UNIX
Severity levels	Low	1 through 5
	Medium	
	High	
Signature templates	Yes	No
Configuration versioning	No	Yes
Local logging	Database	Text file
Configuration versioning	No	Yes
Generate SNMP traps	No	Yes

Both Director platforms display the alarms generated by the sensors. Alarm severity in CSPM has three possible levels: Low, Medium, or High. With the Cisco Secure IDS Director for UNIX, alarm severity is a number between 1 and 5. A severity 1 alarm represents the lowest severity, whereas a severity 5 alarm represents the most severe alarm.

When you deploy multiple sensors on your network, you probably want to manage their configurations from your Director platform. With CSPM, you create signature templates for your sensors. These signature templates can be shared between sensors. Furthermore, if you change a template, it is automatically applied to all sensors referencing it. The Cisco Secure IDS Director for UNIX also enables you to save multiple complete configuration versions for the sensors that can be applied as needed through nrConfigure. (For more information on nrConfigure, see Chapter 16, "The Configuration Management Utility (nrConfigure).")

Each Director platform needs to save the alarms generated by your sensors. The logged alarms in CSPM are saved in a database and as text files in the Director for UNIX.

The Cisco Secure IDS Director for UNIX supports two final features that CSPM does not support:

- Configuration versioning
- Generating SNMP traps for alarms

Configuration versioning tracks multiple versions of each sensor configuration. Every time you change a configuration, the current configuration is saved as a previous version. Therefore, if necessary, you can easily roll back to any of these saved configuration versions. When the Cisco Secure IDS Director for UNIX receives alarms, it can also generate SNMP traps.

Cisco Secure IDS and the PostOffice Protocol

The Director platform and sensors must communicate with each other to relay alarms, configurations, messages, and so on. Cisco Secure IDS services communicate with each other by using the PostOffice protocol (not to be confused with e-mail, SMTP, or other mail delivery protocols). These services are the IDS software daemons that exist on the sensors and Director platform. The following are some of the major daemons:

- postofficed
- sapd
- loggerd
- fileXferd

NOTE   These daemons are explained in Appendix B, "Cisco Secure IDS Architecture."

The following sections examine the aspects of the Cisco Secure IDS communications infrastructure:

- PostOffice protocol
- PostOffice features
- PostOffice identifiers
- PostOffice addressing scheme

PostOffice Protocol

The proprietary PostOffice protocol provides a communication vehicle between your sensors and your Director platform. It uses the UDP transport on port 45000. The following types of messages are sent using the PostOffice protocol:

- Command
- Error
- Command log
- Alarm
- IP log
- Redirect
- Heartbeat

PostOffice Features

The PostOffice protocol provides a critical communication link between your Director platform and your IDS sensors. Being the primary method of communication, the PostOffice protocol must support certain necessary functionality:

- Reliability
- Redundancy
- Fault tolerance

Reliability

When a sensor generates an alarm, it transmits this information to the Director platform. The sensor needs to guarantee that the Director received the alarm information. The PostOffice protocol supports guaranteed delivery by requiring an acknowledgment for every message sent (see Figure 4-8). When the sensor sends a message to the Director, the Director must reply with an acknowledgment within a predetermined length of time. If the acknowledgment is not received, the sensor retransmits the message repeatedly until the acknowledgment is received.

Figure 4-8 *PostOffice Protocol Reliability*

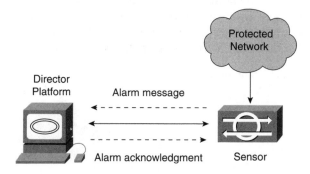

Redundancy

In many network topologies, you want a sensor to transmit alarm messages to multiple Directors. Notifying multiple Directors enables you to inform multiple personnel when sensors detect intrusive activity on your network. The PostOffice protocol enables sensors to propagate messages up to 255 destinations (see Figure 4-9). This feature allows for redundant alarm notifications, which ensures that the appropriate personnel are notified when an alarm is received.

Figure 4-9 *PostOffice Protocol Redundancy*

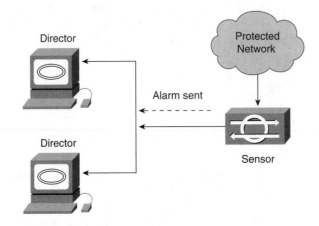

Fault Tolerance

With the PostOffice protocol, you can have up to 255 alternate IP addresses for a single host (see Figure 4-10). These alternate IP addresses represent different network interface cards (NICs) on your multihomed Director. The alternate routing protocol automatically switches to the next IP address on your Director whenever the current connection fails. It also uses a system watchdog to detect when a connection to the preferred IP address is reestablished, at which time the sensor reverts to the primary address.

Figure 4-10 *PostOffice Protocol Fault Tolerance*

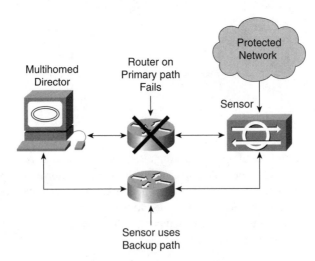

By placing multiple NICs into your Director, you make it a *multihomed system*. It can then receive traffic from multiple networks. By configuring the IP addresses for all the NICs into the PostOffice protocol, your sensors can contact your Director via any of the alternate IP addresses. The sensor uses these backup addresses, however, only if the primary address programmed into the sensor is inaccessible.

Using a multihomed Director increases the fault tolerance of your Cisco Secure IDS by increasing availability to the Director. However, using multiple NICs is not the only key to fault tolerance. To obtain the highest fault tolerance, you also need to ensure that multiple paths exist to the different NICs on your Director. Therefore, a single network failure is unlikely to prevent your sensor from communicating with your Director.

Multihomed Systems

Many machines have a single NIC. These machines can send and receive network traffic only through this one interface and are known as single-homed devices. To route traffic between different networks, routers usually have multiple NICs. (At a minimum, a router must have two NICs.) A router is a good example of a multihomed device. Sometimes, you want a regular system, such as a server, to also be multihomed for network accessibility. By placing multiple NICs on your server, you connect that system to multiple networks. Each of these NICs has a separate IP address for the network to which it is connected. Traffic that needs to reach your server can go to any of the IP addresses for the server. If a router fails on one network, users can still reach your server by using another path and network interface. By multihoming your Director, you gain the same fault tolerance by providing multiple paths between your sensors and your Director.

PostOffice Identifiers

You must assign each Cisco Secure IDS device a unique numeric identifier. This unique numeric identifier is a combination of host identification components and organization identification components. Associated with the host identifier is an alphanumeric host name. Similarly, associated with the organization identifier is an alphanumeric organization name. The following are the individual PostOffice identifiers. (See Figure 4-11 for an illustration of the main parameters used by the PostOffice protocol to identify Cisco Secure IDS components.)

- Host ID
- Organization ID
- Host name
- Organization name

Figure 4-11 *Cisco Secure IDS PostOffice Identifiers*

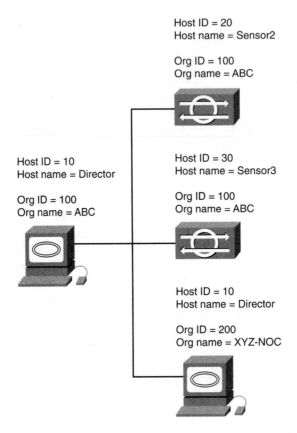

Host ID = 20
Host name = Sensor2

Org ID = 100
Org name = ABC

Host ID = 10
Host name = Director

Org ID = 100
Org name = ABC

Host ID = 30
Host name = Sensor3

Org ID = 100
Org name = ABC

Host ID = 10
Host name = Director

Org ID = 200
Org name = XYZ-NOC

Host ID

Each device with the same organization ID requires a unique host identifier (host ID). The host ID is a numeric value greater than zero for each Cisco Secure IDS device.

Organization ID

An organization identifier (organization ID) groups each collection of Cisco Secure IDS devices. The organization ID, like the host ID, is a numeric value greater than zero. It can be used to group a number of Cisco Secure IDS devices under the same number for easy identification purposes.

Host Name

Each Cisco Secure IDS device is labeled with an alphanumeric identifier. The name chosen is typically one that contains the word *sensor* or *director*, which enables you to easily identify the device type.

Organization Name

Each group of Cisco Secure IDS devices is associated with an alphanumeric identifier. The name chosen is typically one that describes the name of the company where the device is installed or the name of the department within the company where the device is installed.

PostOffice Addressing Scheme

Now that you understand the PostOffice identifiers, it is time to explain how these identifiers are used in the Cisco Secure IDS addressing scheme. This addressing scheme is composed of three components. The host and organization identifiers represent the first two components of the PostOffice proprietary addressing scheme. The third component of the addressing scheme is a unique application identifier. The PostOffice protocol uses all three of these unique identifiers to route command and control communications.

Figure 4-12 illustrates an example in which the sensor (20.100) is transmitting a PostOffice message to the Director platform (10.100). The packetd service on the sensor (application ID 10008) generates the alarm message destined for the smid service (application ID 10006) on the Director platform. When the Director receives the alarm message, the Director platform's postofficed service (application ID 10000) sends an acknowledgment (ACK) message to the postofficed service on the sensor (application ID 10000).

Figure 4-12 *PostOffice Addressing Parameters*

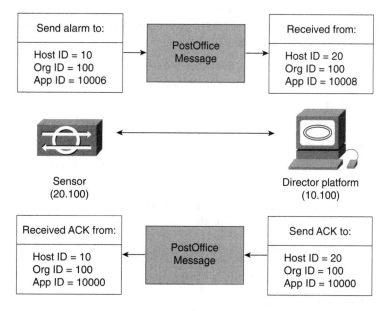

Summary

Cisco Secure IDS is a network-based intrusion detection system that uses a signature database to trigger intrusion alarms. Cisco Secure IDS is composed of the following two major components:

- Sensor platform
- Director platform

Interaction between these two components is accomplished via a communication infrastructure based on the proprietary PostOffice protocol.

Each Cisco Secure IDS Sensor has a monitoring interface and a command and control interface. Using the monitoring interface, the sensor compares network traffic against the signatures in its signature database. If unauthorized activity is detected, the sensor uses the command and control interface to inform the Director platform of the activity. Cisco Secure IDS supports two different sensor platforms:

- 4200 Series Sensors
- IDS Module for the Catalyst 6000 family of switches

The 4200 Series Sensors are PC appliances that can be placed at various locations through-out your network. The 4200 Series Sensors come in two varieties: IDS-4210 and IDS-4230.

IDSM is an actual integrated line card that operates directly on the Catalyst switch. It receives packets directly from the switch's backplane. The switch's performance is not impacted, however, because the IDSM operates on copies of the network packets. It is not located in the switch-forwarding path.

All of these sensors communicate with a Director platform that supplies a single GUI management interface for the end user. Cisco Secure IDS currently supports two Director platforms:

- Cisco Secure Policy Manager (CSPM)
- Cisco Secure Intrusion Detection Director

CSPM provides a management interface that supports many different Cisco products. IDS sensors are only one of these products. It runs on the Windows NT operating environment.

Cisco Secure IDS Director for UNIX uses HP OpenView to provide the GUI interface. The base operating system is Solaris or HPUX.

To communicate messages between the Director platform and the sensor platform, Cisco Secure IDS uses a proprietary protocol called the PostOffice protocol. This protocol pro-vides numerous necessary features, such as the following:

- Reliability
- Redundancy
- Fault tolerance

Review Questions

The following questions test your retention of the material presented in this chapter. The answers to the Review Questions are in Appendix K, "Answers to Review Questions."

1 What are the two main components of the Cisco Secure IDS?

_____

_____

_____

2 Is Cisco Secure IDS a network-based IDS?

_____

_____

_____

3 What is intrusion detection?

_____

_____

_____

4 What are the two Cisco Secure IDS Director platforms?

_____

_____

_____

5 What are the features of the PostOffice protocol?

_____

_____

_____

6 What is the IDS triggering mechanism used by Cisco Secure IDS?

_____

_____

_____

7 How many different types of sensor platforms are supported by Cisco Secure IDS?

_____

_____

_____

8 What are the two 4200 Series Sensors?

_____

_____

_____

9 What are the three types of responses that a sensor can perform in reply to an attack?

_____

_____

_____

10 How do Cisco Secure IDS devices communicate with each other?

_____

_____

_____

11 What three identifiers are used to construct a unique addressing scheme for Cisco Secure IDS?

_____

_____

_____

12 Can multiple systems share the same host ID?

_____

_____

_____

PART III

CSIDS Installation

## CHAPTER 5

Cisco Secure IDS Sensor Deployment

Being a network-based intrusion detection system (IDS), Cisco Secure IDS relies on one or more sensors to monitor network traffic at selected locations throughout your network. These sensors represent the eyes of Cisco Secure IDS. Therefore, deployment of the sensors is crucial to a successful Cisco Secure IDS installation.

NOTE   An individual sensor contains two separate network interfaces. The sensor uses one of these interfaces to passively *sniff* all the network packets by placing the interface in Promiscuous mode. When an interface "sniffs," it captures all the network packets that travel on the wire, not just the packets addressed to the system that do the sniffing. The sensor uses the other network interface for command and control traffic. To detect attacks, the sensor maintains a database of attack signatures. As packets traverse the network, the sensor examines each packet, attempting to match one of the signatures in its signature database. Whenever the network traffic matches one of the signatures, the sensor generates an alarm on its command and control interface.

In this chapter, you learn the following:

- To effectively deploy sensors in your network, you must analyze your network topology completely.

- After determining potential sensor installation points within your network, you need to decide how you want to configure those sensors. You can deploy each sensor in one of several different installation configurations, depending on the specific level of protection and capabilities needed.

Preparing for Deployment: Analyzing Your Network Topology

Attackers can launch exploits against any available resources on your network. Analyzing your network topology is crucial to defining all of your resources. Furthermore, deciding what information and resources you want to protect is the first step to creating a sensor deployment plan. Unless you understand your network topology thoroughly, you cannot comprehensively identify all the network resources that need protection. When examining your network topology, you must consider many factors:

- Entry points into your network
- Critical network components
- Remote networks
- Size and complexity of your network
- Security policy restrictions

Entry Points into Your Network

All the points where data enters your network represent potential locations at which an attacker can gain access to your network. You need to verify that each entry point is adequately monitored. Not monitoring an entry point into your network allows an attacker to penetrate your network undetected by your IDS. Common entry points into most networks include the following:

- Internet
- Extranets
- Intranets
- Remote access configurations

Internet Entry Points

Your network's Internet connection makes your network visible to the entire Internet. Hackers worldwide can attempt to gain access to your network through this entry point. With most corporate networks, access to the Internet is directed through a single router. This device is known as a *perimeter router.* By placing a sensor behind this device, you can monitor all traffic (including attacks) destined for your corporate network. If your network contains multiple perimeter routers, you might need to use multiple sensors, one to watch each Internet entry point into your network.

NOTE   As of January, 2001, current estimates project that 100 million hosts are connected to the Internet, with more than 350 million Internet users worldwide. Any of these users can potentially attack your network through your Internet connection. (The source of these numbers is "Study Finds 100 Million Internet Hosts" by John Rendleman, *InformationWeek,* January 10, 2001. http://www.techweb.com/wire/story/TWB20010110S0020.)

Extranet Entry Points

Many corporate networks have special connections to business partners' networks. Traffic from these business partners' networks does not always travel through your network's perimeter device; therefore, it is important to make sure that these entry points are also monitored effectively. By penetrating your business partners' networks, an attacker can use the extranet to infiltrate your network. You usually have little or no control over the security of your business partners' networks. Furthermore, if an attacker penetrates your network and then uses the extranet link to attack one of your business partners, you are faced with a potential liability issue.

Intranet Separation Points

Intranets represent internal divisions within your network. These divisions might be organizational or functional. Sometimes, different departments within your network require different security considerations, depending on the data and resources that they need to access or protect. Usually, these internal divisions are already separated by a firewall, signaling different security levels between the different networks. Other times, the network administrator uses access control lists (ACLs) on the router between network segments to enforce separate security zones. Placing a sensor between these networks (in front of the firewall or router) enables you to monitor the traffic between the separate security zones and verify compliance with your defined security policy.

Sometimes, you also might want to install a sensor between network segments that have complete access to each other. In this situation, you want the sensor to monitor the types of traffic between the different networks, even though by default you have not established any physical barriers to traffic flow. However, any attacks between the two networks are quickly detected.

Remote Access Entry Points

Most networks provide a means to access the network through a dial-up phone line. This access allows corporate users to access network functionality, such as e-mail, when away from the office. Although this enhanced functionality is useful, it also opens up another avenue for an attacker to exploit. You probably need to use a sensor to monitor the network traffic from your remote access server, just in case a hacker can defeat your remote access authentication mechanism.

Many remote users use home systems that connect continuously through high-speed Internet connections, such as cable modems. Because these systems are usually minimally protected, attackers frequently target and compromise these home systems, which might also lead to a compromise of your remote access mechanism. Other times, stolen laptops reveal a wealth of information on how to access your network. Therefore, even if you trust your users and remote access mechanisms, it is beneficial to monitor your remote access servers with IDS sensors.

Critical Network Components

Determining critical components on your network is vital to a comprehensive analysis of your network topology. A hacker usually views your critical network components as trophies. Compromising a critical component also poses a significant threat to the entire network. Critical components fall into several categories:

- Servers (DNS, HTTP, CA, NFS, and so on)
- Infrastructure (routers, switches, hubs, and so on)
- Security components (firewalls, IDS components, and so on)

Sensors need to be deployed throughout your network to ensure that attacks against these critical components can be detected, and in certain situations halted through blocking (also known as device management).

NOTE   *Blocking*, or *device management*, refers to the process whereby the IDS sensor can dynamically update the access control lists on a router to block current and future traffic coming to the router from an attacking host.

Servers

Network servers represent the workhorses in your network. Typical services provided by your servers include name resolution, authentication, e-mail, and corporate Web pages. Monitoring access to these valuable network components is vital to a comprehensive security policy.

Many servers exist on a typical network. Some of those servers are as follows:

- Domain Name System (DNS) servers
- Dynamic Host Configuration Protocol (DHCP) servers
- Hypertext Transfer Protocol (HTTP) servers
- Windows domain controllers
- Certificate Authority (CA) servers
- E-mail servers
- Network File System (NFS) servers

Infrastructure

The network infrastructure represents the devices that transfer data or packets between the hosts on the network. Common infrastructure devices include routers, switches, gateways, and hubs. Without these devices, the individual hosts on your network are isolated entities that are incapable of communicating with each other.

Routers transfer traffic between different network segments. When a router stops functioning, traffic flow between connected networks ceases. Your network is probably composed of several internal routers and one or more perimeter routers.

Switches transfer traffic between hosts located on the same network segment. Switches provide minimal security by sending nonbroadcast traffic to only specific ports on the switch. If a switch is disabled, it can cease to send traffic, resulting in a denial of service (DoS). In other situations, a switch can fail in an open state. In this open state, it sends all network packets to every port on the switch, essentially converting the switch into a hub.

NOTE   Hubs also transfer traffic between hosts located on the same network. Unlike switches, however, hubs pass all the traffic to every port on the switch. Not only does this generate performance problems, it also reduces the security of the network by enabling any host on the segment to watch the traffic going to other hosts on the network.

Security Components

Security components enhance the security of the network by limiting traffic flow and watching for attacks against the network. Common security devices include firewalls, IDS sensors, IDS management devices, and routers with access control lists.

Firewalls establish a security barrier between multiple networks. Normally, a firewall is installed to protect an internal network from unauthorized access. This makes them a prime target for attack.

Similarly, the IDS components continually monitor the network looking for signs of an attack. Hackers continually hunt for new methods to confuse and disrupt the operation of common intrusion detection systems. By disabling the intrusion detection system, an attacker can penetrate the network unseen (without raising the alarms that indicate an attack is in progress).

Remote Networks

Many networks are composed of a central corporate network and multiple remote offices that communicate with the corporate network through WANs. Security at these remote facilities needs to be considered in your network analysis. Depending on the security posture of the remote sites, you might want to place a sensor to monitor the traffic traveling across the WAN links. Sometimes, remote facilities have independent connections to the Internet. All Internet connections definitely need to be monitored.

Size and Complexity of Your Network

The more complex your network is, the more likely it is that you need to deploy multiple sensors at various locations throughout your network. A large network also usually dictates the use of multiple sensors because each sensor is limited by a maximum amount of traffic that it can monitor. If your Internet network connection is a multi-gigabit pipe, a single sensor cannot currently handle all the traffic that your fully loaded Internet connection can deliver to your network.

Considering Security Policy Restrictions

Sometimes, sensors are placed in your network to verify compliance with your defined security policy. An excellent example of this is placing a sensor on the inside and the outside of a firewall.

The sensors labeled Sensor 1 and Sensor 5 in Figure 5-1 illustrate this setup. Sensor 1 monitors all traffic that is headed to the protected network. It detects all the attacks sent toward the protected network, even though most of the attacks can be prevented by the firewall. Sensor 5, however, monitors all the internal traffic. This represents traffic that manages to make it through the firewall from the outside, as well as traffic generated by internal hosts. Both sensors can detect security policy violations. Sensor 5 monitors traffic that makes it into the protected network, whereas Sensor 1 monitors the traffic that leaves the protected network.

Figure 5-1   *Deploying Sensors at Common Functional Boundaries*

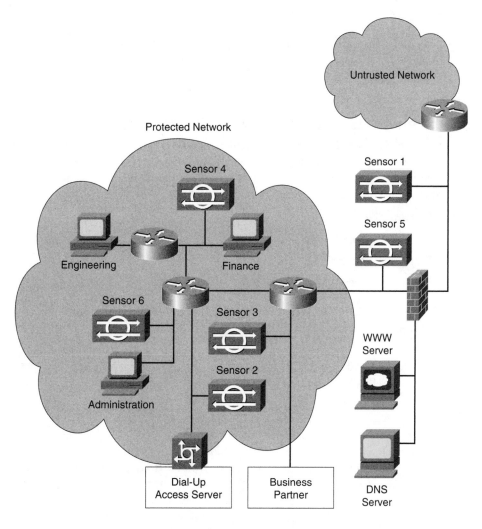

Executing the Deployment: Sensor Installation Considerations

Now that you have a thorough understanding of your network's resources and topology, it is time to start locating potential sensor placements within your network. Ideally, your network analysis has highlighted the areas that you think need sensors. If so, that is great. You can begin to decide the types of sensor configurations that you require. If you are still not sure about where to place the sensors, all is not lost.

Even though each network is unique, system administrators tend to gravitate toward several common sensor installation locations, over and over again, on almost all networks. These locations focus on some common functional boundaries. If you are unsure about where to place your sensors, examining the common functional boundaries in your network is an excellent place to start. After you understand those common functional boundaries, you can concentrate on installation configurations.

Sensor Placement Based on Network Functions

If you refer back to Figure 5-1, you see that it shows a sample network that illustrates the common functional boundaries where you can locate sensors to effectively monitor traffic entering your network, as well as traffic traveling between intranets within your network. Specifically, the network illustrates the following:

- Perimeter protection
- Extranet connections
- Intranet connections
- Remote access server connections

Perimeter Protection

Sensor 1 in Figure 5-1 monitors the perimeter of the network. All traffic traveling to and from the untrusted network is visible to this sensor. In most networks, the perimeter protection refers to the link between your network and the Internet.

NOTE   Be sure to locate all Internet connections to your network. Many times, administrators forget that remote sites contain Internet connections. Sometimes, departments within your network have their own Internet connection (separate from the corporate Internet connection). Any connection to the Internet needs to be properly monitored.

Connections to Business Partners (Extranets)

Sensor 3 in Figure 5-1 is positioned so that it can monitor the traffic traversing the link between your network and your business partner's network. This extranet link is only as strong as the security applied to both of the networks that it connects. If either network has weak security, the other network becomes vulnerable as well. Therefore, extranet connections need to be monitored. Because the IDS sensor monitoring this boundary can detect attacks in either direction, you might consider sharing the expense of this sensor with your business partner.

Intranet Connections

Sensor 4 in Figure 5-1 monitors traffic between the engineering network and the finance network. This is an example of a sensor monitoring traffic between separate network segments within your network. Many times, you use intranets to divide your network into functional areas, such as engineering, research, finance, and human resources. At other times, organizations drive the boundary definitions. Sometimes, both of these classifications define intranet boundaries.

In this example, the engineering network is separated from the finance network (and the router that separates the other networks) by its own router. For more protection, a firewall is also commonly used. In either situation, you can use a sensor to monitor the traffic between the networks and verify that the security configuration (for the firewall or router) is defined correctly. Traffic that violates the security configuration generates IDS alarms, which you can use as a signal to update the configuration of the firewall or router because it is enforcing the security policy.

Remote Access Server (Dial-Up Modem Lines)

Sensor 2 in Figure 5-1 monitors traffic coming from the dial-up access server. Numerous war-dialers are freely available on the Internet. Therefore, do not think that dial-up lines are safe by assuming a hacker cannot determine the phone numbers of your dial-up modems. Furthermore, many remote users use home computers that are continuously connected to the Internet through high-speed Internet connections. If an attacker compromises one of these home systems, it can easily lead to an attack through your remote access server.

Threats Posed by War-Dialers

A *war-dialer* is a tool that dials a specified range of phone numbers looking for modem connections. An attacker can start a war-dialer on her computer and let it run for days, attempting to locate potential modem connections. Later, the hacker attempts to connect to the phone numbers that are listed as modems from the output of her war-dialer program. If any of these modem connections has weak authentication mechanisms, the attacker easily infiltrates the network.

Installation Configurations

You understand your network topology and determined several locations at which to deploy Cisco Secure IDS Sensors. The next step is to decide on the type of sensor configurations to use at each location you identified. Several different installation configurations are common, each providing a different level of functionality:

- Standalone configuration
- Device management configuration

- Firewall sandwich configuration
- Remote sensor configuration

NOTE   After you understand the various installation configurations, you need to complete the "Cisco Secure Communications Deployment Worksheet" in Appendix I. This worksheet provides a convenient location to record the various communication parameters that you need to reference during the installation of your various Cisco Secure IDS components.

Standalone Configuration

Installing sensors without device management is also sometimes referred to as a *standalone configuration*. Figure 5-2 shows a simple Cisco Secure IDS installation that contains a single sensor that monitors the perimeter of the protected network.

Figure 5-2   *Standalone Sensor Installation*

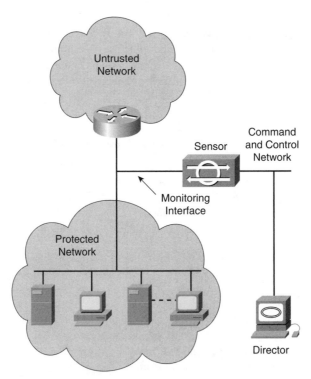

The sensor uses a separate command and control network connection to send alarms and other information, generated by the sensor, to a management console or Director. In this configuration, the sensor's reactive capacity is limited to the resetting of TCP connections and IP logging.

This configuration assumes that the amount of network traffic entering the protected network does not exceed the capacity of the sensor.

Device Management Configuration

The simple standalone installation enables the effective monitoring for attacks against the protected network, but it is limited to a mostly passive role. The sensor can reset TCP connections, but an attacker can still launch more attacks. Furthermore, not all attacks can be halted using TCP resets (such as UDP-based attacks).

Many customers want a more robust reaction capability. One common reactionary technique is for Cisco Secure IDS to automatically update the access control lists on a router in the network, based on the attacks detected by the sensor. By adjusting the access control lists on the router to drop all traffic from the attacker's host, future attacks are blocked as well from that specific IP address. Dynamically updating the access control lists in response to attacks on your network is known as IP blocking or device management. Figure 5-3 shows a sensor configuration that enables device management.

With the device management installation, the sensor monitors the incoming traffic for potential attacks. If an attack is detected (matching a signature that is configured for blocking), it can update the access control lists on the perimeter router to block traffic from the attacker's IP address for a specified period of time. So long as the attacker's IP address is blocked at the perimeter router, he cannot launch any more attacks against your network from that host.

For blocking to function correctly, you first must enable Telnet on the router. Second, you need to add the router to the sensor's device management list. For detailed instructions on setting up device management, refer to Chapter 13, "IP Blocking Configurations."

Command and Control Network Isolation

When deploying your Cisco Secure IDS, you need to minimize the hosts on your command and control network to reduce the ability of an attacker to directly attack your IDS components. Ideally, this command and control network needs to contain only IDS components, such as your Cisco Secure IDS Director and Cisco Secure IDS Sensors.

Figure 5-3   *Sensor Installation Using Device Management*

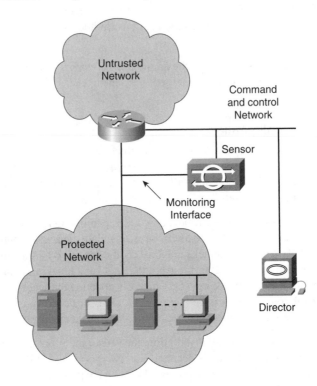

Firewall Sandwich Configuration

Network administrators use firewalls to limit traffic flow to and from a protected network or group of networks. Placing a sensor with the monitoring interface in front of the firewall and the command and control network behind the firewall is known as a *firewall sandwich* (see Figure 5-4). The firewall sandwich configuration uses the firewall to protect the command and control network for Cisco Secure IDS. This is the preferred installation for Cisco Secure IDS Sensors used in conjunction with a firewall.

NOTE   The command and control interface can connect directly into the network behind the firewall. In this configuration, however, internal users can potentially attack the Cisco Secure IDS. A more secure installation places the command and control interface on a separate interface behind the firewall (by using an isolated DMZ interface). The dotted network lines connecting to the inside of the firewall indicate these two options (see Figure 5-4).

Figure 5-4   *Firewall Sandwich Installation*

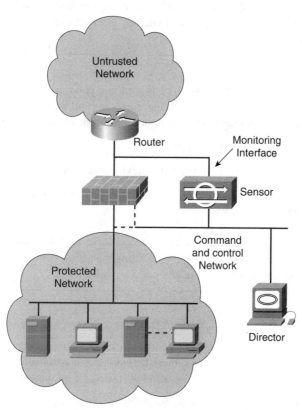

The deployment of a firewall indicates that the network administrator is concerned about the type of traffic that is allowed to enter the protected network(s) behind the firewall. It definitely makes sense, therefore, to deploy a sensor to monitor the traffic that is attempting to enter the protected network(s).

The firewall is effective at limiting traffic flow, but it does not monitor attacks as extensively. Although the firewall should stop the attacks against the protected network, the Cisco Secure IDS Sensor generates alarms for all the attacks that an attacker launches at your protected network.

Understanding the types of exploits that attackers launch at your network is crucial to continually enhancing your network's security. Furthermore, the Cisco Secure IDS Sensor can dynamically update the access control lists on the router to block future attacks (refer back to Figure 5-4). This setup provides device management on the router without requiring another interface on the router (refer back to Figure 5-3). Command traffic to update the access control lists traverses through the firewall to the router, while the firewall prevents unauthorized traffic from accessing your sensor.

NOTE   Appendix A, "Deploying Intrusion Detection: Case Studies," provides a detailed explanation of the steps necessary to deploy a sensor in a firewall sandwich sensor configuration.

When using the firewall sandwich configuration, you must allow certain traffic through the firewall and turn on certain features on the router and the sensor to enable device management. Enabling blocking in this configuration can be broken down into the following steps:

Step 1 Enable Telnet on the router.

Step 2 Add the router to the sensor's device management list.

Step 3 Permit the Telnet traffic (only from the sensor to the router) to pass through the firewall.

NOTE   Currently, the sensor is incapable of updating the access control lists on a PIX Firewall, but in the future this might become an option as well.

Remote Sensor Configuration

Sometimes, you need to deploy a sensor to monitor a network but the Director, or management interface, is located on a remote network that is reachable only through an untrusted network. Figure 5-5 shows a typical remote sensor deployment.

In a remote sensor configuration, the traffic traveling across the untrusted network (from the sensor to the director, and vice versa) *must be* encrypted. Without the confidentiality provided through the encryption, an attacker can potentially monitor and manipulate traffic between the sensor and the Director from the untrusted network. A simple way to enable encryption of the traffic is to define an IPSec tunnel across the untrusted network. In Figure 5-5, the IPSec tunnel runs from router to router. Using PIX Firewalls, you can establish the IPSec tunnel from firewall to firewall, or firewall to router.

IPSec

The *Internet Protocol Security Architecture (IPSec)* outlines a blueprint for performing security on the Internet at the IP layer. Basically, IPSec is a suite of protocols that define a mechanism whereby you can add confidentiality (via encryption) and integrity to your IP-based traffic. IPSec is the heart of VPNs and other software that requires both confidentiality and integrity.

Figure 5-5   *Remote Sensor Installation*

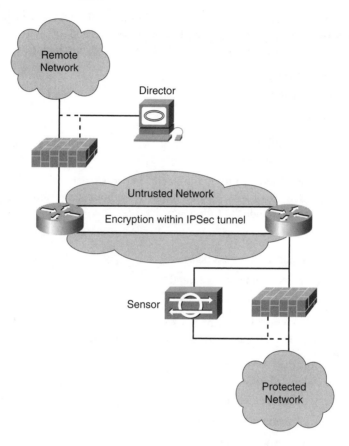

You need to perform several tasks to successfully set up a remote sensor. Some steps enable blocking, whereas other steps enable traffic to flow through the IPSec tunnel. The tasks include the following:

- Enable Telnet services on the router for the sensor.
- Add the router to the sensor's device management list.
- Configure the firewall to allow the following traffic:
    — Telnet traffic from the sensor to the router
    — UDP 45000 traffic from the sensor to the director
- Configure the IPSec tunnel on the routers.

Summary

Cisco Secure IDS relies on sensors to monitor network traffic at designated locations in your network. Understanding your network resources and topology is crucial to defining effective sensor locations. Key network factors to consider include the following:

- Network entry points
- Critical network components
- Remote networks
- Size and complexity of your network
- Restrictions imposed by your security policy

Across various Cisco Secure IDS-protected networks, network administrators locate Cisco Secure IDS Sensors at some common functional boundaries, repeatedly. These typical sensor locations include the following:

- At network entry points
- On extranets to business partners
- Between internal network boundaries
- In front of remote access servers

After deciding where in your network to locate your Cisco Secure IDS Sensors, you need to decide how to configure those sensors. Common sensor configurations include the following:

- Standalone configuration
- Device management configuration
- Firewall sandwich configuration
- Remote sensor configuration

Developing a sensor deployment plan is a major step in the overall Cisco Secure IDS installation process; and thoughtful placement of sensors is vital to the success of the Cisco Secure IDS installation.

Review Questions

The following questions test your retention of the material presented in this chapter. The answers to the Review Questions are in Appendix K, "Answers to Review Questions."

1 What are the common entry points into your network?

_____

_____

_____

2 When analyzing your network topology to determine sensor deployment, what are the main issues that you need to examine?

_____

_____

_____

3 What are some common network boundaries that you can monitor with your Cisco Secure IDS Sensors?

_____

_____

_____

4 What are the four common sensor deployment configurations?

_____

_____

_____

5 Where is your perimeter router typically located?

_____

_____

_____

6 What are intranets?

_____

_____

_____

7 What is IP blocking?

_____

_____

_____

8 What are some common servers that are frequently targeted by attackers?

_____

_____

_____

9 What is a firewall?

_____

_____

_____

10 In a firewall sandwich sensor configuration with device management, which features must you enable?

_____

_____

_____

11 When deploying Cisco Secure IDS Sensors remotely across an untrusted network, what security concepts do you need to employ to protect the traffic from attackers?

_____

_____

_____

12 What is a war-dialer?

_____

_____

_____

13 Why is it important to restrict the hosts on the command and control network to only Cisco Secure IDS components and a few infrastructure devices?

_____

_____

_____

## CHAPTER 6

Cisco Secure Policy Manager Installation

Cisco Secure Policy Manager (CSPM) is one of the two supported Director platforms for Cisco Secure IDS. Although CSPM manages a variety of Cisco security products, this book focuses only on using CSPM to manage Cisco Secure IDS Sensors.

To install CSPM, you must build a system that conforms to a set of hardware and software requirements. These requirements ensure optimal performance of CSPM, which uses Windows NT 4.0 as its base operating system. Running on the Windows NT 4.0 operating system, the installation of CSPM is a straightforward menu-driven process. You must know the type of CSPM installation you are installing, the account that accesses CSPM, and the basic Cisco Secure PostOffice parameters.

After installing CSPM, you can view some multimedia presentations to become familiar with CSPM. These presentations provide you with a series of lessons that introduce you to the various tasks that you must perform in CSPM.

This chapter breaks the process down into these discrete sections:

- CSPM overview
- CSPM installation requirements
- CSPM installation settings and options
- Starting CSPM

CSPM Overview

CSPM is a Windows NT 4.0-based application that provides scalable, comprehensive security policy management for the following:

- Cisco Secure PIX Firewalls
- Cisco IOS Firewalls with the Cisco Secure Integrated VPN Software
- Cisco Secure IDS Appliance Sensors
- IDSM for the Catalyst 6000 family of switches

It would take more than an entire book to explain all the functionality provided by CSPM. This book focuses on the management software CSPM uses to configure, log, and display alarms generated by Cisco Secure IDS Sensors. Signature templates, which enable you to manage the configurations of your Cisco Secure IDS Sensors, also are examined in thorough detail. To learn about any other features of CSPM, you need to refer to the CSPM documentation.

Your CSPM installation is defined by the following:

- Software feature sets
- Deployment configuration

Software Feature Sets

CSPM provides numerous software capabilities. It can collect audit records, update configuration files for managed devices, generate on-demand and scheduled reports, and so on. These capabilities are divided into the following feature sets:

- Policy Server
- Policy Administrator
- Policy Proxy
- Policy Proxy-Monitor
- Policy Monitor

Policy Server Feature Set

The Policy Server is a core feature set. In each deployment configuration, the Policy Server resides on a central system within your network. This feature set includes the Database subsystem that stores all system configuration data and audit records. The Policy Server feature set is composed of the following main components:

- **Database subsystem**—Stores all system configuration data and audit records
- **Reporting subsystem**—Generates on-demand and scheduled reports
- **Generation subsystem**—Compiles global policy into a set of device-specific policies and adjusts the addresses for NAT

When you install the Policy Server feature set, it also automatically installs the following feature sets:

- Policy Administrator
- Policy Proxy
- Policy Monitor

Policy Administrator Feature Set

The Policy Administrator feature set includes the graphical user interface (GUI), which provides the primary interface for policy definition, enforcement, and auditing for your CSPM system. You install this feature set on hosts used for remote administration only. Installation of the Policy Administrator feature set is explained in the CSPM documentation.

Policy Proxy Feature Set

The Policy Proxy feature set includes the Proxy subsystem necessary for mapping and translating your intermediate policy into a device-specific rule set required by the managed devices on your network. This feature set also includes a secondary database that maintains a local copy of the intermediate policies and stores the system events generated by the Proxy subsystem. This secondary database exchanges data with the primary database on the Policy Server host. The Policy Administrator feature set is also included when you install the Policy Proxy feature set.

Policy Monitor Feature Set

The Policy Monitor feature set includes the Monitoring subsystem responsible for collecting audit records from the managed devices and generating notification alerts regarding audit events. You define the conditions necessary to generate notification messages through e-mail, pager, or pop-up window. The Policy Monitor feature set includes its own secondary database. This database exchanges status and summary audit records with the primary database (located on the Policy Server host). The Policy Administrator feature set is installed in conjunction with the Policy Monitor feature set.

Policy Proxy-Monitor Feature Set

The Policy Proxy-Monitor feature set combines the functionality of the Proxy subsystem and the Monitoring subsystem. If your network resources are limited, you can use this feature set when building a distributed CSPM environment. The Policy Proxy-Monitor feature set includes a secondary database that exchanges status and summary audit records with the primary database on the Policy Server system. The Policy Administrator feature set is also included because it is installed in conjunction with the Policy Monitor feature set.

Deployment Configurations

You can install your CSPM in several different configurations:

- Standalone
- Client-Server
- Distributed

The main distinction between these different configurations is the way you distribute your feature sets and databases throughout your network.

NOTE   Currently, only the Standalone and Client-Server configurations are supported for Cisco Secure IDS. The distributed configuration introduces a complex problem of replicating alarm information between the multiple databases distributed across your network. Therefore, the distributed configuration is not currently supported for Cisco Secure IDS.

Standalone Configuration

With the Standalone configuration, you install the Policy Server feature set on a single host. This is the only feature set you need to install in this configuration. This host carries out all database, generation, proxy, monitoring, and reporting functionality. Local administration of CSPM also occurs on the standalone system.

NOTE   Although you only install the Policy Server feature set, this feature set also includes the Policy Administrator, Policy Proxy, and Policy Monitor feature sets.

Client-Server Configuration

With the Client-Server configuration, you also install the Policy Server on a single host (similar to the Standalone configuration). The Policy Administrator, however, is installed on one or more hosts throughout your network. This arrangement enables you to administer the Policy Server system locally or from any of the Policy Administrator hosts on your network.

Distributed Configuration

The final configuration also revolves around the installation of the Policy Server on a single host that serves as the focus point for the administration of your network. Other feature sets (Policy Proxy, Policy Proxy-Monitor, and Policy Monitor), however, can be installed on additional computers that serve as secondary and tertiary systems spread throughout your physical network. Each secondary and tertiary system supplies the monitoring and proxy functionality for a specific segment of your enterprise network. You also can distribute your Policy Administrators across various hosts to support remote administration.

Database Key

When building a distributed CSPM, you must always install the Policy Server feature set first. Installation of the Policy Server generates a database key. You must export this key and use it during the installation of the other feature sets.

CSPM Installation Requirements

CSPM is a set of software modules that need to be installed on one or more computer systems. To install these modules, you must build base computer systems that adhere to certain software and hardware requirements.

One last installation requirement—licensing—depends on the number of devices that your CSPM manages.

Software Requirements

CSPM has certain software requirements to operate efficiently. These requirements fall into two basic categories:

- Operating system
- Supporting applications

Operating System

CSPM needs to be installed on a disk partition formatted with the Windows NT File System, commonly known as NTFS. NTFS supports numerous security features that are not available on a standard *DOS FAT file system*. More specifically, you must install Windows NT 4.0 Service Pack 6a.

DOS FAT File System and Security

The FAT file system is a holdover from the original Disk Operating System (DOS). DOS was designed for a single-user environment. All the file security features are designed for this single-user environment. Therefore, it has no provisions for multiple users. File security is limited to simple passwords, compared to NTFS, which provides access control lists based on individual users as well as other features.

One final requirement is that you must install the TCP/IP protocol stack on your network interface card (NIC). Communication between CSPM and your Cisco Secure IDS Sensors uses TCP/IP protocols. Furthermore, you need to assign a static IP address to your CSPM machine, as opposed to using a dynamic address generated by DHCP. Without a static IP address, you cannot configure your Cisco Secure IDS Sensors to communicate with your CSPM host because one of the key identifiers used in the PostOffice protocol is the Director IP address (see Chapter 4, "Cisco Secure IDS Overview").

In summary, the basic operating system requirements for CSPM are as follows:

- NTFS disk partition
- Windows NT 4.0 operating system
- Windows NT 4.0 Service Pack 6a
- TCP/IP protocol stack
- DHCP disabled (recommended)

Supporting Applications

Other than the basic operating system components, CSPM also requires a few support applications:

- **Internet Explorer 5.x**—Internet Explorer 5.x displays the reports created by CSPM. CSPM provides you with two reporting formats: Hypertext Markup Language (HTML) and plain text.

- **TAPI/MAPI (optional for pager notifications)**—If you want to configure CSPM to generate pager notifications for specific events, you must enable the TAPI/MAPI interface. The Messaging Application Programming Interface (MAPI) provides the capability for CSPM to generate a notification to a pager through a modem on the system.

- **Cisco Secure VPN Client (optional)**—The Cisco Secure VPN Client enables a CSPM host to act as an IPSec tunnel endpoint for secure command distribution to an IPSec-enabled managed gateway device. If you want to use this client, you must install it before you install CSPM on your system.

TAPI/MAPI

The Telephony Application Programming Interface (TAPI) was developed jointly by Microsoft and Intel with input from a number of telephony companies. Microsoft released the initial version of TAPI in 1994. This interface enables Windows applications to share telephony devices with each other and provides a common means of handling different media (voice, data, fax, video, and so on) on a wide range of hardware platforms. Over the years, the interface expanded to provide increased functionality. Today, complementing TAPI is a powerful collection of other Windows APIs and software functions including the Messaging API (MAPI), the Speech API (SAPI), and Media Control Interface (MCI),

Communication, and Wave Audio functions. For more information on TAPI/MAPI, refer to Microsoft's communication Web site at http://www.microsoft.com/ntserver/commserv/default.asp.

Hardware Requirements

To ensure optimal performance, it is recommended that you install CSPM on hosts that meet specific minimum hardware requirements. For example, the Policy Server is a multithreaded application that benefits from multiple CPUs and a large amount of available memory on a single host, whereas enhancing the Policy Administrator host would not necessarily optimize GUI client performance.

Table 6-1 identifies the minimum hardware requirements for various CSPM systems.

Table 6-1 *Minimum Hardware Requirements for Various CSPM Installations*

Standalone and Server Installations	Client Installations
600 MHz Pentium III Processor	400 MHz Pentium II Processor
256 MB of RAM memory	96 MB of RAM memory
8 GB free hard drive space	2 GB free hard drive space
10 Mbps network interface card	10 Mbps network interface card
1024 × 768 video adapter card capable of at least 256 K color	1024 × 768 video adapter card capable of at least 256 K color
Sound card with external speakers (for tutorial videos)	Sound card with external speakers (for tutorial videos)
CD-ROM drive (preferably Autorun-enabled)	CD-ROM drive (preferably Autorun-enabled)
Modem (optional for pager notifications)	Modem (optional for pager notifications)
Mouse	Mouse
SVGA color monitor	SVGA color monitor

Licensing Options

CSPM uses a licensing scheme that enables you to align your purchasing goals with the size of your operational requirements. Essentially, the license you purchase determines the total number of supported devices you can manage. CSPM presently supports management of Cisco Secure PIX Firewalls, Cisco IOS VPN Routers, and Cisco Secure IDS Sensors.

Currently, Cisco provides two permanent licensing options for CSPM:

* Lite License (SEC-POL-MGR-LITE)
* Unlimited License (SEC-POL-MGR-2.0)

Another licensing option is a temporary Demo license. This option provides limited functionality and is provided only to allow you to examine the GUI provided by CSPM.

Lite License

The Lite License is SEC-POL-MGR-LITE. This version of CSPM can manage a maximum of three devices. These three devices can be a combination of any of the security devices that CSPM can manage. The software functionality provided is the same as that for the unlimited license.

Unlimited License

The Unlimited License is SEC-POL-MGR-2.0. You can manage an unlimited number of security devices (from the lists of devices that CSPM supports) by using this CSPM licensing option. If you have more than three security devices that you plan to manage with CSPM, this is the CSPM license you need to purchase.

CSPM Installation Settings and Options

When you install CSPM, you must complete the following general steps:

Step 1 Complete the Cisco Secure Communications Deployment Worksheet.

Step 2 Build a Windows NT 4.0 host.

Step 3 Define installation settings.

Step 4 Verify installation settings.

Step 5 Perform TechSmith Screen Capture Codec (TSCC) installation.

Step 6 Perform PostOffice installation.

Step 7 Finalize installation.

Step 8 Enable Telnet on the router.

Step 9 Add the router to the sensor's Device Management list.

The following sections discuss the first seven steps in detail.

Complete the Cisco Secure Communications Deployment Worksheet

During the installation of your Cisco Secure IDS components, you need to enter various PostOffice parameters. These parameters enable the Cisco Secure IDS components to communicate with each other. For this communication to occur successfully, however, the parameters on your Director must match the values that you configure on your sensors. Appendix I, "Cisco Secure Communications Deployment Worksheet," provides a Cisco Secure Communications Deployment worksheet. By completing this worksheet, you can outline all the PostOffice parameters that you use during the installation process in a single location. Then, during the installation of your Director and sensors, you have a handy reference to help you configure all of your PostOffice parameters.

Build a Windows NT 4.0 Host

After defining your PostOffice communications parameters for your deployment, you need to build your CSPM host by using the hardware and software specifications listed previously in this chapter. Next, you need to log on to your system with an account that has Administrator privileges. Finally, to start the auto-installation process, insert the CSPM CD-ROM into the CD drive on your computer.

NOTE   The NT account that you run the installation script from will also be the account that you use to access CSPM. Refer to the "Account Information" section later in this chapter for more information on choosing this account.

If you never installed the *Cisco Secure VPN Client* software on your system, you see a screen like the one shown in Figure 6-1.

Figure 6-1   *Cisco Secure VPN Client Message*

Cisco Secure VPN Client

If you plan to install the Cisco Secure VPN Client software on your CSPM system, you need to exit the CSPM installation at this point. The Cisco Secure VPN Client software needs to be installed before you install the CSPM software. The Cisco Secure VPN Client enables a CSPM host to act as an IPSec tunnel endpoint for secure command distribution to an IPSec-enabled managed gateway device.

If you do not plan to install the Cisco Secure VPN Client, you can continue with the CSPM installation.

Define Installation Settings

Next, you need to define various settings to be used during the installation of the software, including the following:

- License acceptance
- CSPM installation type
- Account information
- Basic settings

To begin entering these items, you need to click Install Product and then click the Next button (see Figure 6-2).

Figure 6-2   *Start CSPM Installation*

License Acceptance

Before you can start installing CSPM, you need to review the conditions stipulated by the license agreement. By using the scrollbars on the right side of the license agreement screen, you can read the entire license agreement (see Figure 6-3). To accept the license agreement and continue with the installation process, click the I accept the agreement button, and then click the Next button.

Figure 6-3 *License Acceptance*

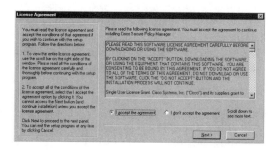

Besides accepting the basic license agreement for CSPM, you also must specify the location of your operational license that you purchased for CSPM.

Your permanent license determines the number of devices that you can manage with your CSPM environment. First, specify the disk location of the license file (see Figure 6-4). You can either type in the license file location or click the Browse button to locate the license file location. To prevent unauthorized use of your license file, it is also protected by a password. Enter the password just below the license file location (see Figure 6-4). This password is provided to you along with CSPM software. After specifying the license file and password, you can click the Next button to continue.

Figure 6-4 *CSPM License Disk*

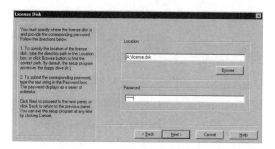

CSPM Installation Type

You can install CSPM in three different modes:

- Standalone installation
- Client-Server installation
- Distributed installation

NOTE	Currently, only the Standalone and Client-Server configurations are supported for Cisco Secure IDS. The Distributed configuration introduces a complex problem of replicating alarm information between the multiple databases distributed across your network. Therefore, the Distributed configuration is not currently supported for Cisco Secure IDS.

Each of these installation modes provides specific functionality to CSPM by spreading feature sets across various hosts throughout your network. With both the Client-Server and Distributed installations, the Policy Server feature set is installed on a primary host. Other feature sets are then installed on additional hosts as needed for remote administration. The Standalone installation places all the feature sets on a single host.

The following sections in this chapter explain the steps necessary to configure a Standalone CSPM installation to monitor your Cisco Secure IDS Sensors. First, select the Standalone CPSM installation option button (see Figure 6-5). By choosing the Standalone option, you specify that your CSPM operates from a single host.

Figure 6-5   *CSPM Installation Type*

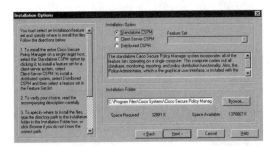

Client-Server Installation

You can also use the Client-Server installation to monitor your Cisco Secure IDS Sensors. The main advantage over the Standalone installation is that it enables you to spread the remote administration functionality across numerous hosts. For more information on establishing a Client-Server installation, refer to the CSPM documentation.

In addition to specifying the CSPM installation configuration, you also need to specify the disk folder where you want to install the CSPM files. The default location is C:\Program Files\Cisco Systems\Cisco Secure Policy Manager. If you want to change this location, type in an alternate directory path (see Figure 6-5). You can also click the Browse button to enter a different directory location. After you make your selections, click the Next button to proceed with the installation process.

Account Information

You must define an account to log on to CSPM (see Figure 6-6). When accessing CSPM, you log on using this account. This account is the Windows NT account that you used to run the installation program. You must provide the current password below your account name, which is already supplied for you.

You should create a specific account (other than the regular administrator account) to use to access CSPM. By creating a specific account for CSPM, you can help control access to CSPM (even from the normal Administrator account). Then, after installing CSPM, you can configure other accounts within CSPM itself that you can use to enable different people to access the software.

Figure 6-6 *CSPM Account Information*

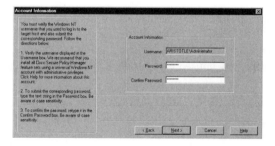

Basic Settings

Finally, you must enter a few basic settings (see Figure 6-7):

- Local IP address
- Service port
- Primary Policy database key export file

Figure 6-7 *CSPM Basic Settings*

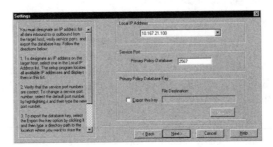

The local IP address specifies the location which all inbound and outbound traffic destined for your CSPM system uses. This field cannot be entered using the keyboard. You can select an IP address that corresponds only to a defined network interface card on your system. If the address shown is not correct, you can click the down arrow at the end of the Local IP Address field to pick another address.

The service port specifies the port that the Policy database listens on for communication requests. The IANA-assigned port number for database communications is 2567. To change the port number, delete the existing one in the Primary Policy Database field, and then enter the new unused port number.

NOTE   Altering the service port has no effect on IDS communications or operations. If you install CSPM strictly for IDS use, keep the default setting.

You also can export the Primary Policy Database key. You do not need to do this for the Standalone installation. You use this key in other installation configurations to install feature sets on hosts beside the Policy Server host. After entering all the basic settings, click the Next button to continue with the installation process.

Verify Installation Settings

At this point in the installation, you see the items you defined (see Figure 6-8). If these options are acceptable, click the Copy Files button to continue; you can click the Back button to alter the settings that you want to change.

Figure 6-8   *Verify Installation Settings*

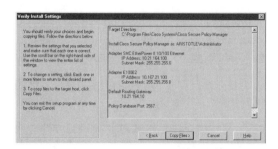

The Optional TechSmith Screen Capture Codec Installation

CSPM comes with several introductory videos on operating CSPM. To view these training aids, you must install the TechSmith Screen Capture Codec on your system (see Figure 6-9). This decompression software is required if you plan to use these "Getting Started" videos (refer to the "Getting Started Videos" section later in this chapter). To install the TechSmith software, click the Install button. If you do not plan to view these multimedia presentations, you can skip the installation of this software by clicking the Cancel button.

Figure 6-9   *TechSmith Screen Capture Codec Installation*

NOTE   If you skip the installation of the TechSmith software, you can always view the videos by running the videoex.exe program separately. Furthermore, when you access the Wizards, Getting Started menu option from the main CSPM screen, you need to insert your CSPM installation CD in your CD drive.

The PostOffice Installation

At this point, the installation process initiates a separate process to install Cisco Secure PostOffice if it is not already installed on your system (see Figure 6-10). The Cisco Secure PostOffice protocol is required for your Cisco Secure IDS components to communicate with each other. The installation occurs in four stages, as discussed in the following sections.

Figure 6-10 *Cisco Secure PostOffice Installation*

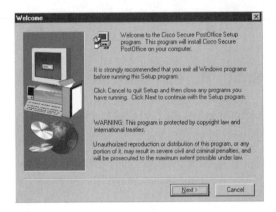

License Acceptance

Like CSPM, Cisco Secure PostOffice has a general license agreement. You need to review the conditions of the license by using the scroll bars on the right of the screen to move through the entire agreement (see Figure 6-11). Click the Yes button to continue with the Cisco Secure PostOffice installation.

Figure 6-11 *Cisco Secure PostOffice License Agreement*

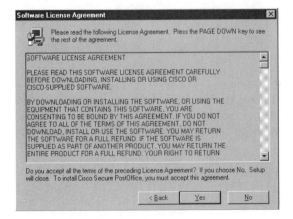

User Information

To complete the User Information screen, you need to enter your name and company name (see Figure 6-12). After entering your name and company name, click the Next button to proceed with the PostOffice installation.

Figure 6-12 *Cisco Secure PostOffice User Information*

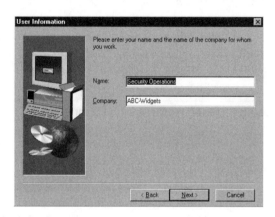

Cisco Secure PostOffice Install Location

You must enter the directory location where you want to install Cisco Secure PostOffice. If you want to change the default location, click the Browse button and select an alternative folder (see Figure 6-13). Otherwise, just click the Next button to continue with the installation process.

Figure 6-13 *Cisco Secure PostOffice Install Location*

NOTE	The default folder for Cisco Secure PostOffice is C:\Program Files\Cisco Systems\Cisco Secure PostOffice.

Configure Communication Properties

The communication parameters are crucial to the correct operation of the Cisco Secure PostOffice protocol. The communication properties you define are used to define the PostOffice identification for this host (see Table 6-2). These values should be listed in the worksheet you fill out in Appendix I.

Table 6-2   *Cisco Secure PostOffice Communication Parameters*

PostOffice Setting	Parameters	Description
Host ID	(1–65536)	Numeric identifier identifying CSPM.
Organization ID	(1–65536)	Numeric identifier that further identifies CSPM, which can be used to group a number of Cisco Secure IDS devices under the same number for easy identification purposes.
IP Address	<IP address>	IP address of CSPM host.
Host Name	<host name>	Alphanumeric identifier for your Director (for example, director0). The name chosen here is typically one that contains the word *director* so that you can easily identify that it is a Director.
Organization Name	<organization name>	Alphanumeric identifier that further identifies CSPM (for example, ABC-Widgets). It can be used to group a number of Cisco Secure IDS devices under the same name for easy identification purposes.

After entering the PostOffice parameters, click the Next button to start copying the PostOffice installation files. After the files are copied, the PostOffice Setup Complete window opens (see Figure 6-14).

Finalize Installation Programs

Click the Finish button to finalize the PostOffice installation. The installation program for CSPM continues and the setup program copies all files to the specified installation folder and creates the necessary Registry keys. During this installation process, you see a screen similar to Figure 6-15.

Figure 6-14 *PostOffice Setup Complete*

Figure 6-15 *CSPM Installation Progress*

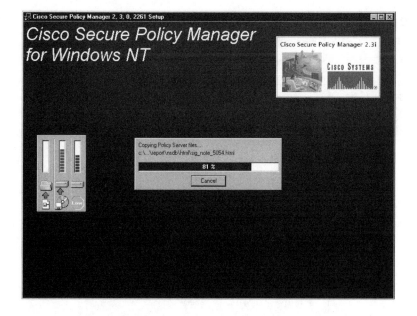

After the installation process finishes copying the files and performing all the installation requirements, the CSPM Setup Complete window opens (see Figure 6-16). CSPM is now installed on the host. Click the Finish button to finalize the CSPM installation.

Figure 6-16 *CSPM Setup Complete*

Starting CSPM

Now that you have installed your CSPM, it is time to run it. After launching CSPM, you need to log on. When inside CSPM, it displays a Getting Started pop-up window where you can learn about the operation of the CSPM software.

CSPM Logon

To start CSPM, choose Start, Programs, Cisco Systems, Cisco Secure Policy Manager, Cisco Secure Policy Manager.

This will launch CSPM, bringing up the Cisco Secure Policy Manager logon window (see Figure 6-17). At this screen, you need to enter the username and password of the privileged account that you specified during the installation process. Then click the Connect button or press the Enter key to enter CSPM.

Figure 6-17 *CSPM Logon*

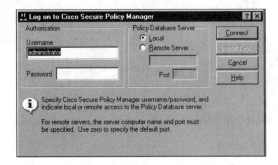

NOTE   The Local or Remote Server option buttons (see Figure 6-18) within the Policy Database
Server group box are used based on the initial CSPM installation option. If you install
CSPM in Standalone mode, always use the Local Server option. In the Client-Server
configuration, use the Remote Server option when connecting to your CSPM host from
your remote administration host.

Getting Started Videos

In addition to reading through the online help and printed documentation, you can learn
important concepts about CSPM by viewing the "Getting Started" videos. These videos
consist of a series of lessons that introduce you to the high-level tasks that you must
perform in CSPM.

These videos are included on the CSPM CD-ROM. If you downloaded the CSPM software,
you need to install the TechSmith Compression Codec (TSCC) by running the program
videoex.exe. This program is included with the software that you can download.

TechSmith Compression Codec (TSCC)

TechSmith has created a proprietary compression code called Camtasia. The "Getting
Started" videos are encoded with Camtasia. Therefore, before you can view the videos, you
must install TechSmith's Camtasia on your computer. This is just another step during the
installation process when installing from the CSPM CD-ROM. If you download the CSPM
software, you must install Camtasia manually by running the videoex.exe program
separately.

After logging on to CSPM, you see a Getting Started pop-up window (see Figure 6-18).
This window provides you with several options to become familiar with CSPM. You can
review the latest release notes and work through a tutorial. Finally, you can view some
multimedia presentations that explain how to configure CSPM.

NOTE   When you initially start CSPM, you might not see the CSPM Getting Started pop-up
window. Instead, you might see a window similar to Figure 6-19. This happens if you
installed from the CSPM CD-ROM and the CD-ROM is not in the drive. You can insert the
CSPM CD-ROM into the drive and select the CD-ROM drive from the Folder drop-down
menu. You can also copy the files from the root directory of the CSPM CD-ROM to a folder
on your hard disk. Then you can select this folder as the location of the installation
CD-ROM image (see Figure 6-19).

Figure 6-18 *CSPM Getting Started*

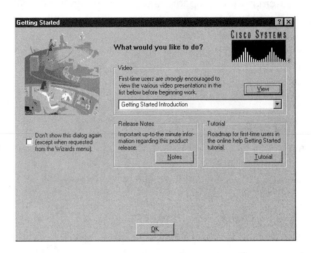

Figure 6-19 *Locate Installation CD-ROM Image*

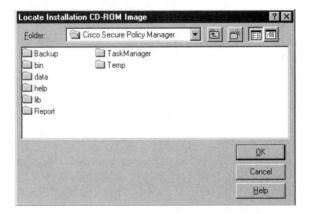

To view a "Getting Started" lesson, select that lesson from the drop-down list and click View (refer back to Figure 6-18). Your default AVI player (commonly, Windows Media Player) opens and plays the video.

NOTE   The Getting Started pop-up window appears every time that you enter CSPM. You can click the OK button to dismiss the window and start using CSPM. Performing this step every time you initiate CSPM can become annoying. Therefore, if you no longer want to see the Getting Started pop-up window, click the Don't show this dialog again (except when requested from the Wizards menu) check box at the left side of the window. This prevents the Getting Started pop-up window from appearing when you start CSPM. You can still view the Getting Started pop-up window at any time by accessing it from the Wizards pull-down menu.

Summary

CSPM manages a wide variety of security devices. You can establish an enterprisewide security policy and audit that policy from CSPM. CSPM is composed of the following software feature sets:

- Policy Server
- Policy Administrator
- Policy Proxy
- Policy Proxy-Monitor
- Policy Monitor

When deploying CSPM, you have three different configurations from which to choose:

- Standalone
- Client-Server
- Distributed

Both the Standalone configuration and the Client-Server configuration can be used to manage your Cisco Secure IDS Sensors.

CSPM runs on a Windows NT 4.0 system with the following software requirements:

- Windows NT Service Pack 6a
- NTFS disk partition
- TCP/IP protocol stack
- DHCP disabled (recommended)
- Internet Explorer 5.x
- TAPI/MAPI (optional for pager notifications)
- Cisco Secure VPN Client (optional)

To ensure optimal performance, your CSPM installation must meet the minimum hardware requirements specified in Table 6-1.

Your permanent license determines the maximum number of devices that your CSPM installation can manage throughout your network.

Installing CSPM is a straightforward process. You must specify the CSPM installation configuration, the administrative account used to access CSPM, and some basic parameters (such as IP address and service port).

Your Cisco Secure IDS Sensors communicate with CSPM by using the Cisco Secure PostOffice protocol. Therefore, you must also configure Cisco Secure PostOffice on your CSPM system. The main parameters needed to configure Cisco Secure PostOffice are as follows:

- Host ID
- Organization ID
- IP address
- Host name
- Organization name

To become acquainted with the CSPM software, you can view several videos that illustrate basic configuration tasks that you need to perform within CSPM. These videos are encoded with the TechSmith Compression Codec (TSCC). You must install a decoder (included with CSPM) to view these videos.

When starting CSPM, you need to enter the account that you used to install CSPM to access CSPM. In addition to supplying the correct account credentials, you need to connect to your CSPM using the Local or Remote Server option button depending on whether you installed CSPM in Standalone or Client-Server mode.

Review Questions

The following questions test your retention of the material presented in this chapter. The answers to the Review Questions are in Appendix K, "Answers to Review Questions."

   1 Which CSPM installation configurations support Cisco Secure IDS Sensor management?

   _____

   _____

   _____

2 How many permanent license options does CSPM support?

_____

_____

_____

3 Why do you have to install Cisco Secure PostOffice on your CSPM system?

_____

_____

_____

4 What is the difference between the Lite License and the Unlimited License?

_____

_____

_____

5 On what operating system does CSPM run?

_____

_____

_____

6 What is the minimum processor speed recommended for a CSPM host?

_____

_____

_____

7 What is the minimum amount of RAM recommended on a CSPM client host?

_____

_____

_____

8 What is the minimum recommended free space for a CSPM server installation?

_____

_____

_____

9 What formatting must you use for your CSPM disk partition?

_____

_____

_____

10 Why is the TechSmith Screen Capture Codec needed?

_____

_____

_____

11 Can you change the account name used to access CSPM during the installation process?

_____

_____

_____

## CHAPTER 7

4200 Series Sensor Installation Within CSPM

The 4200 Series represents the PC appliances that serve as IDS sensors. These appliances perform the monitoring function within your Cisco Secure IDS. Two categories of 4200 Series Sensors are currently supported: IDS-4230 and IDS-4210.

Your Director platform communicates with your sensors by using the PostOffice protocol. Multiple mechanisms exist through which you can directly manage your Cisco Secure IDS Sensors. When managing your sensors directly, you log on to the sensor by using a couple of predefined system accounts.

When you first set up a 4200 Series Sensor, you need to run a script that defines the basic operational parameters. Then, you need to also finalize the sensor installation through your Director platform.

This chapter explains the steps necessary to add a 4200 Series Sensor if you use Cisco Secure Policy Manager (CSPM) as your Director platform. If you use Cisco Secure ID Director for UNIX, you need to refer to Chapter 16, "The Configuration Management Utility (nrConfigure)," which outlines the procedures necessary to install 4200 Series IDS Sensors in that environment.

Specifically, this chapter covers the following:

- Understanding the sensor appliance
- Configuring the sensor bootstrap
- Adding a sensor to a CSPM Director

Understanding the Sensor Appliance

The 4200 Series Sensors are the network appliances that serve as IDS sensors. These appliances are standalone devices that can be connected at various locations throughout your network. Cisco Secure IDS supports two categories of standalone IDS sensor appliances: IDS-4230 and IDS-4210.

The following sections cover these sensors. In addition, you learn about the following:

- Management access
- Logon accounts

IDS-4230

The IDS-4230 is the high-end sensor in the 4200 Series and provides the following features:

- **Performance:** 100 Mbps
- **Processor:** Dual Pentium III 600 MHz
- **Memory:** 512 MB
- **Monitoring NIC:** FE/SFDDI/DFDDI

Like most sensors, it comes with a front panel and a back panel.

Front Panel

The IDS-4230 Sensor is a rack-mountable device that is four rack units (RUs) high. The lockable front access panel protects the sensor from unauthorized tampering (see Figure 7-1). A floppy drive and CD-ROM drive are standard components of the default system.

Figure 7-1 *IDS-4230 Sensor Front Panel*

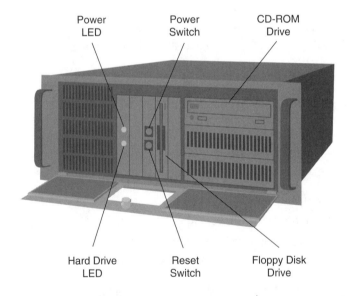

Power
LED

Power
Switch

CD-ROM
Drive

Hard Drive
LED

Reset
Switch

Floppy Disk
Drive

Rack Units

When installing equipment in a lab environment, space is a major concern. Normally, you use racks, which have numerous mounting holes, to efficiently install equipment in your lab. Because the width of the racks is fixed, rack-mountable equipment is usually measured by its height. The measurement used is known as rack units (RUs), where one RU equals approximately 1.75 inches. Therefore, the 4-RU IDS-4230 is approximately 7 inches high.

Back Panel

The IDS-4230 Sensor supports installation in five different network environments. Each of these network environments represents a different model of the IDS-4230 Sensor. The location of the monitoring (sniffing) connection depends on the model of sensor—whether it is an Ethernet, a Fast Ethernet, Token Ring, and so on. Table 7-1 lists types of network environments and the corresponding monitoring interface device names.

Table 7-1   *4230 Monitoring Interface Device Names for Different Network Environments*

Network Connections	Device Name
Ethernet	/dev/spwr0
Fast Ethernet	/dev/spwr0
Token Ring	/dev/mtok0
Single FDDI	/dev/ptpci
Dual FDDI	/dev/ptpci

Regardless of the model, some connections are common to all sensors, such as the keyboard, monitor, and command and control network interface connection. Most users prefer to perform the initial configuration by using the keyboard and monitor connections. Figure 7-2 shows the back of an IDS-4230 Sensor configured with multiple Ethernet interfaces.

Figure 7-2   *IDS-4230 Sensor Back Panel*

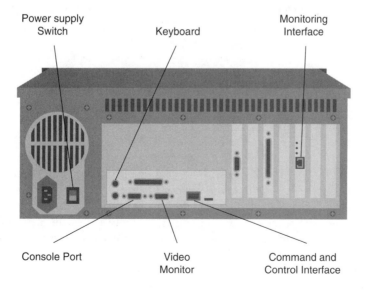

NOTE	Before you install your IDS sensors, you need to read and understand all safety requirements listed in the *Cisco Secure IDS User Guide*.

IDS-4210

The IDS-4210 is a compact sensor that provides the following features:

- **Performance:** 45 Mbps
- **Processor:** Single Celeron 566 MHz
- **Memory:** 256 MB
- **Monitoring NIC:** Ethernet only

The following sections discuss the front panel and back panel specifications.

Front Panel

The 4210 Sensor is a 1-RU, rack-mountable device (see Figure 7-3). Like the IDS-4230, it comes equipped with a floppy drive and a CD-ROM drive. Access to these drives is obtained by removing the front cover. However, this front access panel is not lockable.

Figure 7-3   *IDS-4210 Sensor Front Panel*

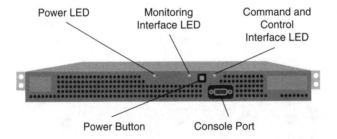

Back Panel

The back of the IDS-4210 Sensor has two Ethernet interfaces. The top interface is the command and control interface, and the bottom interface is the monitoring interface. The IDS-4210 Sensor supports only installation into an Ethernet network environment. Table 7-2 shows the device name corresponding to the monitoring interface Ethernet network connection.

Table 7-2   *Device Name for 4210 Monitoring Interface*

Network Connection	Device Name
Ethernet	/dev/iprb0

In addition to the Ethernet interfaces, the 4210 Sensors give you access to the keyboard port, the console access port, and the video monitor port (see Figure 7-4).

Figure 7-4   *IDS-4210 Sensor Back Panel*

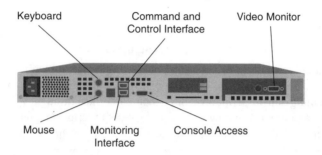

As with the IDS-4230, you need to read and understand all safety requirements listed in the *Cisco Secure IDS User Guide* before you install your IDS-4210 Sensors.

Management Access

To access your sensors for management, you have four options:

- Console port using an RS-232 cable
- Monitor and keyboard on sensor
- Telnet to sensor's IP address
- Configuration through your Director platform

Initially, you will probably utilize the monitor and keyboard connections on your Cisco Secure IDS Sensors to set up your sensors. These connections are directly connected to your sensor and do not need to be configured.

After your sensor is operational, you can use either the serial interface or Telnet to manage your sensors. Furthermore, you can perform many configuration tasks directly through your Director platform without needing to access the sensor directly.

Logon Accounts

By default, a couple of different logon accounts are created on the sensors. You use these logon accounts to accomplish specific functions on the sensor. The default logon accounts are root and netrangr.

root

Use the root account to perform operating system–level functions. When first setting up your sensor, you must use the root account to run the **sysconfig-sensor** script to define the basic configuration settings for your sensor.

---

sysconfig-sensor

When initially installing your sensor, you need to define numerous basic operational parameters. These values are stored in multiple configuration files throughout the system. The **sysconfig-sensor** script provides a single interface through which you can configure all these parameters. Running the **sysconfig-sensor** script is a prerequisite before continuing with the installation of the sensor from your Director platform.

Another situation in which you use the root account is when you perform Solaris operating system–level tasks. These tasks might involve installing an operating system patch or update or updating your IDS software. When troubleshooting the operation of your Cisco Secure IDS Sensor, you might need to run **snoop** to examine raw network traffic. The **snoop** command can be executed only from the root account.

---

snoop

The Solaris operating system provides a command-line tool named **snoop**. This tool enables you to examine the network traffic on any of the network interface cards (NICs) on your sensor. By placing your NIC in Promiscuous mode, **snoop** can capture all the packets on that specific network interface. Sometimes, by using **snoop** to verify the network traffic, you can debug operational problems with your sensor by verifying that traffic is actually getting to the NIC on your sensor.

The default password for the root account is *attack*. You need to change this to prevent unauthorized access to your sensor. The password that you choose must be difficult for an attacker to guess or obtain through a dictionary or brute-force, password-cracking program (see Chapter 1, "Need for Network Security").

netrangr

To obtain Cisco Secure IDS–level access to your sensor, you need to use the *netrangr* account. You can run all the Cisco Secure IDS commands (except **sysconfig-sensor**) by using this account. Some of the basic commands include the following:

- **nrstatus**
- **nrvers**
- **nrstop**
- **nrstart**

NOTE   Appendix B, "Cisco Secure IDS Architecture," provides a detailed explanation of what these commands do and when you use them.

Similar to the root account, the default password for the netrangr account is *attack*. Again, to prevent unauthorized modification of your sensor, you need to change this password to something else. The new password that you choose needs to be difficult for an attacker to guess or obtain through a dictionary or brute-force, password-cracking program.

Configuring the Sensor Bootstrap

During the initial setup of your sensor, you need to define a minimal set of operational parameters. These parameters identify the sensor and the Director that manage it. The PostOffice protocol requires these values to enable communication between the sensor and the Director. In addition to PostOffice parameters, you also need to configure certain IP parameters for your sensor.

To configure the basic parameters on your sensor, you run **sysconfig-sensor** (a Cisco Secure menu-driven configuration script). You must log on to the sensor by using the root account to run the **sysconfig-sensor** script.

This section takes you through the configuration process by overtly presenting the following:

- **sysconfig-sensor**
- IP configuration
- Network access control
- Configuring communication parameters
- Creating initial configuration files
- Configuring system date, time, and timezone
- Changing passwords
- Exiting **sysconfig-sensor**
- Setting up secure communications

sysconfig-sensor

At the command prompt on the sensor, enter **sysconfig-sensor** and press Enter. You see a menu with nine different parameters that you can configure (see Figure 7-5).

Figure 7-5   **sysconfig-sensor** *Menu*

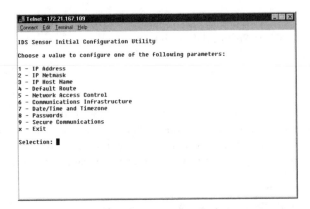

IP Address

The *IP Address* (option 1 in Figure 7-5) is the network address that other hosts use to communicate with your sensor.

IP Netmask

An IP address is composed of two components: Network address and Host address.

The network address defines a group of machines that all belong to the same broadcast domain. Whenever a machine on the network generates a broadcast packet, all the hosts on the network receive this packet.

The host address uniquely identifies all the machines that are located on a single network.

The *IP Netmask* (option 2 in Figure 7-5) defines the boundary between the network address and the host address. This boundary can vary depending on the subnetting used in your network environment.

IP Host Name

The *IP Host Name* (option 3 in Figure 7-5) is an alphanumeric name for your sensor. This name is easier to remember than the regular IP address when referencing your sensor.

Default Route

Whenever your sensor needs to send traffic to other hosts, it needs to know how to reach those hosts. The *default Route* (option 4 in Figure 7-5) defines a single path through which all traffic (other than local network traffic) can be sent. The default route is usually a router that knows where to send your packets so that they can reach their destination.

Network Access Control

Option 5 in Figure 7-5, *Network Access Control*, enables you to set any number of IP addresses—either by host or network—that are allowed to connect through Telnet or FTP to your sensor. In most cases, you need to limit access to the sensor through these protocols to a single trusted host. This single trusted host is typically your Director. Each device that can access your Cisco Secure IDS Sensor represents a potential path that an attacker can use to take control of your sensor. By allowing numerous hosts to access your sensor through these protocols, you increase the chances that your sensor can be compromised by an attack.

Network access to your sensor enables you to perform several useful functions:

- Troubleshooting
- Moving signature update files to the sensor
- Moving product update files to the sensor

Sometimes, you might need to log on to your sensor to troubleshoot problems with the operation of the sensor. This access is usually performed using Telnet. Updating your sensor might involve using FTP to transfer signature and product update files to your sensor.

Communications Infrastructure

Option 6 in Figure 7-5, the *Communications Infrastructure* menu option, enables you to input the data necessary for communications between the sensor and Director (see Figure 7-6). Table 7-3 contains the parameters you need to enter, along with a description of each parameter.

Figure 7-6   *Communications Infrastructure Configuration Menu*

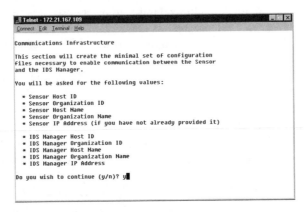

Table 7-3   *Communications Infrastructure Parameters*

Cisco Secure IDS Settings	Parameters	Description
Sensor Host ID	1-65535	Numeric identifier for each sensor.
Sensor Organization ID	1-65535	Numeric identifier for a collection of IDS devices. It can be used to group a number of sensors and Directors under the same number for easy identification purposes.
Sensor Host Name	<Host Name>	Alphanumeric identifier for each sensor. The name chosen here is typically one that contains the word *sensor* so that you can easily identify that it is a sensor (for example, sensor1).
Sensor Organization Name	<Org Name>	Alphanumeric identifier for a collection of IDS devices. The name chosen here is typically one that describes the name of the company where the sensor is installed or the name of the department within the company where the sensor is installed (for example, Cisco).
Sensor IP Address	<IP Address>	The IP address of the sensor.
Director Host ID	1-65535	Numeric identifier for each Director.
Director Organization ID	1-65535	Numeric identifier for a collection of IDS devices. It can be used to group a number of sensors and Directors under the same number for easy identification purposes.

Table 7-3   *Communications Infrastructure Parameters (Continued)*

Cisco Secure IDS Settings	Parameters	Description
Director Host Name	\<Host Name\>	Alphanumeric identifier for each Director. The name chosen here is typically one that contains the word *director* so that you can easily identify that it is a Director (for example, director1).
Director Organization Name	\<Org Name\>	Alphanumeric identifier for a collection of IDS devices. The name chosen here is typically one that describes the name of the company where the Director is installed or the name of the department within the company where the Director is installed (for example, Cisco).
Director IP Address	\<IP Address\>	The IP address of the Director.

NOTE   You need to remember the sensor's host name and organization name, the sensor's ID and organization ID, and the sensor's IP address. This information is required during the completion of the sensor installation on your Director platform. Furthermore, the Director ID, Director organization ID, and Director organization name need to match the values that you used during the configuration of your Director platform. If you completed the worksheet in Appendix I, "Cisco Secure Communications Deployment Worksheet," this information is consolidated in a single location.

You must be careful when entering the communication infrastructure parameters (see Figure 7-6). The information you enter is included in each packet that travels between the sensor and Director and must be error-free. Exercise extreme caution not to confuse the sensor information for the Director information, and vice versa (refer to the worksheet that you filled out in Appendix I).

After you enter all the information for the Cisco Secure IDS communications infrastructure configuration, you are prompted to create the initial configuration files (see Figure 7-7). Examine the information that you entered carefully. If you made an error, just enter **n** and press the Enter key to reenter the information that needs to be corrected. If the information is correct, enter **y** and press the Enter key to create the initial configuration files.

When all files have been successfully created, you are prompted to continue. Press the Enter key to proceed to the Cisco Secure IDS notes page. Read the information presented and then press the Enter key to continue.

Figure 7-7 *Creating Initial Configuration Files*

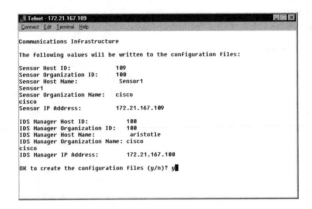

Configuring System Date, Time, and Timezone

Option 7 in Figure 7-5, the system *Date/Time and Timezone* Menu, enables you to enter the date, time, and timezone for your sensor appliance (see Figure 7-8). You also can synchronize the date and time with another time service–enabled host on your network. Synchronizing the time used by your security devices throughout your network enables you to easily compare these various sources of information. Without a common time source, this consolidation of logged information is difficult because the same event occurs at different times on each of your devices.

Figure 7-8 *Configuring System Date, Time, and Timezone*

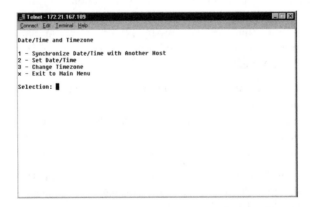

Table 7-4 contains the values you can enter, along with a description for each parameter, when configuring the system date, time, and timezone.

Table 7-4   *Cisco Secure IDS Settings and Their Parameters*

Cisco Secure IDS Settings	Parameters	Description
Option 1: Synchronize Date/ Time with Another Host	\<Host Name>	Enables you to synchronize the sensor's date and time with a reachable host, with the time the service is running. The date and time is set to that of the remote host. (This uses the UNIX **rdate** command.)
Option 2: Set Date/Time	\<Year>, \<Month>, \<Day>, \<Hour>, \<Minutes>	Enables you to set or change any date or time setting manually.
Option 3: Change Timezone.	\<Time Zone>	Enables you to select the sensor's timezone setting from a list of choices.
Option x: Exit to Main Menu		Enables you to exit the System Date, Time, and Timezone menu and return to the sysconfig-sensor menu.

Changing Passwords

Option 8 in Figure 7-5, *Passwords*, enables you to change the password for any account on the sensor (see Figure 7-9). The two default sensor accounts are netrangr and root.

To change the password for an account, you must enter the account name to select the appropriate account for which you want to change the password. Next, you need to enter the new password. After you do this, you need to reenter the password for verification purposes (to make sure that you did not mistype the password value). When the password is changed, the old password is discarded without being saved.

Figure 7-9   *Passwords*

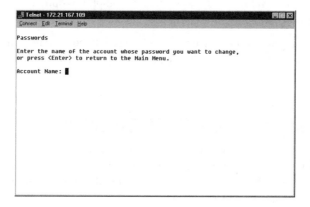

Setting Up Secure Communications

Option 9 in Figure 7-5, *Secure Communications*, enables you to define the parameters necessary to set up encrypted communications with your sensor. After selecting Option 9, you see the Secure Communications screen (see Figure 7-10).

Figure 7-10 *Configuring Secure Communications*

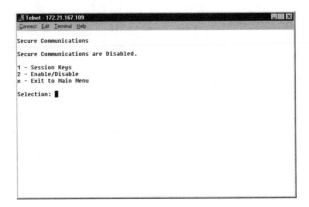

To set up secure communications, you need to enter your session keys and then you need to enable secure communications.

Exiting sysconfig-sensor

Option x in Figure 7-5, *Exit*, enables you to exit from **sysconfig-sensor**. If options 1 through 5 (the IP configuration settings) are modified, you are prompted to reboot the system. Enter **y** at the prompt to reboot the sensor. For options 6 and 8, the system is not required to re-boot, so you are returned to the command prompt. For option 7, you are not required to reboot unless the Timezone setting is changed.

After running **sysconfig-sensor**, Cisco Secure IDS communications are now ready for the Director to establish a connection with your sensor and enable intrusion detection through the sensor.

Adding a Sensor to a CSPM Director

This section describes how to add a sensor to your Director platform. Before you can add a sensor to the Director platform, however, you must define the initial bootstrap parameters on the sensor. This is accomplished by running the **sysconfig-sensor** script (discussed previously in this chapter).

This chapter addresses only the installation of an IDS Sensor to Cisco Secure Policy Manager. If you use Cisco Secure ID Director for UNIX, refer to Chapter 16 for instructions on installing a Cisco Secure IDS Sensor in that environment.

To add a sensor in your Network Topology tree (NTT), use the Add Sensor Wizard. The Add Sensor Wizard helps you create a sensor object and gives you the option of extracting and saving a sensor's configuration information into a signature template.

This part of the chapter walks you through the following actions:

- Starting the Add Sensor Wizard
- Entering the sensor's PostOffice identification parameters
- Entering the sensor's default gateway
- Selecting the sensor version and signature template
- Verify settings

Then you need to go through the following steps to complete the installation of your Cisco Secure IDS Sensor:

Step 1   Add the CSPM host to the topology.

Step 2   Select the policy distribution point.

Step 3   Save and Update the configuration.

Step 4   Push the configuration files to the sensor.

Step 5   Check for errors.

Start the Add Sensor Wizard

Inside of CSPM, choose Add Sensor from the Wizards drop-down menu to start the Add Sensor wizard, which displays the Sensor Identification window (see Figure 7-11).

Enter Sensor's PostOffice Identification Parameters

The Sensor Identification dialog box enables you to enter the PostOffice configuration parameters for the sensor that you are adding (see Figure 7-12). The lower-left corner of the window contains two check boxes:

- Check here to verify Sensor's address.
- Check here to capture the Sensor's configuration.

Figure 7-11 *Starting the Add Sensor Wizard*

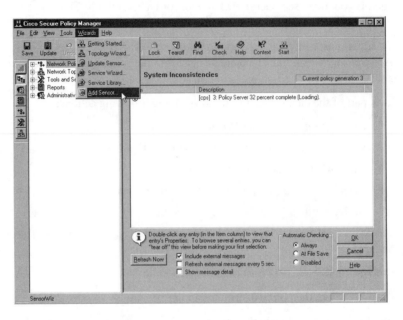

Figure 7-12 *Sensor's PostOffice Identification Parameters*

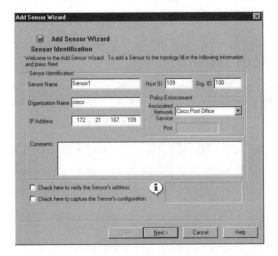

These options enable you to cause CSPM to communicate with the sensor before you proceed with the sensor configuration. By verifying the sensor's address, you can confirm that your CSPM host has network connectivity with the sensor. Capturing the sensor's configuration enables you to cause CSPM to poll the sensor for its current software version and configuration files.

The PostOffice parameters that you need to enter are contained in Table 7-5.

Table 7-5   *Required PostOffice Parameters*

PostOffice Settings	Parameters	Description
Sensor Name	\<Host Name\>	Alphanumeric identifier for each sensor. The name chosen here is typically one that contains the word *sensor* so that you can easily identify that it is a sensor (for example, sensor1).
Organization Name	\<Org Name\>	Alphanumeric identifier for a collection of IDS devices. The name chosen here is typically one that describes the name of the company where the sensor is installed or the name of the department within the company where the sensor is installed (for example, Cisco).
Host ID	1-65535	Numeric identifier for each sensor.
Organization ID	1-65535	Numeric identifier for a collection of IDS devices. It can be used to group a number of sensors and Directors under the same number for easy identification purposes.
Associated Network Service		Leave as Cisco PostOffice.
Comments	\<Comments\>	Alphanumeric field to enter any user comments about the sensor.

After you enter all the parameters, click the Next button to proceed to the definition of the sensor's default gateway.

Enter Sensor Object's Default Gateway

The next information that you need to enter is the default gateway (see Figure 7-13). The default gateway represents the next hop device for the network object that is created by CSPM.

After entering the default gateway, click the Next button to continue with the installation of the sensor by specifying the sensor software version and signature template.

Figure 7-13 *Sensor Object's Default Gateway*

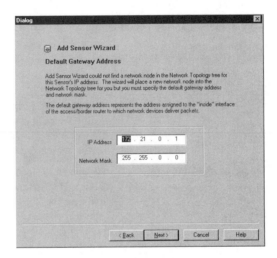

Select Sensor Version and Signature Template

Finally, you need to enter the following parameters:

- Sensor software version
- Signature template

You can select the sensor's software version by using the pull-down menu next to the Sensor Version field (see Figure 7-14). The signature template defines which signatures the sensor looks for, along with their associated severity. You can select the correct template by using the pull-down menu next to the Signature Template field (see Figure 7-14). For more information on signature templates, refer to Chapter 12, "Signature and Intrusion Detection Configuration."

NOTE   If you selected the Check here to capture the Sensor's configuration check box on the Sensor Identification dialog box (refer back to Figure 7-12), the software version and configuration must already be set to the correct values because CSPM polled the sensor to obtain this information.

After you enter the sensor's software version and signature template, you can click the Next button to review all the settings that you have defined so far during the sensor installation.

Figure 7-14 *Sensor Version and Signature Template*

Verify Sensor Settings

After you have entered all the sensor's basic operational settings, a screen similar to Figure 7-15 displays. This screen displays all the sensor parameters that you entered. If these parameters are all correct, click the Finish button to complete the sensor installation. The appropriate objects are added to the NTT, and any saved templates are added to the Tools and Services tree.

Figure 7-15 *Verify Sensor Settings*

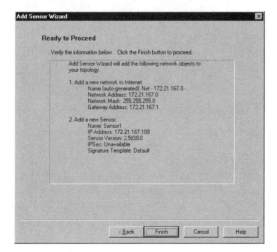

NOTE   Figure 7-15 shows that CSPM creates a new network object as well as a new sensor object. This occurs because the network to which the command and control interface on the sensor is connected was not previously defined in CSPM's Network Topology tree. If you add a sensor to a network that is already defined in your NTT, you see only a new sensor object.

Add the CSPM Host to the Topology

You successfully added your sensor to your NTT. The sensor, however, must communicate with the CSPM. Therefore, you also need to add your CSPM host to your NTT. To add a host to an existing network object in CSPM, right-click the network object and point to New from the first drop-down menu and Host from the second drop-down menu (see Figure 7-16).

Figure 7-16 *Add the CSPM Host to Topology*

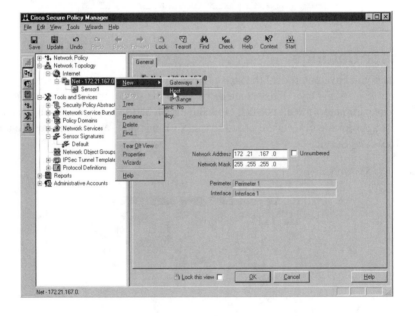

NOTE   If this is not your first sensor, or you have previously defined your CSPM host, you do not need to add your CSPM host to your network topology. You just need to add your hosts into your NTT one time.

At this point, CSPM notices that it has an interface on the network where you are adding a host. Therefore, it displays a window asking whether your CSPM host is the host that you want to add to the network (see Figure 7-17). Because this is the host that you want to add, click the Yes button to add your CSPM host to your NTT.

Figure 7-17 *Object Automatically Detected*

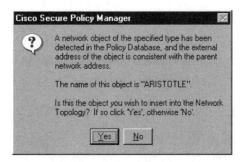

NOTE   After clicking the Yes button to add your CSPM host to your NTT, a pop-up window displays (see Figure 7-18). This pop-up window appears every time that you add a new object to your NTT. It is a reminder that you need to reference this new object in your Network Policy tree under the Security Policy Enforcement branch, if you plan to make network policy decisions based on this object. You can prevent this reminder from popping up by clicking the Don't show this message again check box in the lower-left corner of the window.

Figure 7-18 *Network Policy Reminder Pop-Up Window*

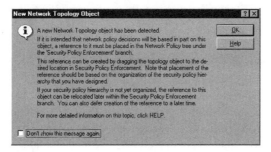

Selecting the Policy Distribution Point

Your sensor enforces your security policy. Updates to your sensor's policy definition must come from a defined source known as the *policy distribution point (PDP)* for the sensor object. The CSPM host is the PDP.

To configure the PDP for your sensor object, you must first highlight the sensor object from the NTT and then select the Control tab (see Figure 7-19).

Figure 7-19 *Selecting the Policy Distribution Point*

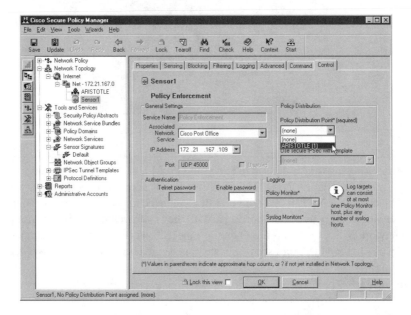

Within the Control tab, select the CSPM host itself from the Policy Distribution Point drop-down menu. Click the OK button to accept this new PDP.

Saving and Updating the Configuration

The Save and Update buttons on the toolbar are responsible for generating the configuration files that can then be pushed to the sensor, as well as updating the database on your CSPM host. After you successfully do this, you can view the generated command set by using the Command tab on sensor object (see Figure 7-20). When you manage devices other than sensors, the Save and Update operations generate commands for each device identified in the Network Topology tree. In addition, they include all the routing and mapping rules that are either derived by CSPM or manually entered by you as part of these rule sets.

Figure 7-20 *Pushing the Configuration Files to the Sensor*

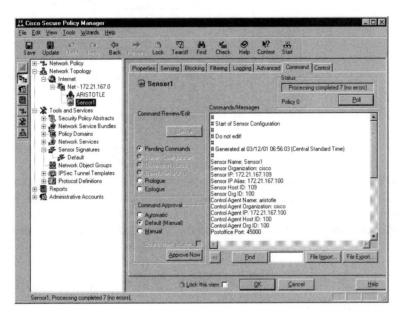

NOTE   The Save button updates the database files on your CSPM host. The Update button updates the database files on your CSPM host and generates the updated configuration files that you need to push down to the devices that your CSPM is managing.

Pushing the Configuration Files to the Sensor

After you generate and view the commands by using the Save and Update buttons and the Command tab on the sensor, you need to push the updated files to the sensor. You can use three methods to push the updated files to your sensors:

- Automatic
- Default (manual)
- Manual

The default (manual) publishing method requires you to manually push the updated files to your sensor by using the Approve Now button on the sensor object's Command tab (see Figure 7-20). You also can configure CSPM to automatically publish the command sets to all the *policy enforcement points (PEPs)* that you administer each time you click Save and Update on the File menu.

Default (Manual)

The Default update selection currently operates the same as the Manual selection. This selection enables you to define whether the default update method is either manual or automatic. To change the default from manual to automatic, you need to access the Tools, Options screen from the main CSPM window. On this screen you can choose from either Automatic or Manual as your update preference.

Policy Enforcement Points

The policy enforcement points (PEPs) on your network are the devices that actually monitor your network and enforce your defined security policy. These devices can be your IDS sensors, PIX Firewalls, and IOS Firewall routers. Your CSPM host centrally manages these PEPs, by acting as a PDP. Your PDP updates the policies on each of your PEP devices.

The following steps are required to apply a signature template to a sensor in CSPM by using the Default (Manual) method:

Step 1   Select the sensor from the NTT.

Step 2   Select the Command tab in the Sensor view panel.

Step 3   Click the Approve Now button in the Command Approval section. Wait for the configuration files to download to the sensor.

Checking for Errors

After pushing updated files to your sensors, you want to confirm that the transfer occurred without any errors. You can check for errors by looking at the Status group box under the Command tab (see Figure 7-20). After an update is complete, the Refresh button is no longer grayed out (see Figure 7-21). You can then click the Refresh tab to update information in the Commands, Messages window. You can select Distribution Status under Command Review, Edit to see any errors that might have been generated during the transfer of files (see Figure 7-22).

Figure 7-21 *Refresh Command Message Window*

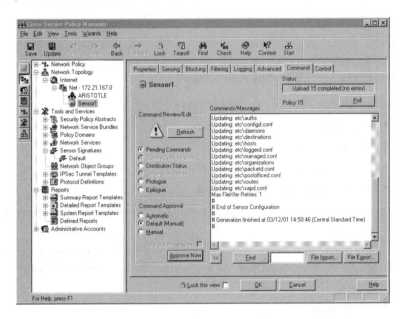

Figure 7-22 *Checking for Errors*

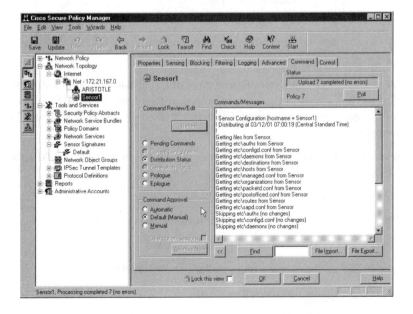

Summary

The 4200 Series Sensor comes in two different hardware platforms: IDS-4230 and IDS-4210.

Both platforms are rack-mountable network appliances. The features are similar with the IDS-4230 supplying slightly more features.

To manage your sensors, you have four options:

- Console port using an RS-232 cable
- Monitor and keyboard on sensor
- Telnet to sensor's IP Address
- Configuration through the Director platform

When directly managing your sensors, you use two different logon accounts: root and netrangr.

The first step to install your sensor is to configure the sensor bootstrap parameters. You perform this by logging on with the root account on your sensor and running the **sysconfig-sensor** script. This script defines the following:

- IP configuration
- Network access control
- Configuring communication parameters
- Creating initial configuration files
- Configuring system date, time, and timezone
- Changing passwords

After you have run the **sysconfig-sensor** script, continue the configuration on your Director platform. Each platform has its own procedure to configure a 4200 Series Sensor. However, both Director platforms communicate with the sensors by using the same PostOffice protocol.

When using CSPM, you need to go through the following steps to add your Cisco Secure IDS Sensors:

Step 1 Start the Add Sensor Wizard.

Step 2 Enter the sensor's PostOffice identification parameters.

Step 3 Enter the sensor object's default gateway.

Step 4 Select the sensor version and signature template.

Step 5 Verify the entered settings.

Step 6 Add the CSPM host to the NTT (only if it has not already been added).

Step 7   Select the PDP for the sensor object (the CSPM host).

Step 8   Use the Save button to write the new configuration to the CSPM database.

Step 9   Use the Update button to generate the configuration files for the sensor.

Step 10 Push the configuration files to the sensor.

Review Questions

The following questions test your retention of the material presented in this chapter. The answers to the Review Questions are in Appendix K, "Answers to Review Questions."

  1 How many different types of the 4200 Series Sensor exist?

\
\
\

  2 What is the **sysconfig-sensor** script?

\
\
\

  3 What are the management options available for accessing your Cisco Secure IDS Sensor?

\
\
\

  4 What account do you need to be logged on to the sensor with to execute the **sysconfig-sensor** script?

\
\
\

  5 What are the default accounts on the 4200 Series Sensors?

\
\
\

6 Besides setting up the initial parameters on the sensor, for what reason is the root account used?

_____

_____

_____

7 What are the differences between the IDS-4230 and IDS-4210 Sensors?

_____

_____

_____

8 What is a policy enforcement point (PEP)?

_____

_____

_____

9 What is a policy distribution point?

_____

_____

_____

10 What are the IP configuration parameters that you must set on your sensor by using **sysconfig-sensor**?

_____

_____

_____

11 What are the primary PostOffice parameters that you need to know when installing your sensor?

_____

_____

_____

12 When changing your sensor configuration by using **sysconfig-sensor**, which options require you to reboot your sensor?

_____

_____

_____

## PART IV

Alarm Management and Intrusion Detection Signatures

Working with Cisco Secure IDS Alarms in CSPM

Each of the sensors in the network reports alarms and other events to your CSPM host. These alarms have a severity associated with them to help you understand their potential impact on your network. To protect your network, you must understand how to view these alarms using the *CSPM Event Viewer*. More importantly, you must understand the significance of the alarms that occur. Chapter 9, "Understanding Cisco Secure IDS Signatures," provides an in-depth explanation for most of the signatures that your Cisco Secure IDS Sensors are looking for on your network.

CSPM Event Viewer

The CSPM Event Viewer is a graphical interface through which you can view the information being forwarded to your CSPM host by the Cisco Secure IDS Sensors spread throughout your network. This information includes alarms and other status events. The Event Viewer represents your primary tool to analyze the information being generated by your sensors.

Although many people use the CSPM Event Viewer to view their alarms, some people prefer to utilize their own programs for alarm processing. The **cvtnrlog.exe** program enables you to extract alarm entries from the CSPM database and place them into text files (see Appendix B, "Cisco Secure IDS Architecture"). You then can process these text files using your own custom programs.

Before you start digging into the fine details of the different attack signatures that can generate alarms on your system, you must understand how to manipulate the alarms in CSPM with fine precision. This requires a thorough understanding of the CSPM Event Viewer. During an attack on your network, alarms can appear very quickly. If you are unfamiliar with the operation of the CSPM Event Viewer, you can easily become overwhelmed as the alarms accumulate.

This chapter discusses four major areas:

- Managing Alarms
- Customizing the Event Viewer
- Preference Settings
- Connection Status Pane

Each of the categories deals with a different aspect of the overall task of efficiently operating your CSPM Event Viewer. Efficient operation of your Event Viewer enables you to effectively analyze the information that your sensors are telling you about the state of your network.

Managing Alarms

Your sensors are continually looking for attack signatures and forwarding alarms to your CSPM host when a signature is matched. This information is stored in a database on your CSPM host. You gain access to this information through the CSPM Event Viewer. Understanding the Event Viewer is crucial to managing the intrusion alarms on your network.

Managing alarms on your CSPM host involves the following:

- Opening the Event View
- Understanding alarm fields
- Resolving host names
- Viewing the context buffer
- Opening the NSDB
- Understanding exploit signature information
- Understanding related vulnerability information
- Deleting alarms
- Suspending and resuming the alarm display

This discussion begins with accessing your CSPM Event Viewer.

Opening the Event Viewer

Intrusion alarms generated by your sensors are sent to your CSPM host, which stores this information into a database. To view the information in this database, you use the Event Viewer. The Event Viewer provides a graphical window of the alarms stored in the CSPM database. To open the Event Viewer, choose **View Sensor Events**, **Database** from the Tools drop-down menu of the CSPM main window (see Figure 8-1).

Figure 8-1   *Opening the CSPM Event Viewer*

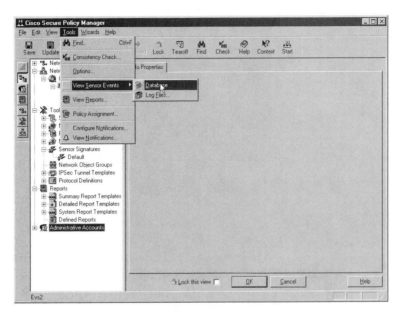

Viewing Log Files with Event Viewer

In addition to using the Event Viewer to view the CSPM database, you can use the Event Viewer to display alarm events that you saved to a log file. These log files can be created from the log files on your sensors or your CSPM database using a conversion utility.

Before you can actually see the Event Viewer, you must specify which alarms you want to view in the Event Viewer (see Figure 8-2). The default is to display all the Cisco Secure IDS alarm records in the CSPM database. You can alter the settings based on your needs. Therefore, you can open several Event Viewer windows, each with a different set of alarms from your CSPM database.

After opening an Event Viewer window, you will see a table of entries similar to Figure 8-3. Furthermore, you can open multiple Event Viewer windows simultaneously. Once you open an Event Viewer window, you can modify its display characteristics independently of all the other Event Viewer windows that are currently opened. Therefore, you can customize each window to display events based on specific operational criteria as required by your operating environment.

Figure 8-2 *Specifying Records for Event Viewer*

Figure 8-3 *CSPM Event Viewer*

Alarm Fields

Each alarm in the Event Viewer is represented as a row entry in the table (see Figure 8-3). This table is composed of numerous fields (represented by separate columns) that provide you with information about the alarm entry. Not all the alarm fields are initially visible onscreen. You can view these other fields by manipulating or customizing the Event Viewer. In this section, however, the focus is on describing the actual alarm fields. These alarm fields fall into the following categories:

- General information fields
- Source information fields
- Destination information fields
- Signature information fields

General Information Fields

The general information fields are as follows:

- Count
- Name
- Local Date
- Local Time
- Organization Name
- Sensor Name
- Application Name

The Count field informs you how many alarm entries are represented by that row in the table. By default, the alarm entries are consolidated by the first two columns in the Event Viewer. This is probably explained more clearly with an actual example. If the host whose IP address is 172.21.130.10 conducts a TCP port scan against three separate systems (172.21.131.10, 172.21.131.15, and 172.21.131.20), your Cisco Secure IDS Sensor detects this as three signature matches, generating three alarms:

- TCP Port Sweep from 172.21.130.10 to 172.21.131.10
- TCP Port Sweep from 172.21.130.10 to 172.21.131.15
- TCP Port Sweep from 172.21.130.10 to 172.21.131.20

In the Event Viewer (with the default field expansion), all three of these alarms consolidate on a single row with the following characteristics:

- **Count:** 3
- **Name:** TCP Port Sweep
- **Source address:** 172.21.130.10

If you expand the destination address field, each alarm is now represented as a separate row in the table, each with a count of 1. Expanding collapsed columns is explained later in this chapter in the "Customizing the Event Viewer" section.

The Name field just provides you with a descriptive name of the alarm event that the sensor detected. The Local Date and Local Time fields indicate the date and time that the sensor generated the alarm. These values are determined by the time and date values on the sensor.

The final three general information fields describe the identity of your IDS sensor itself. The Sensor Name and Organization Name represent the fields that you configured when setting up the PostOffice communication parameters on the sensor. The Application Name is the final parameter used by the PostOffice protocol to uniquely identify an information source. It provides the name of the application that actually generated the alarm or other informational message. Common application names are as follows:

- postofficed
- packetd
- managed
- loggerd
- smid
- eventd

Source Information Fields

The source information fields provide you with information that helps you identify the source of the intrusive traffic. This information includes the following:

- Source address
- Source port
- Source location

The Source Address just defines the source IP address associated with the alarm, whereas the Source Port indicates the TCP or UDP source port from which the traffic originated. These two pieces of information tell you which host or device originated the unauthorized traffic. Sometimes, your Cisco Secure IDS may generate false positives, and knowing where the traffic originated from might help you determine whether an alarm is a potential false positive or an actual attack.

False Positives

False positives are explained in Chapter 3, "Intrusion Detection Systems." As a quick review, however, you need to note that false positives represent a situation in which a signature generates an alarm based on normal user traffic rather than an actual attack.

The Source Location is a little more complicated. When you set up your Cisco Secure IDS, you can define what addresses constitute your internal network. When an alarm occurs, if the address is within this internal network, the value of source location becomes IN. If the address is not on your internal network, the value of source location becomes OUT.

Internal Network

Your sensor might have access to traffic from various networks. It is sometimes helpful to have a quick indication as to whether an alarm entry involves a host on your internal protected network or just hosts that are on your network but not being directly protected by your sensor. For more details on defining your internal network addresses, refer to Chapter 11, "Sensor Configuration Within CSPM."

Destination Information Fields

The destination information fields are essentially identical to the source information fields, except these fields represent the target of the intrusive traffic:

- Destination Address
- Destination Port
- Destination Location

Again, the Destination Address defines the destination IP address associated with the alarm, whereas the Destination Port indicates the TCP or UDP destination port to which the intrusive traffic was sent. In most situations, these two pieces of information tell you which host or device received the unauthorized traffic on your network. In most situations, this host represents the target at which the attack is directed.

The Destination Location can be either IN or OUT. If the destination is on your internal network, the value of the destination location is IN. Otherwise, the destination location receives a value of OUT.

NOTE   You also can use the Source Location and Destination Location to alter your response to specific alarms (refer to Chapter 12, "Signature and Intrusion Detection Configuration"). Traffic coming from a system within your internal network to another internal host that generates an alarm may be acceptable (a potential false positive), whereas, you might consider this same traffic, originating from an external host or the Internet, totally unacceptable.

Signature Information Fields

The signature information fields tell you which signature on your sensor generated the alarm entry. The signature fields also give you an indication of the severity associated with the alarm entry. These fields are as follows:

- Signature ID
- Subsignature ID

- Severity
- Level
- Details

The Signature ID field provides you with the numeric identifier assigned to the signature that generated the alarm. Chapter 10 provides an in-depth explanation of numerous Cisco Secure IDS signatures and defines the various categories of signatures.

Some signatures have a secondary identification field known as a Subsignature ID. This field further defines which signature generated the alarm when multiples events can all trigger the same signature ID. Most of the Cisco Secure IDS signatures do not have a subsignature ID.

The Severity and Level fields help you understand the seriousness of the event that triggered the alarm. The Severity has three possible values: Low, Medium, and High, with High the most severe. Level, however, is a numeric rating from 1 to 5. The Severity value is assigned by mapping each of the alarm level values to one of the three severity possibilities. Table 8-1 shows the default mapping from Level values to Severity values.

Table 8-1   *Assigned Severity Values*

Alarm Level	Associated Severity
1 or 2	Low
3 or 4	Medium
5	High

The Details field provides information unique to the current alarm entry. For a signature that matches a specific text string, the Details field contains the matched string. Only some of the signatures use the Details field.

Resolving Host Names

The entries in the Event Viewer indicate the IP addresses associated with alarm entries. Although this information is useful, you probably do not know all the hosts on your network by their IP addresses. Instead, you usually reference your hosts using an alphanumeric name. From the Event Viewer, you can quickly and easily identify the name of the host that triggered the alarm, as well as the name of the host being attacked.

To resolve the names of the hosts associated with an alarm, right-click the alarm that you want to examine, and then choose **Resolve Hostnames** from the drop-down menu (see Figure 8-4).

Figure 8-4   *Selecting Resolve Hostnames for an Alarm Entry*

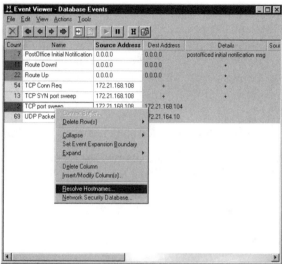

Clicking **Resolve Hostnames** brings up a window that shows the source and destination IP addresses and their respectively resolved host names, for the selected alarm entry (see Figure 8-5). If either host name cannot be resolved, the **Cannot be resolved** message is displayed instead of a host name.

Figure 8-5   *Resolved Hostnames Window*

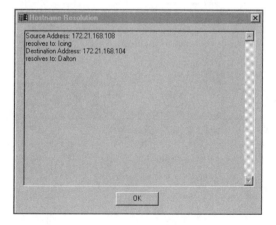

Resolving Host Names

CSPM has two mechanisms with which to resolve host names. You can manually build a C:\WINNT\system32\drivers\etc\hosts file that defines the host name-IP address combinations for the hosts about which you are interested. Another option is to configure your CSPM to use DNS to resolve host names. You can use either or both of these approaches depending on your operational environment and security requirements.

Other ways to open the Host Name Resolution window are as follows:

- Select the alarm to examine and choose **Resolve Hostnames** from the Event Viewer **Tools** drop-down menu (see Figure 8-6).

- Select the alarm to examine and click the Resolve Hostnames button on the top of the Event Viewer toolbar (see Figure 8-7).

Figure 8-6 *Event Viewer Tools Drop-Down Menu*

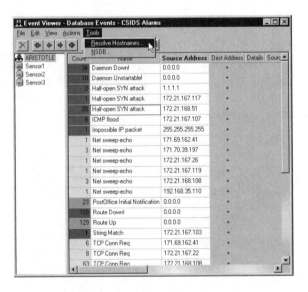

Figure 8-7   *Event Viewer Toolbar Icon Buttons*

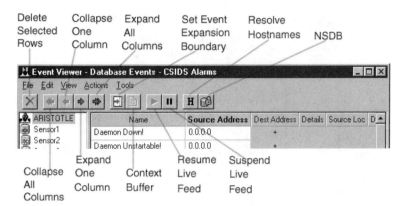

Viewing the Context Buffer

Many TCP-based connections transmit data in human-readable form. When a signature generates an alarm on one of these TCP streams, it is useful to examine the data around the data that actually triggered the alarm. Therefore, for many TCP-based signatures, the sensor captures up to 255 characters from the TCP stream, which can be examined using the Event Viewer. These 255 characters (maximum) are called the *context buffer* and contain keystrokes, data, or both from the connection stream. The context buffer data is captured around the string of characters that triggered the alarm. This feature proves useful for determining whether the triggered alarm is from a deliberate attack or whether it is an accidental set of keystrokes. For actual attacks, it provides you with some insight as to what the attacker did after the alarm fired.

To view the captured context buffer, right-click the alarm you want to examine, and then choose **Context Buffer** from the drop-down menu (see Figure 8-8).

Viewing the Context Buffer selection displays a window showing the context data buffer (see Figure 8-9). When an alarm entry has no context buffer data, the Context Buffer option in the drop-down menu is grayed out (refer back to Figure 8-4).

Figure 8-8 *Accessing the Context Buffer*

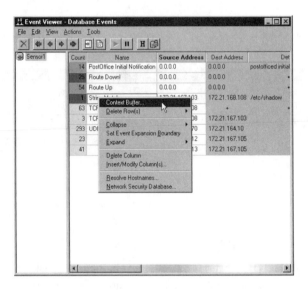

Figure 8-9 *Context Buffer for Alarm Entry*

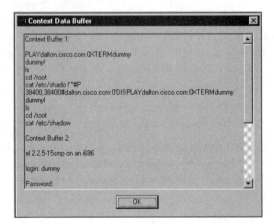

NOTE   The context buffer information is divided into two separate sections (see Figure 8-9).
Context Buffer 1 shows the information sent from the source IP address of the alarm,
whereas Context Buffer 2 shows the information received by the source IP address of
the alarm.

You also can open the Context Buffer window in the following ways:

- Select the alarm to examine and choose **Context Buffer** from the **View** drop-down menu (see Figure 8-10).

- Select the alarm to examine and click the Context Buffer button on the top of the Event Viewer toolbar (refer back to Figure 8-7).

Figure 8-10 *Event Viewer View Pull-Down Menu*

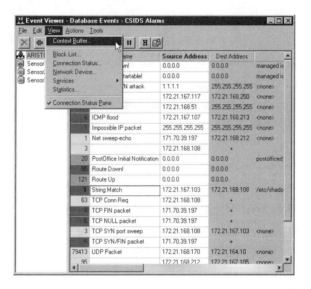

Opening the NSDB

The Network Security Database (NSDB) is Cisco's HTML-based encyclopedia of network vulnerability information. This database provides you with a wealth of information on the attacks that attackers use against your network. Furthermore, each alarm entry is linked to this database so that you can easily bring up the NSDB information for that entry. To do this, right-click the alarm that you want to examine, and then choose **Network Security Database** from the drop-down menu (see Figure 8-11). This will access the exploit signature information from the NSDB.

Other ways to open the NSDB window are as follows:

- Select the alarm to examine and then choose **NSDB** from the Event Viewer Tools drop-down menu (refer back to Figure 8-6).

- Select the alarm to examine and click the Network Security Database button on the top of the Event Viewer toolbar (refer back to Figure 8-7).

Figure 8-11 *Accessing the Network Security Database*

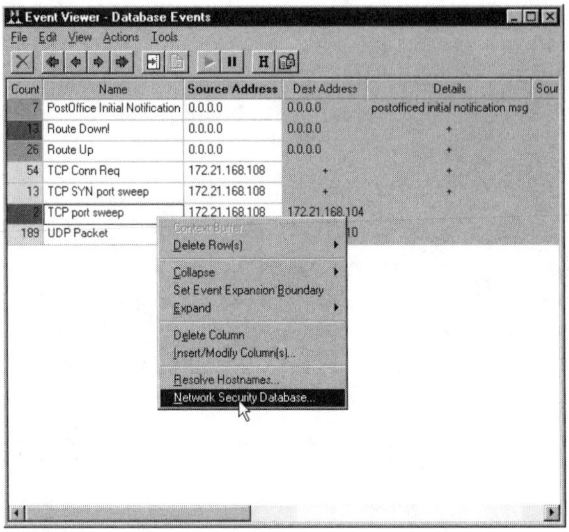

Understanding Exploit Signature Information

A typical NSDB Exploit Signature page contains the following information about the signature that triggered the alarm (see Figure 8-12):

- Signature name
- Signature ID
- Subsignature ID
- Recommended alarm level
- Signature type
- Signature structure
- Implementation
- Signature description
- Benign trigger(s)
- Related vulnerability
- User notes

Signature Name

The signature name provides a short descriptive name of the signature. This name is easier to remember than the signature ID.

Figure 8-12 *NSDB Exploit Signature Page*

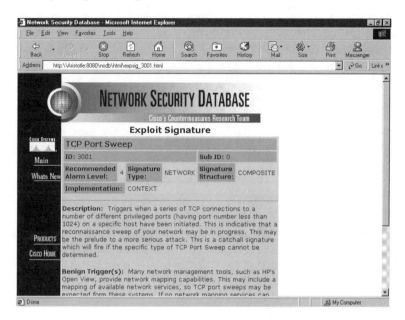

Signature ID

Each signature is assigned a unique identification number or ID. Your sensors watch for hundreds of individual signatures on your network. Remembering each signature ID quickly becomes infeasible. Therefore, blocks of numbers are assigned to each category of intrusive traffic. By just knowing these attack categories, you can quickly identify a signature (even if the number is unfamiliar). The Cisco Secure IDS signatures are explained thoroughly in Chapter 9.

Subsignature ID

For some attack signatures, a single signature ID can represent multiple attacks. An excellent example of this is a 3000 connection alarm. Many types of connections can generate this alarm. You need more information to understand the impact of these connection alarms. Therefore, another identifier is required. This identifier is called a subsignature ID. With the 3000 connection alarm, the subsignature ID is the port number of the connection. For example, a connection to TCP port 23 generates a 3000 alarm with a Subsignature ID of 23.

Recommended Alarm Level

The alarm level can assume a value from 1 to 5, with 5 being the most severe. Cisco's Signatures and Exploits Team (SETI) determines recommended alarm levels after extensively researching each alarm. This recommended alarm level helps you understand the potential impact of the alarm on your network's operation.

Signature Type

The signature type indicates the type of signature that generates the alarm. Currently, for Cisco Secure IDS, this is mainly NETWORK because the sensors detect all the signatures by passively monitoring network traffic.

Signature Structure

The signature structure indicates whether the signature structure is either atomic or composite. Atomic signatures occur in a single packet, whereas composite signatures can be spread across multiple packets. (See Chapter 9 for a detailed explanation of the Cisco Secure IDS signature structure.)

Implementation

The implementation indicates whether the signature implementation is either content or context. Content signatures are based on information in the data portion of a network packet, whereas context signatures are based on information in the packet headers. (See Chapter 9 for a detailed explanation of how signatures are implemented in Cisco Secure IDS.)

Signature Description

The signature description provides you with a concise explanation of the signature. This explanation includes the exploits that the signature detects.

Benign Trigger(s)

One of the problems with monitoring network traffic is false positives. Benign triggers indicate situations or network configurations that are known to generate false positives with the signature. If these benign triggers are present on your network, you *will* experience false positives. Understanding the benign triggers helps you weed out false positives from actual attacks.

Related Vulnerability

Each vulnerability information page provides background information on the vulnerability and a link to any available countermeasures. The countermeasures help you harden your network against future attacks. The link to the related vulnerability is located near the bottom of the NSDB Exploit Signature page (see Figure 8-13).

Figure 8-13 *Bottom of the NSDB Exploit Signature Page*

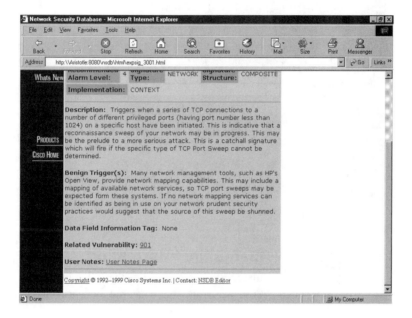

User Notes

You can enter unique information related to this signature with respect to your specific installation and implementation. This information is accessed from the User Notes field at the bottom of the NSDB Exploit Signature page (see Figure 8-13). The User Notes page is similar to Figure 8-14.

The User Notes pages provide you with a location at which to save specific information for each of the Cisco Secure IDS signatures. This information is available only on your copy of CSPM, but the information is preserved during Cisco Secure IDS product updates. Blank User Notes pages are supplied with Cisco Secure IDS, and you need to use an HTML editor to enter your site-specific information into the blank User Notes pages.

Figure 8-14 *User Notes Page*

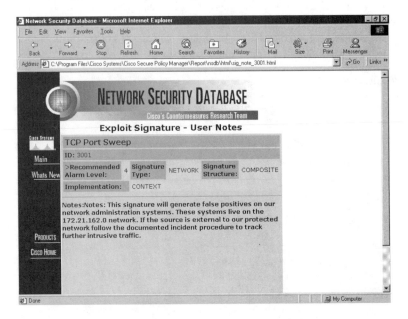

Understanding Related Vulnerability Information

A typical NSDB Related Vulnerability page contains the following information about the vulnerability associated with the signature that triggered the alarm (see Figure 8-15):

- Vulnerability name
- Alias
- Vulnerability ID
- Severity level
- Vulnerability type
- Exploit type
- Affected system(s)
- Affected program(s)
- Vulnerability description
- Consequence(s)
- Countermeasure(s)
- Advisory/related info link(s)
- Fix/upgrade/patch link(s)

- Exploit links
- User notes

Figure 8-15 *Related Vulnerability Information Page*

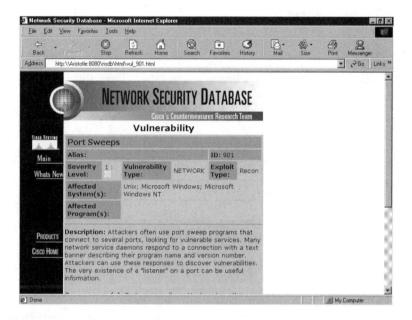

Vulnerability Name

The Vulnerability Name field is just a short descriptive name of the vulnerability being exploited.

Alias

Many vulnerabilities are known by several different names or aliases. The Alias field lists any other names used to refer to this vulnerability or exploit.

Vulnerability ID

A unique identification number, or ID, identifies each vulnerability in the Vulnerability ID field. These vulnerability IDs are not related to the signature IDs. Besides the unique Cisco Secure IDS vulnerability ID, the NSDB is being enhanced also to provide you with Common Vulnerability and Exposure (CVE) identifiers (see http://cve.mitre.org). These CVE identifiers provide a cross-vendor unique identifier for security vulnerabilities.

Severity Level

The Severity Level field identifies how severe the vulnerability is. The severity level is associated with the damage that the vulnerability enables an attacker to inflict on your network. The severity level of the vulnerability, however, may or may not match the recommended alarm level.

Vulnerability Type

The Vulnerability Type field indicates whether the vulnerability is a host or network vulnerability.

Exploit Type

The Exploit Type field indicates the type of exploit. Exploits are categorized as follows:

- Reconnaissance
- Relay
- Access
- Denial of service

Affected System(s)

The Affected System(s) field provides a list of operating systems and versions affected by this vulnerability.

Affected Programs(s)

The Affected Program(s) field supplies a list of the applications and versions affected by this vulnerability.

Vulnerability Description

The Vulnerability Description field provides a concise explanation of the vulnerability and ways that an attacker can exploit it.

Consequence(s)

The Consequence(s) field defines the damage that an attacker can inflict on your network by the exploiting this vulnerability.

Countermeasure(s)

Attackers exploit vulnerabilities to gain access to your network. The Countermeasures field provides a detailed description of things that can be done to protect systems against this vulnerability.

Advisory/Related Information Links

Manufacturers release security advisories defining known security vulnerabilities with their products. Security Web sites also provide information on the security vulnerabilities and exploits that can impact your network. The Advisory/Related Information Links field provides you with a list of links that you can use to find further information on this vulnerability.

Fix/Upgrade/Patch Links

After security vulnerabilities become known, manufacturers release software patches and fixes. The Fix/Upgrade/Patch Links field supplies you with sites on the Web that contain fixes, upgrades, or patches for the vulnerability.

Exploit Link(s)

The Exploit Link(s) field indicates sites on the Web where exploits for the vulnerability might be found.

User Notes

The User Notes field provides a link to a page with user-entered information unique to this installation and implementation.

Deleting Alarms

When an alarm has been acknowledged, dealt with, or both, you might want to remove it from the Event Viewer grid or from the CSPM database altogether. To do this, right-click the alarm you want to delete, and then choose the appropriate deletion type (see Figure 8-16). You have three deletion options from which to choose:

- From This Grid
- From All Grids
- From Database

Figure 8-16 *Options for Deleting an Alarm Entry*

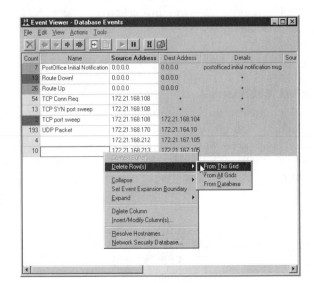

From This Grid

Choosing the **From This Grid** deletion option deletes the alarms from the Event Viewer where the action is performed. It does not delete alarms from other Event Viewers or from the CSPM database.

From All Grids

Selecting the **From All Grids** deletion option deletes the alarms from all Event Viewers, including other Event Viewers that might be open. It does not delete alarms from the CSPM database.

From Database

Picking the **From Database** deletion option deletes the alarms from all the open Event Viewers as well as the CSPM database. If you use this option, the alarm is completely gone and you might not display it in the Event Viewer again, even if you open another Event Viewer.

NOTE   When deleting alarms on your CSPM console, you do not affect the alarms that are logged in the sensor's log files. These log files still contain entries for all the alarms that the sensor generated provided you enabled the logging of alarms on your sensors.

Deleting All Rows

If the Count cell of the top row of the Event Viewer is selected when using any of the delete options, the delete option is applied to all the rows in the Event Viewer.

Other ways to delete alarms are as follows:

- Select the alarm to delete and choose one of the delete options from the Edit drop-down menu (see Figure 8-17).

- Select the alarm to delete and click the Delete Selected Rows button on the top of the Event Viewer toolbar (refer back to Figure 8-7)

Figure 8-17 *Deleting an Alarm Entry by Using the Edit Drop-Down Menu*

NOTE	Using the Delete Selected Rows button on the Event Viewer toolbar removes the alarm entries from the current Event Viewer grid only.

Suspending and Resuming Alarm Display

Sometimes, you might want to freeze the Event Viewer display and temporarily not display any more alarms. This might happen during a flood of alarms. If alarms keep updating the Event Viewer, you might have difficulty analyzing what is happening. At that point, it is nice to freeze your Event Viewer window so that you can research the alarms that you already have in your window.

CSPM enables you to suspend the Event Viewer from displaying new alarms. To suspend the Event Viewer, choose **Suspend New Events** on the **Edit** drop-down menu (see Figure 8-18). To resume alarms, choose **Resume New Events** on the **Edit** drop-down menu. Only one of the options is available at a time. When you suspend alarms, for example, the resume option becomes available. (It is no longer grayed out.) Furthermore, suspending alarms does not prevent new alarms from being added to the CSPM database. It only prevents them from being displayed in your current Event Viewer.

Figure 8-18 *Suspending and Resuming Alarm Display*

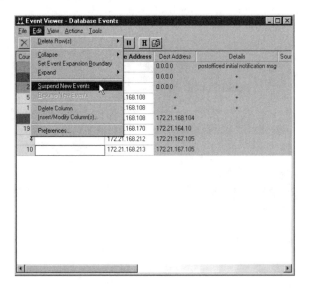

Other ways to suspend or resume the Event Viewer are as follows:

- To suspend an alarm, click the Suspend Live Feed button on the top of the toolbar. This button is on the top toolbar of the Event Viewer and looks like two vertical bars, similar to the pause button on most CD players (refer back to Figure 8-7).

- To resume displaying new alarms, click the Resume Live Feed button on the top toolbar. This button is just to the left of the Suspend Live Feed button and looks like the play button on most CD players (refer back to Figure 8-7).

The Suspend feature is best used while you are analyzing the current alarms being displayed. By suspending alarms, you prevent new alarms from being displayed and shuffling the positions of the current alarms that you are examining. You also might find it beneficial to use the Suspend feature when you are deleting alarms.

Customizing the Event Viewer

This section discusses the different options that enable you to customize the Event Viewer to meet the operational needs of your network environment. All of these customizations, except setting the fields to display, are not persistent. They apply only to the Event Viewer that you are currently using. Therefore, if you open another Event Viewer, you have to reapply the customizations. The customizations that you can perform are as follows:

- Expanding One Column on the Selected Alarm Entry
- Expanding All Columns on the Selected Alarm Entry
- Collapsing One Column on the Selected Alarm Entry
- Collapsing Columns up to the Currently Selected Column
- Changing the Alarm Expansion Boundary
- Moving Columns
- Deleting Columns
- Selecting Columns to be Displayed

Expanding One Column on the Selected Alarm Entry

By default, the Event Viewer consolidates or "collapses" alarms based on the first two column fields. The rest of the fields in the alarm entry have a gray background to indicate that they have been collapsed. (The collapsed fields might indicate actual field values or a plus sign, +). To view these collapsed fields, you must expand the collapsed columns until the fields that you are interested in are shown. To expand fields one column at a time, select the row that you want to expand and then click the Expand One Column button on the top toolbar (see Figure 8-7).

NOTE   When expanding columns in your Event Viewer, you increase the number of row entries being displayed. The Count field shows how many entries are consolidated onto a single row in the Event Viewer. This consolidation is based on the columns currently expanded. As you expand fields, less of the alarm entries have the same values for all of the expanded columns. When you expand all the columns, each row probably represents only one alarm entry (count equal to 1), because it is unlikely that two separate alarm entries have the exact same values for every column.

Other ways to expand alarms one column at a time to the right are as follows:

- Select the row to expand and choose **Expand**, **One Column** on the Event Viewer **Edit** drop-down menu (see Figure 8-19).
- Double-click the row you want to expand.

Figure 8-19 *Expanding Columns Using the Edit Drop-Down Menu*

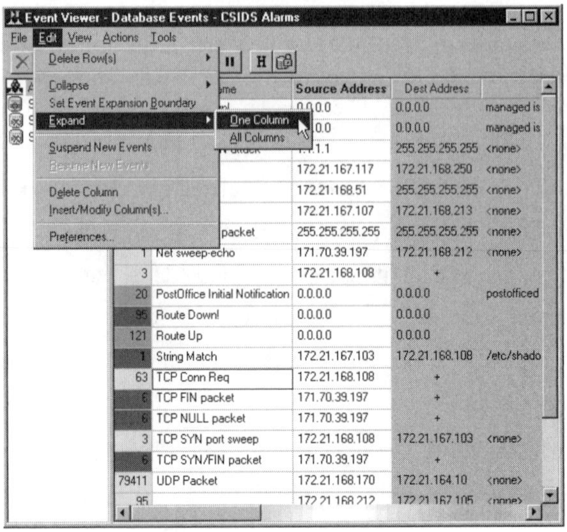

NOTE This is not a persistent change. This means that closing the Event Viewer and reopening it brings back the default settings and expansion boundary.

Expanding All Columns on the Selected Alarm Entry

Expanding an alarm entry one row at a time can be tedious, especially if the column that you are interested in is many fields away. In one click, you can expand all the fields for the currently selected row. To expand all the columns for the current alarm entry, click the Expand All Columns button on the top toolbar (refer back to Figure 8-7).

Another way to expand all the columns for an alarm entry is to select the row to expand and then choose **Expand**, **All Columns** from the **Edit** drop-down menu (see Figure 8-19).

NOTE This is not a persistent change. This means that closing the Event Viewer and reopening it brings back the default settings and expansion boundary.

Collapsing One Column on Selected Alarm Entry

To consolidate alarm details, you must collapse the columns until only the fields that you are interested in are expanded. When you collapse columns, however, the process begins with the column (that is not already collapsed) farthest to the right on the Event Viewer display. You cannot collapse specific columns only.

To collapse one column, select the row that you want to consolidate and then click the Collapse One Column button on the top toolbar (refer back to Figure 8-7).

Another way to collapse alarms one column at a time is to select the row to consolidate, and then choose **Collapse**, **One Column** from the Event Viewer **Edit** drop-down menu (see Figure 8-20).

Figure 8-20 *Collapsing Columns Using the Edit Drop-Down Menu*

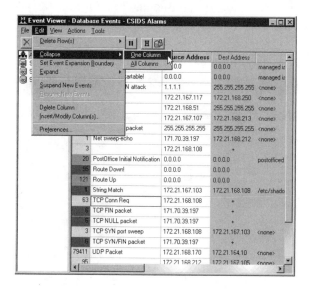

NOTE   This is not a persistent change. This means that closing the Event Viewer and reopening it brings back the default settings and expansion boundary.

Collapsing Columns up to the Currently Selected Column

Instead of collapsing a row one column at a time, you can collapse the row down to a specific column in a single operation. To do this, select the column you want to collapse to (in the row that you want to collapse), and then click the Collapse All Columns button on the top Event Viewer toolbar (refer back to Figure 8-7).

Another way to collapse alarms all the way to the column currently selected is to select the column that you want to collapse to, and then select **Collapse**, **All Columns** on the **Edit** drop-down menu (see Figure 8-20).

NOTE	This is not a persistent change. This means that closing the Event Viewer and reopening it brings back the default settings and expansion boundary.

Changing the Alarm Expansion Boundary

By default, the Event Viewer expands the first two columns of the grid. If you want to automatically expand more fields than this, you need to change the expansion boundary. To alter the expansion boundary, right-click on the last column that you want to expand, and then choose **Set Event Expansion Boundary** (see Figure 8-21). From this point forward, any new alarms that come in expand up to the column set to be the new expansion boundary.

Figure 8-21 *Changing the Alarm Expansion Boundary*

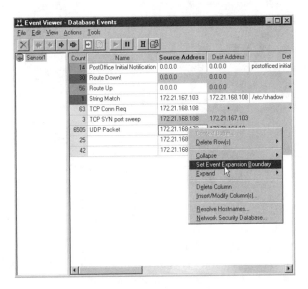

Expansion Boundary

The expansion boundary represents the block of columns that automatically expand when a new alarm entry comes into the table. The block of columns is contiguous and starts at the first column in the Event Viewer. By default, the expansion boundary expands the first two fields of an alarm entry. When setting a new expansion boundary, you have to specify only the last column to be expanded. All columns from the first column to the column that you specify now expand for new alarm entries.

Other ways to set the new expansion boundary are as follows:

- Select the column that you want to expand to, and choose **Set Event Expansion Boundary** from the Event Viewer **Edit** drop-down menu (refer back to Figure 8-18).

- Select the column that you want to expand to, and click the **Set Event Expansion Boundary** button on the top toolbar (refer back to Figure 8-7).

NOTE   This is not a persistent change. This means that closing the Event Viewer and reopening it brings back the default expansion boundary.

Moving Columns

The default order of fields within an alarm entry might not suit your operational environment. You can change the order in which the columns display in the Event Viewer. To move a column, click-and-drag the column header of the column that you want to move to the new position where you want it to be.

NOTE   This is not a persistent change. This means that closing the Event Viewer and reopening it brings back the default column ordering.

Deleting Columns

Instead of moving columns around to get the needed information at the beginning of the alarm entries, you might just want to remove certain columns from the Event Viewer.

NOTE   Deleting a column from the Event Viewer affects only the current Event Viewer window. If you open another Event Viewer window, all the fields are again available.

To delete columns from the Event Viewer, right-click the column that you want to delete, and then choose **Delete Column** from the pop-up menu (see Figure 8-22).

Another way to delete columns from the Event Viewer is to click anywhere on the column that you want to delete, and then choose **Delete Column** on the **Edit** drop-down menu (refer back to Figure 8-18).

Figure 8-22 *Selecting Delete Column*

NOTE

This is not a persistent change. This means that closing the Event Viewer and reopening it brings back the previously deleted columns.

Caution

Removing certain columns can affect the features available in your Event Viewer. The following table illustrates the effects of removing specified columns.

Column	Feature Affected
Source Address	Block, Remove Block (except all)
Sensor Name	View Block List, List Connection Status, View Network Device, View Services, View Statistics, Block, Remove Block, Reset Statistics, Enable Future Blocks, Disable Future Blocks
Org Name	View Block List, List Connection Status, View Network Device, View Services, View Statistics, Block, Remove Block, Reset Statistics, Enable Future Blocks, Disable Future Blocks
App Name	View Statistics, Reset Statistics

Selecting Columns to Be Displayed

You can customize which field columns display in the Event Viewer. To do this, choose **Insert, Modify Column(s)** on the **Edit** drop-down menu (refer back to Figure 8-18). This opens the Insert, Modify Columns window.

The Insert, Modify Columns window shows all the available fields (see Figure 8-23). To select or deselect a field to display, click the selection box in the Show column for that field. To choose the default sort order choose ↑ or ↓ in the Sort column for that field by clicking the sort field and toggling between ↑ or ↓.

Figure 8-23 *Insert/Modify Columns Window*

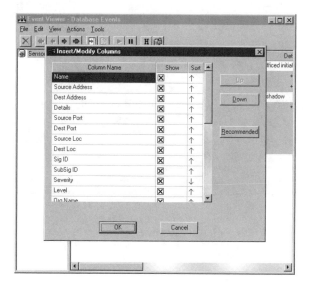

To change the order in which the fields display, you can use the **Up** or **Down** buttons to move the field location up or down. If you click the **Recommended** button, the field settings are reverted back to their default settings.

After you customize the view settings for the fields, you must click **OK** to accept your changes. If you choose to revert to the previous settings and ignore your changes, click **Cancel**. Choosing either of these options will take you back to the Event Viewer.

NOTE   This is a persistent change. This means that closing the Event Viewer and reopening it will bring back the same columns in the Event Viewer display.

Preference Settings

This section describes the different preference settings that you can use to customize in the Event Viewer. To access the Preferences window, click the **Preferences** option from the **Edit** drop-down menu (refer back to Figure 8-18). This will display the Preferences pop-up window (see Figure 8-24).

Figure 8-24 *Event Viewer Preferences Window*

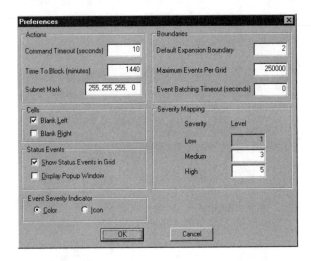

These settings fall into six basic categories:

- Actions
- Cells
- Status events
- Boundaries
- Event severity indicator
- Severity mapping

Actions

The Actions group box in the Preferences window enables you to set the following values (see Figure 8-24):

- Command Timeout [seconds]
- Time To Block [minutes]
- Subnet Mask

Command Timeout

The Command Timeout [seconds] value determines how long, in seconds, the Event Viewer waits for a response from the sensor before it concludes that it has lost communication with the sensor. In most cases, you do not need to modify this value. If you find that you are experiencing frequent command timeout errors, you might consider increasing the Command Timeout value or diagnosing the reason that your Event Viewer is experiencing such a slow response time.

The Command Timeout value applies to all functions that require communication through the PostOffice infrastructure. For example, functions such as retrieving sensor statistics, viewing sensor block lists, and requesting that the sensor blocks a particular IP address all must be completed within the Command Timeout. This timeout value is not used for non-PostOffice functions, such as DNS queries. The default value is 10 seconds, with an allowable range between 1 to 3600 seconds (one hour).

Time To Block

The Time To Block [minutes] specifies how long (in minutes) the sensor blocks traffic from the specified source when you issue a Block command from the Event Viewer. The block duration value that can be specified for the sensor in the Network Topology tree (NTT) applies only to blocks that are generated automatically by that sensor. The Time To Block value in the Preferences dialog box applies only to manually generated blocks from the Event Viewer. The default value is 1440 minutes (one day). The allowable range is from 1 to 525,600 minutes (one year).

Subnet Mask

The Subnet Mask value defines the network portion of the IP address that blocks a range of addresses. Your sensors use this information when they publish a blocking rule to the blocking devices on your network. The Subnet Mask value is applied only to the **Block**, **Network** and **Remove Block**, Network options from the Event Viewer Actions drop-down menu. The default value 255.255.255.0 represents a Class C address range.

Cells

The Blank Left and Blank Right check boxes in the Cells section of the Preferences window enable you to specify whether certain cells will be blank or filled in (refer back to Figure 8-24):

- Blank Left
- Blank Right

Blank Left

Choosing the Blank Left check box controls whether values that are suggested by a cell above a row are filled in on following rows in the Event Viewer. For example, consider the TCP Conn Req alarms shown in Figure 8-25. Because the Blank Left check box is selected, many of the fields are blank. This indicates that the field is the same as the previously filled in field. For instance, TCP Conn Req is listed only on the first alarm entry. The same thing happens after the 172.21.168.108 source address. The next two entries are the same address, so they are left blank.

Figure 8-25 *Example of Blank Left Selected*

1	String Match	172.21.167.103	172.21.168.108	/etc/shad
3	TCP Conn Req	171.69.162.41	172.21.168.106	
3			172.21.168.108	
8		172.21.167.22	172.21.168.170	
9		172.21.168.108	172.21.167.103	
36			172.21.168.104	
18			172.21.168.212	
3		172.21.168.206	172.21.168.106	6969
7	TCP FIN packet	171.70.39.197	172.21.168.106	<none>

If the Blank Left box is not selected, the grid appears as shown in Figure 8-26. Here all the fields are filled in.

Figure 8-26 *Example of Blank Left Not Selected*

1	String Match	172.21.167.103	172.21.168.108	/etc/shad
3	TCP Conn Req	171.69.162.41	172.21.168.106	
3	TCP Conn Req	171.69.162.41	172.21.168.108	
8	TCP Conn Req	172.21.167.22	172.21.168.170	
9	TCP Conn Req	172.21.168.108	172.21.167.103	
36	TCP Conn Req	172.21.168.108	172.21.168.104	
18	TCP Conn Req	172.21.168.108	172.21.168.212	
3	TCP Conn Req	172.21.168.206	172.21.168.106	6969
7	TCP FIN packet	171.70.39.197	172.21.168.106	<none>
1	TCP FIN packet	171.70.39.197	172.21.168.180	<none>

Blank Right

Choosing Blank Right also affects how the collapsed cells display in the Event Viewer, but with respect to the fields on the right side of the expansion boundary. When cells are collapsed, their background color is gray and if the collapsed values are different, a plus sign (+) displays. When Blank Right is selected, a plus sign displays in a collapsed cell regardless of whether the cell values differ (see Figure 8-27).

Figure 8-27 *Example of Blank Right Selected*

1	Impossible IP packet	255.255.255.255	+
1	Net sweep-echo	171.69.162.41	+
3	Net sweep-echo	171.70.39.197	+
1	Net sweep-echo	172.21.167.26	+
1	Net sweep-echo	172.21.167.119	+
3	Net sweep-echo	172.21.168.108	+
1	Net sweep-echo	192.168.35.110	+
23	PostOffice Initial Notification	0.0.0.0	+

The default setting is for Blank Right not to be selected. In this state, a plus sign displays in collapsed cells only if the values in the cells differ. If the values in the collapsed cell are the same, the actual value displays in the Event Viewer (see Figure 8-28).

Figure 8-28 *Example of Blank Right Not Selected*

1	Impossible IP packet	255.255.255.255	255.255.255.255	<none>
1	Net sweep-echo	171.69.162.41	172.21.168.213	<none>
3	Net sweep-echo	171.70.39.197	+	
1	Net sweep-echo	172.21.167.26	172.21.168.213	<none>
1	Net sweep-echo	172.21.167.119	172.21.168.250	<none>
3	Net sweep-echo	172.21.168.108	+	
1	Net sweep-echo	192.168.35.110	172.21.168.213	<none>
23	PostOffice Initial Notification	0.0.0.0	0.0.0.0	postoffice

Status Events

The Status Events group box enables you to determine how status events display in your Event Viewer (refer back to Figure 8-24). There are three possible status events:

- PostOffice Initial Notification
- Route Down
- Route Up

The PostOffice Initial Notification status event occurs when a sensor's PostOffice service is started. Notification of the event is sent to your CSPM host.

The final two status events indicate the state of the communication between devices on your network. When communication with another device is lost, a Route Down message is generated. When the communication is restored, a Route Up message is generated.

You have two options that you can choose from as to how these three status messages display in the Event Viewer:

- Show Status Events in Grid
- Display Popup Window

Show Status Events in Grid

Show Status Events in Grid is the default setting. This option displays the status events in the actual grid of the Event Viewer. These status events appear similar to other alarm entries in the Event Viewer grid (refer back to Figure 8-3). The following are common status events:

- Route Down
- Route Up
- PostOffice Initial Notification

Display Popup Window

If you do not want the status events to appear in the Event Viewer grid, choose Display Popup Window. With this option, only the Route Down status events appear as a pop-up window. The other two status events do not display.

Boundaries

The Boundaries group box in the Preferences enables you to set the following values (refer back to Figure 8-24):

- Default Expansion Boundary
- Maximum Events Per Grid
- Event Batching Timeout

Default Expansion Boundary

The Default Expansion Boundary field specifies the default number of columns in which the cells of a new event are expanded. By default, the first two columns of an event are expanded.

Maximum Events Per Grid

The Maximum Events Per Grid field defines the maximum number of alarms that can display in a single Event Viewer. When the maximum value is reached, an error message appears. The default value is 250,000 alarms. The allowable range is from 1 to 4,000,000,000 alarms.

Warning

Setting the Maximum Events Per Grid field to its maximum value of 4,000,000,000 requires an extremely large database. If your database is too small, you run the risk of exceeding its capacity.

Event Batching Timeout

The Event Batching Timeout [seconds] field specifies how often (in seconds) the Event Viewer is updated during an alarm flood. The default value is 0 seconds, indicating that the Event Viewer is continually updated as your sensors generate alarms.

Event Severity Indicator

You have two options to choose from in the Event Severity Indicator area of the Preferences screen (refer back to Figure 8-24): Color and Icon.

Color

The default setting is for the severity to be indicated in the Event Viewer with colors. The color affects the background of the Count field. The following colors are used to indicate alarm severity:

- High severity displays in red.
- Medium severity displays in yellow.
- Low severity displays in green.

Icon

In addition to the default color severity indicator, you also can choose to display the severity of your alarms using icons. The following icons display alarm severity:

- High severity is a red exclamation point.
- Medium severity is a yellow flag.
- Low severity receives no icon.

Severity Mapping

The values under the Severity Mapping group box of the Preferences window (refer back to Figure 8-24) map a range of an alarm's severity level (a number that usually ranges from 1 to 5) to a severity of Low, Medium, or High.

By default, events at levels 1 and 2 are Low, levels 3 and 4 are Medium, and levels 5 and higher are High. By changing the starting level value for any option, you can change the associated range of severities. This changes the associated color and icon to the events that fall within that range within the Event Viewer grids.

A few constraints apply to the numbers you can specify. The Medium level must be greater than or equal to the Low level, and the High level must be greater than or equal to the Medium level. The start value for the Low level range is fixed at 1. Also, all values must be between 1 to 255. If they are not, you are notified, and the values are adjusted for you.

Connection Status Pane

This section discusses the sensor status reporting options in the Event Viewer. You can choose to display the Connection Status pane in your Event Viewer. The Connection Status pane displays icons for all the sensors reporting to CSPM and provides options to get status information from the sensors. To view the Connection Status pane, choose **Connection Status Pane** from the **View** drop-down menu (see Figure 8-29). If the Connection Status pane is already displayed, a check mark appears before the menu choice (refer back to Figure 8-10). The Event Viewer without the Connection Status pane active can be seen in Figure 8-29. This status pane displays the names of your sensors that are communicating with your CSPM host.

Figure 8-29 *Selecting the Connection Status Pane Option*

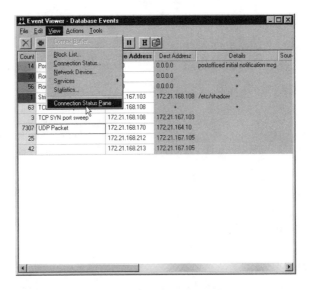

The Connection Status pane provides you with several types of sensor status:

- Connection status
- Service status
- Service versions
- Statistics
- Reset statistics

Connection Status

From the Connection Status pane, you can get information on the status of the connection between your CSPM host and the sensors reporting to it. To do this, right-click the sensor you want connection status information about on the Connection Status pane and choose **Connection Status** (see Figure 8-30). This opens the Connection Status window, which indicates the status of the connection for the selected sensor.

Figure 8-30 *Displaying Sensor Connection Status Information*

In the Connection Status window, you see one of two possible connection status messages (see Figure 8-31): Established and Not established.

Figure 8-31 *Connection Status Window*

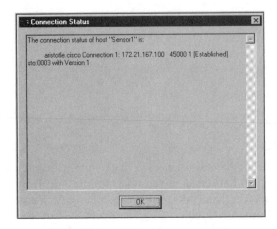

Other ways to open the Connection Status window are as follows:

- Select the sensor you want connection status information about from the Connection Status pane and choose **Connection Status** from the **View** drop-down menu (refer back to Figure 8-10).

- Select a row in the Event Viewer and choose **Connection Status** from the **View** drop-down menu (refer back to Figure 8-10). You receive connection status information for the sensor that reported the alarm you selected in the Event Viewer. If the row has consolidated alarms from multiple sensors, the connection status of all sensors is reported.

Service Status

From the Connection Status pane, you can get information on the status of the services running on the sensors reporting to your CSPM host. To do this, choose **Service Status** from the Connection Status pane for the appropriate sensor (see Figure 8-30). This opens the Daemon Status window, which indicates the status of the services running on the selected sensor.

The Daemon Status window indicates the status of the services running on your sensor (see Figure 8-32).

Figure 8-32 *Daemon Status Window*

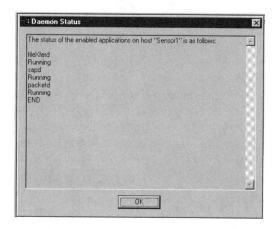

Other ways to open the Daemon Status window are as follows:

- Select the sensor you want service status information about on the Connection Status pane, and choose **Services**, **Status** from the **View** drop-down menu (see Figure 8-33).

- Select a row in the Event Viewer and choose Services, Status from the View drop-down menu (see Figure 8-33). You receive service status information for the service that generated the selected alarm only, typically packetd.

Figure 8-33 *Choosing Service Information from the View Drop-Down Menu*

NOTE	If the App Name column is not displayed in the Event Viewer, Services, Status will be grayed out in the View drop-down menu, indicating the option is not available.

Service Versions

From the Connection Status pane, you can get the version information of the services running on the sensors reporting to your CSPM host. To do this, choose **Service Versions** from the Connection Status pane for the sensor in question (refer back to Figure 8-30). This opens the Daemon Versions window, which indicates the versions of the services running on the selected sensor.

The versions of the services running on your sensor display in a Daemon Versions window (see Figure 8-34).

Figure 8-34 *Daemon Versions Window*

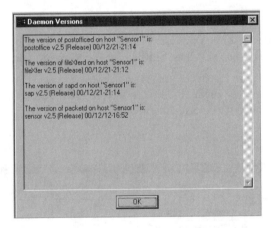

Other ways to open the Daemon Versions window are as follows:

- Select the sensor you want service version information about from the Connection Status pane and choose **Services**, **Version** on the **View** drop-down menu (see Figure 8-33).

- Select a row in the Event Viewer and choose **Services**, **Version** from the **View** drop-down menu (see Figure 8-33). You receive service version information for the service that generated the selected alarm only, typically packetd.

NOTE	If the App Name column is not being displayed in the Event Viewer, Services, Status is grayed out in the View drop-down menu, indicating the option is not available.

Statistics

The sensor keeps track of statistics regarding the processing of network packets, such as the number of packets viewed since the sensor's services were last started. To view the statistics for a sensor, select the sensor you want statistics information about on the Connection Status pane and choose **Statistics** from the **View** drop-down menu (refer back to Figure 8-10). This opens the Sensor Statistics window.

In the Sensor Statistics window, you see the statistics for the selected sensor (see Figure 8-35).

Figure 8-35 *Sensor Statistics Window*

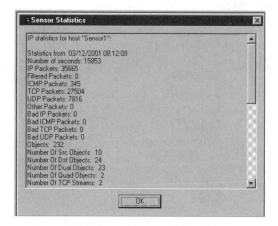

The Sensor Statistics window provides you statistical information related to the traffic that your sensor examined and transmitted. These statistics are broken down into three categories:

- IP statistics
- Packet statistics (Monitoring interface)
- SYSLOG statistics

These statistics enable you to get a feel for the amount of traffic that your sensor is processing. It also shows you the breakdown for the types of traffic that your sensor needs to process. It is helpful to know whether the majority of the traffic on your network is TCP, UDP, or ICMP-based. Furthermore, these statistics give you insight into the types of objects that your sensor is tracking. These objects enable your sensor to detect various alarms, but these objects also take up valuable space in your sensor's memory.

Another way to open the Sensor Statistics window is to select a row in the Event Viewer and choose **Statistics** from the **View** drop-down menu (refer back to Figure 8-10). Statistic information for the sensor that generated the selected alarm will display.

NOTE	If the Sensor Name column is not displayed in the Event Viewer, **Statistics** in the **View** drop-down menu are grayed out, indicating the option is not available.

Reset Statistics

You can reset the counts back to 0 for the statistics kept for a sensor. To reset the statistic counts for a sensor, select the sensor you want to reset statistics for on the Connection Status pane and choose **Reset Statistics** from the **Actions** drop-down menu (see Figure 8-36).

Figure 8-36 *Event Viewer Action Drop-Down Menu*

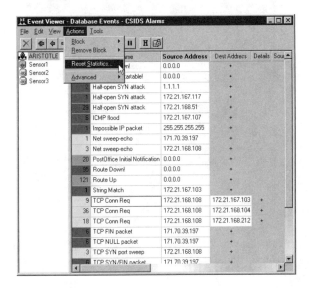

This resets the statistics for the selected sensor and opens the Resetting Statistics status window (see Figure 8-37).

The Resetting Statistics window indicates the success of your attempt to reset the statistical counters on your sensor. If no errors occurred, each statistical category should show a success indicating that the reset occurred without an error.

Another way to reset the sensor statistics is to select a row in the Event Viewer and choose **Reset Statistics** on the **Actions** drop-down menu (see Figure 8-36). You reset the statistics for the sensor that generated the selected alarm.

Figure 8-37 *Reset Statistics Window*

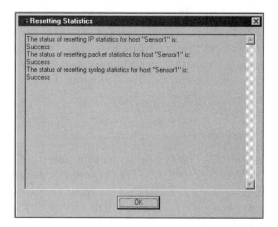

NOTE   If the Sensor Name column is not displayed in the Event Viewer, **Reset Statistics** in the
Actions drop-down menu appear grayed out, indicating the option is not available.

Summary

Understanding the operation of the CSPM Event Viewer is vital to the efficient analysis of
the alarms that your sensors generate. The Event Viewer is a graphical interface into the
database of alarms being maintained by your CSPM host. Operating your Event Viewer
requires a detailed understanding of the various features that you can modify within the
Event Viewer to accommodate your operational environment. This chapter discussed
features that fall into the following four areas:

- Managing alarms
- Customizing the Event Viewer
- Preference settings
- Connection Status pane

As discussed, to manage alarms effectively, you must focus on the numerous functions
related to analyzing the alarms displayed by the Event Viewer.

The alarm entries are composed of various fields. These fields supply the information
needed to analyze the impact of the alarm on your network. Basically, these fields fall into
the following four categories:

- General information fields
- Source information fields

- Destination information fields
- Signature information fields

The Event Viewer displays the IP addresses of the hosts involved in an alarm. Most people remember the names of the hosts on their network more easily than the actual IP addresses. You can determine the names of the hosts associated with an alarm by right-clicking the alarm in question and choosing **Resolve Hostnames** from the drop-down menu.

Some signatures create a context buffer that provides you with up to 255 bytes worth of data that is collected around the time that the signature triggered. The context buffer contains keystrokes, data, or both from the connection stream.

To help you analyze the impact of alarms on your network, Cisco has developed its Network Security Database (NSDB). Each signature is described in this database and is linked to the vulnerability that an attacker is exploiting to trigger the signature. The basic signature information is presented in an NSDB Exploit Signature page. This Web page consists of the following fields:

- Signature Name
- Signature ID
- Subsignature ID
- Recommended Alarm Level
- Signature Type
- Signature Structure
- Implementation
- Signature Description
- Benign Triggers
- Related Vulnerability
- User Notes

The Related Vulnerability field links the exploit information to an NSDB Related Vulnerability page. This Web page provides information about the vulnerability that an attacker is exploiting to cause a specific signature to fire. This vulnerability page consists of the following fields:

- Vulnerability Name
- Alias
- Vulnerability ID
- Severity Level
- Vulnerability Type
- Exploit Type

- Affected System(s)
- Affected Program(s)
- Vulnerability Description
- Consequence
- Countermeasures
- Advisory/Related Link(s)
- Fix/Upgrade/Patch Link(s)
- Exploit Links
- User Notes

To reduce clutter and the shear amount of alarms on your screen, you frequently need to remove or delete alarm entries from the Event Viewer. When you delete alarms from the Event Viewer, you have three options:

- From This Grid
- From All Grids
- From Database

In addition to deleting alarms from the Event Viewer, sometimes you need to stop new alarms from appearing on the screen so that you can analyze the alarms that you already have. You can do this by stopping and resuming the live feed to the Event Viewer. Even though you stop the live feed to the Event Viewer, new alarms are still collected by the CSPM database.

To effectively manage alarms, you also must understand how to customize the Event Viewer. By default, only some of the columns on each alarm entry are expanded in the Event Viewer. Entries with identical expanded columns are automatically consolidated onto a single row. You can customize the appearance of your Event Viewer in the following ways:

- Expand or Collapse Single Columns
- Expand or Collapse All Columns
- Change the Order of Columns
- Move Columns
- Delete Columns
- Setting the Columns to be Displayed

You also have access to a Preferences window that enables you to control the following six areas:

- Actions
- Cells

- Status Events
- Boundaries
- Event Severity Indicator
- Severity Mapping

The Actions section enables you to configure the length of time that your Director waits (without a response) before indicating that your sensor is unreachable. You also can configure the default blocking duration and network mask used for manually initiated blocks.

The Cells section enables you to configure how the Event Viewer handles the display of cells for contiguous records with identical fields. You can turn these two options on and off: Blank Left and Blank Right.

The Status Events section enables you to configure how the Event Viewer handles the following three message types:

- PostOffice Initial Notification
- Route Down
- Route Up

These messages indicate the status of the link between your Director and your sensor. You can control how these events display by choosing one of the following two options:

- Show Status Events in Grid
- Display Popup Window

The Boundaries section enables you to set limits on your Event Viewer display by configuring the following parameters:

- Default Expansion Boundary
- Maximum Events Per Grid
- Event Batching Timeout

The Event Severity Indicator section enables you to configure the color and icon type for your different alarm levels. It also enables you to map your numeric alarm levels to an alarm severity.

The final area that affects your management of alarms is the Connection Status pane. These options in this pane examine the current status of the connections with your sensor, along with the status of service applications on your sensor. Furthermore, through the Connection Status pane, you can obtain statistics about the types of traffic that your sensor is processing. These options are as follows:

- Connection Status
- Service Status

- Service Versions
- Statistics
- Reset Statistics

Review Questions

The following questions test your retention of the material presented in this chapter. The answers to the Review Questions are in Appendix K, "Answers to Review Questions."

1 What serves as the interface to the alarms in the CSPM database?

_____

_____

_____

2 What is the NSDB?

_____

_____

_____

3 What is the context buffer?

_____

_____

_____

4 What is a subsignature ID?

_____

_____

_____

5 When you expand more columns on an alarm entry, are those changes present when you open another Event Viewer?

_____

_____

_____

6 How do you change the default order of columns for new Event Viewers?

_____

_____

_____

7 What are your two options for indicating event severity?

_____

_____

_____

8 What values can the alarm level assume?

_____

_____

_____

9 What values can the alarm severity assume?

_____

_____

_____

10 Which fields can remove CSPM features if they are deleted from your Event Viewer?

_____

_____

_____

11 How do you determine the amount of TCP traffic that one of your sensors regularly examines?

_____

_____

_____

12 Which customizations to the Event Viewer are persistent?

_____

_____

_____

13 When deleting alarm entries from the Event Viewer, what are your three options?

_____

_____

_____

14 What two techniques can you use to enable your CSPM host to resolve host names?

_____

_____

_____

15 Is the signature ID equal to the vulnerability ID of the related vulnerability for each signature?

_____

_____

_____

16 If you delete the Source Address field from the Event Viewer, what functions can you no longer perform from the Event Viewer?

_____

_____

_____

17 What menu selection do you need to use to view the running status of the daemons on your sensor?

_____

_____

_____

18 If you delete the App Name field from the Event Viewer, what functions are no longer available?

_____

_____

_____

19 If the Blank Right preference option is selected, what will the field to the right of the expansion boundary contain?

_____

_____

_____

## CHAPTER 9

Understanding Cisco Secure IDS Signatures

Your Cisco Secure IDS Sensors continually monitor the traffic at key locations throughout your network. Their job is to detect intrusive activity on your network and then report this activity to your Director platform so that you can take the appropriate action to protect your network resources. Your sensors detect attacks against your network by checking network traffic against defined attack signatures in its database. These signatures form the core of your Cisco Secure IDS. Understanding these signatures enables you to more effectively use your IDS to defend critical network components. To aid your understanding, this chapter contains the following categories:

- Signature definition
- Signature classes
- Signature types
- Signature severity

Signature Definition

A *signature* is a set of rules that your sensor uses to detect typical intrusive activity. These rules are based on various criteria. Some of these criteria include the following:

- IP protocol parameters (IP addresses, IP options, fragmentation, and so on)
- Transport protocol parameters (TCP flags, port numbers)
- Packet data

Your Cisco Secure IDS Sensors examine the traffic on your network by using the rule sets in its database. If your sensor observes traffic that matches a signature (a specific set of rules), it triggers an event. This event represents a unique response for the specific signature that the sensor detected. The two characteristics that define a Cisco Secure IDS signature are as follows:

- Signature implementation
- Signature structure

Signature Implementation

The Cisco Secure IDS signatures must locate intrusive activity by monitoring the traffic traversing the network. The only information available to the sensor is the Ethernet frames that it captures with its monitoring interface. Inside these frames are encapsulated IP packets. These IP packets are composed of different headers and, potentially, application data. Sensor signatures can examine the information in the various headers or the packet's data. Therefore, the sensor signatures are implemented in one of two ways (depending on whether the signature is examining packet headers or packet data):

- Context
- Content

Context

Context-based signatures are triggered by the data contained in packet headers. The rules for these signatures focus on IP protocol parameters and transport protocol parameters. The common transport protocols are TCP, UDP, and ICMP. Data for context signatures comes from the control structure used to communicate between hosts and other devices on a network. Some of the information examined for context-based signatures includes the following:

- Port numbers
- IP options
- IP fragmentation parameters
- TCP flags
- IP protocol field
- IP, TCP, and UDP checksums
- IP addresses

A sample context signature is TCP SYN Port Sweep (Signature ID 3002). This signature triggers when an attacker scans multiple ports on a host. The sensor is checking the TCP headers from multiple packets traveling across the network.

Content

Content-based signatures are triggered by information contained in the data portion of the packets traveling across the network. This data portion of the packet is also known as the *packet payload* and is information being sent to an application on another host on the network.

A sample content signature is Sendmail Reconnaissance (Signature ID 3103). This signature locates IP packets with either a **VRFY** or **EXPN sendmail** command. An attacker can use these commands to locate account names on the mail server.

Signature Structure

Signature implementations involve examining packet headers and packet data. Now it is time to examine the structure of a signature. The structure of signatures revolves around the number of packets that the sensor must examine to detect the signature. Signature structures fall into two distinct categories:

- Atomic
- Composite

Atomic

Some attacks can be conducted with a single packet. With other attacks, a specific attack string must occur in a single packet. Each of these attacks falls into the *atomic* signatures category because the attack can be detected by observing a single network packet. Therefore, atomic signatures do not require any state information. An example of an atomic signature is the SYN-FIN packet (Signature ID 3041).

NOTE   TCP connections use several flags to control the connection (SYN, FIN, ACK, RST, and PSH). A SYN is used during the initiation of a connection, whereas a FIN is used to signal the end of a connection. If both the SYN and FIN flags are set in the same IP packet, this is an invalid combination. Furthermore, an invalid combination is a suspicious activity that probably indicates a scan against your network.

Composite

Composite signatures are triggered by a series of multiple packets. Unlike atomic signatures, a sensor needs to potentially examine multiple packets to detect a composite signature. Furthermore, because your sensor has to examine multiple data packets to identify composite signatures, these signatures also require the sensor to save information about packets seen so far (known as *state information*). When your sensor sees the first packet that might be part of a composite signature, it must save this information while it checks for other packets that potentially complete the signature.

A sample composite signature is IP fragments overlap (Signature ID 1103). To trigger this signature (as the name implies), you need at least two fragmented IP packets (making the signature composite). The sensor checks each IP fragment for a single packet to determine whether any of the individual fragments overlap.

Signature Classes

The Cisco Secure IDS signatures fall into several categories, depending on the goal of the attacker. These signature classes are as follows:

- Reconnaissance
- Informational
- Access
- Denial of service

Reconnaissance Signatures

Before conducting a robbery, robbers usually case their target to determine potential weaknesses in the target's security. These weaknesses might be open windows or an antiquated alarm system.

Computer attackers also case your network before conducting their actual attack. The *reconnaissance class signatures* trigger on network activity that potentially represents an attacker attempting to locate systems, services, and vulnerabilities on your network. Examples of potential reconnaissance activity include the following:

- **Ping sweeps**—Searching for active machines in a range of IP addresses
- **Port scans**—Checking multiple ports on a system in search of active services
- **DNS queries**—Retrieving information from DNS about the topology of your network

Informational Signatures

Information class signatures are signatures that trigger on normal network activity that in itself is not considered to be malicious, but can be used to determine the validity of an attack or for forensics purposes. Examples of information activity include the following:

- **ICMP echo requests**—A packet used to check network connectivity to a system
- **TCP connection requests**—A TCP packet with the SYN flag set that is sent to a specific TCP port on a system (indicates a new connection attempt)
- **UDP connections**—Packets sent to a specific UDP port on a system (indicates use of a UDP service)

Access Signatures

Access class signatures are signatures that trigger on network activity that is known to be or might lead to unauthorized data retrieval, system access, or privileged escalation. Examples of access activity include the following:

- UNIX Tooltalk Database server attack (Signature ID 6191)
- Internet Information Services (IIS) Unicode attack (Signature ID 5114)
- BackOrifice (Signature ID 4053)

Denial of Service Signatures

Sometimes, an attacker's goal is to disrupt the operation of a network. This might be denying access to an e-commerce Web server. It might be preventing access to a mail server. All of these attacks are known as *denial of service attacks*.

The *denial of service class signatures* trigger on network traffic that is known to disable or disrupt systems or services on your network. Examples of denial of service activity include the following:

- Ping of Death (Signature ID 2154)
- Tribe Flood Network (TFN) attacks (Signature IDs 6501 and 6502)
- Trinoo attacks (Signature IDs 6505 and 6506)

Signature Types

Besides categorizing signatures by the goals of the attacker, sometimes it is helpful to break down the signatures by the types of network traffic involved. This more closely relates the intrusive traffic to the type of network traffic that your sensor is observing. The signature types are as follows:

- General
- Connection
- String
- Access control list

General

The general signatures detect a wide range of intrusion attempts. These signatures are spread across various protocols (IP, ICMP, TCP, and UDP). Many of these signatures are context-based because they examine protocol control information and look for abnormalities; whereas others, such as many of the Web signatures, are content-based because they look for abnormalities in the data portion of HTTP protocol packets (an application layer protocol). The general signatures include the following Cisco Secure IDS signature series:

- Series 1000 signatures (IP signatures)
- Series 2000 signatures (ICMP signatures)
- Series 5000 signatures (Web/HTTP signatures)
- Series 6000 signatures (cross-protocol signatures)

Some examples of general signatures include the following:

- IP fragments overlap (Signature ID 1103)
- ICMP echo request (Signature ID 2004)
- DNS zone transfer request (Signature ID 6051)
- WWW IIS Unicode attack (Signature ID 5114)
- TFN client request (Signature ID 6501)

Connection

The connection signatures (as the name implies) detect TCP connections and network traffic to UDP ports. The Cisco Secure IDS signature series that track connections fall into the following two series:

- 3000 Series signatures (TCP signatures)
- 4000 Series signatures (UDP signatures)

If your sensor simply reports that it detects 40 TCP connections and 35 UDP connections, you cannot use this information effectively. First, you might wonder which ports the various connections went to. Knowing the destination port for a TCP or UDP connection usually informs you of the application that the connection is going to (by knowing the well-known port numbers). Therefore, the connection signatures use a subsignature ID to distinguish connections, with the subsignature ID being the port that the connection went to. For instance, a connection request to TCP port 21 alarms with Signature 3000 and Subsignature ID 21. The following are connection signature examples:

- TCP High Port Sweep (3001)
- UDP bomb (4050)

String

The string signatures detect specific textual strings that you consider important. Your sensor examines network traffic by using a standard *regular expression*–matching algorithm to trigger your string signatures. The string signatures fall into one Cisco Secure IDS signature series: 8000 Signature (string-matching signatures).

Regular Expression

A *regular expression* is a mechanism by which you can define how your sensor searches for a specified sequence of characters in the data stream. You can use many features to create an elaborate string search. Many different programs use regular expressions to enable you to create custom string searches. In the UNIX world, the **grep** command is probably the most common program that utilizes regular expressions to search for text. The following is a command example:

```
grep [Aa][Tt][Tt][Aa][Cc][Kk] file.txt
```

In the previously listed example, the **grep** command is used to perform a noncase-sensitive search for the word *attack*.

Each time your sensor triggers on a string signature, the Signature ID is 8000. The signature subID is used to differentiate which string was detected. As an example, you can define an 8000 signature with a SubID equal to 10000 that triggers on the string "hack". In this case, any IP traffic with the string "hack" triggers an alarm. The ID of the alarm is 8000, with a SubID equal to 10000. Some predefined 8000 Series alarms include the following:

- Telnet-/etc/shadow (ID 8000, SubID 2302)
- Rlogin + + (ID 8000, SubID 51303)

Access Control List

You restrict traffic on your network by applying access control lists (ACLs) to the routers on your network. When network traffic attempts to violate these established policies (ACLs), your routers can trigger alarms. The signatures (triggered by violations against your defined Cisco IOS ACLs) fall into a single Cisco Secure IDS signature series, for example, 10000 series signatures (policy violation signatures).

Again, the signature subID is used to differentiate the various ACL signatures because each ACL signature has a Signature ID of 10000.

Signature Severity

Your signature templates assign severity levels to each Cisco Secure IDS signature. The severity of the signature represents the probability that the signature represents an immediate threat to the network.

Cisco network security engineers establish default severity values for each of the Cisco Secure IDS signatures (see Appendix G, "Cisco Secure IDS Signatures and Recommended Alarm Levels"). These default values are adequate for many network environments.

However, the signature severity settings are configurable to enable you to tune the signature severity values to match your operational network environment. The three severity levels are as follows:

- Low
- Medium
- High

Table 9-1 displays a consolidated view of the mappings of severity level to threat level and the probability of an actual attack.

Table 9-1 *Signature Severities*

Severity	Description	Probability of an Actual Attack	Immediate Threat
Low Alarm Level 1–2	Signatures that detect network activity considered to be benign but are detected for informational purposes	Very Low	No
Medium Alarm Level 3–4	Signatures that detect abnormal network activity that might be perceived as malicious	Medium	Low
High Alarm Level 5	Signatures that detect attacks often used to gain access or cause a denial of service	Very High	High

Low Severity (Alarm Level 1–2)

The low-severity signatures are composed of the signatures that pose the lowest threat to your network. These signatures usually detect network activity considered benign that is detected for informational purposes. A low severity is equated to a default alarm level of 1–2. The following are examples of low-severity signatures:

- Unknown IP Protocol (Signature ID 1101)
- FTP SYST Command Attempted (Signature ID 3151)

Benign Signatures

Most of the low-severity signatures are considered benign. These benign signatures trigger on normal network activity, such as ICMP echo requests and TCP connections. By themselves, they do not represent a significant threat to your network and are included to provide a more complete view of activity on your network. Furthermore, during an actual attack, this extra information can prove invaluable.

Medium Severity (Alarm Level 3–4)

The medium-severity signatures are composed of abnormal network activity that you might perceive as malicious. Some of these signatures include legacy vulnerabilities that are not often seen on today's networks because they have been patched by most operating systems. Attacks against these legacy vulnerabilities have a low probability of succeeding, which is why they are categorized with a medium severity. By default, signatures with an alarm level of 3 and 4 are mapped into the medium-severity range. The following are examples of medium-severity signatures:

- ICMP Network Sweep w/Echo (Signature ID 2100)
- TCP SYN Port Sweep (Signature ID 3002)

High Severity (Alarm Level 5)

The final severity level is composed of the most significant threats to your network. These signatures detect attacks that an attacker uses to gain access to resources on your network. The high-severity range also includes DoS attacks because they disrupt the operation of your network. The following are examples of high-severity signatures:

- BackOrifice BO2K TCP Non Stealth (Signature ID 3990)
- WWW IIS Unicode (Signature ID 5114)
- sadmind RPC Buffer Overflow (Signature ID 6194)

NOTE   You can change the mapping of alarm level to severity value by altering the Severity Mapping on the Preferences menu (see Chapter 8, "Working with Cisco Secure IDS Alarms in CSPM," for details). The default values are as follows:

- **Low severity:** 1
- **Medium severity:** 3
- **High severity:** 5

This means signatures with an alarm level of 1 and 2 map to a low severity. Alarm levels of 3 and 4 map to medium severity. Only signatures with an alarm level of 5 map to high severity.

Summary

Signatures form the heart of your Cisco Secure IDS. Understanding how these signatures are structured and the various signature series that they fall into is vital to obtaining the optimum protection from your Cisco Secure IDS.

Each IDS signature represents a specific set of rules that define potentially intrusive network activity. If your sensor detects the traffic specified by one of these rule sets (signature), it fires an alarm.

Signatures can be constructed through one of two implementation categories:

- Context
- Content

The implementation method used depends on where the sensor needs to look for the specific traffic. If the sensor needs to examine the IP headers, the signature is context. However, if the sensor needs to examine the payload or data in a packet, the signature is content-based.

Besides the implementation, each signature also has an associated structure. This structure defines how many network packets your sensor needs to examine to potentially trigger the signature. The two possible signature structures are as follows:

- Atomic
- Composite

With atomic signatures, your sensors need to look only at a single packet to determine whether to trigger the signature. Composite signatures, however, require your sensor to examine multiple packets before observing all the intrusive activity and determining whether to trigger an alarm. Furthermore, with composite signatures, your sensor needs to maintain state information. This state information must be maintained from the time that your sensor receives the first packet that can be part of an attack signature until it observes either a packet that completes the attack signature or a packet that indicates that the attack signature cannot be completed.

The Cisco Secure IDS signatures fall into several categories, depending on the goal of the attacker. These signature classes are as follows:

- Reconnaissance
- Informational
- Access
- Denial of service

Reconnaissance signatures are indicative of an attacker casing your network (potentially preparing for a more severe attack). Informational signatures represent activity on your network that in and of itself does not pose a significant threat, but these signatures are included in Cisco Secure IDS to provide a more complete picture of the activity on your network. This supporting information is useful during an actual attack. The attack signatures are composed of network traffic that is indicative of actual attacks, whereas the DoS signatures are composed of activity that is indicative of an attacker attempting to disrupt the operation of your network resources.

In addition to categorizing signatures by the goals of the attacker, sometimes it is helpful to break down the signatures by the types of network traffic involved. The signature types are as follows:

- General
- Connection
- String
- ACL

Finally, each Cisco Secure IDS signature is associated with a severity that indicates the criticality of the signature. This criticality is measured by the probability that the traffic represents an attack against your network and the immediacy of the threat. The three severity levels are as follows:

- Low
- Medium
- High

The high-severity signatures represent the most significant threats against your network.

Review Questions

The following questions test your retention of the material presented in this chapter. The answers to the Review Questions are in Appendix K, "Answers to Review Questions."

1   What are the two signature implementation categories?

_____

_____

_____

2   What are the three severity levels associated with Cisco Secure IDS signatures?

_____

_____

_____

3   What are the classes of signatures?

_____

_____

_____

4 What does a content signature examine?

_____

_____

_____

5 Alarms with which severity represent the most significant threat to your network?

_____

_____

_____

6 What are the four signature classes that break down signatures based on the goal of the attacker?

_____

_____

_____

7 What is a port scan?

_____

_____

_____

8 What are the four categories of signatures based on network traffic?

_____

_____

_____

9 What is a Cisco Secure IDS signature?

_____

_____

_____

10 What are the two structure types for Cisco Secure IDS signatures?

_____

_____

_____

11 What does it mean to say that a signature is composite?

_____

_____

_____

12 What are the major areas of an IP packet that are examined by context signatures?

_____

_____

_____

## CHAPTER 10

Signature Series

For easier identification, Cisco Secure IDS organizes its signatures in numeric series. Each numeric series defines a collection of related signatures. Even though you might not recognize a specific signature ID, you can readily identify the type of signature that it is by knowing the signature series into which it falls. The current eight series, along with the associated signature type, are as follows:

- IP signatures (1000 Series)
- ICMP signatures (2000 Series)
- TCP signatures (3000 Series)
- UDP signatures (4000 Series)
- Web/HTTP signatures (5000 Series)
- Cross-protocol signatures (6000 Series)
- String-matching signatures (8000 Series)
- Policy-violation signatures (10000 Series)

This chapter discusses each in turn.

IP Signatures (1000 Series)

The 1000 Series signatures include the signatures that are based on examining components of the IP header (see Figure 10-1). These signatures fall into the following categories:

- IP options
- IP fragmentation
- Bad IP packets

Figure 10-1 *IP Packet*

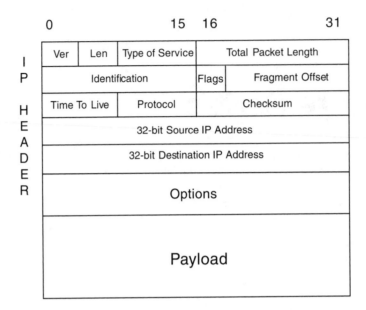

IP Options

The IP datagram header is normally 20 bytes long. The IP protocol allows for up to 40 additional bytes of optional fields. Only 8 options are considered valid in IP version 4. The IP option structure and fields are illustrated in Figure 10-2.

The Cisco Secure IDS signatures related to IP options are as follows:

- 1000 Bad Option List
- 1001 IP Options-Record Packet Route
- 1002 IP Options-Timestamp
- 1003 IP Options-Provide s, c, h, and tcc
- 1004 IP Options-Loose Source Route
- 1005 IP Options-SATNET ID
- 1006 IP Options-Strict Source Route

Figure 10-2 *IP Option Structure*

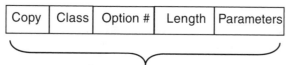

| Copy | Class | Option # | Length | Parameters |

Option Entry

Copy (1 bit long)

    0—Do not include options in packet fragments
    1—Include options in packet fragments

Class (2 bits long)

    0—Network Control
    2—Debugging

Option# (5 bits long)

    0—End of Options
    1—No Operation
    2—Security
    3—Loose Source Route
    4—Timestamp
    7—Record Route
    8—Stream ID
    9—Strict Source Route

Length (8 bits long)

Parameters (Variable)

1000 Bad Option List

- **Default Severity**—Low.
- **Structure**—Atomic.
- **Implementation**—Context.
- **Class**—Information.

- **Description**—This signature triggers on receipt of an IP datagram where the list of IP options in the IP datagram header is incomplete or malformed. No known exploits purposely incorporate this option. This does not preclude the possibility that exploits do exist outside of the realm of the Cisco Systems knowledge domain or that poorly written hacker code might produce malformed datagrams.

- **Benign Triggers**—There is no legitimate use for malformed datagrams. This might indicate systems that are experiencing problems with their kernel or network interface cards (NICs). This is unusual traffic and warrants investigation. When nonspecific network traffic of this type is encountered, the most prudent action from a security perspective is to block or disallow it.

1001 IP Options-Record Packet Route

- **Default Severity**—Low.

- **Structure**—Atomic.

- **Implementation**—Context.

- **Class**—Information/reconnaissance.

- **Description**—Triggers on receipt of an IP datagram where the IP option list for the datagram includes option 7 (Record Packet Route). This option records the route a packet travels to reach a destination. This information might be requested by just using a *ping -R <target>* command. The target machine responds to the echo request with an echo reply whose payload contains the recorded route of the request. This alarm might indicate a reconnaissance attack is in progress against your network.

- **Benign Triggers**—Although network troubleshooting might require the legitimate use of this feature, this is unusual traffic that warrants investigation. When nonspecific network traffic of this type is encountered, the most prudent action from a security perspective is to block or disallow it.

1002 IP Options—Timestamp

- **Default Severity**—Low.

- **Structure**—Atomic.

- **Implementation**—Context.

- **Class**—Information.

- **Description**—This signature triggers on receipt of an IP datagram where the IP option list for the datagram includes option 4 (Timestamp). This option might be used in addition to the Record Route option to determine the length of time the packet spends in transit between hops. This alarm indicates that a reconnaissance attack might be in progress against your network.

- **Benign Triggers**—Although network troubleshooting might require the legitimate use of this feature, this is unusual traffic that warrants investigation. When nonspecific network traffic of this type is encountered, the most prudent action from a security perspective is to block or disallow it.

1003 IP Options—Provide s, c, h, tcc

- **Default Severity**—Low.
- **Structure**—Atomic.
- **Implementation**—Context.
- **Class**—Information.
- **Description**—This signature triggers on receipt of an IP datagram where the IP option list for the datagram includes option 2 (Security Options). No known exploit exists. This does not preclude the possibility that exploits do exist outside of the realm of the Cisco Systems knowledge domain.
- **Benign Triggers**—This signature triggers if you implemented IP security options on your network. However, IP security options are rarely, if ever, implemented. When nonspecific network traffic of this type is encountered, the most prudent action from a security perspective is to block or disallow it.

1004 IP Options—Loose Source Route

- **Default Severity**—High.
- **Structure**—Atomic.
- **Implementation**—Context.
- **Class**—Access.
- **Description**—This signature triggers on receipt of an IP datagram where the IP option list for the datagram includes option 3 (Loose Source Route). The Loose Source Route option might be used to specify specific routers that must be traversed along a packet's path, thereby defeating authentication mechanisms that rely on IP addresses as their basis for trust relationships.
- **Benign Triggers**—Although network troubleshooting might require the legitimate use of this feature, this type of traffic is rarely, if ever, noted and needs to comprise much less than 1 percent of network traffic.

1005 IP Options—SATNET ID

- **Default Severity**—Low.
- **Structure**—Atomic.

- **Implementation**—Context.
- **Class**—Information.
- **Description**—This signature triggers on receipt of an IP datagram where the IP option list for the datagram includes option 8 (SATNET Stream Identifier). This signature is included for completeness. No known exploit exists. This does not preclude the possibility that exploits do exist outside of the realm of the Cisco Systems knowledge domain.
- **Benign Triggers**—This option is obsolete and should not be encountered. When nonspecific network traffic of this type is encountered, the most prudent action from a security perspective is to block or disallow it.

1006 IP Options—Strict Source Route

- **Default Severity**—High.
- **Structure**—Atomic.
- **Implementation**—Context.
- **Class**—Access.
- **Description**—This signature triggers on receipt of an IP datagram in which the IP option list for the datagram includes option 9 (Strict Source Route). The Strict Source Route option can be used to specify the exact path a packet must traverse enroute to its destination. This option might be misused to defeat authentication mechanisms that rely on IP addresses as their basis for trust relationships. The limited number of routes (9 hops total) that can be stored in the Options field minimizes the usefulness of this option as a mode of attack across a large Internet.
- **Benign Triggers**—Although network troubleshooting might require the legitimate use of this feature, this type of traffic is rarely, if ever, noted and needs to comprise much less than 1 percent of network traffic.

IP Fragmentation

IP fragmentation involves breaking a single IP packet into multiple segments that are all below the maximum transmission size for the network.

MTU

The *maximum transmission unit (MTU)* represents the maximum packet size that a network segment can handle. These sizes vary depending on underlying network, such as Ethernet, FDDI, Token Ring, and so on.

When IP packets are broken into fragments, only the first packet contains complete header information. Many routers filter packets based on this header information. Because not enough information is in the secondary fragments, many routers automatically let them through.

NOTE   The fragment signatures fall into two categories. One set begins with 11xx and the other set begins with 12xx. These fragment signature sets overlap; they are not both active at the same time. If you enable fragment reassembly, the 12xx signatures are used. If you disable fragment reassembly, the 11xx signatures are used.

The following fragment signatures are active when you have IP fragment reassembly disabled:

- 1100 IP Fragment Attack
- 1103 IP Fragments Overlap

These are discussed next. Then the discussion turns to the fragment signatures that are active when you have IP fragment reassembly enabled:

- 1200 IP Fragmentation Buffer Full
- 1201 IP Fragment Overlap
- 1202 IP Fragment Overrun - Datagram Too Long
- 1203 IP Fragment Overwrite - Data Is Overwritten
- 1204 IP Fragment Missing Initial Fragment
- 1205 IP Fragment Too Many Datagrams
- 1206 IP Fragment Too Small
- 1207 IP Fragment Too Many Frags
- 1208 IP Fragment Incomplete Datagram
- 1220 Jolt2 Fragment Reassembly DoS attack

1100 IP Fragment Attack

- **Default Severity**—Medium.
- **Structure**—Atomic.
- **Implementation**—Context.
- **Class**—Access.

- **Description**—This signature triggers when any IP datagram is received with a small offset indicated in the Offset field. This indicates that the first fragment is unusually small, and is most likely an attempt to defeat packet-filter security policies.

- **Benign Triggers**—IP datagrams might be fragmented normally as they are transported across the network, but they will normally not be fragmented into sizes smaller than 256 bytes. Investigation of this traffic is especially important if a packet-filtering firewall is protecting the network.

1103 IP Fragments Overlap

- **Default Severity**—High.

- **Structure**—Composite.

- **Implementation**—Context.

- **Class**—Denial of service.

- **Description**—This signature identifies that two fragments contained within the same IP datagram have offsets that indicate that they share positioning within the datagram. Fragment A might completely overwrite Fragment B, or Fragment A might only partially overwrite Fragment B. Some operating systems do not properly handle overlapping fragments and might throw exceptions or behave in other undesirable ways upon receipt of overlapping fragments. Teardrop is a widely available attack tool that exploits this vulnerability.

- **Benign Triggers**—Fragment overlaps can occur normally in network traffic because of retransmissions of datagrams. If a packet is retransmitted and the packet requires fragmentation, the fragmentation might be performed differently if the retransmitted packet takes a different route than the originally transmitted packet. Fragmented traffic is in itself unusual. Overlapping of fragments is rarely, if ever, seen. A large number of overlapping fragments is not to be expected at all and is most probably an active attack.

1200 IP Fragmentation Buffer Full

- **Default Severity**—Low.

- **Structure**—Composite.

- **Implementation**—Content.

- **Class**—Access.

- **Description**—This signature identifies when an extraordinary amount of incomplete fragmented traffic is detected on your protected network. This might be because of an excessive number of incomplete fragmented datagrams, a large number of fragments for individual datagrams, or a combination of incomplete datagrams and size/number of fragments in each datagram. This type of traffic is most likely an attempt to bypass security measures or intrusion detection systems by intentional fragmentation of attack activity.

- **Benign Triggers**—IP datagrams might be fragmented normally as they are transported across the network. Although some fragmentation might be normal, a large number of incomplete datagrams or a large number of fragments per datagram is suspicious. Investigation of this traffic is especially important if a packet-filtering firewall is protecting the network.

1201 IP Fragment Overlap

- **Default Severity**—High.
- **Structure**—Composite.
- **Implementation**—Content.
- **Class**—Access.
- **Description**—This signature identifies that two fragments contained within the same IP datagram have offsets that indicate that they share positioning within the datagram. Fragment A might completely overwrite Fragment B, or Fragment A might only partially overwrite Fragment B. Some operating systems do not properly handle overlapping fragments and might throw exceptions or behave in other undesirable ways upon receipt of overlapping fragments. Teardrop is a widely available attack tool that exploits this vulnerability.
- **Benign Triggers**—Fragment overlaps can occur normally in network traffic because of retransmissions of datagrams. If a packet is retransmitted and the packet requires fragmentation, the fragmentation might be performed differently if the retransmitted packet takes a different route than the originally transmitted packet. Fragmented traffic is in itself unusual. Overlapping fragments are a rare occurrence, and a large number of overlapping fragments indicates a probable active attack.

1202 IP Fragment Overrun—Datagram Too Long

- **Default Severity**—High.
- **Structure**—Atomic.
- **Implementation**—Content.
- **Class**—Denial of service.
- **Description**—Triggers when a reassembled fragmented datagram exceeds the declared IP data length or the maximum datagram length. By definition, no IP datagram should be larger than 65,535 bytes. Systems that try to process these large datagrams might crash. This type of fragmented traffic might indicate a denial of service attempt.

- **Benign Triggers**—None

1203 IP Fragment Overwrite—Data Is Overwritten

- **Default Severity**—High.
- **Structure**—Atomic.
- **Implementation**—Content.
- **Class**—Access.
- **Description**—Overlapping fragments might be used in an attempt to bypass intrusion detection systems. In this scenario, part of an attack is sent in fragments along with additional random data. Future fragments might overwrite the random data with the remainder of the attack. If the completed datagram is not properly reassembled at the IDS, the attack is undetected. This signature triggers when a fragment overlap occurs that results in existing data being overwritten.
- **Benign Triggers**—None.

1204 IP Fragment Missing Initial Fragment

- **Default Severity**—Low.
- **Structure**—Atomic.
- **Implementation**—Content.
- **Class**—Access.
- **Description**—Triggers when a datagram cannot be reassembled because of missing initial data. This is most likely an attempt to defeat packet-filter security policies.
- **Benign Triggers**—None

1205 IP Fragment Too Many Datagrams

- **Default Severity**—Low.
- **Structure**—Composite.
- **Implementation**—Content.
- **Class**—Access.
- **Description**—This signature identifies when an excessive number of incomplete fragmented datagrams are detected on the network. This is most likely either a denial of service attack or an attempt to bypass security measures.
- **Benign Triggers**—Although some fragmentation might be normal, a large number of incomplete datagrams is suspicious. Investigation of this traffic is especially important if a packet-filtering firewall is protecting the network.

1206 IP Fragment Too Small

- **Default Severity**—Low
- **Structure**—Atomic.
- **Implementation**—Content.
- **Class**—Access.
- **Description**—Triggers when any fragment other than the final fragment is fewer than 400 bytes, indicating that the fragment is likely intentionally crafted. Small fragments might be used in denial of service attacks or in an attempt to bypass security measures or detection.
- **Benign Triggers**—IP datagrams might be fragmented normally as they are transported across the network, but they are normally not fragmented into sizes smaller than 400 bytes. Investigation of this traffic is especially important if a packet-filtering firewall is protecting the network.

1207 IP Fragment Too Many Frags

- **Default Severity**—Low.
- **Structure**—Composite.
- **Implementation**—Content.
- **Class**—Access.
- **Description**—This signature identifies when a given datagram has an excessive number of fragments. This is most likely either a denial of service attack or an attempt to bypass security measures.
- **Benign Triggers**—Although some fragmentation might be normal, a large number of fragments per datagram is suspicious. Investigation of this traffic is especially important if a packet-filtering firewall is protecting the network.

1208 IP Fragment Incomplete Datagram

- **Default Severity**—Low.
- **Structure**—Composite.
- **Implementation**—Content.
- **Class**—Access.
- **Description**—Triggers when a datagram cannot be fully reassembled because of missing data. This might indicate a denial of service attack or an attempt to defeat packet-filter security policies.

- **Benign Triggers**—Some fragmentation might occur normally in network traffic. Additionally, some fragments might be dropped enroute to their destination causing the data to be eventually retransmitted. Fragmented traffic is in itself unusual, but a large number of incomplete datagrams is not expected and is most probably an active attack.

1220 Jolt2 Fragment Reassembly DoS Attack

- **Default Severity**—High.
- **Structure**—Composite.
- **Implementation**—Content.
- **Class**—Denial of Service.
- **Description**—This alarm fires when multiple fragments are received, all claiming to be the last fragment of an IP datagram. It continues to provide summary data periodically while the attack is underway.
- **Benign Triggers**—None.

Bad IP Packets

Various settings in the IP header represent illegal or invalid packets based on RFC 791. An excellent example of this is a packet that has the source address equal to the destination address. The signatures related to bad IP packets are as follows:

- 1101 Unknown IP Protocol
- 1102 Impossible IP Packet
- 1104 IP Localhost Source Spoof

1101 Unknown IP Protocol

- **Default Severity**—Low.
- **Structure**—Atomic.
- **Implementation**—Context.
- **Class**—Information.
- **Description**—This signature triggers when an IP datagram is received with the protocol field set to 134 or greater. These protocol types are undefined or reserved and should not be used. Use of undefined or reserved protocol types might indicate establishment of a proprietary communication channel. No known exploits implement this concept. This does not preclude the possibility that exploits do exist outside of the realm of the Cisco System knowledge domain.

- **Benign Triggers**—Locally developed protocols that might use unknown IP protocol types trigger this signature. The use of these protocol types is highly unusual and needs to be investigated. When nonspecific network traffic of this type is encountered, the most prudent action from a security perspective is to block or disallow it.

1102 Impossible IP Packet

- **Default Severity**—High.
- **Structure**—Atomic.
- **Implementation**—Context.
- **Class**—Denial of service.
- **Description**—This triggers when an IP packet arrives with the source IP address equal to the destination IP address. This signature catches the so-called Land Attack.
- **Benign Triggers**—This packet should never occur in legitimate traffic.

1104 IP Localhost Source Spoof

- **Default Severity**—High.
- **Structure**—Atomic.
- **Implementation**—Context.
- **Class**—Access.
- **Description**—This signature triggers when an IP packet with a source address of 127.*x.x.x* is detected. This is a local host IP address and should never be seen on the network. This might indicate someone trying to take advantage of local host trust relationships to either gain access to or in some other way subvert a target machine.
- **Benign Triggers**—None.

ICMP Signatures (2000 Series)

RFC 792 defines the Internet Control Message Protocol (ICMP). These messages enable a system administrator to check basic network connectivity and systems to generate basic connectivity error messages. ICMP signatures can be divided into the following categories:

- ICMP query messages
- ICMP error messages
- Ping sweeps
- ICMP attacks

ICMP Query Messages

ICMP query messages represent a request for information. These messages vary from a simple *echo request* (used to verify network connectivity between two devices) to an *address mask request*. The types of ICMP messages are as follows:

- Type 0 - Echo Reply
- Type 8 - Echo Request
- Type 13 - Timestamp Request
- Type 14 - Timestamp Reply
- Type 15 - Information. Request
- Type 16 - Information. Reply
- Type 17 - Address Mask Request
- Type 18 - Address Mask Reply

The signatures related to ICMP query messages are as follows:

- 2000 ICMP Echo Reply
- 2004 ICMP Echo Request
- 2007 ICMP Timestamp Request
- 2008 ICMP Timestamp Reply
- 2009 ICMP Information Request
- 2010 ICMP Information Reply
- 2011 ICMP Address Mask Request
- 2012 ICMP Address Mask Reply

2000 ICMP Echo Reply

- **Default Severity**—Disable.
- **Structure**—Atomic.
- **Implementation**—Context.
- **Class**—Information.
- **Description**—This signature triggers when an IP datagram is received with the Protocol field of the IP header set to 1 (ICMP) and the Type field in the ICMP header set to 0 (Echo Reply). ICMP echo replies have been used to bypass packet-filter security policies because they are rarely filtered in either incoming or outgoing traffic. These packets might be used to establish a communication channel or to perform denial of service attacks.

- **Benign Triggers**—The ICMP echo reply is the expected response to an ICMP echo request. This request/reply pair is most commonly implemented through the ping utility. Many network management tools use this mechanism or some derivative. This is extremely common network traffic. Suspicion needs to be raised when a large number of these packets, without a corresponding ICMP request, are found on the network. If no legitimate reason for this traffic can be identified, prudent security practices suggest that the source be blocked.

2004 ICMP Echo Request

- **Default Severity**—Disable.
- **Structure**—Atomic.
- **Implementation**—Context.
- **Class**—Information.
- **Description**—This signature triggers when an IP datagram is received with the Protocol field of the IP header set to 1 (ICMP) and the Type field in the ICMP header set to 8 (Echo Request). ICMP echo requests are commonly used to perform reconnaissance sweeps of networks. These sweeps often are a prelude to attack. Additionally, they might be used to perform denial of service attacks.
- **Benign Triggers**—This is extremely common network traffic. Suspicion needs to be raised when a large number of these packets are found on the network.

2007 ICMP Timestamp Request

- **Default Severity**—Disable.
- **Structure**—Atomic.
- **Implementation**—Context.
- **Class**—Information/reconnaissance.
- **Description**—This signature triggers when an IP datagram is received with the Protocol field of the IP header set to 1 (ICMP) and the Type field in the ICMP header set to 13 (Timestamp Request). ICMP timestamp requests can be used to perform reconnaissance sweeps of networks. These sweeps often are a prelude to attack. Additionally, they might be used to perform denial of service attacks. No known exploits incorporate this option. This does not preclude the possibility that exploits do exist outside of the realm of the Cisco System knowledge domain.
- **Benign Triggers**—The ICMP timestamp request/reply pair can be used to synchronize system clocks on the network. The requesting system issues the timestamp request bound for a destination; the destination system responds with a

timestamp reply message. This is normal network traffic but is uncommon on most networks. Suspicion needs to be raised when a large number of these packets are found on your network.

2008 ICMP Timestamp Reply

- **Default Severity**—Disable.
- **Structure**—Atomic.
- **Implementation**—Context.
- **Class**—Information.
- **Description**—This signature triggers when an IP datagram is received with the Protocol field of the IP header set to 1 (ICMP) and the Type field in the ICMP header set to 14 (Timestamp Reply). ICMP timestamp replies can be used to perform denial of service attacks.
- **Benign Triggers**—The ICMP timestamp request/reply pair can be used to synchronize system clocks on the network. The requesting system issues the timestamp request bound for a destination, the destination system responds with a timestamp reply message. This is normal network traffic but is uncommon on most networks. Suspicion needs to be raised when a large number of these packets are found on the network without a corresponding request.

2009 ICMP Information Request

- **Default Severity**—Disable.
- **Structure**—Atomic.
- **Implementation**—Context.
- **Class**—Information.
- **Description**—This signature triggers when an IP datagram is received with the Protocol field of the IP header set to 1 (ICMP) and the Type field in the ICMP header set to 15 (Information. Request). This signature is included for completeness.
- **Benign Triggers**—This datagram type is obsolete and should not be encountered.

2010 ICMP Information Reply

- **Default Severity**—Disable.
- **Structure**—Atomic.
- **Implementation**—Context.
- **Class**—Information.

- **Description**—This signature triggers when an IP datagram is received with the Protocol field of the IP header set to 1 (ICMP) and the Type field in the ICMP header set to 16 (ICMP Information. Reply). This signature is included for completeness.

- **Benign Triggers**—This datagram type is obsolete and should not be encountered.

2011 ICMP Address Mask Request

- **Default Severity**—Disable.

- **Structure**—Atomic.

- **Implementation**—Context.

- **Class**—Information/reconnaissance.

- **Description**—This signature triggers when an IP datagram is received with the Protocol field of the IP header set to 1 (ICMP) and the Type field in the ICMP header set to 17 (Address Mask Request). ICMP address mask requests can be used to perform reconnaissance sweeps of networks. These sweeps often are a prelude to attack. Additionally, they might be used to perform denial of service attacks.

- **Benign Triggers**—The ICMP address mask request/reply pair can be used to determine the subnet mask used on the network. The requesting system issues the address mask request bound for a destination; the destination system responds with an address mask reply message. This is normal network traffic but is uncommon on most networks. Suspicion needs to be raised when a large number of these packets are found on your network.

2012 ICMP Address Mask Reply

- **Default Severity**—Disable.

- **Structure**—Atomic.

- **Implementation**—Context.

- **Class**—Information.

- **Description**—This signature triggers when an IP datagram is received with the Protocol field of the IP header set to 1 (ICMP) and the Type field in the ICMP header set to 18 (Address Mask Reply). ICMP timestamp replies can be used to perform denial of service attacks.

- **Benign Triggers**—The ICMP address mask request/reply pair can be used to determine the subnet mask used on the network. The requesting system issues the address mask request bound for a destination; the destination system responds with an address mask reply message. This is normal network traffic but is uncommon on most networks. Suspicion needs to be raised when a large number of these packets without a corresponding request are found on the network.

ICMP Error Messages

The ICMP protocol supports numerous error messages that indicate current network connectivity. These error messages, with their ICMP types, are as follows:

- 3 - Destination Unreachable
- 4 - Source Quench
- 5 - Redirect
- 11 - Time Exceeded
- 12 - Parameter Problem

The Cisco Secure IDS signatures related to ICMP error messages are as follows:

- 2001 ICMP Host Unreachable
- 2002 ICMP Source Quench
- 2003 ICMP Redirect
- 2005 ICMP Time Exceeded for a Datagram
- 2006 ICMP Parameter Problem on a Datagram

2001 ICMP Host Unreachable

- **Default Severity**—Disable.
- **Structure**—Atomic.
- **Implementation**—Context.
- **Class**—Information.
- **Description**—This signature triggers when an IP datagram is received with the Protocol field of the IP header set to 1 (ICMP) and the Type field in the ICMP header set to 3 (Destination Unreachable). ICMP destination unreachable datagrams might be used to bypass packet-filter security policies because they are rarely filtered in either incoming or outgoing traffic. These packets might be used to perform denial of service attacks.
- **Benign Triggers**—This is the common response provided to a client when there is no path available to the requested host. This is a very common type of network traffic. A large number of this datagram type on the network indicates network difficulties or might indicate hostile actions.

2002 ICMP Source Quench

- **Default Severity**—Disable.
- **Structure**—Atomic.

- **Implementation**—Context.
- **Class**—Information/denial of service.
- **Description**—This signature triggers when an IP datagram is received with the Protocol field of the IP header set to 1 (ICMP) and the Type field in the ICMP header set to 4 (Source Quench). ICMP source quench datagrams might be used to bypass packet-filter security policies because they are rarely filtered in either incoming or outgoing traffic. This might be used to perform denial of service attacks. No known exploits incorporate this option. This does not preclude the possibility that exploits do exist outside of the realm of the Cisco System knowledge domain.
- **Benign Triggers**—This datagram might be used in network management to provide congestion control. A source quench packet is issued when a router is beginning to lose packets because of the transmission rate of a source. The source quench is a request to the source to reduce the rate of datagram transmission. This datagram type is rarely, if ever, seen on networks, and some systems do not even support it. A large number of this datagram type on the network indicates network difficulties or might indicate hostile actions.

2003 ICMP Redirect

- **Default Severity**—Disable.
- **Structure**—Atomic.
- **Implementation**—Context.
- **Class**—Information.
- **Description**—This signature triggers when an IP datagram is received with the Protocol field of the IP header set to 1 (ICMP) and the Type field in the ICMP header set to 5 (Redirect). ICMP redirects can be used to facilitate system access attempts. No known exploits incorporate this option. This does not preclude the possibility that exploits do exist outside of the realm of the Cisco System knowledge domain.
- **Benign Triggers**—The redirect message might be issued from a router to inform a host of a better route to a requested destination. The host then updates its routing table to include this route. This method of updating routing tables is an uncommon practice today.

2005 ICMP Time Exceeded for a Datagram

- **Default Severity**—Disable.
- **Structure**—Atomic.
- **Implementation**—Context.
- **Class**—Information/denial of service.

- **Description**—This signature triggers when an IP datagram is received with the Protocol field of the IP header set to 1 (ICMP) and the Type field in the ICMP header set to 11 (Time Exceeded for a Datagram). ICMP time exceeded datagrams might be used to bypass packet-filter security policies because they are rarely filtered in either incoming or outgoing traffic. These packets might be used to perform denial of service attacks. No known exploits incorporate this option. This does not preclude the possibility that exploits do exist outside of the realm of the Cisco System knowledge domain.

- **Benign Triggers**—ICMP time exceeded datagrams are issued when a router drops a datagram whose Time-To-Live (TTL) flag has expired. This is a normal and necessary type of network traffic. A large number of this datagram type on the network indicates network difficulties or might indicate hostile actions.

2006 ICMP Parameter Problem on a Datagram

- **Default Severity**—Disable.

- **Structure**—Atomic.

- **Implementation**—Context.

- **Class**—Information.

- **Description**—This signature triggers when an IP datagram is received with the Protocol field of the IP header set to 1 (ICMP) and the Type field in the ICMP header set to 12 (Parameter Problem on Datagram). ICMP parameter problem datagrams might be used to bypass packet-filter security policies because they are rarely filtered in either incoming or outgoing traffic. These packets might be used to perform denial of service attacks. No known exploits incorporate this option. This does not preclude the possibility that exploits do exist outside of the realm of the Cisco System knowledge domain.

- **Benign Triggers**—ICMP parameter problem datagrams are issued when a router drops a datagram because it was malformed. This is a normal and necessary type of network traffic. A large number of this datagram type on the network indicates network difficulties or might indicate hostile actions.

Ping Sweeps

ICMP packets can be utilized to locate hosts on a network. They represent normal traffic that system administrators and various management tools use to verify network connectivity. Attackers, however, can use the same packets to map out your network. These network sweeps can be performed with the following ICMP packet types:

- Type 8 - Echo Request

- Type 8 - Timestamp Request

- Type 8 - Address Request

The signatures that detect ping sweeps are as follows:

- 2100 ICMP Network Sweep with Echo
- 2101 ICMP Network Sweep with Timestamp
- 2102 ICMP Network Sweep with Address Mask

2100 ICMP Network Sweep with Echo

- **Default Severity**—Medium.
- **Structure**—Composite.
- **Implementation**—Context.
- **Class**—Reconnaissance.
- **Description**—This signature triggers when IP datagrams (from the same source IP address) are received directed at multiple hosts on the network with the Protocol field of the IP header set to 1 (ICMP) and the Type field in the ICMP header set to 8 (Echo Request). This indicates that a reconnaissance sweep of your network might be in progress. This might be the prelude to a more serious attack.
- **Benign Triggers**—Many network management tools, such as HP OpenView, provide network-mapping capabilities. Many times this mapping is at least partially accomplished through a ping sweep of the network address space. Ping uses ICMP echo requests to check connectivity with hosts on your network.

2101 ICMP Network Sweep with Timestamp

- **Default Severity**—High.
- **Structure**—Composite.
- **Implementation**—Context.
- **Class**—Reconnaissance.
- **Description**—This signature triggers when IP datagrams are received directed at multiple hosts on the network with the Protocol field of the IP header set to 1 (ICMP) and the Type field in the ICMP header set to 13 (Timestamp Request). This indicates that a reconnaissance sweep of your network might be in progress. This might be the prelude to a more serious attack.
- **Benign Triggers**—None.

2102 ICMP Network Sweep with Address Mask

- **Default Severity**—High.

- **Structure**—Composite.
- **Implementation**—Context.
- **Class**—Reconnaissance.
- **Description**—This signature triggers when IP datagrams are received directed at multiple hosts on the network with the Protocol field of the IP header set to 1 (ICMP) and the Type field in the ICMP header set to 17 (Address Mask Request). This indicates that a reconnaissance sweep of your network might be in progress. This might be the prelude to a more serious attack.
- **Benign Triggers**—None.

ICMP Attacks

Besides using ICMP packets to collect reconnaissance information about your network, attackers can also use ICMP traffic to attack your network. These attacks are as follows:

- 2150 Fragmented ICMP Packet
- 2151 Large ICMP Packet
- 2152 ICMP Flood
- 2153 ICMP Smurf Attack
- 2154 Ping of Death Attack

2150 Fragmented ICMP Packet

- **Default Severity**—Disable.
- **Structure**—Atomic.
- **Implementation**—Context.
- **Class**—Access/Denial of service.
- **Description**—This signature triggers when an IP datagram is received with the Protocol field of the IP header set to 1 (ICMP) and either the more fragments flag is set to 1 or an offset is indicated in the Offset field. The Boolean equation that describes this is ICMP AND (MFFLAG OR OFFSET). Fragmented ICMP traffic might indicate a denial of service attempt.
- **Benign Triggers**—IP datagrams might be fragmented normally as they are transported across the network, but ICMP is rarely fragmented. The traffic needs to be investigated.

2151 Large ICMP Packet

- **Default Severity**—Disable.
- **Structure**—Atomic.
- **Implementation**—Context.
- **Class**—Denial of service.
- **Description**—This signature triggers when an IP datagram is received with the Protocol field of the IP header set to 1(ICMP) and the IP Length field is set to a value greater than 1024. A large ICMP packet might indicate a denial of service attack.
- **Benign Triggers**—Although it is possible to receive ICMP datagrams that have a size greater than 1024 bytes, this is an unusual occurrence that warrants investigation.

NOTE   Stacheldraht (Signature IDs 6503 and 6504) traffic might also trigger the large ICMP traffic signature because of a bug by which it sends out large (> 1000 byte) ICMP packets.

2152 ICMP Flood

- **Default Severity**—High.
- **Structure**—Composite.
- **Implementation**—Context.
- **Class**—Denial of service.
- **Description**—This signature triggers when multiple IP datagrams are received directed at a single host on the network with the Protocol field of the IP header set to 1 (ICMP). This indicates that a denial of service attack might be in progress against your network.
- **Benign Triggers**—Someone using ping in its Recursive mode can generate this traffic pattern. However, it should not be a common occurrence. This might indicate some type of network problem or attack and needs to be investigated.

2153 ICMP Smurf Attack

- **Default Severity**—High.
- **Structure**—Composite.
- **Implementation**—Context.
- **Class**—Denial of service.

- **Description**—This triggers when a large number of ICMP echo replies is targeted at a machine. They can be from one or many sources. This catches the attack known as Smurf. Because this attack can come from many sources, automatic blocking of individual hosts is not effective.

- **Benign Triggers**—Any programs, such as network administration tools, that use broadcast ICMP requests can potentially trigger this signature.

2154 Ping of Death Attack

- **Default Severity**—High.
- **Structure**—Atomic.
- **Implementation**—Context.
- **Class**—Denial of service.
- **Description**—This signature triggers when an IP datagram is received with the Protocol field of the IP header set to 1(ICMP), the Last Fragment bit is set, and the IP offset is greater than the maximum size for an IP packet (65,535 bytes). The IP offset is represented in 8-byte units. Therefore, the IP offset times 8 indicates the amount of data previously sent for this fragmented IP packet. This amount plus the IP data length of the current packet is used to check whether the fragmented IP datagram exceeds the 65,535 byte limit. This indicates a denial of service attack.

- **Benign Triggers**—This signature has no known benign triggers. Blocking on the source of this attack is of questionable value because the source IP of this attack can be spoofed.

TCP Signatures (3000 Series)

The 3000 Series signatures cover TCP-based signatures. These TCP-based signatures can be subdivided into the following categories:

- TCP traffic records
- TCP port scans
- TCP host sweeps
- Abnormal TCP packets
- Mail attacks
- FTP attacks
- Legacy Cisco Secure IDS Web attacks
- NetBIOS attacks
- SYN Flood and TCP Hijack attacks
- TCP applications

TCP Traffic Records (Signature 3000)

TCP traffic records monitor connections to various TCP ports. Each of these ports represents a well-known service or application. These signatures trigger frequently; therefore, the majority of them are disabled by default. All the traffic records trigger with a signature ID of 3000. The individual signatures are differentiated by the signature subID that is equal to the destination port of the connection, and they all have the following characteristics:

- **Default Severity**—Disable.
- **Structure**—Atomic.
- **Implementation**—Context.
- **Class**—Reconnaissance.
- **3000/0**—TCP default connection signature.

The TCP connection signatures defined by default include the following:

- 3000/1 - Connection request-tcpmux
- 3000/7 - Connection request-echo
- 3000/9 - Connection request-discard
- 3000/11 - Connection request-systat
- 3000/13 - Connection request-daytime
- 3000/15 - Connection request-netstat
- 3000/19 - Connection request-Chargen
- 3000/20 - Connection request-ftp-data
- 3000/21 - Connection request-ftp
- 3000/23 - Connection request-telnet
- 3000/25 - Connection request-smtp
- 3000/37 - Connection request-time
- 3000/43 - Connection request-whois
- 3000/53 - Connection request-dns
- 3000/70 - Connection request-gopher
- 3000/79 - Connection request-finger
- 3000/80 - Connection request-www
- 3000/87 - Connection request-link
- 3000/88 - Connection request-kerberos-v5
- 3000/95 - Connection request-supdup

- 3000/101 - Connection request-hostnames
- 3000/102 - Connection request-iso-tsap
- 3000/103 - Connection request-x400
- 3000/104 - Connection request-x400-snd
- 3000/105 - Connection request-Csnet-ns
- 3000/109 - Connection request-pop-2
- 3000/110 - Connection request-pop3
- 3000/111 - Connection request-sunrpc
- 3000/117 - Connection request-uucppath
- 3000/119 - Connection request-nntp
- 3000/123 - Connection request-ntp
- 3000/137 - Connection request-netbios
- 3000/138 - Connection request-netbios
- 3000/139 - Connection request-netbios
- 3000/143 - Connection request-imap2
- 3000/144 - Connection request-NeWS
- 3000/177 -- Connection request-xdmcp
- 3000/178 - Connection request-nextstep
- 3000/179 - Connection request-bgp
- 3000/194 - Connection request-irc
- 3000/220 - Connection request-imap3
- 3000/372 - Connection request-ulistserv
- 3000/515 - Connection request-printer
- 3000/530 - Connection request-Courier
- 3000/540 - Connection request-uucp
- 3000/600 - Connection request-pcserver
- 3000/750 - Connection request-kerberos-v4

Three of the connection request signatures represent connections to services that have an extensive history of security vulnerabilities. These signatures, commonly known by their recognizable names of rexec, rlogin and rsh, are as follows:

- 3000/512 - Connection request-exec (severity 3, access)
- 3000/513 - Connection request-login (severity 3, access)
- 3000/514 - Connection request-shell (severity 3, access)

These signatures share the following signature characteristics:

- **Default Severity**—Medium.
- **Structure**—Atomic.
- **Implementation**—Context.
- **Class**—Access.

TCP Port Scans

TCP port scans are detected when a single host searches for multiple running services on another single host or target machine. There are common scans that use normal TCP-SYN (connection request) to determine that a service is running. There are stealth scans that use FIN, SYN-FIN, null, or PUSH flags and fragmented packets to determine that a service is running. The TCP flags and their meanings are as follows:

- **SYN**—Synchronize sequence numbers to initiate a connection. Each time a new connection is established, the SYN flag is turned on.
- **FIN**—When set, this flag implies that the sender has finished sending data.
- **ACK**—When the ACK flag is set, the acknowledgment number in the corresponding field is valid. The acknowledgment number contains the next sequence number that the sender of the acknowledgment expects to receive.
- **RST**—This flag is used to reset the TCP connection.
- **URG**—The urgent pointer is valid when this flag is set. This pointer is a positive offset that must be added to the Sequence Number field of the segment to yield the sequence number of the last byte of urgent data.
- **PSH**—Indicates that the receiver should pass this data to the application as soon as possible.

The Cisco Secure IDS signatures related to TCP port scans are as follows:

- 3001 TCP Port Sweep
- 3002 TCP SYN Port Sweep
- 3003 Fragmented TCP SYN Port Sweep
- 3005 TCP FIN Port Sweep
- 3006 Fragmented TCP FIN Port Sweep
- 3010 TCP High Port Sweep
- 3011 TCP FIN High Port Sweep
- 3012 Fragmented TCP FIN High Port Sweep
- 3015 TCP Null Port Sweep

- 3016 Fragmented TCP Null Port Sweep
- 3020 TCP SYN-FIN Port Sweep
- 3021 Fragmented TCP SYN-FIN Port Sweep
- 3045 Queso Sweep

3001 TCP Port Sweep

- **Default Severity**—High.
- **Structure**—Composite.
- **Implementation**—Context.
- **Class**—Reconnaissance.
- **Description**—This signature triggers when a series of TCP connections to a number of different privileged ports (having port number less than 1024) on a specific host have been initiated. This indicates that a reconnaissance sweep of your network might be in progress. This might be the prelude to a more serious attack. This is a catchall signature, which fires if the specific type of TCP port sweep cannot be determined.
- **Benign Triggers**—Many network management tools, such as HP OpenView, provide network-mapping capabilities. This might include a mapping of available network services, so TCP port sweeps might be expected from these systems.

3002 TCP SYN Port Sweep

- **Default Severity**—Medium.
- **Structure**—Composite.
- **Implementation**—Context.
- **Class**—Reconnaissance.
- **Description**—This signature triggers when a series of TCP SYN packets have been sent to a number of different destination ports on a specific host. This indicates that a reconnaissance sweep of your network might be in progress. This might be the prelude to a more serious attack.
- **Benign Triggers**—Many network management tools, such as HP OpenView, provide network-mapping capabilities. This might include a mapping of available network services, so TCP port sweeps might be expected from these systems.

3003 Fragmented TCP SYN Port Sweep

- **Default Severity**—High.
- **Structure**—Composite.

- **Implementation**—Context.
- **Class**—Reconnaissance.
- **Description**—This signature triggers when a series of fragmented TCP SYN packets are sent to a number of different destination ports on a specific host. This indicates that a reconnaissance sweep of your network might be in progress. The fragmentation indicates an attempt to conceal the sweep. This might be the prelude to a more serious attack.
- **Benign Triggers**—Although network management tools can generate port sweeps, they should not generate fragmented sweeps, unless a misconfigured router is somewhere in the path that has an extremely low MTU setting.

3005 TCP FIN Port Sweep

- **Default Severity**—High.
- **Structure**—Composite.
- **Implementation**—Context.
- **Class**—Reconnaissance.
- **Description**—This signature triggers when a series of TCP FIN packets are sent to a number of different privileged ports (having a port number less than 1024) on a specific host. This indicates that a reconnaissance sweep of your network might be in progress. The use of FIN packets indicates an attempt to conceal the sweep. This might be the prelude to a more serious attack.
- **Benign Triggers**—Although network management tools can generate port sweeps, they should not generate FIN sweeps, so such a tool is extremely unlikely to be a cause of this alarm.

3006 Fragmented TCP FIN Port Sweep

- **Default Severity**—High.
- **Structure**—Composite.
- **Implementation**—Context.
- **Class**—Reconnaissance.
- **Description**—This signature triggers when a series of fragmented TCP FIN packets are sent to a number of different privileged ports (having a port number less than 1024) on a specific host. This indicates that a reconnaissance sweep of your network might be in progress. The use of fragmentation and of FIN packets indicates an attempt to conceal the sweep. This might be the prelude to a more serious attack.

- **Benign Triggers**—Although network management tools can generate port sweeps, they should not generate FIN sweeps, so such a tool is extremely unlikely to be a cause of this alarm. In addition, these sweeps should not be fragmented, unless a misconfigured router is somewhere in the path that has an extremely low MTU setting.

3010 TCP High Port Sweep

- **Default Severity**—Disable.
- **Structure**—Composite.
- **Implementation**—Context.
- **Class**—Reconnaissance.
- **Description**—This signature triggers when a series of TCP connections to a number of different high-numbered ports (having port number greater than 1023) on a specific host are initiated. This indicates that a reconnaissance sweep of your network might be in progress. This might be the prelude to a more serious attack. This is a catchall signature that fires if the specific type of TCP high port sweep cannot be determined.
- **Benign Triggers**—Many network management tools, such as HP OpenView, provide network-mapping capabilities. This might include a mapping of available network services, so high TCP port sweeps might be expected from these systems.

High Ports Versus Low Ports

Original UNIX systems treated the first 1024 ports (low ports) as privileged. Regular users (unprivileged) can create services that use ports 1024 through 65535 (high ports). Therefore, most of the well-known services run in the range of ports from 1 to 1023. You might consider scans in low port range more severe than scans of your high ports. As more new services are created, however, more of them are placed in the high port range, so even high port scans are becoming more critical.

3011 TCP FIN High Port Sweep

- **Default Severity**—High.
- **Structure**—Composite.
- **Implementation**—Context.
- **Class**—Reconnaissance.

- **Description**—This signature triggers when a series of TCP FIN packets are sent to a number of different destination high-numbered ports (having a port number greater than 1023) on a specific host. This indicates that a reconnaissance sweep of your network might be in progress. The use of FIN packets indicates an attempt to conceal the sweep. This might be the prelude to a more serious attack.

- **Benign Triggers**—Although network management tools can generate port sweeps, they should not generate FIN sweeps, so such a tool is extremely unlikely to be a cause of this alarm.

3012 Fragmented TCP FIN High Port Sweep

- **Default Severity**—High.
- **Structure**—Composite.
- **Implementation**—Context.
- **Class**—Reconnaissance.
- **Description**—This signature triggers when a series of fragmented TCP FIN packets are sent to a number of different destination high-numbered ports (having a port number greater than 1023) on a specific host. This indicates that a reconnaissance sweep of your network might be in progress. The use of fragmentation and of FIN packets indicates an attempt to conceal the sweep. This might be the prelude to a more serious attack.

- **Benign Triggers**—Although network management tools can generate port sweeps, they should not generate FIN sweeps, so such a tool is extremely unlikely to be a cause of this alarm. In addition, these sweeps should not be fragmented, unless a misconfigured router is somewhere in the path that has an extremely low MTU setting.

3015 TCP Null Port Sweep

- **Default Severity**—High.
- **Structure**—Composite.
- **Implementation**—Context.
- **Class**—Reconnaissance.
- **Description**—This signature triggers when a series of TCP packets with none of the SYN, FIN, ACK, or RST flags set are sent to a number of different destination ports on a specific host. This indicates that a reconnaissance sweep of your network might be in progress. The use of this type of packet indicates an attempt to conceal the sweep. This might be the prelude to a more serious attack.

- **Benign Triggers**—Although network management tools can generate port sweeps, they should not generate this type of packet, so such a tool is extremely unlikely to be a cause of this alarm.

3016 Fragmented TCP Null Port Sweep

- **Default Severity**—High.
- **Structure**—Composite.
- **Implementation**—Context.
- **Class**—Reconnaissance.
- **Description**—This signature triggers when a series of fragmented TCP packets with none of the SYN, FIN, ACK, or RST flags set are sent to a number of different destination ports on a specific host. This indicates that a reconnaissance sweep of your network might be in progress. The use of this type of packet and of fragmentation indicates an attempt to conceal the sweep. This might be the prelude to a more serious attack.
- **Benign Triggers**—Although network management tools can generate port sweeps, they should not generate this type of packet, so such a tool is extremely unlikely to be a cause of this alarm. In addition, these sweeps should not be fragmented, unless a misconfigured router is somewhere in the path that has an extremely low MTU setting.

3020 TCP SYN-FIN Port Sweep

- **Default Severity**—High.
- **Structure**—Composite.
- **Implementation**—Context.
- **Class**—Reconnaissance.
- **Description**—This signature triggers when a series of TCP packets with both the SYN and FIN flags set are sent to a number of different destination ports on a specific host. This indicates that a reconnaissance sweep of your network might be in progress. The use of both the SYN and FIN flags is abnormal and can indicate an attempt to conceal the sweep. This might be the prelude to a more serious attack.
- **Benign Triggers**—Although network management tools can generate port sweeps, they should not generate this type of packet, so such a tool is extremely unlikely to be a cause of this alarm.

3021 Fragmented TCP SYN-FIN Port Sweep

- **Default Severity**—High.
- **Structure**—Composite.
- **Implementation**—Context.
- **Class**—Reconnaissance.

- **Description**—This signature triggers when a series of fragmented TCP packets with both the SYN and FIN flags set are sent to a number of different destination ports on a specific host. This indicates that a reconnaissance sweep of your network might be in progress. The use of both the SYN and FIN flags is abnormal, as is the use of fragmentation, and can indicate an attempt to conceal the sweep. This might be the prelude to a more serious attack.

- **Benign Triggers**—Although network management tools can generate port sweeps, they should not generate this type of packet, so such a tool is extremely unlikely to be a cause of this alarm. In addition, these sweeps should not be fragmented, unless a misconfigured router is somewhere in the path that has an extremely low MTU setting.

3045 Queso Sweep

- **Default Severity**—High.
- **Structure**—Composite.
- **Implementation**—Context.
- **Class**—Reconnaissance.
- **Description**—This signature triggers after having detected a FIN, SYN-FIN, and a PUSH sent from a specific host bound for a specific host.
- **Benign Triggers**—None.

TCP Host Sweeps

Unlike TCP port scans, which focus on traffic to a single host, TCP host sweeps trigger on traffic destined for multiple systems on your network. Like ICMP sweeps, attackers can use TCP host sweeps to locate systems and services on your network. Many times, an attacker looks for a specific service for which he has a working exploit.

The signatures related to TCP host sweeps are as follows:

- 3030 TCP SYN Host Sweep
- 3031 Fragmented TCP SYN Host Sweep
- 3032 TCP FIN Host Sweep
- 3033 Fragmented TCP FIN Host Sweep
- 3034 TCP NULL Host Sweep
- 3035 Fragmented TCP NULL Host Sweep
- 3036 TCP SYN-FIN Host Sweep
- 3037 Fragmented TCP SYN-FIN Host Sweep

3030 TCP SYN Host Sweep

- **Default Severity**—Low.
- **Structure**—Composite.
- **Implementation**—Context.
- **Class**—Reconnaissance.
- **Description**—This signature triggers when a series of TCP SYN packets are sent to the same destination port on a number of different hosts. This can, for example, be a sweep of many hosts to find out which ones can receive mail or telnet sessions. This indicates that a reconnaissance sweep of your network might be in progress. This might be the prelude to a more serious attack.
- **Benign Triggers**—Host sweep signature 3030 detects behaviors that should not be observed from sources outside the local network but are normal behaviors for sources from within the local network. It is, therefore, important to define the appropriate internal IP ranges to keep local machines from triggering this signature.

3031 Fragmented TCP SYN Host Sweep

- **Default Severity**—High.
- **Structure**—Composite.
- **Implementation**—Context.
- **Class**—Reconnaissance.
- **Description**—This signature triggers when a series of fragmented TCP SYN packets are sent to the same destination port on a number of different hosts. This can, for example, be a sweep of many hosts to find out which ones can receive mail or Telnet sessions. This indicates that a reconnaissance sweep of your network might be in progress. This might be the prelude to a more serious attack. The use of fragmentation is abnormal and can indicate an attempt to conceal the sweep.
- **Benign Triggers**—None

3032 TCP FIN Host Sweep

- **Default Severity**—High.
- **Structure**—Composite.
- **Implementation**—Context.
- **Class**—Reconnaissance.

- **Description**—This signature triggers when a series of TCP FIN packets are sent to the same destination port on a number of different hosts. This can, for example, be a sweep of many hosts to find out which ones can receive mail or Telnet sessions. This indicates that a reconnaissance sweep of your network might be in progress. This might be the prelude to a more serious attack.

- **Benign Triggers**—Host sweep signature 3032 detects behaviors that should not be observed from sources outside the local network but are normal behaviors for sources from within the local network. It is, therefore, important to define the appropriate internal IP ranges to keep local machines from triggering this signature.

3033 Fragmented TCP FIN Host Sweep

- **Default Severity**—High.
- **Structure**—Composite.
- **Implementation**—Context.
- **Class**—Reconnaissance.
- **Description**—This signature triggers when a series of fragmented TCP FIN packets have been sent to the same destination port on a number of different hosts. This can, for example, be a sweep of many hosts to find out which ones can receive mail or Telnet sessions. This indicates that a reconnaissance sweep of your network might be in progress. This might be the prelude to a more serious attack. The use of fragmentation is abnormal and can indicate an attempt to conceal the sweep.
- **Benign Triggers**—None

3034 TCP NULL Host Sweep

- **Default Severity**—High.
- **Structure**—Composite.
- **Implementation**—Context.
- **Class**—Reconnaissance.
- **Description**—This signature triggers when a series of TCP packets with none of the SYN, FIN, ACK, or RST flags set are sent to the same destination port on a number of different hosts. This can, for example, be a sweep of many hosts to find out which ones can receive mail or Telnet sessions. This indicates that a reconnaissance sweep of your network might be in progress. This might be the prelude to a more serious attack. The use of this packet is abnormal and can indicate an attempt to conceal the sweep.
- **Benign Triggers**—None

3035 Fragmented TCP NULL Host Sweep

- **Default Severity**—High.
- **Structure**—Composite.
- **Implementation**—Context.
- **Class**—Reconnaissance.
- **Description**—This signature triggers when a series of fragmented TCP packets with none of the SYN, FIN, ACK, or RST flags set are sent to the same destination port on a number of different hosts. This can, for example, be a sweep of many hosts to find out which ones can receive mail or Telnet sessions. This indicates that a reconnaissance sweep of your network might be in progress. This might be the prelude to a more serious attack. The use of this packet is abnormal, as is the use of fragmentation, and can indicate an attempt to conceal the sweep.
- **Benign Triggers**—None

3036 TCP SYN-FIN Host Sweep

- **Default Severity**—High.
- **Structure**—Composite.
- **Implementation**—Context.
- **Class**—Reconnaissance.
- **Description**—This signature triggers when a series of TCP packets with both the SYN and FIN flags set are sent to the same destination port on a number of different hosts. This can, for example, be a sweep of many hosts to find out which ones can receive mail or Telnet sessions. This indicates that a reconnaissance sweep of your network might be in progress. The use of both the SYN and FIN flags is abnormal and can indicate an attempt to conceal the sweep.
- **Benign Triggers**—None.

3037 Fragmented TCP SYN-FIN Host Sweep

- **Default Severity**—High.
- **Structure**—Composite.
- **Implementation**—Context.
- **Class**—Reconnaissance.
- **Description**—This signature triggers when a series of fragmented TCP packets with both the SYN and FIN flags set are sent to the same destination port on a number of different hosts. This can, for example, be a sweep of many hosts to find out which ones can receive mail or Telnet sessions. This indicates that a reconnaissance sweep of your

network might be in progress. This might be the prelude to a more serious attack. The use of both the SYN and FIN flags is abnormal, as is the use of fragmentation, and can indicate an attempt to conceal the sweep.

- **Benign Triggers**—None.

Abnormal TCP Packets

Abnormal TCP packets usually indicate attacks against your network. These packets are usually packets that are not allowed by RFC 793 (Transmission Control Protocol), therefore, normal programs usually do not generate them. The signatures related to abnormal TCP packets are as follows:

- 3038 Fragmented NULL TCP Packet
- 3039 Fragmented Orphaned FIN packet
- 3040 NULL TCP Packet
- 3041 SYN/FIN Packet
- 3042 Orphaned FIN Packet
- 3043 Fragmented SYN/FIN Packet

3038 Fragmented NULL TCP Packet

- **Default Severity**—High.
- **Structure**—Atomic.
- **Implementation**—Context.
- **Class**—Reconnaissance.
- **Description**—Triggers when a single fragmented TCP packet with none of the SYN, FIN, ACK, or RST flags set are sent to a specific host. This indicates that a reconnaissance sweep of your network might be in progress. The use of this type of packet indicates an attempt to conceal the sweep. This might be the prelude to a more serious attack. This should never occur in legitimate traffic.
- **Benign Triggers**—None.

3039 Fragmented Orphaned FIN Packet

- **Default Severity**—High.
- **Structure**—Atomic.
- **Implementation**—Context.
- **Class**—Reconnaissance.

- **Description**—Triggers when a single fragmented orphaned TCP FIN packet is sent to a privileged port (having port number less than 1024) on a specific host. This indicates that a reconnaissance sweep of your network might be in progress. The use of a single fragmented FIN packet, when no other alarms fire, indicates an attempt to conceal the sweep by slowly scanning the network in an effort to beat port or host scan detectors. This might be the prelude to a more serious attack.

- **Benign Triggers**—None.

Orphaned FIN packet

A TCP packet with the FIN flag set (FIN packet) indicates the normal close of a TCP connection between two hosts. Because it signals the end of a connection, other packets need to be sent during the connection before the FIN packet is sent. A FIN packet observed without any initial packets is known as an *orphaned FIN packet*, and normally indicates an attacker who is searching for services on your network.

3040 NULL TCP Packet

- **Default Severity**—High.
- **Structure**—Atomic.
- **Implementation**—Context.
- **Class**—Reconnaissance.
- **Description**—Triggers when a single TCP packet with none of the SYN, FIN, ACK, or RST flags set are sent to a specific host. This indicates that a reconnaissance sweep of your network might be in progress. The use of this type of packet indicates an attempt to conceal the sweep. This might be the prelude to a more serious attack. This should never occur in legitimate traffic.
- **Benign Triggers**—None.

3041 SYN/FIN Packet

- **Default Severity**—High.
- **Structure**—Atomic.
- **Implementation**—Context.
- **Class**—Reconnaissance.

- **Description**—Triggers when a single TCP packet with the SYN and FIN flags set is sent to a specific host. This indicates that a reconnaissance sweep of your network might be in progress. The use of this type of packet indicates an attempt to conceal the sweep. This might be the prelude to a more serious attack. This should never occur in legitimate traffic.

- **Benign Triggers**—None.

3042 Orphaned FIN Packet

- **Default Severity**—High.

- **Structure**—Atomic.

- **Implementation**—Context.

- **Class**—Reconnaissance.

- **Description**—Triggers when a single orphaned TCP FIN packet is sent to a privileged port (having port number less than 1024) on a specific host. This indicates that a reconnaissance sweep of your network might be in progress. The use of a single FIN packet, when no other alarms fire, indicates an attempt to conceal the sweep by slowly scanning the network in an effort to beat port scan detectors. This might be the prelude to a more serious attack.

- **Benign Triggers**—Although network management tools can generate port sweeps, they should not generate FIN sweeps, so such a tool is extremely unlikely to be a cause of this alarm.

3043 Fragmented SYN/FIN Packet

- **Default Severity**—High.

- **Structure**—Atomic.

- **Implementation**—Context.

- **Class**—Reconnaissance.

- **Description**—Triggers when a single fragmented TCP packet with the SYN and FIN flags set is sent to a specific host. This indicates that a reconnaissance sweep of your network might be in progress. The use of this type of packet indicates an attempt to conceal the sweep. This might be the prelude to a more serious attack. This should never occur in legitimate traffic.

- **Benign Triggers**—None.

Mail Attacks

Simple Mail Transfer Protocol (SMTP) has a long history of vulnerabilities. Attackers continually attempt to gain access to networks through their mail servers. The Cisco Secure IDS signatures related to SMTP are as follows:

- 3100 Smail Attack
- 3101 Sendmail Invalid Recipient
- 3102 Sendmail Invalid Sender
- 3103 Sendmail Reconnaissance
- 3104 Archaic Sendmail Attacks
- 3105 Sendmail Decode Alias
- 3106 Sendmail SPAM Attack
- 3107 Majordomo Exec Bug
- 3108 MIME Overflow Bug
- 3109 Qmail Length Crash

3100 Smail Attack

- **Default Severity**—High.
- **Structure**—Composite.
- **Implementation**—Content.
- **Class**—Access.
- **Description**—This signature triggers on the common smail attack against e-mail servers. This attack attempts to cause e-mail servers to execute programs on the attacker's behalf. Successful execution of a smail attack might result in the mail server being compromised.
- **Benign Triggers**—For security reasons, users should not be allowed to execute programs through e-mail servers. This is a serious indication that your network might be under attack, and the source must be blocked immediately.

3101 Sendmail Invalid Recipient

- **Default Severity**—High
- **Structure**—Composite.
- **Implementation**—Content.
- **Class**—Access.

- **Description**—This signature triggers on any mail message with a pipe (|) symbol in the recipient field. This attack attempts to cause e-mail servers to execute programs on the attacker's behalf. Successful execution of this attack might result in your mail server being compromised.

- **Benign Triggers**—For security reasons, users should not be allowed to execute programs through e-mail servers. This is a serious indication that your network might be under attack, and the source must be blocked immediately.

3102 Sendmail Invalid Sender

- **Default Severity**—High.
- **Structure**—Composite.
- **Implementation**—Content.
- **Class**—Access.
- **Description**—This signature triggers on any mail message with a pipe symbol (|) in the From field. This attack attempts to cause e-mail servers to execute programs on the attacker's behalf. Successful execution of this attack might result in your mail server being compromised.
- **Benign Triggers**—For security reasons, users should not be allowed to execute programs through e-mail servers. This is a serious indication that your network might be under attack, and the source must be blocked immediately.

3103 Sendmail Reconnaissance

- **Default Severity**—Low.
- **Structure**—Composite.
- **Implementation**—Content.
- **Class**—Reconnaissance.
- **Description**—This signature triggers when **EXPN** or **VRFY** commands are issued to the SMTP port. This indicates that your network might be under a reconnaissance attack.
- **Benign Triggers**—These commands are commonly used to verify that a user mail account exists on the server or to expand an alias to determine the actual recipients of a message. Users that use the **EXPN** and **VRFY** commands for legitimate purposes trigger this signature. The information obtained is useful but not dangerous on its own. Monitoring future traffic for patterns of misuse is recommended.

3104 Archaic Sendmail Attacks

- **Default Severity**—Low.
- **Structure**—Composite.
- **Implementation**—Content.
- **Class**—Information.
- **Description**—This signature triggers when **wiz** or **debug** commands are sent to the SMTP port. This indicates that a student of computer security history decided to make a feeble attempt at compromising your system.
- **Benign Triggers**—This type of traffic should not be seen on modern networks. There is little chance that there will be any adverse effects from someone attempting these "old" hacks.

3105 Sendmail Decode Alias

- **Default Severity**—Medium.
- **Structure**—Composite.
- **Implementation**—Content.
- **Class**—Access.
- **Description**—This signature triggers on any mail message with **=decode@** in the header. This might indicate an attempt to illegally access system resources. System compromise is possible.
- **Benign Triggers**—The decode alias is used to uudecode files and is primarily implemented as a convenience for system administrators. For security purposes, this should not be allowed, and the service needs to be disabled. If allowed, users who mail to the alias can trigger this signature.

3106 Sendmail SPAM Attack

- **Default Severity**—Medium.
- **Structure**—Composite.
- **Implementation**—Content.
- **Class**—Denial of service.
- **Description**—Counts number of Rcpt to lines in a single mail message and alarms after a user-definable maximum has been exceeded (default is 250).
- **Benign Triggers**—Some mailing list software might trigger this signature.

NOTE   Currently, the SPAM and MIME thresholds (signature IDs 3106 and 3108) are configurable only on the IDSM line card through the signature-tuning parameters (see Chapter 11, "Sensor Configuration Within CSPM"). With Cisco IDS version 3.0, these parameters are also user configurable on the appliance sensor through customizable signatures (see Chapter 18, "Planned Cisco Secure IDS Enhancements").

3107 Majordomo Exec Bug

- **Default Severity**—High.
- **Structure**—Composite.
- **Implementation**—Content.
- **Class**—Access.
- **Description**—A bug in the Majordomo program allows remote users to execute arbitrary commands at the privilege level of the server.
- **Benign Triggers**—None.

3108 MIME Overflow Bug

- **Default Severity**—High.
- **Structure**—Composite.
- **Implementation**—Content.
- **Class**—Access.
- **Description**—Fires when an SMTP mail message has a MIME Content.- field that is excessively long. The token MimeContent.MaxLen defines the longest valid header length for MIME Content.-. header tokens. It defaults to 200 and can be set to any value greater or equal to 76.
- **Benign Triggers**—It is possible, but unlikely, that a legitimate MIME Content.- field might be longer than the MimeContent.MaxLen token. The RFC 2045 recommends that fields be no longer than 72 characters, for readability, but this is not a requirement. A vendor can choose to make an application that uses longer fields. If this signature fires, the offending mail message needs to be examined to check the long field. In a typical exploit, it is a repeated character, such as AAA...AAA.

3109 Qmail Length Crash

- **Default Severity**—High.
- **Structure**—Composite.

- **Implementation**—Content.
- **Class**—Denial of service.
- **Description**—This signature triggers when an attempt is made to pass an overly long command string to a mail server.
- **Benign Triggers**—None.

FTP Attacks

FTP is a common file transfer mechanism. Users and system administrators commonly use FTP to transfer files between various systems on their network. Like many other protocols, FTP has a long history of security vulnerabilities. The Cisco Secure IDS signatures related to FTP are as follows:

- 3150 FTP Remote Command Execution
- 3151 FTP SYST Command Attempt
- 3152 FTP CWD ~root Command
- 3153 FTP Improper Address Specified
- 3154 FTP Improper Port Specified
- 3155 FTP RETR Pipe Filename Command Execution
- 3156 FTP STOR Pipe Filename Command Execution
- 3157 FTP PASV Port Spoof

3150 FTP Remote Command Execution

- **Default Severity**—Low.
- **Structure**—Composite.
- **Implementation**—Content.
- **Class**—Reconnaissance.
- **Description**—This signature triggers when someone tries to execute the FTP **SITE** command. This might indicate an attempt to illegally access system resources.
- **Benign Triggers**—The FTP **SITE** command enables a user to execute a limited number of commands through the FTP server on the host machine. No authentication is required to execute this command. The commands that might execute vary from system to system, and on many systems, the **SITE** command is not even implemented. It is recommended that the **SITE** command be disabled on FTP servers if possible. If this signature is triggered from a source outside of your network, prudent security practices suggest that the source needs to be blocked.

3151 FTP **SYST** Command Attempt

- **Default Severity**—Disable.
- **Structure**—Composite.
- **Implementation**—Content.
- **Class**—Information.
- **Description**—Triggers when someone tries to execute the FTP **SYST** command. This indicates that your network might be under reconnaissance.
- **Benign Triggers**—The FTP **SYST** command returns the type of operating system that the FTP server is running. Authentication is not required to execute this command. **SYST** provides information that might be used to refine attack methods. FTP from Linux causes **SYST** signature to fire. Some proxies, such as the TIS Toolkit, also issue the **SYST** command.

3152 FTP **CWD ~root** Command

- **Default Severity**—High.
- **Structure**—Composite.
- **Implementation**—Content.
- **Class**—Access.
- **Description**—This signature triggers when someone tries to execute the **CWD ~root** command. This might indicate an attempt to illegally access system resources.
- **Benign Triggers**—There is no known reason that this command should ever be executed. If this signature is triggered from a source outside of your network, prudent security practices suggest that the source needs to be blocked.

3153 FTP Improper Address Specified

- **Default Severity**—High.
- **Structure**—Atomic.
- **Implementation**—Content.
- **Class**—Access.
- **Description**—This signature triggers if a **port** command is issued with an address that is not the same as the requesting host.
- **Benign Triggers**—None.

3154 FTP Improper Port Specified

- **Default Severity**—High.
- **Structure**—Atomic.
- **Implementation**—Content.
- **Class**—Access.
- **Description**—This signature triggers if a **port** command is issued with a data port specified that is less than 1024 or greater than 65535.
- **Benign Triggers**—None.

3155 FTP RETR Pipe Filename Command Execution

- **Default Severity**—High.
- **Structure**—Atomic.
- **Implementation**—Content.
- **Class**—Access.
- **Description**—The FTP client can be tricked into running arbitrary commands supplied by the remote server. When the remote file begins with a pipe symbol (|), the FTP client processes the contents of the remote file as a shell script.
- **Benign Triggers**—None.

3156 FTP STOR Pipe Filename Command Execution

- **Default Severity**—High.
- **Structure**—Atomic.
- **Implementation**—Content.
- **Class**—Access.
- **Description**—The FTP client can be tricked into running arbitrary commands supplied by the remote server. When the remote file begins with a pipe symbol (|), the FTP client processes the contents of the remote file as a shell script.
- **Benign Triggers**—None.

3157 FTP PASV Port Spoof

- **Default Severity**—High.
- **Structure**—Composite.
- **Implementation**—Content.

- **Class**—Access.

- **Description**—A possible attempt has been made to open connections through a firewall to a protected FTP server to a non-FTP port. This happens when the firewall incorrectly interprets an FTP **227**, or **Entering Passive Mode** command, by opening an unauthorized connection.

- **Benign Triggers**—None.

Legacy Cisco Secure IDS Web Attacks

In a later version of Cisco Secure IDS, Web attacks are organized into the 5000 class signatures. Originally, this was not the case. Therefore, the original legacy Web attacks do not fall into the 5000 signatures. These signatures fall into the signature range from 3200 through 3233. These legacy Web signatures are as follows:

- 3200 WWW Phf Attack
- 3201 WWW General cgi-bin Attack
- 3202 WWW .url File Requested
- 3203 WWW .lnk File Requested
- 3204 WWW .bat File Requested
- 3205 HTML File Has .url Link
- 3206 HTML File Has .lnk Link
- 3207 HTML File Has .bat Link
- 3208 WWW campas Attack
- 3209 WWW Glimpse Server Attack
- 3210 WWW IIS View Source Attack
- 3211 WWW IIS Hex View Source Attack
- 3212 WWW NPH-TEST-CGI Attack
- 3213 WWW TEST-CGI Attack
- 3214 IIS DOT DOT VIEW Attack
- 3215 IIS DOT DOT EXECUTE Bug
- 3216 IIS Dot Dot Crash Attack
- 3217 WWW php View File Attack
- 3218 WWW SGI Wrap Attack
- 3219 WWW PHP Buffer Overflow
- 3220 IIS Long URL Crash Bug
- 3221 WWW cgi-viewsource Attack

- 3222 WWW PHP Log Scripts Read Attack
- 3223 WWW IRIX cgi-handler Attack
- 3224 HTTP WebGais
- 3225 HTTP Gais Websendmail
- 3226 WWW Webdist Bug
- 3227 WWW Htmlscript Bug
- 3229 Website Win-C-Sample Buffer Overflow
- 3230 Website Uploader
- 3231 Novell Convert Bug
- 3232 Finger Attempt
- 3233 WWW count-cgi Overflow

3200 WWW Phf Attack

- **Default Severity**—High.
- **Structure**—Composite.
- **Implementation**—Content.
- **Class**—Access.
- **Description**—This signature triggers when the phf attack is detected. This might indicate an attempt to illegally access system resources. A flaw in the CGI library function **escape_shell_cmd** can provide attackers with the ability to execute commands and access files. Numerous programs incorporate this library function, including a program named phf.
- **Benign Triggers**—This cgi program introduces significant security problems and needs to be removed. No valid reason to access the phf CGI file exists. Hosts that attempt to access this file, especially from outside your network, must be blocked.

3201 WWW General cgi-bin Attack

- **Default Severity**—High.
- **Structure**—Composite.
- **Implementation**—Content.
- **Class**—Access.
- **Description**—This alarms triggers when any **cgi-bin** script attempts to retrieve password files on various operating systems, such as the /etc/passwd (SubID 1), /etc/shadow (SubID 2), /etc/master.passwd (SubID 3), /etc/master.shadow (SubID 4),

/etc/security/passwd (SubID 5), and /etc/security/opasswd (SubID 6). This might indicate an attempt to illegally access system resources and be the prelude to a more serious attack. No valid reason to access these files through this mechanism exists. Hosts that attempt to access these files, especially from outside your network, must be blocked.

- **Benign Triggers**—None.

3202 WWW .url File Requested

- **Default Severity**—High.
- **Structure**—Composite.
- **Implementation**—Content.
- **Class**—Access.
- **Description**—This signature triggers when a user attempts to get any URL file. A flaw in Microsoft Internet Explorer might allow illegal access to system resources when files of type URL are accessed through the HTTP **GET** command.
- **Benign Triggers**—There are no known legitimate reasons for files of type URL to be placed on Web sites for user access. You need to investigate the source of this alarm and thoroughly review the suspect file.

3203 WWW .lnk File Requested

- **Default Severity**—High.
- **Structure**—Composite.
- **Implementation**—Content.
- **Class**—Access.
- **Description**—This signature triggers when a user attempts to get any LNK file. A flaw in Microsoft Internet Explorer might allow illegal access to system resources when files of type LNK are accessed through the HTTP **GET** command.
- **Benign Triggers**—There are no known legitimate reasons for files of type LNK to be placed on Web sites for user access. You need to investigate the source of this alarm and thoroughly review the suspect file.

3204 WWW .bat File Requested

- **Default Severity**—High.
- **Structure**—Composite.
- **Implementation**—Content.

- **Class**—Access.
- **Description**—This signature triggers when a user attempts to get any BAT file. A flaw in Microsoft Internet Explorer might allow illegal access to system resources when files of type BAT are accessed through the HTTP **GET** command.
- **Benign Triggers**—There are no known legitimate reasons for files of type BAT to be placed on Web sites for user access. You need to investigate the source of this alarm and thoroughly review the suspect file.

3205 HTML File Has .url Link

- **Default Severity**—Disable.
- **Structure**—Composite.
- **Implementation**—Content.
- **Class**—Access.
- **Description**—This signature triggers when a file has a URL link. This signature warns before a user has a chance to click the potentially damaging link. Cisco Secure IDS Signature 3202 alarms on any attempt to click the link, but it might do its damage before any defensive action can be taken. A flaw in Microsoft Internet Explorer might allow illegal access to system resources when files of type URL are accessed through the HTTP **GET** command.
- **Benign Triggers**—There are no known legitimate reasons for files of type URL to be placed on Web sites for user access. You need to investigate the source of this alarm and thoroughly review the suspect file.

3206 HTML File Has .lnk Link

- **Default Severity**—Disable.
- **Structure**—Composite.
- **Implementation**—Content.
- **Class**—Access.
- **Description**—This signature triggers when a file has a LNK link. This signature warns before a user has a chance to click the potentially damaging link. Cisco Secure IDS Signature 3203 alarms on any attempt to click the link, but it might do its damage before any defensive action can be taken. A flaw in Microsoft Internet Explorer might allow illegal access to system resources when files of type LNK are accessed through the HTTP **GET** command.
- **Benign Triggers**—There are no known legitimate reasons for files of type LNK to be placed on Web sites for user access. You need to investigate the source of this alarm and thoroughly review the suspect file.

3207 HTML File Has .bat Link

- **Default Severity**—Disable.
- **Structure**—Composite.
- **Implementation**—Content.
- **Class**—Access.
- **Description**—This signature triggers when a file has a BAT link. This signature warns before a user has a chance to click the potentially damaging link. Cisco Secure IDS Signature 3204 alarms on any attempt to click the link, but it might do its damage before any defensive action can be taken. A flaw in Microsoft Internet Explorer might allow illegal access to system resources when files of type BAT are accessed through the HTTP **GET** command.
- **Benign Triggers**—There are no known legitimate reasons for files of type BAT to be placed on Web sites for user access. You need to investigate the source of this alarm and thoroughly review the suspect file.

3208 WWW campas Attack

- **Default Severity**—High.
- **Structure**—Composite.
- **Implementation**—Content.
- **Class**—Access.
- **Description**—This signature triggers when an attempt is made to pass commands to the CGI program **campas**. A problem in the CGI program **campas**, which is included in the NCSA Web Server distribution, enables an attacker to execute commands on the host machine. These commands execute at the privilege level of the HTTP server.
- **Benign Triggers**—This signature indicates abuse and the source should be blocked.

3209 WWW Glimpse Server Attack

- **Default Severity**—High.
- **Structure**—Composite.
- **Implementation**—Content.
- **Class**—Access.
- **Description**—This alarm triggers when an attempt is made to pass commands to the Perl script **GlimpseHTTP**. These commands can allow an attacker to execute commands on the host machine. **GlimpseHTTP** is an interface to the Glimpse search tool.
- **Benign Triggers**—There are no legitimate reasons to pass commands to a Glimpse server.

3210 WWW IIS View Source Attack

- **Default Severity**—Medium.
- **Structure**—Composite.
- **Implementation**—Content.
- **Class**—Access.
- **Description**—If a request to a Microsoft Internet Information Server is formatted in a certain way, executable files are read instead of being executed. This can reveal executable scripts and sensitive database information, including passwords. An attacker might be able to analyze these scripts for vulnerabilities. This signature triggers when a request is made to an HTTP server attempting to view the source.
- **Benign Triggers**—There should be no valid reason for a user to enter a request terminated with a dot.

3211 WWW IIS Hex View Source Attack

- **Default Severity**—Disable.
- **Structure**—Composite.
- **Implementation**—Content.
- **Class**—Access.
- **Description**—If a request to Microsoft IIS is formatted in a certain way, executable files are read instead of being executed. This can reveal executable scripts and sensitive database information, including passwords. An attacker might be able to analyze these scripts for vulnerabilities. This signature triggers when a request is made to an HTTP server attempting to view the source.
- **Benign Triggers**—It is possible that a Web page might be served with a **%2E** embedded in a hyperlink. Following this link might cause a Web browser client to trigger this alarm.

3212 WWW NPH-TEST-CGI Attack

- **Default Severity**—Medium.
- **Structure**—Composite.
- **Implementation**—Content.
- **Class**—Access.
- **Description**—This signature triggers when an attempt is made to view directory listings with the script **nph-test-cgi**. Some HTTP servers include this script, which can be used to list directories on a server. It is a test script and needs to be removed on an operational server.

- **Benign Triggers**—An attempt to access this script from outside is suspicious.

3213 WWW TEST-CGI Attack
- **Default Severity**—Medium.
- **Structure**—Composite.
- **Implementation**—Content.
- **Class**—Access.
- **Description**—This signature triggers when an attempt is made to view directory listings with the script **test-cgi**. Some HTTP servers contain this script, which can be used to list directories on a server. It is a test script and needs to be removed on an operational server.
- **Benign Triggers**—An attempt to access this script from outside is suspicious.

3214 IIS DOT DOT VIEW Attack
- **Default Severity**—Disable.
- **Structure**—Composite.
- **Implementation**—Content.
- **Class**—Access.
- **Description**—This signature triggers on any attempt to view files above the chrooted directory using Microsoft's Internet Information Server. This can result in viewing files that are not intended to be publicly accessible. The chroot directory is supposed to be the topmost directory to which HTTP clients have access.
- **Benign Triggers**—None

3215 IIS DOT DOT EXECUTE Bug
- **Default Severity**—High.
- **Structure**—Composite.
- **Implementation**—Content.
- **Class**—Access.
- **Description**—This signature triggers on any attempt to cause Microsoft's Internet Information Server to improperly execute commands using a URL that includes the dot dot (**..**) directory traversal directive.
- **Benign Triggers**—None

3216 IIS Dot Dot Crash Attack

- **Default Severity**—High.
- **Structure**—Composite.
- **Implementation**—Content.
- **Class**—Denial of service.
- **Description**—This signature triggers when an attempt is made to crash an IIS server by requesting a URL beginning with ./.
- **Benign Triggers**—None.

3217 WWW php View File Attack

- **Default Severity**—High.
- **Structure**—Composite.
- **Implementation**—Content.
- **Class**—Access.
- **Description**—This signature triggers when someone attempts to use the PHP cgi-bin program to view a file. This might indicate an attempt to illegally access system resources.
- **Benign Triggers**—This cgi program introduces significant security problems; you should not use it. Hosts that attempt to access this file, especially from outside your network, need to be blocked.

3218 WWW SGI Wrap Attack

- **Default Severity**—High.
- **Structure**—Composite.
- **Implementation**—Content.
- **Class**—Access.
- **Description**—Illegitimately accessing the wrap program to view or list files triggers this signature. This program is distributed with the IRIX Web Server.
- **Benign Triggers**—Although legitimate circumstances might exist when the wrap program can be used, this signature should not fire when it is used legitimately.

3219 WWW PHP Buffer Overflow

- **Default Severity**—High.
- **Structure**—Composite.

- **Implementation**—Content.
- **Class**—Access.
- **Description**—This signature triggers when an oversized query is sent to the PHP cgi-bin program. This represents an attempt to overflow a buffer and gain system access.
- **Benign Triggers**—None.

3220 IIS Long URL Crash Bug

- **Default Severity**—Disable.
- **Structure**—Composite.
- **Implementation**—Content.
- **Class**—Denial of service.
- **Description**—This triggers when a large URL has been passed to a Web server in an attempt to crash the system.
- **Benign Triggers**—None.

3221 WWW cgi-viewsource Attack

- **Default Severity**—Medium.
- **Structure**—Composite.
- **Implementation**—Content.
- **Class**—Access.
- **Description**—This signature triggers when someone attempts to use the **cgi-viewsource** script to view files above the HTTP root directory.
- **Benign Triggers**—None.

3222 WWW PHP Log Scripts Read Attack

- **Default Severity**—Medium.
- **Structure**—Composite.
- **Implementation**—Content.
- **Class**—Access.
- **Description**—When someone attempts to use the PHP scripts **mlog** or **mylog** to view files on a machine, this signature triggers.
- **Benign Triggers**—None.

3223 WWW IRIX cgi-handler Attack

- **Default Severity**—Medium.
- **Structure**—Composite.
- **Implementation**—Content.
- **Class**—Access.
- **Description**—This signature triggers when someone attempts to use the **cgi-handler** script to execute commands.
- **Benign Triggers**—None

3224 HTTP WebGais

- **Default Severity**—Medium.
- **Structure**—Composite.
- **Implementation**—Content.
- **Class**—Access.
- **Description**—This signature triggers when someone attempts to use the **webgais** script to run arbitrary commands.
- **Benign Triggers**—None.

3225 HTTP Gais Websendmail

- **Default Severity**—Medium.
- **Structure**—Composite.
- **Implementation**—Content.
- **Class**—Access.
- **Description**—This signature triggers when someone attempts to use the script **websendmail** to read the password file on a machine.
- **Benign Triggers**—None.

3226 WWW Webdist Bug

- **Default Severity**—Medium.
- **Structure**—Composite.
- **Implementation**—Content.
- **Class**—Access.

- **Description**—This signature triggers when an attempt is made to use the **webdist** program.
- **Benign Triggers**—Legitimate use of the **webdist** program triggers this signature.

3227 WWW Htmlscript Bug

- **Default Severity**—Medium.
- **Structure**—Composite.
- **Implementation**—Content.
- **Class**—Access.
- **Description**—This signature triggers when an attempt is made to view files above the HTML root directory through a bug in the **htmlscript** program.
- **Benign Triggers**—None.

3228 WWW Performer Bug

- **Default Severity**—Medium.
- **Structure**—Composite.
- **Implementation**—Content.
- **Class**—Access.
- **Description**—This signature triggers when an attempt is made to view files above the HTML root directory. The two scripts that are exploited for this signature are **pfdisplay.cgi** and **pfdispaly.cgi**. The latter is misspelled because the actual script name is spelled incorrectly in the Web software.
- **Benign Triggers**—None.

3229 Website Win-C-Sample Buffer Overflow

- **Default Severity**—High.
- **Structure**—Composite.
- **Implementation**—Content.
- **Class**—Access.
- **Description**—When someone attempts to access the **win-c-sample** program distributed with WebSite servers, this signature triggers.

- **Benign Triggers**—Web or system administrators accessing the **win-c-sample** program as a test of newly installed or upgraded WebSite servers trigger this alarm. The user population in general should not access this program. After testing has been completed by the administrator, you need to delete this program.

3230 Website Uploader

- **Default Severity**—Medium.
- **Structure**—Composite.
- **Implementation**—Content.
- **Class**—Access.
- **Description**—This signature triggers when an attempt is made to access the **uploader** program distributed with WebSite servers.
- **Benign Triggers**—None.

3231 Novell Convert Bug

- **Default Severity**—High.
- **Structure**—Composite.
- **Implementation**—Content.
- **Class**—Access.
- **Description**—This signature triggers when a user attempts to use the **convert.bas** program included with Novell's Web server to illegally view files.
- **Benign Triggers**—None

3232 Finger Attempt

- **Default Severity**—Medium.
- **Structure**—Composite.
- **Implementation**—Content.
- **Class**—Access.
- **Description**—This signature triggers when an attempt is made to run the **finger.pl** program through the HTTP server.
- **Benign Triggers**—This signature can be triggered by legitimate, as well as illegitimate, use of the **finger** script. You need to remove all unnecessary CGI scripts from the cgi-bin directory.

3233 WWW count-cgi Overflow

- **Default Severity**—High.
- **Structure**—Composite.
- **Implementation**—Content.
- **Class**—Access.
- **Description**—When someone attempts to overflow a buffer in the CGI Count program, this signature triggers.
- **Benign Triggers**—None.

NetBIOS Attacks

NetBIOS is a legacy Windows networking protocol. This protocol has a long history of security vulnerabilities. The signatures related to NetBIOS attacks are as follows:

- 3300 NETBIOS OOB Data
- 3301 NETBIOS Stat
- 3302 NETBIOS Session Setup Failure
- 3303 Windows Guest Login
- 3304 Windows Null Account Name
- 3305 Windows Password File Access
- 3306 Windows Registry Access
- 3307 Windows Redbutton Attack
- 3308 Windows LSARPC Access
- 3309 Windows SRVSVC Access

3300 NETBIOS OOB Data

- **Default Severity**—High.
- **Structure**—Atomic.
- **Implementation**—Context.
- **Class**—Denial of service.
- **Description**—This signature triggers when an attempt to send Out of Band data to port 139 is detected. This Out of Band data can be used to crash Windows machines.
- **Benign Triggers**—There is no known reason that you should see this type of traffic. If a source from outside of your network triggers this signature, prudent security practices suggest that the source be blocked.

3301 NETBIOS Stat

- **Default Severity**—Disable.

- **Structure**—Atomic.

- **Implementation**—Content.

- **Class**—Information.

- **Description**—This signature triggers when NBTSTAT is used. The Windows NT program called NBTSTAT displays protocol statistics and current TCP/IP connections by using NetBIOS. An attacker can use this application to list a remote machine's name table. This tool basically allows an intruder to determine legitimate usernames, the Windows domain or workgroup name, and many other facts useful in attacking a Windows network. Furthermore, UNIX tools are also available that perform the same function as NBTSTAT.

- **Benign Triggers**—This is a low-severity alarm that is disabled by default because it can be generated by normal network activity.

3302 NETBIOS Session Setup Failure

- **Default Severity**—Disable.

- **Structure**—Atomic.

- **Implementation**—Context.

- **Class**—Information/access.

- **Description**—When a client connects to an SMB server (Windows NT, Windows 95, Samba, and so on) a TCP connection to port 139 is established. The client then provides the server with its NetBIOS name and the NetBIOS name it wants to connect to. If the name does not exist on the server, the session setup attempt fails and an error message is sent to the client. This session failure can also indicate an attack.

- **Benign Triggers**—The default alarm level for this signature is low because this traffic happens during normal network activity within a Windows network. As an example, when mounting the C: drive from a Windows 95 system to a Windows NT system, numerous session setup failures can occur while browsing the file system.

3303 Windows Guest Login

- **Default Severity**—Low.

- **Structure**—Atomic.

- **Implementation**—Content.

- **Class**—Access.

- **Description**—When a client establishes a connection to an SMB server (Windows NT or Samba), it provides an account name and password for authentication. If the server does not recognize the account name, it might log the user on as a guest. This is optional behavior by the server, and guest privileges should be limited. As a general security precaution, users should not be allowed access as guest.

- **Benign Triggers**—Because you might have a legitimate reason to allow this on your network, and because certain Samba servers allow guest access by default, the recommended alarm severity for this signature is low.

3304 Windows Null Account Name

- **Default Severity**—Disable.

- **Structure**—Atomic.

- **Implementation**—Content.

- **Class**—Information.

- **Description**—When a client establishes a connection to an SMB server (Windows NT or Samba), it provides an account name and password for authentication. This signature triggers when a null account name is passed during session establishment. Some hacking tools are available (Red Button and NetBIOS Auditing Tool) that also use null account names.

- **Benign Triggers**—Some legitimate Microsoft network services provide a null account name. Because these null account names occur within normal network traffic, this signature is given a low default alarm severity.

NOTE   Cisco Secure IDS uses other signatures to specifically detect Red Button and NetBIOS Auditing Tool (NAT) attacks, which also use null account names.

3305 Windows Password File Access

- **Default Severity**—High.

- **Structure**—Atomic.

- **Implementation**—Content.

- **Class**—Access.

- **Description**—This alarm occurs whenever a client attempts to access a PWL file on the server. These files contain user passwords on Windows 95 and other systems. This signature indicates an abnormal attempt to read or copy the PWL file.

- **Benign Triggers**—None.

3306 Windows Registry Access

- **Default Severity**—High.
- **Structure**—Atomic.
- **Implementation**—Content.
- **Class**—Access.
- **Description**—This signature triggers when a client attempts to access the Registry on the Windows server. Microsoft tools such as **regedit** provide the ability to access a server's Registry over the network. Several hacking tools also provide similar abilities. Every attempted access causes an alarm to be sent. An attacker can cause serious damage to a computer system by changing the Registry.
- **Benign Triggers**—This signature triggers if a Windows NT administrator accesses the Registry on servers remotely for legitimate purposes. By defining exclusions in your configuration file, you can prevent this alarm from occurring on the administrator's workstation. (Refer to Chapter 12, "Signature and Intrusion Detection Configuration," for more information on excluding signatures.)

3307 Windows Redbutton Attack

- **Default Severity**—High.
- **Structure**—Composite.
- **Implementation**—Content.
- **Class**—Access.
- **Description**—This alarm occurs when the Red Button tool is run against a server. The tool is designed to demonstrate a security flaw in Windows NT 4.0 that allows remote Registry access without a valid user account. Although Microsoft's NT Service Pack 3 fixes this flaw, the tool can still be run against servers. The seriousness of this attack is indicated by its default high alarm severity.
- **Benign Triggers**—A theoretical possibility exists that a combination of one or more network, system, or connection management tools can make a series of network accesses that trigger this signature. An initial indication warrants a review of the target Windows NT machines to ensure that the appropriate remote Registry access safeguards are in place.

3308 Windows LSARPC Access

- **Default Severity**—Disable.
- **Structure**—Atomic.
- **Implementation**—Content.

- **Class**—Reconnaissance.

- **Description**—This signature indicates that an attempt is made to access the LSARPC service on a Windows system. This service might be used to gain system information that can be useful in launching subsequent attacks. Access and browsing through this service are an integral portion of the so-called Redbutton attack.

- **Benign Triggers**—This is normal traffic on Windows networks and is included as an informational signature. This type of traffic is more suspicious when the source is external to your protected network.

3309 Windows SRVSVC Access

- **Default Severity**—Disable.

- **Structure**—Atomic.

- **Implementation**—Content.

- **Class**—Reconnaissance.

- **Description**—This signature indicates that an attempt is made to access the SRVSVC service on a Windows system. This service might be used to gain system information that can be useful in launching subsequent attacks. Access and browsing through this service are an integral portion of the so-called Redbutton attack.

- **Benign Triggers**—This is normal traffic on Windows networks and is included as an informational signature. This type of traffic is more suspicious when the source is external to your protected network.

SYN Flood and TCP Hijack Attacks

The TCP protocol is prone to several security vulnerabilities. An attacker might attempt to flood your network with SYN requests or try to hijack valid TCP connections. The Cisco Secure IDS signatures that detect these events are as follows:

- 3050 Half-Open SYN Attack

- 3250 TCP Hijacking

- 3251 TCP Hijacking Simplex Mode

3050 Half-Open SYN Attack

- **Default Severity**—High.

- **Structure**—Composite.

- **Implementation**—Context.

- **Class**—Denial of service.

- **Description**—This signature triggers when multiple TCP sessions are improperly initiated on any of several well-known service ports. Detection of this signature is currently limited to FTP, Telnet, WWW, and e-mail servers (TCP ports 21, 23, 80, and 25, respectively). This indicates that a denial of service attack against your network might be in progress.

- **Benign Triggers**—No known sources legitimately generate this traffic pattern. This might indicate some type of network problem and needs to be investigated. To avoid depletion of your network resources, the source needs to be blocked during the course of your investigation.

3250 TCP Hijacking

- **Default Severity**—High.
- **Structure**—Composite.
- **Implementation**—Context.
- **Class**—Access.
- **Description**—This signature triggers when both streams of data within a TCP connection indicate that a TCP hijacking might have occurred. The current implementation of this signature does not detect all types of TCP hijacking, and false positives are possible. Even when hijacking is discovered, little information is available to the operator other than the source and destination addresses and ports of the systems affected. TCP hijacking might be used to gain illegal access to system resources on your network, but the attacker must have network access between the systems involved in the TCP connection.

- **Benign Triggers**—The most common network event that might trigger this signature is an idle Telnet session. The TCP hijack attack is a low-probability, high-level-of-effort event. If it is successfully launched, it can lead to serious consequences, including system compromise. The source of these alarms needs to be investigated thoroughly before any actions are taken.

3251 TCP Hijacking Simplex Mode

- **Default Severity**—High.
- **Structure**—Composite.
- **Implementation**—Context.
- **Class**—Access.
- **Description**—This signature triggers when both streams of data within a TCP connection indicate that a TCP hijacking might have occurred. The current implementation of this signature does not detect all types of TCP hijacking, and false positives

might occur. Even when hijacking is discovered, little information is available to the operator other than the source and destination addresses and ports of the systems being affected. TCP hijacking might be used to gain illegal access to system resources. Simplex mode means that only one command is sent, followed by a connection reset packet, which makes recognition of this signature different from regular TCP hijacking (Signature ID 3250).

- **Benign Triggers**—The most common network event that can trigger this signature is an idle Telnet session. The TCP hijack attack is a low-probability, high-level-of-effort event. If it is successfully launched, it can lead to serious consequences, including system compromise. The source of these alarms needs to be investigated thoroughly before any actions are taken.

TCP Application Exploits

Numerous TCP applications have security exploits associated with them. The Cisco Secure IDS signatures that detect TCP application exploits are as follows:

- 3400 Sun Kill Telnet DoS
- 3401 Telnet-IFS Match
- 3450 Finger Bomb
- 3500 rlogin-froot
- 3525 IMAP Authenticate Overflow
- 3526 IMAP Login Buffer Overflow
- 3530 Cisco Secure ACS Oversized TACACS+ Attack
- 3540 Cisco Secure ACS CSAdmin Attack
- 3550 POP Buffer Overflow
- 3575 INN Buffer Overflow
- 3576 INN Control Message Exploit
- 3600 IOS Telnet Buffer Overflow
- 3601 IOS Command History Exploit
- 3602 Cisco IOS Identity
- 3603 IOS Enable Bypass
- 3650 SSH RSAREF2 Buffer Overflow
- 3990 BackOrifice BO2K TCP Non Stealth
- 3991 BackOrifice BO2K TCP Stealth 1
- 3992 BackOrifice BO2K TCP Stealth 2

3400 Sun Kill Telnet DoS

- **Default Severity**—Medium.
- **Structure**—Composite.
- **Implementation**—Content.
- **Class**—Denial of Service.
- **Description**—The signature fires when someone attempts to cause the telnet server to lock up using a program known as Sun Kill.
- **Benign Triggers**—None.

3401 Telnet-IFS Match

- **Default Severity**—Medium.
- **Structure**—Composite.
- **Implementation**—Content.
- **Class**—Access.
- **Description**—When someone attempts to change the internal field separator (IFS) to / during a Telnet session, this signature triggers. This might indicate an attempt to gain unauthorized access to system resources.
- **Benign Triggers**—No known benign trigger for this signature. Prudent security practices suggest that the source of this attempt needs to be blocked.

3450 Finger Bomb

- **Default Severity**—Medium.
- **Structure**—Atomic.
- **Implementation**—Content.
- **Class**—Denial of service.
- **Description**—This signature triggers when it detects a finger bomb attack. This attack attempts to crash a finger server by issuing a finger request that contains multiple @ symbols. If the finger server allows forwarding, the multiple @ symbols cause the finger server to recursively call itself and use up system resources.
- **Benign Triggers**—None.

3500 rlogin-froot

- **Default Severity**—High.
- **Structure**—Composite.

- **Implementation**—Content.
- **Class**—Access.
- **Description**—When someone attempts to access rlogin with the **-froot** argument, this signature triggers. A flaw in some rlogin processes allows unauthorized root access. Serious system compromise is possible.
- **Benign Triggers**—None.

3525 IMAP Authenticate Overflow

- **Default Severity**—High.
- **Structure**—Composite.
- **Implementation**—Content.
- **Class**—Access.
- **Description**—This signature triggers on receipt of packets bound for port 143 that are indicative of an attempt to overflow a buffer in the IMAP daemon. This might be the precursor to an attempt to gain unauthorized access to system resources.
- **Benign Triggers**—None.

3526 IMAP Login Buffer Overflow

- **Default Severity**—High.
- **Structure**—Composite.
- **Implementation**—Content.
- **Class**—Access.
- **Description**—This signature triggers on receipt of packets bound for port 143 that are indicative of an attempt to overflow the imapd login buffer. This might be the precursor to an attempt to gain unauthorized access to system resources.
- **Benign Triggers**—None.

3530 Cisco Secure ACS Oversized TACACS+ Attack

- **Default Severity**—Medium.
- **Structure**—Atomic.
- **Implementation**—Content.
- **Class**—Access.

- **Description**—It is possible to send an oversized TACACS+ packet that causes certain Cisco Secure ACS for NT versions to crash. This signature triggers on these oversized packets, indicating that an attacker is attempting to crash your TACACS+ server.
- **Benign Triggers**—None

3540 Cisco Secure ACS CSAdmin Attack

- **Default Severity**—High.
- **Structure**—Atomic.
- **Implementation**—Context.
- **Class**—Access.
- **Description**—This signature triggers when a large request is made to the CSAdmin service, which listens on TCP port 2002.
- **Benign Triggers**—None.

3550 POP Buffer Overflow

- **Default Severity**—High.
- **Structure**—Composite.
- **Implementation**—Content.
- **Class**—Access.
- **Description**—This signature triggers on receipt of packets bound for port 110 that are indicative of an attempt to overflow the POP daemon user buffer. This might be the precursor to an attempt to gain unauthorized access to system resources.
- **Benign Triggers**—None.

3575 INN Buffer Overflow

- **Default Severity**—High.
- **Structure**—Composite.
- **Implementation**—Context.
- **Class**—Access.
- **Description**—This signature triggers when an attempt is made to overflow a buffer in the Internet News (INN) server.
- **Benign Triggers**—None.

3576 INN Control Message Exploit

- **Default Severity**—High.
- **Structure**—Composite.
- **Implementation**—Content.
- **Class**—Access.
- **Description**—This signature triggers when an attempt is made to execute arbitrary commands through a control message. This is probably because of an attempt to use the pipe command (l) in the control message.
- **Benign Triggers**—None.

3600 IOS Telnet Buffer Overflow

- **Default Severity**—High.
- **Structure**—Composite.
- **Implementation**—Content.
- **Class**—Denial of service.
- **Description**—This signature triggers on receipt of packets bound for port 23 of a Cisco router that are indicative of an attempt to crash the router by overflowing an internal command buffer. This might be the precursor to an attempt to gain unauthorized access to system resources.
- **Benign Triggers**—None.

3601 IOS Command History Exploit

- **Default Severity**—High.
- **Structure**—Composite.
- **Implementation**—Content.
- **Class**—Access.
- **Description**—This signature triggers on an attempt to force a Cisco router to reveal prior users' command history.
- **Benign Triggers**—None.

3602 Cisco IOS Identity

- **Default Severity**—Low.
- **Structure**—Atomic.

- **Implementation**—Content.
- **Class**—Information.
- **Description**—This signature triggers if someone attempts to connect to port 1999 on a Cisco router. This port is not enabled for access.
- **Benign Triggers**—None.

3603 IOS Enable Bypass

- **Default Severity**—High.
- **Structure**—Composite.
- **Implementation**—Content.
- **Class**—Access.
- **Description**—A successful attempt to gain privileged access (Enable mode) on a Cisco Catalyst switch is detected. Check the configuration on the switch in question and ensure that the latest IOS release is installed.
- **Benign Triggers**—None.

3650 SSH RSAREF2 Buffer Overflow

- **Default Severity**—High.
- **Structure**—Composite.
- **Implementation**—Context.
- **Class**—Access.
- **Description**—A buffer overflow is present in versions of SSH1, up to and including 1.2.27, that are compiled using the **--with-rsaref** option. During a key exchange, the RSAREF2 library does not properly ensure that the length of the key received is less than the maximum allowable key length. A buffer overflow can occur on either the client or server. This occurs when the key is abnormally large, such as more than 1024 bits.
- **Benign Triggers**—None.

3990 BackOrifice BO2K TCP Non Stealth

- **Default Severity**—High.
- **Structure**—Composite.
- **Implementation**—Content.
- **Class**—Access.

- **Description**—BO2K TCP mode is the basic configuration of BackOrifice. This alarm indicates nonstealth traffic for the BO2K toolkit is detected. BackOrifice is a "backdoor" program that can be installed on a Microsoft Windows 95 or Windows 98 system, allowing remote control of the system.

- **Benign Triggers**—None.

3991 BackOrifice BO2K TCP Stealth 1

- **Default Severity**—High.
- **Structure**—Composite.
- **Implementation**—Content.
- **Class**—Access.
- **Description**—The Stealth plug-in for BO2K, STCPIO, scrambles the bo2k-specific protocol header into a form that is not easily detected by a Network IDS. A nontrivial dialog between bo2k client and server, however, has in its conversation enough information for Cisco Secure IDS to recognize this activity. Seeing a Stealth-mode alarm indicates sneaky activity on the part of a legitimate administrator or an illegitimate attacker. Stealth type 1 indicates XOR encryption is used. BackOrifice is a "backdoor" program that can be installed on a Microsoft Windows 95 or Windows 98 system, allowing remote control of the system.
- **Benign Triggers**—None.

3992 BackOrifice BO2K TCP Stealth 2

- **Default Severity**—High.
- **Structure**—Composite.
- **Implementation**—Content.
- **Class**—Access.
- **Description**—The Stealth plug-in for BO2K, STCPIO, scrambles the bo2k-specific protocol header into a form that is not easily detected by a network IDS. A nontrivial dialog between bo2k client and server, however, has in its conversation enough information for Cisco Secure IDS to recognize this activity. Seeing a Stealth-mode alarm indicates sneaky activity on the part of a legitimate administrator or an illegitimate attacker. Stealth type 2 indicates an encryption other than XOR is being used (Blowfish, Cast, Idea, RC6, Serpent, or 3Des). BackOrifice is a "backdoor" program that can be installed on a Microsoft Windows 95 or Windows 98 system, allowing remote control of the system.
- **Benign Triggers**—None

UDP Signatures (4000 Series)

Another major transport mechanism for traffic on your network is UDP. Unlike TCP, UDP is an unreliable transport mechanism and is prone to spoofing. The UDP signatures fall into the 4000 series signatures. These signatures are broken down into the following categories:

- UDP traffic records
- UDP port scan
- UDP attacks
- UDP applications

UDP Traffic Records (4000 Signature)

Similar to TCP traffic records, UDP traffic records monitor connections to specific destination ports on your network. These traffic records can generate a large amount of alarm traffic on your network. Therefore, most of these signatures are disabled by default.

All the UDP traffic records have a Signature ID of 4000. The subID indicates the destination port of the connection. They share the following characteristics:

- **Default Severity**—Disable.
- **Structure**—Atomic.
- **Implementation**—Context.
- **Class**—Reconnaissance.
- **4000/0**—UDP default connection signature.

The default UDP connection signatures include the following:

- 4000/7 - UDP traffic - echo
- 4000/9 - UDP traffic - discard
- 4000/13 - UDP traffic - daytime
- 4000/19 - UDP traffic - chargen
- 4000/37 - UDP traffic - time
- 4000/53 - UDP traffic - dns
- 4000/69 - UDP traffic - tftp
- 4000/70 - UDP traffic - gopher
- 4000/80 - UDP traffic - www
- 4000/88 - UDP traffic - kerberos-v5
- 4000/111 - UDP traffic - sunrpc
- 4000/123 - UDP traffic - ntp

- 4000/177 - UDP traffic - xdmcp
- 4000/179 - UDP traffic - bgp
- 4000/220 - UDP traffic - imap3
- 4000/372 - UDP traffic - Ulistserv
- 4000/512 - UDP traffic - biff
- 4000/513 - UDP traffic - who
- 4000/514 - UDP traffic - syslog
- 4000/515 - UDP traffic - printer
- 4000/517 - UDP traffic - talk
- 4000/518 - UDP traffic - ntalk
- 4000/520 - UDP traffic - route
- 4000/2049 - UDP traffic - nfs

UDP Port Scan

Unlike TCP connections, which have numerous scan types because of the various control flags available, the only option available to search for open UDP ports is to send a packet to the different destination ports. The only UDP port scan signature is 4001 UDP Port Scan.

It has these characteristics:

- **Default Severity**—High.
- **Structure**—Composite.
- **Implementation**—Context.
- **Class**—Reconnaissance.
- **Description**—When a system initiates a series of UDP connections to a number of different destination ports on a specific host, this signature triggers. This indicates that a reconnaissance sweep of your network might be in progress. Furthermore, this traffic might be the prelude to a more serious attack.
- **Benign Triggers**—Many network management tools, such as HP OpenView, provide network-mapping capabilities. This might include a mapping of available network services, so UDP port sweeps might be expected from these systems.

UDP Attacks

Cisco Secure IDS checks for several specific UDP attacks that take advantage of weaknesses in the UDP protocol. These signatures are as follows:

- 4002 UDP Flood
- 4050 UDP Bomb
- 4051 Snork
- 4052 Chargen DoS

4002 UDP Flood

- **Default Severity**—Disable.
- **Structure**—Composite.
- **Implementation**—Context.
- **Class**—Denial of service.
- **Description**—This triggers when a large number of UDP packets are directed at a host. This fires when the Pepsi attack is launched across a protected boundary. This signature is also indicative of a UDP port sweep.
- **Benign Triggers**—Cisco Secure IDS Sensors and Directors can fire this signature and need to be listed in RecordOfExcluded addresses to avoid false positives. Any application that causes heavy UDP traffic can also fire this signature.

4050 UDP Bomb

- **Default Severity**—Medium.
- **Structure**—Atomic.
- **Implementation**—Context.
- **Class**—Denial of service.
- **Description**—This signature triggers when the UDP length specified is less than the IP length specified. This malformed packet type is associated with a denial of service attempt.
- **Benign Triggers**—No legitimate use exists for malformed datagrams. This might indicate systems that experience problems with their kernel or NIC cards. This is unusual traffic and warrants investigation.

4051 Snork

- **Default Severity**—Medium.
- **Structure**—Atomic.
- **Implementation**—Context.
- **Class**—Denial of service.
- **Description**—This signature triggers when a UDP packet is seen with a source port of 135, 7, or 19, and a destination port of 135 is detected.
- **Benign Triggers**—Certain Windows applications use UDP communication between port 135 on both the server and client machines. The user needs to exclude servers that run these applications from this signature. (Refer to Chapter 12 for details on how to exclude hosts.)

4052 Chargen DoS

- **Default Severity**—Medium.
- **Structure**—Atomic.
- **Implementation**—Context.
- **Class**—Denial of service.
- **Description**—This signature triggers when a UDP packet is detected with a source port of 7 and a destination port of 19.
- **Benign Triggers**—None.

UDP Applications

Numerous UDP applications have known security vulnerabilities. The Cisco Secure IDS signatures that detect exploits against UDP applications are as follows:

- 4053 Back Orifice
- 4054 RIP Trace
- 4055 BackOrifice BO2K UDP
- 4100 TFTP Passwd
- 4150 Ascend Denial of Service
- 4600 IOS UDP Bomb

4053 Back Orifice

- **Default Severity**—High.
- **Structure**—Composite.
- **Implementation**—Content.
- **Class**—Access.
- **Description**—This signature triggers when Cisco Secure IDS detects traffic coming from a BackOrifice server that is running on your network. BackOrifice is a "backdoor" program that can be installed on a Microsoft Windows 95 or Windows 98 system, allowing remote control of the system.
- **Benign Triggers**—None.

4054 RIP Trace

- **Default Severity**—High.
- **Structure**—Atomic.
- **Implementation**—Content.
- **Class**—Denial of service.
- **Description**—This alarm triggers when **TRACEON** or **TRACEOFF** commands are enabled for a packet. The commands are related to the Routing Information Protocol (RIP).
- **Benign Triggers**—None.

4055 BackOrifice BO2K UDP

- **Default Severity**—High.
- **Structure**—Composite.
- **Implementation**—Content.
- **Class**—Access.
- **Description**—BO2K UDP mode is a basic configuration of BackOrifice. Seeing this traffic indicates a nonstealth use of the BO2K toolkit. BackOrifice is a "backdoor" program that can be installed on a Microsoft Windows 95 or Windows 98 system, allowing remote control of the system.
- **Benign Triggers**—None.

4100 TFTP Passwd

- **Default Severity**—High.

- **Structure**—Composite.
- **Implementation**—Content.
- **Class**—Access.
- **Description**—This signature triggers on an attempt to access the passwd file through TFTP and indicates an attempt to gain unauthorized access to system resources.
- **Benign Triggers**—System administrators might use this service to update system files. It is a high security risk if this is normal practice and should be avoided. No other benign triggers exist for this signature.

4150 Ascend Denial of Service

- **Default Severity**—Medium.
- **Structure**—Composite.
- **Implementation**—Content.
- **Class**—Denial of service.
- **Description**—This signature triggers when an attempt is made to send a maliciously malformed command to an Ascend router in an attempt to crash the router.
- **Benign Triggers**—None.

4600 IOS UDP Bomb

- **Default Severity**—High.
- **Structure**—Composite.
- **Implementation**—Context.
- **Class**—Denial of service.
- **Description**—This signature triggers on receipt of improperly formed SYSLOG transmissions bound for UDP port 514.
- **Benign Triggers**—None.

Web/HTTP Signatures (5000 Series)

The 5000 Series signatures represent the HTTP or Web signatures that Cisco Secure IDS detects. These signatures all fall into the following category:

- Web attacks

NOTE	The legacy Cisco Secure IDS Web signatures use Signature IDs in the range 3200 through 3233.

Web Attacks

The Cisco Secure IDS Web/HTTP signatures are as follows:

- 5034 WWW IIS newdsn Attack
- 5035 HTTP cgi HylaFAX Faxsurvey
- 5036 WWW Windows Password File Access Attempt
- 5037 WWW SGI MachineInfo Attack
- 5038 WWW wwwsql File Read Bug
- 5039 WWW Finger Attempt
- 5040 WWW Perl Interpreter Attack
- 5041 WWW anyform attack
- 5042 WWW CGI Valid Shell Access
- 5043 WWW Cold Fusion Attack
- 5044 WWW Webcom.se Guestbook Attack
- 5045 WWW xterm Display Attack
- 5046 WWW dumpenv.pl Recon
- 5047 WWW Server Side Include POST Attack
- 5048 WWW IIS BAT EXE Attack
- 5049 WWW IIS Showcode .asp Attack
- 5050 WWW IIS .htr Overflow
- 5051 IIS Double Byte Code Page
- 5052 FrontPage Extensions PWD Open Attempt
- 5053 FrontPage _vti_bin Directory List Attempt
- 5054 WWWBoard Password
- 5055 HTTP Basic Authentication Overflow
- 5056 WWW Cisco IOS %% DoS
- 5057 WWW Sambar Samples
- 5058 WWW info2www Attack
- 5059 WWW Alibaba Attack

- 5060 WWW Excite AT-generate.cgi Access
- 5061 WWW catalog_type.asp Access
- 5062 WWW classifieds.cgi Attack
- 5063 WWW dmblparser.exe Access
- 5064 WWW imagemap.cgi Attack
- 5065 WWW IRIX infosrch.cgi Attack
- 5066 WWW man.sh Access
- 5067 WWW plusmail Attack
- 5068 WWW formmail.pl Access
- 5069 WWW whois_raw.cgi Attack
- 5070 WWW msacds.dll Access
- 5071 WWW msacds.dll Attack
- 5072 WWW bizdb1-search.cgi Attack
- 5073 WWW EZshopper loadpage.cgi Attack
- 5074 WWW EZshopper search.cgi Attack
- 5075 WWW IIS Virtualized UNC Bug
- 5076 WWW webplus Bug
- 5077 WWW Excite AT-admin.cgi Access
- 5078 WWW Piranha Passwd Attack
- 5079 WWW PCCS MySQL Admin Access
- 5080 WWW IBM WebSphere Access
- 5081 WWW WinNT cmd.exe Access
- 5083 WWW Virtual Vision FTP Browser Access
- 5084 WWW Alibaba Attack 2
- 5085 WWW IIS Source Fragment Access
- 5086 WWW WEBactive Logfile Access
- 5087 WWW Sun Java Server Access.
- 5088 WWW Akopia MiniVend Access
- 5089 WWW Big Brother Directory Access
- 5090 WWW FrontPage htimage.exe Access
- 5091 WWW Cart32 Remote Admin Access
- 5092 WWW CGI-World Poll It Access
- 5093 WWW PHP-Nuke admin.php3 Access

- 5095 WWW CGI Script Center Account Manager Attack
- 5096 WWW CGI Script Center Subscribe Me Attack
- 5097 WWW FrontPage MS-DOS Device Attack
- 5099 WWW GWScripts News Publisher Access
- 5100 WWW CGI Center Auction Weaver File Access
- 5101 WWW CGI Center Auction Weaver Attack
- 5102 WWW phpPhotoAlbum explorer.php Access
- 5103 WWW SuSE Apache CGI Source Attack
- 5104 WWW YaBB File Access
- 5105 WWW Ranson Johnson mailto.cgi Attack
- 5106 WWW Ranson Johnson mailform.pl Access
- 5107 WWW Mandrake Linux/Perl Access
- 5108 WWW Netegrity Site Minder Access
- 5109 WWW Sambar Beta search.dll Access
- 5110 WWW SuSE Installed Packages Access
- 5111 WWW Solaris Anwerbook2 Access
- 5112 WWW Solaris Answerbook2 Attack
- 5113 WWW CommuniGate Pro Access
- 5114 WWW IIS Unicode Attack

5034 WWW IIS newdsn Attack

- **Default Severity**—High.
- **Structure**—Composite.
- **Implementation**—Content.
- **Class**—Access.
- **Description**—This signature triggers when an attempt is made to run the **newdsn.exe** command through the HTTP server. The **newdsn.exe** sample application installed with Microsoft's Internet Information Server (IIS) version 3.0 contains a vulnerability that allows a remote attacker to create arbitrary Microsoft Access files (*.mdb) on the Web server using any filenames. A remote attacker can create files on the hard disk of the Web server and eventually fill it up, thereby causing a denial of service. In addition, a well-known exploit causes the Web server to become unresponsive (hang) or generate a General Protection Fault (GPF).
- **Benign Triggers**—None.

5035 HTTP cgi HylaFAX Faxsurvey

- **Default Severity**—High.
- **Structure**—Composite.
- **Implementation**—Content.
- **Class**—Access.
- **Description**—This signature triggers when an attempt is made to pass commands to the CGI program **faxsurvey**. A problem in the CGI program **faxsurvey**, included with the HylaFAX package from SGI, allows an attacker to execute commands on the host machine. These commands execute at the privilege level of the HTTP server. No legitimate reasons exist to pass commands to the **faxsurvey** command. This signature indicates abuse, and the source needs to be blocked.
- **Benign Triggers**—None.

5036 WWW Windows Password File Access Attempt

- **Default Severity**—High.
- **Structure**—Composite.
- **Implementation**—Content.
- **Class**—Access.
- **Description**—This alarm is triggered when an attempt is made to retrieve either the current or backup copy of the Windows NT password file through the Web server.
- **Benign Triggers**—None.

5037 WWW SGI MachineInfo Attack

- **Default Severity**—Medium.
- **Structure**—Composite.
- **Implementation**—Content.
- **Class**—Information.
- **Description**—This signature triggers when an attempt is made to display information about the targeted host with the **MachineInfo** script. Some SGI (Irix) servers include this script, which is intended to show hardware and configuration information about the server. An attempt to access this script from outside your protected network is definitely suspicious.
- **Benign Triggers**—None.

5038 WWW wwwsql File Read Bug

- **Default Severity**—High.
- **Structure**—Composite.
- **Implementation**—Content.
- **Class**—Access.
- **Description**—This alarm triggers when an attempt is made to read files in the cgi-bin directory using the **www-sql** script. This can indicate that a remote attacker is trying to download cgi-bin scripts and access otherwise protected directories under the DocumentRoot directory of the Web server.
- **Benign Triggers**—None.

5039 WWW Finger Attempt

- **Default Severity**—Medium.
- **Structure**—Composite.
- **Implementation**—Content.
- **Class**—Reconnaissance.
- **Description**—This signature triggers when an attempt is made to run the **finger** program through the HTTP server. All unnecessary programs need to be removed from the cgi-bin directory.
- **Benign Triggers**—This signature can be triggered by legitimate and illegitimate use of the **finger** program.

5040 WWW Perl Interpreter Attack

- **Default Severity**—High.
- **Structure**—Composite.
- **Implementation**—Content.
- **Class**—Access.
- **Description**—Triggers when someone attempts to pass and execute Perl commands on your server through a Perl interpreter. These commands execute with the privilege level of the Web server. If successful, an attacker might gain unauthorized access and remotely execute commands. This can lead to further system access (including root access) and malicious activity. The source address for this signature needs to be blocked.
- **Benign Triggers**—None.

5041 WWW anyform Attack

- **Default Severity**—High.
- **Structure**—Composite.
- **Implementation**—Content.
- **Class**—Access.
- **Description**—This alarm triggers when an attacker attempts to execute arbitrary commands through the **anyform** cgi-bin script. The source address for this attack needs to be blocked.
- **Benign Triggers**—None.

5042 WWW CGI Valid Shell Access

- **Default Severity**—High.
- **Structure**—Composite.
- **Implementation**—Content.
- **Class**—Access.
- **Description**—This signature triggers when an attempt is made to access a valid shell or interpreter on the targeted system. These include **bash** (SubID 1), **tcsh** (SubID 2), **ash**, **bsh**, **csh**, **ksh**, **jsh**, or **zsh** (SubID 3), **sh** (SubID 4), Java interpreter (SubID 5), and Python interpreter (SubID 6). This might indicate an attempt to illegally access system resources. The presence of a valid command shell or interpreter of any kind introduces significant security problems and needs to be removed. Hosts that attempt to access these types of files, especially from outside your protected network, need to be blocked.
- **Benign Triggers**—None.

5043 WWW Cold Fusion Attack

- **Default Severity**—High.
- **Structure**—Composite.
- **Implementation**—Content.
- **Class**—Access.
- **Description**—This alarm triggers when an attempt is made to access example scripts shipped with Cold Fusion servers. The source address for this signature needs to be blocked. SubID 1 indicates an attempt to access the **openfile.cfm** script. This script allows an attacker to upload files to the target host or server. SubID 2 indicates an attempt to access **displayopenedfile.cfm**. This can indicate that a remote attacker is trying to access files on the target host or server. SubID 3 indicates an attempt to

upload files to a Cold Fusion server through the **exprcalc.cfm** script. This can be used to overwrite files on the target server or host. These files are part of the documentation system for Cold Fusion. You need to remove documentation and sample scripts for Cold Fusion from production servers.

- **Benign Triggers**—None.

5044 WWW Webcom.se Guestbook Attack

- **Default Severity**—High.
- **Structure**—Composite.
- **Implementation**—Content.
- **Class**—Access.
- **Description**—This alarm triggers when an attacker attempts to execute arbitrary commands through Webcom.se's **rguest.exe** or **wguest.exe** cgi-bin script. The source address for this attack needs to be blocked.
- **Benign Triggers**—None.

5045 WWW xterm Display Attack

- **Default Severity**—High.
- **Structure**—Composite.
- **Implementation**—Content.
- **Class**—Access.
- **Description**—This signature triggers when any cgi-bin script attempts to execute the command **xterm -display**. This might indicate an attempt to illegally log on to your system. This attack can result in the attacker gaining access to your system. Serious system compromise is possible. No valid reason to execute **xterm -display** through this mechanism exists. Hosts that attempt to access execute **xterm -display**, especially from outside your protected network, need to be blocked.
- **Benign Triggers**—None.

5046 WWW dumpenv.pl Recon

- **Default Severity**—Medium.
- **Structure**—Composite.
- **Implementation**—Content.
- **Class**—Information.

- **Description**—Triggers when an attempt is made to display information about the targeted host with the **dumpenv.pl** script. Some Web servers include this script, which is intended to show environmental information about the server. An attempt to access this script from outside your protected network is suspicious, and you need to block the source.
- **Benign Triggers**—None.

5047 WWW Server Side Include POST Attack

- **Default Severity**—High.
- **Structure**—Composite.
- **Implementation**—Content.
- **Class**—Access.
- **Description**—When someone attempts to embed a server side include (SSI) in an HTTP **POST** command, this signature triggers. This traffic might indicate an attempt to illegally access system resources.
- **Benign Triggers**—None.

5048 WWW IIS BAT EXE Attack

- **Default Severity**—High.
- **Structure**—Composite.
- **Implementation**—Content.
- **Class**—Access.
- **Description**—This signature triggers when an attempt is made to execute remote commands on a Microsoft IIS 1.0-2.0b Web server. This might indicate an attempt to illegally access system resources.
- **Benign Triggers**—None.

5049 WWW IIS Showcode .asp Attack

- **Default Severity**—Medium.
- **Structure**—Composite.
- **Implementation**—Content.
- **Class**—Access.

- **Description**—This alarm triggers whenever an attempt is made to access the **showcode.asp** Active Server Page. This script allows for arbitrary access to any file on the target's file system.
- **Benign Triggers**—None.

5050 WWW IIS .htr Overflow

- **Default Severity**—High.
- **Structure**—Composite.
- **Implementation**—Content.
- **Class**—Access.
- **Description**—This signature triggers when an .htr buffer overrun attack is detected, indicating a possible attempt to execute remote commands or cause a denial of service against the targeted Windows NT IIS server. Hosts that cause this type of alarm, especially from outside your protected network, need to be blocked.
- **Benign Triggers**—None.

5051 IIS Double Byte Code Page

- **Default Severity**—Medium.
- **Structure**—Atomic.
- **Implementation**—Content.
- **Class**—Access.
- **Description**—The Internet Information Server (IIS) contains a vulnerability that can allow a Web site visitor to view the source code for selected files on the server if the server's default language is set to Chinese, Japanese, or Korean. An indication of this attack is an HTTP request with a URL terminated by ***.asp[%81-%FE]**.
- **Benign Triggers**—None.

5052 FrontPage Extensions PWD Open Attempt

- **Default Severity**—High.
- **Structure**—Atomic.
- **Implementation**—Content.
- **Class**—Access.

- **Description**—This signature triggers when an attempt is made to open a configuration file on a Microsoft Personal Web Server (for Windows platforms) or FrontPage extensions (for UNIX) Web server.
- **Benign Triggers**—None.

5053 FrontPage _vti_bin Directory List Attempt

- **Default Severity**—High.
- **Structure**—Atomic.
- **Implementation**—Content.
- **Class**—Access.
- **Description**—This signature triggers when an attempt is made to list the directory of binaries from Microsoft Personal Web Server (for Windows platforms) or FrontPage extensions (for UNIX) Web server.
- **Benign Triggers**—None.

5054 WWWBoard Password

- **Default Severity**—Medium.
- **Structure**—Atomic.
- **Implementation**—Content.
- **Class**—Access.
- **Description**—A number of vulnerabilities exist in the WWWBoard package. CGI scanners used in the underground look for the existence of the WWWBoard before mounting any attacks. You need to use this package with extreme caution.
- **Benign Triggers**—Legitimate use of the WWWBoard package triggers this signature.

5055 HTTP Basic Authentication Overflow

- **Default Severity**—High.
- **Structure**—Composite.
- **Implementation**—Content.
- **Class**—Access.
- **Description**—A buffer overflow can occur on vulnerable Web servers if a large username and password combination is used with Basic Authentication. This represents a Basic Authentication base64 query greater than 128 bytes.
- **Benign Triggers**—None.

5056 WWW Cisco IOS %% DoS

- **Default Severity**—Disable.
- **Structure**—Composite.
- **Implementation**—Content.
- **Class**—Denial of service.
- **Description**—An attempt to crash a Cisco IOS-based product using the HTTP management interface is detected. Certain versions of IOS incorrectly interpret the characters % % when passed to the HTTP management interface. This can result in a router crashing, causing the need for the power to be cycled to restore normal operation.
- **Benign Triggers**—It has been observed that the character combinations, which cause a Cisco IOS-based product to crash, are present in normal HTTP traffic. Verify that the suspected victim of this attack is actually a Cisco router or switch. If you receive large amounts of false-positive alarms based on this signature, you need to disable the signature or exclude the addresses involved in the alarms from being processed. (Refer to Chapter 12 for details on excluding alarms from hosts.)

5057 WWW Sambar Samples

- **Default Severity**—Medium.
- **Structure**—Composite.
- **Implementation**—Content.
- **Class**—Access.
- **Description**—Two cgi programs shipped with the Sambar Web server contain vulnerabilities: **echo.bat** and **hello.bat**. An attempt to access either of these cgi programs triggers this signature.
- **Benign Triggers**—None.

5058 WWW info2www Attack

- **Default Severity**—High.
- **Structure**—Composite.
- **Implementation**—Content.
- **Class**—Access.
- **Description**—An attempt has been made to execute commands using the **info2www** cgi program.
- **Benign Triggers**—None.

5059 WWW Alibaba Attack

- **Default Severity**—High.
- **Structure**—Composite.
- **Implementation**—Content.
- **Class**—Access.
- **Description**—An exploit attempt is made to execute commands using one of the following Alibaba Web server cgi programs: **get32.exe**, **alibaba.pl**, or **tst.bat**.
- **Benign Triggers**—None.

5060 WWW Excite AT-generate.cgi Access

- **Default Severity**—Medium.
- **Structure**—Composite.
- **Implementation**—Content.
- **Class**—Access.
- **Description**—An attempt is made to access the CGI program **AT-generate.cgi**. This might result in unauthorized change of the Administrator password for the Excite for Web Servers application. Administrators need to check to ensure that the system affected is not modified.
- **Benign Triggers**—None.

5061 WWW catalog_type.asp Access

- **Default Severity**—High.
- **Structure**—Composite.
- **Implementation**—Content.
- **Class**—Access.
- **Description**—An attempt is made to access the vulnerable sample ASP file **catalog_type.asp**.
- **Benign Triggers**—None.

5062 WWW classifieds.cgi Attack

- **Default Severity**—High.
- **Structure**—Composite.
- **Implementation**—Content.

- **Class**—Access.
- **Description**—An exploit attempt is made to execute commands using the **classifieds.cgi** cgi program.
- **Benign Triggers**—None.

5063 WWW dmblparser.exe Access

- **Default Severity**—Medium.
- **Structure**—Composite.
- **Implementation**—Content.
- **Class**—Access.
- **Description**—An attempt is made to access the **dmblparser.exe** cgi program. This program can be used to provide guestbook and message board services.
- **Benign Triggers**—None.

5064 WWW imagemap.cgi Attack

- **Default Severity**—High.
- **Structure**—Composite.
- **Implementation**—Content.
- **Class**—Access.
- **Description**—An attempt is made to overflow a buffer in the **imagemap.cgi** cgi program. You need to check the system affected to ensure that it is been compromised.
- **Benign Triggers**—None.

5065 WWW IRIX infosrch.cgi Attack

- **Default Severity**—High.
- **Structure**—Composite.
- **Implementation**—Content.
- **Class**—Access.
- **Description**—An attempt is made to execute commands using the IRIX **infosrch.cgi** cgi program.
- **Benign Triggers**—None.

5066 WWW man.sh Access

- **Default Severity**—Medium.
- **Structure**—Composite.
- **Implementation**—Content.
- **Class**—Access.
- **Description**—An attempt is made to access the **man.sh** cgi shell script. **man.sh** is a Web-enabled man page viewer. Because of improper parsing of user input, an attacker can execute arbitrary comments on the Web server.
- **Benign Triggers**—None.

5067 WWW plusmail Attack

- **Default Severity**—High.
- **Structure**—Composite.
- **Implementation**—Content.
- **Class**—Access.
- **Description**—An attempt is made to change the PlusMail administrator password. This can allow an attacker to gain full control of the PlusMail program. You need to check with the administrator of the system to see whether his password is modified.
- **Benign Triggers**—None.

5068 WWW formmail.pl Access

- **Default Severity**—Medium.
- **Structure**—Composite.
- **Implementation**—Content.
- **Class**—Access.
- **Description**—An attempt is made to access the **formmail.pl** cgi program. Depending on the version of the **formmail.pl** script being used, an attacker might execute arbitrary commands with the privilege of the Web server.
- **Benign Triggers**—None.

5069 WWW whois_raw.cgi Attack

- **Default Severity**—High.
- **Structure**—Composite.

- **Implementation**—Content.
- **Class**—Access.
- **Description**—An attempt is made to access and possibly execute commands using the Cdomain **whois_raw.cgi** cgi program.
- **Benign Triggers**—None.

5070 WWW msacds.dll Access

- **Default Severity**—High.
- **Structure**—Composite.
- **Implementation**—Content.
- **Class**—Reconnaissance.
- **Description**—This signature triggers when an attempt is made to access the **msacds.dll** cgi program. This attempt might indicate a reconnaissance session for a later attack to exploit the IIS RDS vulnerability. Although no attempt to execute commands or view files is detected, you must check the system(s) affected to ensure that they were not altered.
- **Benign Triggers**—None.

5071 WWW msacds.dll Attack

- **Default Severity**—High.
- **Structure**—Composite.
- **Implementation**—Content.
- **Class**—Access.
- **Description**—When someone gains privileged access through **msacds.dll** and attempts to execute commands or view secured files, this signature triggers. Administrators must check the affected system(s) to ensure that they were not illicitly modified.
- **Benign Triggers**—None.

5072 WWW bizdb1-search.cgi Attack

- **Default Severity**—High.
- **Structure**—Composite.
- **Implementation**—Content.
- **Class**—Access.

- **Description**—An attempt is made to execute commands or view files with the privileges of the Web server using the **bizdb1-search.cgi** cgi program.
- **Benign Triggers**—None.

5073 WWW EZshopper loadpage.cgi Attack

- **Default Severity**—High.
- **Structure**—Composite.
- **Implementation**—Content.
- **Class**—Access.
- **Description**—An attempt is made to execute commands or view files with the privileges of the Web server using the Ezshopper **loadpage.cgi** cgi program.
- **Benign Triggers**—None.

5074 WWW EZshopper search.cgi Attack

- **Default Severity**—High.
- **Structure**—Composite.
- **Implementation**—Content.
- **Class**—Access.
- **Description**—An attempt is made to execute commands or view files with the privileges of the Web server using the EZshopper **search.cgi** cgi program.
- **Benign Triggers**—None.

5075 WWW IIS Virtualized UNC Bug

- **Default Severity**—Medium.
- **Structure**—Composite.
- **Implementation**—Content.
- **Class**—Access.
- **Description**—This signature triggers when an attempt is made to view the source of an ASP file. A bug exists in certain versions of Microsoft IIS Web server that allows an attacker to view the source of ASP and other files if the IIS virtual directory they reside in is mapped to a UNC share.
- **Benign Triggers**—None.

NOTE   Universal Naming Convention or Uniform Naming Convention is a PC format for specifying the location of resources on a local area network. It uses the following format:

`\\server-name\<path>\resource`

This naming convention creates a unique name for each resource that you share. To access the file sharedfile.txt that is located in the public directory on the server named test, for example, use the following:

`\\test\public\sharedfile.txt`

5076 WWW webplus Bug

- **Default Severity**—Medium.
- **Structure**—Composite.
- **Implementation**—Content.
- **Class**—Access.
- **Description**—An attempt is made to gain access to files outside the Web server directories using the **webplus** cgi program.
- **Benign Triggers**—None.

5077 WWW Excite AT-admin.cgi Access

- **Default Severity**—Medium.
- **Structure**—Composite.
- **Implementation**—Content.
- **Class**—Access.
- **Description**—An attempt is made to access the **AT-admin.cgi** cgi program. Excite for Web Servers 1.1 has a vulnerability that exposes the encrypted Administrator password to all system users (those with shell and nonanonymous FTP access). Using the encrypted password string through the **AT-generate.cgi** cgi program, a user can change the Administrator password and gain control of the Excite for Web Servers application.
- **Benign Triggers**—Normal use of the **AT-generate.cgi** cgi program generates this alarm, but this access should not occur from systems outside your protected network.

5078 WWW Piranha Passwd Attack

- **Default Severity**—High.
- **Structure**—Composite.

- **Implementation**—Content.
- **Class**—Access.
- **Description**—This signature triggers when an attempt is made to access the vulnerable **piranha/secure/passwd.php3** cgi script using suspicious arguments.
- **Benign Triggers**—None.

5079 WWW PCCS MySQL Admin Access

- **Default Severity**—Medium.
- **Structure**—Atomic.
- **Implementation**—Content.
- **Class**—Access.
- **Description**—The PCCS PHP-based MySQL administration tool contains a remotely accessible file that contains the database administrator's username and password. By gaining remote access to this file, an attacker can compromise the database.
- **Benign Triggers**—None.

5080 WWW IBM WebSphere Access

- **Default Severity**—Medium.
- **Structure**—Atomic.
- **Implementation**—Content.
- **Class**—Access.
- **Description**—Triggers when someone attempts to access a JSP file through a URL such as **http://server/servlet/file/login.jsp** potentially revealing the JSP source code.
- **Benign Triggers**—None.

JSP

Java Server Pages (JSPs) are an extension to the Java Servlet technology developed by Sun as an alternative to Microsoft Active Scripting Pages (ASPs). Embedded in an HTML page, Java source code (and extensions) adds functionality such as dynamic database queries. Furthermore, JSPs are platform-independent.

5081 WWW WinNT cmd.exe Access

- **Default Severity**—High.
- **Structure**—Atomic.
- **Implementation**—Content.
- **Class**—Access.
- **Description**—This signature triggers when the use of the Windows NT **cmd.exe** is detected in a URL. A malicious user can cause severe damage to the system hosting the Web site by adding, changing, or deleting data. Furthermore, an attacker can run code already on the server or upload new malicious code to the server and run it.
- **Benign Triggers**—None.

5083 WWW Virtual Vision FTP Browser Access

- **Default Severity**—Medium.
- **Structure**—Atomic.
- **Implementation**—Content.
- **Class**—Reconnaissance.
- **Description**—Triggers when an attempt to traverse directories in a URL (such as **http://server/cgi-bin/ftp/ftp.pl?dir=././etc**) is detected.
- **Benign Triggers**—None.

5084 WWW Alibaba Attack 2

- **Default Severity**—Medium.
- **Structure**—Atomic.
- **Implementation**—Content.
- **Class**—Access.
- **Description**—Triggers when a pipe character (|) is detected in a URL such as **http://server/cgi-bin/post32.exe|echo%20>c:\text.txt** or **http://server/cgi-bin/lsindex2.bat|dir%20c:\[dir]**.
- **Benign Triggers**—None.

5085 WWW IIS Source Fragment Access

- **Default Severity**—Medium.
- **Structure**—Atomic.
- **Implementation**—Content.

- **Class**—Access.
- **Description**—This signature triggers when a URL ending in **+.htr** is detected. A remote attacker can view the contents of ASP, ASA, and other file types on the Web server, which might contain sensitive information such as usernames and passwords.
- **Benign Triggers**—None.

5086 WWW WEBactive Logfile Access

- **Default Severity**—Low.
- **Structure**—Atomic.
- **Implementation**—Content.
- **Class**—Access.
- **Description**—Triggers when an attempt to access the WEBactive log file is detected.
- **Benign Triggers**—None.

5087 WWW Sun Java Server Access

- **Default Severity**—Medium.
- **Structure**—Atomic.
- **Implementation**—Content.
- **Class**—Access.
- **Description**—This signature triggers when an attempt to access URLs such as **http://server/pservlet.html** or **http://server/servlet/sunexamples/RealmDump Servlet** is detected. A remote attacker can identify users and file permissions on the Web server. This knowledge can be used to perform additional probes or attacks to gain further access to the Web server.
- **Benign Triggers**—None.

5088 WWW Akopia MiniVend Access

- **Default Severity**—Medium.
- **Structure**—Atomic.
- **Implementation**—Content.
- **Class**—Access.
- **Description**—Triggers when an attempt to access a URL such as **http://server/view_page.html** is detected.
- **Benign Triggers**—None.

5089 WWW Big Brother Directory Access

- **Default Severity**—Medium.
- **Structure**—Atomic.
- **Implementation**—Content.
- **Class**—Access.
- **Description**—Triggers when an attempt to traverse directories with the Big Brother cgi program **bb-hostsvc.sh** is detected.
- **Benign Triggers**—None.

5090 WWW FrontPage htimage.exe Access

- **Default Severity**—Medium.
- **Structure**—Atomic.
- **Implementation**—Content.
- **Class**—Reconnaissance.
- **Description**—This signature triggers when the FrontPage CGI program is accessed with a filename argument ending with **0,0**. This file is associated with three known vulnerabilities when it is on Windows servers. It allows identification of the Web root path, possibly causes a denial of service when run with a large argument, and allows access to files on the Web server.
- **Benign Triggers**—None.

5091 WWW Cart32 Remote Admin Access

- **Default Severity**—Medium.
- **Structure**—Composite.
- **Implementation**—Content.
- **Class**—Reconnaissance/Access.
- **Description**—This signature triggers when an attempt is made to access the vulnerable **cart32.exe** cgi script with suspicious arguments: **/cart32.exe/cart32clientlist** or **/c32web.exe/changeadminpassword**. A remote user can change the administrative password without knowing the previous password. The remote user can also obtain information such as usernames, passwords, and credit card numbers.
- **Benign Triggers**—None.

5092 WWW CGI-World Poll It Access

- **Default Severity**—Medium.
- **Structure**—Atomic.
- **Implementation**—Content.
- **Class**—Reconnaissance
- **Description**—This signature triggers when an attempt is made to access the **Poll-It** cgi script by using an internal script variable name **data_dir** as an argument in the HTTP request.
- **Benign Triggers**—None.

5093 WWW PHP-Nuke admin.php3 Access

- **Default Severity**—Medium.
- **Structure**—Atomic.
- **Implementation**—Content.
- **Class**—Access.
- **Description**—An attempt is made to access the vulnerable PHP-Nuke **admin.php3** cgi script by using suspicious arguments.
- **Benign Triggers**—None.

5095 WWW CGI Script Center Account Manager Attack

- **Default Severity**—Medium.
- **Structure**—Atomic.
- **Implementation**—Content.
- **Class**—Access.
- **Description**—Triggers when an attempt to change the Administrator password of the CGI Script Center Account Manager is detected.
- **Benign Triggers**—A valid user changing the administrator password can trigger this signature.

5096 WWW CGI Script Center Subscribe Me Attack

- **Default Severity**—Medium.
- **Structure**—Atomic.
- **Implementation**—Content.

- **Class**—Access.
- **Description**—Triggers when an attempt to change the administrative password of the CGI Script Center Subscribe package is detected.
- **Benign Triggers**—A password change performed by a valid user can trigger this signature.

5097 WWW FrontPage MS-DOS Device Attack

- **Default Severity**—Medium.
- **Structure**—Composite.
- **Implementation**—Content.
- **Class**—Denial of service
- **Description**—This alarm triggers when a URL is requested using the **shtml.exe** component of FrontPage that includes an MS-DOS device name. A denial of service can result from this URL request.
- **Benign Triggers**—None.

5099 WWW GWScripts News Publisher Access

- **Default Severity**—Medium.
- **Structure**—Atomic.
- **Implementation**—Content.
- **Class**—Access.
- **Description**—This signature triggers when someone attempts to add an author to the GWScript's News Publisher interface.
- **Benign Triggers**—An authorized user adding an author might trigger this signature.

5100 WWW CGI Center Auction Weaver File Access

- **Default Severity**—Medium.
- **Structure**—Atomic.
- **Implementation**—Content.
- **Class**—Reconnaissance.
- **Description**—This signature triggers when someone attempts to access normally inaccessible files by using the **auctionweaver.pl** cgi script.
- **Benign Triggers**—None.

5101 WWW CGI Center Auction Weaver Attack

- **Default Severity**—Medium.
- **Structure**—Atomic.
- **Implementation**—Content.
- **Class**—Access.
- **Description**—This signature triggers when someone attempts to execute an unauthorized command through the **auctionweaver.pl** cgi script.
- **Benign Triggers**—None.

5102 WWW phpPhotoAlbum explorer.php Access

- **Default Severity**—Medium.
- **Structure**—Atomic.
- **Implementation**—Content.
- **Class**—Reconnaissance.
- **Description**—This signature triggers when an unauthorized attempt to access files using the **explorer.php** cgi script is detected.
- **Benign Triggers**—None.

5103 WWW SuSE Apache CGI Source Attack

- **Default Severity**—Medium.
- **Structure**—Atomic.
- **Implementation**—Content.
- **Class**—Reconnaissance.
- **Description**—This signature triggers when an attempt to access the **/cgi-bin-sdb** directory of a Web server is detected. An attacker can view the contents of cgi scripts and programs that might contain sensitive information, such as database usernames and passwords.
- **Benign Triggers**—None.

5104 WWW YaBB File Access

- **Default Severity**—Medium.
- **Structure**—Atomic.
- **Implementation**—Content.

- **Class**—Reconnaissance.
- **Description**—This signature triggers when an attempt to read unauthorized files using the **YaBB.pl** cgi bulletin board program is detected.
- **Benign Triggers**—None.

5105 WWW Ranson Johnson mailto.cgi Attack

- **Default Severity**—Medium.
- **Structure**—Atomic.
- **Implementation**—Content.
- **Class**—Access.
- **Description**—This signature triggers when someone attempts to execute system commands using the **mailto.cgi** program.
- **Benign Triggers**—None.

5106 WWW Ranson Johnson mailform.pl Access

- **Default Severity**—Medium.
- **Structure**—Atomic.
- **Implementation**—Content.
- **Class**—Access.
- **Description**—This signature triggers when an attempt to access the **mailform.pl** script is detected. The Ranson Johnson MailForm cgi program contains a vulnerability that allows read access to any file to which the Web server has access. The hidden variable **XX-attach_file** can be manipulated to cause the cgi program to e-mail unauthorized files to a remote address.
- **Benign Triggers**—None.

5107 WWW Mandrake Linux/Perl Access

- **Default Severity**—Medium.
- **Structure**—Atomic.
- **Implementation**—Content.
- **Class**—Reconnaissance.

- **Description**—This signature triggers when an attempt to access the URL path **/perl** directly is detected. The **/perl** directory is used by mod_perl to store Perl scripts that can be executed by the Web server. By accessing this directory, a remote user can obtain a directory listing. The knowledge of a script's presence might allow more sophisticated attacks to occur.
- **Benign Triggers**—None.

5108 WWW Netegrity Site Minder Access

- **Default Severity**—Medium.
- **Structure**—Atomic.
- **Implementation**—Content.
- **Class**—Access.
- **Description**—This signature triggers when an unauthorized attempt to access protected content using an authentication bypass method is detected on a Web site that is managed by Netegrity Site Minder. This signature looks for strings such as **/$/somefile.ccc** in a URL. A remote attacker can read or execute protected content on the Web site administered by Site Minder.
- **Benign Triggers**—None.

5109 WWW Sambar Beta search.dll Access

- **Default Severity**—Medium.
- **Structure**—Atomic.
- **Implementation**—Content.
- **Class**—Access.
- **Description**—This signature triggers when an unauthorized attempt to access files or directories using the Sambar Server search.dll cgi program is detected.
- **Benign Triggers**—None.

5110 WWW SuSE Installed Packages Access

- **Default Severity**—Low.
- **Structure**—Atomic.
- **Implementation**—Content.
- **Class**—Reconnaissance.

- **Description**—This signature triggers when an attempt to access the URL **http://*server*/doc/packages** is detected. The Apache RPM package shipped with certain versions of S.u.S.E. Linux contains a misconfiguration, which allows a remote user to list all the RPM-based packages installed on the system.
- **Benign Triggers**—None.

5111 WWW Solaris Anwerbook2 Access

- **Default Severity**—Medium.
- **Structure**—Atomic.
- **Implementation**—Content.
- **Class**—Reconnaissance.
- **Description**—This signature triggers when an attempt to add a user to the AnswerBook interface is detected.
- **Benign Triggers**—This signature might fire as the result of a valid account being added to the AnswerBook interface.

5112 WWW Solaris Answerbook2 Attack

- **Default Severity**—Medium.
- **Structure**—Atomic.
- **Implementation**—Content.
- **Class**—Access.
- **Description**—This signature triggers when an attempt to execute an unauthorized command using the access/error rotation feature of the administrative interface of AnswerBook 2 is detected. A remote attacker can create an AnswerBook administrator account without providing any authentication information, allowing the attacker to gain the ability to execute arbitrary commands with the privileges of the Web server.
- **Benign Triggers**—None.

5113 WWW CommuniGate Pro Access

- **Default Severity**—Medium.
- **Structure**—Atomic.
- **Implementation**—Content.
- **Class**—Reconnaissance.

- **Description**—This signature triggers when an unauthorized attempt to access files using the Communicate Pro Web interface is detected.
- **Benign Triggers**—None.

5114 WWW IIS Unicode Attack

- **Default Severity**—High.
- **Structure**—Atomic.
- **Implementation**—Content.
- **Class**—Access.
- **Description**—This signature triggers when an attempt to exploit the Unicode directory traversal vulnerability (./) is detected. An attacker can add, change, or delete data; run code already on the server; or upload new code to the server and run it.
- **Benign Triggers**—None.

Cross-Protocol Signatures (6000 Series)

The 6000 Series, cross-protocol signatures detect attacks that are independent of IP protocols. For example, RPC-related services can operate on both TCP and UDP. This section covers the following:

- SATAN attacks
- DNS attacks
- RPC services attacks
- Ident attacks
- Authentication failures
- Loki attacks
- Distributed denial of service attacks

SATAN Attacks

The Security Analysis Tool for Auditing Networks (SATAN) is one of the original network scanners that was created to enable system administrators to proactively check the security of their networks. This tool incorporates various modules to examine a host or group hosts from a security perspective. Some of the services that SATAN examines are as follows:

- Finger
- NIS

- FTP
- TFTP
- REXD

Attackers can also use this tool, which was publicly released, to gain access to your network. Cisco Secure IDS incorporates a couple of signatures to look for the use of this scanner. These signatures are as follows:

- 6001 Normal SATAN Probe
- 6002 Heavy SATAN Probe

6001 Normal SATAN Probe

- **Default Severity**—High.
- **Structure**—Composite.
- **Implementation**—Content.
- **Class**—Reconnaissance.
- **Description**—This is a supersignature triggered when a port sweep pattern produced by the SATAN tool is detected. It is tuned to detect an attacker running SATAN in Normal mode. This traffic indicates that a reconnaissance sweep of your network might be in progress and might be the prelude to a more serious attack.
- **Benign Triggers**—Many network management tools, such as HP OpenView, provide network-mapping capabilities. This might include a mapping of available network services, so port sweeps might be expected from these systems. Furthermore, a chance exists that this activity might trigger this signature if it is similar enough to a normal SATAN scan.

6002 Heavy SATAN Probe

- **Default Severity**—High.
- **Structure**—Composite.
- **Implementation**—Content.
- **Class**—Reconnaissance.
- **Description**—This is a supersignature triggered when a port sweep pattern produced by the SATAN tool is detected. It is tuned to detect an attacker running SATAN in Heavy mode. This traffic indicates that a reconnaissance sweep of your network might be in progress and might be the prelude to a more serious attack.

- **Benign Triggers**—Many network management tools, such as HP OpenView, provide network-mapping capabilities. This might include a mapping of available network services, so port sweeps might be expected from these systems. If this mapping is similar enough to the traffic generated by SATAN, this signature incorrectly identifies them as SATAN scans.

DNS Attacks

The Domain Name System (DNS) provides a mechanism by which a human-readable name, such as www.companyx.com, can be easily converted to an IP address. Attackers frequently exploit DNS to perform reconnaissance against your network. Furthermore, DNS Server software has a history of security vulnerabilities. The Cisco Secure IDS signatures related to DNS are as follows:

- 6050 DNS HINFO Request
- 6051 DNS Zone Transfer Request
- 6052 DNS Zone Transfer from High Port
- 6053 DNS Request for All Records
- 6054 DNS Version Request
- 6055 DNS Inverse Query Buffer Overflow
- 6056 BIND NXT Buffer Overflow
- 6057 BIND SIG Buffer Overflow

6050 DNS HINFO Request

- **Default Severity**—Medium.
- **Structure**—Atomic.
- **Implementation**—Content.
- **Class**—Reconnaissance.
- **Description**—This signature triggers on an attempt to access HINFO records from a DNS server. The DNS includes an optional record type that allows for system information to be recorded and retrieved. This information typically includes the OS and hardware platform that the system is running on. There is little utility in including this record in the database, and it provides attackers with valuable targeting information. It is suggested that this record not be included in your DNS database for this reason. Request for these records indicates that your network might be under a reconnaissance attack.

- **Benign Triggers**—The DNS HINFO information field might be accessed for many valid reasons from the network. Common false triggers for this signature are curiosity on the part of a novice user or a system administrator in search of all systems on the network running a particular operating system.

6051 DNS Zone Transfer Request

- **Default Severity**—Low.
- **Structure**—Atomic.
- **Implementation**—Content.
- **Class**—Information.
- **Description**—This signature triggers on normal DNS zone transfers, in which the source port is 53. Zone transfers are the method by which secondary DNS servers update their DNS records. All DNS records are transferred at once from the primary to secondary server. This transfers records only for the zone specified. Zone transfer request from hosts other than a secondary server (especially from systems outside your protected network) indicate that your network is under a reconnaissance attack.
- **Benign Triggers**—This is a normal transaction on networks. If the source of the request is not a secondary server on your network, this might be a reconnaissance effort, and heightened awareness of future security relevant events is suggested.

6052 DNS Zone Transfer from High Port

- **Default Severity**—High.
- **Structure**—Atomic.
- **Implementation**—Content.
- **Class**—Reconnaissance.
- **Description**—This signature triggers on an illegitimate DNS zone transfer, in which the source port is not equal to 53. Zone transfers are the method by which secondary DNS servers update their DNS records. All DNS records are transferred at once from the primary to secondary server. This transfers records only for the zone specified. Because of the access method, this signature indicates that your network probably is under a reconnaissance attack and is a prelude to more serious attacks.
- **Benign Triggers**—There are no benign triggers for this event. Zone transfers performed in this manner are observed only when there is an active attempt to hide the activity. This is probably a reconnaissance effort and heightened awareness of future security relevant events is suggested.

6053 DNS Request for All Records

- **Default Severity**—Low.
- **Structure**—Atomic.
- **Implementation**—Content.
- **Class**—Access.
- **Description**—This signature triggers on a DNS request for all records and is similar to a zone transfer in that it provides a method for transferring DNS records from a server to another requesting host. The primary difference is that all DNS records are transferred, not just those specific to a particular zone. This traffic indicates that your network might be under a reconnaissance attack.
- **Benign Triggers**—This is a normal transaction on networks. If the source of the request is not a secondary server on your network, this might be a reconnaissance effort, and heightened awareness of future security relevant events is suggested.

6054 DNS Version Request

- **Default Severity**—Medium.
- **Structure**—Atomic.
- **Implementation**—Content.
- **Class**—Reconnaissance.
- **Description**s—Triggers when a request for the version of a DNS server is detected. Numerous versions of the popular BIND DNS server software contain buffer overflow vulnerabilities, and scanners exist that detect the presence of vulnerable DNS servers.
- **Benign Triggers**—None.

6055 DNS Inverse Query Buffer Overflow

- **Default Severity**—High.
- **Structure**—Atomic.
- **Implementation**—Content.
- **Class**—Access.
- **Description**—This alarm triggers when an IQUERY request arrives with a data section that is larger than 255 characters.
- **Benign Triggers**—None.

6056 BIND NXT Buffer Overflow

- **Default Severity**—High.
- **Structure**—Composite.
- **Implementation**—Content.
- **Class**—Access.
- **Description**—This alarm triggers when a DNS server response arrives that has a long NXT resource entry where the length of the resource data is greater than 2069 bytes or the length of the TCP stream containing the NXT resource is greater than 3000 bytes.
- **Benign Triggers**—None.

NXT Resource Record

Your DNS server enables you to configure various types of entries known as resource records. The NXT resource record enables you to define resources that do not exist. For instance, you can use NXT resource records to define a range of available DNS names. You also can use these records to define a range of resource records that are not available for an existing DNS name. For more information on NXT entries, refer to RFC 2535, "Domain Name System Security Extensions."

6057 BIND SIG Buffer Overflow

- **Default Severity**—High.
- **Structure**—Composite.
- **Implementation**—Context.
- **Class**—Access.
- **Description**—This alarm triggers when a DNS server response arrives that has a long SIG resource entry where the length of the resource data is greater than 2069 bytes or the length of the TCP stream containing the SIG resource is greater than 3000 bytes.
- **Benign Triggers**—None.

SIG Resource Record

Your DNS server enables you to configure various types of entries known as resource records. The SIG resource record provides authentication for a set of resource records along with defining a signature validity time. These SIG resource records basically define the encryption methods that enable a requesting program to verify the integrity of DNS replies. For more information on SIG entries, refer to RFC 2535, "Domain Name System Security Extensions."

RPC Services Attacks

Remote Procedure Call (RPC) is a protocol that enables one program to request a service from another computer on a network. This protocol does not require the requesting computer to understand the layout of the network. This protocol is based on a client/server model.

Instead of using well-known ports, the remote procedures use ephemeral ports. This requires a program that keeps track of which program is at which ephemeral port (usually referred to as the *port mapper*). The port mapper is located at a well-known port (100000). This program then issues ports for other programs as they register with it.

Attackers frequently attempt to manipulate RPC functionality to gain unauthorized access to your network resources. They either request port information on services directly from the port mapper, or they might scan individual ports looking for RPC services without going through the port mapper. The Cisco Secure IDS signatures related to RPC are as follows:

- 6100 RPC Port Registration
- 6101 RPC Port Unregistration
- 6102 RPC Dump
- 6103 Proxied RPC Request
- 6104 RPC Set Spoof
- 6105 RPC Unset Spoof
- 6110 RPC RSTATD Sweep
- 6111 RPC RUSERSD Sweep
- 6112 RPC NFS Sweep
- 6113 RPC MOUNTD Sweep
- 6114 RPC YPPASSWDD Sweep
- 6115 RPC SELECTION_SVC Sweep
- 6116 RPC REXD Sweep
- 6117 RPC STATUS Sweep
- 6118 RPC ttdb Sweep
- 6150 ypserv Portmap Request
- 6151 ypbind Portmap Request
- 6152 yppasswdd Portmap Request
- 6153 ypupdated Portmap Request
- 6154 ypxfrd Portmap Request
- 6155 mountd Portmap Request

- 6175 rexd Portmap Request
- 6180 rexd Attempt
- 6190 statd Buffer Overflow
- 6191 RPC.tooltalk Buffer overflow
- 6192 RPC mountd Buffer Overflow
- 6193 RPC CMSD Buffer Overflow
- 6194 sadmind RPC Buffer Overflow
- 6195 RPC and Buffer Overflow
- 6500 RingZero Trojan

6100 RPC Port Registration

- **Default Severity**—High.
- **Structure**—Atomic.
- **Implementation**—Content.
- **Class**—Access.
- **Description**—This signature triggers when attempts are made to register new RPC services on a target host. Port registration is the method used by new services to report to the port mapper that they are present and to gain access to a port. This information is then advertised by the port mapper. Do not allow this traffic from a remote host. No known exploit of this function exists. This does not preclude the possibility that exploits do exist outside of the realm of the Cisco System knowledge domain.
- **Benign Triggers**—None.

6101 RPC Port Unregistration

- **Default Severity**—High.
- **Structure**—Atomic.
- **Implementation**—Content.
- **Class**—Denial of service.
- **Description**—This signature triggers when attempts are made to unregister existing RPC services on a target host. Port unregistration is the method used by services to report to the port mapper that they are no longer present and to remove them from the active port map. Do not allow this traffic from a remote host. No known exploit of this function exists. This does not preclude the possibility that exploits do exist outside of the realm of the Cisco System knowledge domain.
- **Benign Triggers**—None.

6102 RPC Dump

- **Default Severity**—High.
- **Structure**—Atomic.
- **Implementation**—Content.
- **Class**—Reconnaissance.
- **Description**—This signature triggers when an RPC dump request is issued to a target host. This is a procedure that might be used to determine the presence and port location of RPC services being provided by a system. This signature can indicate that your network is under reconnaissance attack.
- **Benign Triggers**—This is a common procedure performed by many system administrators and users to determine what RPC services are being offered. It heightens awareness of future security relevant events because this might be a reconnaissance attack.

6103 Proxied RPC Request

- **Default Severity**—Low.
- **Structure**—Atomic.
- **Implementation**—Content.
- **Class**—Access.
- **Description**—This signature triggers when a proxied RPC request is sent to the port mapper of a target host. This method of requesting RPC services involves having the port mapper act as your proxy. This might indicate an attempt to gain unauthorized access to system resources and should not be allowed from hosts outside your protected network.
- **Benign Triggers**—If proxy RPC requests are allowed on your network, those users who employ them trigger the signature. This might be a serious attempt at gaining unauthorized access; and if the source of the attempt is not within your network, it needs to be blocked.

6104 RPC Set Spoof

- **Default Severity**—High.
- **Structure**—Atomic.
- **Implementation**—Content.
- **Class**—Denial of service.
- **Description**—This signature triggers when an RPC set request with a source address of 127.x.x.x is detected.
- **Benign Triggers**—None.

6105 RPC Unset Spoof

- **Default Severity**—High.
- **Structure**—Atomic.
- **Implementation**—Content.
- **Class**—Denial of service.
- **Description**—This signature triggers when an RPC unset request with a source address of 127.x.x.x is detected.
- **Benign Triggers**—None.

6110 RPC RSTATD Sweep

- **Default Severity**—High.
- **Structure**—Composite.
- **Implementation**—Context.
- **Class**—Reconnaissance.
- **Description**—This signature triggers when RPC requests are made to many ports for the RSTATD program.
- **Benign Triggers**—None.

6111 RPC RUSERSD Sweep

- **Default Severity**—High.
- **Structure**—Composite.
- **Implementation**—Context.
- **Class**—Reconnaissance
- **Description**—This signature triggers when RPC requests are made to many ports for the RUSERSD program.
- **Benign Triggers**—None.

6112 RPC NFS Sweep

- **Default Severity**—High.
- **Structure**—Composite.
- **Implementation**—Context.
- **Class**—Reconnaissance.

- **Description**—This signature triggers when RPC requests are made to many ports for the **nfs** program.
- **Benign Triggers**—None.

6113 RPC MOUNTD Sweep

- **Default Severity**—High.
- **Structure**—Composite.
- **Implementation**—Context.
- **Class**—Reconnaissance.
- **Description**—This signature triggers when RPC requests are made to many ports for the **mountd** program.
- **Benign Triggers**—None.

6114 RPC YPPASSWDD Sweep

- **Default Severity**—High.
- **Structure**—Composite.
- **Implementation**—Context.
- **Class**—Reconnaissance.
- **Description**—This signature triggers when RPC requests are made to many ports for the **yppasswdd** program.
- **Benign Triggers**—None.

6115 RPC SELECTION_SVC Sweep

- **Default Severity**—High.
- **Structure**—Composite.
- **Implementation**—Context.
- **Class**—Reconnaissance.
- **Description**—This signature triggers when RPC requests are made to many ports for the **selection_svc** program.
- **Benign Triggers**—None.

6116 RPC REXD Sweep

- **Default Severity**—High.
- **Structure**—Composite.
- **Implementation**—Context.
- **Class**—Reconnaissance.
- **Description**—This signature triggers when RPC requests are made to many ports for the **rexd** program.
- **Benign Triggers**—None.

6117 RPC STATUS Sweep

- **Default Severity**—High.
- **Structure**—Composite.
- **Implementation**—Context.
- **Class**—Reconnaissance.
- **Description**—This signature triggers when RPC requests are made to many ports for the **status** program.
- **Benign Triggers**—None.

6118 RPC ttdb Sweep

- **Default Severity**—High.
- **Structure**—Composite.
- **Implementation**—Content.
- **Class**—Reconnaissance.
- **Description**—This signature triggers on an attempt to access the ToolTalk database daemon on multiple ports on a single host.
- **Benign Triggers**—None.

6150 ypserv Portmap Request

- **Default Severity**—Low.
- **Structure**—Atomic.
- **Implementation**—Content.
- **Class**—Access.

- **Description**—This signature triggers when a request is made to the port mapper for the YP server daemon (ypserv) port. The ypserv daemon is responsible for looking up information maintained in NIS maps. This traffic might indicate an attempt to gain unauthorized access to system resources on your network.

- **Benign Triggers**—If this procedure is allowed on your network, those users who employ it trigger the signature. If the source of the attempt is not within your protected network, this might be a serious attempt to gain unauthorized access and should be blocked.

6151 ypbind Portmap Request

- **Default Severity**—Low.
- **Structure**—Atomic.
- **Implementation**—Content.
- **Class**—Access.
- **Description**—This signature triggers when a request is made to the port mapper for the YP bind daemon (ypbind) port. The ypbind daemon is responsible for maintaining the information needed for a client process to communicate with a ypserv process. This traffic might indicate an attempt to gain unauthorized access to system resources on your network.
- **Benign Triggers**—If this procedure is allowed on your network, those users who employ it trigger the signature. If the source of the attempt is not within your protected network, this might be a serious attempt to gain unauthorized access and should be blocked.

6152 yppasswdd Portmap Request

- **Default Severity**—Disable.
- **Structure**—Atomic.
- **Implementation**—Content.
- **Class**—Access.
- **Description**—This signature triggers when a request is made to the port mapper for the YP password daemon (yppasswdd) port. The YP password daemon allows users to remotely modify password files. This traffic might indicate an attempt to gain unauthorized access to system resources on your network.
- **Benign Triggers**—If this procedure is allowed on your network, those users who employ it trigger the signature. If the source of the attempt is not within your protected network, this might be a serious attempt to gain unauthorized access and should be blocked.

6153 ypupdated Portmap Request

- **Default Severity**—Low.
- **Structure**—Atomic.
- **Implementation**—Content.
- **Class**—Access.
- **Description**—This signature triggers when a request is made to the port mapper for the YP update daemon (ypupdated) port. The YP update daemon is responsible for updating local NIS maps. This traffic might indicate an attempt to gain unauthorized access to system resources on your network.
- **Benign Triggers**—If this procedure is allowed on your network, those users who employ it trigger the signature. If the source of the attempt is not within your protected network, this might be a serious attempt to gain unauthorized access and should be blocked.

6154 ypxfrd Portmap Request

- **Default Severity**—Low.
- **Structure**—Atomic.
- **Implementation**—Content.
- **Class**—Access.
- **Description**—This signature triggers when a request is made to the port mapper for the YP transfer daemon (ypxfrd) port. The YP transfer daemon is responsible for transferring NIS information on behalf of ypserv. This traffic might indicate an attempt to gain unauthorized access to system resources on your network.
- **Benign Triggers**—If this procedure is allowed on your network, those users who employ it trigger the signature. If the source of the attempt is not within your protected network, this might be a serious attempt to gain unauthorized access and should be blocked.

6155 mountd Portmap Request

- **Default Severity**—Disable.
- **Structure**—Atomic.
- **Implementation**—Content.
- **Class**—Access.

- **Description**—This signature triggers when a request is made to the port mapper for the mount daemon (mountd) port. This is the NFS daemon that is responsible for processing mount requests. This traffic might indicate an attempt to gain unauthorized access to system resources on your network.

- **Benign Triggers**—If this procedure is allowed on your network, those users who employ it trigger the signature. If the source of the attempt is not within your protected network, this might be a serious attempt to gain unauthorized access and should be blocked.

6175 rexd Portmap Request

- **Default Severity**—Medium.
- **Structure**—Atomic.
- **Implementation**—Content.
- **Class**—Access.
- **Description**—This signature triggers when a request is made to the port mapper for the remote execution daemon (rexd) port. The remote execution daemon is the server responsible for remote program execution. This traffic might indicate an attempt to gain unauthorized access to system resources on your network.
- **Benign Triggers**—If this procedure is allowed on your network, those users who employ it trigger the signature. If the source of the attempt is not within your protected network, this might be a serious attempt to gain unauthorized access and should be blocked.

6180 rexd Attempt

- **Default Severity**—High.
- **Structure**—Atomic.
- **Implementation**—Context.
- **Class**—Access.
- **Description**—This signature triggers when a call to the **rexd** program is made. The remote execution daemon is the server responsible for remote program execution. This traffic might indicate an attempt to gain unauthorized access to system resources on your network.
- **Benign Triggers**—If this service is being used legitimately, this alarm fires. For security purposes, you probably should not allow this service on your network.

6190 statd Buffer Overflow

- **Default Severity**—High.
- **Structure**—Composite.
- **Implementation**—Context.
- **Class**—Access.
- **Description**—This signature triggers when a large **statd** request is sent. This can be an attempt to overflow a buffer and gain access to system resources.
- **Benign Triggers**—None.

6191 RPC.tooltalk Buffer overflow

- **Default Severity**—High.
- **Structure**—Composite.
- **Implementation**—Content.
- **Class**—Access.
- **Description**—This signature triggers when an attempt is made to overflow an internal buffer in the tooltalk rpc program.
- **Benign Triggers**—None

6192 RPC mountd Buffer Overflow

- **Default Severity**—High.
- **Structure**—Composite.
- **Implementation**—Content.
- **Class**—Access.
- **Description**—This signature triggers on an attempt to overflow a buffer in the RPC **mountd** application. This might result in unauthorized access to system resources.
- **Benign Triggers**—None.

6193 RPC CMSD Buffer Overflow

- **Default Severity**—High.
- **Structure**—Atomic.
- **Implementation**—Content.
- **Class**—Access.

- **Description**—This signature fires when an attempt is made to overflow an internal buffer in the Calendar Manager Service daemon, **rpc.cmsd**. This vulnerability can allow a remote attacker to gain root access on your system.
- **Benign Triggers**—None.

6194 sadmind RPC Buffer Overflow

- **Default Severity**—High.
- **Structure**—Atomic.
- **Implementation**—Content.
- **Class**—Access.
- **Description**—This signature fires when a call to RPC program number 100232 procedure 1 with a UDP packet length greater than 1024 bytes is detected. This vulnerability can allow a remote attacker to gain root access on your system.
- **Benign Triggers**—None.

6195 RPC and Buffer Overflow

- **Default Severity**—High.
- **Structure**—Composite.
- **Implementation**—Content.
- **Class**—Access.
- **Description**—The trigger for this signature is an RPC call to the Berkeley auto-mounter daemon's rpc program (300019) procedure 7 with a UDP length greater than 1024 or a TCP stream length greater than 1024. The TCP stream length is defined by the contents of the two bytes preceding the RPC header in a TCP packet. This vulnerability can allow a remote attacker to gain root access on your system.
- **Benign Triggers**—None.

6500 RingZero Trojan

- **Default Severity**—High.
- **Structure**—Composite.
- **Implementation**—Content.
- **Class**—Reconnaissance.

- **Description**—The RingZero Trojan consists of an information transfer (ITS) agent and a port scanning (PST) agent. A machine infected with the RingZero ITS Trojan will attempt to retrieve a data file called its.dat from phzforum.virtualave.net and zoom.members.com. A machine infected with the RingZero PST Trojan can port scan random IPs for TCP ports 80, 8080, and 3128. When an open port is found, it sends a request on the open port to proxy the IP and port number discovered to www.rusftpsearch.net. OUTBOUND signature traffic indicates an internal machine is infected with RingZero, except if the originating machine is a Web server or proxy, in which case it indicates an internal Web server was scanned by a Trojanized source. INBOUND signature traffic is an indication of a scan from an external Trojanized source. (For more information on Trojan horse programs, refer to Chapter 1, "Need for Network Security.")

- **Benign Triggers**—None.

Ident Attacks

The Identification (Ident) protocol provides a mechanism to prevent host name and address spoofing, as well as identifying false usernames. When a user connects to a specific service on a destination host, the destination host contacts the initiating host through the Ident protocol to confirm the identification of the requesting user. For a detailed explanation of the Ident protocol, refer to RFC 1413.

The Cisco Secure IDS signatures related to the Ident protocol are as follows:

- 6200 Ident Buffer Overflow

- 6201 Ident Newline

- 6202 Ident Improper Request

NOTE   Although the Ident protocol is designed to prevent host name and IP address spoofing, it has limited effectiveness in practice because it assumes that the user does not have *root* access on the machine from which he is connecting. If a user has total control of the originating machine, he can spoof the initial packets and spoof the Ident replies as well.

6200 Ident Buffer Overflow

- **Default Severity**—High.

- **Structure**—Composite.

- **Implementation**—Content.

- **Class**—Access.

- **Description**—This signature triggers when a server returns an ident reply that is too large. This might indicate an attempt to gain unauthorized access to your system resources.

- **Benign Triggers**—Although it is possible that malformed responses from improperly written ident servers can trigger this signature, this is highly unlikely. Prudent security practices suggest that the source of this attempt needs to be blocked.

6201 Ident Newline

- **Default Severity**—High.
- **Structure**—Composite.
- **Implementation**—Content.
- **Class**—Access.
- **Description**—This signature triggers when a server returns an ident reply that includes a newline followed by more data. This might indicate an attempt to gain unauthorized access to your system resources.
- **Benign Triggers**—Although malformed responses from improperly written ident servers can trigger this signature, this is highly unlikely. Prudent security practices suggest that the source of this attempt needs to be blocked.

6202 Ident Improper Request

- **Default Severity**—High.
- **Structure**—Composite.
- **Implementation**—Content.
- **Class**—Access.
- **Description**—This signature triggers when a client's ident request is too long or specifies nonexistent ports. This might indicate an attempt to gain unauthorized access to your system resources.
- **Benign Triggers**—Although malformed responses from improperly written ident servers can trigger this signature, this is highly unlikely. Prudent security practices suggest that the source of this attempt needs to be blocked.

Authentication Failures

A basic security mechanism on your network is user authentication. Your Cisco Secure IDS can identify user authentication failures for various services throughout your network. The signatures that check authentication failures are as follows:

- 6250 FTP Authorization Failure
- 6251 Telnet Authorization Failure
- 6252 Rlogin Authorization Failure
- 6253 POP3 Authorization Failure
- 6255 SMB Authorization Failure

6250 FTP Authorization Failure

- **Default Severity**—Low.
- **Structure**—Composite.
- **Implementation**—Content.
- **Class**—Information/access.
- **Description**—This signature triggers when a user fails to authenticate three times in a row while trying to establish an FTP session. This might indicate a brute-force password-guessing attempt and might be viewed as an attempt to gain unauthorized access to your system resources.
- **Benign Triggers**—Users who have forgotten passwords might trigger this signature.

NOTE   Currently, the three failure thresholds for signature 6250 are not user configurable. With Cisco IDS version 3.0, however, this value can be user-configurable through the *MinHits* custom signature parameter (refer to Chapter 18).

6251 Telnet Authorization Failure

- **Default Severity**—Low.
- **Structure**—Composite.
- **Implementation**—Content.
- **Class**—Information/access.
- **Description**—This signature triggers when a user fails to authenticate three times in a row while trying to establish a Telnet session. This might indicate a brute-force password-guessing attempt, and might be viewed as an attempt to gain unauthorized access to your system resources.
- **Benign Triggers**—Users who have forgotten passwords might trigger this signature.

6252 Rlogin Authorization Failure

- **Default Severity**—Low.
- **Structure**—Composite.
- **Implementation**—Content.
- **Class**—Access.
- **Description**—This signature triggers when a user fails to authenticate three times in a row while trying to establish an rlogin session. This might indicate a brute-force password-guessing attempt and might be viewed as an attempt to gain unauthorized access to your system resources.
- **Benign Triggers**—Users who have forgotten passwords might trigger this signature.

6253 POP3 Authorization Failure

- **Default Severity**—Low.
- **Structure**—Composite.
- **Implementation**—Content.
- **Class**—Information/access.
- **Description**—This signature triggers when a user fails to authenticate three times in a row while trying to establish a POP3 session. This might indicate a brute-force password-guessing attempt and might be viewed as an attempt to gain unauthorized access to your system resources.
- **Benign Triggers**—Users who have forgotten passwords might trigger this signature.

6255 SMB Authorization Failure

- **Default Severity**—Low.
- **Structure**—Composite.
- **Implementation**—Content.
- **Class**—Information/Access.
- **Description**—This alarm triggers when a client fails Windows NT (or Samba) user authentication three or more consecutive times within a single SMB session. This indicates that the user does not have a valid account name or password, the user has forgotten the password, or a password-guessing attack such as NAT is used against the server. This alarm also triggers on multiple failures to access a Windows 95 share. Share-level access disregards the provided username and uses only the provided password.
- **Benign Triggers**—This might indicate a user has forgotten his password but needs to be investigated by your network administrators.

Loki Attacks

Loki is a software package that enables an attacker to tunnel information from one machine to another machine in a covert channel. Loki passes the tunneled information as data in seemingly innocuous ICMP packets. The Cisco Secure IDS signatures that detect Loki are as follows:

- 6300 Loki ICMP Tunneling
- 6302 General Loki ICMP Tunneling

6300 Loki ICMP Tunneling

- **Default Severity**—High.
- **Structure**—Composite.
- **Implementation**—Context.
- **Class**—Access.
- **Description**—Loki is a tool designed to run an interactive session that is hidden within ICMP traffic. An attacker needs to first gain root on a system but can then set up a Loki server (lokid) as a backdoor. This can provide future command-line access hidden as ICMP traffic, which can be encrypted. This signature fires if the original Loki that was distributed in Phrack Issue 51 is installed on your system.
- **Benign Triggers**—No benign trigger is known for this alarm. This alarm indicates that your system is compromised. The source needs to be blocked, and incident control and recovery procedures need to be followed.

6302 General Loki ICMP Tunneling

- **Default Severity**—High.
- **Structure**—Composite.
- **Implementation**—Context.
- **Class**—Access.
- **Description**—Loki is a tool designed to run an interactive session that is hidden within ICMP traffic. An attacker needs to first gain root access on a system but can then set up a Loki server (lokid) as a backdoor. This can provide future command-line access hidden as ICMP traffic, which can be encrypted. This signature triggers on Loki even if certain user-configurable options are modified.
- **Benign Triggers**—No benign trigger is known for this alarm. This alarm indicates that your system is compromised. The source needs to be blocked, and incident control and recovery procedures need to be followed.

Distributed Denial of Service Attacks

A distributed denial of service (DDoS) attack is a form of a DoS attack in which the attack launched against a victim host or network is launched from multiple attacking hosts. The attacking hosts are controlled from a master host. The Cisco Secure IDS Signatures watching for DDoS attacks are as follows:

- 6501 TFN Client
- 6502 TFN Server Reply
- 6503 Stacheldraht Client Request
- 6504 Stacheldraht Server Reply
- 6505 Trinoo Client Request
- 6506 Trinoo Server Reply
- 6507 TFN2K Control Traffic
- 6508 mstream Control Traffic

6501 TFN Client

- **Default Severity**—High.
- **Structure**—Composite.
- **Implementation**—Content.
- **Class**—Denial of service.
- **Description**—Tribe Flood Network (TFN) is a distributed denial of service tool. TFN clients and servers by default communicate using ICMP echo reply packets. This signature looks for ICMP echo reply packets containing potential TFN commands sent from a TFN CLIENT to a TFN SERVER. The ICMP reply does not have an associated ICMP echo request packet.
- **Benign Triggers**—None.

NOTE   Loki ICMP tunneling might also be incorrectly detected as TFN traffic.

6502 TFN Server Reply

- **Default Severity**—High.
- **Structure**—Composite.
- **Implementation**—Content.
- **Class**—Denial of service.

- **Description**—Tribe Flood Network (TFN) is a distributed denial of service tool. TFN clients and servers by default communicate using ICMP echo reply packets. This signature looks for ICMP echo reply packets containing potential TFN commands sent from a TFN SERVER to a TFN CLIENT. The ICMP reply does not have an associated ICMP echo request packet.

- **Benign Triggers**—None.

NOTE   Loki ICMP tunneling might also be incorrectly detected as TFN traffic.

6503 Stacheldraht Client Request

- **Default Severity**—High.
- **Structure**—Composite.
- **Implementation**—Content.
- **Class**—Denial of service.
- **Description**—Stacheldraht clients and servers, by default, communicate using ICMP echo reply packets. This signature looks for ICMP echo reply packets containing potential commands sent from a Stacheldraht CLIENT to a Stacheldraht SERVER. The ICMP reply does not have an associated ICMP echo request packet.
- **Benign Triggers**—None.

NOTE   Loki ICMP tunneling might also be incorrectly detected as Stacheldraht traffic. Furthermore, Stacheldraht traffic might also trigger the large ICMP Traffic (Signature ID 2151) because of a bug by which it sends out a large (greater than 1000 byte) ICMP packet.

6504 Stacheldraht Server Reply

- **Default Severity**—High.
- **Structure**—Composite.
- **Implementation**—Content.
- **Class**—Denial of service.
- **Description**—Stacheldraht clients and servers, by default, communicate using ICMP echo reply packets. This signature looks for ICMP echo reply packets containing potential commands sent from a Stacheldraht SERVER to a Stacheldraht CLIENT. The ICMP reply does not have an associated ICMP echo request packet.

- **Benign Triggers**—None.

NOTE   Loki ICMP tunneling might also be incorrectly detected as Stacheldraht traffic. Further-more, Stacheldraht traffic might also trigger the large ICMP Traffic (Signature ID 2151) because of a bug by which it sends out a large (greater than 1000 byte) ICMP packets.

6505 Trinoo Client Request

- **Default Severity**—High.
- **Structure**—Composite.
- **Implementation**—Content.
- **Class**—Denial of service.
- **Description**—Trinoo clients communicate by default on UDP port 27444 using a default command set. This signature looks for UDP packets containing potential commands from a Trinoo CLIENT to a Trinoo SERVER.
- **Benign Triggers**—None.

6506 Trinoo Server Reply

- **Default Severity**—High.
- **Structure**—Composite.
- **Implementation**—Content.
- **Class**—Denial of service.
- **Description**—Trinoo servers reply to clients by default on UDP port 31335 using a default command set. This signature looks for UDP packets containing potential command replies from a Trinoo SERVER to a Trinoo CLIENT.
- **Benign Triggers**—None.

6507 TFN2K Control Traffic

- **Default Severity**—High.
- **Structure**—Composite.
- **Implementation**—Content.
- **Class**—Denial of service.

- **Description**—TFN2K is a distributed denial of service tool that is used to launch coordinated attacks against one or more targets. Servers (zombies) are created when a system is compromised and the TFN2K daemon is installed. They are called servers (zombies) because they are "sleeping," waiting for a command to tell them to wake up and start a DOS attack (usually a flood) against the victim. The hacker issues the "wake up" control command from a remote client console and specifies what victim to attack, how to attack it, and for what duration. TFN2K is a more robust and flexible version of the original Tribe Flood Network (TFN). This signature identifies the control traffic from the attacker's client console and the server (zombie) machine.

- **Benign Triggers**—None.

6508 mstream Control Traffic

- **Default Severity**—High.

- **Structure**—Composite.

- **Implementation**—Content.

- **Class**—Denial of service.

- **Description**—mstream is a UNIX-based distributed denial of service tool similar to Trinoo, TFN, and Stacheldraht. mstream uses the Stream (stream.c) DoS as its method of assault. This distributed attack involves an attacker running client software on numerous compromised systems. This system is the server (agent) that controls all the clients (handlers). This signature identifies the control traffic between both the attacker's server and a client, and between a client and the attacker's server.

- **Benign Triggers**—None.

String-Matching Signatures (8000 Series)

The 8000 Series, string-match signatures, enable the network security administrator to create custom TCP signatures to detect specific string patterns. This flexibility provides the network security administrator the ability to implement and deploy on-the-fly signatures. Custom signatures are commonly used as follows:

- To act as a temporary signature for newly discovered vulnerabilities until an official Cisco Secure IDS signature is released

- To detect misuse based on offending keywords

- To protect specific network applications for which Cisco Secure IDS does not have current signatures to detect possible attacks

You can configure custom signatures by specifying the following parameters:

- TCP port number

- Traffic direction (to or from port)
- Number of occurrences
- String (specified as a regular expression)

These string signatures fall into the following two major categories:

- Custom string matches
- TCP applications signatures

Custom String Matches

String signatures use a regular-expression IDS engine. You can enter a UNIX-like regular expression as the string to match. An example custom string entry is as follows:

```
[/]etc[/]shadow 2302 23 TO 1
```

This example string signature matches attempts to grab a UNIX shadow password file. Furthermore, this example is composed of the following fields:

- String ([/]etc[/]shadow)
- Signature SubID (2302)
- Port (23)
- Direction (TO)
- Number of occurrences (1)

Therefore, this custom string signature looks for occurrences of /etc/password that go to port 23. After one occurrence, your sensor fires a string signature (8000) with a SubID of 2302.

TCP Applications

TCP application signatures are attacks against various TCP applications. They are implemented here as an example of regular-expression formats. The default string signatures distributed with Cisco Secure IDS show users how to create their own custom string signatures (see Chapter 12).

Because all the string signatures are Signature ID 8000, it is helpful to try and create self-documenting subIDs. For example, you might want to adopt a convention in which you create the subID by making the first four digits the port number and the next digit a uniqueness identifier. By using this convention, you can quickly determine which port (and probably which service) a string signature triggered on.

The default string signatures (listed by subID) are as follows:

- 2101 FTP RETR passwd
- 2301 Telnet IFS=/
- 51301 Rlogin IFS=/
- 2303 Telnet + +
- 51303 Rlogin + +
- 2302 Telnet /etc/shadow
- 51302 Rlogin /etc/shadow

2101 FTP RETR passwd

- **Default Severity**—High.
- **Structure**—Composite.
- **Implementation**—Content.
- **Class**—Access.
- **Description**—This signature triggers on string **passwd** issued during an FTP session. It might indicate someone attempting to retrieve the password file from a machine to crack it and gain unauthorized access to your system resources.

2301 Telnet IFS=/

- **Default Severity**—High.
- **Structure**—Composite.
- **Implementation**—Content.
- **Class**—Access.
- **Description**—This signature triggers when an attempt to change the IFS to / is done during a Telnet session. This might indicate an attempt to gain unauthorized access to your system resources.

51301 Rlogin IFS=/

- **Default Severity**—High.
- **Structure**—Composite.
- **Implementation**—Content.
- **Class**—Access.

- **Description**—This signature triggers when an attempt to change the IFS to **/** is done during an rlogin session. This might indicate an attempt to gain unauthorized access to your system resources.

2303 Telnet + +

- **Default Severity**—Low.
- **Structure**—Composite.
- **Implementation**—Content.
- **Class**—Access.
- **Description**—This signature triggers on the string **+ +** issued during a Telnet session. The **+ +** might indicate someone trying to update a RHOSTS file to enable an attacker to gain access to the system without authentication.

51303 Rlogin + +

- **Default Severity**—Low.
- **Structure**—Composite.
- **Implementation**—Content.
- **Class**—Access.
- **Description**—This signature triggers on string **+ +** issued during an rlogin session. The **+ +** might indicate someone trying to update a RHOSTS file to enable an attacker to gain access to the system without authentication.

2302 Telnet /etc/shadow

- **Default Severity**—High.
- **Structure**—Composite.
- **Implementation**—Content.
- **Class**—Access.
- **Description**—This signature triggers on string **/etc/shadow** issued during a Telnet session. This might indicate an attempt to gain unauthorized access to your system resources.

51302 Rlogin /etc/shadow

- **Default Severity**—High.
- **Structure**—Composite.

- **Implementation**—Content.
- **Class**—Access.
- **Description**—This signature triggers on string **/etc/shadow** issued during an rlogin session. This might indicate an attempt to gain unauthorized access to your system resources.

Policy-Violation Signatures (10000 Series)

The 10000 Series signatures enable you to monitor traffic that attempts to violate the ACLs that you configured on one of your Cisco routers. Whenever your router detects a packet that attempts to violate your ACL, it generates a SYSLOG message. Your Cisco Secure IDS Sensor then takes this information and converts it into a 10000 Series alarm.

These signatures are not enabled by default. You need to configure your router and sensor to enable policy-violation detection. Refer to Chapter 12 for more information on configuring policy-violation signatures.

Summary

Signatures are divided into different series based on the general type of intrusive activity. These series span an easily recognizable range of signature IDs. The signature series currently used by Cisco Secure IDS are as follows:

- IP signatures (1000 Series)
- ICMP signatures (2000 Series)
- TCP signatures (3000 Series)
- UDP signatures (4000 Series)
- Web/HTTP signatures (5000 Series)
- Cross-protocol signatures (6000 Series)
- String-matching signatures (8000 Series)
- Policy-violation signatures (10000 Series)

Knowing these signature series enables you to quickly identify the type of alarm detected, even if the specific signature ID is unfamiliar to you.

Review Questions

The following questions test your retention of the material presented in this chapter. The answers to the Review Questions are in Appendix K, "Answers to Review Questions."

1 If you notice a 4xxx signature, what do you know immediately (even if you don't know the exact signature that triggered)?

_____

_____

_____

2 If you enable IP fragment reassembly, which fragmentation signatures does Cisco Secure IDS use?

_____

_____

_____

3 If your sensor detects a TCP attack, what range does the signature ID fall into?

_____

_____

_____

4 Into which signature series (range of signature IDs) does ICMP fall?

_____

_____

_____

5 Which signatures fall into the 1000 series of signatures?

_____

_____

_____

6 Besides the string to search for, what other parameters do you need to specify for a custom string signature?

_____

_____

_____

7 What types of signatures fall into the 6000 Series signatures?

_____

_____

_____

8 How are string signatures identified?

_____

_____

_____

9 What is a host sweep?

_____

_____

_____

10 What is fragmentation?

_____

_____

_____

CSIDS Configuration

## CHAPTER 11

Sensor Configuration Within CSPM

Your sensors monitor actual network traffic to find intrusive activity on your network. Therefore, optimizing the configurations on your sensors is crucial for you to achieve peak performance from your Cisco Secure IDS. Cisco Secure Policy Manager (CSPM) enables you to alter numerous features of your Cisco Secure IDS Sensors. The main sections addressed in this chapter are as follows:

- CSPM Sensor configuration screens
- Basic configuration changes
- Log file configuration
- Advanced configuration changes
- Pushing a new configuration to your sensor

Within these sections, the explanation initially focuses on the eight separate configuration screens that you use to modify the configuration of your sensors. Understanding the sensor features that you can change with each configuration screen gives you a thorough understanding of the configuration options available to you. It also enables you to readily view the current configuration settings for your sensors.

Then the focus shifts to some practical configuration changes that you need to perform while setting up and operating your Cisco Secure IDS. The practical configuration changes involve items such as the following:

- Defining your internal networks
- Altering sensor identification parameters
- Setting up logging
- Specifying additional alarm destinations
- Configuring IP fragment reassembly
- Configuring TCP stream reassembly

CSPM Sensor Configuration Screens

When altering the configuration of your sensors through CSPM, you first make a change to the configuration on the screen. Next, you need to update the information in the CSPM database and then push that updated information to your sensor.

Access to your sensor's configuration is available through eight separate configuration screens that appear after you select a sensor from the Network Topology tree (see Figure 11-1):

- Properties
- Sensing (This chapter discusses the unique screens for both the Intrusion Detection System Module, IDSM, Sensor, and the 4200 Series Sensor.)
- Blocking
- Filtering
- Logging
- Advanced
- Command
- Control

Figure 11-1 *Sensor Properties Configuration Screen*

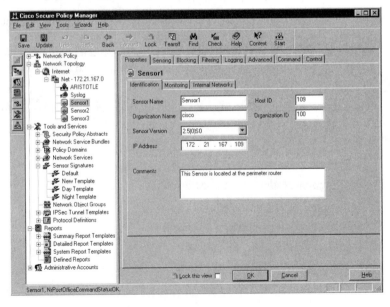

Each of these configuration tabs enables you to alter a different aspect of your sensor's configuration.

Properties Configuration Screen

The Properties tab enables you to alter some basic properties of your sensor (see Figure 11-1). These properties fall into three basic categories:

- Identification
- Monitoring
- Internal networks

Identification Parameters

The Identification tab under the Properties configuration screen enables you to change the basic PostOffice protocol parameters for your sensor (refer back to Figure 11-1). To receive alarms on your CSPM host from your sensors, the PostOffice communication protocol between your CSPM host and sensor must be operating correctly. For the PostOffice protocol to work, the identification parameters must be configured the same on both your sensor and CSPM host (refer to Appendix I, "Cisco Secure Communications Deployment Worksheet"). The configurable parameters under the Identification tab are as follows:

- Host name
- Organization name
- Host ID
- Organization ID
- Sensor version
- IP address
- Comments

Correctly configuring these parameters is vital for successful communication between your sensor and your CSPM host. For detailed descriptions of these identification fields, see Chapter 7, "4200 Series Sensor Installation Within CSPM."

Monitoring Parameters

The Monitoring tab under the Properties configuration screen provides you with an interface to configure multiple SYSLOG data sources (see Figure 11-2). Each SYSLOG data source defines a device that supplies your sensor with SYSLOG event information. A SYSLOG data source is defined by the following:

- IP address
- Subnet mask

Figure 11-2 *Sensor Monitoring Configuration Screen*

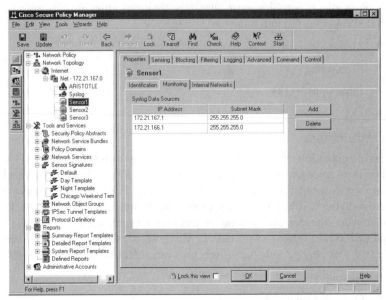

Policy Violation Signatures

To use the policy violation signatures (10000 Series), you need to configure SYSLOG data sources. The policy violation signatures trigger when a packet attempts to violate a defined access control list (ACL) on one of your routers. This triggers an event to SYSLOG on the router. If your sensor is not monitoring these SYSLOG events, it cannot detect that a policy violation occurred.

Internal Networks Configuration

You use the Internal Networks tab under the Properties configuration screen to configure which networks represent your internal networks (see Figure 11-3).

When your sensors generate alarm events, the events include two location fields:

- Source
- Destination

Figure 11-3 *Sensor Internal Networks Configuration Screen*

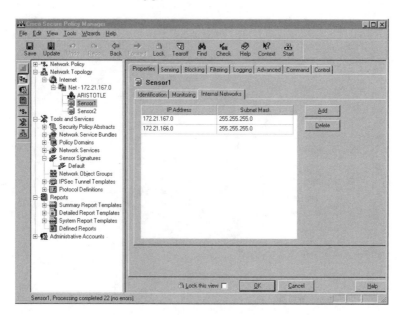

The configuration of your internal networks impacts the value of these two location fields. Each location field can assume one of two values: IN or OUT.

The determination of IN or OUT is based on the networks that you define using the Internal Networks tab. If an IP address is located within one of your internal networks, the location value is IN. Otherwise, the value of the location field is OUT.

4200 Series Sensing Configuration Screen

The Sensing configuration tab shows you the current settings for how your sensor monitors network traffic (see Figure 11-4). The way in which your 4200 Series Sensor monitors network traffic is defined by the following parameters:

- Active Configuration
- Packet Capture Device
- Advanced Sensor Settings

Figure 11-4 *4200 Series Sensor Sensing Configuration Screen*

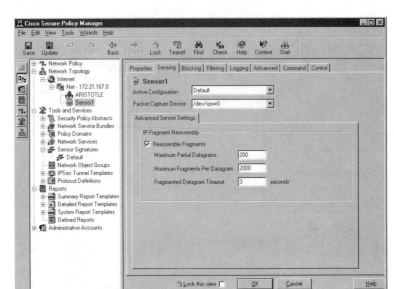

Active Configuration

The Active Configuration field indicates the current configuration that your sensor uses to generate alarm events. This configuration defines the signatures that your sensor actively checks for while observing traffic on your network. Each signature also has an associated severity that defines the potential seriousness of the signature when detected on your network. You can build multiple configurations for different operational needs, such as one for normal working hours and one for after hours. These active configurations are known as *templates* and are explained in Chapter 12, "Signature and Intrusion Detection Configuration."

Packet Capture Device

The Packet Capture Device field indicates the interface on your sensor that examines network traffic. This interface represents the eyes of your sensor. All network traffic is examined through this interface. The name of this interface also indicates the type of network that the sensor monitors (see Table 11-1).

Table 11-1   *Packet Capture Devices*

Packet Capture Device	Description
/dev/spwr0	Use with 4220-E and 4230-FE Sensors.
/dev/mtok	Use with 4220-TR Sensors with NICs not labeled 100/16/4.
/dev/mtok36	Use with 4220-TR Sensors with NICs labeled 100/16/4.
/dev/ptpci0	Use with 4230-SFDDI and 4230-DFDDI Sensors.
/dev/iprb0	Use with 4210 Sensors.

Advanced Sensor Settings

The final section on the 4200 Series Sensor Sensing configuration screen determines how your sensor handles fragmented data packets. Many attackers attempt to obfuscate their attacks by sending their attacks in a stream of *fragmented data*.

Fragmented Data

A network has a limit on the size of network packets that it transports. The maximum size is known as the *maximum transmission unit (MTU)*. If a computer wants to send a packet that is larger than the MTU, it must break the packet up into multiple Ethernet frames. These frames are sent to the destination host, which then reconstructs the fragments into the original packet.

Some attackers might fragment packets that are smaller than the MTU in an attempt to bypass your IDS. At other times, they use overlapping fragments in an attempt to achieve the same goal. With fragments that overlap, the order in which the packets are reassembled affects the reconstructed contents of the data packet. Depending on how your IDS performs fragment reconstruction, intrusive traffic can potentially slip by undetected.

If you enable IP fragment reassembly, your sensor reassembles fragmented IP packets before they are compared against intrusion signatures. In other words, you can improve the capability of your sensor to rebuild incomplete IP packets before it checks for intrusive activity. The drawback is that reconstruction consumes memory and processing power.

The Advanced Sensor Settings area under the Sensing screen dictates the manner in which your sensor deals with fragmented IP data packets. You can configure whether your sensor processes fragmented data by checking or clearing the Reassemble Fragments check box (see Figure 11-4). Furthermore, after you turn on processing for fragmented packets, you can configure the following IP fragment reassembly parameters:

- Maximum Partial Datagrams
- Maximum Fragments Per Datagram
- Fragmented Datagram Timeout

The Maximum Partial Datagrams defines the maximum number of partial datagrams that your sensor tracks. A partial datagram is a fragmented datagram that still has missing fragments or pieces. Essentially, this parameter defines how many separate packets that the sensor attempts to reconstruct at one time.

The Maximum Fragments Per Datagram defines the maximum number of fragments that your sensor tracks for a specific datagram. Normal fragmented packets have a limited number of fragments. By limiting the maximum number of fragments per datagram, you help limit the impact of an attacker who floods your network with a never-ending stream of fragments.

The Fragmented Datagram Timeout specifies the maximum length of time that can elapse between fragments. If this value is set too high, valuable sensor memory is taken up waiting on fragments that might never arrive. This parameter enables your sensor to free up resources in a timely manner when an attacker floods your network with a random stream of IP fragments. Without a reasonable timeout value, maintaining state on these random fragments quickly consumes all the sensor's memory.

WARNING   The reassembly settings work in conjunction with each other to ensure that the sensor has adequate system resources available to analyze network traffic. Unless you understand your network traffic thoroughly, including the likelihood of fragmented datagrams occurring over a specified period of time, you should not modify the default values. The supplied values for these settings are configured to optimize the utilization of network resources on your sensor.

IDSM Sensing Configuration Screen

Currently, the IDSM Sensor has different sensing capabilities compared to the 4200 Series Sensor. This is apparent from the IDSM Sensing Configuration screen (see Figure 11-5).

With the IDSM Sensor, the following configuration tabs are on the Sensing configuration screen:

- Advanced Sensor Settings
- Signature Tuning Parameters
- Port Mapping

Figure 11-5 *IDSM Sensing Configuration Screen*

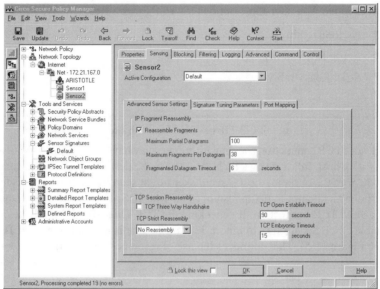

Advanced Sensor Settings

The Advanced Sensor Settings screen enables you to control your reassembly options and active configuration. This includes both IP Fragment Reassembly and TCP Session Reassembly.

TCP Session Reassembly

A TCP session is composed of numerous packets that are ordered by sequence numbers. However, these packets do not always traverse the network in order. If your IDS checks for attacks in a TCP session without reassembling the packets based on their sequence numbers, attacks can be missed if the packets arrive out of sequence.

The control over IP Fragment Reassembly and Active Configuration for the IDSM Sensor involves the same settings and parameters as the 4200 Series Sensor. These topics are explained previously in this chapter.

Unlike the 4200 Series Sensor, however, the IDSM Sensor also supports TCP Session Reassembly. Like IP fragment reassembly, TCP Session Reassembly reconstructs data stream packets before they are compared against intrusion signatures. These settings ensure that valuable system resources are not wasted maintaining state for sessions that are no longer active. You have three options for TCP Stream Reassembly:

- No Reassembly
- Loose Reassembly
- Strict Reassembly

TCP Three-Way Handshake Check Box

All valid TCP connections begin with a three-way handshake composed of a SYN from the initiating host, followed by a SYN-ACK from the destination host, and concluding with an ACK from the initiating host. An attacker might send traffic that appears to be valid TCP traffic in an attempt to tie up resources on your IDS. This bogus traffic is not usually part of a valid TCP connection. By checking the TCP Three-Way Handshake check box, you enable Cisco Secure IDS to ignore TCP traffic that is not part of a valid TCP connection (see Figure 11-5). This optimizes the use of resources on your IDS.

No Reassembly immediately processes packets in the order that they arrive at the sensor. No attempt is made to place the packets in the correct order based on sequence numbers. This option is not recommended because it can lead to false positives, as well as false negatives.

False Positives and Negatives

False positives are alarms generated based on normal user activity, whereas *false negatives* are situations when your IDS fails to trigger a signature when actual intrusive activity is present. False negatives are severe because you have no indication that the intrusive activity was not detected.

Loose Reassembly attempts to reconstruct a TCP stream, but it allows for gaps in the sequence number stream. Your sensor queues the packets for each TCP stream and then periodically processes groups of packets looking for intrusive activity. When the processing occurs, any missing packets represent gaps in the TCP stream. These gaps can lead to false positives. However, the packets that are available for reconstruction are assembled in the correct order based on their sequence numbers.

Strict Reassembly does not allow any missing packets in a TCP session. If the sensor misses a single packet from a TCP session, it starts queuing packets waiting on the missing packet. Eventually, the TCP session exceeds a timeout value for the session and the sensor removes it. At that point, your sensor no longer checks for intrusive activity against traffic for the deleted session.

Of the three options, Loose Reassembly is probably the most optimum choice. No Reassembly can easily miss attacks because all packets are examined based on their arrival time, not their sequence number. Strict Reassembly prevents examination of sessions that have any missing packets, therefore completely missing any intrusive activity in those sessions. With Loose Reassembly, received packets are examined in their sequence number order, but missing packets do not prevent the analysis of the packets that are received.

Signature Tuning Parameters

Specific signatures for the IDSM Sensor have one or two configurable parameters (see Figure 11-6). By using these parameters, you can determine how often you are notified of a particular attack. These tuning parameters are based on how often an attack occurs and the length of time that transpired since the attack was initially detected. For more information on tuning signatures for IDSM, refer to Chapter 12.

Port Mapping Settings

Many of the attacks that your sensors detect are based on examining traffic to specific TCP ports. These port numbers represent the ports used by standard services when they are initially installed on your network. Sometimes, however, you might want to check for intrusive activity on other ports than the standard ones. Therefore, the IDSM Sensor enables you to add custom ports for certain advanced attack signatures. This feature is called *port mapping* and you can access it by clicking on the Port Mapping tab (refer back to Figure 11-5).

Clicking the Port Mapping tab brings up the Port Mapping configuration screen (see Figure 11-7).

The Port Mapping configuration screen enables you to configure the TCP ports that are examined for the following advanced signatures:

- TCP hijack signatures
- TCP SYN-Flood signatures
- Telnet signatures
- HTTP (Web) signatures

Figure 11-6 *Signature Tuning Parameters Screen*

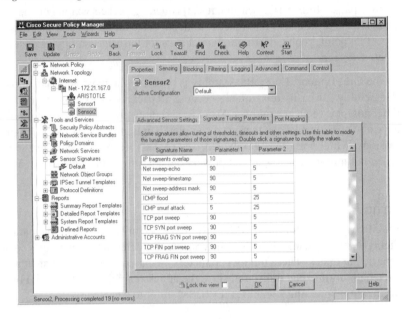

Figure 11-7 *Port Mapping Configuration Screen*

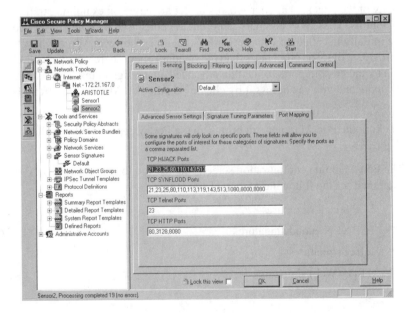

For example, the default HTTP ports are 80, 3128, and 8080. This means that you sensor checks for HTTP attack signatures on all those ports. Suppose that you run your HTTP servers on port 9400. By default, your sensor is not going to check for known HTTP attacks against your HTTP servers. If you add 9400 to the HTTP Ports text box (see Figure 11-7), however, your sensor knows that it also needs to examine traffic going to port 9400 when checking for HTTP attacks.

This was an overview of port mapping. For more detailed information concerning port mapping, refer to Chapter 12.

Blocking Configuration Screen

Only the 4200 Series Sensor supports blocking. Therefore, none of the blocking configuration options are available on your IDSM Sensors. Clicking the Blocking tab for an IDSM Sensor brings up a screen that states that blocking is currently not supported. In future releases of the IDSM software, this will probably be supported (see Chapter 18, "Planned Cisco Secure IDS Enhancements").

The Blocking configuration tab controls the blocking parameters that your sensor uses to block traffic from specific hosts because of intrusive activity detected on your network (see Figure 11-8). The Block Duration defines the length of time (in minutes) that a host is blocked after a blocking signature fires. Furthermore, three subconfiguration tabs enable you to completely define the role of blocking in your Cisco Secure IDS environment. (For detailed information on using blocking on your network, refer to Chapter 13, "IP Blocking Configurations.")

- Never Block Addresses
- Blocking Devices
- Master Blocking Sensor

WARNING   If you choose to implement blocking as a component of your overall Cisco Secure IDS security plan, you need to implement it carefully. Failure to exercise caution can enable an attacker to use your own IDS blocking to disrupt the operation of your network. By generating spoofed network traffic, an attacker can fool your IDS into blocking traffic from key components on your network (such as your CSPM host, your sensors, and other critical network resources).

Figure 11-8 *Sensor Blocking Configuration Screen*

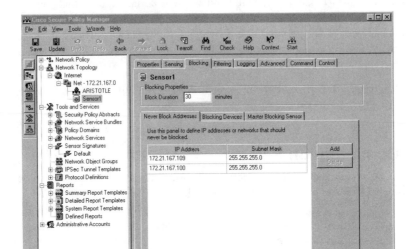

Never Block Addresses

To prevent your Cisco Secure IDS from disrupting the operation of your IDS, you might want to configure the key components of your IDS (CSPM host, Cisco Secure IDS Sensors, and so on) as Never Block Addresses (see Figure 11-8). This prevents your sensors from blocking these hosts. An attacker might spoof traffic so that it appears to originate from your key IDS components in an attempt to make it appear as if those devices are attacking your network. If you do not have those devices configured as Never Block Addresses and you have blocking enabled, your Cisco Secure IDS can see this bogus traffic and attempt to block the operational components of your IDS. If your sensor blocks traffic from your CSPM host, for example, you no longer can receive alarm events on your CSPM host.

NOTE   You might want to define other key components on your network, and possibly critical hosts on your partner's networks, as Never Block Addresses to prevent your sensors from blocking these systems. Otherwise, an attacker might attempt to use your own IDS to generate an effective denial of service attack against these resources that are vital to the operation of your network.

Blocking Devices

Use the Blocking Devices tab under the Blocking configuration screen to configure the devices that you use to perform the actual blocking of network traffic. ACLs on these devices actually restrict the flow of traffic on your network. To update these ACLs, your sensor needs to automatically log on to your blocking devices. For your sensor to automatically update these ACLs, you must supply the information necessary for your sensors to log on to your blocking devices (see Figure 11-9). These required fields include the following:

- Telnet IP Address
- Telnet Username
- Telnet Password
- Enable Password
- Blocking Interface

Figure 11-9 *Sensor Blocking Devices Configuration Screen*

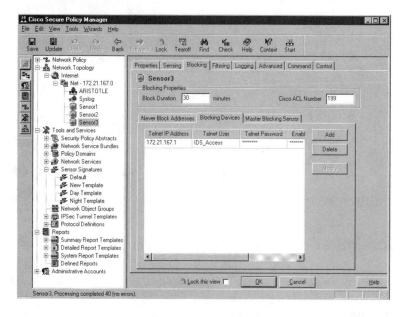

Your sensor uses these values to establish a Telnet session with the blocking device. Then it updates the ACL configuration on the device to block the necessary IP addresses. Your sensor also needs to log on to the device to remove the blocking after the blocking duration has expired. For detailed information on blocking devices, refer to Chapter 13.

Master Blocking Sensor

Depending on your network topology, you might have multiple entry points into your networks. When one of your sensors initiates a blocking event, it prevents the intrusive traffic from entering your network at specific entry points. To accomplish this on routers that are controlled by other sensors, however, you need to define a *master blocking sensor* (see Figure 11-10). The master blocking sensor essentially commands other sensors to initiate blocking actions whenever it initiates a blocking action. By commanding another sensor to initiate the action, it prevents multiple sensors from attempting to modify the same device simultaneously. The master blocking sensor is explained in detail in Chapter 13.

Figure 11-10 *Master Blocking Sensor Configuration Screen*

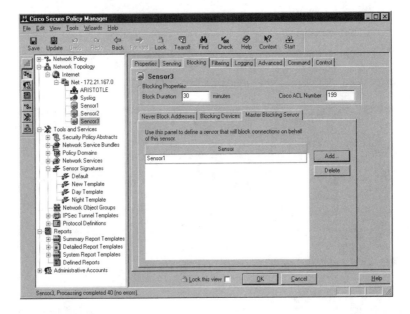

Filtering Configuration Screen

After examining the traffic on your network, you might determine that certain signatures routinely generate false positives. You can use the Filtering configuration tab to define the filtering rules necessary to customize the response of your IDS to these specific signatures (see Figure 11-11). By altering your filtering rules, you can prevent these known signatures from generating false positives on your CSPM console by excluding these alarms from specific hosts throughout your network. (For detailed filtering examples, see Chapter 12.) Filtering is broken into three sections:

- Minimum event level
- Simple Filtering
- Advanced Filtering

Figure 11-11 *Sensor Filtering Configuration Screen*

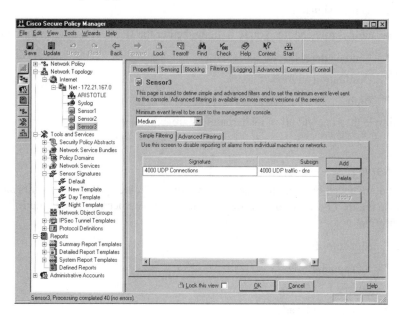

Minimum Event Level

The minimum event level defines the lowest alarm severity that the Cisco Secure IDS Sensor forwards to the Director platform. By filtering alarms below a specified severity level, you can reduce the amount of alarm traffic on your CSPM host. Therefore, instead of spending valuable resources examining minor alarm traffic, you can spend your time with more serious issues.

Simple Filtering

The Simple Filtering tab enables you to filter or disable specific signatures from each of your sensors (see Figure 11-11). To filter a specific signature, click the Add button and supply the following information:

- Signature ID
- Subsignature ID
- IP address
- Subnet mask
- Address role

The signature and subsignature IDs identify the alarm that you want to exclude.

The IP address and subnet mask define the host that you want to exclude from triggering the specified signature.

The address role enables you to define whether the IP address applies to the following:

- Source address
- Destination address
- Both

Simple filtering and all of its parameters are explained in detail in Chapter 12.

Advanced Filtering

The Advanced Filtering tab also enables you to disable specific signatures on your sensors (see Figure 11-12). To filter a specific signature, you need to supply the following information:

- Signature ID
- Subsignature ID
- Source IP address
- Destination IP address

The main difference between using simple filtering and advanced filtering is that advanced filtering enables you to specify both the source and destination addresses. This provides you with a finer degree of control over the filtering process. (Refer to Chapter 12 for more information on using advanced filtering.)

Logging Configuration Screen

On the Logging configuration tab, you can enable and control data management on your sensors (see Figure 11-13). Although you might not want to see all events on your CSPM host, a complete history of alarm events (including low-severity alarms) often proves useful after an attack. By enabling logging on your sensors, you can log more events than you want to display on your Director platform. Then, you can always refer to these log files whenever necessary. (More information on logging is provided later in this chapter.) If you want your sensor to automatically archive your log files on another host, you need to supply the following values:

- Target FTP server
- Username
- Password

Periodically, your sensor logs on to the target FTP server by using the supplied username and password. It then transfers the log files to the FTP server for archiving.

Figure 11-12 *Sensor Advanced Filtering Configuration Screen*

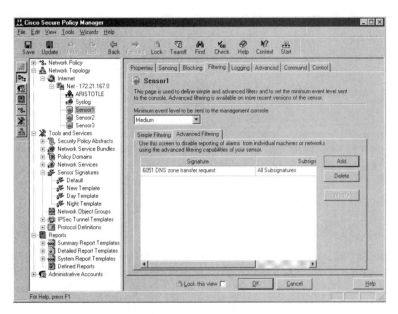

Figure 11-13 *Sensor Logging Configuration Screen*

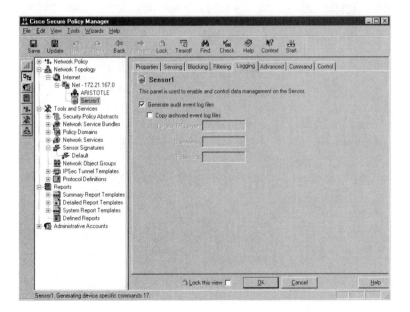

Advanced Configuration Screen

The Advanced configuration tab provides you access with some miscellaneous advanced configuration values that you can change for your sensors (see Figure 11-14). These parameters are broken down into two separate subconfiguration tabs:

- PostOffice Settings
- Additional Destinations

WARNING   You rarely need to change these parameters. Furthermore, altering these parameters incorrectly can disrupt the operation of your Cisco Secure IDS. Therefore, manipulate these values with caution.

PostOffice Settings

You can configure various advanced PostOffice features to help you customize communications in your environment. You can access these PostOffice settings by clicking the Advanced configuration tab and then clicking the Postoffice Settings subtab (see Figure 11-14).

Figure 11-14   *Sensor Advanced Configuration Screen*

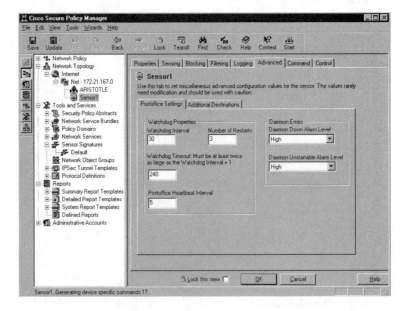

The Watchdog feature in PostOffice queries the services running on the local host, Cisco Secure IDS Sensor, or Director platform to ensure that they are running. If Watchdog detects a service that is not running, it issues a Daemon Down alarm and it tries to restart the service. After it tries to restart the service a configurable number of times, it then issues a Daemon Unstartable alarm.

The PostOffice Heartbeat feature queries other PostOffice services on remote hosts, Cisco Secure IDS Sensor, or Director platform with which it must communicate. If the local PostOffice service does not get a response from a remote PostOffice service, it issues a Route Down alarm.

You can configure the following advanced PostOffice features:

- **Watchdog Interval**—Specifies how often Watchdog queries the local services that need to be running. The default is 30 seconds.

- **Watchdog Timeout**—Specifies how long Watchdog waits for a response from a queried service. If this time is exceeded, a Daemon Down alarm is issued, and PostOffice tries to restart the service. This value must be at least two times greater than the value specified in the Watchdog Interval box. The default is 240 seconds.

- **Number of Restarts**—Specifies the number of times that PostOffice attempts to restart a downed service. If this value is exceeded, a Daemon Unstartable alarm is issued. The default is 3 restarts for the 4200 Series Sensors and 0 for the IDSM. Currently, the daemons running on IDSM cannot be restarted easily; therefore, the default is 0 so that a restart is not even attempted.

- **Daemon Down Alarm Level**—Specifies the alarm level that PostOffice generates when a queried service fails to respond to the Watchdog query. You can specify one of the following values: High (default), Medium, or Low.

- **Daemon Unstartable Alarm Level**—Specifies the alarm level that PostOffice generates when it fails to restart a downed service the number of times identified in the Number of Restarts box. You can specify one of the following values: High (default), Medium, or Low.

- **PostOffice Heartbeat Interval**—Specifies how often PostOffice queries a remote PostOffice with which it needs to be communicating. If PostOffice does not receive a response, it issues a Route Down alarm. The default is 5 seconds.

Additional Destinations

Through the Additional Destinations configuration tab on the Advanced configuration screen, you can configure your sensor to forward alarm events to multiple destinations (see Figure 11-15). These destinations can be services on other hosts or other services on the sensor itself. When configuring an additional destination, you must click the Add button and then specify the following parameters:

- Sensor name
- Organization name
- Organization ID
- Sensor ID
- Service name
- Minimum event level
- IP address
- Heartbeat timeout
- Port

Figure 11-15 *Additional Destinations Configuration Screen*

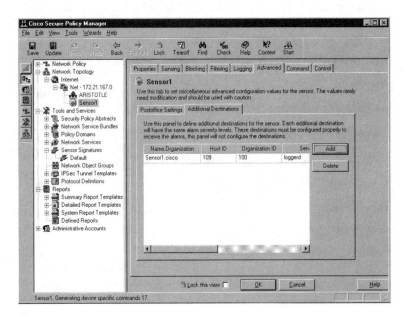

Command Screen

The Command configuration tab enables you to update the configuration files on your sensors (see Figure 11-16). Whenever configuration changes on your CSPM host affect your sensor's configuration, you must push the new configuration file(s) to your sensor by using the **Approve Now** button. The Command configuration screen has the following buttons that you can use to manipulate your sensor's configuration files:

- Approve Now
- Refresh
- Poll
- File Import and File Export

Approve Now

The **Approve Now** button initiates the transfer of updated configuration files to your sensor. Whenever updated configuration files are available to be pushed down to your sensor, the **Approve Now** button is solid and not grayed out. If the configuration in your CSPM database matches the configuration on your sensor, the **Approve Now** button is grayed out, indicating that no new configuration data needs to be transferred to the sensor.

Figure 11-16 *Sensor Command Configuration Screen*

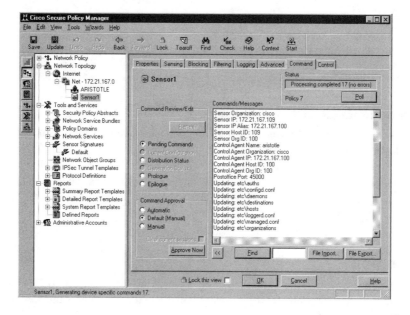

Refresh

The **Refresh** button enables you to check the status of the sensor configuration file update. Initially, the **Refresh** button is grayed out, indicating that the current status information is displayed on the screen. When new status information is available, the **Refresh** button is no longer grayed out. At that point, you can click the **Refresh** button to display the latest status information on the screen. During a configuration update, the **Refresh** button remains grayed out until the update has completed.

In conjunction with the **Refresh** button, you have several option check boxes:

- Pending Commands
- Current Configuration
- Distribution Status
- Generation Status
- Prologue
- Epilogue

When you click the **Refresh** button, you see the status for the associated option check box that you selected. With your sensors, the only two check boxes that are currently used are Pending Commands and Distribution Status. Pending Commands enables you to check on the status of pushing a new configuration to the sensor, whereas Distribution Status shows the names of the actual configuration files that are transferred.

Poll

You can click the **Poll** button to determine the status of your sensor. The window above the **Poll** button indicates the current status of communication with your sensor.

File Import and File Export

The **File Import** button enables you to read in a list of commands from a file and then send those commands to the device for execution. The **File Export** button is just the reverse process in that it saves the commands from the screen into a file on your hard disk. Devices such as firewalls are more suited to these types of operations. Therefore, these buttons are not currently used to configure your Cisco Secure IDS Sensors. For more information on this capability, refer to the *CSPM Configuration Guide*.

Control Screen

The final sensor configuration tab is the Control tab (see Figure 11-17). Through the Control configuration screen, you can manipulate the parameters that define policy enforcement with respect to your sensor.

Policy enforcement involves updating signature information on your sensors. These parameters are divided into four main sections:

- General Settings
- Authentication
- Policy Distribution
- Logging

Figure 11-17 *Sensor Control Configuration Screen*

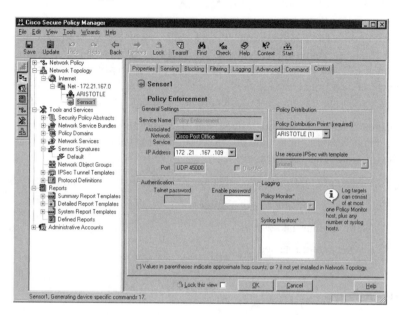

From the Control screen, however, you are currently only able to define the policy distribution point and the mechanism by which it communicates with your sensor. The other parameters are not currently used for Cisco Secure IDS Sensors. (For more information on how the other parameters are used with other devices, refer to the *CSPM Configuration Guide*.)

Policy Distribution Point

The *policy distribution point* identifies the host that disperses policy information. The role of the policy distribution point is critical to the operation of your security system. It defines a single entity that generates and distributes commands to your policy enforcement points within your network. A thorough explanation of the policy distribution point is beyond the scope of this book, but more information can be obtained from the *CSPM Configuration Guide*.

Basically, your CSPM host updates the configuration on your sensor, so it is your policy distribution point. Furthermore, it communicates with your sensor by using the Cisco PostOffice protocol.

Basic Configuration Changes

During the initial configuration (running **sysconfig-sensor**) of your sensors, you specify most of the basic configuration values to build a working sensor (see Chapter 7 for more information). You also must use the same values when you add the sensor to your CSPM database. These values remain fairly static on most networks. As your network evolves, however, you might need to modify these parameters. Therefore, it is useful to understand how to configure your sensor's identification parameters and packet capture device.

One parameter not defined during the initial configuration is your internal networks. You definitely need to understand how to configure this parameter because it is used to define the location fields for alarm events.

The basic configuration options that are addressed in this section are as follows:

- Changing identification parameters
- Defining internal networks
- Packet capture device

Identification Parameters

When you first added your sensor node to CSPM by using the Add Sensor Wizard (see Chapter 7 for more information on this wizard), you defined various identification settings. The PostOffice protocol uses these parameters to communicate between your Cisco Secure IDS Sensor and CSPM host. Although these settings do not change frequently, you might need to alter the values as your network topology changes. Therefore, CSPM enables you to alter these identification parameters as required. You can change these basic identification settings:

- Host name
- Organization name
- Host ID
- Organization ID
- Sensor version
- IP address
- Comments

For detailed descriptions of these identification fields, see Chapter 7.

To change the identification settings for one of your sensors through CSPM, perform the following steps:

Step 1 Select the sensor.

Step 2 Access the identification data.

Step 3   Alter and save the identification data.

Step 4   Push the new configuration to the sensor.

Before you can change the sensor's identification parameters, you must highlight the sensor in the Network Topology tree. The Network Topology tree is located in the left window of the main CSPM screen (see Figure 11-18). To select a sensor, click the appropriate sensor's name.

After you select the correct sensor, CSPM displays a sensor configuration window on the right of your CSPM screen (refer back to Figure 11-1). You can then access the identification data by clicking the **Properties** configuration tab.

Next, you need to update the necessary identification fields. After you make all of your changes, click the **OK** button to save your changes (refer back to Figure 11-1). If you do not want to save your updates, click the **Cancel** button.

Finally, you need to update the configuration files on your sensor. Refer to the "Pushing a New Configuration to Your Sensor" section later in this chapter for details on how to update the configuration files on your sensor.

Figure 11-18 *Main CSPM Screen*

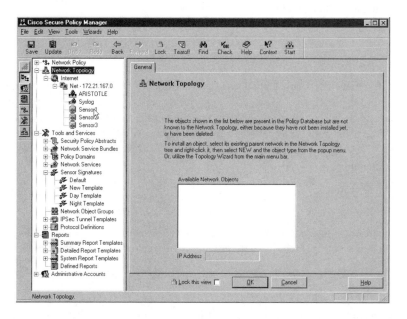

NOTE   Before changing the communications parameters for the sensor through CSPM, you must first change them on the sensor itself by using **sysconfig-sensor**. Failure to do this prevents your sensor from communicating with your CSPM host by using the PostOffice communication protocol.

Internal Networks

You can designate that your sensor treats specific network IP addresses as internal for reporting and logging purposes. IP addresses that do not match the internal network definitions are considered to be external IP addresses. When alarms are generated by the sensor, the location of the source and destination IP addresses of the attack are logged as either internal (IN) or external (OUT) to help you easily identify the origin and destination of the attack with respect to your network.

NOTE   The internal network definition does not affect the intrusion detection capabilities of the sensor. If no internal network entries are added, the sensor logs all alarms as outside (OUT) to outside (OUT) attacks.

Adding an Internal Network

To designate a network as internal, you must add it to your sensor's configuration. The first step in this process is to select the appropriate sensor from the Network Topology tree by clicking the sensor name. Next, you must select the Properties configuration tab. Finally, you must select the Internal Networks configuration tab from the Properties configuration screen (refer back to Figure 11-3). Each internal network entry is identified by two parameters:

- IP Address
- Subnet Mask

To add a new internal network entry, click the Add button (refer back to Figure 11-3). This action inserts a new internal network entry with the following properties (see Figure 11-19):

- IP Address: 0.0.0.0
- Subnet Mask: 255.255.255.0

You need to enter the correct values for these two fields and then click the OK button to save the new internal network entry. Finally, you need to update the configuration files on your sensor. Refer to the "Pushing a New Configuration to Your Sensor" section later in this chapter for details on how to update the configuration files on your sensor.

Figure 11-19 *Adding a New Internal Network*

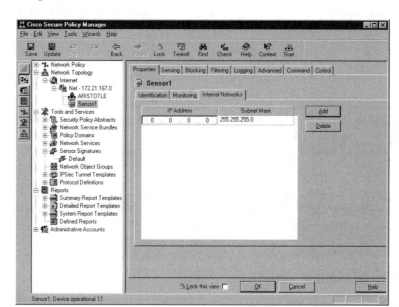

Deleting an Internal Network

To delete an internal network entry, you must remove it from your sensor's configuration. The first step in this process is to select the appropriate sensor from the Network Topology tree by clicking the sensor name. Next, you must select the **Properties** configuration tab. Finally, you must select the Internal Networks configuration tab from the Properties configuration screen (refer back to Figure 11-3). Each internal network entry is listed onscreen.

Select the internal network that you want to delete by clicking the IP address. Then you can delete the highlighted internal network entry by clicking the **Delete** button. Next, you must click the **OK** button to save your changes.

Finally, you need to update the configuration files on your sensor. Refer to the "Pushing a New Configuration to Your Sensor" section later in this chapter for details on how to update the configuration files on your sensor.

Packet Capture Device

The *packet capture device* identifies the device name of the monitoring interface on your Cisco Secure IDS Sensor. The first step in changing the packet capture device is to select the appropriate sensor from the Network Topology tree by clicking the sensor name. Next, you must select the **Sensing** configuration tab (refer back to Figure 11-4).

At this point, you change the value of the packet capture device by selecting the correct device name from the Packet Capture Device pull-down menu. Table 11-1 describes the various acceptable packet capture devices.

After selecting the correct packet capture device name, click the **OK** button to save your changes.

NOTE   The packet capture device applies only to the 4200 Series Sensors. The IDSM does not have a packet capture device because it is tied directly into your switch's backplane.

Finally, you need to update the configuration files on your sensor. Refer to the "Pushing a New Configuration to Your Sensor" section later in this chapter for details on how to update the configuration files on your sensor.

Log File Configuration

This section discusses how to configure your sensor to generate log files locally and how to configure the sensor to automatically transfer these log files to an FTP server. Specifically, this section discusses the following:

- Enabling sensor generation of log files
- Configuring automatic log file transfer

Enabling Sensor Generation of Log Files

Cisco Secure IDS Sensors can be configured to generate a log file locally on the sensor. By default, the sensors are configured to send alarms of severity of medium and higher to CSPM. When logging to a local log file, however, you can specify a different minimum severity level. Therefore, you can log more alarms by specifying a lower minimum severity. This expanded set of alarm information usually proves helpful if you experience an attack on your network but does not clutter up your CSPM event viewer.

The sensor creates a new log file every time its services are restarted. This means that every time a new configuration is pushed to the sensor, a new configuration file is created and the old log file is closed and transferred to a temporary directory. A new log file also is created whenever the active one has been opened for more than one hour or it has reached 1 GB of data.

The sensor log file has the properties shown in Table 11-2. (Refer to Appendix D, "Cisco Secure IDS Log Files," for a detailed explanation of Cisco Secure IDS Log Files.)

Table 11-2 *Sensor Log File Properties*

Property	Setting
File Name	log.YYYYMMDDHHMM
	where:
	YYYY = 4-digit year
	MM = 2-digit month
	DD = 2-digit day
	HH = 2-digit hour
	MM = 2-digit minutes
Active Log File Location	/usr/nr/var
Closed Log File Location	/usr/nr/var/new

To enable your sensor to generate a local log file, you first must select the appropriate sensor from the Network Topology tree by clicking the sensor name (refer back to Figure 11-18). Next, you must select the **Logging** configuration tab (refer back to Figure 11-13).

To turn on logging on your sensor, check the Generate audit event log files option on the Logging screen. Then click the **OK** button to save your changes.

Finally, you need to update the configuration files on your sensor. Refer to the "Pushing a New Configuration to Your Sensor" section later in this chapter for details on how to update the configuration files on your sensor.

Configuring Automatic Log File Transfer

You also can configure the sensor to automatically perform an FTP transfer of closed local log files to a designated FTP server. The FTP transfer is triggered when the file is closed and moved to the /usr/nr/new directory on the sensor.

The first thing you must do to set up this automatic transfer is select the appropriate sensor from the Network Topology tree by clicking the sensor name (refer back to Figure 11-18). Next, you must select the **Logging** configuration tab (refer back to Figure 11-13).

If logging is not turned on, check the Generate audit event log files option on the Logging screen to turn on logging on your sensor. Then check the **Copy archived event log files** option and fill out the following fields:

- Target FTP Server
- Username
- Password

The Target FTP Server field identifies the IP address of the system to which you want to send the log files. The Username and Password fields provide the account information necessary for your sensor to log on to the target FTP server.

After you have made all of your changes, click **OK** to save those changes. Finally, you need to update the configuration files on your sensor. Refer to the "Pushing a New Configuration to Your Sensor" section later in this chapter for details on how to update the configuration files on your sensor.

Advanced Configuration Changes

This section discusses how to configure the advanced configuration options on the sensor:

- IP fragment reassembly
- TCP session reassembly
- Additional destinations

NOTE   IP fragment reassembly is currently available in the 2.2.1.5, 2.5(X), and 2.5(X) IDSM software versions.

IP Fragment Reassembly

You can specify that your sensor reassemble fragmented IP packets before they are compared against intrusion signatures. In other words, you can specify the extent to which the sensor attempts to reconstruct a single datagram from multiple network frames before checking for intrusive activity. This reconstruction, however, consumes memory and processing power.

The ultimate goal for defining the reassembly settings is to ensure that the sensor does not allocate all its resources to datagrams that cannot be completely reconstructed, either because some frame transmissions are missing or because an attacker is intentionally generating random fragmented datagrams.

WARNING   The reassembly settings work in conjunction with each other to ensure that the sensor has adequate system resources available to analyze network traffic. Unless you understand your network traffic thoroughly, including the potential frequency of fragmented datagrams, you do not need to modify the default values provided for these settings.

To configure your sensor to perform IP fragment reassembly, select the appropriate sensor from the Network Topology tree by clicking the sensor name (refer back to Figure 11-18). Then select the **Sensing** configuration tab (refer back to Figure 11-4).

To turn on IP fragment reassembly on your sensor, check the **Reassemble Fragments** check box in the IP Fragment Reassembly section of the Sensing screen (refer back to Figure 11-4).

IP fragment reassembly is controlled by three parameters:

- Maximum Partial Datagrams
- Maximum Fragments Per Datagram
- Fragmented Datagram Timeout

Table 11-3 defines these parameters.

Table 11-3   *Parameters for IP Fragment Assembly*

Parameter	Description
Maximum Partial Datagrams	Maximum number of partial datagrams that the sensor can attempt to reconstruct at any given time
Maximum Fragments Per Datagram	Maximum number of fragments that can be accepted for a single datagram
Fragmented Datagram Timeout	Maximum number of seconds that can transpire before the sensor stops tracking a particular exchange for which it is trying to reassemble a datagram

The recommended guidelines for determining the maximum partial datagrams (MPD) and the maximum fragments per datagram (MFPD) are as follows:

- For 4200 Series Sensors running the 2.2.1.5 or 2.5(X) software versions, MPD multiplied by MFPD should be less than 2,000,000.
- For Catalyst 6000 IDS modules running the 2.5(X) IDSM software version, MPD multiplied by MFPD should be less than 5,000.

After you have entered all your changes, click the OK button to accept the changes. This also closes the sensor window.

Finally, you need to update the configuration files on your sensor. Refer to the "Pushing a New Configuration to Your Sensor" section later in this chapter for details on how to update the configuration files on your sensor.

Understanding TCP Session Reassembly

You can specify that the sensor reassembles TCP data stream packets before they are compared against intrusion signatures. Like the IP fragment reassembly settings, these settings ensure that valuable system resources are not needlessly reserved for sessions that are no longer active.

NOTE TCP session reassembly is currently available only in the 2.5(X) IDSM software version.

You can choose three options for TCP session reassembly, as discussed in the following sections.

No Reassembly

Do not perform TCP session reassembly. The sensor immediately processes all packets in a stream. This option is recommended only in environments with high packet loss. The drawback of this option is that it permits out-of-order processing, which can lead to false positives and false negatives.

Loose Reassembly

The sensor permits sequence gaps when it attempts to reassemble all packets into a composite session record. This option can lead to false positives because the session record is incomplete. This option does ensure that the packets are reassembled in order.

Strict Reassembly

The sensor does not process TCP sessions for which it cannot track every packet in the session's sequence. In other words, if a single packet of a stream is dropped, the sensor does not analyze any packets belonging to that session.

NOTE In addition to the TCP session reassembly options, you can configure your sensor to track only those sessions for which the three-way handshake is completed. Furthermore, the TCP open established timeout and TCP embryonic timeout values can also be configured.

Configuring TCP Session Reassembly

To configure the sensor to perform TCP session reassembly, select the appropriate sensor from the Network Topology tree by clicking the sensor name (refer back to Figure 11-18). Then select the **Sensing** configuration tab (refer back to Figure 11-5).

Select the **TCP Three-Way Handshake** box in the TCP Session Reassembly section of the Sensing configuration screen if you want the sensor to track only those sessions for which the three-way handshake is completed. Next, you must choose your TCP Session Reassembly method from the drop-down menu.

Finally, you need to define values for the following:

- TCP Open Establish Timeout
- TCP Embryonic Timeout

Table 11-4 defines these two fields.

Table 11-4   *Defined Values for TCP Session Reassembly*

Option	Description
TCP Open Establish Timeout	Specifies the number of seconds that can transpire before the sensor frees the resources allocated to a fully established TCP session. Default is 90 seconds. Range is 1 to 120 seconds. (It is recommended that this value not be set below 30 seconds.)
TCP Embryonic Timeout	Specifies the number of seconds that can transpire before the sensor frees the resources allocated for an initiated, but not fully established, TCP session. Default is 15 seconds. Range is 0 to 15 seconds.

Now that you entered all your changes, click on the OK button to save your changes. For your sensor to recognize your changes, you need to update the configuration files on your sensor. Refer to the "Pushing a New Configuration to Your Sensor" section later in this chapter for details on how to update the configuration files on your sensor.

Additional Destinations

The sensor can be configured to send its alarms to other locations other than the main Director platform to which it is reporting. These additional destinations can be services on other Directors or Cisco Secure IDS Sensors, as well as services within the sensor itself.

The first step in configuring an additional destination is to select the sensor from the Network Topology tree (refer back to Figure 11-18). This brings up the CSPM configuration information for your sensor. Clicking the **Advanced** tab brings up the Advanced configuration screen (refer back to Figure 11-14). By clicking the **Additional Destinations** tab, you gain access to the Additional Destinations configuration screen (refer back to Figure 11-15). Each additional destination occupies a single line on the screen.

To add an additional destination, click the **Add** button. This opens a new entry on the screen. You must fill in the fields, as described in Table 11-5. You also can delete an additional destination by highlighting an entry and clicking the **Delete** button.

Table 11-5 *Required Fields for Additional Alarm Destinations*

Field	Description
Name.Organization	The PostOffice host name and organization name of the additional destination host.
	The format for this setting must be Hostname.OrgName. Use a dot between the host name and the organization name, for example, **aristotle.cisco**.
Host ID	The PostOffice host ID of the additional destination host.
Organization ID	The PostOffice organization ID of the additional destination host.
Service	Identifies the additional destination Director or sensor service. You can specify one of the following services to which to send the alarms:
	smid (default)—Use this service when you want to send the alarms to other Directors to be displayed in the Event Viewer.
	eventd—Use this service when you want to execute user-defined scripts. This service is supported only in Directors for UNIX or the 4200 Series Sensors. eventd itself is not configurable from CSPM.
	loggerd—Use this service when you want to log the alarms locally on the host to which you are sending the alarms.
IP Address	The IP address of the additional destination host.

Pushing a New Configuration to Your Sensor

Whenever you make changes to your CSPM host, you must transfer your changes to the actual Cisco Secure IDS Sensor for them to take effect. The process to push updated configuration information to your sensor involves the following steps:

Step 1 Save and update your CSPM configuration.

Step 2 Update the sensor configuration.

Step 3 Check the sensor configuration update.

NOTE   If you have your sensor configured for automatic command approval, you do not need to manually transfer the new configuration data to the sensor. After you click the **Update** button, your new configuration changes are automatically transferred to your sensor as part of the update process.

Save and Update Your CSPM Configuration

After making changes to your CSPM configuration, you need to save the new configuration in the CSPM database. Then, you need to generate new configuration files for your sensors. The Update button on the main CSPM screen enables you to perform both of these operations (refer back to Figure 11-17). It writes changed information into the CSPM database and then builds new configuration files that you can then use to update your sensors.

Updating Sensor Configuration

After building new sensor configuration files by using the **Update** button, you need to transfer these new configuration files to your actual Cisco Secure IDS Sensors. The first step in updating the configuration on your sensor is to access the sensor's information by clicking the sensor in the Network Topology tree (refer back to Figure 11-18).

This accesses the CSPM information for the selected Cisco Secure IDS Sensor; then click the Command tab to bring up the Command screen (refer back to Figure 11-16). The **Approve Now** button needs to be solid, indicating that new configuration files need to transfer to your sensor. Clicking the **Approve Now** button initiates the transfer of the updated configuration information to the sensor.

Checking Sensor Configuration Update

While the configuration information is being transferred to your sensor, the **Refresh** button is grayed out (refer back to Figure 11-16). This indicates that no new information exists for command and message windows. When the sensor's configuration update is complete, the **Refresh** button is no longer grayed out. At this point, you can click the **Refresh** button to check the status of the configuration update. The commands/messages window now displays the status of the configuration update.

Summary

Your CSPM software enables you to configure numerous parameters on your Cisco Secure IDS Sensors. When you select one of your sensors in the Network Topology tree, you have eight separate tabs to view and change information with respect to your sensor's configuration. These eight tabs provide you with access to the following configuration screens:

- Properties
- Sensing
- Blocking
- Filtering

- Logging
- Advanced
- Command
- Control

Each of the screens enables you to configure a different aspect of your sensor's configuration. Some of the main features that you can configure through the CSPM interface are as follows:

- Sensor identification parameters
- IP fragment reassembly parameters
- TCP session reassembly parameters (IDSM only)
- Sensor logging parameters
- Blocking devices (4200 Series only)
- SYSLOG data sources

After changing any of your sensor's configuration parameters, you need to transfer this new information to your Cisco Secure IDS Sensor for the changes to become active. The first step is to save the changes into the CSPM database; then you need to create updated configuration files for your sensor. The Update button enables you to perform both of these operations.

Finally, you need to transfer the updated configuration files to your sensor. To transfer the new configuration data to your sensor, select the Command screen for your sensor and click the Approve Now button. This transfers the updated configuration files to the sensor.

Review Questions

The following questions test your retention of the material presented in this chapter. The answers to the Review Questions are in Appendix K, "Answers to Review Questions."

1 What is IP fragment reassembly?

_____

_____

_____

2 Which Cisco Secure IDS Sensors support TCP session reassembly?

_____

_____

_____

3 What is the Watchdog process?

_____

_____

_____

4 What are the eight major configuration tabs that you use to configure your sensor parameters?

_____

_____

_____

5 Where do you configure the TCP stream reassembly parameters?

_____

_____

_____

6 Where do you configure the advanced PostOffice parameters?

_____

_____

_____

7 Which screen enables you to transfer updated configuration files to your sensor?

_____

_____

_____

8 What are the advanced PostOffice parameters?

_____

_____

_____

9 What are the three options for TCP stream reassembly?

_____

_____

_____

10 What is the TCP Embryonic Timeout?

_____

_____

_____

11 What are the main feature differences between the 4200 Series Sensor and the IDSM Sensor?

_____

_____

_____

12 What is the function of the Additional Destinations feature?

_____

_____

_____

13 What does the Maximum Partial Datagrams field regulate?

_____

_____

_____

14 What is the PostOffice Heartbeat Interval?

_____

_____

_____

Signature and Intrusion Detection Configuration

To obtain the optimum performance from your Cisco Secure IDS, you need to correctly configure its sensors with respect to your operational environment. One of the major areas that you need to concentrate on is the signature templates that the different sensors use to analyze network traffic. Creating and applying customized signature templates is essential to achieving the peak capability from your Cisco Secure IDS. By using signature templates, you can alter various signature parameters, such as the following:

- Enabling or disabling signatures
- Defining signature severity
- Setting signature actions
- Modifying connection signature configurations
- Modifying string signature configurations
- Modifying ACL signature configurations

Minimizing traffic on your CSPM Director is also addressed to help you understand how to reduce the amount of alarm traffic forwarded to CSPM from your Cisco Secure IDS Sensors. Limiting the traffic to CSPM enables you to focus on the more serious threats to your network, as well as limiting the number of false positives that you need to examine.

The structure of this chapter divides into the following major topics:

- Basic signature configuration
- Signature templates
- Signature filtering
- Advanced signature configuration
- Creating ACL signatures

NOTE   Signature templates are supported only for CSPM. If you use the Cisco Secure Intrusion Detection Director (CSIDD), refer to Chapter 16, "The Configuration Management Utility (nrConfigure)" for configuration in that environment.

Basic Signature Configuration

CSPM enables you to configure multiple signature templates for use on your Cisco Secure IDS Sensors. To view a signature template, you need to select the signature template. In the left window on the main CSPM screen, you see a Sensor Signatures section. This section is under the Tools and Services heading (see Figure 12-1). Under this section, the names of all the sensor templates that you currently defined appear. The Default signature template is created automatically by CSPM and includes the signatures detected by all known Cisco Secure IDS versions.

Figure 12-1 *Sensor Signatures Screen*

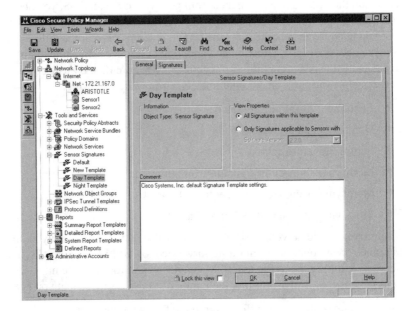

The Sensor Signatures screen provides two configuration tabs (see Figure 12-1):

- General
- Signatures

After you become familiar with these tabs in the following sections, the text covers signature settings and related configurations.

General Tab

The **General** tab displays the name and description of the template. Also included on this screen is a View Properties section. This section enables you to configure the signatures that you can see and configure when you view the template. You have two options from which to select:

- All Cisco Secure IDS Signatures
- Signatures applicable to specific sensor software versions

By default, the **All Signatures within this template** check box is selected. If you want to limit the viewable signatures to those associated with a specific sensor software version only, click the **Only Signatures applicable to Sensors with** check box. Furthermore, you must then specify the software version that you are using.

NOTE   All templates contain all the signatures up to the latest Cisco Secure IDS Sensor software version that CSPM knows about. Only the signatures that are appropriate for a specific sensor software version are actually sent to the sensor when the signature template is applied to the sensor. By clicking the **Only Signatures applicable to Sensors with** check box, you can limit the display within the CSPM signature template to only the signatures that apply to your sensor's software version.

Signatures Tab

Selecting the Signatures tab displays the Cisco Secure IDS signatures associated with this template (see Figure 12-2). Listing all the signatures on a single screen makes it difficult for you to locate signatures. Therefore, to facilitate access to specific signatures, you can view signatures in blocks based on four signature classes:

- General
- Connection
- String
- ACL

Besides improving access, by dividing the signatures into separate classes, each class can have slightly different configuration parameters. Each signature class has a basic set of configurable parameters, as well as class-specific characteristics for each individual signature. Therefore, to configure a specific signature's properties, you must first select the appropriate class. If you need to configure a connection signature, for example, you first must select the Connection Signatures subtab. Then, scroll down to the appropriate connection signature and make your changes.

Figure 12-2 *Sensor Signature Configuration Screen*

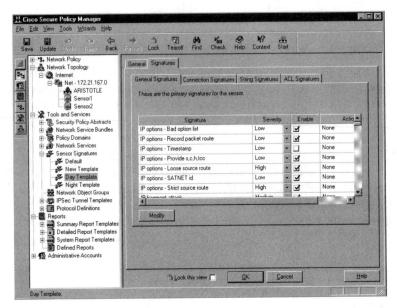

Viewing the Signature Settings

Each Cisco Secure IDS signature has three basic configurable properties. These properties are explained in the following sections:

- Defining Signature Severity
- Enabling and Disabling Signatures
- Setting Signature Actions

NOTE   Some Cisco Secure IDS signatures have more settings based on the signature class. For example, connection signatures also have Port and Protocol fields in addition to the basic properties.

Defining Signature Severity

Cisco Network Security Engineers predefine a default severity for each signature. However, you can change the severity for any of the signatures in your template. By clicking the **Severity** drop-down list, you can assign a severity value from Table 12.1.

Table 12-1   *Available Severity Values*

Severity Name	Default Severity Value
Low	1
Medium	3
High	5

To change the signature severity for one of the signatures in your signature template, follow these steps:

Step 1   Select a Signature template by clicking its name in the Sensor Signatures section of the main CSPM screen (refer back to Figure 12-1).

Step 2   Select the **Signatures** tab (refer back to Figure 12-2).

Step 3   Select the appropriate signature class by clicking the correct subtab: **General**, **Connection**, **String**, or **ACL**.

NOTE   If you are uncertain as to which class the signature is in, refer to Chapter 9, "Understanding Cisco Secure IDS Signatures," which provides a detailed explanation of the various signatures and which classes they fall into.

Step 4   Scroll down to the signature that you want to configure using the vertical scroll bars on the right of the Signatures tab screen.

Step 5   Choose the severity level from the **Severity** drop-down menu (see Figure 12-3).

Step 6   Click **OK** in the Sensor view panel.

Step 7   Click **Update** on the toolbar.

Step 8   Apply the updated configuration to the sensor (see the "Applying the Signature Template to the Sensor" section later in this chapter).

Enabling and Disabling Signatures

For each signature in your template, you can choose whether the signature is enabled or disabled. To optimize the performance of your sensors, you can choose to disable certain signatures to reduce the processing load on your sensors. This can also reduce the workload on your security analyst. By default, some signatures are already disabled, such as TCP connections (ID 3000) to various ports. Simple TCP connections to ports occur normally with regular user traffic. Therefore, having these signatures enabled adds unnecessary processing unless you have a specific operational need to trigger on these events—not to mention the time spent by your security analyst who must analyze all the alarms triggered by Cisco Secure IDS.

Figure 12-3 *Setting Signature Severity*

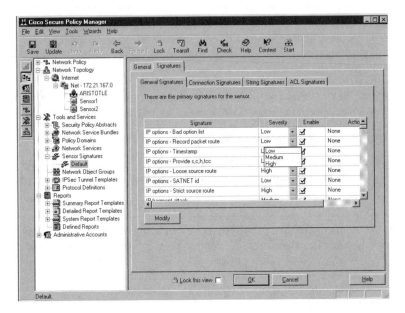

You also might want to temporarily disable a specific signature because it is generating false positives. Although you are debugging while the signature is triggering on normal user traffic, you probably do not want the false positives popping up on your Director platform.

The **Enable** check box for a signature controls whether the signature is enabled or disabled (refer back to Figure 12-2). To enable or disable a signature, follow these steps:

Step 1   Select a signature template by clicking its name in the Sensor Signatures section of the main CSPM screen (refer back to Figure 12-1).

Step 2   Select the **Signatures** tab (refer back to Figure 12-2).

Step 3   Select the appropriate signature class by clicking the correct subtab: **General Signatures**, **Connection Signatures**, **String Signatures**, or **ACL Signatures**.

NOTE   If you are uncertain as to which class the signature is in, refer to Chapter 10 for a detailed explanation of the various signatures and which classes they fall into.

Step 4   Scroll down to the signature that you want to configure using the vertical scroll bars on the right of the Signatures tab screen.

Step 5   Select the **Enable** check box to enable or deselect the **Enable** check box to disable the signature (refer back to Figure 12-2).

Step 6   Click **OK** in the Sensor view panel.

Step 7   Click **Update** on the toolbar.

Step 8   Apply the updated configuration to the sensor (see "Applying the Signature Template to the Sensor" section later in this chapter).

Setting Signature Actions

Every time that a signature triggers on one of your Cisco Secure IDS Sensors, the sensor generates an alarm event and potentially forwards the alarm information to your Director if the severity matches your defined minimum severity for alarms on your Director. Besides generating this alarm event, you also can configure your sensor to take some action when a signature triggers. CSPM enables you to individually define the signature actions in Table 12.2 for each of the signatures in your signature template.

Table 12-2   *Available Sensor Signature Actions*

Action	Description
None	No action is taken.
Block	Generates an IOS ACL to stop the attack to the host.
TCP reset	Sends a TCP reset to terminate the connection from the attacking host.
IP log	Creates a log session of IP traffic after the initial detection occurs. IP log files are stored on the sensor in /usr/nr/var/iplog directory.

NOTE   When changing the action for a signature, all the possible actions might not be valid for the signature. For example, TCP reset is not valid for UDP signatures. Any invalid actions appear grayed out in the Signature Action dialog box to indicate that you cannot select them for the currently selected signature.

To configure the actions taken by your sensor when a signature triggers, follow these steps:

Step 1   Select a Signature template by clicking its name in the Sensor Signatures section of the main CSPM screen (refer back to Figure 12-1).

Step 2   Select the **Signatures** tab (refer back to Figure 12-2).

Step 3 Select the appropriate signature class by clicking the correct subtab: **General Signatures**, **Connection Signatures**, **String Signatures**, or **ACL Signatures**.

Step 4 Scroll down to the signature that you want to configure using the vertical scroll bars on the right of the Signatures tab screen.

Step 5 Double-clicking the **Actions** field for the signature that you want to change open the Signature Actions pop-up window (see Figure 12-4).

Step 6 Select the actions to take (see Figure 12-4).

Step 7 Click **OK** in the Signature Actions window.

Step 8 Click **OK** in the Sensor view panel.

Step 9 Click **Update** on the toolbar.

Step 10 Apply the updated configuration to the sensor (see "Applying the Signature Template to the Sensor" section later in this chapter).

Figure 12-4 *Setting Signature Action*

NOTE   You also can change the action settings by clicking the **Modify** button. Using the **Modify** button is the same as double-clicking the signature Action field. It brings up the same Signature Actions pop-up window.

Connection Signature Type and Port Configuration

The connection signatures (as the name implies) detect TCP connections and network traffic to UDP ports. Connection signatures have two additional parameters that you can configure:

- **Type**—IP protocol type (TCP or UDP)
- **Port**—IANA port number associated with a network service

The **Type** field is used to specify the IP Protocol associated with the connection. You have two transport protocols to pick from: TCP and UDP. TCP is a reliable connection-oriented transport protocol. UDP is a connectionless transport mechanism that does not guarantee delivery of datagrams.

The **Port** parameter identifies the port number associated with the service. The Internet Assigned Numbers Authority (IANA) assigns port numbers to specific network services. By assigning standard port numbers to network services, it makes it easier to locate these network programs on an operational network.

Assigned Port Numbers

The IANA has published numerous Request For Comments (RFCs) outlining the mapping of network services to port numbers. The RFCs are titled, "Assigned Numbers," with the current standard being RFC 1700.

The default signature list includes numerous connection signatures for various network services. The Signature ID distinguishes whether connection signatures are TCP or UDP. The signature ID is 3000 for TCP connection signatures and 4000 for UDP connection signatures. Next, the subsignature ID is used to indicate the port or network service to which the signature is associated. (Refer to Appendix G, "Cisco Secure IDS Signatures and Recommended Alarm Levels," to see the list of defined TCP and UDP connection signatures.)

Adding a Connection Signature

Although numerous connection signatures are already available, you might need to add new connection signatures to support specific network services on your operational network. You also need to add connection signatures if you want to monitor connections to network services on nonstandard ports.

NOTE   If your sensor platform supports port mapping, you also can use this to have certain specific signatures trigger when the monitored service is on a nonstandard port. Refer to the "Signature Port Mapping" section later in this chapter.

To add a new connection signature, follow these steps:

Step 1   Select a Signature template by clicking its name in the Sensor Signatures section of the main CSPM screen (refer back to Figure 12-1).

Step 2   Select the **Signatures** tab (refer back to Figure 12-2).

Step 3   Select the **Connection Signatures** subtab (see Figure 12-5).

Step 4   Click the **Add** button. This adds a new signature entry.

Step 5 Enter a description of the new signature in the Signature text box.

Step 6 Choose the protocol type (TCP or UDP) of the port from the **Type** drop-down menu.

Step 7 Select the **Port** field and enter the numeric value of the port.

Step 8 Configure the basic signature parameters discussed previously in this chapter.

Step 9 Click **OK** in the Sensor view panel.

Step 10 Click **Update** on the toolbar.

Step 11 Apply the updated configuration to the sensor (see the "Applying the Signature Template to the Sensor" section later in this chapter).

Figure 12-5 *Connection Signatures Configuration*

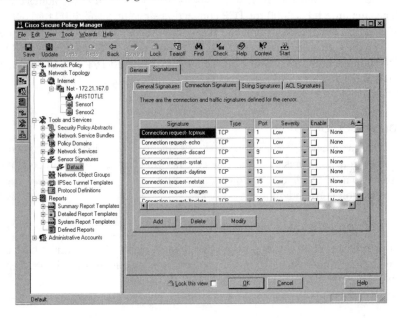

Modifying a Connection Signature

To alter the characteristics of a connection signature, follow these steps:

Step 1 Select a Signature template by clicking its name in the Sensor Signatures section of the main CSPM screen (refer to Figure 12-1).

Step 2 Select the **Signatures** tab (refer back to Figure 12-2).

Step 3 Select the **Connection Signatures** subtab.

Step 4   Scroll down to the signature that you want to configure using the vertical scroll bars on the right of the Signatures tab.

Step 5   To change the signature actions, double-click the **Actions** field for the signature that you want to change. This displays the Signature Actions pop-up window where you can change the actions for the specific signature.

Step 6   Choose the protocol type (TCP or UDP) of the port from the **Type** drop-down menu.

Step 7   Select the **Port** field and enter the numeric value of the port.

Step 8   Configure the basic signature parameters discussed previously in this chapter.

Step 9   Click **OK** in the Sensor view panel.

Step 10   Click **Update** on the toolbar.

Step 11   Apply the updated configuration to the sensor (see the "Applying the Signature Template to the Sensor" section later in this chapter).

String Signatures Configuration

String signatures trigger when a specific text pattern is observed in network traffic going to or from certain TCP network ports. In addition to the basic signature properties, string signatures have the changeable parameters listed in Table 12.3.

Table 12-3   *Changeable Parameters for String Signatures*

Setting	Value
String	The specific characters Cisco Secure IDS is to detect. Cisco Secure IDS uses a regular expression matching algorithm.
Port	The number of the TCP service where you want to search for the string.
Direction	From—Cisco Secure IDS searches for the specific string when it leaves the specified port. The port is the source.
	To—Cisco Secure IDS searches for the specific string when it enters the specified port. The port is the destination.
	To & From—Cisco Secure IDS searches for the specific string when it enters or leaves the specific port.
Occurrences	This setting determines how many times the string has to appear before an alarm is generated.

All the string signatures have a Signature ID of 8000. The subsignature ID defines the various string signatures. Several string signatures are defined by default. (Refer to Appendix G for a list of the default string signatures).

To create a new string subsignature with CSPM, follow these steps:

Step 1   Select a Signature template by clicking its name in the Sensor Signatures section of the main CSPM screen (refer back to Figure 12-1).

Step 2   Select the **Signatures** tab (refer back to Figure 12-2).

Step 3   Select the **String Signatures** subtab (see Figure 12-6).

Step 4   Click **Add**. A new string subsignature entry is created.

Step 5   Enter the string you want detected in the **String** text box.

Step 6   Select the **Port** field and enter the TCP port number. The default is 21.

Step 7   Choose the direction from the **Direction** drop-down menu. The default is To.

Step 8   Enter the number of occurrences the string needs to appear. The default is 1.

Step 9   Choose the severity from the **Severity** drop-down menu. The default is High.

Step 10 To select the signature actions, double-click in the **Actions** field. The Signature Actions pop-up window appears, and you can select the actions that you want taken for the new string signature. (Figure 12-4 shows the Signature Actions pop-up window.) The default is for no actions to be taken for the new string signature.

Step 11 Click **OK** in the Sensor view panel.

Step 12 Click **Update** on the toolbar.

Step 13 Apply the updated configuration to the sensor (see the "Applying the Signature Template to the Sensor" section later in this chapter).

Figure 12-6 *String Signature Configuration*

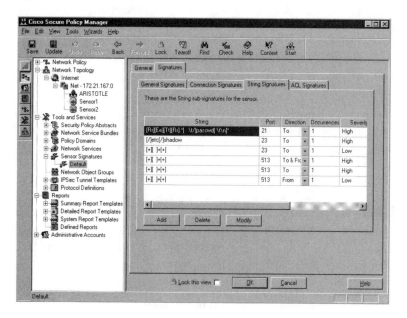

Signature Templates

Understanding signature templates is crucial to configuring your sensors to efficiently
monitor the traffic in your operational environment. This section discusses the following:

- What is a signature template?
- Creating new signature templates
- Assigning the signature template used by the sensor
- Applying the signature template to the sensor

What Is a Signature Template?

CSPM uses templates to enforce security policies on your network devices. Signature
templates enable you to easily manage, assign, and apply signatures to your sensors. By
default, CSPM creates a default signature template that contains all known Cisco Secure
IDS signatures and their settings.

You can create various different signature templates and apply them to your sensors as necessary. For example, you can create a signature template named *Business Hours* with signature settings that are optimized for the high-peak network traffic that occurs during normal business hours. You also can create a signature template named *After Hours* with signature settings optimized for network traffic that occurs after 7 p.m. Because the *After Hours* template has a reduced traffic load, you can scrutinize your network traffic more closely.

After creating these two templates, you can easily assign and apply the *Business Hours* template to your sensors during high-peak hours. Furthermore, after 7 p.m., you can then easily change the configuration of your sensors by assigning and applying the *After Hours* template.

Creating New Signature Templates

CSPM enables you to create signature templates that you can then assign and apply to your sensors. The newly created template is a duplicate of the default template. You can then modify the template, configuring the signature settings for your specific network environment.

To create a new CSPM signature template, follow these steps:

Step 1   Right-click **Sensor Signatures** (see Figure 12-7).

Step 2   Choose **New, Sensor Signature** (see Figure 12-7).

Step 3   Rename the new signature template by typing in a more meaningful name than the default of Sensor Signature 1.

Step 4   Click **Save** on the main CSPM toolbar.

NOTE   CSPM defaults to naming the new template **Sensor Signature 1**. You need to rename the template to reflect its purpose. If a template is created for all sensors at your Chicago office, for example, you might want to name it Chicago Sensors. Initially, you can rename the new signature template by just typing in another name (while Sensor Signature 1 is highlighted). If you accidentally accept the default name, or you need to change the name of previously created signature template, you can right-click the template name and select **Rename** (see Figure 12-8).

Figure 12-7 *Creating a New Signature Template*

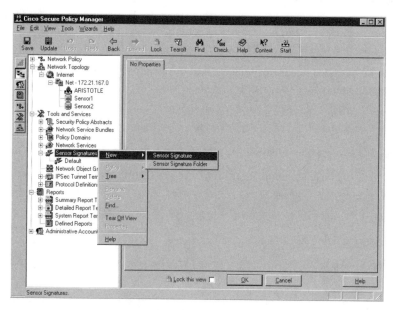

Figure 12-8 *Renaming a Signature Template*

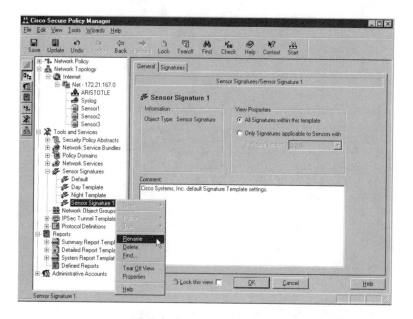

Assigning the Signature Template Used by the Sensor

You must assign each sensor a signature template. This template defines the signatures that the sensor uses to search for intrusive activity on your network. Initially, CSPM assigns the default signature template to your sensors as you add them.

To change the signature template that your sensor uses, you need to assign a different signature template. To do so, follow these steps:

Step 1 Select the sensor from the Network Topology tree (NTT) by clicking the name of the sensor that you want to change.

Step 2 Select the **Sensing** tab in the Sensor view panel.

Step 3 Choose the template from the **Active Configuration** drop-down menu (see Figure 12-9).

Step 4 Click **OK** in the Sensor view panel.

Step 5 Click **Update** on the toolbar.

Step 6 Apply the signature template to the sensor (see the following section).

Figure 12-9 *Assigning a Signature Template*

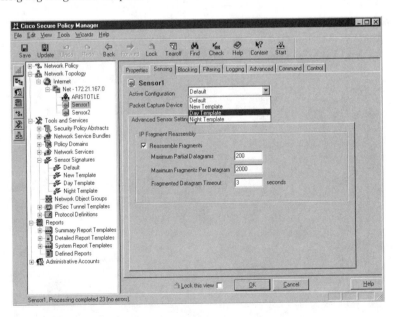

Applying the Signature Template to the Sensor

Cisco Secure IDS configuration files generated by CSPM are not pushed to a sensor until they are applied. The configuration files generated include sensor settings and signature settings associated with the sensor's assigned signature template. These configuration files are generated when you click the Update **button** on the main CSPM toolbar.

To push the updated configuration files to your sensor (including a new signature template), follow these steps:

Step 1   Select the sensor from the NTT by clicking the name of the sensor on which you want to update the configuration files.

Step 2   Select the **Command** tab in the Sensor view panel (see Figure 12-10).

Step 3   Click the **Approve Now** button in the Command Approval section. Wait for the configuration files to be downloaded to the sensor. When the download is complete, you can click the **Refresh** button to refresh the Commands/Messages window. This window indicates the success of the transfer of configuration files to your sensor.

Figure 12-10   *Sensor Command Window*

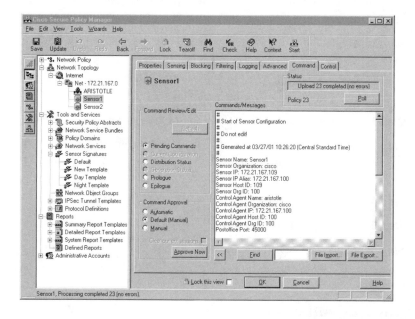

NOTE   You must update the configuration files on your sensor each time a configuration change is made to either the sensor settings or signature settings. You can perform numerous configuration changes, however, before you update the configuration files on your sensor.

Signature Filtering

Signature filtering enables you to exclude certain hosts from triggering specific signatures. You also can use filtering to define the minimum severity required for an alarm to be forwarded to the CSPM Director. This section is divided into three parts that discuss the following:

- Setting the minimum level to send to the Director
- Simple signature filtering
- Advanced signature filtering

Setting the Minimum Level to Send to the Director

CSPM enables you to configure the minimum event level that is sent from a sensor to the Director. This feature can help reduce the number of alarms CSPM has to log and display. By reducing the alarms sent to your Director, you can concentrate your resources on investigating the intrusive traffic that represents the most significant threat to your network.

To configure the minimum event level that the sensor sends to the Director, follow these steps:

Step 1   Select the sensor from the NTT by clicking the name of the sensor on which you want to set the minimum event level.

Step 2   Select the **Filtering** tab in the Sensor view panel.

Step 3   Choose the severity level from the Minimum event level to be sent to the management console through the **Minimum event list to be sent to the management console** drop-down menu (see Figure 12-11).

Step 4   Click **OK** in the Sensor view panel.

Step 5   Click **Update** on the toolbar.

Step 6   Apply the updated configuration to the sensor (see the "Applying the Signature Template to the Sensor" section in this chapter).

Simple Signature Filtering

CSPM enables you to perform simple and advanced signature filtering (see Figure 12-12). Simple signature filtering excludes signatures based on a source or destination IP address or network.

Figure 12-11   *Setting Minimum Severity Level*

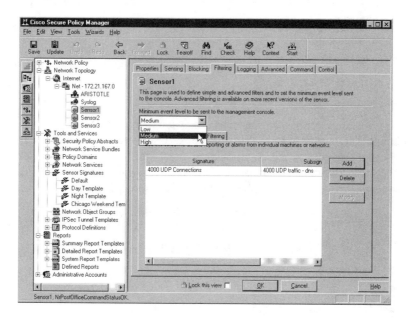

Figure 12-12   *Sensor Filtering Configuration Screen*

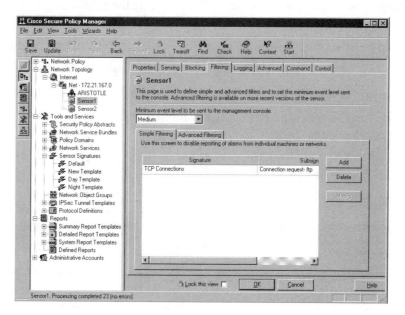

When defining a simple filter, you need to configure the following fields:

- Signature
- Subsignature
- IP Address
- Network Mask
- Address Role

The signature identifies the alarm that you want to exclude. You pick this entry from the **Choose a signature to be excluded** list box. Associated with a signature is a subsignature indicator. This entry is chosen by picking an entry from the Subsignature to be excluded list box. Some signatures do not have a subsignature, and in that case, you need to choose **All Subsignatures** from the **Subsignature to be excluded** list box.

The IP address and network mask indicate the address that is excluded by your filter, and the address role determines whether this address is applied to the source or destination address. The possible values for the address role are as follows:

- Destination address
- Source address
- Source or destination address

To create a simple signature filter, follow these steps:

Step 1 Select the sensor from the NTT by clicking the name of the sensor for which you want to create a simple signature filter.

Step 2 Select the **Filtering** tab in the Sensor view panel (see Figure 12-12).

Step 3 Select the **Simple Filtering** subtab. (This is selected by default.)

Step 4 Click **Add**. The Create Filter pop-up window opens (see Figure 12-13).

Step 5 Choose the signature to exclude from the **Choose a signature to be excluded** list box.

Step 6 Choose the subsignature to exclude from the **Subsignature to be excluded** list box.

NOTE You must select a subsignature for each signature that you are filtering. If the signature does not have any subsignature options, you need to select All Subsignatures as your subsignature.

Step 7 Enter the **IP address** in the IP Address field.

Step 8 Enter the network mask in the **Network Mask** field.

Step 9 From the Create Filter pop-up window, select the address role (see Figure 12-14).

Step 10 Click **OK** in the Create Filter pop-up window.

Step 11 Click **OK** in the Sensor view panel.

Step 12 Click **Update** on the toolbar.

Step 13 Apply the updated configuration to the sensor (see the "Applying the Signature Template to the Sensor" section in this chapter).

Figure 12-13 *Simple Create Filter Pop-Up Window*

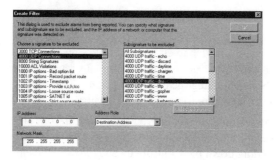

Figure 12-14 *Setting Filter Address Role*

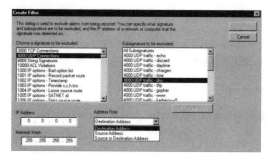

Advanced Signature Filtering

The advanced signature filtering feature section provides you greater flexibility when excluding signatures. Unlike simple signature filtering, advanced signature filtering can exclude signatures based on the different values for the source and destination addresses of the connection. Furthermore, you can include multiple signatures in a single filter.

NOTE	To specify an internal or external IP address, an internal network must be defined.

When defining an advanced signature filter, you need to configure the following fields:

- Signature
- Subsignature
- Source Address
- Destination Address

In the Signature field, you need to identify the alarm(s) that you want to exclude. You pick your entries from the **Choose one or more signatures to be excluded** list box.

Selecting Multiple Signatures

You have two ways in which to choose multiple signatures in an advanced filter. After clicking a signature, you can include a contiguous range of signatures by holding down the Shift key before clicking the ending signature. This selects all the signatures from the originally chosen signature to the current signature.

If the signatures are not contiguous, you can select multiple signatures by holding down the Control key before selecting your signatures. You also can remove entries that are already selected by holding down the Control key and clicking the entry.

Associated with each signature is a subsignature indicator. This entry is chosen by picking an entry from the **Choose one or more subsignatures** list box. Some signatures do not have a subsignature. In such a case, you must choose All Subsignatures from the **Choose one or more subsignatures** list box. If you choose multiple signatures to be excluded in a single filter, you need to select All Subsignatures from the **Choose one or more subsignatures** list box.

The source and destination addresses determine which network traffic the filter excludes. Your choices, which can be different for the source and destination addresses, are as follows:

- Any IP address
- Any internal or external IP address
- A single IP address
- A range of IP addresses
- An IP network

To create an advanced filter, follow these steps:

Step 1 Select the sensor from the NTT by clicking the name of the sensor for which you want to create an advanced signature filter.

Step 2 Select the **Filtering** tab.

Step 3 Select the **Advanced Filtering** subtab (see Figure 12-15).

Step 4 Click **Add**. The Create Filter pop-up window opens (see Figure 12-16).

Step 5 From the Create Filter pop-up window, choose one or more signatures to exclude from the **Choose one or more signatures to be excluded** list box.

Step 6 Choose the subsignature to exclude from the **Choose one or more subsignatures** list box.

NOTE You must select a subsignature for each signature that you are filtering. If the signature does not have any subsignature options, select **All subsignatures** as your subsignature.

Step 7 From the Create Filter pop-up window, select an exclude option from the **Source Address** group box.

Step 8 From the Create Filter pop-up window, select an exclude option from the **Destination Address** group box.

NOTE You might need to enter a start address and end address or just a single address depending on the options that you choose for your source address and destination address. If these fields are required, they appear below your address choices (see Figure 12-17).

Step 9 Click **OK** from the Create Filter pop-up window.

Step 10 Click **OK** in the Sensor view panel.

Step 11 Click **Update** on the toolbar.

Step 12 Apply the updated configuration to the sensor (see the "Applying the Signature Template to the Sensor" section in this chapter).

Figure 12-15 *Advanced Filtering Configuration Screen*

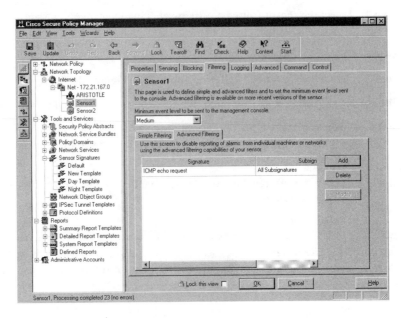

Figure 12-16 *Advanced Create Filter Pop-Up Window*

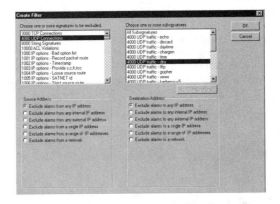

Figure 12-17 *Advanced Filter Address Fields*

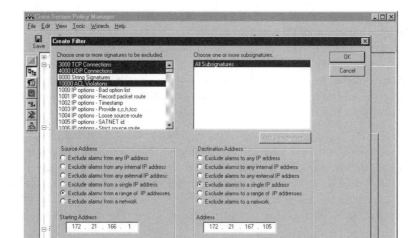

Advanced Signature Configuration

Advanced signature settings are signature version-dependent and are configured per sensor. Not every sensor platform supports advanced signature configuration parameters. The IDSM Sensor currently supports two advanced signature features:

- Signature Tuning
- Signature Port Mapping

NOTE   These advanced features are currently available only on the IDSM Sensor platform.

Signature Tuning

The *Signature Tuning* feature enables you to assign values to certain parameters for common Cisco Secure IDS signatures (see Figure 12-18). These parameters enable you to further customize the characteristics of signatures on your sensors. For example,

ICMP Flood (ID 2152) has two configurable parameters: *Expiration* and *Threshold*. The Expiration parameter defines the duration (after the signature triggers) for which your sensor expects to observe that same signature again. During this expiration time, the signature does not fire again for the same host (thus limiting the number of alarms generated). The Threshold parameter defines the number of occurrences of the signature that your sensor must observe prior to the expiration before triggering an alarm. These parameters enable you to configure the frequency and quantity of an event that must occur to trigger an alarm. Furthermore, configuring these parameters according to your network environment and security policy provides you significant control over the operation of your sensors.

The ICMP Flood signature has a default expiration of 5 and a default threshold of 25. This means that your sensor needs to observe at least 25 ICMP messages destined for a single host before it triggers. Furthermore, for 5 seconds after the alarm triggers, the ICMP Flood signature does not trigger again for that same host. The expiration value helps limit the number of alarms being sent to your Director during an attack. In this example, for example, the ICMP Flood can only be triggered every 5 seconds for a specific host.

Figure 12-18   *Signature Tuning Parameters Subtab*

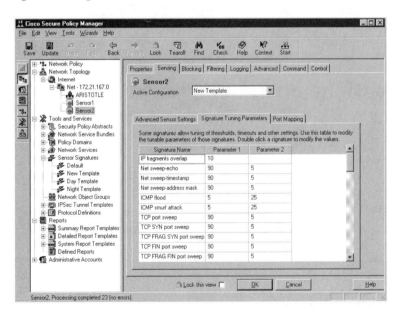

When viewing the signatures in the Signature Tuning window, each signature has one or two parameters: **Parameter 1** and **Parameter 2**. These names are not very descriptive. By double-clicking a signature, however, the Signature Parameter Editor displays (see Figure 12-19).

Figure 12-19 *Signature Parameter Editor*

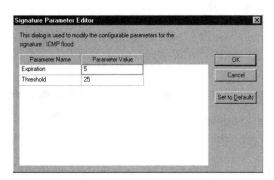

The Signature Parameter Editor provides more descriptive names for the generic **Parameter 1** and **Parameter 2** fields. These descriptive names indicate what the parameters control with respect to the signature.

To tune your signatures for your sensors that support tuning, follow these steps:

Step 1   Select the sensor from the NTT by clicking the name of the sensor on which you want to tune signatures.

Step 2   Select the Sensing tab.

Step 3   Select the Signature Tuning Parameters subtab (refer back to Figure 12-18).

Step 4   Scroll down to the signature that you want to tune using the vertical scroll bars on the right of the Signature Tuning Parameters subtab.

Step 5   Double-click the Cisco Secure IDS signature that you want to tune. This displays the Signature Parameter Editor (see Figure 12-19)

Step 6   In the Signature Parameter Editor window, modify the parameter values to meet your operational requirements.

Step 7   Click **OK** in the Signature Parameter Editor subtab.

Step 8   Click **OK** in the Sensor view panel.

Step 9   Click **Update** on the toolbar.

Step 10 Apply the updated configuration to the sensor (see the "Applying the Signature Template to the Sensor" section in this chapter).

Port Mapping

The Port Mapping feature enables you to assign different port numbers to signatures that normally detect attacks only on predefined ports (see Figure 12-20). For example, Web signatures normally analyze only Web traffic on port 80. The signature port mapping feature provides you with a mechanism to analyze Web traffic on other ports, such as 81, 8080, 8888, and thus provides you with more complete coverage. This feature is beneficial because on many networks, services such as HTTP are run on nonstandard ports.

Figure 12-20 *Port Mapping*

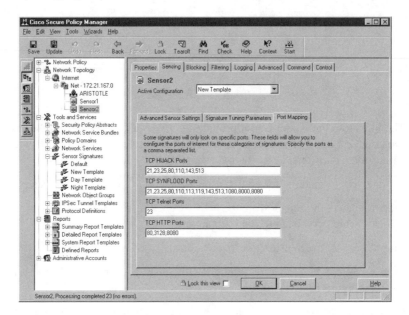

Cisco Secure IDS has four signature groupings that allow for port mapping:

- TCP HIJACK
- TCP SYNFLOOD
- TCP Telnet
- TCP http

To change the Port Mapping configuration, follow these steps:

Step 1 Select the sensor from the NTT by clicking the name of the sensor on which you want to configure Port Mapping.

Step 2 Select the **Sensing** tab in the Sensor view panel.

Step 3 Select the **Port Mapping** subtab (see Figure 12-20).

Step 4 Add or remove port numbers from one or more of the signature groups.

NOTE   The list of port numbers is a comma-separated list. Do not use any spaces. If you use spaces, CSPM does not accept the data when you click OK.

Step 5   Click **OK** in the Sensor view panel.

Step 6   Click **Update** on the toolbar.

Step 7   Apply the updated configuration to the sensor (see the "Applying the Signature Template to the Sensor" section in this chapter).

Creating ACL Signatures

You can configure access control lists (ACLs) on the routers in your network. ACL signatures enable your sensor to trigger an alarm if traffic attempts to violate these ACLs. This section discusses how you can create and manage your ACL signatures.

The first step in using ACL signatures is to create the ACLs on your routers. Furthermore, you need to configure the router to generate SYSLOG messages when traffic matching the ACLs is detected.

After your ACLs are in place, you must do the following to create ACL signatures:

- Select the ACL to monitor using an ACL signature.
- Configure the sensor to monitor SYSLOG messages from the network devices on your network.

Create the ACL Signature

To create an ACL signature, you need to identify the ACL that your sensor needs to monitor. To do so, follow these steps:

Step 1   Select a signature template by clicking its name in the Sensor Signatures section of the main CSPM screen (refer back to Figure 12-1).

Step 2   Select the **Signatures** tab (refer back to Figure 12-2).

Step 3   Select the **ACL Signatures** subtab (see Figure 12-21).

Step 4   Click **Add**. A new ACL signature is created.

Step 5   Enter the ACL number or name corresponding to the ACL that you defined on your network device.

Step 6   Enter in the **Comment** field a comment that describes the ACL.

Step 7 Configure the basic signature parameters discussed previously in this chapter.

Step 8 Click **OK** in the Sensor view panel.

Step 9 Click **Update** on the toolbar.

Step 10 Apply the updated configuration to the sensor (see the "Applying the Signature Template to the Sensor" section in this chapter).

Figure 12-21 *ACL Signature Window*

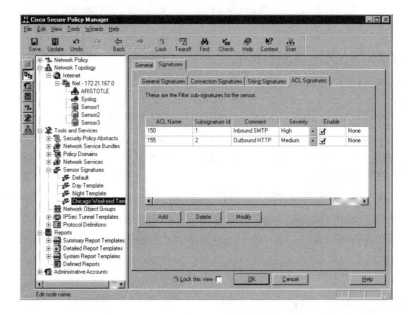

Defining SYSLOG Sources

Now that you created your ACL signatures, you need to have your sensor monitor the SYSLOG messages from your network device(s) with the ACLs. By monitoring the SYSLOG output from your network devices, your sensor can trigger alarms when network traffic attempts to violate the ACLs on your network.

To configure the sensor to accept SYSLOG messages from a network device, follow these steps:

Step 1 Select the sensor from the NTT by clicking the name of the sensor for which you want to define a SYSLOG source.

Step 2 Select the **Properties** tab in the Sensor view panel.

Step 3 Select the **Monitoring** subtab in the Properties window (see Figure 12-22).

Step 4   Click **Add**. A new SYSLOG source entry is created.

Step 5   Enter the IP address and network mask of the network device.

Step 6   Click **OK** in the Sensor view panel.

Step 7   Click **Update** on the toolbar.

Step 8   Apply the updated configuration to the sensor (see "Applying the Signature Template to the Sensor" in this chapter).

Figure 12-22   *Sensor Properties Monitoring Screen*

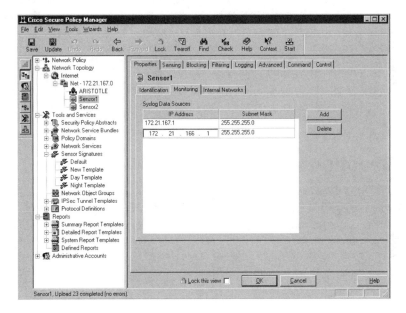

Summary

Optimizing the performance of your Cisco Secure IDS requires you to correctly configure your sensors with respect to your operational environment. With CSPM, signature templates enable you to configure how your sensors analyze network traffic. Creating and applying customized signature templates is essential to achieving the peak capability from your Cisco Secure IDS. Some of the parameters that you can control through signature templates include the following:

- Defining signature severity

- Enabling or disabling signatures

- Setting signature actions

- Adding and modifying connection signature configurations
- Modifying string signature configurations

Filtering the amount of traffic that your CSPM Director receives enables you to concentrate on the most significant threats to your network. You can filter traffic through the following:

- Setting the minimum event level to the Director
- Simple signature filtering
- Advanced signature filtering

Sometimes, you want to monitor attempts to violate the ACLs that are helping to enforce your network security policy. Usually, this policy is enforced by ACLs. You can create ACL signatures that trigger when network traffic attempts to violate these defined ACLs. To create ACL signatures, you need to do the following:

- Create the ACL(s) on your network device(s).
- Create the ACL signature(s).
- Define the SYSLOG source(s) that your sensor monitors.

Review Questions

The following questions test your retention of the material presented in this chapter. The answers to the Review Questions are in Appendix K, "Answers to Review Questions."

1 What are the four classes of signatures?

_____

_____

_____

2 What are the basic configurable parameters for all signatures in your signature template?

_____

_____

_____

3 What three actions can your sensor take when a signature triggers?

_____

_____

_____

4 Are advanced signature configuration options available on all sensor platforms?

_____

_____

_____

5 What advanced signature configuration options does the IDSM Sensor provide?

_____

_____

_____

6 What is the _default_ template?

_____

_____

_____

7 What options are available for both the source and destination addresses when using advanced filtering?

_____

_____

_____

8 What three mechanisms can you use to filter traffic to the CSPM host?

_____

_____

_____

9 What is a SYSLOG data source?

_____

_____

_____

10 What parameters do you need to configure specifically for string signatures?

_____

_____

_____

11 What features do advanced filters provide that are not available for simple filters?

_____

_____

_____

12 What are the two methods for accessing the Signature Actions pop-up window?

_____

_____

_____

13 How do you rename a signature template?

_____

_____

_____

14 Which sensor configuration tab enables you to add simple and advanced filters?

_____

_____

_____

15 How do you access the Signature Parameter Editor?

_____

_____

_____

16 Can you use spaces when specifying port numbers for port mapping?

_____

_____

_____

17 How do you specify an address for a simple filter?

_____

_____

_____

18 What is the address role?

_____

_____

_____

19 Can you specify a range of IP addresses for both the source and destination of an advanced filter?

_____

_____

_____

20 Where do you configure the minimum event level?

_____

_____

_____

21 Through CSPM, what values can you configure for the minimum event level?

_____

_____

_____

22 What category does the Sensor Signatures section fall under on the main CSPM window?

_____

_____

_____

23 Where do you assign a signature template to a sensor?

_____

_____

_____

24 How do you push updated configuration files to your sensor?

_____

_____

_____

## CHAPTER 13

IP Blocking Configurations

IP blocking is an important component of your Cisco Secure IDS. By halting future traffic from an attacker's host or network after an attack is detected, you can limit his ability to attack your network.

NOTE   In earlier versions of Cisco Secure IDS, IP blocking was known as *shunning*. Although the use of the term *shunning* is obsolete, you might still find it used in some configuration files or configuration screens. Eventually, these instances will be completely phased out of Cisco Secure IDS.

Be aware, however, that configuring IP blocking incorrectly enables an attacker to potentially trick your IDS into blocking legitimate traffic on your network, and therefore conduct a successful denial of service attack.

IP Blocking

IP blocking refers to applying access control lists (ACLs) on network devices to restrict traffic flow on your network. Your Cisco Secure IDS Sensors can automatically install ACLs in response to identifying specific attack signatures on your network. You also can manually apply ACLs through CSPM to prevent traffic from a host or network that generated an alarm. These ACLs remain in effect for your default blocking duration.

When using IP blocking, you need to understand the impact of placing your ACLs on outbound versus inbound traffic, as well as internal versus external interfaces. You must decide which signatures warrant blocking when detected. Finally, you must configure your sensors to perform IP blocking. Essentially, this chapter is broken down into the following three categories:

- Understanding ACLs
- ACL placement considerations
- Configuring the sensor for IP blocking

Understanding ACLs

ACLs are part of the Cisco IOS architecture. ACLs enable you to restrict traffic flow on your network by associating a set of restrictions with a physical interface on the routers within your network. You can define two types of ACLs on your network devices:

- Standard
- Extended

Extended ACLs

Extended ACLs enable you to create fine-tuned filtering policies. Whereas standard ACLs enable you to restrict traffic based on the source IP address only, extended ACLs enable you to create filters based on the source IP address, destination IP address, protocol (such as UDP, TCP, and ICMP), and port number. You also can specify items such as established TCP connections.

Cisco IOS allocates specific numeric ranges to each type of ACL. Furthermore, all the ACLs enable you to permit or deny passage of data packets through the physical interfaces on your network devices. Table 13-1 shows the ACL numeric ranges for standard and extended IP ACLs.

Table 13-1   *IOS ACL Numeric Ranges*

ACL Number	Type of ACL
1–99	IP standard access list
100–199	IP extended access list
1300–1999	IP standard access list expanded range
2000–2699	IP extended access list expanded range

You can apply an ACL to your physical interface (external or internal) in two ways:

- Inbound traffic
- Outbound traffic

Basically, applying an ACL to inbound traffic causes it to check data packets when they come into the interface, whereas an outbound ACL checks data packets as they attempt to leave or go out the physical interface. Furthermore, filtering packets on your internal interface means that your router still must process the packets when they come into the router from outside of your network.

By default, your Cisco Secure IDS Sensor creates an ACL numbered 199 (an extended ACL). When this ACL needs to be rewritten, your sensor builds a new ACL numbered 198 (an extended ACL). Your sensor then replaces ACL 199 with 198. The sensor continues to apply the new ACL by swapping between 198 and 199.

It might seem confusing why the sensor uses two ACLs instead of just updating the same ACL over and over again. The reason behind this is quite simple. By using only a single ACL, there is potentially a small window in which your network is unprotected while your sensor updates the ACL. This occurs because you cannot update the characteristics of a numbered ACL so long as it is applied to an interface on your router. You must unapply it from the interface, update it, and then reapply it to the interface. By using two different ACLs, however, your network always remains protected, because your sensor can apply the new ACL after it is constructed. The replaced ACL still exists on the router; it is just no longer applied to an interface.

The rest of this section focuses on the following topics that give you a strong understanding of how to utilize IP blocking in your environment:

- Device management
- Device management requirements
- IP blocking guidelines
- IP blocking at the router
- Master blocking sensors

Device Management

Device Management refers to your sensor's capability to dynamically reconfigure the ACLs on your Cisco IOS network devices. After detecting intrusive traffic, your sensor can use device management to block the source of the attack in real time. By halting the attacker's access to your network, you minimize her ability to continue with her attack. Furthermore, while the attacker is blocked, you can examine your network and strengthen your security policy as necessary to prevent similar attacks in the future.

To dynamically update the ACL on your Cisco IOS network device, your sensor telnets to the device by using its command and control interface. Therefore, your command and control interface must have a route to the network device on which you want to place the ACL.

Device Management Requirements

Numerous Cisco devices support ACLs. The following series of routers have been approved and tested with respect to sensors and device management:

- 1600 Series
- 2500 Series
- 2600 Series

- 3600 Series
- 4500 Series
- 4700 Series
- 7200 Series
- 7500 Series

Your sensor must communicate with the router to use device management. Therefore, the sensor must have a route to or exist on the same subnet as the managed router. To implement IP blocking, you must enable Telnet on the router so that the sensor can access it. Enabling Telnet on your router requires the following:

- Configuring the appropriate vty lines
- Setting the enable password

IP Blocking Guidelines

The Cisco Secure IDS IP blocking feature is a powerful feature that must be implemented only through well-thought-out planning. The IP blocking feature generates ACLs based solely on the IP addresses of the hosts that generate the alarms. Cisco Secure IDS does not determine whether the attacking host is considered a friend or foe. Consequently, it is quite possible that the IP blocking feature can block legitimate network traffic.

Keep in mind the following key points when designing and implementing IP blocking:

- Anti-spoofing mechanisms
- Critical hosts
- Entry points
- Signature selection
- Blocking duration

Anti-Spoofing Mechanisms

Attackers can forge packets with IP addresses that are either private addresses (refer to RFC 1918) or addresses of your internal network. The attacker's goal is to have Cisco Secure IDS block valid IP addresses, therefore causing a denial of service. By implementing proper anti-spoofing mechanisms, Cisco Secure IDS does not block these valid addresses.

An excellent reference on IP address filtering is RFC 2827, "Network Ingress Filtering: Defeating Denial of Service Attacks Which Employ IP Source Address Spoofing." This reference explains how you can apply basic filtering to your router interfaces. Although these recommendations are not foolproof, they significantly help reduce the IP spoofing attacks against your network.

Basically, you need to make sure that all the traffic leaving your protected network comes from a source IP address that represents a valid address on your protected network. Consequently, for traffic entering your protected network, you need to make sure that the source IP address is not one of your valid internal addresses. Addresses that violate these conditions are probably spoofed and need to be dropped by your router.

Critical Hosts

Each network has critical hosts that do not need to be blocked. You need to identify these hosts to prevent possible network disruptions. The following are some common critical hosts:

- Cisco Secure IDS Sensors
- Cisco Secure IDS Director
- Windows domain controllers
- DNS servers

If you choose to utilize IP blocking, you must decide which systems on your network are too critical to be blocked. Although Cisco Secure IDS protects these critical hosts, they still need to have tight local security configurations to protect them from attack.

Entry Points

Today's networks have several entry points to provide reliability, redundancy, and resilience. These entry points also represent different avenues for the attacker to attack your network. You must identify all the entry points into your network and decide whether they need to also participate in IP blocking.

To effectively block an attacker, you must initiate IP blocking on all entry points into your network. A good analogy is locking the doors to your house. If you lock only your front door, a burglar can go in through your unlocked back door. If all the doors are locked, he might slip in through an open window. To secure your house, you must lock all the entry points into it.

Similarly, you need to be diligent in your search for all the entry points into your network. If you miss any, it is almost certain that an attacker will attempt to take advantage of them.

Signature Selection

Cisco Secure IDS contains several hundred signatures that can be configured to perform IP blocking (see Appendix F, "Cisco Secure IDS Signature Structures and Implementations"). It is not feasible to perform blocking on all these signatures. You need to identify which Cisco Secure IDS signatures are best suited to perform IP blocking in your network environment. If you allow only Web traffic to your server farm, for example, you need to concentrate on identifying the Cisco Secure IDS Web-related signatures that specifically apply to your Web server software. From this reduced signature list, you then need to identify those signatures whose severity is High and can potentially lead to an attacker gaining access to one of your systems. These signatures are the best candidates to configure with IP blocking.

Blocking Duration

By default, Cisco Secure IDS performs automatic blocking for 30 minutes. This value works for many networks. You must examine your specific operational requirements to determine the appropriate time for your network environment.

The blocking duration that you choose depends on several factors. One of the factors is how quickly you can analyze attacks against your network. This depends on how large your network is, the experience of your security staff, and the hours that they work. Using the default blocking duration for severe alarms might be inadequate for your weekend and evening configuration if your security staff does not work on evenings and weekends. You might want to use a longer blocking duration for time periods that are not monitored by your security staff.

Another factor that you need to consider when choosing a blocking duration is the severity of the alarm being blocked. You need to ensure adequate time to analyze traffic that represents a potentially serious attack on your network. Therefore, you probably want to increase the blocking duration for alarms that represent a serious attack against your network.

IP Blocking at the Router

IP blocking at the router is a three-step process (see Figure 13-1).

The first step in this process is for an attacker to launch an attack against your network from the untrusted network. The goal of this attack is usually to run an exploit that provides the attacker with access to data or resources on your protected network. Furthermore, these attack signatures usually have a High severity associated with them.

In the second step, as your sensor observes this intrusive activity on the network through its monitoring interface, it triggers a specific signature from its signature database. Associated with this signature are the actions that you configured your sensor to take when the signature fires. These actions are explained in Chapter 12, "Signature and Intrusion Detection Configuration." In conjunction with just notifying the sensor through an alarm event, however, you also can perform a combination of the following actions:

- None
- TCP reset
- Block
- IP log

Figure 13-1 *IP Blocking at the Router*

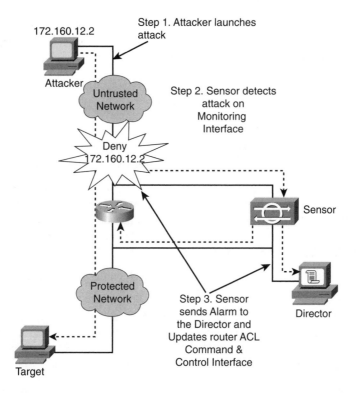

The example illustrated in Figure 13-1 assumes that the sensor is configured to initiate
blocking when the signature in question triggers.

Finally, in the third step, the sensor forwards an alarm event to the Director. At the same
time, the sensor automatically builds a new ACL on the managed router to deny traffic
whose source address matches the attacker's host. After this ACL is established, your
managed router denies all future traffic from the attacking host until the following
occurs:

- You manually remove the block.
- The default blocking duration is exceeded.

Default Block Time

Whenever your sensor establishes a blocking ACL, the blocking is not permanent. The sensor starts a timer by using the default blocking duration. The ACL remains in effect until the default blocking duration expires. This value is set through the **Blocking** tab on the sensor view panel.

Master Blocking Sensors

In some configurations, you must have a proxy sensor perform the IP blocking action for another sensor on your network. This proxy sensor is referred to as a *master blocking sensor*.

It is perhaps easiest to explain the master blocking sensor through an example. Figure 13-2 illustrates a network that connects to the Internet through multiple Internet service providers (ISPs). A Cisco Secure IDS Sensor monitors each of the entry points into this network. Furthermore, each of the sensors is configured to perform device management on its associated border or perimeter router.

First, an attacker attempts to compromise a host on the protected network (step 1 in Figure 13-2). This usually involves the attacker launching an exploit against the target machine.

When Sensor A detects the attack, it fires one of the signatures in its database (step 2 in Figure 13-2). Because the signature is configured for blocking, Sensor A telnets into Router A and creates or updates an ACL to block the traffic from the attacker's host, along with sending the alarm event to the Director (step 3 in Figure 13-2).

The ACL on Router A prevents the attacker from sending any traffic into the network through ISP X's network (see Figure 13-2). Because the network has two entry points, however, the attacker can reroute his traffic through ISP Y because it is still currently allowing traffic from the attacker's host. Therefore, to completely protect the network from the attacker, Sensor B is configured as a master blocking sensor.

After blocking the attacker's traffic at Router A, Sensor A tells Sensor B to also block the attacker's traffic. Because Sensor B is configured as the master blocking sensor, Sensor B accepts Sensor A's request and telnets into Router B to create or update the ACL to also block the attacker's traffic. At this point, both entry points into the network are now protected from the attacker.

NOTE   A savvy network security administrator configures Sensor A to command Sensor B to block Provider Y's router. This protects from attacks initiated through Provider X's network. Then to complete the security configuration, he also needs to configure Sensor A as the master blocking sensor for Sensor B. Therefore, if an attacker comes from either Provider X or Provider Y, both entry points into the network are protected.

Figure 13-2 *Master Blocking Sensor*

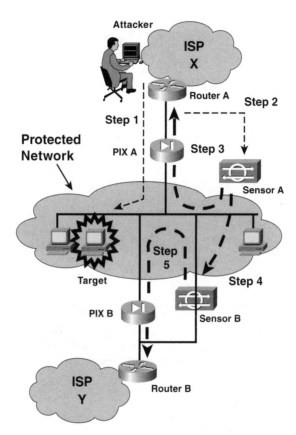

ACL Placement Considerations

When applying ACLs on your network, consider your operational requirements and network topology. You have several options when applying ACLs to one of your network devices. The ACL might be applied on either the external or internal interface of the router. It also can be configured for inbound or outbound traffic on each of these two interfaces. Although you can choose inbound or outbound (with respect to the router interface, not your network) on each physical interface, the most common combinations are illustrated in Figure 13-3.

Figure 13-3 *ACL Placement*

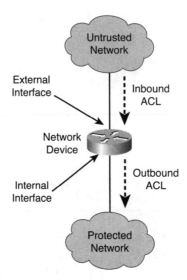

You also must consider that the sensor must have full control of the interface/direction on which the blocking ACL is applied. Because only one ACL is allowed on the given interface/direction, manually entered ACLs are not allowed on this interface/direction, but might be applied to other interfaces. If you configured a manual ACL on your external inbound interface, for example, you can still apply blocking using the internal outbound interface.

NOTE   If you have an ACL manually applied to the interface/direction that your sensor uses, it is unapplied as soon as the sensor takes control of the interface. If the ACL number you used for your ACL is the same that the sensor tries to apply, your ACL is cleared and overwritten by the sensor-generated ACL. The sensor does not make any attempt to merge your ACL into the new ACL that it creates.

Where to Apply ACLs

When deciding where to apply your ACLs, you need to understand the various options available to you. These options are as follows:

- Traffic direction
- External interface
- Internal interface

Traffic Direction

The traffic direction specifies whether the ACL is applied to traffic entering or leaving the specified interface. You can allow certain traffic into an interface while denying this same traffic from leaving the interface. You must apply a traffic direction when creating an ACL for a given interface on your network device.

External Interface

The external interface is located on the unprotected side of your network device (see Figure 13-3). Applying your ACL to your external interface results in the following advantages:

- Denies host before it enters the router
- Provides the best protection against an attacker
- User-defined ACLs on the internal interface are allowed.

Internal Interface

Your internal interface resides on the protected side of your network device (see Figure 13-3). Applying your ACL to your internal interface results in the following advantages:

- The block does not apply to the router itself.
- User-defined ACLs on the external interface are allowed.

Applying ACLs on the External Versus Internal Interface

Applying the ACL to the external interface in the inward direction denies a host access before your router processes the packets. If an attacker generates a large amount of traffic, this reduces the performance impact on your router.

Applying the ACL to the internal interface in the outbound direction denies traffic from a host to the protected network but allows packets to be processed by the router. This scenario is less desirable but might be required if outside inbound ACLs are already used.

Each network configuration has it own specific requirements. You must decide, based on your unique network architecture, which configuration meets your needs for security and user functionality.

Configuring the Sensor for IP Blocking

To take advantage of IP blocking, you must configure your sensor appropriately. This involves the following:

- Defining which signatures warrant blocking
- Specifying your blocking devices
- Possibly setting up master blocking sensors

You must decide which signatures must be configured for blocking. This requires you to examine your network environment and to determine the types of services and traffic that your network provides. The services provided by your environment determine the attacks that an attacker can use to compromise your environment. Finally, you must configure specific signatures to perform blocking. Configuring specific signatures with the blocking action is explained in Chapter 12.

After configuring certain signatures to perform blocking, you must define the blocking device(s) that your sensor uses to block attackers.

Blocking Device

A *blocking device* is a Cisco IOS device. Your Cisco Secure IDS Sensor communicates with the blocking device through Telnet to establish an ACL that prevents IP-based traffic. Signature actions are limited to restricting traffic from a single-source IP address. Through manual blocking (described later in this chapter), however, you also can restrict an entire network.

Finally, if your network has multiple entry points monitored by multiple sensors, you need to configure master blocking sensors. Your blocking is less effective if you do not configure them. Without master blocking sensors, an attacker can attack your network through one entry point while being blocked at another. Eventually, she might be blocked at all the entry points, but only after she has initiated multiple attacks against your network.

WARNING   Because your sensor accesses your router through Telnet, you must verify that this process is done securely and according to your security policy. The best approach is to have the sensor communicate with the router across a completely separated network. If this is not possible, you need to definitely use ACLs to limit Telnet access to the router to only authorized systems.

The remainder of this chapter discusses how to configure the sensor for IP blocking. The first thing you must do is set the blocking device properties.

Setting the Blocking Device Properties

To specify the information about the Cisco IOS router (blocking device) that the sensor uses to block detected attacks, follow these steps:

Step 1 Select the sensor from the Network Topology tree (NTT) by clicking the name of the sensor for which you want to define a block device.

Step 2 Select the **Blocking** tab in the sensor view panel (see Figure 13-4).

Step 3 Select the **Blocking Devices** subtab from within the Blocking tab (see Figure 13-5).

Step 4 Click **Add** to open the Blocking Device Properties pop-up window (see Figure 13-6). This window enables you to configure the properties of your blocking device.

Step 5 Configure the basic identification parameters:

— **Telnet IP Address**—Identifies the router's IP address that the sensor telnets to when applying ACLs

— **Telnet Username**—Identifies the username that the sensor uses when logging on to the router

— **Telnet Password**—Identifies the password that the sensor uses to log on to the router

— **Enable Password**—Identifies the password that the sensor needs to access Privileged or Enable mode on the router

NOTE   Some routers are not configured to have multiple username accounts. These routers prompt you for a password only when you log on to them. If your router is configured this way, you must leave the Telnet Username field blank.

Step 6 Besides the basic parameters, you also must define on which interface the ACL is applied. Click **Add** on the Blocking Device Properties pop-up window to add a line in the Blocking Interfaces section of the Blocking Device Properties pop-up window (see Figure 13-6).

Step 7 Configure the interface parameters:

— **Interface Name**—Each interface on your router is identified by a specific name (such as Ethernet0, Eth1/0, FastEthernet0/0, Serial0, and so on). Your sensor applies the blocking ACL to this interface.

> — **Interface Direction**—You must specify which direction the ACL
> is applied on the interface. Your two options are inbound and
> outbound.

WARNING   Do not add a space between the interface name and the interface number. If you do, the
sensor does not recognize the interface when the sensor attempts to build the ACL.

Step 8   If you want to apply ACLs to multiple interfaces on your router, you need
to keep clicking the **Add** button until you have defined all the interfaces
to which the sensor applies blocking ACLs.

Step 9   Click **OK** on the Blocking Device Properties pop-up window to accept
your configuration changes.

Step 10   Click **OK** in the sensor view panel to accept your changes.

Step 11   Click **Save** on the top toolbar to save your changes.

Step 12   Finally, you must transfer the updated configuration to your sensor (see
"Pushing a New Configuration to Your Sensor" in Chapter 11, "Sensor
Configuration Within CSPM.").

Figure 13-4   *Blocking Tab in the Sensor View Panel*

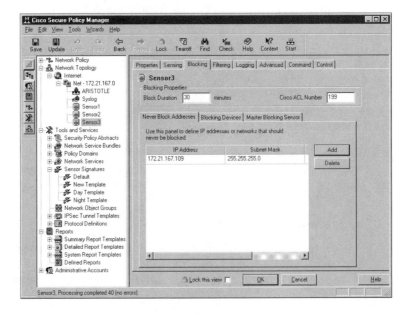

Figure 13-5 *Blocking Devices Configuration Screen*

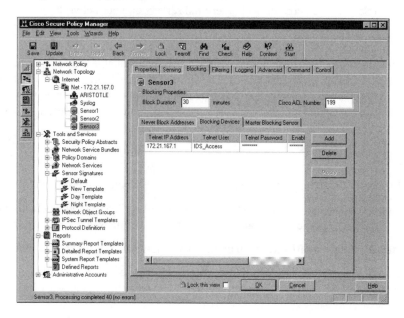

Figure 13-6 *Blocking Device Properties Window*

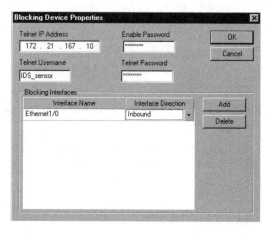

Setting Never to Block IP Addresses

Blocking traffic prevents all traffic from a specified host from passing through your network device in the direction (inbound or outbound) that the ACL is applied. This can be devastating if the blocking is performed on critical components of your own network. Some of the components that probably do not need to be blocked are your Cisco Secure IDS Sensors, Cisco Secure IDS Director, and other vital servers on your network.

NOTE   Blocking occurs because of network traffic. Sometimes, this traffic represents an actual attack. Other times, a signature fires because of a false positive. An attacker might even send *spoofed* traffic that appears to come from systems on your own network. Therefore, if you plan to implement blocking on your network, you need to carefully consider which hosts on your network must never be blocked.

To specify IP addresses that the sensor never blocks, follow these steps:

Step 1   Select the sensor from the Network Topology tree (NTT) by clicking the name of the sensor on which you want to define Never Block Addresses.

Step 2   Select the **Blocking** tab in the sensor view panel (refer back to Figure 13-4).

Step 3   The default tab is the **Never Block Addresses** subtab (refer back to Figure 13-4). If this screen is not displayed, click the Never Block Addresses subtab to display it.

Step 4   The current Never Block Addresses are shown on the screen. To add more entries, click the **Add** button. This inserts another Never Block Address entry that you need to configure.

Step 5   Configure the Never Block Address entry by defining the following parameters:

— **IP Address**—Identifies the IP address for the system that you never want your sensor to block

— **Subnet Mask**—Identifies the subnet mask associated with the specified IP address

Step 6   Keep clicking the **Add** button and defining hosts until you have specified all the hosts that you want to prevent from being blocked by your sensor.

NOTE   You must configure a list of Never Block Addresses for each Cisco Secure IDS Sensor in your network that uses IP blocking.

Step 7   Click **OK** in the sensor view panel to accept your changes.

Step 8   Click **Save** on the top toolbar to save your changes.

Step 9   Finally, you must transfer the updated configuration to your sensor (see "Pushing a New Configuration to Your Sensor" in Chapter 11).

NOTE   If your sensor blocked its own IP address, it might never be able to undo the ACL. Therefore, the IP address of the Cisco Secure IDS Sensor is automatically added as a Never Block Address, even though it is not displayed on the Never Block Addresses subtab. This does not prevent one sensor from potentially blocking another sensor. Therefore, depending on your network topology, you might want to add other sensors into your Never Block Addresses.

Blocking Through a Master Blocking Sensor

If your network has multiple entry points monitored by different Cisco Secure IDS Sensors, you need to configure master blocking sensors, as well as your basic blocking devices.

To configure the master blocking sensor that your sensor uses to block detected attacks at other entry points in your network, follow these steps:

Step 1   Select the sensor from the Network Topology tree (NTT) by clicking the name of the sensor for which you want to define a master blocking sensor.

Step 2   Select the **Blocking** tab in the sensor view panel (refer back to Figure 13-4).

Step 3   Select the **Master Blocking Sensor** subtab within the Blocking tab (see Figure 13-7).

Step 4   Click **Add** to open the Blocking Sensor Selection pop-up window (see Figure 13-8). Select the sensor name, which you want to make the master blocking sensor, from the list and click **OK**.

Step 5   Click **OK** in the sensor view panel to accept your changes.

Step 6   Click **Save** on the top toolbar to save your changes.

Step 7   Finally, you must transfer the updated configuration to your sensor (see "Pushing a New Configuration to Your Sensor" in Chapter 11).

Figure 13-7 *Master Blocking Sensor Screen*

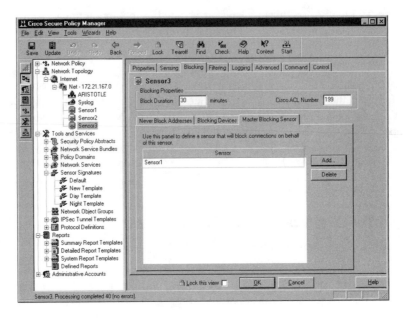

Figure 13-8 *Master Blocking Sensor Selection Screen*

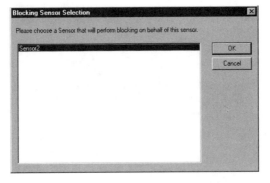

Viewing the List of Blocked IP Addresses

If you implement IP blocking on your network, you probably want to periodically know which hosts are currently blocked. You can discover this information by logging on to your router and checking the ACL that is applied, but this approach is inefficient. However, you can also access this information directly through your CSPM Director.

To view the list of IP addresses blocked by your sensor, as well as the time remaining for that IP address on the block list, follow these steps:

Step 1   Open the Event Viewer - Database Events pop-up window (see Figure 13-9). The Event Viewer is explained in detail in Chapter 8, "Working with Cisco Secure IDS Alarms in CSPM."

NOTE   When you open the Event Viewer, you can open a list of your sensors by clicking the **View**, **Connection Status Pane**. The list of sensors appears on the left portion of the Event Viewer window (see Figure 13-9).

Step 2   On the Event Viewer - Database Events pop-up window, select the sensor on the Connection Status pane or select an alarm generated by the sensor on which you want to view the block information.

Step 3   Choose **View**, **Block List** from the Event Viewer - Database Events main menu. A Shun pop-up window showing the list of blocked IP addresses and the time remaining before they are removed from the block list opens (see Figure 13-10). The time remaining on the block is indicated in seconds and is listed after each host or network entry.

Figure 13-9   *Event Viewer*

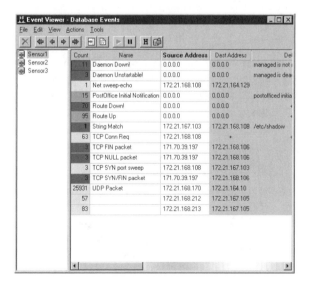

Figure 13-10 *Shun List Window*

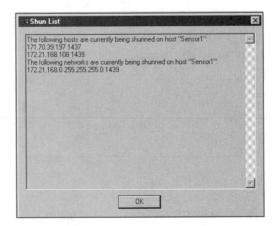

Viewing the Managed Network Devices

To view the list of network devices managed by a sensor and their associated device information, follow these steps:

Step 1 Open the Event Viewer - Database Events pop-up window (see Figure 13-9). The Event Viewer is explained in detail in Chapter 8.

Step 2 On the Event Viewer - Database Events pop-up window, select the sensor from the Connection Status pane or select an alarm generated by the sensor on which you want to view the information.

Step 3 Choose **View, Network Device** from the Event Viewer - Database Events main menu bar. A Network Device Info pop-up window showing the managed device and the device's current time, status, type, and software version opens (see Figure 13-11).

Manually Blocking a Host or Network

Some people prefer to block traffic only after an operator determines conclusively that someone is attacking her network. At other times, you might want to block an entire network address range. These operations are available to you through manual blocking operations. CSPM enables you to manually block either a specific host or an entire network.

NOTE The default value for the blocking duration when initiating blocking manually is 1440 minutes. You can modify this value through the Event Viewer by selecting Edit, Preferences and changing Time To Block (minutes) value in the Actions section.

Figure 13-11   *Network Device Information Window*

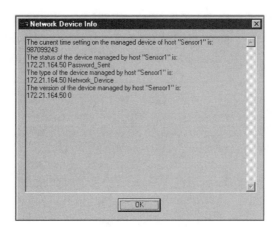

To manually block a host or network, perform the following steps:

Step 1   Open the Event Viewer - Database Events pop-up window (see Figure 13-9). The Event Viewer is explained in detail in Chapter 8.

Step 2   Select an alarm representing the source IP address that you want to block.

Step 3   Choose **Actions**, **Block**, **Host** or **Actions**, **Block**, **Network** from the Event Viewer - Database Events pop-up window main menu (see Figure 13-12).

Step 4   A Shunning Hosts pop-up window showing the status of the block command opens (see Figure 13-13). If the status of the operation is Success, the blocking operation worked correctly.

NOTE   If the status of your operation is something other than Success, such as "Error timeout waiting for response," the blocking operation did not complete successfully. If this happens, you need to investigate why the manual blocking attempt failed. Refer to Appendix C, "Cisco Secure IDS Director Basic Troubleshooting," for some basic troubleshooting tips.

Removing a Blocked Host or Network

Sometimes, when a host gets blocked automatically, you might want to remove the block if you determine that the initial traffic detected did not represent an actual attack. You also might want to remove a manually blocked host or network after investigating a potential problem.

Figure 13-12 *Manually Blocking a Host or Network*

Figure 13-13 *Shunning Window*

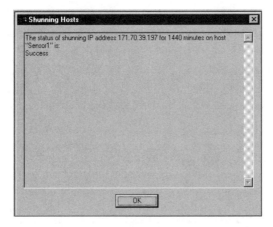

To remove a blocked host or network, you need to perform the following steps:

Step 1 Open the Event Viewer - Database Events pop-up window (see Figure 13-9). The Event Viewer is explained in detail in Chapter 8.

Step 2 Select an alarm that has the appropriate source address (the address currently blocked). You might first need to select the appropriate sensor from the Connection Status pane to view the necessary alarms.

Step 3   Choose **Actions**, **Remove Block**, **Host** or **Actions**, **Remove Block**,
Network from the Event Viewer menu. A Removing Shun of Hosts pop-
up window showing the status of the **remove block** command opens (see
Figure 13-14).

Figure 13-14   *Removing Shun of Hosts Window*

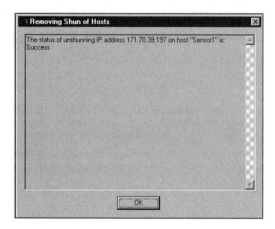

Summary

IP blocking is a useful tool in minimizing an extended attack against your network. This
blocking can be implemented automatically when signatures trigger, or you can manually
apply blocking after you examine alarms on your Director and decide that blocking is
appropriate. Although IP blocking is a powerful tool, if it is not configured correctly, it can
be used against your network by a skilled attacker to cause a denial of service attack.

To implement IP blocking, you need to configure several items:

* Define which signatures warrant the IP blocking action.
* Configure your blocking devices.
* Possibly configure your master blocking sensors.

Each signature can be configured to block traffic by enabling the IP block action for that
signature (refer to Chapter 12 for more information on definable signature actions). You
need to configure only certain signatures for blocking. The exact signatures that fall into
this category vary depending on your operational requirements and network topology.

Your sensor implements IP blocking by logging on to a router (through Telnet) and creating
a blocking ACL. Therefore, your sensor needs to know the IP address of the router along
with the logon credentials necessary to gain privileged access on the router. Furthermore,
your sensor needs to know which interfaces on the router have the ACL applied to them.

If you have multiple entry points into your network that are protected by different sensors, you need to configure master blocking sensors to maximize the protection of your network through IP blocking.

Review Questions

The following questions test your retention of the material presented in this chapter. The answers to the Review Questions are in Appendix K, "Answers to Review Questions."

1 When a signature is configured to block fires, what does it block?

_____

_____

_____

2 What is the only way in which to block an entire network?

_____

_____

_____

3 What is a blocking device?

_____

_____

_____

4 How does your sensor block attacking traffic?

_____

_____

_____

5 Which two ACL numbers do your sensors use to block traffic by default?

_____

_____

_____

6 What is the default automatic blocking duration?

_____

_____

_____

7 Where do you view the current IP addresses and networks that are being blocked?

_____

_____

_____

8 Where do you establish manual blocking?

_____

_____

_____

9 What is the default manual blocking duration?

_____

_____

_____

10 Where do you change the default manual blocking duration?

_____

_____

_____

11 Where do you change the default automatic blocking duration value?

_____

_____

_____

## CHAPTER 14

Catalyst 6000 IDS Module Configuration

The Intrusion Detection System Module (IDSM) for the Catalyst 6000 family of switches tightly integrates security into a switched network environment by placing the IDS sensor on a switch line card. This line card offers the network administrator many features with which to examine the traffic on his network.

Configuring the IDSM involves not only setting up the sensor so that it can communicate with your Director Platform, but also requires you to configure your switch to copy selected traffic to your IDSM line card. You can monitor traffic on your Catalyst switch by using two different methods:

- The Switch Port Analyzer (SPAN) feature
- VACLs

Overall, the IDSM represents an integral component in your complete Cisco Secure IDS environment.

To guide you through the process of configuration, this chapter is divided into the following sections:

- Understanding the Catalyst 6000 IDS Module
- IDSM Ports and Traffic Flow
- Capturing Traffic
- Configuration Tasks
- Updating IDSM Components
- Troubleshooting

Understanding the Catalyst 6000 IDS Module

The Intrusion Detection System Module (IDSM) for the Catalyst 6000 family of switches is a switch line card (see Figure 14-1). This line card is designed specifically to address switched environments by integrating the IDS functionality directly into the switch and taking traffic right off the switch backplane, thus bringing both switching and security functionality into the same chassis.

Figure 14-1 *Catalyst 6000 Intrusion Detection System Module*

Key Features

In switched network environments, traffic must be copied to a monitoring port to capture traffic for intrusion detection analysis. The Catalyst 6000 IDSM offers network and security administrators many capabilities to overcome the problems associated with intrusion detection in switched environments.

Hubs broadcast all traffic to every port. Switches monitor which port a host is located on and only send traffic destined for that host to that specific port. This improves the performance of the switch and provides a modest increase in security.

One of the most difficult problems associated with switched network environments is capturing the traffic on the network so that your Cisco Secure IDS Sensors can analyze it. The IDSM line card has two different mechanisms with which to capture selected network traffic:

- The SPAN feature
- The VACL feature

SPAN ports enable you to direct traffic from various ports and VLANs on your switch to a specific destination port. They are limited, however, by a specific number of ports and VLANs that can be configured. Therefore, the Catalyst 6000 IDSM overcomes this limitation by also providing you the ability to capture traffic off the switch backplane by using the Catalyst Operation System (OS) VLAN ACL (VACL) feature.

Even though the Catalyst 6000 IDSM captures data directly from the backplane, the performance of the switch is not affected because the Catalyst 6000 IDSM is not in the switch-forwarding path.

Switch-Forwarding Path

The switch-forwarding path is the critical path that packets take to travel in on one port and out on another. All steps in the switch-forwarding path affect the performance of the switch because these operations are performed on all packets traversing the switch. The packet-capture mechanisms used by the IDSM make copies only of the packets traversing the switch. The downside to this approach is that the IDSM cannot actually halt an individual packet from going through the switch.

The attacks and signatures detected by the IDSM parallels the 4200 Series Appliance Sensor. Furthermore, the tight integration of the Catalyst 6000 IDSM with your switch makes it an integral part of the Cisco Secure IDS family of products.

Feature Comparison

Whenever multiple components are available that perform similar functions, the question always arises as to which component is better. This also applies to the multiple sensor platforms available for the Cisco Secure IDS environment.

Defining which sensor platform is better, however, is difficult at best. Each network is unique and has its own operational requirements. One network environment might be better suited to one platform, whereas another operates better with another sensor platform. If your current infrastructure already incorporates Catalyst family 6000 switches, for example, you might lean toward deploying IDSM. You can, however, compare the features available on the different sensor platforms. By doing so, you can make an educated decision as to which sensor works best in your specific environment.

The major differences between the Catalyst 6000 IDSM and the traditional appliance are as follows:

- The monitoring port for the Catalyst 6000 IDSM is by default a trunking port, thus allowing visibility into traffic from multiple VLANs.

- The sensor appliance can create Cisco IOS router ACLs to block malicious activity.

- The sensor appliance can use IP Logging to capture associated network traffic from a specific IP address after a predefined attack is detected.

- The sensor appliance can be managed securely with IPSec.

- Various Catalyst 6000 IDSM signature parameters can be configured to enable the security administrator to tune signature triggers. For example, you can set the number of ICMP echo requests to 10 before the ICMP Echo Request alarm triggers.

- The Catalyst 6000 IDSM has the flexibility of associating several ports with signatures or a specific network service. This feature provides a broader range of coverage to detect protocol specific attacks. For example, HTTP (Web) traffic occurs by default on port 80. Other HTTP ports often seen on the Internet are 81, 82, 88, 8080, and 8888. By associating all these ports with HTTP, HTTP attacks against these nonstandard ports can be detected.

- The VACLs available on IDSM enable granular traffic capturing functionality.

This feature comparison is summarized in Table 14-1.

Table 14-1   *Feature Comparison Between IDSM and Appliance*

Feature	IDSM	Appliance
Multi-VLAN Traffic Capturing	Yes	No
IP Blocking	No	Yes
IP Logging	No	Yes
String Matching	Yes	Yes
IPSec Secure Communications	No	Yes
Signature Tuning Parameters	Yes	No
Signature Port Mapping	Yes	No

NOTE   This feature comparison is based on the currently available features on each platform. Refer to Chapter 18, "Planned Cisco Secure IDS Enhancements," to see what is planned for each sensing platform in the future.

Catalyst 6000 Requirements

The Catalyst 6000 IDSM line card tightly integrates with your Catalyst 6000 family switch. A successful integration, nevertheless, requires specific functionality on your switch. To achieve the required functionality, your Catalyst 6000 family switch must meet the following requirements:

- Catalyst OS 6.1(1) or higher. You cannot run CAT IOS on the Supervisor module.
- PFC for VACL Capture feature functionality.
- Supervisor 1A or 2.
- Multilayer Switch Feature Card (MSFC) or MSFC2 (optional).

MSFC Versus Standalone Router

Figure 14-2 shows a typical scenario in which two VLANs are connected by a router. The two possible methods to perform the routing functionality between these VLANs are an external router and the onboard MSFC.

When a connection from the host on VLAN20 is established with the Web server on VLAN30, the initial packets traverse paths 1 and 2 for both the onboard MSFC and an external router. VACLs are applied each time the packet traverses the switch's backplane. Therefore, if you have a VACL applied to VLAN20 and VLAN30, this can result in two copies of the same packet being forwarded to the capture port (once for path 1 and once for path 2).

Figure 14-2 *MSFC Versus Standalone Router*

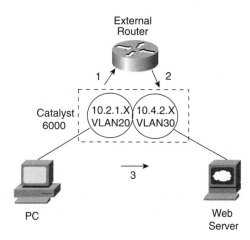

With the onboard MSFC, packets can be routed using path 3 after the MSFC has enough information to establish a flow between the two hosts. Because the packets traverse the switch's backplane only once, this results in a single packet being forwarded to the capture port. Packets routed with the external router always must traverse paths 1 and 2.

The double packet capture is important because it can result in duplicate alarms. Some signatures have thresholds that can be reached quicker because of the duplicate captured packets. Utilizing an MSFC can definitely help reduce the duplicated packets forwarded to your IDSM line cards for analysis.

IDSM Ports and Traffic Flow

Like the traditional appliance, the Catalyst 6000 IDSM has a monitoring port and a command and control port. Understanding how these ports operate is vital to deploying your IDSM line cards effectively. This section discusses the ports on the Catalyst 6000 IDSM, as well as how traffic is captured for intrusion detection analysis.

Ports

The Catalyst 6000 IDSM has two ports that are tied directly into the switch's backplane:

- Monitoring port
- Command and control port

Unlike the monitoring ports on the appliance, the IDSM ports are *not* physically visible.

Monitoring Port

Port 1 on your IDSM line card is the monitoring port. Through this monitoring port, your IDSM receives captured network traffic for intrusion detection analysis. By default Port 1 is a trunking port for all VLANs on your switch and assigned as the destination capture port for VLAN ACLs.

Command and Control Port

Port 2 on your IDSM line card is the command and control port. All communication between the Director Platform and the IDSM occurs through this interface. During the initial IDSM setup procedure (described later in this chapter), you must assign this port an IP address. Your Director software communicates with your IDSM through this IP address.

Traffic Flow

Unlike the traditional appliance, the traffic flow to the IDSM line card requires a little more explanation (see Figure 14-3). Furthermore, understanding this traffic flow is an important aspect of effectively utilizing your Catalyst IDSM to capture and analyze specific traffic on your network. Although the IDSM receives traffic directly from your switch's backplane, your Catalyst 6000 family switch must be configured to enable traffic to flow to both ports on your IDSM line card. If this is not done, your IDSM does not have visibility into the network traffic, and your CSPM host cannot communicate with your IDSM line card on its command and control interface.

Traffic enters the Catalyst 6000 switch destined for a host or network. A copy of this traffic is then diverted through the switch backplane to your IDSM for intrusion detection analysis. Besides analyzing this captured traffic, the IDSM performs certain defined actions like other sensors do. These actions include sending alarms to your Cisco Secure Policy Manager (CSPM) host and receiving commands from your CSPM host.

Figure 14-3 *Traffic Flow*

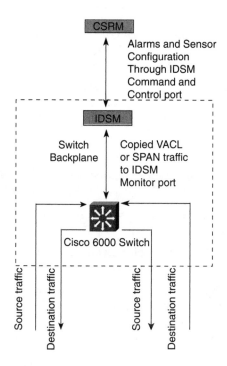

Capturing Traffic

The Catalyst 6000 IDSM can monitor a full 100 Mbps of network traffic, based on the minimum Ethernet packet size of 64 bytes. As the size of the packets captured increases, the performance of the IDSM also increases. Therefore, you might capture more than 100 Mbps from your IDSM because your network traffic is probably composed of a variety of packet sizes.

Network traffic is captured off the switch backplane to be analyzed by the IDSM line card. The methods available to capture traffic depend on the features on your Catalyst 6000 family switch. All switches can use the SPAN feature. For those switches equipped with a PFC, you also can use the VACL feature. The following sections discuss both of these features.

SPAN Feature

The SPAN feature is one method of capturing network traffic for intrusion detection analysis. This functionality is available on all Catalyst 6000 family switches. SPAN mirrors traffic from one or more source locations to a specific destination port for analysis. You have two options for the source location of your SPAN:

- Spanning ports
- Spanning VLANs

Spanning Ports

When using specific ports as the source location for your SPAN association, you have three ways to determine which traffic is copied to your destination port:

- **Ingress**—SPAN session copies network traffic received *(rx)* by the source ports for analysis at the destination port.

- **Egress**—SPAN session copies network traffic transmitted *(tx)* from the source ports for analysis at the destination port.

- **Both**—SPAN session copies network traffic transmitted and received from the source ports for analysis at the destination port.

Spanning VLANs

Instead of using specific ports, sometimes it is more effective to use specific VLANs as the source location for your SPAN association. A VLAN-based SPAN session is known as a VSPAN. Like using source ports, VSPAN has three ways to determine the traffic that is be copied to your destination port:

- **Ingress**—VSPAN copies network traffic received *(rx)* by the source VLAN for analysis at the destination port.

- **Egress**—VSPAN copies network traffic transmitted *(tx)* from the source VLAN for analysis at the destination port.

- **Both**—VSPAN copies network traffic transmitted and received from the source VLAN for analysis at the destination port.

NOTE   For traffic where the source and destination are on the same VLAN, the Both option for spanning behaves differently depending on your type of supervisor engine:

- With the WS-X6K-SUP1A-PFC,WS-X6K-SUP1A-MSFC engine, two packets are forwarded to the SPAN destination port.

- With the WS-X6K-SUP1-2GE,WS-X6K-SUP1A-2GE engine, only one packet is forwarded to the SPAN destination port.

SPAN Limitations

A SPAN session is an association of a destination port with a set of source ports or VLANs, configured with parameters that specify the monitored network traffic. The number of SPAN sessions allowed is limited based on the method of SPAN deployed. Table 14-2 represents the SPAN session limits on the Catalyst 6000 family of switches. The total number of SPAN sessions is 6, of which four are tx and 2 are either rx or both.

Table 14-2   *SPAN Session Limits*

SPAN Session	Number of Sessions
rx or both	2
tx	4

VACLs Feature

VACL access controls *all* packets on a Catalyst 6000 switch through a PFC. VACLs are strictly for security packet filtering and redirecting traffic to specific physical switch ports. Unlike IOS ACLs, VACLs are not defined by the direction of the traffic (inbound or outbound).

VACLs are mainly provided to filter traffic on the switch. The **capture** keyword enables you to use a VACL to mirror matched traffic to a designated capture port. This capture option specifies that packets that match the specified *flows* are switched normally but are also captured and transmitted to the capture ports. Only permitted traffic is sent to the capture ports. The Catalyst 6000 IDSM uses this feature to capture traffic for intrusion detection analysis.

Flows

A flow comprises a traffic stream between a source and destination IP address; a source port and destination port; or a combination of source IP address and source port in conjunction with a destination IP address and destination port. Your VACLs essentially define the flows that represent the interesting traffic on which you want your IDSM to perform intrusion detection analysis. Furthermore, your MSFC utilizes flows to effectively send packets between different VLANs by crossing the switch's backplane only once.

Defining Interesting Traffic

Intrusion detection analysis requires examining specific network traffic. VACLs provide you with granular control over the network traffic that you consider interesting. This interesting traffic is captured by your VACL and passed to your IDSM's monitoring interface. You can capture traffic based on the following:

- Source or destination IP addresses
- Source or destination ports
- A combination of IP addresses and ports

For example, on a Web farm, port 80 (HTTP) and potentially port 21 (FTP) represent the services required for Internet users to access the Web servers and retrieve data. Attackers launch software exploits against these ports. You can create a VACL that captures only traffic destined to these two ports, thereby reducing the amount of traffic sent to the IDSM for intrusion detection analysis.

NOTE	In reality, you need to monitor more ports than 80 to watch for attacks against Web server software. Several ports are commonly used for these services, such as 80, 8080, and 3128. To effectively examine traffic for Web server exploits, you need to at least create VACLs to capture traffic destined for all the ports on which you run your Web servers. Capturing traffic for all the commonly used Web server ports enables you to learn about misdirected attacks (attacks against ports on which you do not even run Web servers).

VACL Limitations

VACLs overcome the limitations of the SPAN feature by having the capability to capture packets that match a specified flow.

Only one VACL per protocol can be applied to a single VLAN. Cisco Secure IDS examines only IP traffic, so you are limited to one IP VACL per VLAN. This IP VACL, however, can be applied across multiple VLANS.

Configuration Tasks

Installing your Catalyst 6000 IDSM line card requires you to configure your IDSM, as well as your Catalyst 6000 family switch. The operations required are as follows:

- Initialize IDSM line card
- Configure the switch for ID analysis
- Verify the IDSM configuration
- Add the IDSM to CSPM

Initialize IDSM

The Catalyst 6000 family switch can be accessed either through a console management session or through Telnet. Some switches might even support ssh access. After an interactive session is established with the switch, you must session into the IDSM line card. This is the only way to gain command-line access to the IDSM. Log in as the *ciscoids* user with the default password *attack*. You are logged in as a privileged user and can initialize the IDSM with the Setup command facility.

---

session Command

Your Catalyst 6000 family switch can have several devices that require console access. Normally, you gain console access by plugging a cable directly into the console port on the device. With devices such as your MSFC and IDSM line card, the devices do not have their own console port. Therefore, to access the console port on these devices, you use the **session** switch command. The syntax for the **session** command is as follows:

```
Console> (enable) session mod_num
```

mod_num represents the slot for the device on which you want to connect to the console port. If your IDSM line card is in slot 9, the **session** command to access the IDSM console is the following:

```
Console> (enable) session 9
```

Assign and Apply Initial Configuration

Before you can add your IDSM to your Cisco Secure IDS, you need to assign and apply an initial configuration. To apply this initial configuration, follow these steps:

Step 1   Use the **session** command to access the IDSM (see Figure 14-4).

Step 2   Run the **setup** IDSM command to begin the System Configuration dialog box (see Figure 14-4).

Step 3   Press Enter or type **Yes** to continue with the configuration dialog box (see Figure 14-4).

Step 4   Enter the PostOffice parameters for the IDSM (see Figure 14-5).

Step 5   Enter **yes** to apply the initial configuration and cause the IDSM to reset. The IDSM is then initialized and can communicate with the Director platform (see Figure 14-5).

IDSM Setup

The IDSM Setup utility is a program that enables you to configure the parameters that you need to define for your ISDM to operate (see Figure 14-4). This is similar to running the

sysconfig-sensor command on the sensor appliance (refer to Chapter 7, "4200 Series Sensor Installation Within CSPM"). The parameters that you define with the IDSM Setup utility are divided into parameters for the IDSM itself and parameters for the Director platform.

Figure 14-4 *IDSM Setup Utility*

Figure 14-5 *Configuring IDSM PostOffice Parameters*

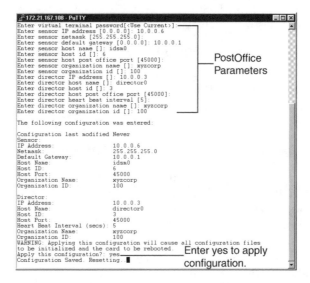

The IDSM-specific parameters are as follows:

- Virtual terminal password
- IP address
- Network mask
- Default gateway
- Host name
- Host ID
- Host port
- Organization name
- Organization ID

Correspondingly, you also need to enter the following parameters that define characteristics of your Director:

- IP address
- Host name
- Host ID
- Heartbeat interval (secs)
- Organization name
- Organization ID

All these parameters, except the virtual terminal password, represent the PostOffice parameters that are required to enable communication between your Director platform and your IDSM. (See Chapter 7 for a detailed explanation of these PostOffice parameters.)

Configure the Switch for ID Analysis

In addition to setting up the basic parameters on your IDSM line card, you need to configure your Catalyst switch to support your IDSM. This section covers the commands used to configure your Catalyst 6000 family switch for intrusion detection analysis. You need to perform the following operations when setting up your switch for ID analysis.

- Assign the command and control port
- Set up SPAN and/or VACL feature(s)
- Clear unwanted VLAN traffic (optional)

Assign the Command and Control Port

You defined an IP address for your IDSM line card's command and control interface when you ran the IDSM **setup** command. For the switch to pass traffic to this IP address, you must place port 2 (the command and control interface) on the IDSM line card onto the correct VLAN. This VLAN represents the network that matches the IP address assigned to your IDSM command and control interface.

NOTE   You can place your IDSM line card and CSPM host on the same VLAN or you can place them on different VLANs. If you choose to place them on different VLANs, you need to make sure that you have configured your routing to allow them to communicate with each other.

To define the VLAN for a port on your Catalyst switch, you use the **set vlan** command. This command sets a group of ports into a single VLAN. You also can use this command to set the private VLAN type or to unmap VLANs. These extra features are explained in the Catalyst switch documentation. The syntax for the basic **set vlan** command is as follows:

```
set vlan vlan_num mod/ports
```

The parameters for the **set vlan** command are explained in Table 14-3.

Table 14-3   set vlan *Parameters*

Parameter	Description
vlan_num	Number identifying the VLAN
mod/ports	Number of the module and ports on the module belonging to the VLAN

NOTE   The IDSM command and control port (port 2) must be assigned to a VLAN that can communicate with CSPM. Otherwise, you cannot complete the installation of your IDSM line card.

To assign ports 5 through 10 on module 4 to VLAN 130, use the following command:

```
Console> (enable) set vlan 130 4/5-10
VLAN 130 modified.

VLAN  Mod/Ports

----  ----------------------

130   4/5-10

Console> (enable)
```

Set Up SPAN or VACL Feature(s)

To analyze traffic, your IDSM must receive traffic on its monitoring interface. You need to configure your Catalyst switch to copy selected traffic to the monitoring port on your IDSM line card. You have two mechanisms with which to capture traffic for the monitoring port on your IDSM line card:

- SPAN ports
- VACLs

To capture traffic by using a SPAN port, you need to use the **set span** switch command. This command enables you to designate the source port(s) and destination port for a SPAN association.

To remove an existing SPAN association, you use the **set span disable** command. The syntax of the **set span** command is as follows:

```
set span src_mod/src_ports | src_vlan dest_mod/dest_port tx | rx | both
    create
set span disable dest_mod/dest_port | all
```

Table 14-4 describes the parameters for the **set span** command.

Table 14-4   **set span** *Parameters*

Parameter	Description
src_mod/src_ports	The module and port numbers of the source traffic to be mirrored.
src_vlan	VLAN number of traffic to be mirrored.
dest_mod/dest_port	The module and port number assigned as the destination for the mirrored traffic.
tx	Copy traffic that is transmitted from the source port or VLAN.
rx	Copy traffic that is received at the source port or VLAN.
both	Copy traffic that is received or transmitted from the source port or VLAN.
create	If you do not specify the keyword **create** with the **set span** command, and you have only one session, the session is overwritten. If a matching destination port exists, the particular session is overwritten (with or without specifying **create**). If you specify the keyword **create** and no matching destination port exists, the session is created.

If you want to configure SPAN so that traffic transmitted and received on port 3/9 (SPAN source) is mirrored on port 3/4 (SPAN destination), you use the following command:

```
Console> (enable) set span 3/9 3/4 both create

Enabled monitoring of Port 3/9 transmit/receive traffic by Port 3/4

Console> (enable)
```

Similarly, if your want to configure SPAN so that traffic received by VLAN 130 (SPAN source) is mirrored on port 3/4 (SPAN destination), use the following command:

```
Console> (enable) set span 130 3/4

Enabled monitoring of VLAN 130 transmit/receive traffic by Port 3/4

Console> (enable)
```

If you choose to use VACLs to capture traffic, the process is a little more complicated than using a SPAN port. To use VACLs to capture traffic, follow these steps:

Step 1 Create the VACL to capture interesting traffic.

Step 2 Commit the VACL to memory.

Step 3 MAP the VACL to VLAN(s).

Step 4 Assign the monitoring port as the VACL capture port. By default, port 1 on the IDSM is assigned as the VACL capture port.

To create a VACL, you need to use the **set security acl ip** switch command. This command creates a VACL to capture IP traffic for intrusion detection analysis by specifying the **capture** keyword. To remove a VACL or VLAN mapping, you need to use the **clear security acl map** switch command.

You build a VACL by defining the traffic that you want copied to your IDSM monitoring port. The system automatically appends an implicit **deny any any** statement to the end of your VACL (this is analogous to regular ACLs). Therefore, any traffic that is not explicitly permitted by your VACL is not allowed through your switch. Traffic flows with the Capture option enabled are copied to IDSM for analysis along with passing through the switch.

The syntax for the **set security acl ip** command is shown using several different examples based on the type of traffic that you want to capture.

The syntax for capturing traffic from a single IP address is as follows:

```
set security acl ip acl_name permit src_ip_spec  capture
```

The syntax for capturing IP traffic between a source IP address and a destination IP address is as follows:

```
set security acl ip acl_name permit [ip | 0] src_ip_spec dest_ip_spec [capture]
```

The syntax for capturing ICMP traffic between a source IP address and a destination IP address is as follows:

```
set security acl ip acl_name permit [icmp | 1] src_ip_spec dest_ip_spec
    [icmp_type] [icmp_code] | [icmp_message] [capture]
```

The syntax for capturing TCP traffic between a source IP address and a destination IP address is as follows:

```
set security acl ip acl_name permit [tcp | 6] src_ip_spec [operator port
    [port]] dest_ip_spec [operator port [port]] [established] [capture]
```

The syntax for capturing UDP traffic between a source IP address and a destination IP address is as follows. Table 14-5 lists the related parameters.

```
set security acl ip acl_name permit [udp | 17] src_ip_spec [operator port
    [port]] dest_ip_spec [operator port [port]] [capture]
```

Table 14-5   **set security acl ip** *Parameters*

Parameter	Description
acl_name	Unique name that identifies the lists to which the entry belongs.
permit	Keyword to allow traffic from the source IP address.
src_ip_spec	Source IP address and the source mask.
protocol	Keyword or number of an IP protocol.
dest_ip_spec	Destination IP address and the destination mask.
capture	Keyword to specify packets are switched normally and captured; permit must also be enabled.
**ip	0**	(Optional) Keyword or number to match any IP packets.
**icmp	1**	(Optional) Keyword or number to match ICMP packets.
icmp-type	(Optional) ICMP message type name or a number.
icmp-code	(Optional) ICMP message code name or a number.
icmp-message	ICMP message type name or ICMP message type and code name.
**tcp	6**	(Optional) Keyword or number to match TCP packets.
operator	(Optional) Operands; valid values include **lt** (less than), **gt** (greater than), **eq** (equal), **neq** (not equal), and **range** (inclusive range).
port	(Optional) Number or name of a TCP or UDP port; valid port numbers are from 0 to 65,535.
established	(Optional) Keyword to specify an established connection; used only for TCP protocol.
**udp	17**	(Optional) Keyword or number to match UDP packets.

Now you can take a look at some actual examples of the **set security acl ip** command. The first example involves capturing traffic that matches the following requirements:

- The source network is the Class C address 172.21.166.0.
- The source ports are 1–1024.
- The destination network is the Class C address 172.21.168.0.
- The destination ports are 60–100.
- The traffic type is UDP.
- The security ACL name is UDPACL1.

The associated **set security acl ip** command is as follows:

```
Console> (enable) set security acl ip UDPACL1 permit udp 172.21.166.0 0.0.0.255
    range 1 1024 172.21.168.0 0.0.0.255 range 60 100 capture

UDACL1 editbuffer modified. Use 'commit' command to apply changes.

Console> (enable)
```

This next example involves capturing traffic that matches the following requirements:

- The source address can be anything.

- The destination IP address is anything.

- The traffic type is ICMP echo reply messages.

- The security ACL name is ICMPACL1.

```
Console> (enable) set security acl ip ICMPACL1 permit icmp any any
    echo-reply capture

ICMPACL1 editbuffer modified. Use 'commit' command to apply changes.

Console> (enable)
```

NOTE   When specifying either the *src_ip_spec* or the *dest_ip_spec*, you need to supply an IP address followed by a netmask. For the netmask, 0 indicates a care bit, and 1 indicates a don't-care bit. Some useful keywords are

- Use the keyword **any** as an abbreviation for an IP address and netmask of 0.0.0.0 and 255.255.255.255, respectively.

- Use **host** *IP address* as an abbreviation for an IP address with a netmask of 0.0.0.0.

After defining the interesting traffic to be captured with the **set security acl ip** command, you need to commit the VACL to hardware. You use the **commit security acl** command. The syntax for this command is as follows:

```
commit security acl acl_name | all
```

You can either commit all the security ACLs by using the **all** keyword or you can specify the name of the specific security ACL to commit to hardware. To commit the sample security ACLs that were shown previously in this chapter, use these commands:

```
cat6k (enable) commit security acl UDPACL1

Hardware programming in progress...

ACL UDPACL1 is committed to hardware.

cat6k (enable) commit security acl ICMPACL1

Hardware programming in progress...

ACL ICMPACL1 is committed to hardware.

cat6k (enable)
```

Next, you need to map your security ACLs to specific VLANs on your switch through the **set security acl map** command. The syntax for this command is as follows:

```
set security acl map acl_name vlan
```

You need to specify which security ACL *(acl_name)* that you want to map to which VLAN *(vlan)*. If you want to map the previously described security ACL ICMPACL1 to VLANs 12 and 14, use the following commands:

```
cat6k (enable) set security acl map ICMPACL1 12

ACL ICMPACL1 mapped to vlan 12

cat6k (enable) set security acl map ICMPACL1 14

ACL ICMPACL mapped to vlan 14

cat6k (enable)
```

Finally, you need to use the **set security acl capture-ports** command to define which ports on your switch receive the traffic captured by your security ACLs. The syntax for this command is as follows:

```
set security acl capture-ports {mod/ports...}
```

The only parameters are a list of ports on your switch to receive the traffic captured by your security ACLs. If your IDSM line card is in slot 4, to define its monitoring port as the capture port for security ACLs, use the following command:

```
cat6k (enable) set security acl capture-ports 4/1

Successfully set 4/1 to capture ACL traffic.

cat6k (enable)
```

Clear Unwanted VLAN Traffic

Clearing unwanted VLAN traffic is optional. By default, port 1 on your IDSM is a trunking port and assigned as the destination capture port for VLAN ACLs. This means that it captures traffic for all the VLANs defined on your Catalyst switch. If you do not want to capture traffic from all the VLANs on your switch, you need to change the trunk parameters associated with port 1 on your IDSM line card. You need to use the following commands to change the trunk parameters associated with a port on your Catalyst switch:

- **set trunk**
- **clear trunk**

You use the **set trunk** command to configure trunk ports and to add VLANs to the allowed VLAN list for existing trunks. The syntax for the **set trunk** switch command is as follows:

```
set trunk mod/port {on | off | desirable | auto | nonegotiate}[vlans] [isl |
    dot1q | negotiate]
set trunk mod/port vlans
set trunk all off
```

The parameters for the **set trunk** command are explained in Table 14-6.

Table 14-6   **set trunk** *Parameters*

Parameter	Description
mod/port	Number of the module and the port on the module.
on	Keyword used to force the port to become a trunk port and persuade the neighboring port to become a trunk port. The port becomes a trunk port even if the neighboring port does not agree to become a trunk.
off	Keyword used to force the port to become a nontrunk port and persuade the neighboring port to become a nontrunk port. The port becomes a nontrunk port even if the neighboring port does not agree to become a nontrunk port.
desirable	Keyword used to cause the port to negotiate actively with the neighboring port to become a trunk link.
auto	Keyword used to cause the port to become a trunk port if the neighboring port tries to negotiate a trunk link.
nonegotiate	Keyword used to force the port to become a trunk port but prevent it from sending DTP frames to its neighbor.
vlans	(Optional) Specifies the VLANs to add to the list of allowed VLANs on the trunk; valid values are from 1 to 1000 and 1025 to 4094.
isl	(Optional) Keyword used to specify an ISL trunk on a Fast or Gigabit Ethernet port.
dot1q	(Optional) Keyword used to specify an IEEE 802.1Q trunk on a Fast or Gigabit Ethernet port.
negotiate	(Optional) Keyword used to specify that the port become an ISL (preferred) or 802.1Q trunk, depending on the configuration and capabilities of the neighboring port.
all off	Keywords used to turn off trunking on all ports.

NOTE   When you first configure a port as a trunk, the **set trunk** switch command always adds all of your switch's VLANs to the allowed VLAN list for the trunk, even if you specify a VLAN range. (The specified VLAN range is ignored.)

If you want to add VLAN 10 and VLAN 12 to your IDSM monitoring port (located on port 4/1), the command is as follows:

```
cat6k (enable) set trunk 4/1 10,12

Adding vlans 10,12 to allowed list.
Port(s) 4/1 allowed vlans modified to 1,10,12,20-22.
cat6k (enable)
```

To remove VLANs from the allowed list of VLANs for a trunk, you need to use the **clear trunk** switch command. The syntax for the **clear trunk** command is as follows:

```
clear trunk mod/port vlans
```

NOTE   Before removing VLANs from a trunk port, you need to know which VLANs are assigned to the trunk port. You can obtain this information by using the **show trunk** *mod/port* **detail** switch command.

Suppose you have a trunk port (3/1) that has 13 VLANs (1, 10–12, 14, 15, 17, 18, 21–24) assigned to it. You want to remove VLANs 10, 11, 15, and 18. The command is as follows:

```
cat6k (enable) clear trunk 3/1 10-11,15,18

Removing Vlan(s) 10-11,15,18 from allowed list.
Port(s) 3/1 allowed vlans modified to 1,12,14,17,21-24.
cat6k (enable)
```

Verify the IDSM Configuration

This section discusses the commands used to verify your IDSM configuration. Analyzing your IDSM line card configuration requires examining the configuration on your Catalyst switch as well as your IDSM line card. When verifying your IDSM configuration, you need to execute commands on both your Catalyst switch and your IDSM line card. The commands used to verify your IDSM configuration fall into two groups:

* Catalyst 6000 family switch commands
* IDSM commands

Catalyst 6000 Family Switch Commands

To configure your Catalyst 6000 family switch to pass network traffic to your IDSM line card, you must configure the appropriate packet capture mechanism. To view the configuration settings on your switch, you can use several commands:

* **show config**
* **show span**
* **show security acl**

A wealth of information about the current configuration of your switch can be obtained through the **show config** switch command. When you execute the **show config**, it displays the nondefault system or module configuration. The syntax for **show config** command is as follows:

```
show config [all]
show config [system | mod] [all]
show config acl location
```

Table 14-7 describes the parameters for the **show config** command.

Table 14-7   show config *Parameters*

Parameter	Description
all	(Optional) Keyword used to specify all module and system configuration information, including the IP address.
system	(Optional) Keyword used to display the system configuration.
mod	(Optional) Keyword used to display module configuration.
acl location	Keyword to display ACL configuration file location.

NOTE   Sometimes, you might want to find specific information within the **show config** output. The **show config** command normally displays one full screen of output at a time, with a -- More -- prompt. By pressing Enter, you can view the next screen of information. To search for specific information in the output, you also can enter the following sequence:

```
/<text> (followed by Enter)
```

This searches the output for the <text> that you specified. If the string is found, the display is positioned so that the line containing the text is two lines from the top of the display. If the <text> string is not found, the following message displays at the bottom of the screen:

```
Pattern Not Found
```

Finally, if you want to search for the same text string again, you can enter the following at the -- More -- prompt:

```
n (followed by Enter)
```

If you want to learn detailed information about you current SPAN configuration, use the **show span** switch command. The syntax for the **show span** command is as follows:

```
show span [all]
```

The parameter for the **show span** command is explained in Table 14-8.

Table 14-8   show span *Parameter*

Parameter	Description
all	(Optional) Keyword to display local and remote SPAN configuration information.

When you issue the **show span** command, the output is composed of numerous fields. A sample execution of the **show span** command is shown in the following code segment:

```
Console> (enable) show span

- - - - - - - - - - - - - - - - - - - - - - - - - - - - - - - - - - - - - - - - - - - - - - - - - - -
Destination      : Port 4/1


Admin Source     : Port 2/2

Oper Source      : Port 2/2

Direction        : transmit/receive

Incoming Packets: enabled

Learning         : disabled

Multicast        : enabled

Filter           : 10,20,30,40,50,60,70,80,90,100

Status           : inactive

Console> (enable)
```

The fields listed in the **show span** output are explained in Table 14-9.

Table 14-9 **show span** *Command Output Fields*

Field	Description
Destination	Destination port for SPAN information
Admin Source	Source port or VLAN for SPAN information
Oper Source	Operator port or VLAN for SPAN information
Direction	Status of whether transmit, receive, or transmit/receive information is monitored
Incoming Packets	Status of whether reception of normal incoming packets on the SPAN destination port is enabled or disabled
Learning	Status of whether learning is enabled or disabled for the SPAN destination port
Multicast	Status of whether monitoring multicast traffic is enabled or disabled
Filter	Monitored VLANs in source trunk ports
Status	Bandwidth limits for SPAN traffic, in Mbps

The final command covered in this section is the **show security acl** switch command. This command displays the contents of the ACL that are currently configured or last committed to NVRAM and hardware. The syntax for **show security acl** command is as follows:

```
show security acl
show security acl [editbuffer]
show security acl info acl_name | all [editbuffer [editbuffer_index]]
```

The parameters for the **show security acl** command are explained in Table 14-10.

Table 14-10 show security acl *Parameters*

Parameter	Description
editbuffer	(Optional) Keyword to display the VACLs in the edit buffer
acl_name	Name of the VACL to be displayed
info	Keyword to display the contents of a VACL that were last committed to NVRAM and hardware
all	Keyword to display all QoS ACL information
editbuffer_index	(Optional) Position of the access control entry (ACE) in the VACL

Now it is time to examine an actual example. For this example, you have three IDSM line cards that you configured to monitor six VLANs on your switch by using three security ACLs (see Appendix A, "Deploying Intrusion Detection: Case Studies"). The following sample outputs indicate the output that you receive from the various **show security acl** commands:

```
cat6k> (enable) show security acl

ACL                              Type VLANS
-----------------------------    ---- -----
IDSM_IP1                         IP   16,17
IDSM_IP2                         IP   18,19
IDSM_IP3                         IP   20,21

cat6k> (enable) show security acl editbuffers

ACL                              Type Status
IDSM_IP1                         IP   Committed
IDSM_IP2                         IP   Committed
IDSM_IP3                         IP   Committed

cat6k> (enable) show security acl info IDSM_IP1

set security acl ip IDSM_IP1
----------------------------------------------------
1. permit ip 172.16.64.0 0.0.0.255 any capture
2. permit ip any 172.16.64.0 0.0.0.255 capture
3. permit ip 172.17.64.0 0.0.0.255 any capture
4. permit ip any 172.17.64.0 0.0.0.255 capture
5. permit ip any any

cat6k> (enable)
```

IDSM Commands

In addition to the switch commands that you use to verify your switch configuration, you also can use commands on your IDSM to verify its configuration. These commands are as follows:

- **clear config**
- **show configuration**

- **show eventfile**
- **resetcount**

If you want to remove the configuration on your IDSM line card, use the **clear config** command. The syntax for **clear config** is as follows:

```
clear config
```

NOTE   The **clear config** command *disables* IDS features on the IDSM line card.

The remaining IDSM commands are diagnostic commands. They must be executed in the Diagnostics mode on the IDSM. To enter Diagnostics mode, use the **diag** command:

```
idsm1# diag
idsm1 (diag)#
```

The **show configuration** is an IDSM diagnostic command that displays your IDSM version and configuration settings. The syntax for the **show configuration** command follows:

```
show configuration
```

Sometimes, you need to view the log files on your IDSM line card. You can use the **show eventfile** IDSM command to display the contents of the IDSM event log files. The syntax for the **show eventfile** command is as follows:

```
show eventfile [current | backup | archive]
```

If you want to view the contents of the current log file, use the following command:

```
idsm1# (diag) show eventfile current
4,0,2000/11/25,01:07:12,2000/11/25,01:07:12,10000,6,100,OUT,OUT,5,997,0,TCP/IP,
    0.0.0.0,0.0.0.0,0,0,0.0.0.0,84.100 route 1 down
4,1,2000/11/25,01:07:29,2000/11/25,01:07:29,10000,6,100,OUT,OUT,1,0,0,TCP/IP,
    0.0.0.0,0.0.0.0,0,0,0.0.0.0,postofficed initial notification msg
```

Your IDSM also maintains a counter of the IP traffic received through the command and control port. To reset this counter, use the **resetcount** IDSM diagnostic command. The syntax for the **resetcount** is as follows:

```
diag resetcount
```

NOTE   To view the IP counter that the **resetcount** command resets, use the **show ip traffic** command.

Add the IDSM to CSPM

Finally, you must add your IDSM to CSPM to complete your IDSM installation. After the IDSM is added to CSPM, CSPM can configure the IDSM and log and display alarms generated by the IDSM. To add a sensor to CSPM, you utilize the Add Sensor Wizard. The procedure to add an IDSM Sensor follows the same procedure outlined in Chapter 7 for the 4200 Series Sensor appliance.

Updating IDSM Components

This section discusses IDSM application and maintenance partitions, service packs, and signatures. You need to understand these components to perform the procedures necessary to update your IDSM partitions, service packs, and signatures. To explain these topics, this section is divided into the following two categories:

- Disk structure
- Updating IDSM images

Disk Structure

IDSM has two independent partitions on its internal hard drive: the application partition (hdd:1) and the maintenance partition (hdd:2). Each of these partitions is 4 GB, contains its own image, and is capable of running even if the other partition becomes corrupted. Only one partition can be active at a time. The application partition contains the IDS engine and is active by default.

NOTE   The Catalyst **set boot device** command can be used to assign the default active partition.

Setting the Active Partition

The IDSM can be booted from either of its internal hard drive partitions. The partition that the IDSM uses to boot is known as the *active partition*. If you need to change the active partition, you need to use the **set boot device** command. This command determines which hard drive on the IDSM is the active partition.

Active Partition

Either of the internal hard drive partitions on the IDSM can be used during the boot process. The partition that is used during the boot process is known as the active partition.

The syntax for the **set boot device** command is as follows:

```
Console> (enable) set boot device hdd:partition mod_num
```

To make the maintenance partition the active partition on your IDSM line card in slot 2, use the following command:

```
Console> (enable) set boot device hdd:2 2
```

Application Partition

The application partition contains the IDS application and is the active partition under normal circumstances. If you need to reinstall or upgrade the application partition, do this from the maintenance partition.

Maintenance Partition

The maintenance partition contains maintenance and diagnostic functions and is not capable of performing intrusion detection.

NOTE   Updating a partition is done while it is not active. For example, if the maintenance partition became corrupt, reinstall the maintenance image from the application partition.

Use the Catalyst switch command **reset** to reboot the IDSM line card and make a specific partition active.

The syntax for the **reset** command is as follows:

```
reset mod_num hdd:partition
```

To boot the IDSM line card in slot 3 of the maintenance partition, you use the following command:

```
cat6k (enable) reset 3 hdd:2
```

Updating IDSM Images

IDSM updates are released as files. The update process requires that the update files exist on an accessible FTP server. The update files can be obtained online from Cisco's Software Center at www.cisco.com. A valid Cisco Connection Online (CCO) account is required.

NOTE   To obtain a CCO account, you need to access http://www.cisco.com/register. Then, to complete the registration process, you need to provide your Cisco Service contract number or Partner Service Agreement number.

Signatures and service packs are distributed as self-extracting executables.

Partition image files are distributed in Microsoft cab format. Two supporting files are required: .lst and .dat. The .lst file contains a list of the cab files required to install the image. The .dat file is a binary file containing installation information.

IDSM Files

Each IDSM software filename is composed of the following parts:

- File type
- IDSM version
- Service pack level
- Signature version
- File extension

A sample IDSM signature update software file is IDSM-sig-2.5-2-S1.exe. How this filename is constructed is discussed in the following section.

The four types of IDSM software files follow:

- **Application (a)**—IDS engine image
- **Maintenance (m)**—IDS maintenance image
- **Service Packs (sp)**—IDS engine fixes
- **Signature (sig)**—IDS signature updates

The IDSM version is represented by a numeric value and is separated by a decimal. The preceding number is the major version and the latter is the minor version. A sample version is 2.5, where the major version is 2 and the minor version is 5.

The service pack level identifies the level at which the IDSM has been patched. The signature version identifies the signatures detected by IDSM.

The filename extension can be one the following:

- **.exe**—Self-extracting executable for signature or service pack updates
- **.cab**—Microsoft cab files for IDSM software images
- **.lst**—Text file containing a list of the cab files required for an IDSM software image
- **.dat**—Binary file containing information required for installation of an IDSM software image

An example of an IDSM software file is IDSM-sig-2.5-2-S1.exe. This filename represents the following:

- **File type**—Signature update
- **IDSM version**—IDSM major version 2, minor version 5

- **Service pack level**—2
- **Signature version**—1
- **File extension**—.exe (self-extracting executable)

Update Signatures and Service Packs

To ensure maximum effectiveness of your Cisco Secure IDS, you need to keep your IDS engine software current, along with your signature database.

To install a signature update or a service pack, use the **apply** IDSM configuration command. The syntax for the **apply** command is as follows:

```
apply [signatureupdate | servicepack] site IP address user username
      dir directory file filename
```

Table 14-11 explains the parameters for the **apply** command.

Table 14-11 **apply** *Parameters*

Parameter	Description
signatureupdate	Keyword to specify a signature update file is to be installed
servicepack	Keyword to specify a service pack file is to be installed
site	Keyword to specify that the files to be installed exist on an FTP server
IP address	IP address or host name of the FTP server
user	Keyword to specify an existing user account on the FTP server used to transfer the files
username	The user name of the account on the FTP server
dir	Keyword to specify that the files are stored in a specified directory
directory	The directory where the files are located
file	Keyword to specify that a file is to be transferred from the FTP server
filename	The filename of the file to be transferred and installed

To apply a signature update to your IDSM in slot 3, follow these steps:

Step 1   Session into your IDSM line card:

```
Cat6k (enable) session 3
login: ciscoids
password:
```

Step 2   Go into Configuration mode:

```
idsm1# configure terminal
idsm1# (config) apply signatureupdate site 10.20.2.10 user idsm dir
  update file
     IDSM-sig-2.5-1-S1.exe
```

Step 3 A warning message displays. Enter **yes** when prompted to continue with the install.

Step 4 Enter the password for the FTP user *idsm* when prompted. Wait for the file to download. When the download is complete, the IDSM shuts down and resets. You are automatically returned to the switch prompt.

Step 5 Session into your IDSM.

Step 6 Verify that the service pack was installed using the **show configuration** IDSM diagnostic command.

Updating IDSM Partitions

Sometime it is necessary for you to update the IDSM partitions. Use the **ids-installer** IDSM configuration command to install an IDSM partition image. The syntax for the **ids-installer** command is as follows:

```
ids-installer system /nw /install /server=ip_address /user=username
    /dir=directory /prefix=update_file /save=yes
```

The parameters for the **ids_installer** command are described in Table 14-12.

Table 14-12 ids-installer *Parameters*

Parameter	Description
system	Keyword to specify a system action is to be performed.
/nw	Keyword to specify the installation of the image is done from the network.
/install	Keyword to specify the system action is an install.
/server=	Keyword to specify the image file exists on an FTP server.
ip_address	IP address of the FTP server.
/user=	Keyword to specify a username is required to download the image file.
username	The username of the account on the FTP server.
/dir=	Keyword to specify that the files are stored in a specified directory.
directory	The directory where the files are located. The single quotes are required.
/prefix	Keyword to specify the prefix of the image file is required.
update_file	Prefix of the image file to be transferred and installed.
/save	Keyword to specify if the image file is saved as the cache copy.
yes | no	If **yes**, the image file is installed and saved as a cached copy. If **no**, the image file is installed but not saved.

Troubleshooting

If you have trouble with your IDSM, you have various options at your disposal to debug the problem. The main things that you can check are as follows:

- IDSM status LED
- Catalyst switch commands
- IDSM commands

IDSM Status LED

The status LED is a quick way to determine the state of your IDSM line card. The status LED is located in the left corner of the module (see Figure 14-6). The status LED colors are explained in Table 14-13.

Figure 14-6 *IDSM Front Panel*

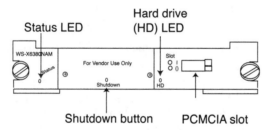

Table 14-13 *IDSM Status LED Colors*

Status Color	Description
Green	IDSM is operational.
Amber	IDSM is disabled or running a boot and self-diagnostics sequence.
Red	Diagnostic other than an individual port test failed.
Off	IDSM power is off.

Catalyst Switch Commands

Several switch commands are available to help you troubleshoot the operation of your IDSM line card. These commands are as follows:

- **show module**
- **show port**
- **reset**

show module

The **show module** Catalyst switch command displays the status and other information related to modules that you installed on your Catalyst 6000 family switch. The syntax for the **show module** command is as follows:

```
show module [mod]
```

The parameter for the **show module** command is explained in Table 14-14.

Table 14-14   **show module** *Parameter*

Parameter	Description
mod	Number of the module on which you want to see the status

show port

To examine the status of ports on your switch, including the counters associated with the port, you need to use the **show port** switch command. The syntax for the **show port** command is as follows:

```
show port [mod[/port]]
```

Table 14-15 explains the single parameter for the **show port** command.

Table 14-15   **show port** *Parameter*

Parameter	Description
mod/port	Number of the module and optionally, the number of the port on the module on which you want to see the status

reset

To restart your Catalyst switch or reset individual modules installed on your switch, you need to use the **reset** switch command. This command enables you to restart the system, reset individual modules, schedule a system reset, or cancel a scheduled reset. The syntax for the **reset** command is as follows:

```
reset mod_num hdd:partition
reset [mod_num | system | mindown]
reset [mindown] at {hh:mm} [mm/dd] [reason]
reset [mindown] in [hh:] {mm} [reason]
reset [cancel]
reset {mod} [bootdevice[,bootdevice]]
```

The parameters for the **reset** command are explained in Table 14-16.

Table 14-16 reset *Parameters*

Parameter	Description
mod_num	Number of the module to reset.
hdd:	Keyword used to specify the boot image is on a hard disk.
partition	Number of the partition on the hard disk that becomes active after the module is reset.
system	(Optional) Keyword used to reset the system.
mindown	(Optional) Keyword used to perform a reset as part of a minimal downtime software upgrade in a system with a redundant supervisor engine.
at	Keyword used to schedule a system reset at a specific future time.
hh:*mm*	Hour and minute of the scheduled reset.
mm/*dd*	(Optional) Month and day of the scheduled reset.
reason	(Optional) Reason for the reset.
in	Keyword to schedule a system reset a specific number of hours and minutes from now.
hh	(Optional) Number of hours into the future to reset the switch.
mm	Number of minutes into the future to reset the switch.
cancel	(Optional) Keyword used to cancel the scheduled reset.
bootdevice	(Optional) Keyword used to indicate that you are specifying a boot device to be reset.
bootdevice	(Optional) Boot device identification. For format guidelines, see the "Usage Guidelines" section of Catalyst switch documentation.

IDSM Commands

Several IDSM commands are available to help you troubleshoot the operation of your IDSM line card. These commands are executed in Diagnostics mode. To enter Diagnostics mode, you need to enter **diag** at the IDSM console prompt. The diagnostic troubleshooting commands are as follows:

- **nrconns**
- **diag bootresults**
- **report systemstatus**
- **show errorfile**

nrconns

The **nrconns** IDSM command displays the current IDS communication service status. This command is the same as the **nrconns** command used to display the communication service status on the appliance sensor. The syntax for the **nrconns** command is as follows:

```
nrconns
```

diag bootresults

The **diag bootresults** IDSM command displays the boot time diagnostic results. The syntax for the **diag bootresults** command is as follows:

```
diag bootresults
```

report systemstatus

You can transfer the system status to an FTP server by using the **report systemstatus** IDSM command. The file transferred is formatted using HTML and contains the diagnostic information for your IDSM Sensor, as well as the IDSM configuration files. The name of the file created is as follows:

<*IDSM Sensor Name*>**SystemStatusReport.html**

If the name of your IDSM is idsm1, for example, the name of the system status file is this:

idsm1SystemStatusReport.html

The syntax for the **report systemstatus** command is as follows:

```
report systemstatus site ip_address user username dir directory
```

The parameters for the **report systemstatus** command are explained in Table 14-17.

Table 14-17   **report systemstatus** *Parameters*

Parameter	Description
site	Keyword to specify that an FTP server is the destination for the file transfer
ip address	The IP address of the FTP server to be used for file transfer
user	Keyword to specify that a username is required to transfer the file to the FTP server
username	The username of the account on the FTP server
dir	Keyword to specify that the files are stored in a specified directory
directory	The directory where the files are stored

show errorfile

The IDSM maintains error log files that store all the errors that occur on the IDSM. These error log files are divided into a separate file for each service running on the IDSM line card (refer to Appendix B, "Cisco Secure IDS Architecture"). To view these log files, you need to use the **show errorfile** IDSM command. The syntax for the **show errorfile** command is as follows:

```
show errorfile [filexferd | loggerd | packetd | postofficed | sapd]
     [current | backup]
```

Table 14-18 explains the parameters for the **show errorfile** command.

Table 14-18   **show errorfile** *Parameters*

Parameter	Description
fileXferd	Keyword that specifies to display the contents of the fileXferd error log file
loggerd	Keyword that specifies to display the contents of the loggerd error log file
packetd	Keyword that specifies to display the contents of the packetd error log file
postofficed	Keyword that specifies to display the contents of the postofficed error log file
sapd	Keyword that specifies to display the contents of the sapd error log file
current	Keyword to display the contents of the current log file specified
backup	Keyword to display the contents of the archived log file specified

Summary

The Intrusion Detection System Module (IDSM) for the Catalyst 6000 family of switches establishes a new security environment by placing an IDS sensor on a line card. By capturing traffic directly off the switch's backplane, the IDSM line card tightly integrates security into a switched network environment. The following two mechanisms are available to the network administrator to capture the traffic on which an IDSM performs intrusion detection analysis:

- The SPAN feature
- The VACL feature

SPAN ports are available on every Catalyst 6000 family switch in your network. To utilize VACLs, however, you must install a Policy Feature Card (PFC) on your Catalyst switch. Regardless of which capture mechanism you use, the traffic is copied to the IDSM monitoring interface directly from the switch's backplane.

Many aspects of the IDSM line card are the same as the 4200 Series Appliance Sensor. For example, both sensor platforms provide two interfaces: a monitoring interface and a command and control interface. Nevertheless, significant differences exist between these two sensor platforms.

Installation of the IDSM line card is similar to that of the 4200 Series Appliance Sensor, except that the initial setup requires you to configure the IDSM line card, as well as parameters on your Catalyst switch.

When troubleshooting the operation of your IDSM line card, you need to examine the configuration on both your IDSM line card and the Catalyst 6000 family switch that houses it.

The attacks and signatures detected by your IDSM line card parallel the 4200 Series Appliance Sensor. Furthermore, the integration of the Catalyst 6000 IDSM into a switch makes it an integral part of the Cisco Secure IDS family of products.

Review Questions

The following questions test your retention of the material presented in this chapter. The answers to the Review Questions are in Appendix K, "Answers to Review Questions."

1   What is the active partition on the IDSM?

2   How many ports does the IDSM line card have?

3   What IDSM command enables you to configure the PostOffice communication parameters for the IDSM line card?

4   What is the default active partition on the IDSM line card?

5   What operating system is required on your Catalyst 6000 family switch to use an IDSM line card?

6 What hardware is required to use VACLs to capture traffic for your IDSM line card?

_____

_____

_____

7 How much traffic can the IDSM line card process?

_____

_____

_____

8 What switch command is used to set up a VACL?

_____

_____

_____

9 Which port on the IDSM line card is the command and control interface?

_____

_____

_____

10 What are the two mechanisms used to capture traffic for the IDSM line card?

_____

_____

_____

11 How many VACLs can you have per protocol?

_____

_____

_____

12 What does an amber status LED indicate on your IDSM line card?

_____

_____

_____

13 What command do you use to access the console on the IDSM line card?

_____

_____

_____

14 What is the default username/password for console access to the IDSM line card?

_____

_____

_____

15 What switch command do you use to set up a SPAN association on your switch?

_____

_____

_____

16 What are the four types of IDSM software files?

_____

_____

_____

## PART VI

Cisco Secure Intrusion Detection Director (CSIDD)

## CHAPTER 15

Cisco Secure ID Director Installation

You can use Cisco Secure Intrusion Detection Director (CSIDD) to manage your Cisco Secure IDS. This Director runs on the Solaris or HPUX operating systems and is integrally tied to *HP OpenView Network Node Manager (NNM)*. Installing the Cisco Secure ID Director requires you to define your Cisco Secure IDS Sensors.

HP OpenView Network Node Manager (NNM)

HP OpenView NNM is a network management application developed and sold by Hewlett-Packard Company. The Cisco Secure ID Director uses this Network Node Management software for its graphical user interface (GUI). This GUI displays the alarms and other information received from your sensors so that your operators can monitor the status of your Cisco Secure IDS.

The installation of the CSIDD requires three phases:

- Installation of the Director software
- Starting the Director
- Configuring the sensors

The following sections discuss each of these phases.

Director Software Installation

The Director software needs to be installed on a hardware platform that has Solaris or HPUX and HP OpenView NNM installed. Solaris or HPUX is the base operating system and HP OpenView NNM serves as the base GUI. The installation process involves the following:

- Running the install script
- Setting netrangr password
- Configuring Director identification parameters

- Creating the initial configuration files
- Rebooting the system

Running the Install Script

Log on to the Director system as user *root* and insert the Director CD-ROM into the CD-ROM drive. Many systems are configured to mount the CD-ROM automatically. If your system does not automatically mount the CD-ROM, you must mount it yourself by using the following command:

```
mount -F hsfs <device_name> <mount_point>
```

<device_name> represents the name of your CD-ROM device and *<mount_point>* represents the empty directory that you want to use as the root directory for the CD-ROM. A sample mount command is

```
# mount -F hsfs -r /dev/dsk/C1t0d0s0 /cdrom
```

Provided you use **cdrom** as your mount point, you can run the Cisco Secure IDS installation script by entering **/cdrom/cdrom0/install**. Alternatively, you can double-click the Install icon from the Solaris File Manager. Both options launch the Director installation program.

NOTE   When running the install script from the Solaris file manager, no parameters need to be passed to it, so click OK when prompted to enter the parameters.

Setting netrangr Password

The Director installation script creates an account or user named *netrangr*. You use the netrangr account to operate your Cisco Secure IDS. After the Director installation script writes all the required files to the hard disk, it prompts you to enter a password for the netrangr account (see Figure 15-1). Set the password for the user netrangr by entering a password once and then reentering it again when prompted. You are prompted for the password twice to ensure that you did not accidentally mistype the password the first time that you entered it.

Configuring Director Identification Parameters

You need to define numerous identification parameters for your Director. These parameters are stored in various configuration files on the Director. To configure the identification parameters for your Director, you need to run a configuration utility called *sysconfig-director*. This utility enables you to enter the values necessary for your Cisco Secure ID Director to operate properly and communicate with your Cisco Secure IDS Sensors.

Figure 15-1 *Setting the netrangr Password*

The Director installation script prompts you to run the **sysconfig-director** utility after you set the netrangr account password (see Figure 15-2). To initiate the **sysconfig-director** utility, enter **y** at the prompt.

Figure 15-2 *Initiating the sysconfig-director Utility*

NOTE   You must run the **sysconfig-director** utility before you can launch the HP OpenView NNM user interface to view Cisco Secure IDS information. This script defines your Cisco Secure IDS communication infrastructure.

After the **sysconfig-director** utility is launched, the script tells you the values that you need to enter and confirms that you want to continue (see Figure 15-3). You must enter **y** before you can begin entering the parameters for the Cisco Secure IDS communications infrastructure.

Figure 15-3   *sysconfig-director Utility*

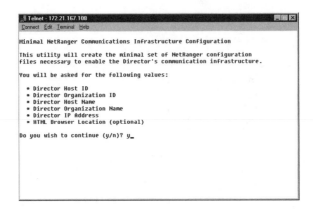

Table 15-1 contains the values you need to enter and a description of each parameter.

Table 15-1   *sysconfig-director Utility Parameters*

CSIDS Settings	Parameters	Description
Director Host ID	(1-65535)	Numeric identifier for each Director.
Director Organization ID	(1-65535)	Numeric identifier for a collection of Directors. It can be used to group a number of Directors under the same identifier for easy identification purposes.
Director Host Name	*<Host Name>* Example: Director1	Alphanumeric identifier for each Director. The name chosen here is typically one that contains the word *director* so that you can easily identify that it is a Director.
Director Organization Name	*<Org Name>* Example: Training	Alphanumeric identifier for a group of Directors. The name chosen here is typically one that describes the name of the company where the Director is installed or the name of the department within the company where the Directors are installed.
Director IP Address	*<IP Address>*	IP address of the Director.
HTML Browser Location	*<Filename>* Example: /opt/netscape/netscape	The Director automatically finds Netscape in /opt/netscape/netscape. If you do not have Netscape or have installed it in another directory, however, you need to enter the file path to your browser in this field.

Creating the Initial Configuration Files

After you finish entering all the communication and operation settings, you are prompted with the following question:

```
OK to create the Cisco Secure IDS configuration files (y/n)?
```

Check the values that you entered for various parameters to ensure that everything was entered correctly. This information needs to match the values that you recorded on the worksheet in Appendix I, "Cisco Secure Communications Deployment Worksheet." Then enter **y** and press the Enter key to generate the Director's configuration files.

NOTE   If you make an error while entering the information, enter **n** and then press the Enter key when prompted. Then select the incorrect parameter number again and enter the correct information.

Rebooting the System

After the installation script generates the configuration files, you are prompted to reboot the system (see Figure 15-4). The changes that the installation process makes to the system kernel do not take effect until you reboot your system. Therefore, at the prompt, enter **y** and press the Enter key to cause your system to reboot.

Figure 15-4 *Rebooting the System*

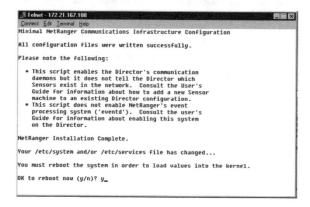

Starting the Director

After the system finishes rebooting, you can log on as user netrangr. From this account, you need to do the following:

- Verify daemons are running.
- Start HP OpenView.
- Configure the HP OpenView NNM environment.

You also need to take the time to become familiar with the HP OpenView NNM navigation buttons.

Verifying Daemons Are Running

When you log on as user netrangr, your home directory is /usr/nr. Each time that you log on, you are automatically placed in this directory.

Before you start HP OpenView to configure the HP OpenView NNM environment, you need to verify that all the Director daemons are operating. To view that status of the Cisco Secure IDS dameons, use the **nrstatus** command. When you enter the **nrstatus** command at the command prompt, the Director displays a list of services that are started and are running (see Figure 15-5).

Figure 15-5 **nrstatus** *Command*

```
Telnet - 172.21.167.108
Connect  Edit  Terminal  Help

netrangr@director:/usr/nr
>nrstatus
netrangr    457     1   0 17:50:49 ?      0:05 /usr/nr/bin/nr.loggerd
netrangr    334     1   0 17:50:41 ?      0:10 /usr/nr/bin/nr.postofficed
netrangr    458     1   0 17:50:49 ?      0:00 /usr/nr/bin/nr.sapd
netrangr    456     1   0 17:50:48 ?      0:15 /usr/nr/bin/nr.configd
netrangr    468     1   0 17:50:51 ?      0:04 /usr/nr/bin/nr.fileXferd
netrangr    465     1   0 17:50:49 ?      0:00 /usr/nr/bin/nr.smid

netrangr@director:/usr/nr
>_
```

| NOTE | You can also use the **nrstatus** command on your sensors to verify that all the required daemons are running. |

The following are the processes that you see and that are enabled by default after running **sysconfig-director**:

- **nr.loggerd**
- **nr.postofficed**
- **nr.sapd**
- **nr.configd**
- **nr.filexferd**
- **nr.smid**

Starting HP OpenView

The Director uses HP OpenView's NNM as its graphical user interface. Not all the daemons shipped with HP OpenView are needed for the Director to work. You can disable the unnecessary daemons to increase the Director's performance and response time and make managing and using HP OpenView easier. Refer to the *Cisco Secure IDS User Guide* for a list of daemons that might be disabled and instructions for disabling them.

To start HP OpenView, run the following command from the netrangr account:

```
ovw &
```

| NOTE | The **&** on the command causes Solaris and HPUX to run HP OpenView in the background. This means that you can still execute commands at the command line in your xwindow. HP OpenView runs in another xwindow that also appears on your screen. |

Initializing the HP OpenView NNM Environment

The Director displays real-time security information sent from your Cisco Secure IDS Sensors. HP OpenView NNM represents this information as icons that display on one or more network security *submaps*.

Submaps

A *submap* is a collection of icons that are grouped based on some common similarities. These submaps are grouped hierarchically. As an example, a top-level submap might represent your company. By expanding your company icon you bring up a submap that displays all the networks in your company. You can expand a network icon to bring up a submap composed of icons for all the hosts on that network.

The Director arranges icons into hierarchical security submaps based on HP OpenView's NNM user interface. You can double-click an icon to view the next lower submap in the hierarchy.

Each icon, whether it represents a machine, an application, or an alarm, has a state, which is expressed in the form of textual and graphical attributes. The most visible indication of an icon's state is its color. The color of the icon directly relates to the severity of the event. The meanings associated to the icon colors are as follows:

- **Green**—The icon state is normal. The alarm level is 1 or 2.
- **Yellow**—The icon state is marginal. The alarm level is 3.
- **Red**—The icon state is critical. The alarm level is 4 or 5.

The color of an icon at a higher level in the submap hierarchy can be used to indicate the most severe icon that is below the icon in the hierarchy. By using this capability, you can quickly determine the worst severity in each hierarchy by just examining the icons at the top submap. Then when an icon indicates that a severe alarm has occurred under it, you can drill down and locate which alarm was detected.

To make an icon take the color of the most severe icon state under it, choose **Map**, **Maps**, **Describe/Modify** from the menu bar. This displays the Map Description window (see Figure 15-6). From the Compound Status area of the Map Description window, select **Propagate Most Critical**, and click OK.

NOTE   When installing the Director on HP OpenView 6.x, the option is Map, Properties from the menu bar rather than Map, Maps, Describe/Modify.

Cisco Secure IDS hosts display in the Collection submap in HP OpenView. To set the Collection submap as the Cisco Secure IDS Home submap, double-click the Cisco Secure IDS icon to display the Collection submap. From the menu choose **Map**, **Submap**, **Set This Submap As Home**. By marking the Collection submap as home, you can use the HP OpenView navigation buttons to quickly return to the Collection submap.

Figure 15-6 *Map Description Window*

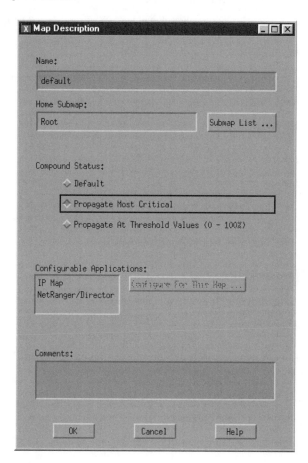

HP OpenView Navigation Buttons

Efficiently using your Director requires you to understand how to move through the HP OpenView NNM graphical user interface. To move through the HP OpenView environment, you use several navigation buttons. Table 15-2 illustrates the major navigation buttons.

Table 15-2   *HP OpenView NNM Navigation Buttons*

HP OpenView Button	Button Function
Close Map	Closes the submap you are currently working in
Home Map	Opens the Cisco Secure IDS Home submap, as set earlier in this chapter
Root Map	Opens the Cisco Secure IDS Root submap
Up One Level	Opens the submap one level above the submap you are currently in

Sensor Configuration

Besides initializing your Director, you also need to install your sensors. Without any Cisco Secure IDS Sensors, your Director does not have any devices to monitor your network.

To configure a Cisco Secure IDS Sensor, you need to perform some operations on the sensor itself along with configuring the sensor on your Director. To initialize a sensor, follow these steps:

1 Run **sysconfig-sensor**.

2 Add a sensor to your Director.

3 Finish the sensor configuration.

Running sysconfig-sensor

The initial step in configuring your sensor involves defining its basic operational parameters. These parameters are stored in various configuration files on your sensor. Instead of editing all the individual configuration files to define the basic identification and communication parameters, you need to run the **sysconfig-sensor** script. This script enables you to enter all the basic identification parameters, as well as update all of the appropriate configuration files on your sensor.

To run the **sysconfig-sensor** script, you first log on to your sensor by using the root account. Then you run the following command:

```
# sysconfig-sensor
```

The first thing that the **sysconfig-sensor** script does is display a list of all the parameters that you can configure (see Figure 15-7).

Figure 15-7 *Output of* **sysconfig-sensor**

```
Telnet - 172.21.167.109
Connect  Edit  Terminal  Help

IDS Sensor Initial Configuration Utility

Choose a value to configure one of the following parameters:

1 - IP Address
2 - IP Netmask
3 - IP Host Name
4 - Default Route
5 - Network Access Control
6 - Communications Infrastructure
7 - Date/Time and Timezone
8 - Passwords
9 - Secure Communications
x - Exit

Selection:
```

NOTE   The default password for the root account on your sensor is *attack*. You can change this password, as well as the password for the netrangr account through the **sysconfig-sensor** script.

For a complete description of the sensor identification parameters, refer to Chapter 7, "4200 Series Sensor Installation Within CSPM."

Adding a Newly Initialized Sensor

Adding a sensor to your Director involves more than a few steps. These steps are accomplished through the Add Host Wizard, which is available via the nrConfigure window. After you add your sensor to your Director, you can use your Director to view the alarms detected by your sensor.

To add your newly initialized sensor to your Director, follow these steps:

1 Start the Configuration Management Utility (nrConfigure).

2 Create the initial Director entry (one-time only).

3 Start the Add Host Wizard.

4 Enter sensor identification settings.

5 Select the host type.

6 Enter IP session logging and blocking duration.

7 Enter the interface name and protected network addresses.

8 Define blocking characteristics.

9 Observe the Add Host Wizard Finished screen.

Starting the Configuration Management Utility

To add your newly initialized sensor to your Director, you need to return to HP OpenView NNM on the Director and start the Add Host Wizard. To access the Add Host Wizard, start the Cisco Secure IDS Configuration File Management Utility (nrConfigure). Refer to Chapter 16, "The Configuration Management Utility (nrConfigure)," for a complete description of the nrConfigure utility.

To start nrConfigure, choose Security, Configure from the Cisco Secure IDS Home submap (see Figure 15-8). This opens the Cisco Secure IDS Configuration File Management Utility (nrConfigure) window (see Figure 15-9).

Figure 15-8 *Starting nrConfigure*

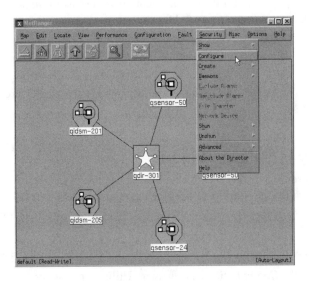

Creating the Initial Director Entry

If this is your first sensor, an Information dialog box opens along with the Cisco Secure IDS Configuration File Management Utility window. Cisco Secure IDS detected that this is the first time you have configured the Director. When you click OK, Cisco Secure IDS adds specific local configuration files and creates the initial entry for your Director in the browser.

Figure 15-9 *Cisco Secure IDS Configuration File Management Utility*

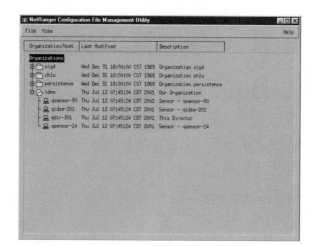

Starting the Add Host Wizard

Now you need to add the sensor to the Director so that it can receive alarm information from your sensor. To do this, choose **File, Add Host** from the menu bar to initiate the Add Host Wizard.

The first window that appears is an initial information window that explains what the Add Host Wizard enables you to configure and how your Director uses this information to communicate with your sensor (see Figure 15-10).

Entering Sensor Identification Settings

You need to configure several identification parameters for your new sensor (see Figure 15-11).

These parameters identify your sensor to your Director and enable your sensor to communicate with your Director. The major parameters are as follows:

- Organization name
- Organization ID
- Host name
- Host ID
- Host IP address

Figure 15-10 *Add Host Wizard Information Window*

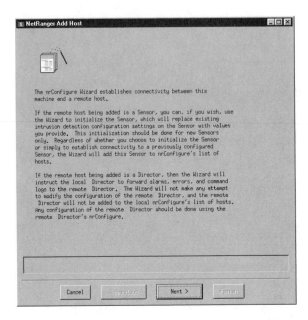

Figure 15-11 *Sensor Identification Parameters Window*

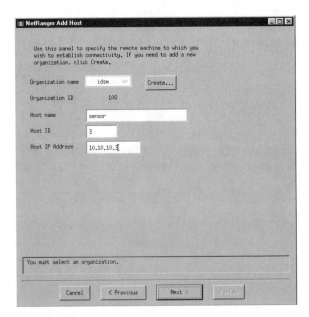

The Add Host Wizard automatically fills in the sensor's organization name and ID by using the organization name for your Director. You can change the organization name by clicking the drop-down menu next to the current organization name. This enables you to choose any organization name that your Director already knows about. If the organization name that you want to use is not listed, you need to create it by clicking the Create button.

NOTE   You do not need to enter the organization ID. The software automatically enters this value based on the organization name that you select. You need to enter the organization ID only if you create a new organization name by clicking the Create button.

Enter the sensor's host name, host ID, and host IP address in the corresponding fields. These entries must be error-free to enable the sensor and Director to communicate. These values need to match the values that you used when you initially ran **sysconfig-sensor** on your sensor, as well as the values listed on the worksheet that you completed in Appendix I.

Click the Next button to continue.

Selecting Host Type

In the Host Type window, you can indicate what type of host is added: a newly initialized sensor, a preconfigured sensor, or a secondary Director for alarm forwarding (see Figure 15-12). You are configuring a newly initialized sensor, so you need to select Initialize a newly installed sensor.

Selecting Connect to a previously configured Sensor enables you to download the configuration of a sensor that was already configured. This is covered in greater detail in Chapter 16. If you select Forward alarms to a secondary Director, the wizard creates host identification entries. The Director can then forward all or some of the alarms received by it to a second Director.

Click the Next button to continue.

NOTE   You can add only one sensor or host at a time. For additional hosts, you must rerun the Add Host Wizard.

Figure 15-12 *Host Type Window*

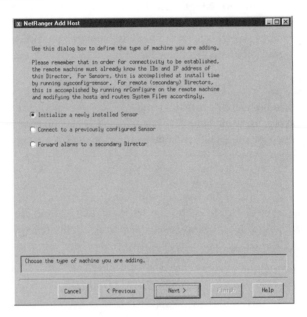

Entering IP Session Logging and Blocking Duration

In the Intrusion Detection Information window, you can set the time for automatic logging of an IP session and the blocking of an IP address (see Figure 15-13). The default time settings for both logging and blocking are 10 minutes. Table 15.3 explains these two parameters.

Table 15-3 *Shunning and Logging Parameters*

CSIDS Settings	Parameters	Description
Number of minutes to log on an event	1–1440 minutes	This field sets the amount of time the sensor logs an event when an alarm is generated. The default setting is 10 minutes.
Number of minutes to shun an event	1–1440 minutes	This field sets the amount of time the sensor shuns an event when an alarm is generated. The default setting is 10 minutes.

Figure 15-13 *IP Session Logging and Shunning Duration Window*

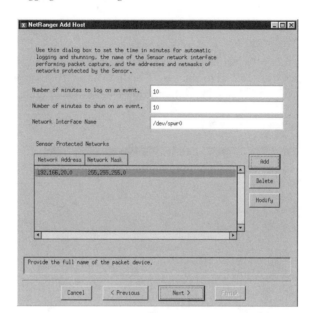

Entering the Interface Name and Protected Network Addresses

The Network Interface Name setting in this window is for the device name of the monitoring interface of the sensor (see Figure 15-13). (The command and control interface is always a Fast Ethernet interface.) The device name used varies depending on the type of sensor being installed (Ethernet, Fast Ethernet, Token Ring, FDDI, or Dual FDDI). You can find this information in the *Cisco Secure IDS User Guide* and on the Quick Start card that comes with every sensor. The different interface values are also listed in Chapter 7.

Your protected networks are those networks that you are protecting with your Cisco Secure IDS. These networks are usually inside defined perimeter boundaries. Cisco Secure IDS flags IP addresses originating in any of these protected networks as inside addresses. IP addresses not originating in the protected networks are flagged as outside addresses. These inside and outside values are used in the alarm entries reported by your sensors. Refer to Chapter 8, "Working with CSIDS Alarms in CSPM," for a detailed explanation of the various alarm fields.

NOTE   Your Cisco Secure IDS Sensors perform intrusion detection on all traffic that they see through their monitoring interfaces. Setting a protected network address (or not) does not have any effect on the capability of Cisco Secure IDS to detect and react to intrusion events.

Click the **Next** button to continue.

Shunning Initialization Window

From the Add Host Wizard, you can enable Cisco Secure IDS to manage a Cisco router's access control lists (ACLs) to shun an IP address as a response to an alarm. You enable shunning through the shunning initialization window (see Figure 15-14).

Figure 15-14 *Shunning Initialization Window*

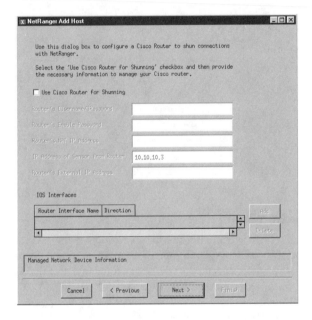

If you want to enable your sensor to shun IP addresses in response to certain alarms, select Use Cisco Router for Shunning on the shunning initialization window. If you select Use Cisco Router for Shunning, you need to configure the following parameters for the router that you want to use to block the IP addresses by using an ACL created by your sensor:

- Router's username/password
- Router's enable password
- Router's NAT IP address
- IP address of sensor from router
- Router's external IP address

Furthermore, you need to configure which interface(s) on the router the ACL is applied on, along with the direction of the ACL (either in or out). Chapter 13, "IP Blocking Configurations," is entirely devoted to IP blocking.

Even if you choose not to implement shunning (not selecting the Use Cisco Router for Shunning check box), your sensor can still respond to attacks through alarm generation and notification to the Director, and through the use of TCP resets and IP session recording.

Click the **Next** button to continue.

Add Host Wizard Finished Screen

You have now added all the information necessary to add the sensor to the Director. The required configuration files that need to be changed on both the Director and the sensor are generated, and then the initial configuration version is created in nrConfigure's Configuration Library.

Click **Finish** to accept your new host configuration. The Director begins trying to establish communication with the sensor. When communication between the Director and sensor is established, the Cisco Secure IDS begins intrusion detection by using the default configuration.

Finishing the Sensor Configuration

The Cisco Secure IDS Configuration File Management Utility (nrConfigure) window now displays the sensor under the correct folder. This folder corresponds to the sensor's organization name.

To exit nrConfigure, choose **File**, **Exit** from the menu. Click **Yes** when you are prompted to quit.

At this point, the Director and sensor icons both display in the Cisco Secure IDS Home submap. The sensor and Director are both online and operating in their default configurations.

Summary

In addition to using CSPM as your Director platform, you also can use Cisco Secure Intrusion Detection Director (CSIDD) to manage your Cisco Secure IDS. Unlike CSPM, which runs under Windows NT, CSIDD uses Solaris or HPUX and HP OpenView Network Node Manager (NNM) to provide a graphical user interface.

To build your CSIDD, you first run an install script on the CSIDD software CD-ROM. This program installs the CSIDD software and creates a netrangr account on the Director.

Using the netrangr account, you define the basic Director parameters by running the **sysconfig-director** script. This script enables you to configure the following Director parameters:

- Director host ID
- Director organization ID
- Director host name
- Director organization name
- Director IP address
- HTML browser location (optional)

Understanding HP OpenView NNM is crucial to effectively operating CSIDD. Understanding HP OpenView's navigation buttons enables your operators to efficiently monitor your Cisco Secure IDS. Furthermore, you can customize your HP OpenView environment to meet your operational environment.

In addition to configuring your Director, you also need to add at least one sensor to your Director to monitor your network for intrusive activity. Adding a sensor requires configuring the sensor with the **sysconfig-sensor** script and then adding the sensor to the Director by using the Add Host Wizard. By using the Add Host Wizard, you can define the following parameters for your sensor:

- Sensor identification settings
- Sensor host type
- IP session logging and shunning duration
- Interface name and protected network addresses
- Shunning characteristics

Review Questions

The following questions test your retention of the material presented in this chapter. The answers to the Review Questions are in Appendix K, "Answers to Review Questions."

1 How can you determine which Cisco Secure IDS processes are currently running on your CSIDD?

_____

_____

_____

2 How do you initially define the basic configuration parameters on your CSIDD?

_____

_____

_____

3 What logon account is created by the CSIDD installation program?

_____

_____

_____

4 How do you define the basic identification parameters on your sensor?

_____

_____

_____

5 What three host types can you add using the Add Host Wizard?

_____

_____

_____

6 A yellow icon corresponds to what alarm level(s)?

_____

_____

_____

7 Does defining a protected network prevent your Cisco Secure IDS Sensor from detecting intrusive activity from hosts on the protected network?

_____

_____

_____

8 What alarm level(s) does a red icon represent?

_____

_____

_____

9 Do you need to reboot your Director after running the **sysconfig-director** script during the installation process?

_____

_____

_____

10 What is Cisco Secure ID Director (CSIDD)?

_____

_____

_____

11 What software is required to install CSIDD?

_____

_____

_____

## CHAPTER 16

The Configuration File Management Utility (nrConfigure)

Cisco Secure ID Director provides you with a central management facility for your Cisco Secure IDS: nrConfigure. You use nrConfigure to manage the configuration of your Director as well as your remote sensors that are distributed across your network.

NOTE When Cisco Secure IDS was first created, it was called NetRanger. Although the NetRanger name has been replaced with Cisco Secure IDS, all references to NetRanger have not been eliminated. Names, such as nrConfigure, nrstart, and nrstop, still refer to the original NetRanger name. Some of the initial configuration screens might still use NetRanger, instead of Cisco Secure IDS. These instances are becoming fewer and fewer, however, with each update to Cisco Secure IDS.

Through nrConfigure, you can add sensors, delete sensors, and update the configuration files for both your Director and your sensors. In addition, in conjunction with the Configuration Library, you can maintain and manage multiple configuration files for the sensors in your Cisco Secure IDS.

Topics explaining the nuances of nrConfigure in this chapter are as follows:

- Working with nrConfigure
- Host types for the Add Host Wizard
- Connecting to a previously configured sensor
- Verifying that the sensor is added to nrConfigure
- Verifying that the sensor is added to the Cisco Secure IDS submap
- Deleting a sensor
- Removing the sensor icon
- Working with the Configuration Library

Working with nrConfigure

To effectively use nrConfigure, you need to understand a few things:

- How nrConfigure is used
- How to start nrConfigure
- nrConfigure screen characteristics
- Setting the HTML browser
- Hiding the status line

How nrConfigure Is Used

Cisco Secure IDS uses nrConfigure to manage the configuration of your Director and the remote sensors distributed across your enterprise network when you use CSIDD as your Director platform. nrConfigure uses a Java-based graphical user interface (GUI) that is launched from the **Security** menu in HP OpenView.

nrConfigure enables you to maintain a number of configuration versions that can be applied as needed. This functionality enables you to keep current and prior configurations. You can "roll back" a sensor or Director to a previous configuration. You can also use this functionality to apply different versions for day and night, or weekdays and weekends.

nrConfigure enables security personnel to manage the configuration of your Cisco Secure IDS for the entire network from a centrally located console.

How to Start nrConfigure

To start nrConfigure, choose **Configure** from the Cisco Secure IDS Home Security drop-down menu on CSIDD (see Figure 16-1).

nrConfigure Screen Characteristics

The nrConfigure screen displays the local Director and all the sensors known by it (see Figure 16-2). If a sensor has a different organization name than the Director, another organization folder is created and that sensor appears under its own organization's folder, rather than under the Director's organization folder.

Figure 16-1 *Starting nrConfigure*

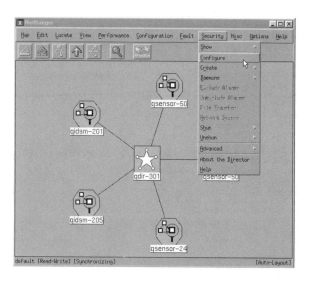

Figure 16-2 *nrConfigure Screen*

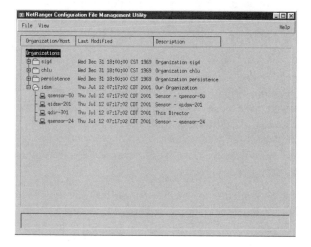

NOTE   Remember that the Director can manage and control sensors even if they belong to a different organization.

The nrConfigure screen displays three categories of information for each item listed (sensors, Directors, and organization folders):

- Organization/Host
- Last Modified
- Description

The Organization/Host column identifies the organization and host name for each entry displayed. All hosts under a specific organization folder are grouped together.

The Last Modified column shows the last day and time when the host's configuration was modified. If your security policy requires periodic updates and checks, you can use this field to verify that you are updating your sensor and Director configuration files on a regular basis.

The Description column provides a user-definable description for the host entry. This field enables you to define easily recognizable names for the various components of your Cisco Secure IDS.

Setting the HTML Browser

You use an HTML browser to view the Network Security Database (NSDB). The browser is automatically opened whenever you attempt to view the description of a specific signature. It is also used when you attempt to view the entire NSDB document. For more information on the NSDB, refer to Chapter 8, "Working with Cisco Secure IDS Alarms in CSPM."

During a Director's initial configuration, you configure several Director parameters by using the **sysconfig-director** script. One of these parameters is the location of the HTML browser that you want to use. You might, however, install a new browser that is located in a different location. In addition, in some instances, your system might not have had a browser installed on the system when you built your Director. In either of these situations, you need to configure the location of your browser if you want to view NSDB information about the alarms on your Director.

Setting the location of your browser is a simple task. First, you must determine the location of your browser's executable file; then, choose Preferences from the File drop-down menu on the nrConfigure screen (see Figure 16-3). The Preferences window (see Figure 16-4) displays. You define the browser location by entering the filename of your browser's executable, including the complete path to this executable.

Figure 16-3 *File Drop-Down Menu*

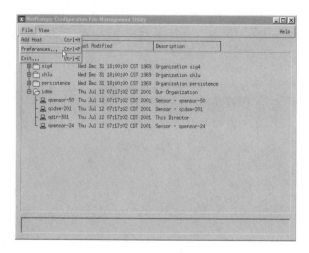

Figure 16-4 *Preferences Screen*

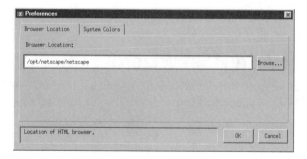

Hiding the Status Line

Whenever you select one of your devices on the nrConfigure screen, a status line appears at the bottom of the screen. This status line displays information about the selected organization or host (see Figure 16-5). You can decide whether you want this status line to display. Choose **Status** from the **View** drop-down menu to hide or display the status line at the bottom of the nrConfigure screen. This option is a toggle switch. If the status line is currently displaying, selecting **Status** from the **View** drop-down menu turns it off. If it is currently off, selecting this option turns it on again.

Figure 16-5 *nrConfigure Status Line*

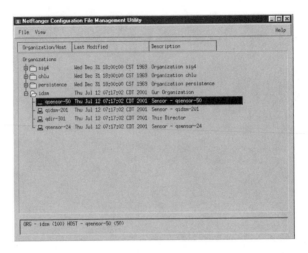

NOTE Instead of using the **View** drop-down menu, you can toggle the status line setting by using the Ctrl-S key sequence.

Host Types for Add Host Wizard

To add a sensor to your Director's configuration, use the Add Host Wizard. Through the Add Host Wizard, you can add any of the following three host types:

- Newly installed sensor
- Secondary Director for alarm forwarding
- Previously configured sensor

Newly Installed Sensor

The Initialize a Newly Installed Sensor option adds a sensor to the Director and initializes a newly installed sensor to the factory default configuration for the sensor. The factory default settings assume that you ran **sysconfig-sensor** on the sensor itself.

When installing a Cisco Secure IDS Sensor, you first need to execute the **sysconfig-sensor** script on the sensor. This script establishes the sensor identification and communication parameters, which brings the sensor to Communications-Only mode (no intrusion detection configuration). When the Director adds the sensor, it initializes it with a default intrusion detection configuration. For complete details on how to initialize newly installed sensors, refer to Chapter 15, "Cisco Secure ID Director Installation."

Secondary Director for Alarm Forwarding

Sometimes, you want your Director to forward its alarms to another Director. This is common when you have multiple Directors deployed throughout your environment, but you want all the Directors to report alarm information to a single master Director. You can configure this master Director to receive only a subset of the total alarms generated by your Cisco Secure IDS, such as alarms that are greater than Level 3 in severity.

If you select the **Forward alarms to a secondary Director** option when using the Add Host Wizard, you need to identify the secondary Director that you want to receive alarms from the current Director. You also need to identify the minimum alarm level that is forwarded to this secondary Director. In most instances, you probably want to minimize the alarms that your secondary Director receives by forwarding only the more severe alarm levels.

NOTE	When a secondary Director is added to the local Director, it appears on the Cisco Secure IDS Home submap. It is *not* displayed under nrConfigure and cannot be configured remotely from the local Director.

Previously Configured Sensor

You also can use the Add Host Wizard to connect to a previously configured sensor. In this situation, you are inserting the sensor into your Director's configuration, but you do not want the Director to initialize the sensor's configuration. When inserting a sensor, the assumption is that the sensor was already configured, including the intrusion detection processes. This is the case if you manually configured the sensor or need to add a previously deleted sensor.

Instead of having the Director initialize your sensor by downloading a set of configuration files, you want the Director to upload your current configuration from your sensor. Then the Director can start receiving alarms from your added sensor, but the sensor's configuration is not changed.

Connecting to a Previously Configured Sensor

This section explains the steps necessary to add a previously configured sensor to your Director. The first step in this process is to choose **Add Host** from the nrConfigure **File** drop-down menu (see Figure 16-6). This initiates the Add Host Wizard.

Figure 16-6 *Starting the Add Host Wizard*

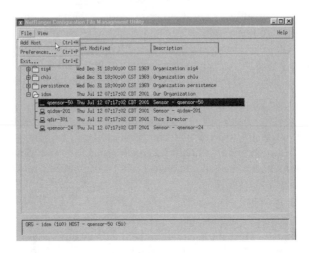

Add Host Initial Window

When the Add Host Wizard starts, it displays an initial information window (see Figure 16-7). After reading the information on this screen, click **Next** to continue with the addition of the host.

Figure 16-7 *Add Host Initial Information Window*

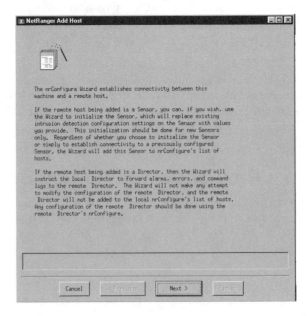

Entering Sensor Identification Settings

You must enter some basic parameters about your sensor so that your Director can communicate with it. The parameters that you need to configure for the sensor are its identification settings (see Figure 16-8). You need to define the following items:

- Organization name
- Organization ID
- Host name
- Host ID
- Host IP address

Figure 16-8 *Sensor Identification Settings*

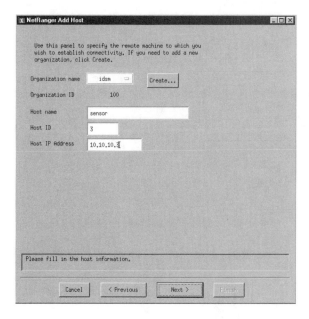

The Add Host Wizard assumes the sensor's organization name and ID to be the same as that of the Director. If you need to create a new organization, click **Create**.

NOTE   The organization ID is one of the sensor's basic identification parameters. You do not need to enter this value, however, because the Add Host Wizard determines this value from the organization name. If you create a new organization name, you need to supply both an organization name and an organization ID.

Enter the sensor's host name, host ID, and host IP Address in the corresponding fields. These entries must be error-free to enable the sensor and Director to communicate. Furthermore, these values must correspond to the values that you entered on your sensor when you ran the **sysconfig-sensor** script (refer to the worksheet that you created in Appendix I, "Cisco Secure Communications Deployment Worksheet").

Click **Next** to continue.

Selecting the Host Type

Next, you must choose the type of machine that you want to add (see Figure 16-9).

Figure 16-9 *Add Wizard Host Type Screen*

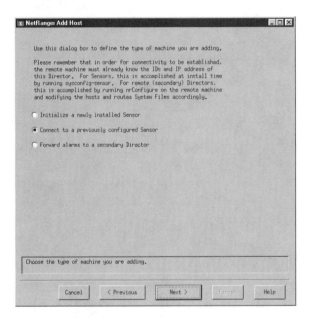

Because the sensor already has a working configuration, you need to choose **Connect to a previously configured Sensor**. This option causes your Director to upload the configuration from your already configured sensor.

Click **Next** to continue.

Add Host Wizard Finished Window

You have now entered all the information necessary to insert the sensor into the Director's configuration. The Add Host Wizard Finished window appears onscreen (see Figure 16-10). When you click **Finish**, the wizard uploads the sensor's configuration to the Director and modifies the Director's configuration to account for the newly inserted sensor. These changes are generated and an initial sensor configuration version is created in nrConfigure's Configuration Library.

Figure 16-10   *Add Host Wizard Finished Window*

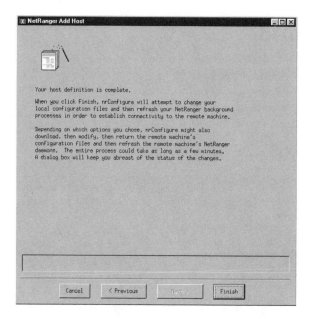

Furthermore, after you click **Finish**, the Director begins trying to establish communications with the sensor. After communication between the Director and sensor is established, the sensor starts reporting alarms to the Director.

Verifying That the Sensor Is Added to nrConfigure

The Cisco Secure IDS Configuration File Management Utility (nrConfigure) window now displays the sensor under the folder that corresponds to the organization name that you specified for the inserted sensor.

To exit nrConfigure, choose **Exit** from the **File** drop-down menu. Click **Yes** when you are prompted to quit.

Verifying That the Sensor Is Added to the Cisco Secure IDS Submap

At this point, the Director and sensor icons are both displayed in the Cisco Secure IDS Home submap. The sensor and Director should both be online and operating properly.

Deleting a Sensor

Sometimes, you need to remove a sensor from your Director's configuration. To remove a sensor from your Director's configuration, you must use the Configuration File Management Utility. While viewing the nrConfigure screen, right-click the sensor's name and choose **Delete Host** from the **Host Menu** drop-down menu to delete the sensor from the Director (see Figure 16-11).

Figure 16-11   *Deleting a Sensor*

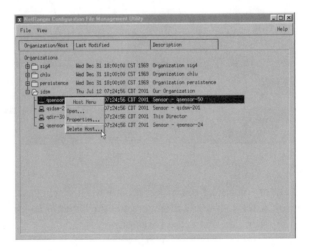

After you choose to delete a sensor from your Director, a confirmation window appears (see Figure 16-12). If you are sure that you want to delete the sensor, click **Yes** to complete the deletion. This removes all sensor configuration information from the Director but does not remove the sensor's icon from the Cisco Secure IDS Home submap.

Figure 16-12   *Sensor Deletion Confirmation Window*

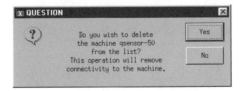

NOTE   After deleting a sensor, you can recover the configuration information on the sensor by
            reinserting the sensor into the Director's configuration. You use the **Connect to a**
            previously configured Sensor option of the Add Host Wizard to reinsert the sensor into the
            Director's configuration.

CAUTION   Do not use this function to delete the Director. Doing so causes the system to stop working
            and requires reinitializing the Director with **sysconfig-director**.

Removing the Sensor Icon

After the sensor is deleted from your Director's configuration by using nrConfigure, you
also must remove its icon from the Cisco Secure IDS Home submap.

To remove the sensor icon, right-click the sensor icon to display the Symbol: *sensor* drop-
down menu (see Figure 16-13). Choose **Delete Symbol** to remove the sensor icon.

NOTE   The sensor icon removed must be green, indicating that no alarms are under it in any
            submap. If it is not green, you must remove the alarms before you can remove the icon.

Figure 16-13   *Deleting the Sensor Icon*

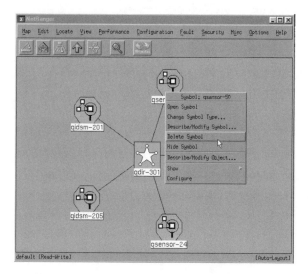

Working with the Configuration Library

The Configuration File Management Utility enables you to maintain multiple configurations for your various Cisco Secure IDS components. These multiple configurations enable you to "roll back" to a previous version if necessary. It also enables you to apply different sensor configurations, such as day and night or weekdays and weekends.

The following sections show you how to work with the Configuration Library. You learn how to do the following:

- Open the Configuration Library
- Work within the Configuration Library
- Close the Configuration Library

Opening the Configuration Library

To open the Configuration Versions window for a given host, double-click or right-click the host and choose **Open** from the **Host Menu** drop-down menu (see Figure 16-14).

Figure 16-14 *Opening the Configuration Library*

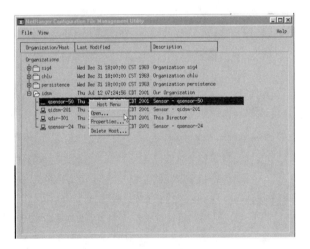

NOTE	If a sensor or Director icon is selected when starting nrConfigure, the Configuration Library for the selected host automatically opens.

Working Within the Configuration Library

Cisco Secure IDS maintains a Configuration Library for the local Director and all sensors reporting to it. The Configuration Library enables you to do the following:

- Configure the local Director and all of its sensors

- Maintain copies of alternative configurations that can be applied at any given time

The active configuration is denoted by **bold** typeface of the version number line (see **Version 2** in Figure 16-15).

Figure 16-15 *Configuration Library Screen*

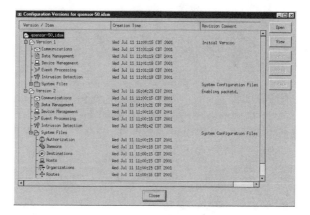

The following sections discuss the versioning and modification of existing configurations (transient versions) within the Configuration Library.

Transient Versions

When opening any of the configuration options, nrConfigure automatically opens a transient version. A transient version is shown as a red folder with a *T* on the Configuration Library. During the onscreen display of Figure 16-16, you see this red folder for Version 3. With the black-and-white presentation in this book, however, you cannot see the color. Therefore, the entry has been highlighted for you in this book.

Any changes to one or more of the configuration options are made from the transient version. This ensures that the original version is not modified and can be reverted to if necessary.

Figure 16-16 *Transient Configuration Version*

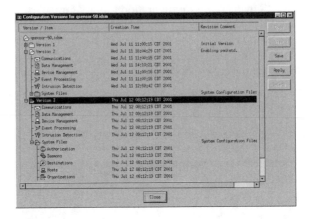

Until a transient version is saved or applied, Cisco Secure IDS does not maintain it. When closing the Configuration Library with any opened transient versions, Cisco Secure IDS displays a warning dialog box indicating that you have unsaved transient versions (see Figure 16-17). If you are sure you want to close the Configuration Library, click **Yes** to discard the transient version(s). Otherwise, you need to click **No** to return to the Configuration Library.

Figure 16-17 *Unsaved Transient Versions Dialog Box*

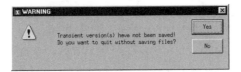

Version Numbering

When a configuration option is opened from a saved version, Cisco Secure IDS creates a transient version that is one number higher than the version from which it is being opened. If that number is already in use, Cisco Secure IDS adds a point version number, starting at one (for example, Version $X.1$). Subsequently, when opening saved point versions, Cisco Secure IDS creates a transient version that is one point number higher than the version from which it is being opened. Again, if the point version is already in use, an additional point version is added to the version number, starting at one (for example, Version $X.1.1$).

When opening a saved version with a lower version number than any that already exist, Cisco Secure IDS adds a point version number with a 0, if necessary, to obtain the correct number of point versions (for example, Version $X.0.1$).

Table 16-1 illustrates examples of how version numbering occurs.

Table 16-1   *Transient Configuration Versioning*

Saved Version to Open	Other Existing Versions	Transient Versions
Version 1	None	Version 2
Version 1	Version 2	Version 1.1
Version 1.1	Version 1	Version 1.2
Version 1	Version 1.1	Version 1.0.1

Saving a Transient Version

To save a transient version, select the version number line you want to save and click the **Save** button located on the right side of the Configuration Library screen (Figure 16-15).

NOTE   In Figure 16-15, the Save, Apply, and Delete buttons are grayed out because no configuration version was selected. These options are available only when you highlight a specific configuration version.

Applying a Transient Version

Applying a version makes that version the active configuration version in your Cisco Secure IDS. When applying a transient version, Cisco Secure IDS saves the version and makes it active.

To apply a transient version, select the version number line you want to apply, and click the **Apply** button located on the upper-right corner of the Configuration Library screen (refer back to Figure 16-15).

Applying a Saved Version

To apply a saved version, select the version number line you want to apply, and click the **Apply** button located on the upper-right corner of the Configuration Library screen (refer back to Figure 16-15).

Deleting a Version

To delete a saved version, select the version number line you want to delete, and click the **Delete** button located on the upper-right corner of the Configuration Library screen (refer back to Figure 16-15).

WARNING   Deleting a version completely erases all configuration information for that version. After a version is deleted, its configuration information cannot be recovered.

NOTE   When selecting a transient version, the **Delete** button is not available (dimmed) because transient versions are not saved until you click **Save** or **Apply**.

Closing the Configuration Library

To close the Configuration Library, click **Close**. If any transient versions have not been saved or applied, you are prompted as to whether you want to quit without saving them (refer back to Figure 16-17). If you click **No**, you are returned to the Configuration Library where you can save or apply transient configurations as needed. If you click **Yes**, the Configuration Library closes and you are returned to the nrConfigure window.

Summary

nrConfigure provides you with a central management facility for your Cisco Secure IDS when you use a Cisco Secure ID Director. You use nrConfigure to manage the configuration of your remote sensors that are distributed across your network as well as your Director itself.

Through nrConfigure, you can do the following:

- Add new hosts to your Director
- Access the Configuration Library

The Add Host Wizard enables you to add the following three types of hosts to your Director's configuration:

- Initialize a newly installed sensor
- Connect to a previously configured sensor
- Add secondary Director information for alarm forwarding

If you have a previously configured sensor, you can add this sensor to your Director without overwriting its configuration. The steps to this process are as follows:

Step 1   Start the Add Host Wizard.

Step 2   Enter the sensor identification settings.

Step 3   Select the host type.

Step 4   Upload the configuration from your sensor.

The Configuration Library enables you to maintain multiple configuration versions for each of your Cisco Secure IDS components. Whenever you change the configuration for one of your IDS components, the Configuration Library creates a transient configuration version. The original version remains unmodified, and the transient version is not officially maintained by the Configuration Library until you save or apply it.

Review Questions

The following questions test your retention of the material presented in this chapter. The answers to the Review Questions are in Appendix K, "Answers to Review Questions."

1 What is a transient version?

2 What is the Configuration Library?

3 What is the Cisco Secure IDS Configuration File Management Utility or nrConfigure?

4 When you delete a sensor through nrConfigure, is its icon on the Cisco Secure IDS Home submap also deleted?

5 If your only saved configuration versions are 1 and 2, and you modify version 1, what is the version of the transient configuration?

6 If your only saved configuration versions are 1, 1.1, and 2, and you modify version 1, what is the version of the transient configuration?

_____

_____

_____

## CHAPTER 17

Cisco IOS Firewall Intrusion Detection System

The Cisco IOS Firewall IDS provides firewall and intrusion detection capabilities to a variety of Cisco IOS routers. It acts just like a Cisco Secure IDS Sensor from an intrusion detection perspective and can be added to the Cisco Secure ID Director map as another icon to provide a consistent view of all intrusion detection sensing devices throughout your network. The Cisco IOS Firewall IDS also has an enhanced reporting mechanism that permits logging to the router's SYSLOG service in addition to the Cisco Secure ID Director (see Figure 17-1).

Figure 17-1 *Cisco IOS Firewall IDS*

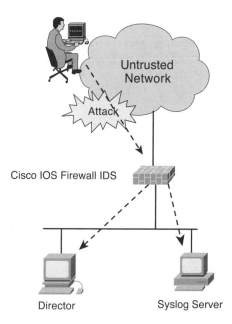

The Cisco IOS Firewall IDS provides a level of protection beyond just a firewall by protecting the network from internal and external attacks and threats. This technology enhances perimeter firewall protection by taking appropriate action on packets and flows that violate the security policy or that represent malicious network activity.

To best present the nuances of how you can integrate Cisco IOS Firewall IDS into your network environment, this chapter is divided into the following sections:

- Cisco IOS Firewall IDS and Intrusion Detection
- Supported Router Platforms
- Deployment Issues
- Signatures
- Configuration Tasks

Cisco IOS Firewall IDS and Intrusion Detection

The Cisco IOS Firewall IDS capabilities are ideal for providing additional visibility at intranet, extranet, and branch-office Internet perimeters (see Figure 17-2). Network administrators now have more robust protection against attacks on the network and can automatically respond to threats from internal or external hosts.

Cisco IOS Firewall IDS can be deployed alongside or independently of other Cisco IOS Firewall features. Existing Cisco Secure IDS customers can deploy the Cisco IOS Firewall IDS signatures to complement their current protection. This allows IDS to be deployed to areas that cannot support a traditional Cisco Secure IDS Sensor. The downside is that the Cisco IOS Firewall IDS incorporates a much smaller set of signatures than other Cisco Secure IDS Sensors, such as the 4200 Series Appliance Sensors.

The Cisco IOS Firewall IDS is intended to satisfy the security goals of all Cisco's customers and is particularly appropriate for the following:

- Enterprise customers
- Service providers
- Small and medium-sized businesses

Enterprise Customers

Enterprise customers have large networks with multiple network boundaries that all require security protection, specifically branch-office, intranet, and extranet perimeters. These numerous boundaries require a cost-effective security solution. Combined with other Cisco Secure IDS Sensors, you can establish a comprehensive IDS that effectively monitors all aspects of their network.

Figure 17-2   *Cisco Secure IOS Router Deployment Points*

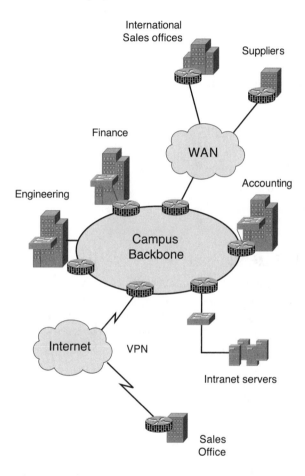

Service Providers

Many service provider customers want to set up managed services, providing firewalling and intrusion detection to their customers. To complement their network architecture, they need all this functionality to be housed within a router.

Small and Medium-Sized Businesses

Small and medium-sized businesses have smaller networks. They do not have massive Information Technology (IT) budgets. Therefore, they need to find cost-effective ways in which to deploy firewall and IDS functionality on their networks. The Cisco IOS Firewall

IDS enables them to use a cost-effective router, while gaining the extra functionality of an integrated firewall with intrusion detection capabilities.

Supported Router Platforms

Cisco IOS Firewall IDS capability is integrated with the Cisco IOS on the following platforms:

- Cisco 1720 Router
- Cisco 2600 Series
- Cisco 3600 Series
- Cisco 7100 Series
- Cisco 7200 Series

Deployment Issues

Although the Cisco IOS Firewall IDS provides you with a cost-effective security solution, it does have various issues to consider before you implement it on your operational network. The following issues need to be considered when you decide to incorporate Cisco IOS Firewall IDS as a component of your network security model:

- Memory usage and performance impact
- Signature coverage
- Signature updates

Memory Usage and Performance Impact

The performance impact of intrusion detection depends on the number of signatures enabled, the level of traffic on the router, the router platform, and other individual features enabled on the router, such as encryption, source route bridging, and so on. Because this router is being used as a security device, no packet is allowed to bypass the security mechanisms. The IDS process in the Cisco IOS Firewall IDS router sits directly in the packet path and, therefore, searches each packet for signature matches. In some cases, the entire packet needs to be searched, and state information—and even application state and awareness—must be maintained by the router.

Signature Coverage

The Cisco IOS Firewall IDS identifies 59 of the most common attacks (see Appendix H, "Cisco IOS Firewall IDS Signature List," for a listing of these signatures) by using signatures to detect patterns of misuse in network traffic. The intrusion detection signatures were chosen from a broad cross-section of overall intrusion detection signatures available on a regular Cisco Secure IDS Sensor. The signatures represent severe breaches of security and the most common network attacks, as well as information-gathering scans. However, the dedicated Cisco Secure IDS 4200 Series Appliance Sensors audit more than 300 signatures, providing the most comprehensive coverage on network attacks. (See Chapter 10, "Signature Series," and Appendix F, "Cisco Secure IDS Signature Structures and Implementations.")

Signature Updates

Whereas signatures on the Cisco Secure IDS Sensor appliance are updated about every other month, the Cisco IOS Firewall IDS signatures are not updated frequently. If signatures are updated for the Cisco IOS Firewall IDS, you need to update the actual IOS image on all your Cisco IOS Firewall IDS routers to incorporate those changes into your network.

Signatures

Any security solution that you plan to use on your network is measured by its capability to check for intrusive activity on your network. This measurement usually revolves around two factors:

- Signature implementations
- Response options

Signature Implementations

Atomic signatures are those that trigger on a single packet. For auditing atomic signatures, there is no traffic-dependent memory requirement. These signatures also minimally impact the router's performance.

Compound signatures are those that trigger on multiple packets. For auditing compound signatures, Cisco IOS Firewall IDS allocates memory to maintain the state of each session for each connection. Memory is also allocated for the configuration database and for internal caching.

Response Options

The Cisco IOS Firewall IDS acts as an inline intrusion detection device, watching packets as they traverse the router's interfaces and acting upon them in a definable fashion. When a packet, or a number of packets in a session, match a signature, the Cisco IOS Firewall IDS might perform one or more of the following configurable actions:

- Generate alarms
- Reset TCP sessions
- Drop packets

Generate Alarms

By defining your Cisco IOS Firewall to generate alarms for IDS signatures, your router can send alarms to a Cisco Secure ID Director, SYSLOG server, and router console. Furthermore, if no other actions are specified, the offending packet(s) is forwarded through the router.

Reset TCP Sessions

For TCP-based IDS signatures, you have the option of configuring your Cisco IOS Firewall IDS to reset the TCP session in which the offending packet(s) occur. The router sends packets with the TCP reset flag set to both session participants. The router still forwards the offending packet(s).

Drop Packets

The final configurable option is to drop the offending packets. If you choose this option, your router immediately drops the offending packets.

NOTE   You can assign various combinations of actions to trigger when an IDS signature is detected, but you need to use the drop and reset actions together to ensure that the attack is terminated.

Configuration Tasks

To configure the Cisco IOS Firewall IDS on a router and to have it report alarms to a Cisco Secure ID Director, you need to perform the following tasks:

- Initialize Cisco IOS Firewall IDS on the router.
- Configure, disable, or exclude signatures.
- Create and apply audit rules.
- Verify the configuration.
- Add the Cisco IOS Firewall IDS to the Director configuration.

NOTE	To perform the configuration changes on your Cisco IOS Firewall IDS, you need to log in to the router. Then, you need to gain privileged access by running the **enable** command. Finally, you need to enter the Configuration mode by using the **configure terminal** command.

Initialize Cisco Secure IOS Firewall IDS on the Router

To customize your Cisco IOS Firewall IDSs to your operational environment, you need to configure various IDS parameters on your router. These configuration steps are as follows:

- Set the notification type.
- Configure the router's PostOffice parameters.
- Configure the router's Director PostOffice parameters.
- Define protected network(s).
- Set the notification queue size.

Set Notification Type

You use the **ip audit notify** global configuration command to specify the methods of alarm notification on your Cisco IOS Firewall IDS.

NOTE	To disable event notifications, just insert a **no** at the beginning of a valid notification command (as in **no ip audit notify log**).

The syntax for the **ip audit notify** command is as follows:

```
ip audit notify {nr-director | log}
no ip audit notify {nr-director | log}
```

The arguments and descriptions are contained in Table 17-1.

Table 17-1   **ip audit notify** *Parameters*

Argument	Description
nr-director	Sends messages in PostOffice format to the CSIDD or sensor
log	Sends messages in SYSLOG format to router's console or a remote SYSLOG server

The following are some actual command-line examples:

```
Router (config)# ip audit notify nr-director
Router (config)# ip audit notify log
Router (config)# no ip audit notify log
```

The first example specifies that the router needs to send alarm events to your CSIDD. The second example sends the alarms to a sensor SYSLOG service, and the third example disables the logging of alarms to the SYSLOG service on the router.

Default Settings

If you do not specify a notify destination (**nr-director** or **log**), the default setting logs the events to the router's SYSLOG service.

Configure the Router's PostOffice Parameters

Before your Cisco IOS Firewall IDS can send alarm notifications to your CSIDD, you need to configure the router's PostOffice parameters. You use the **ip audit po local** global configuration command to specify the local PostOffice parameters used when sending alarm notifications to the CSIDD.

NOTE   To reset any of the PostOffice configuration commands to their default values, insert a **no** at the beginning of the configuration command that you want to reset (for example, **no ip audit po local hostid 10 orgid 1**).

The syntax for the **ip audit po local** command is as follows:

```
ip audit po local hostid host-id orgid org-id
no ip audit po local [hostid host-id orgid org-id]
```

The arguments and descriptions are contained in Table 17-2.

Table 17-2   *Local PostOffice Parameters*

Argument	Description
hostid	Keyword that designates a PostOffice host ID.
host-id	Unique integer in the range 1 to 65,535 used in PostOffice communications to identify the local host. Use with the **hostid** keyword.
orgid	Keyword that designates a PostOffice organization ID.
org-id	Unique integer in the range 1 to 65,535 used in PostOffice communications to identify the group to which the local host belongs. Use with the **orgid** keyword.

The following are some actual command-line examples:

```
Router (config)# ip audit po local hostid 16 orgid 2
Router (config)# no ip audit po local hostid 10 orgid 1
```

The first example defines your router's host ID to be 16 and its organization ID to be 2. The second example removes the router's local PostOffice parameters (resetting them to a default of 1 for the host ID and a 1 for the organization ID).

Default Settings

If you do not specify any local PostOffice parameters *(host-id* or *org-id)*, the default setting is to assign a value of 1 to both the organization ID and the host ID.

Configure the Router's Director PostOffice Parameters

Configuring your router's local PostOffice parameters is only half the task. You also must identify the router's Director PostOffice parameters so that your router knows how to communicate with your CSIDD.

You use the **ip audit po remote** global configuration command to specify one or more sets of PostOffice parameters for the Cisco Secure ID Director receiving alarm notifications from the router.

NOTE   To reset any of the Director PostOffice parameters to their default values, insert a **no** at the beginning of the configuration command that you want to reset (for example, **no ip audit po remote hostid 10 orgid 2 rmtaddress 10.0.1.1**).

The syntax for the **ip audit po remote** command is as follows:

```
ip audit po remote hostid host-id orgid org-id rmtaddress ip-addr localaddress
    ip-addr [port port-num] [preference preference-num] [timeout seconds]
    [application {director I logger}]
no ip audit po remote hostid host-id orgid org-id rmtaddress ip-address
```

The arguments and descriptions are contained in Table 17-3.

The following are some actual command-line examples:

```
Router (config)# ip audit po remote hostid 20 orgid 1 rmtaddress 10.0.3.4
    localaddress 10.0.1.2 preference 1
Router (config)# ip audit po remote hostid 10 orgid 2 rmtaddress 10.0.1.1
    localaddress 10.0.2.2
```

Table 17-3   *Remote PostOffice Parameters*

Argument	Description
host-id	Unique integer in the range 1 to 65,535 used in PostOffice communications to identify the remote host. Use with the **hostid** keyword. The default is 1.
org-id	Unique integer in the range 1 to 65,535 used in PostOffice communications to identify the group to which the remote host belongs. Use with the **orgid** keyword. The default is 1.
rmtaddress	Keyword that designates the IP address of the remote Cisco Secure ID Director.
localaddress	Keyword that designates the IP address of the Cisco IOS Firewall IDS.
ip-addr	IP address of the Cisco Secure IDS Director or Cisco IOS Firewall IDS router's interface. Use with the **rmtaddress** and **localaddress** keywords.
port-num	Integer representing the UDP port on which the Cisco Secure IDS Director is listening for alarm notifications. Use with the **port** keyword. The default UDP port is 45000.
preference-number	Integer representing the relative priority of an IP address to a Cisco Secure IDS Director, if more than one IP address exists. Use with the **preference** keyword. The default preference value is 1 because lower numbers receive a higher priority.
seconds	Integer representing the heartbeat timeout value for PostOffice communications. Use with the **timeout** keyword. The default timeout is 5 seconds.
director	Specifies that the receiving application is a Cisco Secure IDS Director. Use with the **application** keyword. **director** is the default application.
logger	Specifies that the receiving application is a Cisco Secure IDS Sensor. Use with the **application** keyword.

In the first example, the Director's IP address is defined a 10.0.3.4. The router's IP is 10.0.1.2. PostOffice traffic flows between these two addresses. Furthermore, the host ID of the Director is assigned to 20, and the organization ID is assigned a value of 1.

The second example is similar except that the preference field is omitted. Therefore, it defaults to a value of 1.

Default Settings

If you do not specify any remote PostOffice parameters, the following default settings are used:

- **Organization ID:** 1
- **Host ID:** 1

- **UDP port number:** 45000
- **Preference:** 1
- **Heartbeat timeout:** 5 Seconds
- **Default application: Director**

Define Protected Network(s)

The protected networks identify which networks are protected by your Cisco Secure IDS. Defining these networks, however, does not impact intrusion detection functionality. It only enables an IN and OUT designator to be assigned to IP addresses that are part of an alarm notification. (See Chapter 8, "Working with Cisco Secure IDS Alarms in CSPM," for more information on alarm fields.)

To configure the protected networks in your environment, you use the **ip audit po protected** global configuration command to specify whether an IP address is on a protected network.

NOTE   To remove network addresses from the protected network list, append a **no** to the command used to add protected network address initially. If you specify an IP address for removal, that address is removed from the list. If you do not specify an address, all IP addresses are removed from the list.

The syntax for the **ip audit po protected** command is as follows:

```
ip audit po protected ip-addr [to ip-addr]
no ip audit po protected [ip-addr]
```

The arguments and descriptions are contained in Table 17-4.

Table 17-4   *Protected Network Parameters*

Argument	Description
to	Keyword that designates the ending IP address of a range of IP addresses
ip-addr	IP address of a network host

The following are some actual command-line examples:

```
Router (config)# ip audit po protected 10.0.0.1 to 10.0.0.254
Router (config)# no ip audit po protected
```

The first example assigns the IP addresses from 10.0.0.1 through 10.0.0.254 as IP addresses on your protected network. The second example removes all the protected network entries because no specific IP address was included. If you have multiple network ranges to protect, you can issue multiple **ip audit po protected** commands.

Default Settings

If you do not assign any protected addresses, the default setting is to consider all IP addresses as outside the protected network.

Set the Notification Queue Size

The alarm notification queue specifies the maximum number of alarm entries that your router tracks at one time. When setting this parameter, you need to consider the following issues:

- The router has limited persistent storage.
- Each alarm uses 32 KB of memory.
- The default queue size is 100 alarms.
- If the queue fills up, alarms are lost on a first-in first-out (FIFO) basis.

You use the **ip audit po max-events** global configuration command to specify the maximum number of event notifications that are placed in the router's event queue.

NOTE   If you insert a **no** at the beginning of the command to set the maximum queue size, the router reverts to its default maximum queue size setting of 100 alarms.

The syntax for the **ip audit po max-events** command is as follows:

```
ip audit po max-events num-of-events
no ip audit po max-events
```

The arguments and descriptions are contained in Table 17-5.

Table 17-5   **PostOffice Events** *Parameter*

Argument	Description
number-of-events	Integer in the range of 1 to 65,535 that designates the maximum number of events allowable in the event queue. Use with the **max-events** keyword.

The following are some actual command-line examples:

```
Router (config)# ip audit po max-events 200
Router (config)# no ip audit po max-events
```

The first example sets the maximum notification queue size to 200 entries, whereas the second example removes the current maximum setting that causes the maximum notification queue size to revert to the default of 100.

Configure, Disable, or Exclude Signatures

Although your Cisco IOS Firewall IDS has a limited signature database, you can still configure these signatures to obtain the best performance for your specific operational network. You can perform the following configuration changes to customize how your Cisco IOS Firewall IDS handles specific signatures:

- Configure SPAM attack
- Disable signatures globally
- Exclude signatures by host or network

Configure SPAM Attack

The SPAM signature (Signature ID 3106) detects a mail message that has an unusually large number of recipients in a single mail message. The definition of a large number of recipients depends entirely on your network environment. Therefore, you need to configure the threshold that you use to trigger the SPAM signature.

When configuring the SPAM signature threshold, use the **ip audit smtp spam** global configuration command to specify the number of recipients in a mail message over which a SPAM attack is suspected.

NOTE   If you insert a **no** at the beginning of the command to set the SPAM signature threshold, the router reverts to its default threshold of 250 recipients.

The syntax for the **ip audit smtp spam** command is as follows:

```
ip audit smtp spam num-of-recipients
no ip audit smtp spam
```

The argument and description are contained in Table 17-6.

Table 17-6   **smtp spam** *Parameter*

Argument	Description
num-of-recipients	Integer in the range of 1 to 65,535 that designates the maximum number of recipients in a mail message before a spam attack is suspected. Use with the **spam** keyword.

The following are some actual command-line examples:

```
Router (config)# ip audit smtp spam 350
Router (config)# no ip audit smtp
```

The first example sets the SPAM signature so that any mail messages with more than 350 recipients cause the Cisco IOS Firewall IDS to execute its programmed response to the SPAM signature. The second example removes the current SPAM setting that causes the threshold to revert to the default setting of 250 recipients.

Disable Signatures Globally

Sometimes, you might want to disable signatures from alarming. You might do this for performance reasons or because normal traffic keeps generating false alarms, and it is too difficult to exclude the signatures on a specific host or network basis. For whatever reason, you can easily disable any of the router's IDS signatures.

To disable router signatures on a global scope, use the **ip audit signature** global configuration command to globally disable a signature.

NOTE   If you insert a **no** at the beginning of the command to disable a specific IDS signature, you re-enable the signature.

The syntax for the **ip audit signature** command is as follows:

```
ip audit signature sig-id disable
no ip audit signature sig-id
```

The second command might seem a little confusing at first glance. The **no** at the beginning of a command normally turns off a feature. In this instance, the **no** is actually enabling a signature that has previously been disabled.

The arguments and descriptions are contained in Table 17-7.

Table 17-7   *Disabling Signature Parameters*

Argument	Description
sig-id	Unique integer specifying a signature as defined in the Cisco Secure IDS Network Security Database (NSDB)
disable	Keyword used to globally disable a signature from being audited by the Cisco IOS Firewall IDS router

The following are some actual command-line examples:

```
Router (config)# ip audit signature 1004 disable
Router (config)# ip audit signature 3102 disable
Router (config)# no ip audit signature 1004
```

The first two examples disable IDS Signatures 1004 and 3102, respectively. The third example re-enables IDS Signature 1004, which had previously been disabled.

Default Settings
By default, all the router's IDS signatures are enabled.

Exclude Signatures by Host or Network

Sometimes, you want to exclude only certain hosts or networks from triggering a specific router IDS signature. Unlike globally disabling a signature, excluding signatures provides you more control over your security environment.

To exclude signatures on your router, use a combination of two router commands. First, use the **ip audit signature** global configuration command to associate a signature with a specific access list. Then use the **access-list** global configuration command to stop the signature from triggering when generated from a given host or network.

NOTE   If you insert a **no** at the beginning of the command to associate a specific IDS signature with an access list, you remove the exclusion for the signature.

The syntax for the **ip audit signature** command is as follows:

```
ip audit signature sig-id list acl-num
no ip audit signature sig-id
```

The arguments and descriptions are contained in Table 17-8.

Table 17-8   *Signature ACL Parameters*

Argument	Description
sig-id	Unique integer specifying a signature as defined in the Cisco Secure IDS NSDB.
acl-num	Unique integer specifying a configured ACL on the router. Use with the **list** keyword.

The following are some actual command-line examples:

```
Router (config)# ip audit signature 3100 list 92
Router (config)# ip audit signature 3102 list 92
Router (config)# no ip audit signature 1006
```

The first two examples assign the IDS Signatures 3100 and 3102 to access list 92. The third example removes IDS Signature 1006 from the exclusion list.

The syntax for the **access-list** command is as follows:

```
access-list acl-num deny |permit [host]  ip-addr [wildcard]
no access-list acl-num
```

The arguments and descriptions are contained in Table 17-9.

Table 17-9   **access-list** *Parameters*

Argument	Description
acl-num	Number of an access list. This is a decimal number from 1 to 99.
deny	Keyword that denies signature trigger if the conditions are matched.
permit	Keyword that permits signature trigger if the conditions are matched.
host	Keyword that identifies that the following IP address is that of a host.
ip-addr	IP address of the network or host from which the packet is being sent. You can specify the source in two alternative ways: Use a four-octet, dotted-decimal IP address. Use keyword **any** as an abbreviation for an IP address and a wildcard of 0.0.0.0 255.255.255.255.
wildcard	Wildcard bits to be applied to the IP address. You can specify the source wildcard in two ways: Use a four-octet, dotted-decimal format. Place 1s in the bit positions you want to ignore. Use keyword **any** as an abbreviation for an IP address and a wildcard of 0.0.0.0 255.255.255.255.

The following are some actual command-line examples:

```
Router (config)# access-list 92 deny host 10.0.0.25
Router (config)# access-list 92 deny 10.2.2.0 255.255.255.0
Router (config)# access-list permit any
```

The first example line excludes the host whose IP address is 10.0.0.25 from triggering Signatures 3100 and 3102. The second example line excludes the Class C network 10.2.2.0 from triggering Signatures 3100 or 3102. The final example line causes the signatures to trigger for all other IP addresses.

NOTE   All IOS access lists have an implicit **deny any** as their last line. In a normal security setting, this causes the access list to deny any traffic that you have not explicitly allowed. With IDS signature exclusion, however, a **deny** statement prevents an IP address from triggering the signatures associate with the access list. Therefore, if you forget to include the **permit any** clause at the end of your access list, the implicit **deny any** actually excludes all IP addresses from triggering the signatures associated with the access list.

Default Settings

By default, no exclusions are applied to any of the signatures on your Cisco IOS Firewall IDS.

Create and Apply Audit Rules

The audit rules enable you to configure how your router responds when it detects intrusive activity on your network. You have three actions that you can apply to a signature:

- Generate an alarm.

- Drop the packet.

- Reset a TCP Connection (applies only to TCP-based signatures).

You build your audit rule and then apply that rule to a specific interface on your router. This audit rule can apply to all IP addresses or you can create an audit rule that excludes certain hosts or networks. This discussion of audit rules is divided into the following sections:

- Packet Auditing Process

- Setting Default Action for Signatures

- Creating an IDS Audit Rule with Excluded Addresses

Packet Auditing Process

Before you begin configuring an audit rule and applying it to a specific interface on your router, you need to understand the packet auditing process. This section explains the five steps in the packet auditing process on a Cisco IOS Firewall IDS.

- Set default actions.

- Create an audit rule.

- Apply the audit rule.

- Packets are compared against audit rule.

- Signature matches trigger user-configured actions.

The first step in using a packet auditing rule is to define the default action(s) for both your router's information signatures and its attack signatures.

NOTE   The IDS signatures on your Cisco IOS Firewall IDS are divided into two categories: information signatures and attack signatures. Information signatures are normal reconnaissance-type signatures that an attacker uses to collect information on your network structure. Attack signatures are potentially severe attacks against your network. Instead of defining signature actions on a per-signature basis, you define actions per signature groups. Therefore, you need to decide what actions to take for information signatures and what actions to take for attack signatures.

Next you need to create an audit rule. This rule needs to specify which signatures apply to the packets examined by the rule. You have two signature options: information signatures and attack signatures.

Applying your audit rule requires some careful consideration. You must decide which interface on your router to apply the audit rule, and you must decide whether to apply the audit rule to inbound packets or outbound packets. Two issues to consider when deciding whether to apply your audit rule to inbound or outbound traffic are as follows:

- If the audit rule is applied to the *in* direction on the interface, packets passing through the interface are audited before any inbound ACL has a chance to discard them. This allows an administrator to be alerted if an attack or reconnaissance activity is underway, even if the router normally rejects the activity.

- If the audit rule is applied to the *out* direction on the interface, packets are audited after they enter the router through another interface. In this case, the inbound ACL of the other interface might discard packets before they are audited. This might result in the loss of IDS alarms, even though the attack or reconnaissance activity was thwarted.

After examining these two options, you create and apply your audit rule. Packets going through the specified router interface (in the right direction) that match the audit rules are examined by a series of modules. The examination process starts with IP, followed by the transport layer (ICMP, TCP, or UDP), and ending with the application layer.

If a signature match is found in a module, the user-configured action(s) are triggered.

Setting Default Action for Signatures

You need to decide what default actions you want to apply to both the information signatures and the attack signatures. You need to consider your operational environment and security policy when making this decision.

You can configure the default actions for your information and attack signatures globally by using the **ip audit info** and **ip audit attack** commands. These commands define the default signature response options for all audit policies (unless overridden with the **ip audit name** command during the creation of the audit rule).

The syntax for the **ip audit info** command is as follows:

```
ip audit info {action [alarm][drop][reset]}
```

The syntax for the **ip audit attack** command is as follows:

```
ip audit attack {action [alarm][drop][reset]}
```

Table 17-10 explains the parameters for both of these commands.

Table 17-10 *Signature Action Parameters*

Parameter	Description
alarm	Causes the router to send an alarm to the console, Cisco Secure IDS Director, or a SYSLOG server when a signature fires. Use with the **action** keyword. This is the default action.
drop	Causes the router to drop the offending packet(s) when a signature fires. Use with the **action** keyword.
reset	Causes the router to reset the offending TCP connection when a signature fires. Use with the **action** keyword.

Creating and Applying IDS Audit Rules

First, you use the **ip audit name** global configuration command to create audit rules for information and attack signature categories.

Next you need to use the **ip audit** interface configuration command to apply an audit specification (created with the **ip audit name** command) to a specific router interface and traffic in a specific direction.

NOTE   Insert a **no** in front of your **ip audit name** command to delete the audit rule. You also can insert a **no** in front of your **ip audit** command to remove an audit rule from a specific router interface.

The syntax for the **ip audit name** command is as follows:

```
ip audit name audit-name {info | attack} [action [alarm] [drop] [reset]]
no ip audit name audit-name {info | attack}
```

The arguments and descriptions are contained in Table 17-11.

The following are some actual command-line examples:

```
Router (config)# ip audit name AUDIT10 info action alarm
Router (config)# ip audit name AUDIT10 attack action alarm drop reset
Router (config)# no ip audit name AUDIT1 info
```

Table 17-11 ip audit name *Parameters*

Argument	Description
audit-name	Name for an audit specification. Use with the **name** keyword.
info	Keyword that specifies that the audit rule is for information signatures.
attack	Keyword that specifies that the audit rule is for attack signatures.
alarm	Causes the router to send an alarm to the console, Cisco Secure IDS Director, or a SYSLOG server when a signature fires. Use with the **action** keyword. This is the default action.
reset	Causes the router to reset the offending TCP connection when a signature fires. Use with the **action** keyword.
drop	Causes the router to drop the offending packet(s) when a signature fires. Use with the **action** keyword.

The first example specifies only the *alarm* action for the information signatures and assigns this setting to the audit rule named AUDIT10. The second example specifies all three alarm actions (alarm, drop, and reset) for the attack signatures and assigns this setting to the audit rule named AUDIT10. The third example removes the information signatures from the audit rule named AUDIT1.

Default Settings

If you do not specify an action, the default is to assign an action of alarm only.

The syntax for the **ip audit** command is as follows:

```
ip audit audit-name {in | out}
no ip audit audit-name {in | out}
```

The arguments and descriptions are contained in Table 17-12.

Table 17-12 ip audit *Command Parameters*

Argument	Description
audit-name	Name for an audit specification
in	Keyword to apply audit rule to inbound traffic
out	Keyword to apply audit rule to outbound traffic

The following are some actual command-line examples:

```
Router (config)# interface e0
Router (config-if)# ip audit AUDIT10 in
```

The first example line places you in the Interface Configuration mode for interface e0. The second line then assigns the audit rule named AUDIT10 to the inbound direction of interface e0.

Creating an IDS Audit Rule with Excluded Addresses

Similar to excluding signatures from triggering for specific hosts or networks, you also can use the same process to exclude hosts and networks from your audit rule. To create an IDS audit rule with excluded addresses, combine the **access-list** command to the audit rule commands that were explained previously in this chapter. This process involves the following steps:

Step 1   Use the **ip audit name** global configuration command to create your audit rule for both information and attack signatures. With this command, you also associate the audit rule with a specified access list.

Step 2   Use the **ip access-list** global configuration command to exclude the specific hosts and networks that you do not want to trigger your audit rule actions.

Step 3   Use the **ip audit** interface configuration command to apply your audit rule to a specified interface on your router.

The syntax for the **ip audit name** command is as follows:

```
ip audit name audit-name {info | attack} [list acl-num] [action [alarm]
    [drop] [reset]]
no ip audit name audit-name {info | attack}
```

The arguments and descriptions are contained in Table 17-13.

Table 17-13   **ip audit name** *Parameters*

Argument	Description
audit-name	Name for an audit specification.
info	Keyword that specifies that the audit rule is for info signatures.
attack	Keyword that specifies that the audit rule is for attack signatures.
acl-num	Unique integer specifying a configured ACL on the router. Use with the **list** keyword.
alarm	Causes the router to send an alarm to the console, Cisco Secure IDS Director, or a SYSLOG server when a signature fires. Use with the **action** keyword. This is the default action.
reset	Causes the router to reset the offending TCP connection when a signature fires. Use with the **action** keyword.
drop	Causes the router to drop the offending packet(s) when a signature fires. Use with the **action** keyword.

Now it's time to walk through an actual command-line example. For this example, the following requirements apply:

- Information signatures generate only alarms.

- Attack signatures generate alarms, drop offending packets, and reset offending TCP connections.

- The access list (92) needs to prevent the signatures from triggering on traffic from the host with the IP address 10.0.0.25, and the Class C network 10.2.2.0.

- The audit rule needs to be applied to the ethernet0 interface on the inbound direction.

To create this example IDS audit rule with excluded addresses, follow these steps:

Step 1 Define the default actions and associated access list.

```
Router (config)# ip audit name AUDIT10 info list 92 action alarm
Router (config)# ip audit name AUDIT10 attack list 92 action alarm drop reset
```

Step 2 Define the access list 92:

```
Router (config)# ip access-list standard 92
Router (config-std-nacl)# deny host 10.0.0.25
Router (config-std-nacl)# deny 10.2.2.0 255.255.255.0
Router (config-std-nacl)# permit any
```

Step 3 Apply the audit rule to the ethernet0 interface:

```
Router (config)# interface ethernet0
Router (config-if)# ip audit AUDIT10 in
```

Verify the Configuration

You can use several command types to verify the current configuration of your Cisco IOS Firewall IDS configuration. These commands fall into three categories:

- Show
- Clear
- Debug

Show Commands

Several **show** commands enable you to examine the current IDS configuration on your Cisco IOS Firewall IDS. These commands are as follows:

- **show ip audit statistics**
- **show ip audit configuration**
- **show ip audit interface**
- **show ip audit debug**

You use the **show ip audit statistics** command to display the number of packets audited and the number of alarms sent, along with other information. The syntax for the **show ip audit statistics** command is as follows:

```
show ip audit statistics
```

A sample output from the **show ip audit statistics** command is as follows:

```
Signature audit statistics [process switch:fast switch]
  Signature 2000 packets audited  [0:5]
  Signature 2001 packets audited  [11:11]
  Signature 2002 packets audited  [0:5]
  Signature 3151 packets audited  [0:14]
Interfaces configured for audit
Session creations since subsystem startup or last reset 11
Current session counts (estab/half-open/terminating) [0:0:0]
Maxever session counts (estab/half-open/terminating) [2:1:0]
Last session created 16:12:47
Last Statistic Reset never

HID:1000 OID:100 S:128 A:3 H:14085 HA:7114 DA:0 R:0
```

The **show ip audit configuration** command enables you to display additional configuration information, including default values that might not display using the standard **show running-config** command that you normally use to view the current configuration of your router. The syntax for the **show ip audit configuration** command is as follows:

```
show ip audit configuration
```

A sample output from the **show ip audit configuration** command is as follows:

```
Event notification through syslog is enabled
Event notification through Net Director is enabled
Default action(s) for info signatures is alarm
Default action(s) for attack signatures is alarm drop reset
Default threshold of recipients for spam signature is 25
PostOffice:HostID:55 OrgID:123 Msg dropped:0
        :Curr Event Buf Size:100  Configured:100
HID:14 OID:123 S:1 A:2 H:82 HA:49 DA:0 R:0 Q:0 ID:1 Dest:10.1.1.99:45000
    Loc:172.16.58.99:45000 T:5 S:ESTAB *

Audit Rule Configuration
 Audit name AUDIT.10
    info actions alarm
    attack actions alarm drop reset
```

NOTE   The cryptic line in the output of the **show ip audit configuration** command indicates the PostOffice connection with your Director. The *HID* and *OID* are the host ID and organization ID for your director. *Dest* indicates the IP address and port number that your router uses to communicate with the Director. *Loc* indicates these settings on your router. Finally, *ESTAB* indicates that PostOffice connection to the Director is active.

Use the **show ip audit interface** command to display the interface configuration. The syntax for the **show ip audit interface** command is as follows:

```
show ip audit interface
```

A sample output from the **show ip audit interface** command is as follows:

```
Interface Configuration
 Interface Ethernet0
  Inbound IDS audit rule is AUDIT.1
    info actions alarm
    attack actions alarm drop reset
  Outgoing IDS audit rule is not set
 Interface Ethernet1
  Inbound IDS audit rule is AUDIT.1
    info actions alarm
    attack actions alarm drop reset
  Outgoing IDS audit rule is not set
```

The **show ip audit debug** command enables you to display the currently enabled debug flags. These debugging options are enabled by the debug commands discussed later in the "Debug Commands" section of this chapter. The syntax for the **show ip audit debug** command is as follows:

```
show ip audit debug
```

A sample output from the **show ip audit debug** command is as follows:

```
IDS Object Creations debugging is on
IDS Timer events debugging is on
IDS FTP commands and responses debugging is on
IDS FTP tokens debugging is on
```

Clear Commands

You can use a couple of clear commands to clear or disable features of your Cisco IOS Firewall IDS. These commands are as follows:

- **clear ip audit statistics**

- **clear ip audit configuration**

You use the **clear ip audit statistics** command to reset statistics on packets analyzed and alarms sent. The syntax for the **clear ip audit statistics** command is as follows:

```
clear ip audit statistics
```

The **clear ip audit configuration** command enables you to disable the IDS functionality on your router. It removes all intrusion detection configuration entries and releases dynamic resources. The syntax for the **clear ip audit configuration** command is as follows:

```
clear ip audit configuration
```

Debug Commands

You can use a plethora of debug commands to troubleshoot and test your Cisco Secure IOS Firewall IDS configuration. The following list shows the available **debug** commands:

- **debug ip audit timers**
- **debug ip audit object-creation**
- **debug ip audit object-deletion**
- **debug ip audit function trace**
- **debug ip audit detailed**
- **debug ip audit ftp-cmd**
- **debug ip audit ftp-token**
- **debug ip audit icmp**
- **debug ip audit ip**
- **debug ip audit rpc**
- **debug ip audit smtp**
- **debug ip audit tcp**
- **debug ip audit tftp**
- **debug ip audit udp**

NOTE	To turn off the debugging commands, you can either attach a **no** to the beginning of the **debug** command or use the **undebug** keyword on your command.

Add the Cisco IOS Firewall IDS to the Director Configuration

When you finish configuring your Cisco IOS Firewall IDS, the IDS-enabled router appears as another sensor on the Cisco Secure IDS Home submap. To get to that stage, however, you need to complete two configuration steps:

- Add the router's host name and host ID to the host's configuration.
- Add the router's IP address to the route's configuration.

Both of these operations need to be performed on your CSIDD.

Add the Router's Host Name and Host ID to the Host's Configuration

To allow communication between CSIDD and your Cisco IOS Firewall IDS, you need to complete the following steps to enter the router's host name and host ID information into the Director's configuration using the Configuration File Management Utility (nrConfigure):

Step 1 From the Director, start nrConfigure by choosing **Configure** from the **Security** menu in HP OpenView.

Step 2 Double-click the name of your Director machine on the displayed list of devices. The Configuration Library screen displays (see Figure 17-3).

Step 3 On the currently applied configuration version (the one that is bold), expand the System Files by clicking the plus sign (+) to the left of the folder (see Figure 17-3). After expansion, the plus sign becomes a minus sign (–).

Step 4 Double-click **Hosts** under System Files. The Hosts dialog box opens (see Figure 17-4).

Step 5 Click the **Add** button in the upper-right corner of the Hosts dialog box. The Hosts - Add dialog box opens (see Figure 17-5).

Step 6 Enter the host name and host ID for the Cisco IOS Firewall IDS in the proper fields. You configured these parameters with the **ip audit po local** on your router.

Step 7 Click **OK**. The Hosts - Add dialog box closes.

Step 8 Click **OK**. The Hosts dialog box closes.

Figure 17-3 *Configuration Library Screen*

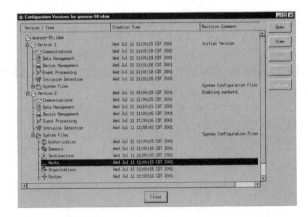

Figure 17-4 *Hosts Dialog Box*

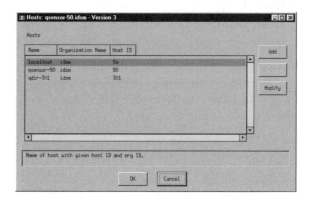

Figure 17-5 *Hosts - Add Dialog Box*

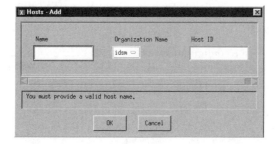

Add the Router's IP Address to the Route's Configuration

To finalize the configuration in the Cisco Secure ID Director and add the Cisco IOS Firewall IDS, you need to complete the following steps to enter the IP address for the router into the Director's configuration by using nrConfigure:

Step 1 From the Director, start nrConfigure by choosing **Configure** from the **Security** menu in HP OpenView.

Step 2 Double-click the name of your Director machine on the displayed list of devices. The Configuration Library screen displays (refer back to Figure 17-3).

Step 3 On the currently applied configuration version (the one that is bold), expand the System Files by clicking the plus sign (+) to the left of the folder (refer back to Figure 17-3). The plus sign becomes a minus sign (–) after expansion.

Step 4 Double-click **Routes** under System Files. The Routes dialog box opens (see Figure 17-6).

Step 5 Click the **Add** button in the upper-right corner of the Routes dialog box. The Routes - Add dialog box opens (see Figure 17-7).

Step 6 Choose the host name for the Cisco IOS Firewall IDS from the Name drop-down menu. You added this name when you added the router's host name and host ID to the Director's configuration. These steps were explained previously in this chapter.

Step 7 Enter the IP address for the Cisco IOS Firewall IDS in the proper field. Leave all the other settings at their default.

Step 8 Click **OK**. The Routes - Add dialog box closes.

Step 9 Click **OK**. The Routes dialog box closes.

Step 10 Select the newly created configuration transient version and click **Apply**.

Step 11 In the Version Comment pop-up window, enter a description for the new configuration version, such as **Added IOS-IDS router**.

Step 12 Click **OK**.

Step 13 Wait for the configuration to be applied. (The configuration version turns bold after the configuration is applied.) The Cisco IOS Firewall IDS now has a sensor icon displayed in the Director's Home submap.

Figure 17-6 *Routes Dialog Box*

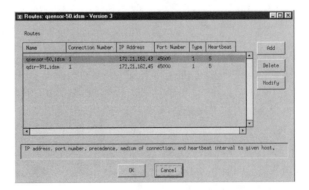

Figure 17-7 *Routes - Add Dialog Box*

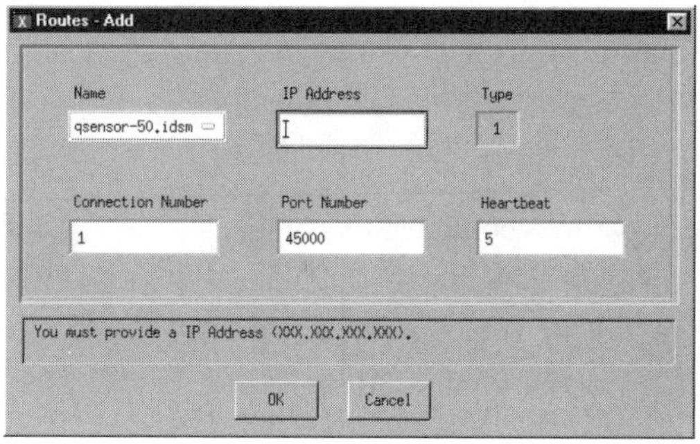

Summary

The Cisco Secure IOS IDS software enables you to improve your network's security in a cost-effective manner. This solution adds firewall and IDS functionality to the routers in your infrastructure. Furthermore, this Cisco IOS Firewall IDS can be deployed in environments that are not suited for the 4200 Series Appliance Sensors.

The Cisco IOS Firewall IDS is intended to satisfy the security goals of all Cisco's customers, and is particularly appropriate for the following:

- Enterprise customers with numerous network boundaries
- Service providers that want to provide managed services such as firewalling and intrusion detection
- Small and medium-sized businesses with limited IT budgets

Although the Cisco IOS Firewall IDS provides a cost-effective security solution that can be implemented on numerous router platforms, you must consider several issues before you actually deploy the IOS IDS software:

- Memory usage and performance impact
- Signature coverage
- Signature updates

You must weigh each of these issues against your operational requirements and security policy.

The signatures on the Cisco IOS Firewall IDS are divided into two groups:

- Information signatures
- Attack signatures

Furthermore, you have three user-configurable actions that you can apply to these two signature groups:

- Generate alarm.
- Reset TCP session.
- Drop packets.

You can assign the various combinations of the user-configurable actions to each signature category. It is recommended, however, that the TCP reset and drop actions be used in tandem to completely block an attack.

When configuring your Cisco IOS Firewall IDS, you need to perform the following operations:

- Initialize the Cisco IOS Firewall IDS on the router.
- Decide whether any signatures need to be disabled.
- Configure which hosts/networks will be excluded from various signatures.
- Create and apply your audit rules.
- Verify your configuration using various commands on your router.
- Add your Cisco IOS Firewall IDS to your CSIDD configuration.

Review Questions

The following questions test your retention of the material presented in this chapter. The answers to the Review Questions are in Appendix K, "Answers to Review Questions."

1 Does the Cisco IOS Firewall IDS support as many signatures as the regular sensor appliance? If not, how many does each support?

2 What are the three response actions that you can configure?

3 What are some deployment issues that must be considered before deploying the Cisco IOS Firewall IDS on your network?

_____

_____

_____

4 What is the command to globally disable an IDS signature on your Cisco IOS Firewall IDS?

_____

_____

_____

5 What command do you use to turn off the IDS functionality on your Cisco IOS Firewall IDS?

_____

_____

_____

6 What is the command to set the router's Director PostOffice parameters?

_____

_____

_____

7 What is the command to set the router's local PostOffice parameters?

_____

_____

_____

8 What command do you use in conjunction with the **ip audit signature** command to exclude a host or network from triggering a specific alarm?

_____

_____

_____

9 What command do you use to show your IDS configuration on your router?

_____

_____

_____

10 What destinations can you configure for alarms on your router?

_____

_____

_____

PART VII

Cisco Secure IDS Upcoming Releases

## CHAPTER 18

Planned Cisco Secure IDS Enhancements

The current version of Cisco Secure IDS is 2.5. By the time this book is on the shelves, however, another major version of Cisco Secure IDS will have been released. The Cisco Secure IDS product is continually evolving. Therefore, this chapter is devoted to explaining some of the new features planned for Cisco Secure IDS in the immediate future.

NOTE The features and enhancements explained in this chapter are subject to change. This chapter is intended to give only an indication of the kinds of new improvements being incorporated into Cisco Secure IDS.

This chapter covers the following:

- Version 3.0
- Version 4.0
- Enhancements to the sensor and Director platforms

This chapter ends with a quick overview of the new user-definable signature capability introduced in Cisco IDS Version 3.0.

NOTE Improvements are continually being considered for inclusion into Cisco Secure IDS. To give developers a clear goal, a set of improvements is agreed upon for a specific software release. At the same time, other features are being considered. These features can be included in future planned software releases. By planning multiple releases in advance, customers are given a clearer indication of how the product functionality is growing.

Version 3.0

The next major software release for Cisco Secure IDS is version 3.0. This version will add numerous enhancements to Cisco Secure IDS. These enhancements can be divided into the following three categories:

- Installation and configuration enhancements
- Signature enhancements
- Blocking enhancements

NOTE   When this book appears on shelves, Cisco IDS Version 3.0 will probably be the current release. Starting with version 3.0, Cisco Secure IDS is being renamed to Cisco IDS.

Installation and Configuration Enhancements

Simplifying the Cisco Secure IDS initial installation and regular upgrades is always a prominent customer concern. Furthermore, customers are always looking for more efficient ways to configure their Cisco Secure IDS. The upcoming installation and configuration enhancements are as follows:

- Sensor login through SSH
- Software determines monitoring interface name
- Alarm when monitoring interface is disconnected
- Simplified signature and application software upgrade

Sensor Login Through SSH

Currently, remote in-band access to the Cisco Secure IDS Sensors is provided through Telnet. Telnet is not secure, especially over WAN links because it transmits login credentials unencrypted. For some customers, this is not a significant issue. Managed service providers and large enterprise customers that have a multiple-site deployment, however, require a more secure mechanism to remotely access their Cisco Secure IDS Sensors. Therefore, Secure Shell (SSH) is going to be added as a remote access mechanism for the Cisco Secure IDS Sensors. This will provide you with a more secure mechanism with which to manage the Cisco Secure IDS Sensors that you deploy on your network.

NOTE   The capability to log on to your sensor through SSH applies only to the appliance sensors.

Software Determines Monitoring Interface Name

Presently, you are required to enter the device name for the monitoring interface (for example, /dev/spwr0) when initializing a Cisco Secure IDS Sensor. Many customers find this confusing, and it is a common source of error. Therefore, Cisco Secure IDS is being modified so that you do not need to specify the device name for the monitoring interface.

Alarm When Monitoring Interface Is Disconnected

One of the current capabilities of Cisco Secure IDS is to generate an alarm when the command and control link goes down. Driven by customer requests, this alarm capability is being expanded to include the monitoring interface on the sensor as well. The alarming on the monitoring interface will provide two levels of functionality:

- Trigger when link goes down
- Trigger when unicast message is not received in specified time period

Only the Cisco Secure IDS 4210 Sensor appliance will support alarming in the event that the monitoring link goes down. However, all the sensors will support alarming when they fail to receive a unicast message within a specified time period. This functionality will be extremely helpful in determining when a sensor that is connected to a SPAN port is no longer receiving traffic.

Simplified Signature and Application Software Upgrade

With Cisco Secure IDS 2.5 and earlier, every time a signature update was released, you needed to manually download the file and FTP this file to all of your Cisco Secure IDS Sensors. Then, you needed to run an install script on all of your sensors as well. That is a time-consuming and cumbersome task, especially if your network environment is large. Furthermore, running the FTP server on the sensors themselves represents a service that can potentially be exploited by an attacker.

Simplifying this process is a concern for many customers. Therefore, Cisco IDS Version 3.0 will incorporate a mechanism that helps automate the process of deploying signature and application software updates. This automated process will be based on executing the **update** command remotely or scheduling the update to occur at a specific time. Furthermore, this new process will not require a persistent server, such as FTP, on your sensors.

NOTE   Automating the update process is not a trivial task. Significant improvements will be made in Cisco IDS 3.0. This process might continue to be improved in other future releases as well.

Signature Enhancements

The second category of enhancements includes features that are being implemented to increase the capability of your Cisco Secure IDS to detect attacks on your network. This category also includes improving your ability to customize IDS signatures to match your specific operational environment.

The signature enhancements for Cisco IDS 3.0 fall into the following categories:

- Network denial of service (DoS) attacks
- Tuning signature thresholds
- Custom connection signatures
- User-defined signatures
- Monitoring ISL/802.1Q traffic
- Host includes
- IP session log format

Network Denial of Service (DoS) Attacks

A number of recent DOS attacks are targeted at consuming network resources, such as bandwidth. These attacks are not always targeted at a specific host. Functionality is being added to detect attacks that are targeted at consuming network resources. In particular, a signature to detect SYN Flood DoS attacks is being implemented.

Tuning Signature Thresholds

Signature thresholds are currently hard-coded into signatures, preventing customers from modifying them. For certain signatures, customers prefer to have the ability to modify specific signature thresholds to match their particular environment.

Certain signatures are being modified to enable you to adjust the threshold parameters. This will enable you to have more control over the fidelity of your Cisco Secure IDS.

Signature Threshold

A signature threshold is a parameter within a signature that is used to trigger the signature. An example of a signature threshold is the number of ports that constitutes a port scan. Another example of a threshold is the number of hosts that constitutes a ping sweep.

Custom Connection Signatures

Many customers want their Cisco Secure IDS to alert them when certain traffic is detected between specific source and/or destination IP addresses. The only mechanism currently available to accomplish this task is to use a 3000 or 4000 connection signature. These signatures, however, generate large volumes of information by logging every connection to a specified port. Furthermore, you must sift through this large amount of log information to locate the specific hosts in which you are interested.

Therefore, Cisco Secure IDS is being modified to enable you to create custom connection signatures. With these custom signatures, you will be able to define a connection signature based on source IP address, destination IP address, source port, destination port, and protocol. These more granular connection signatures will reduce the amount of log data that needs to be collected and processed, and will improve the performance of your sensors. Furthermore, each of the parameters can be wildcarded to provide even more functionality.

User-Defined Signatures

Some IDSs enable their users to develop their own signatures. Network Flight Recorder (NFR) currently provides this functionality. This functionality enables customers to enhance their IDS by adding signatures unique to their operational environment.

Based on customer requests, Cisco Secure IDS is being modified to enable you to write your own signatures. You will be able to generate these signatures by specifying attributes of ISO network layers two to seven. Later in this chapter, a quick overview of this new functionality is presented, along with some actual custom signature examples.

Monitoring Inter-Switch Link (ISL)/802.1Q Traffic

You can use ISL and 802.1Q trunking protocols to interconnect multiple VLAN-capable devices. All Cisco switches, by definition, are VLAN-capable. Furthermore, all Cisco routers from the 2600 and higher support VLANs.

Traffic between multiple VLAN-capable devices can utilize trunk lines to transport traffic from multiple VLANs across the same physical connection. To provide more options for sensor placement throughout your network, the Cisco Secure IDS Sensors are being enhanced to add the capability to monitor both ISL and 802.1Q trunk lines.

NOTE   The IDSM can already capture traffic from multiple VLANs, but this capability is available only on the Catalyst 6000 family of switches. The capability to monitor trunk lines is targeted at other sensor platforms.

NOTE	Implementation of this feature might be affected by problems on existing NIC cards with packets that exceed the maximum Ethernet frame size of 1514 bytes.

Host Includes

Cisco Secure IDS enables you to exclude certain hosts from triggering specific alarms. This functionality works great when you know the specific hosts for which you want to exclude the signatures. This can be cumbersome if you need to exclude a large number of hosts.

Based on customer requests, Cisco Secure IDS is being enhanced to enable you to define *inclusions*. An inclusion basically enables you to specify a limited number of hosts for which a signature will trigger. The signature will not fire for any host not listed in the inclusion. You might want to use this capability to cause certain Web signatures to be checked only against traffic to hosts that you specifically know to be Web servers.

An example of where this feature will be helpful is the Cisco IOS HTTP Server %% Vulnerability. The signature is noisy (high false positive rate) if you alarm on all Web traffic because of the nature of the vulnerability. By enabling you to configure this signature to alarm only on traffic destined for your Cisco routers, you will eliminate the false positives. Without this Include feature, customers are forced to Exclude all nonrouter Web traffic, which is counterintuitive and cumbersome.

IP Session Log Format

The current IP Session log feature captures only TCP data and the Transcript log viewer provides only limited functionality. Based on customer requests, IP Session logging is being expanded to capture all IP packet data along with the application layer data (for example, IP and TCP header information). Furthermore, this data will be stored in a common format such as tcpdump. This common format will enable you to re-create (or replay) these collected packet streams on a test network for forensic and post-mortem analysis by using tools such as TCPReplay.

---

tcpdump

tcpdump is a common sniffing program available on almost all Linux systems. Other sniffing programs can usually import data saved by tcpdump, such as ethereal.

Shunning Enhancements

To halt an attack against your network, one action that your Cisco Secure IDS can take is to block traffic from the attacking host. Enhancements to improve the capability of Cisco

Secure IDS to block or shun attacking hosts in Cisco Secure IDS Version 3.0 include the following:

- Blocking with the PIX
- Enhanced ACL block handling
- Blocking with Catalyst 5000 Route Switch Module (RSM)
- Blocking with Catalyst 6000 Security ACLs

Blocking with the PIX

After an attack is detected, your Cisco Secure IDS Sensor is capable of shunning/blocking the attacker on various router platforms. This capability is being extended to include the PIX Firewall. In addition, a capability to notify CSPM that the sensor commanded the PIX to block will be developed to permit CSPM to synchronize its knowledge of the configuration of the PIX with what is actually running on the PIX.

NOTE   It is presently unclear when the associated functionality will be incorporated into CSPM to process the notification message being sent by the sensor.

NOTE   This functionality is being incorporated into PIX Version 6.0. Therefore, to take advantage of this new functionality, your PIX will have to be running 6.0 or higher.

Enhanced ACL Block Handling

The current implementation of blocking through ACLs uses a "brute-force" approach of total ownership and completely reapplies the entire ACL. This prevents you from adding your own user-defined ACL rules to the same interface/direction combination. By enhancing the ACL block handling functionality, you will not have to devote a specific interface/direction for blocking.

Blocking with Catalyst 5000 Route Switch Module (RSM)

It is currently unknown whether the ACL blocking capability works correctly with the Catalyst 5000 RSM. Many customers connect Cisco Secure IDS Sensors to a SPAN port on a Catalyst 5000 switch. In this configuration, it is desirable to have your Cisco Secure IDS Sensor block on the Catalyst 5000 RSM. This enhancement will enable you to connect a sensor to a SPAN port on your Catalyst 5000 switch and then block on the RSM that is installed in the same chassis.

Blocking with Catalyst 6000 Security ACLs

Many customers install the Catalyst 6000 IDS Module (IDSM) in their Catalyst 6000 switches. Other customers have appliance sensors connected to a SPAN port on these switches. In these configurations, you might want to block using the Security ACL capability on your switch. This functionality is being added for both the IDSM and the appliance sensors.

Version 4.0

Cisco Secure IDS Version 4.0 builds on the improvements started in version 3.0. The enhancements planned for inclusion into Cisco Secure Version 4.0 can be grouped into three distinct categories as well:

- Installation and configuration enhancements
- Signatures enhancements
- Blocking enhancements

Installation and Configuration Enhancements

Simplifying the Cisco Secure IDS initial installation and regular upgrades is always a prominent customer concern. Furthermore, customers are always looking for more efficient ways to configure their Cisco Secure IDS. Cisco IDS Version 3.0 provides several enhancements in this arena. The upcoming installation and configuration enhancements for Cisco IDS Version 4.0 are as follows:

- Fully functional CLI on sensor
- Integrate scanner feedback
- Alarm destination/director failover
- Sensor "stateful" failover
- Monitor full-duplex and multiple segments
- Time synchronization
- Sensor console redirection

Fully Functional CLI on Sensor

A number of customers, for one reason or another, cannot use nrConfigure to configure their sensors. These customers require a robust sensor command-line interface (CLI) for configuring their sensors. Currently, these customers are either manually editing the configuration files or using **nrset** commands, both of which are complex operations that are error prone.

In addition, current appliances look and operate like PCs running a UNIX application. All the host operating system commands and features are available to the user. This introduces an opportunity for you to run commands or use features that can potentially adversely affect the operation of your sensor. In some circumstances, these commands can cause your sensor to become inoperable. Furthermore, troubleshooting the sensor is much more complicated.

Therefore, a CLI is being implemented that enables you to configure the functionality on your sensor. These configuration commands will probably mimic classic IOS command-line interface behavior and follow IOS syntax for similar commands.

Integrate Scanner Feedback

Configuring a sensor initially can take a considerable amount of time and energy. Reducing the effort required to configure sensors reduces the operational cost of your IDS. The Cisco Secure Scanner can assist in solving this problem because it collects data that can be used to configure Cisco Secure IDS Sensors. Furthermore, integrating scan data will enable you to more finely tune your sensors, which will improve your sensor's performance.

Therefore, one of the enhancements of Cisco IDS Version 4.0 is to integrate Cisco Secure Scanner data into the IDS Sensor to assist in establishing an initial configuration. There is also a feature to enable you to manually rescan to update your sensor's configuration. The scanner data will be used to configure various items, such as the following:

- Setting signature severity levels
- Disabling signatures that are not relevant for the specific environment (for example, turn off UNIX signatures in an NT-only environment)

Alarm Destination/Director Failover

Because the alarm database on the current Director platform is stored locally on the platform, the only way to implement a failover strategy is to have sensors send alarms to multiple Directors simultaneously. This results in your sensor sending out a number of unnecessary and duplicate alarms. You have to manually analyze and clear the duplicate alarms on your "backup" Director to keep the alarm repository from filling up and crashing.

NOTE   The only other failover feature currently supported involves using multiple NICs on your Director. If the route to the primary NIC fails, your sensors can send alarms to the secondary NIC. This failover deals only with network connectivity and does not enable you to run multiple instances of your Director software on different machines.

To fill this deficiency, the capability to send alarms to a backup destination if and when the primary destination fails is being incorporated into Cisco Secure IDS. Furthermore, the sensor will automatically begin sending alarms to the primary when connectivity is restored, thereby ceasing the alarm transmittal to the backup destination. Future releases might also incorporate redundancy and data concurrency as well.

Sensor "Stateful" Failover

Currently, no way exists to implement a "transparent stateful" sensor failover configuration. The only option is to have two sensors monitoring the same segment, sending duplicate alarms to the management platform. This scheme can generate a lot of extraneous data, and the sensors will appear to the user as individual sensors rather than a single entity. Many customers are asking for stateful sensor failover functionality.

"Transparent Stateful" Sensor Failover

Stateful sensor failover enables you to have two sensors monitoring the same traffic, with the backup taking over if the primary sensor fails (without losing state or missing any alarms). Even though two sensors are monitoring the same traffic, alarms are generated only by one of the sensors. Being transparent means that you do not need to intervene during the failover process.

To accommodate various customer requests, a stateful sensor failover capability is being integrated into Cisco Secure IDS. This capability will enable you to configure two sensors to monitor the same network segment but act as a single sensor. These two sensors will operate with the following characteristics:

- One sensor will be the primary and the other will be the backup.
- Only one alarm will be sent to the Director from the primary.
- Both sensors will have the same identification parameters.
- You will configure a single virtual sensor (not both sensors separately).
- The backup can become the primary without losing state.

Monitor Full-Duplex and Multiple Segments

Many customers have requested the capability to monitor full-duplex and multiple network segments simultaneously with a single appliance by installing multiple NICs. Therefore, the packetd software is being modified to enable you to use multiple NIC cards in your sensor. This will enable your sensors to monitor multiple network feeds simultaneously through the separate NIC cards.

NOTE	The Cisco Secure IDS Sensor software is being modified to provide the functionality to monitor full-duplex and multiple segments. It is presently unclear, however, when the appropriate sensor hardware platform that takes advantage of this feature will be supported.

Time Synchronization

Currently, no method exists for handling clock drift on the individual sensors. Time synchronization is being added to Cisco Secure IDS to enable cross-correlation of multiple events from various sensors throughout your network. Furthermore, this time synchronization is being implemented securely to prevent spoofing, because event time is a critical analysis and correlation attribute.

Sensor Console Redirection

With the Cisco Secure IDS 2.2.1 release, users were able to connect and log on to sensors through the COM1 port by using a Laplink cable and a PC running HyperTerminal. In this configuration, COM1 is a TTY port and the console is still mapped to a directly connected keyboard and monitor. Numerous customers have requested the capability to redirect the console to the COM port connected to a modem in order to view the sensor operating system boot sequence for remote maintenance and troubleshooting. Therefore, this capability is being incorporated into Cisco Secure IDS.

Signature Enhancements

The second category of enhancements includes features that are being implemented to increase the capability of your Cisco Secure IDS to detect attacks on the network. This category also includes improving your ability to customize IDS signatures to your specific operational environment. Some of the features build on functionality that is being incorporated into Cisco IDS Version 3.0.

The signature enhancements for Cisco Secure IDS 4.0 fall into the following categories:

- Tune signature thresholds
- User-defined signatures
- Transmit alarms through SNMP and SYSLOG

Tune Signature Thresholds

Beginning in version 3.0, Cisco began converting many hard-coded signature thresholds into settings that you can modify to accommodate your network environment. Cisco IDS Version 4.0 will convert all thresholds into user-configurable settings. The goal of this endeavor is to provide you with more granular control over the fidelity and operational characteristics of your Cisco Secure IDS.

User-Defined Signatures

Some IDSs allow their users to develop their own signatures. Network Flight Recorder (NFR) currently provides this functionality. This functionality enables customers to enhance their IDS by adding signatures that are unique to their operational environment.

Beginning in Cisco IDS Version 3.0, Cisco began implementing the capability to enable you to develop your own custom signatures. This release will build on that initial capability, enhancing your capability to create custom signatures that you develop to fit your unique operational environment.

Transmit Alarms Through SNMP and SYSLOG

To consolidate data into a single console interface, some customers are using the SNMP trap feature in eventd on the current Director to send alarms to other SNMP management applications. For the Cisco Secure ID Director, you can leverage the *trap* capability in HP OpenView to provide this functionality. This functionality is not currently supported, however, on the CSPM Director.

Furthermore, many customers are also requesting the ability to transmit alarms through SYSLOG. SYSLOG is the de facto standard for logging system events in the UNIX world. It provides both local and remote logging over the network through standard protocols to multiple vendor systems.

NOTE   Both SNMP and SYSLOG have a history of security-related vulnerabilities. Before using these transport mechanisms, you need to understand their weaknesses and how they might impact your overall security policy.

Therefore, the Cisco Secure IDS Sensor software is being modified to permit the transmission of alarms in multiple formats, such as SNMP traps, SYSLOG, and potentially even XML messages. The highest priority is on adding SNMP trap functionality. Other formats will probably be incorporated, but at a lower priority.

Blocking Enhancements

To halt an attack against your network, one action that your Cisco Secure IDS can take is to block traffic from the attacking host. Enhancements to improve the capability of Cisco

Secure IDS to block or shun attacking hosts in Cisco IDS Version 4.0 include blocking with extended ACLs.

The current blocking mechanism uses only standard ACL, which blocks all traffic from the attacking source IP address. Because of potential false positives and unintended DoS concerns, it is useful to provide you with the option to apply an ACL that just prevents the offending traffic, rather than all traffic from a source host or network address.

Therefore, the existing ACL handling capability is being expanded to provide you with more granular control over the blocking configuration. You will be able to block by port and IP address, in addition to the existing capability to block all the traffic from a host or IP subnet.

Sensor Enhancements

Your Cisco Secure IDS Sensors represent the components of your IDS that actually analyze your network traffic. Increasing the amount of traffic that a single sensor can monitor provides you greater flexibility in deploying sensors throughout your network. The two main sensor platforms are as follows:

- Sensor appliance
- Catalyst 6000 Family IDSM

This chapter also covers the following specific sensor enhancements:

- Gigabit IDSM
- Sensor Device Manager (SDM)

Sensor Appliance

The sensor appliance is a network appliance that you can deploy at various locations throughout your network. Currently, the fastest sensor appliance can capture and process up to 100 Mb of network traffic through its network interface. New sensors, however, will be capable of exceeding this barrier.

Currently, Cisco plans to release a sensor appliance in 2001 that is capable of processing network traffic in the 1 gigabit range. This represents a tenfold increase from the previous 100 Mb sensor appliance.

Catalyst 6000 Family IDSM

The Catalyst 6000 Family IDS Module (IDSM) is a line card that resides in your Catalyst 6000 switch. It receives traffic directly from the switch's backplane, even though it is not in the switch's fast path. Some of the planned enhancements for IDSM Version 3.0 include the following:

- Saturation indicator
- Signature response actions
- SAPD functionality
- Host includes
- Network DOS signatures
- Modify PostOffice port
- Direct Telnet to IDSM

Saturation Indicator

Currently, no way exists for you to determine when the IDSM is reaching saturation and will begin to drop packets. Because no way exists to constrain the volume of traffic that you can configure the IDSM to monitor, you can either mistakenly or knowingly exceed the 100 Mbps recommendation. A feature that provides an indication of whether the IDSM is reaching saturation is required to assist you while configuring your IDSM.

When the IDSM reaches a saturated condition at any time during a customer-defined period (for example, n seconds), an alarm will be generated to provide you with an indication of the saturation condition. This alarm also includes information about how long the IDSM was in a saturated condition within the your customer-defined period.

Signature Response Actions

Signature response actions were identified as a desired feature in the initial IDSM product requirements document. However, this functionality was not provided in the 2.5 release. Customers and magazine reviewers have identified this as a product deficiency that must be addressed. Therefore, the blocking capability is being expanded for IDSM so that it matches that of the 3.0 release for the appliance sensor. This includes blocking with Catalyst 6000 RACLs/VACLs, router IOS ACLs, and PIXs.

NOTE   TCP resets will not be implemented as a response action on the IDSM.

SAPD Functionality

Currently, you can enable event logging on IDSM and view the log file through the IDSM CLI. No mechanism exists, however, for you to export these logs to another platform. This limitation makes local logging minimally useful. Therefore, functionality equivalent to what is available on the appliance sensors for log file management and transfer is being incorporated into IDSM 3.0.

Host Includes

Host includes enables you to configure alarms to trigger only when offending traffic involves specified IP addresses. This functionality is the opposite of the exclude capability that is already supported. Basically, this functionality matches the capabilities that are being incorporated into the appliance sensor. For more information on the host inclusion capability, refer to the features for Cisco IDS Version 3.0 explained earlier in this chapter.

Network DoS Signatures

A number of recent DoS attacks were targeted at consuming network resources, such as bandwidth, instead of targeted directly at hosts. The same functionality being added into the appliance sensor is being incorporated into IDSM.

Modify PostOffice Port

The current IDSM 2.5 image does not enable you to modify the PostOffice UDP port number. The capability to enable you to configure the PostOffice service to listen on any valid UDP port number (as with appliance sensors) will be implemented through the IDSM **setup** CLI command.

Direct Telnet to IDSM

Logging on to the IDSM remotely requires the customer to Telnet to the switch supervisor, log on to the switch, and then use the **session** command to access IDSM. Many Customers have separate security and network operations groups that prefer not to provide the security personnel logon access to their switches, to maintain a clear-cut separation of duties between the two groups. To satisfy this requirement, the capability to allow you to Telnet directly to the IP address assigned to the IDSM command and control interface is being implemented. To control access through Telnet, however, packet filtering will also be implemented on IDSM.

Gigabit IDSM

Similar to the gigabit appliance, a gigabit IDSM blade is being developed. The current release date for this product has not been firmly established yet.

Sensor Device Manager (SDM)

The Sensor Device Manager (SDM) will provide Web-based basic configuration, management, provisioning, and monitoring capability as well as some general device "health" information about your sensors. SDM is required to ease setup and to aid in smaller installations of IDS devices, and serve as a troubleshooting option in larger deployments.

Cisco IDS-User-Defined Signatures

Beginning with Cisco IDS Version 3.0, you have the ability to create custom signatures. This section briefly examines this new functionality and provides you with some sample custom signature definitions. This overview is divided into the following sections (for a more detailed explanation, refer to the Cisco Secure IDS documentation):

- Signature Engines
- Master Signature Parameters
- Engine Specific Parameters
- Sample User-Defined Signatures

Signature Engines

Beginning in Cisco Secure IDS Version 3.0, signature processing is divided between various *signature engines*. A signature engine is a component of the Cisco Secure IDS Sensor designed to support many signatures within a certain category. Table 18-1 shows the signature engines:

Table 18-1 *Signature Engines*

Engine	Description
ATOMIC.ICMP	Simple ICMP alarms based on the following parameters: • Type • Code • Sequence • ID
ATOMIC.IPOPTIONS	Simple Layer 3 alarms
ATOMIC.L3.IP	Simple Layer 3 IP alarms
ATOMIC.TCP	Simple TCP packet alarms based on the following parameters: • Port • Destination • TCP flags

Table 18-1   *Signature Engines (Continued)*

Engine	Description
ATOMIC.UDP	Simple UDP packet alarms based on the following parameters: • Port • Direction • DataLength
FLOOD.HOST.ICMP	ICMP floods directed at a single host
FLOOD.HOST.UDP	UDP floods directed at a single host
FLOOD.NET	Multiprotocol floods directed at a network segment
FLOOD.TCPSYN	Connections to multiple ports using TCP SYN packets
SERVICE.DNS.TCP	DNS packet analyzer on TCP port 53 (includes compression handler)
SERVICE.DNS.UDP	UDP-based DNS signatures
SERVICE.PORTMAP	RPC program number sent to port mapper
SERVICE.RPC	Simple RPC alarms based on the following parameters: • Program • Procedure • Length
STRING.HTTP	Specialized STRING.TCP alarms for Web traffic (includes anti-evasive and URL deobfuscation)
STRING.ICMP	Generic ICMP-based string search engine
STRING.TCP	Generic TCP-based string search engine
STRING.UDP	Generic UDP-based string search engine
SWEEP.HOST.ICMP	A single host sweeping a range of nodes using ICMP
SWEEP.HOST.TCP	A single host sweeping a range of nodes using TCP
SWEEP.PORT.TCP	TCP connections to multiple destination ports between two nodes
SWEEP.PORT.UDP	UDP connections to multiple destination ports between two nodes
SWEEP.RPC	Connections to multiple ports with RPC requests between two nodes

Each signature engine is composed of a parser and an inspector. Signature definitions are read from a configuration file. These signature definitions are constructed by specifying a set of signature parameters that define the intrusive activity that you want to detect. These parameters fall into the following two categories:

- Master signature parameters
- Engine-specific parameters

Master Signature Parameters

The *master signature parameters* are composed of signature parameters that are common to all the signature engines. Table 18-2 shows some of the master signature parameters. (For a complete list, refer to the *Cisco IDS Signature Engine Supplement*.)

Table 18-2   *Assorted Master Signature Parameters*

Parameter	Description
AlarmThrottle	Parameter that you use to limit alarm firings with the following options: • **FireAll**—Always sends alarms when the signature alarm condition is met. • **FireOnce**—Sends only the first alarm and then will not alarm on this particular address set. • **Summarize**—Sends two alarms per ThrottleInterval per address set. The first alarm is sent normally. Subsequent alarms are counted until the end of the ThrottleInterval, when a SUMMARY ALARM is sent. • **GlobalSummarize**—Sends only two alarms per ThrottleInterval for all address sets currently being monitored. Alarms in a ThrottleInterval are limited to two per signature across the whole sensor, so you can reduce the alarm bandwidth of flood attacks.
MaxInspectLength	Maximum number of bytes to inspect.
MinHits	Minimum number of signature hits needed before the alarm message is sent. This is a throttle for firing the alarm only after seeing the signature trigger traffic a specified number of times on the same address set.
ResetAfterIdle	Number of seconds to wait before resetting signature counters after the host(s) are idle.
SIGID	Signature Identifier **1000–19,999** Range for default Cisco Secure IDS signature **20,000–50,000** Range for user-defined signatures
SubSig	Subsignature ID.
ThrottleInterval	Number of seconds defining an alarm throttle interval. It is used with the AlarmThrottle parameter to tune the rate at which your signatures generate alarms.

Engine-Specific Parameters

Each signature engine has its own unique set of parameters. These parameters enable you to customize the signatures controlled by that specific signature engine. Refer to the *Cisco IDS Signature Engine Supplement* for a complete listing of the engine specific parameters.

Sample User-Defined Signatures

Defining custom signatures involves creating a *signature definition* for the appropriate signature engine. A signature definition is an entry in your configuration file that uses the master- and engine-specific parameters to define a signature. A sample signature definition is

```
Engine STRING.TCP SIGID 3450 RegexString @@@ ServicePorts 79 Direction
     ToService
```

The discussion now turns to custom signature definitions more closely in the following sections:

- Sample User-Defined Sweep Signature
- Sample User-Defined String Signature
- Sample User-Defined Flood Signature

Sample User-Defined Sweep Signature

You can create sweep signatures by using any of the five sweep signature engines. A sweep involves a host checking for active services on multiple ports on a single system.

For an example, examine a sweep signature that uses the SWEEP.TCP.PORT signature engine. For a sample signature, to create a signature definition that triggers when a host gets five TCP packets with only the RST flag set (out of the flag list of SYN, FIN, and RST), the sample signature definition is as follows:

```
Engine SWEEP.PORT.TCP SIGID 30001 Unique 5 WantFrag FALSE TcpFlags =RST
     Mask =SYN¦FIN¦RST PortRange 1 InvertedSweep TRUE
```

- **SIGID 30001**—The master signature parameter sets the Signature ID to 30001. (The user-definable signature range is from 20,000–50,000.)
- **Unique 5**—This SWEEP.PORT.TCP engine-specific parameter sets the maximum number of port connections needed to trigger the alarm at 5.
- **WantFrag FALSE**—This master signature parameter indicates that this signature needs to be applied only to packets that are not fragmented.
- **TcpFlags =RST**—This SWEEP.PORT.TCP engine-specific parameter indicates that the signature is looking for packets where only the RST flag is set.
- **Mask =SYN|FIN|RST**—This SWEEP.PORT.TCP engine-specific parameter indicates all the TCP flags in which you are interested.

NOTE   The Mask parameter indicates the TCP flags in which you are interested. (Any flags not listed will not appear in the final comparison between the Mask and the flags set in the packet.) The TcpFlags parameter indicates the TCP flags needed to trigger the signature. A bitwise comparison of the Mask parameter and the TCP flags set in the packet is compared against the TcpFlags parameter. If they match, the signature triggers. If the packet has the RST|ACK flags set, for example, and the Mask parameter has the SYN|FIN|RST flags, the comparison yields RST. This triggers the sample signature. However, if the packet has the SYN|ACK flags set and your Mask parameter includes the SYN|RST|FIN|ACK flags, the comparison yields SYN|ACK, which do not trigger the sample signature.

- **PortRange 1**—This SWEEP.PORT.TCP engine-specific parameter indicates that only ports less than 1024 (low ports) are capable of triggering this signature. A *2* indicates only ports greater than 1024 can trigger the signature, whereas a *0* enables all ports to trigger the signature.

- **InvertedSweep TRUE**—This SWEEP.PORT.TCP engine-specific parameter indicates that the signature needs to use the source port rather than the destination port for determining the unique count.

Sample User-Defined String Signature

You can create string signatures by using any of four string engines. String signatures use a regular expression pattern-matching algorithm to search for specific textual patterns.

For an example, we will examine a string signature that uses the STRING.HTTP signature engine. Let us look at a string signature that searches for the word *host* (not case sensitive), followed by any amount of data, followed by the carriage return and linefeed characters. Furthermore, the length of the string matched must be at least 250 characters long. The sample signature definition is as follows:

```
Engine STRING.HTTP SIGID 21000 RegexString [\n][Hh][Oo][Ss][Tt][:].*[\r\n]
    MinMatchLength 250
```

- **SIGID 21000**—The master signature parameter sets the Signature ID to 21000. (The user-definable signature range is from 20,000–50,000.)

- **RegexString [\n][Hh][Oo][Ss][Tt][:].*[\r\n]**—This STRING.HTTP engine-specific parameter defines the string pattern that you are looking for to trigger the signature.

- **MinMatchLength 250**—This STRING.HTTP engine-specific parameter indicates the minimum number of characters (bytes) that the RegexString must match to trigger the signature. Therefore, for this example, there must be a total of 250 characters from the initial "host" to the ending carriage return and linefeed.

Sample User-Defined Flood Signature

You can create flood signatures by using any of the four flood signature engines. Flood signatures look for a large amount of traffic being directed at a specific host or network.

For this example, we will examine a signature created with the FLOOD.NET signature engine. The sample signature checks for ICMP echo requests (pings) that exceed 100 packets per second (pps) without a gap of more than 4 seconds during a 60 second interval. This signature is checking for a flood of traffic against the network. A sample signature definition is as follows:

```
Engine FLOOD.NET SIGID 25000 IcmpType 8 Rate 100 Gap 4 Peaks 3
    ThrottleInterval 60
```

- **SIGID 25000**—The master signature parameter sets the Signature ID to 25000. (The user-definable signature range is from 20,000–50,000.)

- **IcmpType 8**—This FLOOD.NET engine-specific parameter indicates that the signature will be looking for ICMP packets with an ICMP type of 8 (echo request).

- **Rate 100**—This FLOOD.NET engine-specific parameter indicates that after the rate of ping packets exceeds 100 pps, it indicates a suspect second.

- **Gap 4**—This FLOOD.NET engine-specific parameter indicates the length of time (below the Rate) required to reset the peak count to 0. In this example, after 4 seconds below the Rate, the number of Peaks is automatically set to 0.

- **Peaks 3**—This FLOOD.NET engine-specific parameter indicates that, at most, 3 suspect seconds are allowed during the throttle interval without a break at least as long as the Gap setting. If 3 peaks are received (without being reset by the Gap parameter), the signature triggers.

- **ThrottleInterval 60**—This master signature parameter indicates that you have a 60-second window for the signature to trigger. Within a 60-second window, more than 3 Peaks must be detected to trigger this signature.

NOTE   You can also set the Rate to 0, which places the signature in a diagnostic mode. While in the diagnostic mode, the signature generates one alarm per ThrottleInterval. The alarm details string contains "MaxPPS=*max pps seen*". You can then use this information to determine what constitutes normal traffic patterns on your network; and then you can create more accurate flood signatures.

Summary

Cisco Secure IDS is continually evolving and changing. New features are constantly being evaluated. Currently, two major releases of Cisco Secure IDS are in the planning stages:

- Version 3.0
- Version 4.0

Each of these major software releases involves enhancements in the following categories:

- Installation and configuration
- Signatures
- Blocking

The following installation and configuration enhancements planned for version 3.0 include the following:

- Sensor login through SSH
- Director software determines the sensor monitoring interface
- Generate an alarm when the monitoring interface is disabled

Version 4.0 expands on these features by providing the following functionality:

- Fully functional CLI on the sensor
- "Stateful" sensor failover
- Alarm destination/Director failover

The major enhancement with signatures in both versions 3.0 and 4.0 involves more user configuration control over the Cisco Secure IDS signatures. This includes the ability for users to create custom signatures for their own operating environment.

Blocking enhancements involve adding more devices that are supported for blocking. These new devices include the following:

- PIX
- Catalyst 5000 Route Switch Module
- Catalyst 6000 Security ACLs

In addition to the overall enhancements to Cisco Secure IDS, the sensors themselves are continually being enhanced. Soon, a 1 Gb sensor appliance will be available. The Sensor Device Manager (SDM) will provide Web-based basic configuration, management, provisioning, and monitoring capability, as well as some general device "health" information about your sensors.

Some of the enhancements planned for IDSM include the following:

- Saturation indicator
- Signature response actions

- SAPD functionality
- Host includes
- Network DOS signatures
- Modify PostOffice port
- Direct Telnet to IDSM

To support user-defined signatures, Cisco IDS Version 3.0 incorporates signature engines. These signature engines enable you to easily create new signatures by defining a few specific parameters. The five major types of signature engines are as follows:

- Atomic
- Flood
- Service
- String
- Sweep

Each of these types actually consists of several individual signature engines. The parameters for the signature engines are broken down into two categories:

- Master signature parameters
- Engine specific parameters

PART VIII

Appendixes

Deploying Intrusion Detection: Case Studies

Configuring many aspects of Cisco Secure IDS is easier to understand by examining actual examples. This appendix presents different scenarios to help you understand how to deploy intrusion detection technology in a variety of different environments. These scenarios are as follows:

- Using Cisco IOS Firewall IDS
- Sending SYSLOG Data to a Cisco Secure IDS Sensor
- Managing a Router with a Cisco Secure IDS Sensor
- Cisco Secure IDS tiered Director hierarchy
- Setting up multiple IDSM blades in the same chassis

Using Cisco IOS Firewall IDS

The objective of this scenario is to configure the Cisco IOS Firewall IDS on a router. This router operates as a reduced functionality IDS monitoring device within your Cisco Secure IDS. Like other sensors, it forwards alarms to your Cisco Secure IDS Director platform.

The protected subnet contains sensitive research and development systems. The scenario also features various modifications, including signature tuning for false positives and network redesign. This scenario is broken down into the following categories:

- Limitations
- Required equipment
- Network diagram
- General setup
- Common problems and troubleshooting tips

Limitations

Using Cisco IOS Firewall IDS on a router has a couple of limitations:

- Router throughput
- Signature coverage

Router Throughput

Because Cisco IOS Firewall IDS is an inline device, it inspects packets as they traverse the router's interfaces. This examination might impact your network performance to some extent by reducing the total number of packets that your router can process. Also, depending on the speed of the network segment and the processing power of your router, some packets might not trigger signatures reliably.

Signature Coverage

Cisco IOS Firewall IDS has a limited signature set compared to the regular Cisco Secure IDS Appliance Sensor (59 signatures compared to over 300 for the sensor appliance). Therefore, your Cisco IOS Firewall IDS does not detect as many attacks against your network as a normal Cisco Secure IDS Appliance Sensor.

NOTE The signatures for Cisco Secure IDS are described in detail in Chapter 10, "Signature Series." The list of signatures for the Cisco IOS Firewall IDS is provided in Appendix H, "Cisco IOS Firewall IDS Signature List," and the corresponding list for the sensor appliance is provided in Appendix F, "Cisco Secure IDS Signature Structures and Implementations."

Required Equipment

A Cisco 2600, Cisco 3600, Cisco 7100, or Cisco 7200 router with the Cisco IOS Firewall Feature Set and Cisco IOS Firewall IDS enabled is required for this scenario. You also need a Cisco Secure ID Director to receive alarms from the Cisco IOS Firewall IDS platform.

Network Diagram

Figure A-1 illustrates a basic network diagram showing the minimum components required for you to deploy Cisco IOS Firewall IDS on one of your routers. These basic components are as follows:

- Cisco Secure IDS Director
- Cisco router

Figure A-1 *Minimum Components in a Network*

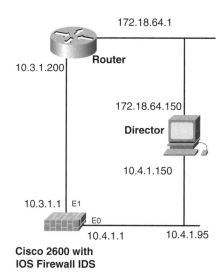

**Cisco 2600 with
IOS Firewall IDS**

General Setup

You must perform the following primary tasks to initially configure your Cisco IOS
Firewall IDS router. (For detailed setup instructions, refer to Chapter 17, "Cisco IOS
Firewall Intrusion Detection System.")

- Initialize Cisco IOS Firewall IDS.
- Add Cisco IOS Firewall IDS information to Cisco Secure IDS.
- Verify the setup.

The Cisco IOS Firewall IDS acts as an inline intrusion detection monitor, watching packets
as they traverse the router's interfaces and acting upon them in a definable fashion. When a
packet, or a number of packets in a session, match a signature, the Cisco IOS Firewall IDS
can perform the following configurable actions:

- **Alarm:** Send an alarm to a SYSLOG server or Cisco Secure ID Director.
- **Drop:** Drop the packet.
- **Reset:** Reset the TCP connection.

In Example A-1, Cisco IOS Firewall IDS is initialized. Notice that the router is set up to use
two routes to communicate with the Cisco Secure ID Director. This configuration is
optional, but provides extra fault tolerance for alarm notifications.

Example A-1 *Cisco IOS Firewall IDS Initialized*

```
ip audit smtp spam 25
ip audit notify nr-director
ip audit notify log
ip audit po local hostid 55 orgid 123
ip audit po remote hostid 14 orgid 123
   rmtaddress 10.4.1.150 localaddress 10.4.1.1
   preference 1
ip audit po remote hostid 14 orgid 123
   rmtaddress 172.18.64.150 localaddress
   10.3.1.1 preference 2
ip audit name AUDIT.1 info action alarm
ip audit name AUDIT.1 attack action alarm
   drop reset

interface e0
ip address 10.4.1.1 255.255.255.0
ip audit AUDIT.1 in

interface e1
ip address 10.3.1.1 255.255.255.0
```

Notice that the Cisco IOS Firewall IDS router's Cisco Secure IDS host ID is assigned to 55, and its organization ID (orgid) matches the Director's organization ID of 123.

These Cisco Secure IDS communication parameters must be added to the Director for the two components to communicate. You use nrConfigure on your Cisco Secure ID Director to add the Cisco IOS Firewall IDS router's information to the Director. This process involves the following steps:

Step 1   On the Director, start nrConfigure by clicking **Configure** on the **Security** drop-down menu.

Step 2   Double-click the name of your Director machine on the displayed list.

Step 3   Double-click the currently applied configuration version (the one that is bolded).

Step 4   Double-click **System Files**.

Step 5   Double-click **Hosts**. The Hosts dialog box opens. Click **Add** and type the host name, host ID, and organization ID for the IDS router.

Step 6   Click **OK** to close the Hosts dialog box.

Step 7   Double-click **Routes**. The Routes dialog box opens.

Step 8   Click **Add** and type the route to the Cisco IOS Firewall IDS router.

Step 9   Click **OK**. The Routes dialog box closes.

Step 10 Select the newly created transient version of the configuration and click **Apply**.

You can verify that the Director has the Cisco IOS Firewall IDS router's information by opening a terminal session on the Director and using the UNIX **more** command to view the actual configuration files (see Example A-2).

Example A-2 *Verifying Cisco IOS IDS on Director*

```
$ more /usr/nr/etc/hosts
14.123 localhost
14.123 director.xyzcorp
55.123 ids2600.xyzcorp
$
$
$ more /usr/nr/etc/routes
ids2600.xyzcorp 1 10.4.1.1 45000 1
ids2600.xyzcorp 2 10.3.1.1 45000 1
$
```

You can verify that Cisco IOS Firewall IDS is properly configured on the router with the **show ip audit configuration** command (see Example A-3). Notice that communication route 1 has a status of established (ESTAB), whereas communication route 2 has a status of listen (LISTEN). If communication route 1 were to go down, communication route 2 automatically becomes active (established). When communication route 1 is re-established, the router automatically reverts to using it rather than route 2.

Example A-3 **Show IP Audit Configuration**

```
ids2600# show ip audit configuration
Event notification through syslog is enabled
Event notification through Net Director is enabled
Default action(s) for info signatures is alarm
Default action(s) for attack signatures is alarm drop reset
Default threshold of recipients for spam signature is 25
PostOffice:HostID:55 OrgID:123 Msg dropped:0
        :Curr Event Buf Size:100  Configured:100
HID:14 OID:123 S:1 A:2 H:82 HA:49 DA:0 R:0 Q:0
 ID:1 Dest:10.4.1.150:45000 Loc:10.4.1.1:45000 T:5 S:ESTAB *
 ID:2 Dest:172.18.64.150:45000 Loc:10.3.1.1:45000 T:5 S:LISTEN

Audit Rule Configuration
 Audit name AUDIT.1
    info actions alarm
    attack actions alarm drop reset

ids2600#
```

You can verify which interfaces have audit rules applied to them with the **show ip audit interface** command (see Example A-4).

Example A-4 Show IP Audit Interface

```
ids2600# show ip audit interface
Interface Configuration
 Interface Ethernet0
  Inbound IDS audit rule is AUDIT.1
    info actions alarm
    attack actions alarm drop reset
  Outgoing IDS audit rule is not set
 Interface Ethernet1
  Inbound IDS audit rule is not set
  Outgoing IDS audit rule is not set
ids2600#
```

Common Problems and Troubleshooting Tips

You need to know some of the common problems and techniques associated with Cisco IOS Firewall IDS, including the following:

- False positives
- Adding an ACL to the audit rule
- Disabling a signature
- Adding an ACL to signatures
- Reorganizing your corporate network

False Positives

One common problem with deploying intrusion detection technologies is false positives. These false positives represent otherwise benign or expected behavior that triggers alarms. Furthermore, determining that these alarms represent benign behavior consumes valuable security resources.

A common situation that generates a false positive is when you run a vulnerability scanner on your network. In Figure A-2, for example, a Cisco Secure Scanner device with an IP address of 10.4.1.95 is mapping out various internal subnets, and the audit rule applied to the router's Ethernet0 interface (10.4.1.1) is detecting this activity and sending alarms to your Cisco Secure ID Director.

Examples that show how to help eliminate false positives are covered in the following sections:

- Adding an ACL to the Audit Rule
- Disabling a Signature
- Adding an ACL to Signatures

This discussion about common problems concludes by covering the topic of reorganizing your corporate network.

Figure A-2   *Vulnerability Scanner Generating False Positives*

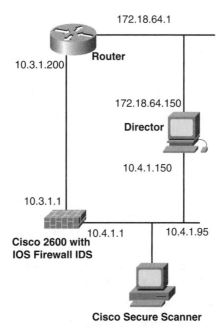

Adding an ACL to the Audit Rule

Because you can configure Cisco Secure Scanner device to scan the internal subnets on a regular basis, you do not need to generate alarms on this activity. To solve this problem, you can add an access control list (ACL) to the audit rule that keeps traffic originating from the Cisco Secure Scanner device from being audited (see Example A-5). ACL 90 prevents any traffic from your scanner at 10.4.1.95 from being processed by the audit rule that examines network traffic for attacks.

Example A-5 *Adding an ACL to the Audit Rule*

```
ip audit smtp spam 25
ip audit notify nr-director
ip audit notify log
ip audit po local hostid 55 orgid 123
ip audit po remote hostid 14 orgid 123 rmtaddress
   10.4.1.150 localaddress 10.4.1.1 preference 1
ip audit po remote hostid 14 orgid 123 rmtaddress
   172.18.64.150 localaddress 10.3.1.1 preference 2

ip audit name AUDIT.1 info list 90 action alarm
ip audit name AUDIT.1 attack list 90 action alarm drop reset

interface e0
ip address 10.4.1.1 255.255.255.0
ip audit AUDIT.1 in

interface e1
ip address 10.3.1.1 255.255.0.0

access-list 90 deny 10.4.1.95
access-list 90 permit any
```

Disabling a Signature

Another way to deal with false positives is to disable the individual signatures that are triggering falsely. Suppose, for example, that you notice that your router is generating a lot of false positives for signatures 3151 (FTP SYST Command Attempt), 6102 (RPC Dump), and 6100 (RPC Port Registration). You know an application on the network is causing Signature 3151 to fire, and it is not an application that causes security concerns. This signature can be disabled using the following command:

```
ip audit signature sigID disable
```

The updated router configuration (including the entry to disable signature 3151) is illustrated in Example A-6.

Example A-6 *Disabling a Signature*

```
ip audit smtp spam 25
ip audit notify nr-director
ip audit notify log
ip audit po local hostid 55 orgid 123
ip audit po remote hostid 14 orgid 123 rmtaddress
    10.4.1.150 localaddress 10.4.1.1 preference 1
ip audit po remote hostid 14 orgid 123 rmtaddress
    172.18.64.150 localaddress 10.3.1.1 preference 2

ip audit signature 3151 disable
```

Example A-6 *Disabling a Signature (Continued)*

```
ip audit name AUDIT.1 info list 90 action alarm
ip audit name AUDIT.1 attack list 90 action alarm drop reset

interface e0
ip address 10.4.1.1 255.255.255.0
ip audit AUDIT.1 in

interface e1
ip address 10.3.1.1 255.255.0.0

access-list 90 deny 10.4.1.95
access-list 90 permit any
```

Adding an ACL to Signatures

Yet another way to stop false positive alarms is to attach an ACL to the signatures in question. Suppose that after further investigation, for example, you discover that the false positives for Signatures 6102 and 6100 are caused by specific applications on hosts 10.4.1.155 and 10.4.1.2, as well as by some workstations using DHCP on the 172.18.64.0 subnet.

By attaching an ACL to a signature, you prevent specific hosts from triggering specific signatures. To attach an ACL to a signature, you need to use the following command:

ip audit signature *SigID* **list** *ACL*

Example A-7 shows the updated router configuration with ACLs attached to the Signatures 6102 and 6100.

Example A-7 *Adding an ACL to Signatures*

```
ip audit smtp spam 25
ip audit notify nr-director
ip audit notify log
ip audit po local hostid 55 orgid 123
ip audit po remote hostid 14 orgid 123 rmtaddress
    10.4.1.150 localaddress 10.4.1.1 preference 1
ip audit po remote hostid 14 orgid 123 rmtaddress
    172.18.64.150 localaddress 10.3.1.1 preference 2

ip audit signature 3151 disable
ip audit signature 6102 list 91
ip audit signature 6100 list 91

ip audit name AUDIT.1 info list 90 action alarm
ip audit name AUDIT.1 attack list 90 action alarm drop reset

interface e0
ip address 10.4.1.1 255.255.255.0
```

continues

Example A-7 *Adding an ACL to Signatures (Continued)*

```
ip audit AUDIT.1 in

interface e1
ip address 10.3.1.1 255.255.0.0

access-list 90 deny 10.4.1.55
access-list 90 permit any
access-list 91 deny host 10.4.1.155
access-list 91 deny host 10.4.1.2
access-list 91 deny 172.18.64.0 0.0.0.255
access-list 91 permit any
```

Reorganizing Your Corporate Network

Other common problems are created when you need to reorganize your networks. In Figure A-3, for example, your network has evolved by adding two subnets and a serial connection to the Internet. Furthermore, you have a new requirement to place only trusted users on the 10.3.0.0 and 10.5.0.0 networks. This reorganization requires you to add audit rules to the 10.3.1.1, 10.5.1.1, and 192.168.1.1 interfaces.

Figure A-3 *Reorganized Network*

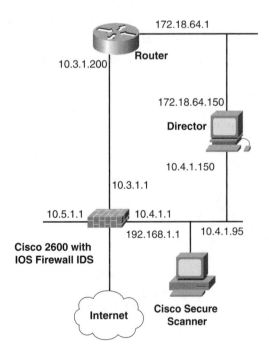

The work done by employees on the trusted network must not be disrupted by the Cisco Firewall IDS, but outside attacks must still be stopped. So, you now apply different actions to the external and internal interfaces. The AUDIT.1 audit rule now alarms only on a match for sessions that originate from the internal router interfaces. The AUDIT.2 rule is created for external attacks. Any attack signature matches (other than the false positive ones that are being filtered out) triggering on traffic from the Internet interface (192.168.1.1) are dealt with in the following manner:

- Send an alarm.
- Drop the packet.
- Reset the TCP session.

This dual-tier method of signature response is accomplished by configuring two different audit specifications (AUDIT.1 and AUDIT.2) and applying each to a different Ethernet interface, as illustrated in Example A-8.

Example A-8 *Dual-Tier Signature Response*

```
ip audit smtp spam 25
ip audit notify nr-director
ip audit notify log
ip audit po local hostid 55 orgid 123
ip audit po remote hostid 14 orgid 123 rmtaddress
      10.4.1.150 localaddress 10.4.1.1 preference 1
ip audit po remote hostid 14 orgid 123 rmtaddress
      172.18.64.150 localaddress 10.3.1.1 preference 2

ip audit signature 3151 disable
ip audit signature 6102 list 91
ip audit signature 6100 list 91

ip audit name AUDIT.1 info list 90 action alarm
ip audit name AUDIT.1 attack list 90 action alarm
ip audit name AUDIT.2 info action alarm
ip audit name AUDIT.2 attack alarm drop reset

interface e0
ip address 10.4.1.1 255.0.0.0
ip audit AUDIT.1 in

interface e1
ip address 10.3.1.1 255.255.255.0
ip audit AUDIT.1 in

interface e2
ip address 10.5.1.1 255.255.255.0
ip audit AUDIT.1 in

interface s0
ip address 192.168.1.1 255.0.0.0
```

continues

Example A-8 *Dual-Tier Signature Response (Continued)*

```
ip audit AUDIT.2 in

access-list 90 deny host 10.4.1.65
access-list 90 permit any
access-list 91 deny host 10.4.1.155
access-list 91 deny host 10.4.1.2
access-list 91 deny 172.18.64.0 0.0.0.255
access-list 91 permit any
```

Sending SYSLOG Data to a Cisco Secure IDS Sensor

You can configure your router to generate a SYSLOG message whenever it receives a packet that is denied by one of your defined ACLs. These packets represent attempts to bypass your security policy. This scenario illustrates the use of SYSLOG messages to report these policy violations to a Cisco Secure IDS Sensor, which can then send the alarm data to your Cisco Secure IDS Director.

The scenario is divided into these sections:

- Limitations
- Required equipment
- General setup
- Common problems and troubleshooting tips

Limitations

The main limitation of this scenario is the number of packets denied by the router's ACL, and consequently, the number of SYSLOG messages sent to the Cisco Secure IDS Sensor. If the volume of packets being denied becomes excessive, your router overloads your Cisco Secure IDS Sensor with SYSLOG messages. This, in turn, generates an excessive number of alarms on your Director platform.

Required Equipment

This scenario requires that you have a Cisco router running any Cisco IOS software version from Release 10.3 through the current release of IOS, and a properly installed and configured Cisco Secure IDS Sensor and Director.

Network Diagram

Figure A-4 illustrates a network configuration in which a router sends SYSLOG messages to a Cisco Secure IDS Sensor. The sensor then forwards alarm data to your Director.

Figure A-4   *Sending SYSLOG to a Cisco Secure IDS Sensor*

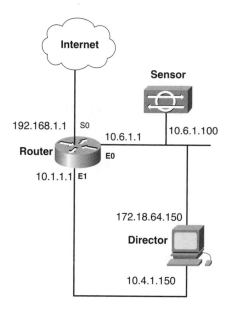

General Setup

The general setup for this configuration involves the following tasks:

- Initializing the Director and sensor
- Setting up SYSLOG on the router
- Configuring the ACLs to log policy violations
- Configuring the sensor to accept SYSLOG messages

Initializing the Director and Sensor

For this scenario, initialize the sensor and Director with the communication parameters listed in Table A-1.

Table A-1   *Sample Communication Parameter Settings*

Parameter	Director	Sensor
IP address	10.6.1.150 10.10.1.150	10.6.1.100
Host ID	150	100
Host name	Director	Sensor
Organization ID	500	500
Organization name	xyzcorp	Xyzcorp

You can verify the parameters on your sensor by examining the contents of the /usr/nr/etc/hosts and /usr/nr/etc/routes files. These contents of these two files are shown in Example A-9:

Example A-9   *Sensor Routes and Hosts Files for the SYSLOG Scenario*

```
$ more /usr/nr/etc/hosts
100.500 localhost
100.500 sensor.xyzcorp
150.500 director.xyzcorp

$ more /usr/nr/etc/routes
director.xyzcorp 1 10.6.1.150 45000 1
director.xyzcorp 2 10.10.1.150 45000 1
```

To verify the identification parameters on your Director, you need to follow the procedure specific to your Director platform.

If you are using CSPM, you can check your sensor's identification parameters by examining the **Identification** subtab under the **Properties** tab for your sensor. (Refer to Chapter 11, "Sensor Configuration Within CSPM," for more information.)

To check the identification parameters if you are using Cisco Secure ID Director, you need to examine the contents of the /usr/nr/etc/hosts and /usr/nr/etc/routes files. The contents of these files are shown in Example A-10.

Example A-10   *Director Routes and Hosts Files for the SYSLOG Scenario*

```
$ more /usr/nr/etc/hosts
150.500 localhost
150.500 director.xyzcorp
100.500 sensor.xyzcorp

$ more /usr/nr/etc/routes
sensor.xyzcorp 1 10.6.1.100 45000 1
```

Setting Up SYSLOG on the Router

To set up SYSLOG notification on the router, enter Configuration mode on the router with the **configure terminal** command and enter the following commands:

```
Router(config)# logging sensor_ip_address
Router(config)# logging trap info
```

where *sensor_ip_address* is the IP address of the sensor's command and control interface.

NOTE   For this scenario, the sensor IP address is 10.6.1.100.

You can exit the Configuration mode on the router by pressing Ctrl-Z. Then, to make your configuration changes permanent on the router, you need to enter the following command:

```
Router# copy running_config startup_config
```

NOTE   You also can use the **write memory** command to make the configuration changes permanent on your router. This is the well-known command that has been replaced with the **copy** command in later IOS releases. The **write memory** command, however, is still used by many users.

Configuring the ACLs to Log Policy Violations

After setting up SYSLOG notification, you need to manually configure the ACLs to log policy violations. In this scenario, an ACL has been applied to the router's Serial0 interface (192.168.1.1) to deny all inbound FTP and Telnet traffic from the Internet. This ACL (199) is listed in the configuration snapshot shown in Example A-11.

Example A-11   *ACL Denying Specific Types of Traffic*

```
interface serial 0
ip address 192.168.1.1 255.255.0.0
ip access-group 199 in

access-list 199 deny tcp any any eq 21
access-list 199 deny tcp any any eq 23
access-list 199 permit ip any any
```

To report violations of this ACL, append the string **log** at the end of each deny rule, as illustrated in Example A-12. This changes the configuration of the router so that any packets that violate the ACL generate a message to the router's SYSLOG service.

Example A-12 *Using the Log Feature*

```
interface serial 0
ip address 192.168.1.1 255.255.0.0
ip access-group 199 in

access-list 199 deny tcp any any eq 21 log
access-list 199 deny tcp any any eq 23 log
access-list 199 permit ip any any
```

Configuring the Sensor to Accept SYSLOG Messages

The final step in sending SYSLOG notifications to a sensor is to configure the sensor to accept the SYSLOG messages that it receives from the router. This process varies depending on the Director platform that you are using. To configure your sensor through CSPM, follow these steps:

Step 1 Select a signature template by clicking its name in the Sensor Signatures section of the main CSPM screen.

Step 2 Select the **Signatures** tab.

Step 3 Select the **ACL Signatures** tab.

Step 4 Click **Add**. A new ACL entry is created.

Step 5 Enter the ACL number or name corresponding to the ACL that you defined on your network device.

Step 6 Enter a comment in the Comment field that describes the ACL.

Step 7 Configure the basic signature parameters.

Step 8 Click **OK** in the Signature Template view panel.

NOTE If your router is already configured as a SYSLOG data source in the configuration for your sensor on CSPM, you do not need to perform Steps 9 through 14.

Step 9 Select the sensor from the Network Topology tree (NTT) by clicking the name of the sensor for which you want to define SYSLOG source.

Step 10 Select the **Properties** tab in the Sensor view panel.

Step 11 Select the **Monitoring** tab in the Properties window

Step 12 Click **Add**. A new SYSLOG source entry is created.

Step 13 Enter the IP address and network mask of the network device.

Step 14 Click **OK** in the Sensor view panel.

Step 15 Click **Update** on the toolbar.

Step 16 Apply the updated configuration to the sensor (see Chapter 11, "Sensor Configuration Within Detection Configuration").

NOTE   Chapter 12 provides a detailed explanation on the configuration of signatures when you are using CSPM.

To configure the sensor to accept SYSLOG traffic from your router through CSIDD, follow these steps:

Step 1 On the Director interface, click the sensor's icon and click **Configure** on the **Security** drop-down menu.

Step 2 In the current configuration version (the folder that is bolded), double-click **Intrusion Detection**.

Step 3 Click the **Data Sources** tab.

Step 4 In the Data Sources field, ensure that the IP address and netmask of the router sending the SYSLOG information are present.

Step 5 Click the **Profile** tab and ensure that Setup Method is set to Manual Configuration.

Step 6 Click **Modify Sensor** and scroll down to the Security Violations signature and click **Expand**.

Step 7 Click **Add** to add the name/number of the Cisco ACL that sends SYSLOG data to the sensor (in this case, 199).

Step 8 Choose an action from the list in response to the policy violation alarm, and enter the alarm's severity level for the destination (the CSIDD).

Step 9 Click **OK** on each dialog box to close them.

Step 10 Select the newly created transient version and click **Apply**.

When you click **Apply**, the CSIDD updates the sensor's configuration. The sensor can now accept SYSLOG traffic from the router and send policy violation alarms to the Director.

Common Problems and Troubleshooting Tips

Using policy violations in this manner as a security mechanism on your network has two drawbacks:

- Insufficient protection
- Large amount of SYSLOG traffic to sensor

Insufficient Protection

A common problem with this type of scenario involves insufficient protection. Although FTP and Telnet traffic is being denied and logged to the sensor, for example, an attacker might try to enter your network through other methods, such as rlogin, HTTP, or TFTP.

In this scenario, other alarms on unauthorized activity are all being generated by a group of hosts on a specific network (hosts 172.31.10.10, 172.31.10.11, 172.31.10.12, and 172.31.10.13). It seems that all the traffic (except the FTP and Telnet attempts) from these specific attackers is getting through the router's interfaces.

The easiest solution is to adjust the ACL to deny the specific hosts (see Example A-13).

Example A-13 *Denying Specific Hosts with an ACL*

```
access-list 199 deny ip host 172.31.10.10 log
access-list 199 deny ip host 172.31.10.11 log
access-list 199 deny ip host 172.31.10.12 log
access-list 199 deny ip host 172.31.10.13 log
access-list 199 deny tcp any any eq 21 log
access-list 199 deny tcp any any eq 23 log
access-list 199 permit ip any any
```

By specifically denying these hosts, any traffic that they send to the router's interface is blocked and, therefore, generates a SYSLOG message.

NOTE   When adding denied hosts to your ACL, remember that every packet received by your router from them generates a SYSLOG message to your sensor. If you choose a large range of addresses that is generating a significant number or packets, you can easily overwhelm your sensor with SYSLOG messages.

Large Amount of SYSLOG Traffic to Sensor

Another problem with this scenario is based largely on the amount of SYSLOG traffic sent to the sensor, as well as the subsequent alarms sent to the Director. If the amount of

SYSLOG notifications is undesirable (either for reasons of performance or alarm management), you have two options:

- Continue to deny traffic, but do not log the policy violations. Remove **log** from the end of any **deny** rule you no longer want logged.

- Reconfigure the ACLs to pinpoint and deny specific traffic instead of denying all traffic of a certain type or source.

Instead of denying traffic from all hosts on a network, for example, deny only certain hosts from that network. In this example, instead of disallowing all incoming FTP and Telnet traffic from the Internet, you can selectively deny this type of traffic from certain hosts or networks known to be hostile.

Managing a Router with a Cisco Secure IDS Sensor

The objective of this scenario is to deploy a Cisco router, PIX Firewall, and sensor in such a way that the sensor can dynamically update the router's ACLs to block attackers.

The case study is divided into the following categories:

- Limitations to consider in advance
- Required equipment
- Network diagram
- General setup
- Common problems and troubleshooting tips

Limitations to Consider in Advance

For this scenario, one limitation applies:

> If an ACL is already in place on a certain interface and direction, the Cisco Secure IDS dynamic ACL might replace it. You need to move the existing ACL to another interface to save it.

NOTE   This limitation of replacing your existing ACL on an interface is being corrected in a future release of Cisco Secure IDS. Refer to Chapter 18, "Planned Cisco Secure IDS Enhancements," for more information.

Required Equipment

The equipment required for this scenario is a Cisco router running any Cisco IOS software version later than Release 10.3, a PIX Firewall, and a Cisco Secure IDS Sensor and Director.

Network Diagram

Figure A-5 depicts a sample configuration that you might deploy in which your sensor manages your router. In this configuration, your Cisco Secure IDS Sensor logs in to the router and establishes ACLs to block traffic from offending hosts after an attacker triggers specific signatures that are configured to initiate blocking.

Figure A-5 *Managed Router Network Configuration*

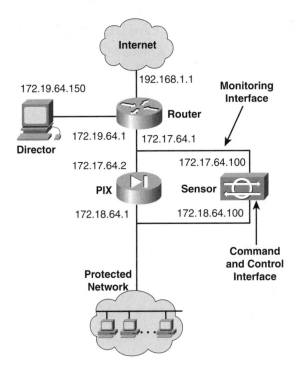

General Setup

The general setup for using your sensor to manage a router involves the following tasks:

- Initializing the Director and sensor
- Configuring the router
- Configuring the firewall
- Setting up device management

Initializing the Director and Sensor

For this scenario, initialize the sensor and Director with the communication parameters listed in Table A-2.

Table A-2   *Communication Parameters for Managed Router Scenario*

Parameter	Director	Sensor
IP address	172.19.64.150	172.18.64.100
Host ID	150	100
Host name	Director	Sensor
Organization ID	500	500
Organization name	xyzcorp	xyzcorp

You can verify the parameters on your sensor by examining the contents of the /usr/nr/etc/hosts and /usr/nr/etc/routes files. These contents of these two files are shown in Example A-14.

Example A-14   *Sensor Routes and Hosts Files for Managed Router Scenario*

```
$ more /usr/nr/etc/hosts
100.500 localhost
100.500 sensor.xyzcorp
150.500 director.xyzcorp

$ more /usr/nr/etc/routes
director.xyzcorp 1 172.19.64.150 45000 1
```

To verify the identification parameters on your Director, you need to follow the procedure specific to your Director platform.

If you are using CSPM, you can check your sensor's identification parameters by examining the **Identification** subtab under the **Properties** tab for your sensor. (Refer to Chapter 11 for more information.)

To check the identification parameters if you are using CSIDD, you need to examine the contents of the /usr/nr/etc/hosts and /usr/nr/etc/routes files on your Director. The contents of these files are shown in Example A-15.

Example A-15   *Director Routes and Hosts Files for Managed Router Scenario*

```
$ more /usr/nr/etc/hosts
150.500 localhost
150.500 director.xyzcorp
100.500 sensor.xyzcorp

$ more /usr/nr/etc/routes
sensor.xyzcorp 1 172.18.64.100 45000 1
```

Configuring the Router

The initial router configuration in this scenario is illustrated in Example A-16.

Example A-16   *Initial Router Configuration*

```
Current Configuration
!
version 12.0
service timestamps debug uptime
service timestamps log uptime
no service password-encryption
!
hostname border-router
!
logging console informational
enable password attack
!
memory-size iomem 10
!
interface ethernet 0
ip address 172.17.64.1 255.255.0.0
!
interface ethernet 1
ip address 172.19.64.1 255.255.0.0
!
interface serial 0
ip address 192.168.1.1 255.255.0.0
```

In this scenario, you need to set up an ACL on the router to deny all traffic outside the 172.18.0.0 Class B network on the router's 172.19.64.1, thereby protecting the Director from any possible outside attacker. The ACL is applied to the outbound direction of the router's Ethernet 1 interface (see Example A-17).

Example A-17   *Applying an ACL to the Ethernet 1 Interface*

```
interface ethernet 1
ip address 172.19.64.1 255.255.0.0
access-group 1 out

access-list 1 permit 172.18.0.0 0.0.255.255
```

Configuring the Firewall

You must configure your PIX Firewall to allow the following traffic:

- Telnet traffic from the sensor's control interface (172.18.64.100) to the router (172.17.64.1)

- Cisco Secure IDS communications (UDP port 45000) between the sensor and the Director

NOTE	Refer to the PIX documentation if you are uncertain as to how to configure your PIX to allow the necessary traffic between your sensor and Director and your sensor and the router.

Setting Up Device Management

Device management refers to the sensor's capability to dynamically reconfigure the filters and ACLs on a router to block an attacker. This functionality is provided by the *managed* service on your sensor. Blocking refers to the sensor's capability to use a network device to deny traffic from a specific network host or in some cases an entire network.

Cisco Secure IDS Sensors can manage the following types of Cisco routers:

- Cisco 1600
- Cisco 2500
- Cisco 3600
- Cisco 4500
- Cisco 4700
- Cisco 7200
- Cisco 7500

The steps required to set up device management depend on the Director platform that you are using. If you utilize CSPM for your Director, you need to execute the following steps to configure device management on your sensor:

Step 1 Select the sensor from the NTT by clicking the name of the sensor for which you want to define a block device.

Step 2 Select the **Blocking** tab in the Sensor view panel.

Step 3 Select the **Blocking Devices** tab from within the Blocking tab window.

Step 4 Click **Add** to open the Blocking Device Properties window. This window enables you to configure the properties of your blocking device.

Step 5 Configure the basic identification parameters:

  — **Telnet IP Address**—Identifies the router's IP address that the sensor telnets to when applying ACLs.

  — **Telnet Username**—Identifies the username that the sensor uses when logging in to the router.

  — **Telnet Password**—Identifies the password that the sensor uses to log in to the router.

  — **Enable Password**—Identifies the password that the sensor needs to access Privileged or Enabled mode on the router.

Step 6 In addition to the basic parameters, you must define the interface on which the ACL is to be applied. Click **Add** on the Blocking Device Properties window to add a line in the Blocking Interfaces section of the screen.

Step 7 Configure the interface parameters:

— **Interface Name**—Each interface on your router is identified by a specific name (such as Ethernet0, Eth1/0, FastEthernet0/0, Serial0, and so on). Your sensor applies the blocking ACL to this interface.

— **Interface Direction**—You must specify which direction the ACL is applied on the interface. Your two options are inbound and outbound.

Step 8 If you want to apply ACLs to multiple interfaces on your router, you need to keep clicking the **Add** button until you define all the interfaces to which the sensor applies blocking ACLs.

Step 9 Select the **Never Block Addresses** tab from within the Blocking tab window.

Step 10 Configure the Never Block entries for your Director, PIX Firewall, and router by defining the following parameters:

— **IP Address**—Identifies the IP address for the system that you never want your sensor to block.

— **Subnet Mask**—Identifies the subnet mask associated with the specified IP address.

NOTE The sensor's IP address is automatically added to the Never Block list.

Step 11 Click **OK** on the Blocking Device Properties window to accept your configuration changes.

Step 12 Click **Save** on the top toolbar to save your changes.

Step 13 Finally, you must transfer the updated configuration to your sensor. (See the "Pushing a New Configuration to Your Sensor" section in Chapter 11.)

NOTE For a detailed explanation of device management with CSPM, refer to Chapter 13, "IP Blocking Configurations."

If you are using CSIDD, follow these steps to configure device management on your sensor:

Step 1 On the Director interface, click the sensor's icon and click **Configure** on the **Security** drop-down menu.

Step 2 In the current configuration version (the folder that is bolded), double-click **Device Management**.

Step 3 Click the **Devices** tab.

Step 4 Add information about the router (such as its IP address, username, password, and enable password).

Step 5 Click the **Interfaces** tab.

Step 6 Add information about each of the managed router's interfaces (such as IP address and interface name).

NOTE The IP address you enter is the IP address of the interface that the sensor uses to communicate with the router. This interface is not necessarily the same interface used for blocking. For this scenario, the sensor communicates with the 172.17.64.1 interface and dynamically blocks on the 192.168.1.1 interface's *in* direction (s0 *in*).

Step 7 Click the **Shunning** tab.

Step 8 Add the Director, sensor, PIX Firewall, and router to the Addresses Never to Shun list.

NOTE Adding the Director, sensor, PIX Firewall, and Router to the Never Shun list keeps the sensor from ever blocking these particular hosts. Therefore, these hosts cannot be blocked, either accidentally or as the result of an attacker's traffic.

Step 9 Set the blocking ACL to 199.

NOTE The sensor uses ACL 199 on the router to dynamically block attackers. The sensor also uses ACL 198 as the second ACL to write to whenever changes need to be made to the original ACL. The sensor then continues to alternate between these two ACLs so that your network is continually protected.

Step 10 Click **OK** to close the Device Management dialog box.

Step 11 Select the newly created transient version and click **Apply**.

When this process is complete, the sensor's /usr/nr/etc/managed.conf file looks something like Example A-18.

Example A-18 *managed.conf File*

```
FilenameOfError               ../var/errors.managed

NetDevice    172.17.64.1  DefaultCisco  password  enable

NeverShunAddress 172.19.64.150 255.255.255.255    #Director
NeverShunAddress 172.18.64.100 255.255.255.255    #Sensor
NeverShunAddress 172.17.64.2 255.255.255.255      #FW--outer
NeverShunAddress 172.18.64.1 255.255.255.255      #FW--inner
NeverShunAddress 172.17.64.1 255.255.255.255      #Router

ShunInterfaceCisco 192.168.1.1 Serial0 in
ShunAclCisco 199
MaxShunEntries 100

FilenameOfError ../var/errors.managed
FilenameOfConfig ../etc/managed.conf
EventLevelOfErrors 1
EventLevelOfCommandLogs 1
EnableACLLogging 0
```

Your Cisco Secure IDS Sensor is now ready to initiate blocking by writing a dynamic ACL to the router's Serial0 interface. The next major step is for you to decide which signatures need to trigger a blocking response. This type of automated response by the sensor needs to be configured only for attack signatures with a low probability of false positive detection, such as an unambiguous SATAN attack. In case of any suspicious activity that does not trigger automatic blocking, you can use a Director menu function to block manually.

Again, the steps you need to perform to configure your signatures to block are specific to your Director platform. If you are using CSPM, follow these steps to set up responses for signatures:

Step 1 Select a signature template by clicking its name in the Sensor Signatures section of the main CSPM screen.

Step 2 Select the **Signatures** tab.

Step 3 Select the appropriate signature class by clicking the correct tab: **General Signatures**, **Connection Signatures**, **String Signatures**, or **ACL Signatures**.

Step 4   By double-clicking the signature that you want to change, you bring up the Signature Actions pop-up window. On this window, you can then select the actions to take when the signature triggers. For this scenario, you need to set the block action on the following signatures:

— 3250 TCP Hijacking

— 3500 rlogin -froot

— 3600 IOS DoS

— 4053 Back Orifice

— 6001 Normal SATAN Probe

— 6002 Heavy SATAN Probe

Step 5   Click **OK** in the Signature Actions window.

Step 6   Click **Update** on the toolbar.

Step 7   Apply the updated configuration to the sensor (see Chapter 11).

NOTE   Chapter 12 provides a detailed explanation on the configuration of signatures when you are using CSPM.

To set up responses for signatures using CSIDD, follow these steps:

Step 1   On the Director interface, click the sensor's icon and click **Configure** on the **Security** drop-down menu.

Step 2   In the current configuration version (the folder that is bolded), double-click **Intrusion Detection**.

Step 3   Click the **Profile** tab.

Step 4   Select **Manual Configuration** and click **Modify Sensor**.

Step 5   In the General Signatures dialog box, you can select blocking for any signature. However, the best candidates for use with blocking are known as Level 5 Signatures, and they are listed in Appendix G, "Cisco Secure IDS Signatures and Recommended Alarm Levels." For this scenario, set the blocking action on the following signatures:

— 3250 TCP Hijacking

— 3500 rlogin -froot

— 3600 IOS DoS

        — 4053 Back Orifice

        — 6001 Normal SATAN Probe

        — 6002 Heavy SATAN Probe

Step 6 Click **OK** to close the General Signatures dialog box.

Step 7 Click **OK** to close the Intrusion Detection dialog box.

Step 8 Select the newly created transient version and click **Apply**.

Common Problems and Troubleshooting Tips

Many security administrators implementing this scenario might prefer to have a dual-homed Director machine so that the sensor can communicate with it directly, instead of through the PIX Firewall and router.

In Figure A-6, the Cisco Secure IDS Director is dual-homed on the 172.19.64.0 and 172.18.64.0 networks.

Figure A-6 *Dual-Homed Director Configuration*

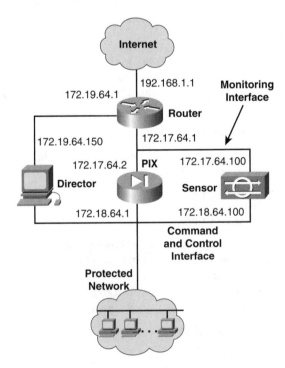

By adding multiple interfaces on your Director, you need to alter the entries in the sensor's /usr/nr/etc/routes file; not only are you adding an entry for the 172.18.64.150 network address, you also decide to make this route the preferred route and the previous route secondary.

To implement this change through CSIDD, you need to use nrConfigure and perform the following tasks:

Step 1 On the Director interface, click the sensor's icon and click **Configure** on the **Security** drop-down menu.

Step 2 In the current configuration version (the folder that is bolded), double-click **System Files**.

Step 3 Double-click **Routes**.

Step 4 Select the second line, which indicates that the route to 172.19.64.150 is a primary route.

Step 5 Click **Modify**.

Step 6 Change the priority of the route to 2.

Step 7 Click **OK**.

Step 8 Click **OK** to close the Routes dialog box.

Step 9 Select the newly created transient version and click **Apply**.

The sensor's routes file now looks like Example A-19.

Example A-19 *Changed /usr/nr/etc/routes File on the Sensor*

```
$ more /usr/nr/etc/routes
director.xzycorp 1 172.18.64.150 45000 1
director.xyzcorp 2 172.19.64.150 45000 1
```

In addition, you have to add this new Director IP address to the sensor's NeverShunAddress list. To do so, follow these steps:

Step 1 On the Director interface, click the sensor's icon and click **Configure** on the **Security** drop-down menu.

Step 2 In the current configuration version (the folder that is bolded), double-click **Device Management**.

Step 3 Click the **Shunning** tab.

Step 4 Add the 172.16.2.200 IP address to the Addresses Never to Shun list.

Step 5 Click **OK** to close the Intrusion Detection dialog box.

Step 6 Select the newly created transient version and click **Apply**.

You can verify this change by looking at the /usr/nr/etc/managed.conf file (see Example A-20).

Example A-20 *Changed /usr/nr/etc/managed.conf File on the Sensor*

```
$ more /usr/nr/etc/managed.conf
FilenameOfError            ../var/errors.managed

NetDevice    172.17.64.1  DefaultCisco  password  enable

NeverShunAddress 172.19.64.150 255.255.255.255
NeverShunAddress 172.18.64.150 255.255.255.255
NeverShunAddress 172.18.64.100 255.255.255.255
NeverShunAddress 172.17.64.2 255.255.255.255
NeverShunAddress 172.18.64.1 255.255.255.255
NeverShunAddress 172.17.64.1 255.255.255.255

ShunInterfaceCisco 192.168.1.1 Serial0 in
ShunAclCisco 199
MaxShunEntries 100

FilenameOfError ../var/errors.managed
FilenameOfConfig ../etc/managed.conf
EventLevelOfErrors 1
EventLevelOfCommandLogs 1
EnableACLLogging 0
```

Many months later, when the corporate network is reconfigured, you decide that outside networks need full access to the 172.19.64.0 network. For this to occur, the ACL on the 172.19.64.1 interface must be removed (see Example A-21). The commands to remove the ACL from the interface are as follows:

```
Router# configure terminal
Enter configuration commands on per line. End with CNTRL/Z.
Router(config)# interface ethernet 1
Router(config-if)# no ip access-group 1 out
Router(config-if)# ^z
```

Example A-21 *Removed ACL from the 172.19.64.1 Interface*

```
interface ethernet 1
ip address 172.19.64.1 255.255.0.0
```

The 172.19.64.0 subnet, however, still has critical servers and systems that an attacker can target. Therefore, to protect these systems, you decide to place another Cisco Secure IDS Sensor on the 172.19.64.0 subnet (see Figure A-7).

Figure A-7 *Sensor Protecting Critical Servers*

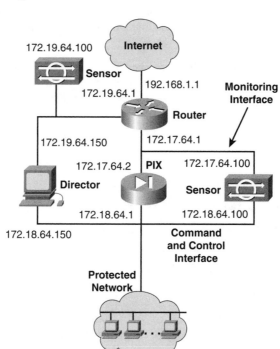

The new sensor at 172.19.64.100 needs to be able to communicate with the Director, and vice versa. You can use CSPM's or nrConfigure's Add Host Wizard to add this sensor, depending on your Director platform. The second sensor's configuration values are listed in Table A-3.

Table A-3   *Second Sensor's Communication Parameters*

Parameter	Sensor
IP address	172.19.64.100
Host ID	300
Host name	sensor2
Organization ID	500
Organization name	xyzcorp

Cisco Secure IDS Tiered Director Hierarchy

The objective of this scenario is to build a hierarchy of sensor and Director systems through the use of message propagation. Instead of broadcasting events from a sensor onto multiple hosts, information can be sent to a single Director, which can then propagate packets onto other platforms defined in its local configuration files. One of the sensors is also configured to propagate messages to more than one Director, thereby demonstrating fault-tolerant communication.

In addition to providing performance benefits and fault tolerance, tiered hierarchies can simplify system management. For example, local Director machines might be responsible for monitoring from 9 a.m. to 5 p.m. and then transfer control onto a central remote Director every evening.

This discussion is divided into the following categories:

- Alarm delay limitations
- Required equipment
- Network diagram
- General setup
- Common problems and troubleshooting tips

Alarm Delay Limitations

Although using a tiered hierarchy provides some benefits of reduced workload, using local Director hosts to forward packets to remote Director hosts might involve delays if the links connecting the segments are slow or heavily trafficked. This might result in slight delays in alarm generation on the "top-level" Director in the tiered hierarchy.

Another limitation involves using the "top-level" Director to configure sensors and act on the copied alarms. These and other issues are discussed in the "Common Problems and Troubleshooting Tips" later in this scenario.

Required Equipment

This scenario involves the use of three sensors and three Directors; however, any number of sensors and Directors can be used.

Network Diagram

The network diagram for this scenario is depicted in Figure A-8.

Figure A-8   *Tiered Hierarchy of Cisco Secure IDS Components*

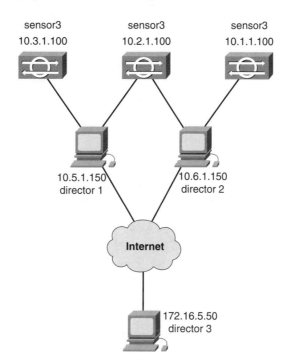

General Setup

The general setup for this scenario involves the following actions:

- Identifying sensor and Director identification parameters
- Configuring Director 3 to receive alarms from Director 1 and Director 2
- Configuring Director 2 and Director 1 to send alarms to Director 3
- Configuring minimum alarm forwarding level on Director 1 and Director 2

Identifying Sensor and Director Identification Parameters

The identification parameters for the different sensors and Directors are shown in Table A-4.

Table A-4   *Tiered Director Communication Parameters*

Host	Host Information	Host Communications
10.5.1.150 (Director)	Host ID: 10 Organization ID: 500 Host name: director1 Organization name: xyzcorp IP address: 10.5.1.150	Primary routes to: sensor3.xyzcorp (10.3.1.100) sensor2.xyzcorp (10.2.1.100) director3.xyzcorp (172.16.5.150)
10.6.1.150 (Director)	Host ID: 20 Organization ID: 500 Host name: director2 Organization name: xyzcorp IP address: 10.6.1.150	Primary routes to: sensor2.xyzcorp (10.2.1.100) sensor1.xyzcorp (10.1.1.100) director3.xyzcorp (172.16.5.150)
172.16.5.150 (Director)	Host ID: 30 Organization ID: 500 Host name: director3 Organization name: xyzcorp IP address: 172.16.5.150	Primary routes to: director1.xyzcorp (10.5.1.150) director2.xyzcorp (10.6.1.150)
10.3.1.100 Sensor	Host ID: 300 Organization ID: 500 Host name: sensor3 Organization name: xyzcorp IP address: 10.3.1.100	Primary route to: director1.xyzcorp (10.5.1.150)
10.2.1.100 Sensor	Host ID: 200 Organization ID: 500 Host name: sensor2 Organization name: xyzcorp IP address: 10.2.1.100	Primary routes to: director1.xyzcorp (10.5.1.150) director2.xyzcorp (10.6.1.150)
10.1.1.100 Sensor	Host ID: 100 Organization ID: 500 Host name: sensor1 Organization name: xyzcorp IP address: 10.1.1.100	Primary route to: director2.xyzcorp (10.6.1.150)

Configuring Director 3 to Receive Alarms from Director 1 and Director 2

After initially configuring Director 3, you need to configure Director 3 to accept the alarms that it receives from both Director 1 and Director 2. To do so, follow these steps:

Step 1 On Director 3's interface, click the Director 3 icon and click **Configure** on the **Security** drop-down menu.

Step 2 Double-click **System Files**.

Step 3 Double-click **Hosts**.

Step 4 Add both Director 1 and Director 2 and click **OK**.

Step 5 Double-click **Routes**.

Step 6 Add the following information about both Director 1 and Director 2:

— Host name

— Connection number

— IP address

— UDP port number (45000)

— Heartbeat, an amount in seconds

Step 7 Click **OK**.

Step 8 Double-click **Authorizations**.

Step 9 Make sure that Director 1 and Director 2 each have the following permissions, at a minimum:

— Get

— Getbulk

Step 10 Click **OK**.

Step 11 Apply your changes by selecting the transient configuration and clicking **Apply**.

Configuring Director 2 and Director 1 to Send Alarms to Director 3

Now that Director 3 is configured to accept alarms from Director 1 and Director 2, the next step is for you to configure Director 1 and Director 2 to forward their alarms to Director 3 by using nrConfigure:

Step 1 On the Director interface, click the Director 1 icon and click **Configure** on the **Security** drop-down menu.

Step 2 On nrConfigure, click **Add Host** on the **File** menu.

Step 3   Read the instructions and click **Next**.

Step 4   Select the organization name to which Director 3 belongs. Then type in Director 3's host name, host ID, and host IP address in the appropriate fields.

Step 5   Click **Next**.

Step 6   Select Forward alarms to secondary Director.

Step 7   Click **Next**.

Step 8   Click **Finish**.

Step 9   Repeat the preceding steps for Director 2.

Configuring a Minimum Alarm Forwarding Level on Director 1 and Director 2

If needed, you can configure the level of alarms sent to Director 3. (By default, this is configured to send only alarms that are greater than or equal to severity level 3.) To configure these levels, follow these steps:

Step 1   On Director 1's interface, click **Configure** on the **Security** drop-down menu.

Step 2   Double-click **Director Forwarding**.

Step 3   Click the **Forwarding** tab.

NOTE   An entry should exist for loggerd on Director 1 and smid for Director 3.

Step 4   To change the level of alarms sent to Director 3, select the Director 3 entry and click **Modify**.

Step 5   For Minimum Level, change the minimum alarm level to 3.

Step 6   Click **OK**.

Step 7   Apply your changes by selecting the transient configuration and clicking **Apply**.

Step 8   Repeat the preceding steps for Director 2, if desired.

The preceding procedures create DupDestination entries in the /usr/nr/etc/smid.conf files for both Director 1 and Director 2. Each of these DupDestination entries matches the following entry:

```
DupDestination director3.xyzcorp smid 3 ERRORS,COMMANDS,EVENTS,IPLOGS
```

These DupDestination tokens provide information on where to send duplicate alarm information. In this scenario, Director 1 and Director 2 send a duplicate copy of the alarms they receive to Director 3.

NOTE	Notice that in each case, only alarms that are Level 3 or higher are forwarded by the sensors because that is the value to which you set the minimum alarm level.

Common Problems and Troubleshooting Tips

With this scenario, you will probably run into the following problems:

- Duplicate alarms
- Director 3's passive role

Duplicate Alarms

The first problem encountered in this scenario is duplicate alarms being sent to Director 3 (172.16.5.150). This duplication is occurring because Sensor 2 (10.2.1.100) is sending alarm data to both Director 1 and Director 2, which are in turn sending Level 3 alarms and higher to Director 3.

Instead of sending alarms to multiple directors for fault tolerance, you can assign multiple Cisco Secure IDS routes to a single director if you are using CSIDD. Only one of these routes is ever used by the sensor to send alarms to the specified director. To define multiple routes to the same director, follow these steps:

Step 1 On the Director 1 interface, click the Sensor 2 icon and click **Configure** on the **Security** drop-down menu.

Step 2 In the current configuration version, double-click **System Files**.

Step 3 Double-click **Routes**.

Step 4 Add a second entry for director1.xyzcorp with a priority of 2.

Step 5 Select the newly created transient version and click **Apply**.

The secondary route for director1.xyzcorp is used only when the primary route to Director 1 fails.

You can verify this change by viewing the routes file on Sensor 2. It needs to have the following entries:

```
director1.xyzcorp 1 10.5.1.150 45000 1
director1.xyzcorp 2 10.7.1.150 45000 1
```

NOTE	Currently, CSPM does not support multiple routes to the Director.

Director 3's Passive Role

The second problem arises when your security personnel try to use Director 3 (172.16.5.150) to act on alarm information sent to it by Director 1 and Director 2. Director 3, in its role as your "top-level" Director of the tiered hierarchy, is only passively receiving alarms, and cannot act on the alarms because it has no entries in its hosts and routes files for the three sensors. Additionally, Director 3 currently has no authority to make changes to any of the sensors' configuration files or to execute commands on them.

First, you need to use nrConfigure to add each sensor's information to Director 3's hosts and routes files. To do so, follow these steps:

Step 1 On the Director interface, click the Director 3 icon and click **Configure** on the **Security** drop-down menu.

Step 2 In the current configuration version, double-click **System Files**.

Step 3 Double-click **Hosts**.

Step 4 Use the **Add** button to add the name, organization name, and host ID for Sensor 1, Sensor 2, and Sensor 3, one at a time.

Step 5 Click **OK** to close the Hosts dialog box.

Step 6 Double-click **Routes**.

Step 7 Use the **Add** button to add the name, connection number, IP address, port number, and type for Sensor 1, Sensor 2, and Sensor 3, one at a time.

Step 8 Click **OK** to close the Routes dialog box.

Step 9 Select the newly created transient version and click **Apply**.

The new hosts file on Director 3 is shown in Example A-22.

Example A-22 *Edited /usr/nr/etc/hosts File on Director 3*

```
$ more /usr/nr/etc/hosts
30.500 localhost
30.500 director3.xyzcorp
20.500 director2.xyzcorp
10.500 director1.xyzcorp
100.500 sensor1.xyzcorp
200.500 sensor2.xyzcorp
300.500 sensor3.xyzcorp
```

The new routes file on Director 3 is shown in Example A-23.

Example A-23 *Edited /usr/nr/etc/routes File on Director 3*

```
$ more /usr/nr/etc/routes
director1.xyzcorp 1 10.5.1.150 45000 1
director2.xyzcorp 1 10.6.1.150 45000 1
sensor1.xyzcorp 1 10.1.1.100 45000 1
sensor2.xyzcorp 1 10.2.1.100 45000 1
sensor3.xyzcorp 1 10.3.1.100 45000 1
```

Next, you need to use nrConfigure to configure your sensor to allow Director 3 to execute commands and make configuration changes on the sensor. To do so, follow these steps:

Step 1   On the Director 3 interface, click the Sensor 1 icon and click **Configure** on the **Security** drop-down menu.

Step 2   In the current configuration version, double-click **System Files**.

Step 3   Double-click **Authorizations**.

Step 4   Click **Add**.

Step 5   Ensure that Get, Get Bulk, Set, Unset, and Execute are all set to Yes.

Step 6   Click **OK** to close the Authorizations dialog box.

Step 7   Select the newly created transient version and click **Apply**.

Step 8   Repeat Steps 1 through 7 for Sensor 2 and Sensor 3.

The preceding process writes entries for Director 3 to each sensor's *auths* files. The updated auths files for the sensors are shown in Example A-24.

Example A-24 *Entries in a /usr/nr/etc/auths File*

```
sensor1 $ more /usr/nr/etc/auths
director2.xyzcorp  GET,GETBULK,SET,UNSET,EXEC
director3.xyzcorp  GET,GETBULK,SET,UNSET,EXEC

sensor2 $ more /usr/nr/etc/auths
director1.xyzcorp  GET,GETBULK,SET,UNSET,EXEC
director2.xyzcorp  GET,GETBULK,SET,UNSET,EXEC
director3.xyzcorp  GET,GETBULK,SET,UNSET,EXEC

sensor3 $ more /usr/nr/etc/auths
director1.xyzcorp  GET,GETBULK,SET,UNSET,EXEC
director3.xyzcorp  GET,GETBULK,SET,UNSET,EXEC
```

The final task is to add Director 3 to each sensor's hosts and routes information, using nrConfigure. To do so, follow these steps:

Step 1   On the Director 3 interface, click the Sensor 1 icon and click **Configure** on the **Security** drop-down menu.

Step 2   In the current configuration version, double-click **System Files**.

Step 3   Double-click **Hosts**.

Step 4   Use the **Add** button to add the name, organization name, and host ID for Director 3.

Step 5   Click **OK** to close the Hosts dialog box.

Step 6   Double-click **Routes**.

Step 7   Use the **Add** button to add the name, connection number, IP address, port number, and type for Director 3.

Step 8   Click **OK** to close the Routes dialog box.

Step 9   Select the newly created transient version and click **Apply**.

Step 10 Repeat Steps 1 through 9 for sensor2 and sensor3.

Setting Up Multiple IDSM Blades in the Same Chassis

IDSM blades provide an effective IDS monitoring platform by seamlessly integrating intrusion detection into your switch infrastructure. Currently these blades are limited to processing 100 Mbps of network traffic. By distributing your network traffic across several IDSM blades, however, you can exceed this 100-Mbps limitation.

This discussion is divided into the following categories:

- 100-Mbps bandwidth limitation per IDSM
- Required equipment
- Network diagram
- VACL definition
- General setup

100-Mbps Bandwidth Limitation per IDSM

Each IDSM is capable of handling only 100 Mbps of network traffic. You need to distribute the traffic capture through the security ACL so that this limitation is not exceeded. The total number of IDSM blades that you can deploy depends on the number of available slots on your Catalyst 6000 family of switches.

NOTE   By the time this book is published, there might be a 1-Gbps version of IDSM (refer to Chapter 18, "Planned Cisco Secure IDS Enhancements," for more information).

Required Equipment

This scenario involves the use of three IDSM blades, a Catalyst 6000 family switch, and a Cisco Secure IDS Director.

NOTE   You can install as many IDSMs in a Catalyst 6000 family switch as you have available card slots. As long as you install at least one supervisor engine, you can fill the rest of the free slots in your Catalyst 6000 family switch with IDSMs.

Network Diagram

The network diagram for this scenario is depicted in Figure A-9.

Figure A-9   *Distributing Network Traffic Across Multiple IDSM Blades*

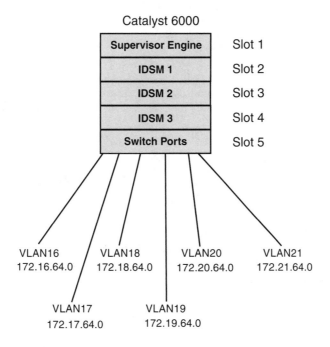

On your switch, you have the following VLANs defined:

- VLAN 16 (172.16.64.0/24)
- VLAN 17 (172.17.64.0/24)
- VLAN 18 (172.18.64.0/24)
- VLAN 19 (172.19.64.0/24)
- VLAN 20 (172.20.64.0/24)
- VLAN 21 (172.21.64.0/24)

Furthermore, your IDSM line cards are located as follows:

- IDSM 1 in switch slot 2
- IDSM 2 in switch slot 3
- IDSM 3 in switch slot 4

VACL Definition

VLAN ACL (VACL) access controls *all* packets on a Catalyst 6000 switch through a Policy Feature Card (PFC). VACLs are strictly for security packet filtering and redirecting traffic to specific physical switch ports. Unlike IOS ACLs, VACLs are not defined by the direction of the traffic (inbound or outbound). You can use VACLs to capture traffic based on individual VLANs.

General Setup

The general setup for this scenario involves the following tasks:

- Initializing each IDSM blade
- Configuring Intrusion Detection settings per IDSM
- Using VACLs for capturing IDS traffic
- Distributing network traffic between multiple IDSMs

Initialize Each IDSM Blade

Before you can use IDSM for intrusion detection analysis, you must log in to the IDSM account (default account *ciscoids*, default password *attack*) and configure the line card using the **setup** command.

NOTE	Enter the **setup** command to configure only a newly installed IDSM. If you use this command on an already configured IDSM, it reverts to its default settings.

The **setup** command prompts you for the basic communications parameters for your IDSM. These parameters are divided into IDSM parameters and Director parameters. The IDSM parameters are as follows:

- IP address
- Netmask
- Default gateway
- Host name
- Host ID
- Host PostOffice port
- Organization name
- Organization ID

The Director parameters are as follows:

- IP address
- Host name
- Host ID
- Host PostOffice port
- Heartbeat interval
- Organization name
- Organization ID

After defining these parameters, the IDSM reboots and is ready to communicate with your IDS Director.

Configuring Intrusion Detection

Like other Cisco Secure IDS Sensors, you can configure many signature parameters, such as the following:

- Signature severity levels
- Signature response options
- Disabling signatures

For more information on configuring your IDSM, refer to Chapter 14, "Catalyst 6000 IDS Module Configuration."

Using VACLs to Capture IDS Traffic

You can set VACLs to capture IDS traffic from a single VLAN or multiple VLANs. Port 1 on the IDSM is set as a trunk port by default and monitors traffic from all VLANs on which a security ACL was applied with the capture feature.

To monitor traffic from only specific VLANs, you need to clear the VLANs that you do not want to monitor from port 1 on the IDSM.

NOTE	By default, port 1 is automatically configured as a security ACL capture port. Port 1 is the monitoring port, and port 2 is the command and control port.

Distributing Network Traffic Between Multiple IDSMs

All capture destination ports in the switch receive the same capture traffic, and filtering of capture traffic by VLAN occurs at the destination port. The IDSM monitoring port (port 1) is a trunk by default. You must configure this port to be a member of only the VLAN(s) that it monitors.

NOTE	To prevent oversubscribing any single IDSM, you need to make sure that the aggregate total of all capture traffic on the VLAN(s) that the IDSM's port 1 belongs to is limited to approximately 100 Mbps

In the example here, you have six different VLANs that need to be monitored. Therefore, assuming that each VLAN has equal traffic volume, you can assign two VLANs to each IDSM. The commands that you use to distribute the captured traffic are listed in Table A-5.

Table A-5 *Switch Traffic-Manipulation Commands*

Task	Command
Clears all of the VLANs associated with the trunk port, or only specified VLANs	**clear trunk** *mod/port* [*vlans*]
Assigns a specific VLAN to an existing trunk port	**set trunk** *mod/port vlans*
Defines the traffic to be captured by your VACL	**set security acl ip** *acl_name* **permit** (...) **capture**

Table A-5   *Switch Traffic-Manipulation Commands (Continued)*

Task	Command
Commits the VACL by writing it to the hardware (must be performed before you map a VLAN to the VACL)	**commit security acl** *acl_name*
Maps the VACL to VLANs	**set security acl map** *acl_name* [*vlans*]
Adds IDSM monitoring port (port 1) to VACL capture list	**set security acl capture** *idsm_mod/1*

The VLANs are divided between the three IDSM line cards, as shown in Table A-6.

Table A-6   *IDSM VLAN Coverage*

IDSM Line Card	VLANs Monitored
IDSM 1	VLAN 16, VLAN 17
IDSM 2	VLAN 18, VLAN 19
IDSM 3	VLAN 20, VLAN 21

IDSM 1 monitors VLAN 16 and VLAN 17. Configuring IDSM 1 to monitor only traffic from these two VLANs requires you to execute various commands on your Catalyst 6000 family switch.

First, you need to clear the VLANs from the default trunk port for your IDSM and assign only the VLANs that you want the IDSM to monitor. You can accomplish this by checking which VLANs are assigned to the trunk with the following command:

```
cat6k> (enable) show trunk 2/1 detail
```

This command displays a wealth of information about the port's trunk configuration. One section of the **show trunk** output shows the VLANs allowed, similar to the following:

```
Port      Vlans allowed on trunk
--------  -----------------------------------------------
2/1       1,16-21
```

Using the list of allowed VLANs, you can remove the ones that you do not want using the following command:

```
cat6k> (enable) clear trunk 2/1 18-21
```

NOTE   The **clear trunk** command cannot be used to remove the default VLAN from a trunk port. On the Catalyst 6000, the default VLAN is 1.

Next, you need to define a security ACL to capture the traffic in which you are interested.
In this case, you configure the security ACL to capture all traffic to and from the two
VLANs assigned to IDSM 1. This requires two separate **permit** commands, as shown in
the following commands:

```
cat6k> (enable) set security acl ip 16_VLAN permit ip 172.16.64.0 0.0.0.255
    any capture
  16_VLAN editbuffer modified. Use 'commit' to apply changes.
cat6k> (enable) set security acl ip 16_VLAN permit ip any 172.16.64.0
    0.0.0.255 capture
  16_VLAN editbuffer modified. Use 'commit' to apply changes.
```

Before you can map this security ACL to specific VLANs, you must commit it to hardware.
You commit your security ACLs to hardware using the **commit security acl** command, as
shown in the following command:

```
cat6k> (enable) commit security acl 16_VLAN
  ACL commit in progress
  ACL '16_VLAN' successfully committed.
```

Now, you must map the security ACL that you created to the appropriate VLAN:

```
cat6k> (enable) set security acl map 16_VLAN 16
  Mapping in progress ...
  ACL 16_VLAN successfully mapped to VLAN 16
```

The steps that you performed for VLAN 16 need to be repeated for VLAN 17:

```
cat6k> (enable) set security acl ip 17_VLAN permit ip 172.17.64.0 0.0.0.255
    any capture
  17_VLAN editbuffer modified. Use 'commit' to apply changes.
cat6k (enable) set security acl ip 17_VLAN permit ip any 172.17.64.0
    0.0.0.255 capture
  17_VLAN editbuffer modified. Use 'commit' to apply changes.
cat6k> (enable) commit security acl 17_VLAN
  ACL commit in progress
  ACL '17_VLAN' successfully committed.
cat6k> (enable) set security acl map 17_VLAN 17
  Mapping in progress ...
  ACL 17_VLAN successfully mapped to VLAN 17
```

Finally, you need to assign IDSM 1's monitoring port be a capture port for the VACL:

```
cat6k> (enable) set security acl capture 2/1
```

NOTE   Refer to Chapter 14 for a detailed description of the preceding switch commands.

At this point, you can verify your configuration changes to the security ACLs using the
following **show security acl** commands:

```
cat6k> (enable) show security acl

ACL                              Type VLANS
-------------------------------- ---- -----
IDSM_IP1                         IP   16,17
IDSM_IP2                         IP   18,19
```

```
IDSM_IP3                          IP   20.21

cat6k> (enable) show security acl editbuffers

ACL                          Type Status
IDSM_IP1                     IP   Committed
IDSM_IP2                     IP   Committed
IDSM_IP3                     IP   Committed

cat6k> (enable) show security acl info IDSM_IP1

set security acl ip IDSM_IP1
------------------------------------------------
1. permit ip 172.16.64.0 0.0.0.255 any capture
2. permit ip any 172.16.64.0 0.0.0.255 capture
3. permit ip 172.17.64.0 0.0.0.255 any capture
4. permit ip any 172.17.64.0 0.0.0.255 capture
5. permit ip any any

cat6k> (enable)
```

You need to repeat the previous steps for each IDSM line card. The only difference is the VLANs that the different IDSM line cards monitor.

Now that you have distributed the traffic on your switch to three different IDSM line cards, you can effectively monitor 300 Mbps of network traffic.

Cisco Secure IDS Architecture

Understanding the Cisco Secure IDS thoroughly requires you to understand many attributes of your Cisco Secure IDS. One of these attributes is the architecture of your Cisco Secure IDS. This appendix illustrates the major facets of the Cisco Secure IDS architecture and is divided into the following topics:

- Cisco Secure IDS software architecture
- Cisco Secure IDS communications
- Cisco Secure IDS commands
- Cisco Secure IDS Directory structure
- Cisco Secure IDS configuration files
- Communications

By understanding these various aspects of the Cisco Secure IDS architecture, you will have a more complete understanding of how your Cisco Secure IDS operates.

Cisco Secure IDS Software Architecture

The sensor and Director each have separate operational software components, often referred to as *daemons* or *services*. Because each major Cisco Secure IDS function is accomplished by a separate service, the result is a security system that is fast, durable, and scalable.

To help understand the flow of information through your Cisco Secure IDS, you need to examine the architecture of its two major components:

- Sensor architecture
- Director architecture

Sensor Architecture

Your Cisco Secure IDS Sensors perform the actual analysis of your network traffic. Understanding the sensor's software architecture is crucial to understanding the processes that the sensor uses to generate the alarms that you monitor on your Director. Figure B-1 outlines the basic sensor architecture.

Figure B-1 *Sensor Architecture*

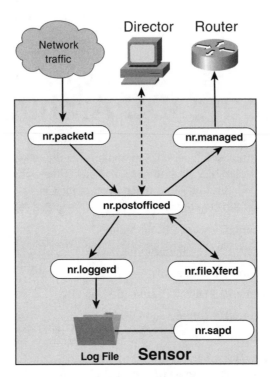

The sensor uses nr.packetd to capture packets directly from the network being monitored. nr.packetd then conducts an intrusion detection analysis on these packets to locate potential intrusive activity. Finally, nr.packetd forwards any intrusion alarms to nr.postofficed for distribution.

nr.postofficed operates as a sort of traffic cop. It distributes messages based on your configured signature settings. If a signature is configured to block an attacking host, for example, nr.postofficed routes the blocking message to nr.managed, which then creates the appropriate ACL and applies it to a specific interface on your Cisco IOS Firewall.

As illustrated in Figure B-1, the major sensor's services or daemons are as follows:

- nr.postofficed
- nr.packetd
- nr.loggerd
- nr.sapd
- nr.managed
- nr.fileXferd

The following sections discuss each of these in turn.

nr.postofficed

nr.postofficed is the traffic cop of Cisco Secure IDS. It handles communications between Cisco Secure IDS services and Cisco Secure IDS nodes. When nr.packetd detects unauthorized activity, it signals nr.postofficed, which then tells nr.loggerd to start logging, alerts nr.smid on the Director (through nr.postofficed on the Director), and communicates blocking commands through nr.managed to a router if the attack signature is configured for blocking.

nr.packetd

nr.packetd serves as the interface between your Cisco Secure IDS Sensor and your network traffic. It captures packets directly from the monitored network(s) and then conducts an intrusion detection analysis on those packets. Intrusion alarms that nr.packetd generates are then forwarded to nr.postofficed for distribution.

nr.loggerd

nr.loggerd is the logging service for Cisco Secure IDS. Its job is to write errors, commands, and alarm entries to various log files on the sensor. For information on where these log files are located, refer to the "Cisco Secure IDS Directory Structure" section later in this appendix. Furthermore, the structure of the log files is explained in Appendix D, "Cisco Secure IDS Log Files."

nr.sapd

nr.sapd is the Security Analysis Package Daemon (SAPD). This service provides data and file management. It is responsible for moving the log files to the database staging areas, performing offline archives, and other routine processes that prevent file systems from filling up and overwriting saved logs.

nr.managed

nr.managed is the process that handles communications between the sensor and your Cisco routers. When nr.packetd identifies that a certain type of attack must be blocked, it sends a block command to nr.managed through nr.postofficed. The router's ACL is then rewritten by nr.managed to prohibit access into the protected network from the attacking host.

nr.fileXferd

        nr.fileXferd is the service that transfers configuration files from the Director to the sensors.

CSPM Director Architecture

The Director platform is the Cisco Secure IDS management system. Director functions include the following:

- Alarm management (graphical display)
- Remote sensor configuration
- Event processing (alarm notification)
- Database functions

The software architecture for the Director is depicted in Figure B-2. The sensor forwards messages to the Director by using its nr.postofficed daemon. The nr.postofficed process on the Director then routes the messages to their appropriate destination.

Figure B-2   *Director Architecture*

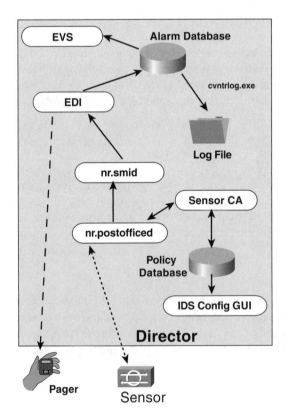

The Director is composed of services that are shown in Figure B-2. These are discussed next.

nr.postofficed

nr.postofficed handles communications between Cisco Secure IDS services and Cisco Secure IDS nodes. When a sensor detects an attack, its passes this information to the Director by using its nr.postofficed daemon. The Director's nr.postofficed service then passes the event to the appropriate destination on the Director, such as nr.smid.

Sensor CA

Sensor CA is a control agent (CA) that pushes out new or updated configuration information to a sensor. It communicates with nr.fileXferd on your sensor through the postOffice daemons on both the Director and the sensor.

nr.smid

nr.smid is the Security Management Interface Daemon (SMID). This service runs only on the Director and is responsible for translating sensor data into meaningful information for nrdirmap. It also enables alarms to be forwarded to other services, such as a secondary Director's nr.smid service.

EDI

The Event Database Interface (EDI) is an nr.smid application. This program receives events from the sensor and places them in the Alarm database. EDI also handles event notifications, such as e-mail, paging, and custom script execution.

EVS

The Event Viewing System (EVS) is the alarm display for sensor alarms. It provides real-time event viewing and correlation in a spreadsheet format.

Cisco Secure IDS Configuration GUI

The Cisco Secure IDS configuration GUI is made up of three major components:

- Sensor configuration
- Signature templates
- Add and Update Wizards

For more information on sensor configuration options, refer to Chapter 11, "Sensor Configuration Within CSPM." Chapter 12, "Signature and Intrusion Detection Configuration," explains signature templates. The Add Wizard is addressed in Chapter 7, "4200 Series Sensor Installation Within CSPM."

cvtnrlog.exe

CSPM stores alarm events in a database. Sometimes, you want to examine alarm data by using your own scripts. At other times, you might want to compare alarm information on the Director with the same data on your sensor. The cvtnrlog.exe program enables you to extract alarm information from the CSPM database and generate a standard Cisco Secure IDS log file. (See Appendix D for more information on Cisco Secure IDS log files.)

The **cvtnrlog.exe** program is a Windows NT command-line utility that extracts data from the Alarm database to create a Cisco Secure IDS log file. The output of the command is sent to the screen. To create a log file from this output, you need to use Windows **redirect** commands to create a file. The syntax for the **cvtnrlog.exe** utility is as follows:

```
cvtnrlog [-d] [-l <level>] [-o]
```

The parameters for the **cvtnrlog** command are explained in Table B-1.

Table B-1   *Parameters for* **cvtnrlog.exe**

Parameter	Description
-d	Delete alarms from a database after converting.
-l <level>	Numeric value from 1 to 255 defining the minimum severity for including context data level. If the -l option is not used, the level defaults to 0.
-o	Converts alarms to Oracle import-compatible format.

Sample output from the **cvtnrlog.exe** utility is as follows:

```
c:\Program Files\Cisco Systems\Cisco Secure Policy Manager\bin\>cvtnrlog.exe

4,3,2001/01/30,16:37:18,2001/01/30,10:37:18,10000,84,100,OUT,OUT,5,997,0,
    TCP/IP,0.0.0.0,0.0.0.0,0,0,0.0.0.0,8.100 route 1 down
4,3,2001/01/30,18:37:18,2001/01/30,12:37:18,10000,84,100,OUT,OUT,5,997,0,
    TCP/IP,0.0.0.0,0.0.0.0,0,0,0.0.0.0,8.100 route 1 up
```

The following example creates a Cisco Secure IDS log file by using the Windows **redirect** command (>) to redirect the output to a file named logfile:

```
c:>\Program Files\Cisco Systems\Cisco Secure Policy Manager\bin\cvtnrlog.exe
    > logfile
```

Cisco Secure IDS Communications

Cisco Secure IDS communications are transferred using the Cisco Secure PostOffice protocol. This protocol transfers the following messages:

- Command
- Error
- Command log
- Alarm
- IP log
- Redirect
- Heartbeat

For more information on the PostOffice protocol, refer to Chapter 4, "Cisco Secure IDS Overview."

Cisco Secure IDS Commands

You can use several commands to start, stop, and troubleshoot your Cisco Secure IDS. These commands are as follows:

- nrstart
- nrstop
- nrconns
- nrstatus
- nrvers

NOTE   These command names are gradually migrating to commands that begin with *ids*. The new commands will be idsstart, idsstop, idsconns, idsstatus, and idsvers.

---

nrstart

To start the Cisco Secure IDS services on your Cisco Secure IDS Sensor, you use the **nrstart** command (see Figure B-3). This command starts the Cisco Secure IDS services that are listed in the /usr/nr/etc/daemons configuration file. (Refer to the "Cisco Secure IDS Configuration Files" section later in this appendix for more information.)

Figure B-3   **nrstart** *Command Output*

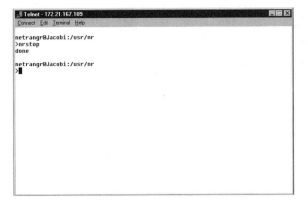

nrstop

Sometimes, you might need to stop the Cisco Secure services on your sensor. You use the **nrstop** command to stop the Cisco Secure IDS services on your sensor (see Figure B-4). This program does not provide much output to the screen.

Figure B-4   *nrstop Command Output*

nrconns

To troubleshoot the connection between your sensor and Director, you need to verify that the communication link between your sensor and Director is operational. The **nrconns** command (see Figure B-5) determines the communication status with a Cisco Secure IDS component (sensor or Director).

Figure B-5 *nrconns Command Output*

If the connection is working, you see a status of **[established]**. Besides **[established]**, you also might see **[SynSent]** if your sensor is trying to establish a TCP connection with your Director.

nrstatus

To verify that all the correct services are running on your sensors, you need to view the processes currently running on the system and then compare this listing with the Cisco Secure services that are required to run your Cisco Secure IDS Sensor. You can use the Solaris **ps** command to obtain this information, but you have to filter through all the other processes that are running on the system. The **nrstatus** command, however, displays only the currently active Cisco Secure IDS services (see Figure B-6).

Figure B-6 *nrstatus Command Output*

```
Telnet - 172.21.167.109
Connect  Edit  Terminal  Help

netrangr@Jacobi:/usr/nr
>nrstatus
netrangr    936    1  1 06:18:49 pts/1    0:01 /usr/nr/bin/nr.loggerd
netrangr    939    1  0 06:18:49 pts/1    0:00 /usr/nr/bin/nr.managed
netrangr    937    1  0 06:18:49 pts/1    0:01 /usr/nr/bin/nr.sapd
netrangr    933    1  0 06:18:49 pts/1    0:00 /usr/nr/bin/nr.fileXferd
netrangr    929    1  0 06:18:48 pts/1    0:00 /usr/nr/bin/nr.postofficed
netrangr    940    1  2 06:18:49 pts/1    0:02 /usr/nr/bin/nr.packetd

netrangr@Jacobi:/usr/nr
>
```

nrvers

To verify the version of Cisco Secure IDS software that you are currently running, you use the **nrvers** command (see Figure B-7). It displays the versions of the currently active Cisco Secure IDS services.

Figure B-7 **nrvers** *Command Output*

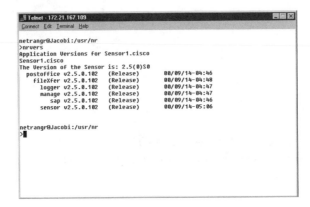

Cisco Secure IDS Directory Structure

Cisco Secure IDS directory structure follows a hierarchy that enables you to quickly locate various system files and data (see Figure B-8). The following are the major Cisco Secure IDS directories:

- Install
- bin
- etc
- var

The first directory is the main installation directory. The last three are major subdirectories. Each of these is discussed in the following sections.

Cisco Secure IDS Install Directory

When you install the Cisco Secure IDS, you need to choose the root installation directory. It is created during the installation phase of Cisco Secure IDS Director and is also the main directory on the sensor. The 4200 Series Appliance Sensors come with the Cisco Secure IDS software already installed, using a default directory of **/usr/nr**. A default CSPM installation install directory is **C:\Program Files\Cisco Systems\Cisco Secure Post Office**.

Figure B-8   *Cisco Secure IDS Directory Hierarchy*

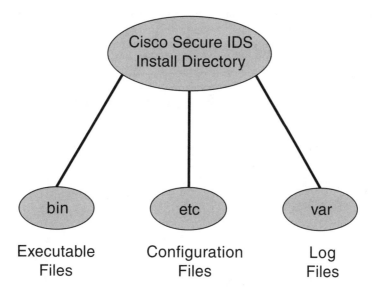

bin Directory

The bin directory is home for all the executable files. It includes all Cisco Secure IDS services, programs, and functions. A sample listing of the bin directory from a 4200 Series Sensor is shown in Figure B-9.

Figure B-9   *bin Directory*

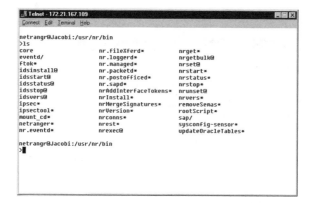

etc Directory

The etc directory is the configuration files directory. It includes all configuration files for all the Cisco Secure IDS services. A sample listing of the etc directory from a 4200 Series Sensor is shown in Figure B-10.

Figure B-10 *etc Directory*

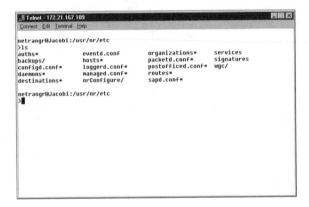

var Directory

The last directory is the var directory, which contains the log and error files. It includes the current and closed log files, IP session recorded files, and error files generated by Cisco Secure IDS services. A sample listing of the var directory from a 4200 Series Sensor is shown in Figure B-11.

Figure B-11 *var Directory*

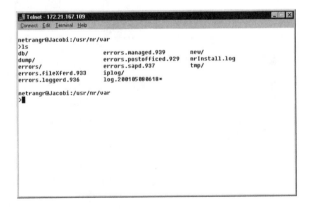

NOTE	If you use CSIDD, the sensor configuration versions being maintained by nrConfigure's Configuration Library are stored in **/usr/nr/var/nrConfigure** on your Director. Each organization name will have its own directory under the nrConfigure directory. Each organization name directory will hold all the configurations being maintained for sensors by the Director belonging to that organization name.

Cisco Secure IDS Configuration Files

To operate correctly and efficiently, you must configure your Cisco Secure IDS to match your specific operational environment. The settings that you enter need to be remembered by your IDS. Therefore, Cisco Secure IDS stores these settings in various text files on the different Cisco Secure IDS components. Understanding where these files are located and how their records are structured enables you to more effectively troubleshoot problems that you might experience.

NOTE	Under most situations, you never need to modify these configuration files directly. CSPM, for example, automatically updates the configuration files for you. Sometimes, however, it is helpful to know which files to check to verify that the correct configuration is in effect, especially during troubleshooting.

This discussion begins by examining the intricacies of configuration files.

What Are Configuration Files?

Configuration files are text files that contain configuration information for each of the daemons that Cisco Secure IDS uses to operate your IDS. These configuration files are constructed with *tokens*. A token is essentially a configurable parameter that enables you to control the operation of Cisco Secure IDS. When you start a Cisco Secure IDS daemon, it uses the tokens specified in its configuration file to determine its operational characteristics. The token entries in the configuration files are structured as follows:

```
[token] [{parameters} {parameters} . . . ]
```

token represents the name of a specific configuration parameter, such as NameOfPacketDevice. This token is then followed by a variable number of parameters depending on the information needed to define the token.

The following is an example entry from packetd.conf:

```
SigOfGeneral 1000 0 1 1
```

In this example, the token is **SigOfGeneral**. The parameters that define **SigOfGeneral** are 1000 0 1 1.

NOTE   To insert comments into a configuration file, you precede the comment with the pound sign (#). You can use these comments to document settings in your configuration files. CSPM, however, rewrites the configuration files when you make configuration changes. This rewrite wipes out any changes you make manually to the configuration files.

Intrusion Detection

The Cisco Secure IDS Sensor's intrusion detection settings are written to the packetd.conf file. The Cisco Secure IDS software service responsible for capturing network traffic and performing intrusion detection analysis is nr.packetd. If this service is not running, your Cisco Secure IDS Sensor is incapable of capturing network traffic and detecting intrusive activity.

The packetd.conf configuration file contains many different tokens that customize the operation of your Cisco Secure IDS. In most examples, you configure these parameters from your Director platform. Nevertheless, it is useful to understand the parameters for these various tokens, especially during troubleshooting. You need to examine the following tokens from the packetd.conf configuration file:

- Packet capture device
- Internal network
- General signature
- TCP or UDP connection
- String signature
- ACL signature
- Monitoring
- Signature filtering

Several of these tokens enable you to define a severity. The first severity setting represents the severity to be sent to destination 1 in the destinations file. The subsequent severities represent destination 2, destination 3, and so on, in the destinations file. Cisco Secure IDS supports a maximum of 32 destinations, and for every destination, a severity level needs to be set.

Destinations File

The destinations file is a configuration file located in the Cisco Secure IDS etc directory. It identifies the multiple locations to which your sensor sends event information. The destinations file is explained later in this appendix.

NOTE   If Cisco Secure IDS is not capturing data as expected, verify that nr.packetd is active on your sensor by using the **nrstatus** command to view the Cisco Secure IDS services that are currently active.

Packet Capture Device Token

The **NameOfPacketDevice** token in the packetd.conf file sets the monitoring interface of the sensor. The following is the token syntax:

```
NameOfPacketDevice [interface name]
```

The *interface name* is the device name of the monitoring interface on the sensor. The following is a list of possible values:

- /dev/sprw0
- /dev/mtok0
- /dev/ptpci
- /dev/iprb0

A sample **NameOfPacketDevice** token in the packetd.conf file is as follows:

```
NameOfPacketDevice /dev/iprb0
```

Refer to Chapter 7 for more information on the various monitoring interfaces available on your sensors.

NOTE   You must have a **NameOfPacketDevice** token in your sensor's packetd.conf. It tells your sensor where it can capture network traffic.

Internal Network Token

Cisco Secure IDS enables you to define internal network(s). The internal network entries are used to associate the source and destination location of alarms. (For more information on alarm fields, refer to Chapter 8, "Working with Cisco Secure IDS Alarms in CSPM.") The keyword **IN** signifies the location in reference to the defined internal network(s). All other locations are assigned the keyword **OUT**. The token syntax for an internal network entry is as follows:

```
RecordOfInternalAddress [IP Address] [Subnet Mask]
```

The *IP Address* is the IP address of the network or host that is part of the inside network Cisco Secure IDS is intended to protect. The *Subnet Mask* is the network mask associated with the IP address of the network or host that is part of the inside network Cisco Secure IDS is intended to protect. A sample internal network token entry is as follows:

```
RecordOfInternalAddress 10.0.2.0 255.255.255.0
```

The preceding sample internal network token indicates that the addresses on the Class C subnet 10.0.2.0 need to be designated as internal addresses. Any alarms with IP addresses on the 10.0.2.0 subnet are marked with the **IN** keyword.

General Signature Token

The **SigOfGeneral** token in the packetd.conf file is associated with Cisco Secure IDS General Signatures tab.

The syntax for the **SigOfGeneral** token is as follows:

```
SigOfGeneral [Signature ID] [Action] [Severity] {[Severity]...}
```

The *Signature ID* is the numeric identification of the signature being configured (1–65535). The *Action* is any one of the following numeric values:

- 0 - None
- 1 - Block
- 2 - IP log
- 3 - Block and IP log
- 4 - TCP reset
- 5 - Block and TCP Reset
- 6 - IP log and TCP reset
- 7 - Block, IP log, and TCP reset

The *Severity* is any one of the following numeric values:

- 0 - Disabled signature
- 1 - Green
- 2 - Green
- 3 - Yellow
- 4 - Red
- 5 - Red

A sample **SigOfGeneral** token entry in the packetd.conf file is as follows:

```
SigOfGeneral 3221 1 3 3 2 2
```

This sample defines the following characteristics for Signature ID 3221:

- Action is block (1).
- Severity is 3 for destination 1, and 2 and 2 for destinations 3 and 4.

TCP or UDP Connection Tokens

The **SigOfTcpPacket** and **SigOfUdpPacket** tokens in the packetd.conf file are associated with Cisco Secure IDS TCP or UDP signatures.

The syntax for the TCP and UDP connection tokens is as follows:

```
SigOfTcpPacket [Port] [Action] [Severity] {[Severity]...}
SigOfUdpPacket [Port] [Action] [Severity] {[Severity]...}
```

The *Port* is a field that represents the port (TCP or UDP) on which you want to assign actions and severities. Connections to the specified port then trigger the actions that you specify. Furthermore, the port number assigned is the subsignature identification for TCP records and UDP packet records. The *Action* is any one of the following numeric values:

- 0 - None
- 1 - Block
- 2 - IP log
- 3 - Block and IP log
- 4 - TCP Reset
- 5 - Block and TCP reset
- 6 - IP Log and TCP reset
- 7 - Block, IP log, and TCP reset

The *Severity* is any one of the following numeric values:

- 0 - Disabled signature
- 1 - Green
- 2 - Green
- 3 - Yellow
- 4 - Red
- 5 - Red

A sample **SigOfTcpPacket** token entry in the packetd.conf file is as follows:

```
SigOfTcpPacket 513 0 3 3 3 3
```

This sample defines the following characteristics for TCP connections to port 513:

- Action is none (0).
- Severity is 3 for destinations 1, 2, 3, and 4.

String Signature Tokens

The **RecordOfStringName** and **SigOfStringMatch** tokens in the packetd.conf file are associated with Cisco Secure IDS string signatures. Each string that you want your Cisco Secure IDS to look for requires both a **RecordOfStringName** and **SigOfStringMatch** token.

The **RecordOfStringName** token identifies items such as the following:

- String to match on (regular expression)
- Port number
- Minimum number of occurrences required to trigger the signature

The **SigOfStringMatch** token associates the actions that the sensor needs to take along with the severity to assign the specific string signature.

The syntax for the **RecordOfStringName** token is as follows:

```
RecordOfStringName [Sub-Signature ID] [Port] [Direction]
    [Num of Occurrences] [String]
```

The *Sub-Signature ID* is the numeric identification of the subsignature being configured (1-65535). The *Port* is the TCP port number that the signature examines for the given string match. The *Direction* is any one of the following three values:

- 1—To the specified port number
- 2—From the specified port number
- 3—Both directions

The *Num of Occurrences* is the number of times the string occurs in the session before an alarm is triggered. The *String* is the actual string to look for. It uses a regular expression format. All string signatures use the Signature ID of 8000. Then, you define a subsignature ID for each string that you want to look for. Along with the string (regular expression), you need to define the port on which the Cisco Secure IDS looks for the string. The port also requires a direction (to the port, from the port, or either direction). Finally, you need to indicate how many occurrences of the string need to be observed before the signature triggers.

A sample **RecordOfStringName** token is as follows:

```
RecordOfStringName 2302 23 1 1 "[/]etc[/]shadow"
```

This sample assigns the following characteristics to string Subsignature 2302:

- Check on port 23 (23).
- Check traffic to port 23 (1).
- Alarm after one occurrence of the string (1).
- Search for /etc/shadow.

The syntax for the **SigOfStringMatch** token is as follows:

```
SigOfStringMatch [Sub-Signature ID] [Action] [Severity] {[Severity]...}
```

The *Sub-Signature ID* is the numeric identification of the subsignature being configured (1-65535). The *Action* is any one of the following numeric values:

- 0 - None
- 1 - Block
- 2 - IP log
- 3 - Block and IP log
- 4 - TCP reset
- 5 - Block and TCP reset
- 6 - IP log and TCP reset
- 7 - Block, IP log, and TCP reset

The *Severity* is any one of the following numeric values:

- 0 - Disabled signature
- 1 - Green
- 2 - Green
- 3 - Yellow
- 4 - Red
- 5 - Red

A sample **SigOfStringMatch** token is as follows:

```
SigOfStringMatch 2302 0 5 5 5 5 5 5 5
```

This sample associates the following characteristics with the 2302 Subsignature ID:

- Action of none (0)
- Alarm severity of 5 for the first 6 destinations

NOTE   You might want to include the port number in the subsignature ID to help remind you what service the signature is related to when it triggers.

ACL Signature Tokens

Each ACL signature is identified by two separate tokens in your packetd.conf file: **RecordOfFilterName** and **SigOfFilterName**. The **RecordOfFilterName** token identifies the ACL used to trigger a policy violation, whereas the **SigOfFilterName** token defines the action(s) to be taken along with assigning a severity per destination. Each ACL signature requires both of these tokens.

The syntax for a **RecordOfFilterName** token is as follows:

```
RecordOfFilterName [Sub-Signature ID] [Violation Name]
```

The *Sub-Signature ID* is the numeric identification of the subsignature being configured (1-65535). The *Violation Name* is the number or name of the ACL list that triggers policy violation alarms.

The syntax for a **SigOfFilterName** token is as follows:

```
SigOfFilterName [Sub-Signature ID] [Action] [Severity] {[Severity]...}
```

The *Sub-Signature ID* is the numeric identification of the subsignature being configured (1-65535). The *Action* is any one of the following numeric values:

- 0 - None
- 1 - Block
- 2 - IP log
- 3 - Block and IP log
- 4 - TCP reset
- 5 - Block and TCP reset
- 6 - IP log and TCP reset
- 7 - Block, IP log, and TCP reset

The *Severity* is any one of the following numeric values:

- 0 - Disabled signature
- 1 - Green
- 2 - Green
- 3 - Yellow
- 4 - Red
- 5 - Red

Examples of the **RecordOfFilterName** and **SigOfFilterName** tokens are as following:

```
RecordOfFilterName 1 199
SigOfFilterName 1 0 5 5 5 5
```

The **RecordOfFilterName** entry assigns the Subsignature ID of 1 to ACL 199. Then, the **SigOfFilterName** entry defines no actions (0) and a severity of 5 for the first four destinations.

Monitoring Tokens

The **RecordOfDataSource** token in the packetd.conf file is also associated with Cisco Secure IDS ACL signatures. This token identifies the IP address of the router that your sensor uses to check for ACL policy violation signatures.

The syntax for the **RecordOfDataSource** token is as follows:

```
RecordOfDataSource [IP Address] [Subnet Mask]
```

The *IP Address* is the IP address of the Cisco router from which the sensor is accepting SYSLOG messages. The *Subnet Mask* is the network mask associated with the IP address of the Cisco router from which the sensor is accepting SYSLOG messages. An example RecordOfDataSource token entry is as follows:

```
RecordOfDataSource 10.20.100.1 255.255.255.0
```

This entry identifies the router's IP address to be the Class C address of 10.20.100.1.

Signature Filtering Tokens

The **Excluded Networks** tab defines a **RecordOfExcludedNetAddress** token in your sensor's packetd.conf file. You use this token to exclude specific host(s) or network(s) from being able to trigger specific alarms.

The syntax for the **RecordOfExcludedNetAddress** token is as follows:

```
RecordOfExcludedNetAddress [Signature ID] [Sub-Signature ID] [IP Address]
    [SubnetMask] [Address Role]
```

The *Signature ID* is the signature identification for which Cisco Secure IDS does not trigger an alarm if the given IP address is the source, destination, or both the source and destination of the traffic.

The Sub-Signature ID is the subsignature ID for which Cisco Secure IDS does not trigger an alarm if the given IP address is the source, destination, or both the source and destination of the traffic.

The *IP Address* is the IP address of the host for which Cisco Secure IDS does not trigger the given alarm if the IP address is the source, destination, or both the source and destination of the traffic.

The *Subnet Mask* is the network mask associated with the IP address of the host for which Cisco Secure IDS does not trigger the given alarm if the IP address is the source, destination, or both the source and destination of the traffic.

The *Address Role* can assume any of the following three values:

- 1 - Source
- 2 - Destination
- 3 - Either

The *Signature ID* and *Sub-signature* ID identify the specific signature that you want to exclude from a host or network. The *IP Address* and *Mask* identify the host or network that are excluded from triggering the specified alarm. Finally, the *Address Role* enables you to specify whether the exclusion applies to traffic from the excluded host (source), traffic to the excluded host (destination), or traffic to and from the excluded host.

A sample **RecordOfExcludedNetAddress** token is as follows:

```
RecordOfExcludedNetAddress 8000 2302 10.200.20.0 255.255.255.0 1
```

This entry excludes IP addresses on the Class C subnet 10.200.20.0 from triggering the string signature (ID 8000) whose subsignature ID is 2302. This exclusion applies only to traffic originating (1) from IP addresses on the excluded subnet.

Device Management and Blocking Tokens

The sensor device management settings are written to the managed.conf file. The nr.managed service generates ACLs to be applied to a Cisco IOS router. Device management tokens exist in managed.conf and packetd.conf files.

The Blocking feature is implemented by several tokens that are located in the managed.conf configuration file. The tokens associated with the Blocking feature are as follows:

- NetDevice
- ShunInterface
- NeverShunAddress
- DupDestination
- MinutesOfAutoShun

The syntax for the **NetDevice** token is as follows:

```
NetDevice [IP Address] CiscoDefault [Telnet Password]|
[Telnet Username/Password] [Enable password]
```

The *IP Address* is the IP address the sensor telnets to on the router, and **CiscoDefault** is the required keyword. The *Telnet Password or Telnet Username/Password* is the password, or username and password combination, used to telnet to the router. The *Enable Password* is the password for the router's Enable mode.

The syntax for the **ShunInterfaceCisco** token is as follows:

```
ShunInterfaceCisco [IP Address] [Interface Name] [Direction]
```

The *IP Address* is the IP address of the managed router. The sensor needs Telnet access to this IP address. The *Interface Name* is the name of the interface where the ACL is applied. No space is allowed between the interface name and its number. The following are some examples:

- ethernet0
- e0
- serial0/1
- s0/1

The *Direction* is the direction to which the blocking ACLs are applied: **in** or **out**.

The syntax for the **NeverShunAddress** token is as follows:

```
NeverShunAddress [IP Address] [Mask]
```

The *IP Address* is the IP address the sensor telnets to on the router. The *Mask* is the network mask associated with the IP address the sensor telnets to on the router.

The syntax for the **DupDestination** token is as follows:

```
DupDestination [Host Name]
```

The *Host Name* is the Cisco Secure IDS host name (host name.organization name) of the other sensor performing blocking on other routers that the user wants to activate when this sensor responds with a block request. This Cisco Secure IDS Sensor block feature is referred to as the master blocking sensor.

The syntax for the **MinutesOfAutoShun** token is as follows:

```
MinutesOfAutoShun [Minutes]
```

The *Minutes* is the number of minutes Cisco Secure IDS blocks an attacking host. Example entries for the blocking tokens are as follows:

```
NetDevice 10.200.10.1 CiscoDefault cisco/pass cisco1
ShunInterfaceCisco 10.200.10.1 e0/1 in
NeverShunAddress 10.200.200.5 255.255.255.255
DupDestination sensor2.security
MinutesOfAutoShun 30
```

These entries define the following blocking characteristics:

- Blocking device is 10.200.10.1.
- Telnet username is *cisco* with a password of *pass*.
- The enable password is *cisco1*.
- The blocking ACL is applied to the e0/1 interface for inbound traffic.
- IP address 10.200.200.5 is marked as an address that cannot be blocked.
- Sensor2.security is informed when blocking activity is initiated.
- Blocking lasts 30 minutes (the default).

Director and Alarm Forwarding

Your Director can forward alarm information to multiple destinations. The configuration settings to enable your Director to forward alarms to multiple destinations are stored in the smid.conf file.

You can also use a **DupDestination** token to specify another destination to which events are forwarded by your Director. These tokens are stored in the smid.conf configuration file.

The syntax for the **DupDestination** token is as follows:

```
DupDestination [Host Name] [Service Name] [Message Level] [Message Type],
    {[Message Type]…}
```

The *Host Name* is the Cisco Secure IDS host name (hostname.organization name) of the host (Director or sensor) that receive the forwarded message. The *Service Name* is the name of the service to which the messages are sent. The possible services are as follows:

- smid
- loggerd
- eventd

The *Message Level* is the minimum severity level that an event must have in order to be forwarded. Values are 1–5 (Low–High). The *Message Type* identifies the following types of messages to be forwarded:

- **ERRORS**—All error messages from any daemon
- **COMMANDS**—All command messages from any daemon to any daemon
- **EVENTS**—All alarms from packetd
- **IPLOGS**—All captured session data from packetd

An example DupDestination token for smid.conf on your Director is as follows:

```
DupDestination Director2.security smid 1 EVENTS,ERRORS,COMMANDS
```

This entry specifies that the Director is to forward all alarms from packetd with a severity greater than or equal to 1 to Director2.security. It also forwards all error and command messages with a severity greater than or equal to 1.

Logging and Logging Settings

The nr.loggerd service is responsible for performing logging functions on Cisco Secure IDS components. The logging settings are stored in the loggerd.conf file.

The Cisco Secure IDS log files are stored in the var directory under the Cisco Secure IDS subdirectory (refer back to Figure B-8). For example, on a 4210 Series Sensor, the log files are stored in **/usr/nr/var**. Cisco Secure IDS maintains subdirectories for the different types of possible log files. These subdirectories are as follows:

- **log**—This directory stores current Cisco Secure IDS log and error files generated by Cisco Secure IDS services.
- **iplog**—This directory stores IP session log files.
- **new**—This directory stores archived Cisco Secure IDS log files.

Refer to Appendix D for information on the structure of Cisco Secure IDS log files.

The active Cisco Secure IDS log file is located in **/usr/nr/var** (refer back to Figure B-11). The IP log files are located in **/usr/nr/var/iplog**. Each Cisco Secure IDS service maintains its own error log file and is located in **/usr/nr/var** (refer back to Figure B-11). These default settings are controlled by the following tokens in the loggerd.conf file:

- FilenameOfLog
- FilenameOfIPLog

Active log files are closed and archived, and new active log files are created when certain file size or time thresholds are exceeded. By default, log files are archived and a new one created when the active log reaches 1 GB or after 60 minutes, whichever comes first. These default settings are controlled by the following tokens in the loggerd.conf configuration file:

- NumberOfSwitchMinutes
- NumberOfSwitchBytes

By default, IP log files remain active for 60 minutes or until the session that triggered the IP log action is terminated. This setting is controlled by the following token in the packetd.conf file:

- MinutesOfAutoLog

Archived log files are located in **/usr/nr/var/new** for Cisco Secure IDS log and error log files and in **/usr/nr/var/iplog/new** for IP session log files. The location of the archived log files is controlled by the following token in the loggerd.conf configuration file: **FilenameOfLogNew**.

NOTE   Refer to Appendix D to understand the manner in which Cisco Secure IDS log filenames are assigned.

FTP Transfer and FTP Transfer Tokens

The FTP transfer settings are written to the sapd.conf file. The nr.sapd service is responsible for performing database functions and offline log file transfers.

The following tokens in sapd.conf are associated with the FTP transfer of sensor log files:

```
DBUser2 [Username]
DBPass2 [Password]
DBAux2  [IP Address]
```

The *Username* is the username for the FTP user. The *Password* is the password for the FTP user. The *IP Address* is the IP address of the target FTP server. The FTP server must have a directory with write permissions assigned.

Example FTP transfer token entries are as follows:

```
DBUser2 ftpuser
DBPass2 ftppass
DBAux2  10.200.200.10
```

These entries define 10.200.200.10 as the address of the FTP server. The login credentials that the Cisco Secure IDS component uses are a username of *ftpuser* and a password of *ftppass*.

Communications

Cisco Secure IDS communications settings are written to the following files:

- postofficed.conf
- organizations
- hosts
- routes
- destinations

These communication settings control many aspects of your Cisco Secure IDS. In this section, the following topics are addressed:

- Fault management
- Cisco Secure IDS organizations
- Cisco Secure IDS hosts
- Cisco Secure IDS routes
- Cisco Secure IDS destinations
- Cisco Secure IDS authorized hosts
- Cisco Secure IDS services
- Cisco Secure IDS applications

Fault Management

Fault management is the mechanism that Cisco Secure IDS uses to continually verify that your Cisco Secure IDS is operating correctly. nr.postofficed constantly queries the various daemons or services on a Cisco Secure IDS component to confirm that the daemons are functioning correctly. The following tokens control fault management:

- WatchDogInterval
- WatchDogResponseTimeOut
- WatchDogNumProcessRestarts
- WatchDogProcTimeOutAlarmLevel
- WatchDogProcDeadAlarmLevel

NOTE   The fault management tokens are all located in the postoffice.conf configuration file.

WatchDogInterval

The **WatchDogInterval** token controls the rate at which nr.postofficed queries the services on a specific component. The syntax for the **WatchDogInterval** token is as follows:

```
WatchDogInterval [Num of Seconds]
```

The *Num of Seconds* is the number of seconds between nr.postofficed's regular status queries of the services running on the said device.

WatchDogResponseTimeout

The **WatchDogResponseTimeOut** token controls the length of time that nr.postofficed waits for a response from the services that it queries. If a response is not received within the timeout period, the service is declared down. The syntax for the **WatchDogResponseTimeOut** token is as follows:

```
WatchDogResponseTimeOut [Num of Seconds]
```

The *Num of Seconds* is the number of seconds that must pass without a given daemon response before declaring that daemon to be down.

WatchDogNumProcessRestarts

The **WatchDogNumProcessRestarts** token controls the number of times that nr.postofficed attempts to restart a down daemon before declaring the down daemon is dead (not startable). The syntax for the **WatchDogNumProcessRestarts** token is as follows:

```
WatchDogNumProcessRestarts [Num of Tries]
```

The *Num of Tries* is the number of times that nr.postofficed tries to restart a downed daemon before declaring it to be dead.

WatchDogProcTimeOutAlarmLevel

The **WatchDogProcTimeOutAlarmLevel** token controls the severity of the alarm event that nr.postofficed generates when it concludes that a daemon is down. (Daemon has not responded within the **WatchDogResponseTimeOut** interval.) The syntax for the WatchDogProcTimeOutAlarmLevel token is as follows:

```
WatchDogProcTimeOutAlarmLevel [Severity]
```

The *Severity* is the severity level of the alarm that is generated when nr.postofficed concludes that a daemon is down.

WatchDogProcDeadAlarmLevel

The **WatchDogProcDeadAlarmLevel** token controls the severity of the alarm event that nr.postofficed generates when it concludes that a daemon is dead. The syntax for the **WatchDogProcDeadAlarmLevel** token is as follows:

```
WatchDogProcDeadAlarmLevel [Severity]
```

The *Severity* is the severity level of the alarm that is generated when nr.postofficed concludes that a daemon is not startable.

The default fault management token entries are as follows:

```
WatchDogInterval 30
WatchDogResponseTimeOut 240
WatchDogNumProcessRestarts 3
WatchDogProcTimeOutAlarmLevel 5
WatchDogProcDeadAlarmLevel 5
```

Cisco Secure IDS Organizations

The organizations file contains PostOffice organization identifications and names. The format for an entry in the organizations file is as follows:

```
[Organization ID] [Organization Name]
```

The *Organization ID* is the numeric identification for a Cisco Secure IDS organization (1-65535). The *Organization Name* is the alphanumeric identification associated with a Cisco Secure IDS organization.

Sample organization definition entries in the Organizations file are as follows:

```
5000 Security
6000 Consulting
```

Cisco Secure IDS Hosts

In UNIX, each machine is identified by both an IP address and name. Cisco Secure IDS uses a more robust addressing scheme. The **/usr/nr/etc/hosts** file, similar to a UNIX

/etc/hosts file, enumerates the organizations and hosts that are recognized by a given sensor or Director system in a Cisco Secure IDS configuration. Each entry has the following form:

```
[host ID].[organization ID] [host name].[organization name]
```

The *host ID* is the numeric identification for the Cisco Secure IDS host (1-65535). The *organization ID* is the numeric identification for the Cisco Secure IDS organization (1-65535).

The *host name* is the alphanumeric identification associated with a Cisco Secure IDS host. The *organization name* is the alphanumeric identification associated with a Cisco Secure IDS organization.

NOTE   The dot between the host identification and organization identification, the host name, and organization name are required. The only exception is the localhost entry.

The combination of the host identification and organization identification must form a unique identifier throughout your entire network of sensors and Directors. The organization identification and name must be the same in all configuration files. This file must have localhost as the first entry. The localhost must have the same host identification and organization identification as the host in which the file is maintained. On the sensor, you need only three entries: localhost, sensor, and Director. On the Director, you have all the sensors and Directors listed.

Sample entries in the Cisco Secure IDS hosts file are as follows:

```
4.5000 localhost
4.5000 sensor.security
3.5000 director.security
```

Cisco Secure IDS Routes

The **routes** file enables you to set the IP address associated with Cisco Secure IDS hosts. For fault tolerance, multiple IP addresses can be defined for a single host. These multiple addresses are then used as alternative IP addresses in case the primary IP address is not responding.

The IP address for each machine known to the host is searched for by nr.postofficed. The **routes** file identifies the actual IP routes that nr.postofficed uses to send messages between different hosts. The format for an entry in the **routes** file is as follows:

```
[hostname].[organization name] [connection #] [IP address] [UDP port] [Type]
{Heartbeat}
```

The *hostname* is the name of the machine to which you want to connect. It must be an entry in the **hosts** file. The *organization name* is the alphanumeric identification associated with the Cisco Secure IDS organization.

The *connection #* is the numeric order in which you want this path to this machine to be tried. The lower the number, the higher the route priority. If multiple entries exist, the higher numbered entries act as backup routes in case the primary route goes down. The *IP address* identifies the IP address of the Cisco Secure IDS device to receive the message.

The *UDP port* identifies the UDP port communication services that are routed through on each host. The default setting is 45000. The *Type* identifies the connection type and is currently not used. It needs to be a 1. The *Heartbeat*, which is optional, is the number of seconds before the routes are considered down.

Sample entries from the **routes** file are as follows:

```
sensor.security 1 10.10.20.5 45000 1 5
director.security 1 10.11.200.3 45000 1 5
director.security 2 10.12.20.4 45000 1 5
director2.security 1 10.15.200.4 45000 1 5
```

In the example entries, the sensor is routing to two different Directors and has a backup route for one of the Directors. Route 1 communicates with director.security at the IP address of 10.11.200.3 until a connection problem is detected. As soon as Cisco Secure IDS detects a problem with the primary route, it automatically switches to Route 2 at IP address 10.12.20.4, while at that same time trying to reestablish the primary route. Cisco Secure IDS automatically reverts to the primary route when the connection is established.

Cisco Secure IDS Destinations

The **destinations** file enables you to add additional destinations to send events generated by Cisco Secure IDS. The routing of the messages to any other host registered in the **hosts** file is handled by postofficed. The **destinations** file identifies the severity of the messages and the type of messages that are routed to a given application on a given host. postofficed can forward messages to the following three services:

- loggerd
- smid
- eventd

A given postofficed can forward messages to a maximum of 32 destinations. The following is the entry format for the **destinations** file:

```
[Destination ID] [host name] [service name] [message level] [message type]
```

The *Destination ID* is the numeric identification (1-32) for each destination. The *host name* is the Cisco Secure IDS name of the host (hostid.orgid) to send the messages. It must already be defined in the **hosts** file. The *service name* is the name of the service to send the messages. The possible services are as follows:

- smid
- loggerd
- eventd

The *message level* is the minimum severity level that an event must have in order to be forwarded. Values range from 1–5 (Low–High). The *message type* identifies the following types of messages to be forwarded:

- **ERRORS**—All error messages from any daemon
- **COMMANDS**—All command messages from any daemon to any daemon
- **EVENTS**—All alarms from packetd
- **IPLOGS**—All captured session data from packetd

Sample entries from the **destinations** file are as follows:

```
1 sensor.security loggerd 1 ERRORS,COMMANDS,EVENTS,IPLOGS
2 Director.security smid 2 EVENTS,ERRORS,COMMANDS
```

In the example **destinations** file entries, the sensor forwards all errors, commands, events, and IP logs with a level of 1 or higher to its loggerd daemon. The sensor has all errors, commands, and events, with a level of 2 or higher forwarded to the smid daemon on the Director.

Cisco Secure IDS Authorized Hosts

The **auths** file enables you to set appropriate permissions for other Cisco Secure IDS hosts to remotely query and configure the current Cisco Secure IDS component, sensor, or Director. The following is the entry format in the **auths** files:

```
[Host Name].[Organization Name] [action]{,[action]. . .}
```

The *Host Name* is the Cisco Secure IDS host name of the host being given permissions. The *Organization Name* is the Cisco Secure IDS organization name associated with the host being given permissions.

The *action* is the allowed actions from the defined host as follows:

- **GET**—Allows access to single pieces of information at a time
- **GETBULK**—Allows access to multiple pieces of information at a time
- **SET**—Allows the remote host to set local attributes
- **UNSET**—Allows the remote host to unset local attributes
- **EXEC**—Allows the remote host to execute Cisco Secure IDS commands

Sample **auths** file entries are as follows:

```
sensor.security GET,GETBULK,SET,UNSET,EXEC
director.security GET,GETBULK,SET,UNSET,EXEC
```

NOTE   The **auths** file needs to contain an entry for the sensor itself.

Cisco Secure IDS Services

The **daemons** file enables you to set which daemons are started every time Cisco Secure IDS is started. The following is the entry format in the **daemons** file:

```
[service name]
```

The *service name* is the name of the daemon to be started every time Cisco Secure IDS is started. Service names can be one or more of the following:

- nr.postofficed
- nr.loggerd
- nr.sapd
- nr.packetd
- nr.fileXferd
- nr.managed
- nr.smid

Sample **daemons** file entries are as follows:

```
nr.postofficed
nr.managed
nr.eventd
nr.loggerd
nr.packetd
```

NOTE   Not all the Cisco Secure IDS service daemons are available on every device. The nr.smid service, for example, runs only on the Director and the nr.packetd service runs only on a sensor.

Cisco Secure IDS Applications

The following is the entry format in the **services** file that defines the application ID for every Cisco Secure IDS daemon:

```
[Application ID] [Service Name]
```

The *Application ID* is the numeric identification assigned to the Cisco Secure IDS daemon. The *Service Name* is the name of the Cisco Secure IDS daemon whose application identification is being set. Cisco Secure IDS application IDs and associated service names are as follows:

- 10000 - postofficed
- 10003 - managed
- 10004 - eventd
- 10005 - loggerd
- 10006 - smid
- 10007 - sapd
- 10008 - packetd
- 10009 – fileXferd

Sample **services** file entries are:

```
10000         postofficed
10003         managed
10004    eventd
10005         loggerd
```

WARNING   Entries in the *services* file must never be changed. Changing entries can cause Cisco Secure IDS to not function properly.

Cisco Secure ID Director Basic Troubleshooting

During the operation of your Cisco Secure IDS, you might sometimes run into problems. This appendix explains some of the basic problems that you might encounter if you use the CSIDD. These problems are divided into the following categories:

- Director problems
- Sensor problems
- Oracle problems
- Data management package problems
- nrConfigure problems
- Online Help and NSDB

Director Problems

While using your CSIDD, you might experience different problems that you need to troubleshoot. Knowing the symptoms of these various problems enables you to effectively troubleshoot your Cisco Secure IDS. The CSIDD problems that you might experience occur in two categories:

- Director not running
- Director running

Director Not Running

If your Director is not running, you might experience the following problems:

- Unable to write to socket.
- Socket buffer is overflowing.
- Inadequate permissions to communicate.
- Semaphore file problems.
- Improperly set LD_LIBRARY_PATH variable.

The following sections discuss each of these in turn.

Unable to Write to Socket

If your Cisco Secure IDS services cannot write to the Director, you might see the following message in one of your service error log files (see Appendix D, "Cisco Secure IDS Log Files"):

```
Cannot write message to Director, errno =2
```

One possible cause of this error is that the nr.smid service is trying to write to a socket that does not exist. This might occur because the OpenView user interface (ovw) is not started. Without the OpenView user interface running, the Director's nrdirmap application cannot create the necessary communication socket (located in /usr/nr/tmp).

If you receive this error, follow these steps:

Step 1 Verify that the underlying Cisco Secure IDS services, such as postofficed and smid, are running by using the **nrstatus** command. (**nrstatus** is explained in Appendix B, "Cisco Secure IDS Architecture.")

Step 2 Use **nrstart** to start services that are not running.

Step 3 Start OpenView by typing **ovw &** at the command line.

Socket Buffer Is Overflowing

Another error that occurs when your Cisco Secure IDS services cannot write to the Director because the UNIX socket is overflowing is as follows:

```
Cannot write message to Director, errno = 233
```

This message will also appear in one of your service error log files (see Appendix D) and occurs when the nr.smid service attempts to write to a socket whose buffer is overflowing. Normally, this occurs when Director's nrdirmap application is not running.

To correct this problem, you need to ensure that the OpenView user interface is running by executing **ovw &** at the command line. Starting the OpenView user interface will automatically start the nrdirmap application.

Inadequate Permissions to Communicate

If the permissions are incorrect on either the **nr.smid** process or the **nrdirmap** application, the following error message might appear in one of your service error log files (see Appendix D):

```
Cannot write message to Director, errno = 239
```

This error message appears when either **nr.smid** or **nrdirmap** do not have adequate permission to communicate via sockets in /usr/nr/tmp. To correct this problem, you need to ensure that nrdirmap is owned by the user netrangr. Furthermore, you need to verify that **nr.smid** runs as *SUID netrangr.*

SUID File Permission Bit

The SUID file permission bit on a program enables a user who is not the owner of the executable file to run the program with the privileges of the owner of the program. For example, a program that is SUID netrangr will run as the user netrangr even if another user invokes the program. Programs that are SUID root will run with root privileges and can pose a security risk to your system if compromised.

```
To verify that nr.smid runs as SUID netrangr, you can use the following commands:
$ cd /usr/nr/bin
$ ls -la nr.smid
-rwsr-s--- 1 netrangr netrangr   668040 Nov 30 2000   nr.smid*
```

The first **netrangr** in the **ls** output indicates that the file is owned by the netrangr account, and the *s* in the Permissions field indicates that the file is SUID.

To verify that **nrdirmap** is owned by netrangr, you can again use the **ls** command, but because it is a link to the actual file, you need to make sure that you examine the actual file.

```
$ cd /usr/nr/bin
$ ls -la nrdirmap
lrwxrwxrwx  1  root  other   20 Nov 30  2000  nrdirmap->/opt/OV/bin/nrdirmap*
$ cd /opt/OV/bin
$ ls -la nrdirmap
-rwxr-xr-x  1  netrangr  netrangr  2868184 Nov 30 2000 nrdirmap*
```

The initial **ls** command indicates that the nrdirmap file in /usr/nr/bin is actually a link to the real nrdirmap file in the /opt/OV/bin directory. An **ls** on the real file indicates that it is owned by netrangr.

Semaphore File Problems

A semaphore file is used to indicate whether a resource is being used (locked) by another process. The semaphore file prevents two processes from attempting to update the same data at the same time. HP OpenView can generate the following error message upon startup:

```
848967818198: WgcSema can't access '/usr/nr/etc/nrdirmap.semaphore'
Error: nrdirmap:main, semaphore initialization failed.
```

A possible cause of the error is the deletion of the *nrdirmap.semaphore* file. This file, which is located in /usr/nr/etc, might also have improper permissions. To correct this problem, follow these steps:

Step 1 Verify that /usr/nr/etc/nrdirmap.semaphore exists.

Step 2 Verify that the netrangr user and group accounts have read access to the file.

Step 3 Ensure that /usr/nr/bin/nrdirmap runs as SUID netrangr.

NOTE If the file /usr/nr/etc/nrdirmap.semaphore does not exist, you can create the file with a text editor, such as **vi**. Add a single character to the file and save it in /usr/nr/etc with the name nrdirmap.semaphore.

Improperly Set LD_LIBRARY_PATH Variable

The LD_LIBRARY_PATH variable identifies the location of various library modules on your system. If your LB_LIBRARY_PATH is set incorrectly, you might see the following error:

```
nrdirmap: fatal: libovw.so.1: can't open file: errno=2
```

This problem commonly appears if you have not logged in to the Director with the correct user. If you have logged in with the correct user, you need to follow the instructions for setting up an HP OpenView environment for user accounts other than netrangr (in the *Cisco Secure IDS Users Guide*). If the account is based on either the Bourne or Korn shell, the following lines need to appear in the user's $HOME/.profile file:

```
if [ -d /opt/OV ] ; then
    . /opt/OV/bin/ov.envvars.sh
    PATH=$OV_BIN:$PATH
    export PATH
    LD_LIBRARY_PATH=$OV_LIB:$LD_LIBRARY_PATH
    export LD_LIBRARY_PATH
fi
```

NOTE If you use a shell other than **ksh** or **sh**, the lines in the preceding code segment must be translated into the appropriate scripting language and placed in the appropriate startup file.

Director Running

Even if your Director is running, you still might experience the following problems:

- No sensor alarms because of incorrect severity status.
- No sensor alarms because of incorrect routing threshold.
- Maximum number of alarms for application.
- Sensor alarm data not logged.
- Show Current Events Utility hangs.

No Sensor Alarms Because of Incorrect Severity Status

Your Director platform displays alarms only that are the same or higher than the minimal alarm level that you have configured for HP OpenView. (This is an HP OpenView setting and has nothing to do with your postofficed configuration.) If your Director's security map contains a Sensor icon but fails to show any alarm events for that sensor, the alarms generated by your sensor might be less than the defined threshold in HP OpenView. To troubleshoot this problem, follow these steps:

Step 1   On the Director interface, select the Sensor icon.

Step 2   Press either Ctrl-O or click **Describe>Modify** on the Edit menu.

Step 3   Select Cisco Secure ID Director and click **View>Modify**.

Step 4   Ensure that Minimum Marginal and Minimum Critical status thresholds are low enough to register events from the sensor in question. (The defaults are 3 for minimum marginal and 4 for minimum critical.)

No Sensor Alarms Because of Incorrect Routing Threshold

In the previous section, the sensor alarms reached the Director, but they were not displayed because of the marginal and minimum critical status thresholds. If that did not solve your problem of no alarm events for your sensor, it is possible that the alarms are not getting forwarded from the sensor. The sensor contains the following file:

```
/usr/nr/etc/destinations
```

This file determines the minimum routing threshold that an alarm must meet or exceed to be forwarded to a destination. You need to verify that the setting in this file is low enough to route alarm information to the Director. The default setting is 2.

Maximum Number of Alarms for Application

Sometimes, one of your submaps will reach 1000 alarm icons. If this happens, you will see the following error message:

```
Application AppId.HostId.OrgId has reached maximum number of alarms.
```

The Director will not create more than 1000 icons on a submap (window) because Open-View can behave unpredictably when this happens. To resolve this problem, you need to delete the alarm icons in the crowded submap.

The Director will resume creating alarm icons on the submap for any new events. To view iconic representations of the events that nrdirmap diverted to /usr/nr/var (after the limit of 1000 alarms was reached), follow these steps:

Step 1   Delete the icons on the submap in question.

Step 2   Shut down and restart the OpenView user interface.

NOTE   The Director saves any additional alarm data (past the 1000 alarm limit) for an application to a file named nrdirmap.buffer.ovw_map_name in the /usr/nr/var directory, where ovw_map_name is the name of the OpenView map.

Sensor Alarm Data Not Logged

Sometimes, your sensor displays alarms correctly on the Director security map, but information on those alarms does not appear in the *Show Current Events* window. Furthermore, the event log file in the Director's /usr/nr/var directory does not contain any records from that sensor.

This might be caused by the Director's loggerd service not being listed as a destination in either of the following:

- Director's configuration files
- Sensor's configuration files

To resolve this problem, you can use nrConfigure to create an entry in the sensor's /usr/nr/etc/destinations file for the Director's loggerd service, or you can create a DupDestination entry in the Director's /usr/nr/etc/smid.conf file to redirect event data to loggerd from smid. (For more information on Cisco Secure IDS services, refer to Appendix B.)

Show Current Events Utility Hangs

Sometimes, when you bring up the Director's Show Current Events window, the information displays properly, but the cursor turns into an hourglass and never changes back. The current events utility continues to pull information from the Director log files as long as the window is up.

Click **Stop** to terminate the filtering application. You can then use the scroll bars and menu options to look at the data. Finally, you can click **Close** to exit the window.

Sensor Problems

Sometimes, you might need to troubleshoot the operation of your sensors. In this section, the following troubleshooting tips are explained:

- Problems starting and stopping the Cisco Secure daemon processes
- Sensor connectivity problems

NOTE   Appendix E, "Advanced Tips," also addresses some problems that you might encounter with your Cisco Secure IDS Sensors.

Problems Starting and Stopping Cisco Secure Daemon Processes

If you are logged in to your sensor and cannot start or stop the Cisco Secure IDS daemon services using the **nrstart** and **nrstop** commands, you are probably logged in to an account that does not have access rights to the sensor daemons. If you experience this problem, you need to ensure that you are logged in to the sensor under the same account that was used to start the daemon services.

NOTE   The default account to start these services is *netrangr.*

Sensor Connectivity Problems

If you are unable to access a sensor or any of the Cisco Secure IDS services running on the sensor's system, this usually indicates that the daemons on the sensor are not running properly (if at all). You need to telnet to the sensor and perform the following steps:

Step 1   Run the **nrstop** command.

Step 2   Examine error files in /usr/nr/var.

Step 3   Restart the sensor daemons by running **nrstart**.

Oracle Problems

The CSIDD can be configured to utilize an Oracle database to record the alarms and other information that it receives. You might experience several problems related to either the installation or operation of your Oracle database software. These problems are divided into the following categories:

- Cannot determine whether Oracle is installed.
- Cannot determine whether Oracle is running.
- Oracle installer did not install Oracle.
- SQLPlus or SQLDR not found.
- SQLPlus does not run.
- Oracle not available.
- LD_LIBRARY_PATH Variable Not Properly Set.
- Oracle Fails to Authorize Connection.
- Oracle Returns a User/Password Error.

Cannot Determine Whether Oracle Is Installed

To verify whether Oracle is installed on your system, you need to check the local and mounted file systems using the following system commands:

- **df**
- **mount**
- **find**

You will be looking for "oracle" in either the name of a remotely mounted disk or as a directory on your local system.

Cannot Determine Whether Oracle Is Running

To determine whether Oracle is running on your system, you need to use the **ps** system command. Because the Oracle process starts with *ora,* you can locate this process with the following command:

```
ps -ef | grep ora
```

The command generates output similar to the following:

```
$ ps -ef | grep ora
oracle 336 1 0 12:07:40 ? 0:00 /usr/apps/oracle/8.1.6/bin/tnslsnr LISTENER
    -inherit
oracle 308 304 0 12:03:28 pts/2 0:00 -ksh
oracle 352 308 0 12:11:23 pts/2 0:00 grep ora
oracle 318 1 0 12:04:19 ? 0:01 ora_pmon_labman
```

```
oracle 320 1 0 12:04:20 ? 0:00 ora_dbw0_labman
oracle 322 1 0 12:04:21 ? 0:00 ora_lgwr_labman
oracle 324 1 0 12:04:22 ? 0:01 ora_ckpt_labman
oracle 326 1 0 12:04:22 ? 0:01 ora_smon_labman
oracle 328 1 0 12:04:23 ? 0:00 ora_reco_labman
oracle 330 1 0 12:04:23 ? 0:00 ora_s000_labman
oracle 332 1 0 12:04:24 ? 0:00 ora_d000_labman
$
```

Your system might not have all the Oracle processes shown in the example, but you should still see several oracle processes running.

Oracle Installer Did Not Install Oracle

If you attempt to install Oracle using the Oracle Installer (**orainst**), it might report that it is unable to find any products to install. If this happens, you probably did not run start.sh prior to running orainst. The **start.sh** script prepares your environment for the orainst program. Therefore, run **/cdrom/cdrom0/orainst/start.sh** and then run the Oracle Installer again.

SQLPlus or SQLDR Not Found

When attempting to run SQLPlus or SQLDR, you might see one of the following messages:

```
sqlplus: not found
sqlldr: not found
```

This usually indicates that the Oracle bin directory is not specified correctly in your execution path. Therefore, you need to change your $PATH variable to include $ORACLE_HOME/bin.

SQLPlus Does Not Run

When attempting to run SQLPlus, you might see the following error message:

```
~~~/oracle/product/7.3.2/bin/sqlplus: cannot open
```

Your shell finds **sqlplus**, but it cannot execute it. This usually occurs when your $PATH includes references to the wrong versions of the Oracle binaries. For example, you have mounted the wrong Oracle directories from a file server. In this situation, you might be trying to execute HP-UX binaries on a SPARC system, for example.

To correct this problem, you need to ensure that the $ORACLE_HOME directory contains the proper binaries for the platform that you are running. Refer to "Installing an Oracle RDBMS" in the *Cisco Secure IDS User Guide*.

Oracle Not Available

When trying to run **sqlplus**, **sqldr**, or **sapx**, you might see the following error message:

```
ERROR: ORA-01034: ORACLE not available
ORA-07200: slsid: oracle_sid not set
```

This indicates that the ORACLE_SID environment variable, which identifies the database instance to use, is not properly set up. This causes the applications to fail with the SID error. You need to set the ORACLE_SID environment variable to the name of your database instance.

NOTE   You can learn your database instance name by running this command:

```
$ ps -ef ¦ grep ora
oracle 336 1 0 12:07:40 ? 0:00 /usr/apps/oracle/8.1.6/bin/tnslsnr LISTENER
     -inherit
oracle 308 304 0 12:03:28 pts/2 0:00 -ksh
oracle 352 308 0 12:11:23 pts/2 0:00 grep ora
oracle 318 1 0 12:04:19 ? 0:01 ora_pmon_labman
oracle 320 1 0 12:04:20 ? 0:00 ora_dbw0_labman
oracle 322 1 0 12:04:21 ? 0:00 ora_lgwr_labman
oracle 324 1 0 12:04:22 ? 0:01 ora_ckpt_labman
oracle 326 1 0 12:04:22 ? 0:01 ora_smon_labman
oracle 328 1 0 12:04:23 ? 0:00 ora_reco_labman
oracle 330 1 0 12:04:23 ? 0:00 ora_s000_labman
oracle 332 1 0 12:04:24 ? 0:00 ora_d000_labman
$
```

The string after the last underscore in returned text is the database instance name. In the previously shown example, the instance name is labman.

LD_LIBRARY_PATH Variable Not Properly Set

When trying to run **sqlplus**, **sqldr**, or **sapx**, you might see an error message resembling the following:

```
libc.so.xxx: can't do something
```

This usually indicates that ORACLE_HOME/lib is not part of your LD_LIBRARY_PATH environment variable. To correct the problem, you need to add ORACLE_HOME/lib to your LD_LIBRARY_PATH environment variable.

You can configure your profile to add ORACLE_HOME/lib to your LB_LIBRARY_PATH every time that you log on to the system. If you are running either a Bourne (**sh**) or Korn (**ksh**) shell, you need to ensure that your $HOME/.profile contains the following entries:

```
LD_LIBRARY_PATH=$LD_LIBRARY_PATH:$ORACLE_HOME/lib
export LD_LIBRARAY_PATH
```

NOTE	If you use a shell other than **ksh** or **sh**, the lines above must be translated into the appropriate scripting language and placed in the appropriate startup file.

Oracle Fails to Authorize Connection

When trying to run sqlplus, sqldr, or sapx, you might see the following error message:

```
ERROR: ORA-12154: TNS: could not resolve service name
```

This error indicates that Oracle cannot understand the name specified in your connect string. To correct this problem, follow these steps:

Step 1 Ensure that the Oracle file tnsnames.ora resides in its proper location (usually $ORACLE_HOME/admin/network).

Step 2 Check its format.

Step 3 Use the **tnsping** utility to test sqlnet connectivity to your remote database.

Oracle Returns a User/Password Error

When trying to run **sqlplus**, **sqldr**, or **sapx**, you might see a TNS or USER/PASSWORD error message. This indicates that you are using an improper connect string. If you are specifying the password on the command line, use the following command:

```
sqlplus user/password@host
```

You also can use the following command:

```
sqlplus user@host
```

By leaving the password off of the command line, **sqlplus** will prompt you to enter the password.

Data Management Package Problems

Your data management package handles many items, including e-mail notifications of alarm events. When using your RDBMS, you might experience difficulties when attempting to retrieve data. Some of the problems that you might encounter during the use of an RDBMS include the following:

- SQL queries do not display data.
- SQL queries do not display correct data.
- No mail notifications sent.
- Database loader fails.

SQL Queries Do Not Display Data

If your SQL queries do not return any data, you might be incorrectly specifying the query. Retry the query using a percentage as your wildcard character.

SQL Queries Do Not Display Correct Data

If you specify @event1, @space1, @time1, or @system1 at the SQLPLUS prompt, you do not receive the proper data. SAP 1.3x requires that you specify @event, @space, @time, or @system. You then are prompted for the desired drill-down level (1, 2, 3, and so on).

No Mail Notifications Sent

If all indications show that successful notifications are happening but your mail notifications are not received, your **mailx** program might not be invokable through the command line. To debug this problem, you need to check several items.

First, you need to ensure that mail can be sent from the command line by using the **mailx** command to send a mail message to yourself. If the mail message is not sent, you need to configure two things:

- Domain name
- Mail server host

To set your domain name, you can use the following command:

```
Domainname <your domain name>
```

NOTE   On Solaris, you can directly add the name of your domain to the /etc/defaultdomain file

---

In addition to having your domain name configured correctly, you need to add your mail server to your /etc/hosts file. The format for the entry in your /etc/hosts file follows:

```
IP Address   Server Name    mailhost
```

In this case, the IP address is the IP address of your mail server and the server name is its DNS name.

Database Loader Fails

If you do not use the NT Oracle 8 database server, you might experience the sapx database loader failing with a JDBC-related error message (ora-1461). To bypass this error, you have three possible options:

- Bypass the default sapx loader by using the alternate loading templates in /usr/nr/bin/sap/sql/skel.

- Use a UNIX Ora7 or Ora8 server. Cisco has successfully tested the server software on Solaris Sparc, x86, and HP-UX.

- Upgrade to NT Ora 8.0.4.0.0 to at least 8.0.4.0.4. This upgrade should solve the JDBC problems, but has not been tested.

nrConfigure Problems

The Configuration Management Utility is known as *nrConfigure*. This program enables you to configure your sensors via your CSIDD. You might encounter the following couple of problems when working with nrConfigure:

- nrConfigure startup problems
- HP-UX performance problems

nrConfigure Startup Problems

During the initial startup, nrConfigure might cause a *core dump*. If this happens, you need to just restart nrConfigure and it will usually restart without an error.

Core Dump

When a program on a UNIX system crashes, it dumps a copy of the current memory contents to a file that is called a *core dump*. This file is named core and is usually written to the directory from which the program is invoked. You can use this file in conjunction with a debugger to determine why the program crashed.

HP-UX Performance Problems

nrConfigure can run slowly on some HP machines. This is because of the lack of availability of a reliable JIT Java Compiler on HP-UX. You can aggravate the problem by initiating actions several times through the sluggish interface. For example, rapid successive mouse clicks can lead to unexpected behavior by nrConfigure. In other examples, scrolling might generate Java errors. Sometimes the Java application screen might crash.

In all of these cases, you probably need to just rerun nrConfigure and repeat your steps with more patience and no extra mouse clicks.

Online Help and NSDB

When launching the NSDB or online help, a new HTML browser window might appear, instead of refreshing the existing HTML browser window. This behavior is controlled by your HTML browser configuration.

If you use Netscape, you can configure Cisco Secure IDS to load all HTML pages into a single browser window by performing the following steps:

Step 1 Open the /usr/nr/etc/nrConfigure.conf file in a text editor.

Step 2 Change the value of the Browser token to the following value:

```
Browser=/usr/nr/bin/director/nrSingleBrowser
```

Step 3 Change the value of the NetscapeLocation token to the following value:

```
NetscapeLocation=/opt/netscape/netscape
```

Step 4 Save your changes and close the editing session.

Cisco Secure IDS Log Files

While monitoring your network for intrusive activity, your Cisco Secure IDS generates a wealth of information. This information is stored in various text files on the different Cisco Secure IDS components. Understanding where these files are located and how they are structured helps with troubleshooting. Furthermore, this information proves useful if you plan to develop your own scripts to pull information from these log files.

Your Cisco Secure IDS generates a lot of information, in conjunction with the expected alarm events. This information is stored in different files on the Cisco Secure IDS components. This appendix examines the following facets of the storage process:

- Levels of logging
- Log file naming conventions
- Log file locations
- Closing active files
- Archived log files
- Event record fields

Levels of Logging

Events are the most well-known items logged by Cisco Secure IDS. The goal of any IDS is to detect intrusive activity and generate alarms when an attack is identified. These alarms, however, represent only one of four types of logging performed by Cisco Secure IDS. The four types of logging provided by Cisco Secure IDS are the following:

- Events (alarms)
- Errors
- Commands
- IP sessions

Events, or alarms, were discussed in the preceding paragraph. Errors, the second item in this list, provide a useful source of troubleshooting information. Whenever a service on one of your Cisco Secure IDS components generates an error, this information is stored as an entry in an error log file. If your Cisco Secure IDS is not functioning correctly, you can save a lot of time by examining your error log file first.

Whenever a Cisco Secure IDS service performs a specific command, this information is also logged, indicating which service executed a command and for whom, as well as other information. This is the third item in the list.

Finally, you can instruct your Cisco Secure IDS to save information on IP sessions that trigger specific alarm signatures. This is the fourth item in the list.

Log File Naming Conventions

Understanding where log files are stored enables you to locate them when needed. Each log filename also indicates information about the contents of the log file along with an indication of when the file was created. Each file type is discussed.

IP Log File

The format for the naming of IP log files conforms to a standard structure that identifies when the file was created. Furthermore, the **iplog** prefix indicates that the file is an IP log file. By understanding this naming format, you can easily determine when a specific log file was created. The structure is

`iplog.XXX.XXX.XXX.XXX.YYYYMMDDHHMM`

where the filename is constructed as follows:

- **iplog**—Keyword identifying the file as a Cisco Secure IDS IP log session file
- *XXX.XXX.XXX.XXX*—The IP address of the attacking host
- *YYYY*—Year the file was created
- *MM*—Month the file was created
- *DD*—Day the file was created
- *HH*—Hour the file was created (using a 24-hour clock)
- *MM*—Minute of the hour the file was created

An example Cisco Secure IDS log file is

`iplog.10.0.0.84.200101301103`

iplog indicates a Cisco Secure IDS IP session log. The IP address of the attacking host is 10.0.0.84. The file was created on January 30, 2001, at 11:03 a.m.

Cisco Secure IDS Log Files

The format for the naming of Cisco Secure IDS log files conforms to a standard structure that identifies them as a Cisco Secure IDS log file and also indicates when the file was created. By understanding this naming format, you can easily determine when a specific log file was created. The structure is

`log.`*YYYYMMDDHHMM*

where the filename is constructed as follows:

* **log**—Keyword identifying the file as a Cisco Secure IDS log file
* *YYYY*—Year the file was created
* *MM*—Month the file was created
* *DD*—Day the file was created
* *HH*—Hour the file was created (using a 24-hour clock)
* *MM*—Minute of the hour the file was created

An example of a Cisco Secure IDS log file is

`log.200101301640`

The **log** prefix indicates a Cisco Secure IDS log. The file was created on January 30, 2001, at 4:40 p.m.

Service Error Log Files

The format for the naming of Service Error log files conforms to a standard structure that identifies which service generated the file. By understanding this naming format, you can easily determine which service generated an error. The structure is

`error.service.processID`

where the filename is constructed as follows:

* **error**—Keyword identifying it as a Cisco Secure IDS Service Error log file
* **service**—Cisco Secure IDS service name
* **processID**—Numeric value of the service process identification number

An example of a Cisco Secure IDS Service Error log file is

`errors.managed.928`

The **errors** prefix indicates a Cisco Secure IDS error log file. The service that generated the error was **managed**. The process identification at the time of the error was **928**.

Log File Locations

The active Cisco Secure IDS log file is located in /usr/nr/var. Each Cisco Secure IDS service maintains its own Service Error log file and is located in /usr/nr/var. The IP log files are located in /usr/nr/var/iplog. Refer to Appendix B, "Cisco Secure IDS Architecture," to see how these file locations fit into the overall file structure of Cisco Secure IDS. Logging information is stored in different types of log files, such as Cisco Secure IDS log files, Service Error log files, and IP log files, and each file type is stored in a different location.

Closing Active Files

For manageability, log files must be closed periodically and a new log file opened. Two factors trigger creation of a new log file:

- File size
- Time threshold

Whenever a log file grows too large, or has been open too long, the active log file is closed and archived. To replace the archived file, a new log file is created.

By default, log files are archived and a new one created when the active log reaches 1 GB or after 60 minutes, whichever comes first. If necessary, you can change the default values to match your requirements by modifying tokens in the loggerd.conf file (see Appendix B).

IP log files, however, remain active for 30 minutes or until the session that triggered the IP log action is terminated. You can lengthen the default value of 30 minutes to match your operational needs.

Archived Log Files

Archived log files are stored in two different locations:

- /usr/nr/var/new
- /usr/nr/var/iplog/new

Cisco Secure IDS archived log and error log files are stored in /usr/nr/var/new, whereas archived IP session log files are stored in /usr/nr/var/iplog/new. When searching through log files, these two directories hold all the information that is not part of the current active log files.

Event Record Fields

Each entry in a Cisco Secure IDS log file represents some event that happened. To understand these events, you must understand the different fields that make up an event record. Each event record is a list of fields delimited by commas. The following two record types are explained in this appendix:

- Alarm event records
- Command log records

Alarm Event Record

Table D-1 lists and explains the fields that make up an event record.

Table D-1   *Event Record Fields*

Field	Description
Record Type	4
Record ID	Numeric value indicating the record number. The value begins at 1,000,000 each time the packetd process is started and is incremented by one.
GMT Date Stamp	Greenwich Mean Time date stamp when the record was generated. Format is YYYY/MM/DD.
GMT Timestamp	Greenwich Mean Time timestamp when the record was generated. Format is HH:MM:SS.
Local Date Stamp	Local date stamp when the record was generated. Format is YYYY/MM/DD.
Local Timestamp	Local timestamp when the record was generated. Format is HH:MM:SS.
Application ID	Cisco Secure IDS service that generated the record. Possible values are as follows:
	10000—postofficed
	10003—managed
	10004—eventd
	10005—loggerd
	10006—smid
	10007—sapd
	10008—packetd
	10009—fileXferd
	10010—iosids
	20001—CSPM
Host ID	PostOffice host identification of the Cisco Secure IDS component that was the source of the record.

continues

Table D-1 *Event Record Fields (Continued)*

Field	Description
Organization ID	PostOffice organization identification of the Cisco Secure IDS component that was the source of the record.
Source Location	The location of the attacking host that caused the record to be generated. The keywords **IN** and **OUT** specify whether the host was inside or outside the defined internal network.
Destination Location	The location of the target host that was the destination of the attack. The keywords **IN** and **OUT** specify whether the host was inside or outside the defined internal network.
Alarm Level	Numeric value of the Cisco Secure IDS alarm severity level. Default Severity values are as follows: 1—Low 3—Medium 5—High
Signature ID	Cisco Secure IDS signature identification number.
Subsignature ID	Cisco Secure IDS subsignature identification associated with the signature identification.
Protocol	TCP/IP is the only protocol supported by Cisco Secure IDS.
Source IP Address	The IP address of the attacking host that caused the record to be generated.
Destination IP Address	The IP address of the target host that was the destination of the attack.
Source Port	Numeric value of the TCP/UDP source port.
Destination Port	Numeric value of the TCP/UDP destination port.
Data Source IP Address	IP Address of a Cisco IOS router that is sending syslog messages to this sensor. The value 0.0.0.0 signifies that the sensor detected the attack.
Optional Event Detail	Additional information associated with certain Cisco Secure IDS signatures.
Optional Event Context	Additional data associated with Cisco Secure IDS signatures.

The majority of the event records are alarm entries. The following is a sample Alarm record. Table D-2 explains the record.

```
4,1000010,2001/01/30,17:03:47,2001/01/30,11:03:47,10008,8,100,OUT,IN,5,8000,
2302,TCP/IP,10.0.0.84,172.30.1.208,1045,23,0.0.0.0,/etc/shadow,
FFFD01FFFD03FFFB0161…0080073776964733E202F6574632F736861646F6F
```

Table D-2   *Breakdown of Sample Event Record*

Field Value	Field Description
4	Event (alarm) record.
1000010	The event record number generated by Cisco Secure IDS.
2001/01/30	The record was generated January 30, 2001.
17:03:47	The record was generated at 5:03:47 p.m. GMT.
2001/01/30	The record was generated January 30, 2001.
11:03:47	The record was generated at 11:03:47 a.m. local time.
10008	packetd generated the event.
8	This is the host identification of the sensor or Director that generated the log record.
100	This is the organization identification of the sensor or Director that generated the log record.
OUT	The source of the attack was outside the defined internal networks.
IN	The destination of the attack was inside the defined internal networks.
5	The alarm has a High severity level.
8000	The Cisco Secure IDS signature that triggered was a string signature.
2302	The Cisco Secure IDS string subsignature identification associated with matching /etc/shadow.
TCP/IP	Indicates TCP/IP network traffic.
10.0.0.84	The source IP address that triggered the event.
172.30.1.208	The destination IP address of the triggered event.
1045	The source port number of the network traffic that triggered the event.
23	The destination port of the attacking host.
0.0.0.0	The sensor specified by the recorded host and organization identification that detected this event.
/etc/shadow	The string /etc/shadow triggered the logging of this event.
FFFD01FFFD03FFFB0161. . . 0080073776964733E202F6574632F73 6861646F6F	Provides detailed context data associated with the signature detected.

NOTE   The detailed context data provides an indication of the traffic that occurred after (and potentially before) the alarm that triggered. This information is presented in hexadecimal notation. To view this data, you must convert the data using a hex data translator.

Command Log Record Fields

When a Cisco Secure IDS service executes a command, it logs this information in a Command log record. The information logged includes the service that executed the command and the service that requested the command to be executed, along with a wealth of other information. Table D-3 lists and explains the fields that make up a Command log record.

Table D-3   *Command Log Record Fields*

Field	Description
Record Type	3
Record ID	Numeric value indicating the record number. The value begins at one for each application every time Cisco Secure IDS is started and is incremented by one. For example, managed and postofficed Command log records both start at one and increment each time the respective service generates a record.
GMT Date Stamp	Greenwich Mean Time date stamp when the record was generated. Format is YYYY/MM/DD.
GMT Timestamp	Greenwich Mean Time timestamp when the record was generated. Format is HH:MM:SS.
Local Date Stamp	Local date stamp when the record was generated. Format is YYYY/MM/DD.
Local Timestamp	Local timestamp when the record was generated. Format is HH:MM:SS.
Application ID	Cisco Secure IDS service that executed the command:
	10000—postofficed
	10003—managed
	10004—eventd
	10005—loggerd
	10006—smid
	10007—sapd
	10008—packetd
	10009—fileXferd
	10010—iosids
	20001—CSPM

Table D-3　*Command Log Record Fields (Continued)*

Field	Description
Host ID	PostOffice host identification of the Cisco Secure IDS component that was the source of the record.
Organization ID	PostOffice organization identification of the Cisco Secure IDS component that was the source of the record.
Application ID	Cisco Secure IDS service that requested the command's execution: 10000—postofficed 10003—managed 10004—eventd 10005—loggerd 10006—smid 10007—sapd 10008—packetd 10009—fileXferd 10010—iosids 20001—CSPM
Host ID	PostOffice host identification of the Cisco Secure IDS component that requested the command's execution.
Organization ID	PostOffice organization identification of the Cisco Secure IDS component that requested the command's execution.
Command	The command executed.

A sample Command log record is

```
3,24,2001/01/30,17:18:35,2001/01/30,11:18:35,10003,8,100,20001,84,100,
EXEC ShunNet 171.69.2.0 255.255.255.0 1440
```

Table D-4 breaks lists and explains the various components of the Command log record.

Table D-4　*Breakdown of Sample Command Log Record*

Field Value	Field Description
3	Command log record.
24	The Command log record number generated by managed.
2001/01/30	The record was generated January 30, 2001.
17:18:35	The record was generated at 5:18:35 p.m. GMT.

continues

Table D-4 *Breakdown of Sample Command Log Record (Continued)*

Field Value	Field Description
2001/01/30	The record was generated January 30, 2001.
11:18:35	The record was generated at 11:18:35 a.m. local time.
10003	managed generated the record.
8	This is the host identification of the sensor or Director that generated the log record.
100	This is the organization identification of the sensor or Director that generated the log record.
20001	Identification number identifying CSPM as the service requesting the command's execution.
84	This is the host identification of the sensor or Director that requested the command's execution.
100	This is the organization identification of the sensor or Director that requested the command's execution.
EXEC ShunNet 171.69.2.0 255.255.255.0 1440	The Cisco Secure IDS component issued a **Block** command to block the network 171.69.2.0 for 1 day.

Advanced Tips

This appendix covers several situations that you might encounter while operating your Cisco Secure IDS, including the following:

- Correcting a sensor that does not sniff
- Using the sensor COM port for console access
- Excluding false-positive alarms

Correcting a Sensor That Does Not Sniff

Your Cisco Secure IDS Sensors form the foundation of your Cisco Secure IDS. If a sensor is not collecting traffic on its monitoring interface, your IDS is blind and cannot see any attacks against your network.

Understanding how to troubleshoot a sensor that does not sniff is an important skill that can help you get your Cisco Secure IDS operational again as quickly as possible. The trouble-shooting process involves the following steps:

- Verify severity of attack scenarios.
- Check packetd process.
- Verify that the monitoring interface is actually seeing network traffic.
- Check the log file to see whether events are being detected.
- Make sure the Director and sensor are communicating.
- Check the sensor's /usr/nr/etc/destinations file to ensure that smid is a defined destination.
- Check whether smid is running on the Director.
- Check the error logs on the Director and sensor.
- Call the Cisco Technical Assistance Center.

Verify Severity of Attack Scenarios

The first step in verifying the operation of your sensor is to generate traffic on your network that triggers alarms on your sensor. Your attacks and test scenarios, however, need to generate alarms with a severity level of 3 or higher.

The default Cisco Secure IDS configuration displays only alarms with a severity level of 3 or higher as an icon or alarm entry on your Director. To view signature severity levels with CSPM, you need to examine your sensor's signature template. (Refer to Chapter 12, "Signature and Intrusion Detection Configuration," for more information on signature templates.)

NOTE	To view signature severity levels with CSIDD, look in the nrConfigure General Signatures dialog box. You can find the currently configured alarm severity level in the Director smid column.

If you have a Windows NT or 95 system on the network, you can use the **ping** command to generate alarms that display on the Director.

You need to enter the following command on your system:

```
ping -l 20000 [IP Address]
```

This **ping** command generates Fragmented ICMP (Signature ID 2150) and Large ICMP (Signature ID 2151) alarms if everything is functioning correctly. If you still don't see any alarms, you need to verify that the packetd daemon is running.

Check the packetd Process

The packetd process performs the actual analysis of traffic on your network (see Appendix B, "Cisco Secure IDS Architecture"). Therefore, you need to confirm that the packetd process is running on the sensor. If it is not running, your sensor cannot examine any network traffic.

To check the Cisco Secure IDS processes currently running on the sensor, you need to log in to the sensor and run **nrstatus** as user netrangr, as follows:

```
netrangr@sensor:/usr/nr
>nrstatus
netrangr 1538    1 0  Jan 29 ?      0:06 /usr/nr/bin/nr.loggerd
netrangr 1404    1 0  Jan 29 console 1:22 /usr/nr/bin/nr.postofficed -r 5000
100 239
netrangr 1565    1 0  Jan 29 console 0:01 /usr/nr/bin/nr.fileXferd
netrangr 1555    1 0  Jan 29 ?      0:00 /usr/nr/bin/nr.sapd
netrangr 1539    1 0  Jan 29 ?      0:00 /usr/nr/bin/nr.configd
netrangr 1596    1 0  Jan 29 ?      0:29 /usr/nr/bin/nr.packetd
```

If the **nrstatus** output contains an entry that lists nr.packetd, the packetd process is running. If packetd is running, you can proceed to the next section where you determine whether the monitoring traffic is actually seeing network traffic.

If packetd is not running, a misconfigured sniffing Network Interface Name entered during the Sensor Add Host process is often the cause. To check the configured Network Interface Name, you need to use the **grep** command to locate the name of your sensor's monitoring interface in the /usr/nr/etc/packetd.conf file. The monitoring interface is defined with the NameOfPacketDevice token:

```
netrangr@sensor:/usr/nr/etc
>grep NameOfPacketDevice /usr/nr/etc/packetd.conf
NameOfPacketDevice /dev/spwr0
```

Depending on the sensor appliance you have, you see one of the interfaces listed in Table E-1.

Table E-1   *Sensor Monitoring Interfaces*

Network You Use	NameOfPacketDevice
Ethernet (2E)	/dev/spwr0
Fast Ethernet (2FE)	/dev/spwr0
Token Ring (TR)	/dev/mtok0
FDDI (SFDDI or DFDDI)	/dev/ptpci0

If your configured interface does not match your network, you need to go back to your Director and correct the name of the packet device in the sensor configuration (see Chapter 11 "Sensor Configuration Within CSPM").

NOTE   For CSIDD, you need to go back on the Director, correct the name of the packet device in the Data Sources tab in the intrusion detection configuration for the sensor and apply the new configuration.

After updating your sensor's configuration, you need to run **nrstatus** on the sensor again to verify that packetd is running. If packetd is running, try your attacks again and see whether you start seeing alarms. If you still don't see any alarms, or if packetd is still not running, go to the next section where you verify that the monitoring interface is actually seeing network traffic.

Verify That the Monitoring Interface Is Actually Seeing Network Traffic

You can manually put the sniffing interface into Promiscuous mode to see whether the interface is seeing network traffic by using the Solaris **snoop** command. The syntax for the **snoop** command is as follows:

```
snoop -d [name_of_interface] .
```

NOTE The *name of interface* matches the name listed in Table E-1 without the leading /dev/.

You also need to switch to the root user to run the **snoop** command. After placing your interface into Promiscuous mode, you see network traffic being displayed. Finally, you use Ctrl-C to break out of the **snoop** command. A sample listing of these steps follows:

```
netrangr@sensor:/usr/nr
>su -
Password:
Sun Microsystems Inc.   SunOS 5.6    Generic August 1997

# snoop -d spwr0
Using device /dev/spwr (promiscuous mode)
   10.1.10.1 -> 224.0.0.10  IP D=224.0.0.10 S=10.1.10.1 LEN=60, ID=0
       ? -> (multicast) ETHER Type=0020 (LLC/802.3), size = 320 bytes
       ? -> *        ETHER Type=9000 (Loopback), size = 60 bytes
   10.1.10.1 -> 224.0.0.10  IP D=224.0.0.10 S=10.1.10.1 LEN=60, ID=0
^C
```

If you still do not see any network traffic, check your connections and cabling and try again. If you see network traffic, you can proceed to examining your log files to see whether any events are being detected.

Check the Log File to See Whether Events Are Being Detected

The active Cisco Secure IDS log file is located in the /usr/nr/var directory. (See Appendix D, "Cisco Secure IDS Log Files," for more information on Cisco Secure IDS log files.) The easiest way to see whether events are being detected is to open and watch the log file while running your sample attacks to see what is being logged. Use **tail -f /usr/nr/var/log*** to open and watch the log file while you rerun your attacks or tests to see whether event records are being appended. Use Ctrl-C to break out of the **tail** command:

```
netrangr@sensor:/usr/nr/var
>tail -f log*
4,1007470,1999/02/02,00:01:29,1999/02/01,18:01:29,10008,200,5000,OUT,IN,1,3000,23,
TCP/IP,10.1.10.20,10.1.9.201,1040,23,0.0.0.0,292107839
4,1007471,1999/02/02,00:01:36,1999/02/01,18:01:36,10008,200,5000,OUT,IN,1,3000,23,
TCP/IP,10.1.10.20,10.1.9.201,1040,23,0.0.0.0,292107839
4,1007472,1999/02/02,00:01:49,1999/02/01,18:01:49,10008,200,5000,OUT,IN,1,3000,2
^C
```

NOTE   Beginning with Cisco Secure IDS version 2.2.1.5, the logging was changed to a memory mapped log file. You cannot use the **tail -f** command with this memory-mapped format because you do not see anything. Instead, you must repeatedly issue the **tail /usr/nr/var/log*** command to view snapshots of the end of the log file.

If new event records are being appended to the log file, and you still do not see any alarm entries or icons, look at the severity Level in the event records. The severity level is the 12th field in the record (see Appendix D). If the severity level is 1 or 2, you need to go back to the beginning and generate alarm traffic with a severity level of 3 or higher. If the severity level is 3 or higher, you need to make sure that your Director and your sensor are communicating correctly.

Make Sure the Director and Sensor Are Communicating

Cisco Secure IDS components use the PostOffice protocol to communicate with each other and to forward alarm information. You can check PostOffice connection status between the sensor and the Director by using the **nrconns** command on your sensor. You see [Established] on each component connection status line.

```
netrangr@sensor:/usr/nr
>nrconns
Connection Status for sensor.cisco
     director.cisco Connection 1: 10.1.9.200    45000 1 [Established]
sto:0000 with Version 1
```

If you do not see the [Established] field in the **nrconns** output, check the /usr/nr/etc/routes file to make sure that your sensor knows how to communicate with the Director. If the Director entry exists (see the bold line in the following sample routes file), make sure the Director IP address is correct. If the Director entry does not exist in the routes file or if the IP address is wrong, add it to the sensor configuration through nrConfigure on the Director. (See "Configuring the System Files" in the *Cisco Secure IDS Users Guide*.)

```
netrangr@sensor:/usr/nr
>more /usr/nr/etc/routes
#--------------------------------------------------------------
# routes
#
# This file contains the listing of routes used by nr.postofficed
# to transport messages between different hosts. Entries are made
#in the form of:
#
# <hostname> <connection#> <IPaddress> <UdpPort> <Type> [<Heartbeat Seconds>]
#
# nr.postofficed will always try to use the lowest connection
# number to transport messages to the remote host. The IP address
# and port number provide the endpoint of communications to the
# remote system.
#--------------------------------------------------------------
sensor.cisco 1 10.1.9.201 45000 1
director.cisco 1 10.1.9.200 45000 1
```

If the Director entry exists and the IP address is correct, see whether you can ping the Director, and start checking cables and routing on the command and control subnet.

If you have connectivity with the Director and you still do not see alarms, you need to verify that the destinations file contains an entry for the smid process on your Director

Check the Sensor's /usr/nr/etc/destinations File to Ensure That smid Is a Defined Destination

The /usr/nr/etc/destinations file on your sensor configures the locations to which your sensor forwards alarm entries. It also configures the minimum severity level. Only alarms (EVENTS) that exceed this minimum severity level forward to each destination. To view the destinations file, you can use the **more** command. A sample viewing of the destinations file follows:

```
netrangr@sensor:/usr/nr
>more /usr/nr/etc/destinations
#-----------------------------------------------------------------
# destinations
#
# This file contains the destinations for the data generated by Cisco Secure IDS.
# Each entry is in the form of:
#
# <ID> <hostname> <service> <minlevel> <datatype>[,<datatype>...]
#
# Valid IDs are in the range of 1-32 for the 32 supported destinations.
# Events must have a level of 'minlevel' or higher or they will not be
# transmitted. The type of data sent are enumerated in the comma separated
# list. Valid data types are:
#
# ERRORS    Cisco Secure IDS errors. Default level is 1.
# COMMANDS  Log of commands sent to Cisco Secure IDS daemons. Default level is 1.
# EVENTS    Events generated by nr.sensord. Default levels in sensord.conf.
# IPLOGS    Binary IP data generated by nr.sensord. Default level is 1.
#-----------------------------------------------------------------

1 sensor.cisco loggerd 1 ERRORS,COMMANDS,EVENTS,IPLOGS
2 director.cisco smid 2 EVENTS,ERRORS,COMMANDS
```

If the Director smid entry does not exist in the destinations file, add it to the sensor configuration through nrConfigure on the Director.

If the smid entry exists in the destinations file, you need to verify that the smid process is running on the Director.

Check Whether smid Is Running on the Director

The smid process handles the display of alarm information on your Director. If smid is not running, you cannot see alarms on your Director. The process that you use to check whether smid is running varies between the two Director platforms. Therefore, each Director platform is explained separately.

CSPM

CSPM does not have an **nrstatus** command that displays the Cisco Secure IDS processes that are currently running. Instead, you need to verify that smid is running by bringing up the Task Manager. You can bring up the Task Manager by first pressing the Ctl-Alt-Del keys simultaneously. This displays a Windows NT Security dialog box, as shown in Figure E-1.

Figure E-1 *Windows NT Security Dialog Box*

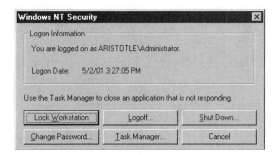

From the Windows NT Security dialog box, click the **Task Manager** button. This displays the Windows NT Task Manager window (see Figure E-2).

Figure E-2 *Windows NT Task Manager Window*

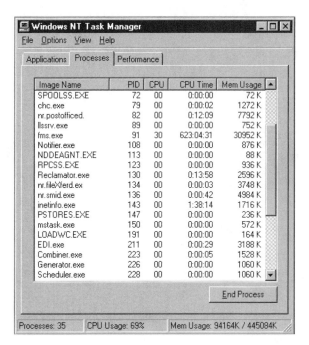

In the task manager process listing, you need to look for a process named nr.smid.exe. If you don't see it, smid is not running. You need to open the Services window and restart the smid process. If smid is running and you still do not see alarms, proceed to checking your error log files.

Cisco Secure ID Director

Run **nrstatus** on the Director and look for the nr.smid line in the output. If you don't see it, smid is not running. Try restarting it by running **nrstop** and then **nrstart**. Run **nrstatus** again and see whether smid has started up. If smid is running and you still do not see alarms, proceed to checking your error log files.

The following sample output is from the **nrstatus** command:

```
netrangr@director:/usr/nr
>nrstatus
netrangr  857   1 0 14:31:33 ?    0:02 /usr/nr/bin/nr.loggerd
netrangr  903   1 0 14:31:35 ?    0:01 /usr/nr/bin/nr.smid
netrangr  864   1 0 14:31:33 ?    0:01 /usr/nr/bin/nr.configd -r 59
netrangr  878   1 0 14:31:34 ?    0:29 /usr/nr/bin/nr.sapd
netrangr  690   1 0 14:31:25 ?    0:53 /usr/nr/bin/nr.postofficed -r 500
0 100 59
netrangr  889   1 0 14:31:34 ?    0:09 /usr/nr/bin/nr.fileXferd
```

Check the Error Logs on the Director and Sensor

The error log files are located in the /usr/nr/var directory on both the sensor and CSIDD. (For CSPM, the directory is \Program Files\Cisco Systems\var.) An error file exists for each Cisco Secure IDS daemon, and the files are named errors.*daemon_name* (see Appendix D). If the file has a 0 length or doesn't exist, there were no logged errors for that service.

This following listing is a sample directory listing of the /usr/nr/var directory:

```
netrangr@sensor:/usr/nr/var
>ls -l
total 1934
drwxr-x---  2 netrangr netrangr   512 Dec 23 11:18 dump/
-rw-r--r--  1 netrangr netrangr     0 Feb  3 09:01 errors.configd
-rw-r--r--  1 netrangr netrangr  4056 Feb  3 09:00 errors.fileXferd
-rw-r--r--  1 netrangr netrangr     0 Feb  3 09:01 errors.loggerd
-rw-r--r--  1 netrangr netrangr  1454 Jan 19 18:01 errors.nrping
-rw-r--r--  1 netrangr netrangr   360 Feb  2 17:20 errors.packetd
-rw-r--r--  1 netrangr netrangr   512 Feb  3 14:37 errors.postofficed
-rw-r--r--  1 netrangr netrangr   256 Jan 29 13:13 errors.sapd
drwxr-x---  2 netrangr netrangr   512 Dec 23 11:17 evidence/
drwxr-x---  2 netrangr netrangr   512 Jan 19 10:14 iplog/
-rw-r--r--  1 netrangr netrangr 38092 Feb  4 11:02 log.199902040902
drwx------  2 root     root     8192 Dec 23 10:31 lost+found/
drwxr-x---  2 netrangr netrangr  5632 Feb  4 09:02 new/
-rw-r--r--  1 root     other   63443 Dec 23 11:20 nrInstall.log
-rw-r--r--  1 root     other  230863 Dec 23 11:16 sensorConfig.log
drwxr-x---  2 netrangr netrangr   512 Dec 23 11:17 tmp/
-rw-r--r--  1 root     other   41486 Dec 23 11:24 verifySensor.log
```

The error files are ASCII text files (human readable) and can be viewed using the **more** command. The syntax for the more command is as follows:

```
more [filename]
```

Viewing these error logs usually provides useful troubleshooting information. Output from a couple of sample error log files follows:

```
netrangr@sensor:/usr/nr/var
>more errors.packetd
02/02/1999 23:20:44UTC E Cannot write message to postoffice
02/02/1999 23:20:45UTC E Cannot write message to postoffice
02/02/1999 23:20:47UTC E Cannot write message to postoffice

netrangr@sensor:/usr/nr/var
>more errors.postofficed

12/29/1998 17:58:24UTC E Network connect using connection 1 to destination
[100.5000]
01/04/1999 14:31:03UTC E Network connect using connection 1 to destination
[100.5000]
01/04/1999 14:31:04UTC E Cannot write message to ApplID [10005] 2 10000 fd 1 sent -
1 exp 124 errno 96 .Destination address required.
01/04/1999 15:18:39UTC E Network connect using connection 1 to destination
[100.5000]
```

Call Cisco Technical Assistance Center

If you attempted all of these steps without success, it's probably time to contact the Cisco Technical Assistance Center (TAC). The TAC Web site (http://www.cisco.com/public/support/tac/home.shtml) provides a wealth of information for troubleshooting problems with Cisco equipment. Furthermore, through the TAC Web site, you can open a trouble case or determine the phone number of the TAC for your area so that you can talk with an expert who can help you locate the source of your problem.

Using the Sensor COM Port for Console Access

On occasion, you need to log directly into a sensor. Initializing a Sensor, for example, requires you to log in to your sensor and run the **sysconfig-sensor** utility as the user *root*. Other tasks requiring you to log in to a sensor include updating signatures, changing the sensor IP address, and troubleshooting certain errors. You can log in to your sensor in one of three ways:

- Through a directly connected keyboard and monitor
- By telneting into the sensor
- Connecting a laptop or PC to the COM port on the sensor and using a communications package

Connecting to your sensor through the first two methods is fairly self-explanatory. Therefore, this section concentrates on the third method. The discussion is divided into the following subtopics:

- root login limitation
- Cable requirement
- Connecting a laptop to the sensor
- Configuring HyperTerminal or another communications package

root Login Limitation

With Cisco Secure IDS, all new sensors are configured at the factory to require you to change the netrangr and root user passwords after the initial login. In addition, you can log in only with the root account at the designated system console, which is the directly connected keyboard and monitor.

If you telnet or log in through the COM port, you have to log in as user netrangr and use the switch user **(su)** command to change to the user root. The combination of the password expiration and only allowing direct root login at the system console requires you to log in through a directly connected keyboard and monitor the first time. After you change the root password, you can log in and switch the user to root when using Telnet or a directly connected laptop. This initial login limitation will be addressed in a future version of Cisco Secure IDS.

Cable Requirement

You need a DB-9 to DB-9 null-modem cable to connect a laptop to the COM port on the sensor. This cable is sold as a serial LapLink or File Transfer Cable. Be careful with null-modem adapters/connectors because they do not always work for this application. You need DB-9 female connectors at each end. The following is the setup for the DB-9 to DB-9 null-modem pinout:

```
1 and 6 to 4
2 to 3
3 to 2
4 to 1 and 6
5 to 5
7 to 8
8 to 7
```

Connecting a Laptop to the Sensor

Using the null-modem cable described previously, connect the appropriate COM port on the laptop to the Console port on the sensor. The Console ports on the 4200 Series Appliance Sensors are shown in Chapter 7, "4200 Series Sensor Installation Within CSPM."

Configuring HyperTerminal or Another Communications Package

After you have the laptop and sensor connected together through the null-modem cable, you can bring up your communications package on the laptop. You need to configure the COM port settings as follows:

- 9600 baud
- 8 data bits
- No parity
- 1 Stop bit
- No flow control

Initiate the connection to the sensor and you see a ttya "login:" prompt. Log in as user netranger and su to root if you need to run commands that the user netrangr is unable to execute.

Excluding False-Positive Alarms

Cisco Secure IDS triggers an alarm when a given packet or sequence of packets matches the characteristics of known attack profiles that are defined in the Cisco Secure IDS signatures. Minimizing false positives and false negatives (refer to Chapter 3, "Intrusion Detection Systems,") is a critical design criterion for any intrusion detection system.

Obviously, a large number of false positives can significantly drain resources, and the specialized skills required to analyze them are costly and difficult to find. False negatives, however, occur when the IDS does not detect and report actual malicious activity. The consequence of this can be catastrophic.

Unfortunately, because of the nature of the signatures that IDSs use to detect malicious activity, it is virtually impossible to completely eliminate false positives and false negatives without severely degrading the effectiveness of the IDS and severely disrupting an organization's computing infrastructure (such as hosts and networks). Customized tuning during the deployment of your Cisco Secure IDS, however, minimizes false positives. Periodic retuning is also required as the computing environment changes (for example, deployment of new systems and applications).

Cisco Secure IDS provides a flexible tuning capability that can minimize false positives during steady-state operations. How you tune your Cisco Secure IDS signatures varies between the two different Director platforms:

- CSPM signature filtering
- Cisco Secure ID Director signature tuning

CSPM Signature Filtering

Tuning signatures with CSPM involves filtering the hosts that you want to prevent from triggering specific alarms. You can apply two types of filtering:

- Simple
- Advanced

Filtering with CSPM is explained in detail in Chapter 12.

Cisco Secure ID Director Signature Tuning

Tuning signatures with Cisco Secure ID Director involves using several features. These features are explained in the following sections:

- Using the Exclude Mechanism
- Globally Disabling Signatures
- Temporarily Excluding Alarms

Using the Exclude Mechanism

Cisco Secure IDS provides the capability to exclude a specific signature from or to a specific host or network address. Excluded signatures neither generate alarm icons nor log records when they are triggered from the hosts or networks that are specifically excluded through this mechanism. To exclude a specific host (a source IP address) from generating a specific signature alarm, select the **Excluded Addresses** tab in the Intrusion Detection configuration window of nrConfigure, click **Add**, and fill in the fields.

You might need to set up various exclusions for different hosts on your network. For example, you normally need to set up an exclusion for your network management station because it periodically does network discovery by running ping sweeps, which triggers the ICMP Network Sweep w/Echo signature (Signature ID 2100). Rather than having to analyze the alarm and delete it every time the network discovery process runs, you can exclude it once and not have to deal with the alarm anymore.

You can configure the following two exclusion types:

- Excluded addresses
- Excluded networks

You can use the **Excluded Addresses** tab to exclude specific signatures based on a specific source network address (see Figure E-3). These exclusions allow you to exclude only a host address as the source for triggering a specific signature.

Figure E-3   *Excluded Addresses Dialog Box*

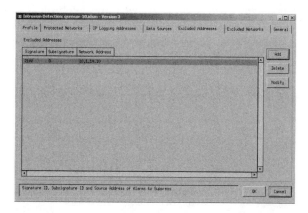

You can use the **Excluded Network** tab to exclude specific signatures based on a specific source or destination network address (see Figure E-4). The Addr Role field enables you to specify whether the defined network address is an alarm source, destination, or both. In addition to specifying networks to exclude, the **Excluded Networks** tab can also be used to exclude individual hosts if you specify a host IP address and use a 32-bit subnet mask.

Figure E-4   *Excluded Networks Dialog Box*

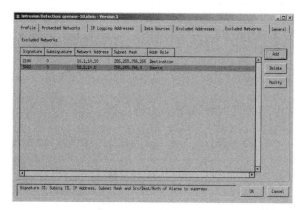

NOTE   Using the **Excluded Networks** tab to exclude hosts enables you to use the Addr Role field to designate the host as an alarm destination, whereas with the Excluded Addresses tab you are limited to only defining alarm sources.

Globally Disabling Signatures

In some instances, you might want to disable a signature from alarming for any host. You can globally disable a signature by specifying a severity level of 0 (zero) in the loggerd and/or smid columns in the General Signatures dialog box (see Figure E-5).

Figure E-5 *General Signatures Dialog Box*

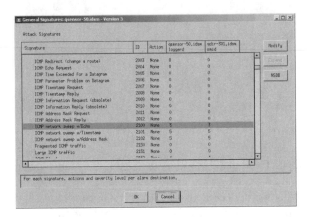

NOTE Disabling signatures with CSPM is explained in Chapter 12.

Temporarily Excluding Alarms

If you right-click an alarm icon (on CSIDD), you notice an **Exclude Alarm** option in the pull-down menu (see Figure E-6). Selecting this option applies an exclusion for that specific signature ID and the source IP address of the alarm in the *running* configuration on the sensor. This exclusion is not written to the sensor configuration files, so it is lost any time the packetd process is restarted (for example, when you apply a new configuration). If you want to make the exclude persistent, you need to use the permanent exclude features described previously. In addition, features to view or delete temporary exclusions do not currently exist, so be careful when using this feature.

Figure E-6   *Exclude Alarm Option*

NOTE   If you mistakenly apply a temporary exclusion (for example, by missing the **Show** option in the pull-down menu), you need to restart packetd on the sensor to remove it. Select the sensor icon in HP OpenView, and then choose **Security**, **Daemons**, **Restart**. You also can right-click the packetd icon in the Machine/Services submap, and choose **Control**, **Stop Daemon**, and then start packetd by selecting **Control**, **Start Daemon**.

Cisco Secure IDS Signature Structures and Implementations

Cisco Secure IDS Signature ID	Cisco Secure IDS Subsignature ID	Cisco Secure IDS Signature Name	Cisco Secure IDS Signature Structure	Cisco Secure IDS Signature Implementation
1000	0	IP options—Bad Option List	Atomic	Context
1001	0	IP options—Record Packet Route	Atomic	Context
1002	0	IP options—Timestamp	Atomic	Context
1003	0	IP options—Provide s, c, h, and tcc	Atomic	Context
1004	0	IP options—Loose Source Route	Atomic	Context
1005	0	IP options—SATNET ID	Atomic	Context
1006	0	IP options—Strict Source Route	Atomic	Context
1100	0	IP Fragment Attack	Atomic	Context
1101	0	Unknown IP Protocol	Atomic	Context
1102	0	Impossible IP Packet	Atomic	Context
1103	0	IP Fragments Overlap	Composite	Context
1104	0	IP Localhost Source Spoof	Atomic	Content
1105	0	Broadcast Source Address	Atomic	Content
1106	0	Multicast IP Source Address	Atomic	Content
1200	0	IP Fragmentation Buffer Full	Atomic	Content
1201	0	IP Fragment Overlap	Atomic	Content
1202	0	IP Fragment Overrun—Datagram Too Long	Atomic	Content
1203	0	IP Fragment Overwrite—Data is Overwritten	Atomic	Content
1204	0	IP Fragment Missing Initial Fragment	Atomic	Content
1205	0	IP Fragment Too Many Datagrams	Atomic	Content

continues

Cisco Secure IDS Signature ID	Cisco Secure IDS Subsignature ID	Cisco Secure IDS Signature Name	Cisco Secure IDS Signature Structure	Cisco Secure IDS Signature Implementation
1206	0	IP Fragment Too Small	Atomic	Content
1207	0	IP Fragment Too Many Frags	Composite	Content
1208	0	IP Fragment Incomplete Datagram	Atomic	Content
1220	0	Jolt2 Fragment Reassembly DoS Attack	Composite	Content
2000	0	ICMP Echo Reply	Atomic	Context
2001	0	ICMP Host Unreachable	Atomic	Context
2002	0	ICMP Source Quench	Atomic	Context
2003	0	ICMP Redirect	Atomic	Context
2004	0	ICMP Echo Request	Atomic	Context
2005	0	ICMP Time Exceeded for a Datagram	Atomic	Context
2006	0	ICMP Parameter Problem on Datagram	Atomic	Context
2007	0	ICMP Timestamp Request	Atomic	Context
2008	0	ICMP Timestamp Reply	Atomic	Context
2009	0	ICMP Information Request	Atomic	Context
2010	0	ICMP Information Reply	Atomic	Context
2011	0	ICMP Address Mask Request	Atomic	Context
2012	0	ICMP Address Mask Reply	Atomic	Context
2100	0	ICMP Network Sweep w/Echo	Composite	Context
2101	0	ICMP Network Sweep w/Timestamp	Composite	Context
2102	0	ICMP Network Sweep w/Address Mask	Composite	Context
2150	0	Fragmented ICMP Traffic	Atomic	Context
2151	0	Large ICMP Traffic	Atomic	Context
2152	0	ICMP Flood	Composite	Context
2153	0	Smurf	Composite	Context
2154	0	Ping of Death Attack	Atomic	Context
3000	0	TCP Ports	Atomic	Context

Cisco Secure IDS Signature ID	Cisco Secure IDS Subsignature ID	Cisco Secure IDS Signature Name	Cisco Secure IDS Signature Structure	Cisco Secure IDS Signature Implementation
3001	0	TCP Port Sweep	Composite	Context
3002	0	TCP SYN Port Sweep	Composite	Context
3003	0	TCP FRAG SYN Port Sweep	Composite	Context
3005	0	TCP FIN Port Sweep	Composite	Context
3006	0	TCP Frag FIN Port Sweep	Composite	Context
3010	0	TCP High Port Sweep	Composite	Context
3011	0	TCP FIN High Port Sweep	Composite	Context
3012	0	TCP Frag FIN High Port Sweep	Composite	Context
3015	0	TCP Null Port Sweep	Composite	Context
3016	0	TCP FRAG Null Port Sweep	Composite	Context
3020	0	TCP SYN FIN Port Sweep	Composite	Context
3021	0	TCP FRAG SYN FIN Port Sweep	Composite	Context
3030	0	TCP SYN Host Sweep	Composite	Context
3031	0	TCP FRAG SYN Host Sweep	Composite	Context
3032	0	TCP FIN Host Sweep	Composite	Context
3033	0	TCP FRAG FIN Host Sweep	Composite	Context
3034	0	TCP NULL Host Sweep	Composite	Context
3035	0	TCP FRAG NULL Host Sweep	Composite	Context
3036	0	TCP SYN FIN Host Sweep	Composite	Context
3037	0	TCP FRAG SYN FIN Host Sweep	Composite	Context
3038	0	Fragmented NULL TCP Packet	Atomic	Context
3039	0	Fragmented Orphaned FIN packet	Atomic	Context
3040	0	NULL TCP Packet	Atomic	Context
3041	0	SYN/FIN Packet	Atomic	Context
3042	0	Orphaned FIN Packet	Atomic	Context
3043	0	Fragmented SYN/FIN Packet	Atomic	Content
3045	0	Queso Sweep	Composite	Context
3050	0	Half—Open SYN Attack	Composite	Context
3100	0	Smail Attack	Composite	Content

continues

Cisco Secure IDS Signature ID	Cisco Secure IDS Subsignature ID	Cisco Secure IDS Signature Name	Cisco Secure IDS Signature Structure	Cisco Secure IDS Signature Implementation
3101	0	Sendmail Invalid Recipient	Composite	Content
3102	0	Sendmail Invalid Sender	Composite	Content
3103	0	Sendmail Reconnaissance	Composite	Content
3104	0	Archaic Sendmail Attacks	Composite	Content
3105	0	Sendmail Decode Alias	Composite	Content
3106	0	Mail Spam	Composite	Context
3107	0	Majordomo Execute Attack	Composite	Content
3108	0	MIME Overflow Bug	Composite	Content
3109	0	Q—Mail Length Crash	Composite	Content
3110	0	Suspicious Mail Attachment	Composite	Content
3150	0	FTP Remote Command Execution	Composite	Content
3151	0	FTP SYST Command Attempt	Composite	Content
3152	0	FTP CWD ~root	Composite	Content
3153	0	FTP Improper Address Specified	Atomic	Content
3154	0	FTP Improper Port Specified	Atomic	Content
3155	0	FTP RETR Pipe Filename Command Execution	Atomic	Content
3156	0	FTP STOR Pipe Filename Command Execution	Atomic	Content
3157	0	FTP PASV Port Spoof	Composite	Content
3200	0	WWW PHF Attack	Composite	Content
3201	0	WWW General cgi—bin Attack	Composite	Content
3202	0	WWW .url File Requested	Composite	Content
3203	0	WWW .lnk File Requested	Composite	Content
3204	0	WWW .bat File Requested	Composite	Content
3205	0	HTML File Has .url Link	Composite	Content
3206	0	HTML File Has .lnk Link	Composite	Content
3207	0	HTML File Has .bat Link	Composite	Content
3208	0	WWW campas Attack	Composite	Content
3209	0	WWW Glimpse Server Attack	Composite	Content

Cisco Secure IDS Signature ID	Cisco Secure IDS Subsignature ID	Cisco Secure IDS Signature Name	Cisco Secure IDS Signature Structure	Cisco Secure IDS Signature Implementation
3210	0	WWW IIS View Source Attack	Composite	Content
3211	0	WWW IIS Hex View Source Attack	Composite	Content
3212	0	WWW NPH-TEST-CGI Attack	Composite	Content
3213	0	WWW TEST-CGI Attack	Composite	Content
3214	0	IIS DOT DOT View Attack	Composite	Content
3215	0	IIS DOT DOT Execute Attack	Composite	Content
3216	0	IIS DOT DOT Crash Attack	Composite	Content
3217	0	WWW PHP View File Attack	Composite	Content
3218	0	WWW SGI Wrap Attack	Composite	Content
3219	0	WWW PHP Buffer Overflow	Composite	Content
3220	0	IIS Long URL Crash Bug	Composite	Content
3221	0	WWW cgi—viewsource Attack	Composite	Content
3222	0	WWW PHP Log Scripts Read Attack	Composite	Content
3223	0	WWW IRIX cgi—handler Attack	Composite	Content
3224	0	HTTP WebGais	Composite	Content
3225	0	HTTP Gais Websendmail	Composite	Content
3226	0	WWW Webdist Bug	Composite	Content
3227	0	WWW Htmlscript Bug	Composite	Content
3228	0	WWW Performer Bug	Composite	Content
3229	0	Website Win-C-Sample Buffer Overflow	Composite	Content
3230	0	Website Uploader	Composite	Content
3231	0	Novell convert	Composite	Content
3232	0	WWW finger Attempt	Composite	Content
3233	0	WWW count—cgi Overflow	Composite	Context
3250	0	TCP Hijack	Composite	Context
3251	0	TCP Hijacking Simplex Mode	Composite	Context
3300	0	NetBIOS OOB Data	Atomic	Context

continues

Cisco Secure IDS Signature ID	Cisco Secure IDS Subsignature ID	Cisco Secure IDS Signature Name	Cisco Secure IDS Signature Structure	Cisco Secure IDS Signature Implementation
3301	0	NetBIOS Stat	Atomic	Content
3302	0	NetBIOS Session Setup Failure	Atomic	Context
3303	0	Windows Guest Login	Atomic	Content
3304	0	Windows Null Account Name	Atomic	Content
3305	0	Windows Password File Access	Atomic	Content
3306	0	Windows Registry Access	Atomic	Content
3307	0	Windows Redbutton Attack	Composite	Content
3308	0	Windows LSARPC Access	Atomic	Content
3309	0	Windows SRVSVC Access	Atomic	Content
3400	0	Sunkill	Composite	Content
3401	0	Telnet—IFS Match	Composite	Content
3450	0	Finger Bomb	Atomic	Content
3500	0	Rlogin—froot Attack	Composite	Content
3525	0	IMAP Authenticate Buffer Overflow	Composite	Content
3526	0	IMAP Login Buffer Overflow	Composite	Content
3530	0	Cisco Secure ACS Oversized TACACS+ Attack	Atomic	Content
3540	0	Cisco Secure ACS CSAdmin Attack	Atomic	Context
3550	0	POP Buffer Overflow	Composite	Content
3575	0	INN Buffer Overflow	Composite	Context
3576	0	INN Control Message Exploit	Composite	Content
3600	0	IOS Telnet Buffer Overflow	Composite	Content
3601	0	IOS Command History Exploit	Composite	Content
3602	0	Cisco IOS Identity	Atomic	Content
3603	0	IOS Enable Bypass	Composite	Content
3650	0	SSH RSAREF2 Buffer Overflow	Composite	Context
3990	0	Back Orifice BO2K TCP Non Stealth	Composite	Content
3991	0	Back Orifice BO2K TCP Stealth 1	Composite	Content
3992	0	Back Orifice BO2K TCP Stealth 2	Composite	Content

Cisco Secure IDS Signature ID	Cisco Secure IDS Subsignature ID	Cisco Secure IDS Signature Name	Cisco Secure IDS Signature Structure	Cisco Secure IDS Signature Implementation
4000	0	UDP Packet	Atomic	Context
4001	0	UDP Port Sweep	Composite	Context
4002	0	UDP Flood	Composite	Context
4050	0	UDP Bomb	Atomic	Context
4051	0	Snork	Atomic	Context
4052	0	Chargen DoS	Atomic	Context
4053	0	Back Orifice	Composite	Content
4054	0	RIP Trace	Atomic	Content
4055	0	Back Orifice BO2K UDP	Composite	Content
4100	0	tftp Passwd File	Composite	Content
4150	0	Ascend Denial of Service	Composite	Content
4600	0	IOS UDP Bomb	Composite	Context
5034	0	WWW IIS newdsn Attack	Composite	Content
5035	0	HTTP cgi HylaFAX Faxsurvey	Composite	Content
5036	0	WWW Windows Password File Access Attempt	Composite	Content
5037	0	WWW SGI MachineInfo Attack	Composite	Content
5038	0	WWW wwwsql file read Bug	Composite	Content
5039	0	WWW finger attempt	Composite	Content
5040	0	WWW Perl Interpreter Attack	Composite	Content
5041	0	WWW anyform Attack	Composite	Content
5042	0	WWW CGI Valid Shell Access	Composite	Content
5043	0	WWW Cold Fusion Attack	Composite	Content
5044	0	WWW Webcom.se Guestbook Attack	Composite	Content
5045	0	WWW xterm display Attack	Composite	Content
5046	0	WWW dumpenv.pl recon	Composite	Content
5047	0	WWW Server Side Include POST Attack	Composite	Content
5048	0	WWW IIS BAT EXE Attack	Composite	Content

continues

Cisco Secure IDS Signature ID	Cisco Secure IDS Subsignature ID	Cisco Secure IDS Signature Name	Cisco Secure IDS Signature Structure	Cisco Secure IDS Signature Implementation
5049	0	WWW IIS showcode.asp Access	Composite	Content
5050	0	WWW IIS .htr Overflow Attack	Composite	Content
5051	0	IIS Double Byte Code Page	Atomic	Content
5052	0	FrontPage Extensions PWD Open Attempt	Atomic	Content
5053	0	FrontPage _vti_bin Directory List Attempt	Atomic	Content
5054	0	WWWBoard Password	Atomic	Content
5055	0	HTTP Basic Authentication Overflow	Composite	Content
5056	0	WWW Cisco IOS %% DoS	Composite	Content
5057	0	WWW Sambar Samples	Composite	Content
5058	0	WWW info2www Attack	Composite	Content
5059	0	WWW Alibaba Attack	Composite	Content
5060	0	WWW Excite AT—generate.cgi Access	Composite	Content
5061	0	WWW catalog_type.asp Access	Composite	Content
5062	0	WWW classifieds.cgi Attack	Composite	Content
5063	0	WWW dmblparser.exe Access	Composite	Content
5064	0	WWW imagemap.cgi Attack	Composite	Content
5065	0	WWW IRIX infosrch.cgi Attack	Composite	Content
5066	0	WWW man.sh Access	Composite	Content
5067	0	WWW plusmail Attack	Composite	Content
5068	0	WWW formmail.pl Access	Composite	Content
5069	0	WWW whois_raw.cgi Attack	Composite	Content
5070	0	WWW msadcs.dll Access	Composite	Content
5071	0	WWW msacds.dll Attack	Composite	Content
5072	0	WWW bizdb1—search.cgi Attack	Composite	Content
5073	0	WWW EZshopper loadpage.cgi Attack	Composite	Content
5074	0	WWW EZshopper search.cgi Attack	Composite	Content

Cisco Secure IDS Signature ID	Cisco Secure IDS Subsignature ID	Cisco Secure IDS Signature Name	Cisco Secure IDS Signature Structure	Cisco Secure IDS Signature Implementation
5075	0	WWW IIS Virtualized UNC Bug	Composite	Content
5076	0	WWW webplus bug	Composite	Content
5077	0	WWW Excite AT—admin.cgi Access	Composite	Content
5078	0	WWW Piranha Passwd Attack	Composite	Content
5079	0	WWW PCCS MySQL Admin Access	Atomic	Content
5080	0	WWW IBM WebSphere Access	Atomic	Content
5081	0	WWW WinNT cmd.exe Access	Atomic	Content
5082	0	WWW Roxen %00 Access	Atomic	Content
5083	0	WWW Virtual Vision FTP Browser Access	Atomic	Content
5084	0	WWW Alibaba Attack 2	Atomic	Content
5085	0	WWW IIS Source Fragment Access	Atomic	Content
5086	0	WWW WEBactive Logfile Access	Atomic	Content
5087	0	WWW Sun Java Server Access	Atomic	Content
5088	0	WWW Akopia MiniVend Access	Atomic	Content
5089	0	WWW Big Brother Directory Access	Atomic	Content
5090	0	WWW FrontPage htimage.exe Access	Atomic	Content
5091	0	WWW Cart32 Remote Admin Access	Composite	Content
5092	0	WWW cgi—world Poll It Access	Atomic	Content
5093	0	WWW PHP—Nuke admin.php3 Access	Atomic	Content
5095	0	WWW CGI Script Center Account Manager Attack	Atomic	Content
5096	0	WWW CGI Script Center Subscribe Me Attack	Atomic	Content
5097	0	WWW FrontPage MS—DOS Device Attack	Composite	Content

continues

Cisco Secure IDS Signature ID	Cisco Secure IDS Subsignature ID	Cisco Secure IDS Signature Name	Cisco Secure IDS Signature Structure	Cisco Secure IDS Signature Implementation
5099	0	WWW GWScripts News Publisher Access	Atomic	Content
5100	0	WWW CGI Center Auction Weaver File Access	Atomic	Content
5101	0	WWW CGI Center Auction Weaver Attack	Atomic	Content
5102	0	WWW phpPhotoAlbum explorer.php Access	Atomic	Content
5103	0	WWW SuSE Apache CGI Source Access	Atomic	Content
5104	0	WWW YaBB File Access	Atomic	Content
5105	0	WWW Ranson Johnson mailto.cgi Attack	Atomic	Content
5106	0	WWW Ranson Johnson mailform.pl Access	Atomic	Content
5107	0	WWW Mandrake Linux /perl Access	Atomic	Content
5108	0	WWW Netegrity Site Minder Access	Atomic	Content
5109	0	WWW Sambar Beta search.dll Access	Atomic	Content
5110	0	WWW SuSE Installed Packages Access	Atomic	Content
5111	0	WWW Solaris Answerbook 2 Access	Atomic	Content
5112	0	WWW Solaris Answerbook 2 Attack	Atomic	Content
5113	0	WWW CommuniGate Pro Access	Atomic	Content
5114	0	WWW IIS Unicode Attack	Atomic	Content
6001	0	Normal SATAN Probe	Composite	Content
6002	0	Heavy SATAN Probe	Composite	Content
6050	0	DNS HINFO Request	Atomic	Content
6051	0	DNS Zone Transfer	Atomic	Content
6052	0	DNS Zone Transfer from High Port	Atomic	Content

Cisco Secure IDS Signature ID	Cisco Secure IDS Subsignature ID	Cisco Secure IDS Signature Name	Cisco Secure IDS Signature Structure	Cisco Secure IDS Signature Implementation
6053	0	DNS Request for All Records	Atomic	Content
6054	0	DNS Version Request	Atomic	Content
6055	0	DNS Inverse Query Buffer Overflow	Atomic	Content
6056	0	BIND NXT Buffer Overflow	Composite	Content
6057	0	BIND SIG Buffer Overflow	Composite	Context
6100	0	RPC Port Registration	Atomic	Content
6101	0	RPC Port Unregistration	Atomic	Content
6102	0	RPC Dump	Atomic	Content
6103	0	Proxied RPC Request	Atomic	Content
6104	0	RPC Set Spoof	Atomic	Content
6105	0	RPC Unset Spoof	Atomic	Content
6110	0	RPC rstatd Sweep	Composite	Content
6111	0	RPC rusersd Sweep	Composite	Content
6112	0	RPC NFS Sweep	Composite	Content
6113	0	RPC mountd Sweep	Composite	Content
6114	0	RPC yppasswdd Sweep	Composite	Content
6115	0	RPC selection_svc Sweep	Composite	Content
6116	0	RPC rexd Sweep	Composite	Content
6117	0	RPC status Sweep	Composite	Content
6118	0	RPC ttdb Sweep	Composite	Content
6150	0	ypserv Portmap Request	Atomic	Content
6151	0	ypbind Portmap Request	Atomic	Content
6152	0	yppasswdd Portmap Request	Atomic	Content
6153	0	ypupdated Portmap Request	Atomic	Content
6154	0	ypxfrd Portmap Request	Atomic	Content
6155	0	mountd Portmap Request	Atomic	Content
6175	0	rexd Portmap Request	Atomic	Content
6180	0	rexd Attempt	Atomic	Context
6190	0	statd Buffer Overflow	Composite	Context

continues

Cisco Secure IDS Signature ID	Cisco Secure IDS Subsignature ID	Cisco Secure IDS Signature Name	Cisco Secure IDS Signature Structure	Cisco Secure IDS Signature Implementation
6191	0	RPC.tooltalk Buffer Overflow	Composite	Content
6192	0	RPC mountd Buffer Overflow	Composite	Content
6193	0	RPC CMSD Buffer Overflow	Atomic	Content
6194	0	sadmind RPC Buffer Overflow	Atomic	Content
6195	0	RPC amd Buffer Overflow	Composite	Content
6200	0	Ident Buffer Overflow	Composite	Content
6201	0	Ident Newline	Composite	Content
6202	0	Ident Improper Request	Composite	Content
6250	0	FTP Authorization Failure	Composite	Content
6251	0	Telnet Authorization Failure	Composite	Content
6252	0	Rlogin Authorization Failure	Composite	Content
6253	0	POP3 Authorization Failure	Composite	Content
6255	0	SMB Authorization Failure	Composite	Content
6300	0	Loki ICMP Tunneling	Composite	Context
6302	0	General Loki ICMP Tunneling	Composite	Context
6500	0	RingZero Trojan	Composite	Content
6501	0	TFN Client Request	Composite	Content
6502	0	TFN Server Reply	Composite	Content
6503	0	Stacheldraht Client Request	Composite	Content
6504	0	Stacheldraht Server Reply	Composite	Content
6505	0	Trinoo Client Request	Composite	Content
6506	0	Trinoo Server Reply	Composite	Content
6507	0	TFN2K Control Traffic	Composite	Content
6508	0	Mstream Control Traffic	Composite	Content
8000	2302	Telnet—/etc/shadow Match	Composite	Content
8000	2101	FTP Retrieve Password File	Composite	Content
8000	2303	Telnet—+ +	Composite	Content
8000	51301	Rlogin—IFS Match	Composite	Content
8000	51302	Rlogin—/etc/shadow Match	Composite	Content
8000	51303	Rlogin—+ +	Composite	Content

Cisco Secure IDS Signatures and Recommended Alarm Levels

This appendix contains recommended Cisco Secure IDS signature alarm levels. The tables are meant *solely* as a reference guide. The recommended alarm levels are as follows:

- **Disable**—The signature needs to be disabled because of the possibility of a large number of alarms generated by normal network traffic. Signatures that fall into this category include the following:
  - — Signature 2000, ICMP Echo Reply
  - — Signature 3205, HTML File Has .url Link

- **Low**—The signature has been determined to be a low threat. Low-severity alarms are triggered by normal network traffic or benign signature. CSIDS Signature IDs 6250-6255 (Failed Login Attempts) and CSIDS Signature ID 3602 (IOS Cisco Identification) are examples of signatures with a recommended low alarm level. Signatures that fall into this category include the following:
  - — Signature 1002, IP Options-Timestamp
  - — Signature 3030, TCP SYN Host Sweep

- **Medium**—The signature has been determined to be an indicator of possible malicious activity. Medium-severity alarms need to be investigated to determine the nature of the traffic that triggered the signature. Signatures that fall into this category include the following:
  - — Signature 3002, TCP SYN Port Sweep
  - — Signature 3106, Mail Spam

- **High**—The signature is associated with a real threat and needs to be taken seriously. High-severity alarms typically indicate an intrusion attempt or a denial of service attack. Signatures that fall into this category include the following:
  - — Signature 1006, IP Options-Strict Source Route
  - — Signature 3005, TCP FIN Port Sweep

The signature types that are covered in this appendix follow:

- General
- Connection
- String
- ACL

General Signatures

The Cisco Secure IDS general signatures detect a wide range of intrusion attempts. These signatures are spread across various protocols (IP, ICMP, TCP, and UDP). Many of these signatures are context-based because they examine protocol control information and look for abnormalities. Others, such as the Web signatures, are usually content-based because they look for abnormalities in the data portion of HTTP protocol packets (an application layer protocol). Table G-1 lists the general signatures.

Table G-1 *Cisco Secure IDS General Signatures*

Signature ID	Signature Name	Recommended Alarm Level
1000	IP Options-Bad Option List	Low
1001	IP Options-Record Packet Route	Low
1002	IP Options-Timestamp	Low
1003	IP Options-Provide s, c, h, and tcc	Low
1004	IP Options-Loose Source Route	High
1005	IP Options-SATNET ID	Low
1006	IP Options-Strict Source Route	High
1100	IP Fragment Attack	Medium
1101	Unknown IP Protocol	Low
1102	Impossible IP Packet	High
1103	IP Fragments Overlap	High
1104	IP Localhost Source Spoof	High
1200	IP Fragmentation Buffer Full	Low
1201	IP Fragment Overlap	High
1202	IP Fragment Overrun - Datagram Too Long	High
1203	IP Fragment Overwrite - Data is Overwritten	High
1204	IP Fragment Missing Initial Fragment	Low

Table G-1   *Cisco Secure IDS General Signatures (Continued)*

Signature ID	Signature Name	Recommended Alarm Level
1205	IP Fragment Too Many Datagrams	Low
1206	IP Fragment Too Small	Low
1207	IP Fragment Too Many Frags	Low
1208	IP Fragment Incomplete Datagram	Low
1220	Jolt2 Fragment Reassembly DoS attack	High
2000	ICMP Echo Reply	Disable
2001	ICMP Host Unreachable	Disable
2002	ICMP Source Quench	Disable
2003	ICMP Redirect	Disable
2004	ICMP Echo Request	Disable
2005	ICMP Time Exceeded for a Datagram	Disable
2006	ICMP Parameter Problem on Datagram	Disable
2007	ICMP Timestamp Request	Disable
2008	ICMP Timestamp Reply	Disable
2009	ICMP Information Request	Disable
2010	ICMP Information Reply	Disable
2011	ICMP Address Mask Request	Disable
2012	ICMP Address Mask Reply	Disable
2100	ICMP Network Sweep w/Echo	Medium
2101	ICMP Network Sweep w/Timestamp	High
2102	ICMP Network Sweep w/Address Mask	High
2150	Fragmented ICMP Traffic	Disable
2151	Large ICMP Traffic	Disable
2152	ICMP Flood	High
2153	Smurf	High
2154	Ping of Death Attack	High
3001	TCP Port Sweep	High
3002	TCP SYN Port Sweep	Medium
3003	TCP Frag SYN Port Sweep	High

continues

Table G-1 *Cisco Secure IDS General Signatures (Continued)*

Signature ID	Signature Name	Recommended Alarm Level
3005	TCP FIN Port Sweep	High
3006	TCP Frag FIN Port Sweep	High
3010	TCP High Port Sweep	Disable
3011	TCP FIN High Port Sweep	High
3012	TCP Frag FIN High Port Sweep	High
3015	TCP Null Port Sweep	High
3016	TCP Frag Null Port Sweep	High
3020	TCP SYN FIN Port Sweep	High
3021	TCP Frag SYN FIN Port Sweep	High
3030	TCP SYN Host Sweep	Low
3031	TCP FRAG SYN Host Sweep	High
3032	TCP FIN Host Sweep	High
3033	TCP FRAG FIN Host Sweep	High
3034	TCP NULL Host Sweep	High
3035	TCP FRAG NULL Host Sweep	High
3036	TCP SYN FIN Host Sweep	High
3037	TCP FRAG SYN FIN Host Sweep	High
3038	Fragmented NULL TCP Packet	High
3039	Fragmented Orphaned FIN Packet	High
3040	NULL TCP Packet	High
3041	SYN/FIN Packet	High
3042	Orphaned Fin Packet	High
3043	Fragmented SYN/FIN Packet	High
3045	Queso Sweep	High
3050	Half-open SYN Attack	High
3100	Smail Attack	High
3101	Sendmail Invalid Recipient	High
3102	Sendmail Invalid Sender	High
3103	Sendmail Reconnaissance	Low
3104	Archaic Sendmail Attacks	Low

Table G-1   *Cisco Secure IDS General Signatures (Continued)*

Signature ID	Signature Name	Recommended Alarm Level
3105	Sendmail Decode Alias	Medium
3106	Mail Spam	Medium
3107	Majordomo Execute Attack	High
3108	MIME Overflow Bug	High
3109	Q-Mail Length Crash	High
3110	Suspicious Mail Attachment	Medium
3150	FTP Remote Command Execution	Low
3151	FTP SYST Command Attempt	Disable
3152	FTP CWD ~root	High
3153	FTP Improper Address Specified	High
3154	FTP Improper Port Specified	High
3155	FTP RETR Pipe Filename Command Execution	High
3156	FTP STOR Pipe Filename Command Execution	High
3157	FTP PASV Port Spoof	High
3200	WWW Phf Attack	High
3201	WWW General cgi-bin Attack	High
3202	WWW .url File Requested	High
3203	WWW .lnk File Requested	High
3204	WWW .bat File Requested	High
3205	HTML File Has .url Link	Disable
3206	HTML File Has .lnk Link	Disable
3207	HTML File Has .bat Link	Disable
3208	WWW campas Attack	High
3209	WWW Glimpse Server Attack	High
3210	WWW IIS View Source Attack	Medium
3211	WWW IIS Hex View Source Attack	Disable
3212	WWW NPH-TEST-CGI Attack	Medium
3213	WWW TEST-CGI Attack	Medium
3214	IIS DOT DOT VIEW Attack	Disable

continues

Table G-1   *Cisco Secure IDS General Signatures (Continued)*

Signature ID	Signature Name	Recommended Alarm Level
3215	IIS DOT DOT EXECUTE Attack	High
3216	IIS Dot Dot Crash Attack	High
3217	WWW PHP View File Attack	High
3218	WWW SGI Wrap Attack	High
3219	WWW PHP Buffer Overflow	High
3220	IIS Long URL Crash Bug	Disable
3221	WWW cgi-viewsource Attack	Medium
3222	WWW PHP Log Scripts Read Attack	Medium
3223	WWW IRIX cgi-handler Attack	Medium
3224	HTTP WebGais	Medium
3225	HTTP Gais Websendmail	Medium
3226	WWW Webdist Bug	Medium
3227	WWW Htmlscript Bug	Medium
3228	WWW Performer Bug	Medium
3229	Website Win-C-Sample Buffer Overflow	High
3230	Website Uploader	Medium
3231	Novell convert	High
3232	WWW finger Attempt	Medium
3233	WWW count-cgi Overflow	High
3250	TCP Hijack	High
3251	TCP Hijacking Simplex Mode	High
3300	NetBIOS OOB Data	High
3301	NETBIOS Stat	Disable
3302	NETBIOS Session Setup Failure	Disable
3303	Windows Guest Login	Low
3304	Windows Null Account Name	Disable
3305	Windows Password File Access	High
3306	Windows Registry Access	High
3307	Windows Redbutton Attack	High
3308	Windows LSARPC Access	Disable

Table G-1   *Cisco Secure IDS General Signatures (Continued)*

Signature ID	Signature Name	Recommended Alarm Level
3309	Windows SRVSVC Access	Disable
3400	Sunkill	Medium
3401	Telnet-IFS Match	Medium
3450	Finger Bomb	Medium
3500	Rlogin-froot Attack	High
3525	IMAP Authenticate Buffer Overflow	High
3526	Imap Login Buffer Overflow	High
3530	Cisco Secure ACS Oversized TACACS+ Attack	Medium
3540	Cisco Secure ACS CSAdmin Attack	High
3550	POP Buffer Overflow	High
3575	INN Buffer Overflow	High
3576	INN Control Message Exploit	High
3600	IOS Telnet Buffer Overflow	High
3601	IOS Command History Exploit	High
3602	Cisco IOS Identity	Low
3603	IOS Enable Bypass	High
3650	SSH RSAREF2 Buffer Overflow	High
3990	BackOrifice BO2K TCP Non Stealth	High
3991	BackOrifice BO2K TCP Stealth 1	High
3992	BackOrifice BO2K TCP Stealth 2	High
4001	UDP Port Sweep	High
4002	UDP Flood	Disable
4050	UDP Bomb	Medium
4051	Snork	Medium
4052	Chargen DoS	Medium
4053	Back Orifice	High
4054	RIP Trace	High
4055	BackOrifice BO2K UDP	High
4100	Tftp Passwd File	High

continues

Table G-1   *Cisco Secure IDS General Signatures (Continued)*

Signature ID	Signature Name	Recommended Alarm Level
4150	Ascend High of Service	Medium
4600	IOS UDP Bomb	High
5034	WWW IIS newdsn Attack	High
5035	HTTP cgi HylaFAX Faxsurvey	High
5036	WWW Windows Password File High Attempt	High
5037	WWW SGI MachineInfo Attack	Medium
5038	WWW wwwsql File Read Bug	High
5039	WWW finger Attempt	Medium
5040	WWW Perl Interpreter Attack	High
5041	WWW anyform Attack	High
5042	WWW CGI Valid Shell Access	High
5043	WWW Cold Fusion Attack	High
5044	WWW Webcom.se Guestbook attack	High
5045	WWW xterm Display Attack	High
5046	WWW dumpenv.pl Low	Medium
5047	WWW Server Side Include POST attack	High
5048	WWW IIS BAT EXE attack	High
5049	WWW IIS showcode.asp Access	Medium
5050	WWW IIS .htr Overflow Attack	High
5051	IIS Double Byte Code Page	Medium
5052	FrontPage Extensions PWD Open Attempt	High
5053	FrontPage _vti_bin Directory List Attempt	High
5054	WWWBoard Password	Medium
5055	HTTP Basic Authentication Overflow	High
5056	WWW Cisco IOS %% DoS	Disable
5057	WWW Sambar Samples	Medium
5058	WWW info2www Attack	High
5059	WWW Alibaba Attack	High
5060	WWW Excite AT-generate.cgi Access	Medium
5061	WWW catalog_type.asp Access	High

Table G-1   *Cisco Secure IDS General Signatures (Continued)*

Signature ID	Signature Name	Recommended Alarm Level
5062	WWW classifieds.cgi Attack	High
5063	WWW dmblparser.exe Access	Medium
5064	WWW imagemap.cgi Attack	High
5065	WWW IRIX infosrch.cgi Attack	High
5066	WWW man.sh Access	Medium
5067	WWW plusmail Attack	High
5068	WWW formmail.pl Access	Medium
5069	WWW whois_raw.cgi Attack	High
5070	WWW msadcs.dll Access	High
5071	WWW msacds.dll Attack	High
5072	WWW bizdb1-search.cgi Attack	High
5073	WWW EZshopper loadpage.cgi Attack	High
5074	WWW EZshopper search.cgi Attack	High
5075	WWW IIS Virtualized UNC Bug	Medium
5076	WWW webplus Bug	Medium
5077	WWW Excite AT-admin.cgi Access	Medium
5078	WWW Piranha passwd Attack	High
5079	WWW PCCS MySQL Admin Access	Medium
5080	WWW IBM WebSphere Access	Medium
5081	WWW WinNT cmd.exe Access	High*
5082	WWW Roxen %00 Access	Low
5083	WWW Virtual Vision FTP Browser Access	Medium
5084	WWW Alibaba Attack 2	Medium
5085	WWW IIS Source Fragment Access	Medium
5086	WWW WEBactive Logfile Access	Low
5087	WWW Sun Java Server Access	Medium
5088	WWW Akopia MiniVend Access	Medium
5089	WWW Big Brother Directory Access	Medium
5090	WWW FrontPage htimage.exe Access	Medium

continues

Table G-1   *Cisco Secure IDS General Signatures (Continued)*

Signature ID	Signature Name	Recommended Alarm Level
5091	WWW Cart32 Remote Admin Access	Medium
5092	WWW CGI-World Poll It Access	Medium
5093	WWW PHP-Nuke admin.php3 Access	Medium
5095	WWW CGI Script Center Account Manager Attack	Medium
5096	WWW CGI Script Center Subscribe Me Attack	Medium
5097	WWW FrontPage MS-DOS Device Attack	Medium
5098	WWW O'Reilly Pro uploader.exe access	Medium
5099	WWW GWScripts News Publisher Access	Medium
5100	WWW CGI Center Auction Weaver File Access	Medium
5101	WWW CGI Center Auction Weaver Attack	Medium
5102	WWW phpPhotoAlbum explorer.php Access	Medium
5103	WWW SuSE Apache CGI Source Access	Medium
5104	WWW YaBB File Access	Medium
5105	WWW Ranson Johnson mailto.cgi Attack	Medium
5106	WWW Ranson Johnson mailform.pl Access	Medium
5107	WWW Mandrake Linux /perl Access	Medium
5108	WWW Netegrity Site Minder Access	Medium
5109	WWW Sambar Beta search.dll Access	Medium
5110	WWW SuSE Installed Packages Access	Low
5111	WWW Solaris Answerbook 2 Access	Medium
5112	WWW Solaris Answerbook 2 Attack	Medium
5113	WWW CommuniGate Pro Access	Medium
5114	WWW IIS Unicode Attack	High
6001	Normal SATAN Probe	High
6002	Heavy SATAN Probe	High
6050	DNS HINFO Request	Medium
6051	DNS Zone Transfer	Low
6052	DNS Zone Transfer from High Port	High
6053	DNS Request for All Records	Low
6054	DNS Version Request	Medium

Table G-1   *Cisco Secure IDS General Signatures (Continued)*

Signature ID	Signature Name	Recommended Alarm Level
6055	DNS Inverse Query Buffer Overflow	High
6056	BIND NXT Buffer Overflow	High
6057	BIND SIG Buffer Overflow	High
6100	RPC Port Registration	High
6101	RPC Port Unregistration	High
6102	RPC Dump	High
6103	Proxied RPC Request	Low
6104	RPC Set Spoof	High
6105	RPC Unset Spoof	High
6110	RPC RSTATD Sweep	High
6111	RPC RUSERSD Sweep	High
6112	RPC NFS Sweep	High
6113	RPC MOUNTD Sweep	High
6114	RPC YPPASSWDD Sweep	High
6115	RPC SELECTION_SVC Sweep	High
6116	RPC REXD Sweep	High
6117	RPC STATUS Sweep	High
6118	RPC ttdb Sweep	High
6150	Ypserv Portmap Request	Low
6151	Ypbind Portmap Request	Low
6152	Yppasswdd Portmap Request	Disable
6153	Ypupdated Portmap Request	Low
6154	Ypxfrd Portmap Request	Low
6155	Mountd Portmap Request	Disable
6175	rexd Portmap Request	Medium
6180	rexd Attempt	High
6190	statd Buffer Overflow	High
6191	RPC.tooltalk Buffer Overflow	High
6192	RPC mountd Buffer Overflow	High

continues

Table G-1 *Cisco Secure IDS General Signatures (Continued)*

Signature ID	Signature Name	Recommended Alarm Level
6193	RPC CMSD Buffer Overflow	High
6194	Sadmind RPC Buffer Overflow	High
6195	RPC amd Buffer Overflow	High
6200	Ident Buffer Overflow	High
6201	Ident Newline	High
6202	Ident Improper Request	High
6250	FTP Authorization Failure	Low
6251	Telnet Authorization Failure	Low
6252	Rlogin Authorization Failure	Low
6253	POP3 Authorization Failure	Low
6255	SMB Authorization Failure	Low
6300	Loki ICMP Tunneling	High
6302	General Loki ICMP Tunneling	High
6500	RingZero Trojan	High
6501	TFN Client Request	High
6502	TFN Server Reply	High
6503	Stacheldraht Client Request	High
6504	Stacheldraht Server Reply	High
6505	Trinoo Client Request	High
6506	Trinoo Server Reply	High
6507	TFN2K Control Traffic	High
6508	Mstream Control Traffic	High

Connection Signatures

The Cisco Secure IDS connection signatures (as the name implies) detect TCP connections and network traffic to UDP ports. The subsignature ID identifies the port number that the traffic is going to and helps you identify the well-known service that the traffic probably represents. Table G-2 shows the default Cisco Secure IDS connection signatures.

Table G-2 *Default Cisco Secure IDS Connection Signatures*

Signature ID	Subsignature ID	Signature Name	Recommended Alarm Level
3000	1	Connection Request - tcpmux	Disable
3000	7	Connection Request - echo	Disable
3000	9	Connection Request - discard	Disable
3000	11	Connection Request - systat	Disable
3000	13	Connection Request - daytime	Disable
3000	15	Connection Request - netstat	Disable
3000	19	Connection Request - chargen	Disable
3000	20	Connection Request - ftp-data	Disable
3000	21	Connection Request - ftp	Disable
3000	23	Connection Request - telnet	Disable
3000	25	Connection Request - smtp	Disable
3000	37	Connection Request - time	Disable
3000	43	Connection Request - whois	Disable
3000	53	Connection Request - dns	Disable
3000	70	Connection Request - gopher	Disable
3000	79	Connection Request - finger	Disable
3000	80	Connection Request - www	Disable
3000	87	Connection Request - link	Disable
3000	88	Connection Request - kerberos-v5	Disable
3000	95	Connection Request - supdup	Disable
3000	101	Connection Request - hostnames	Disable
3000	102	Connection Request - iso-tsap	Disable
3000	103	Connection Request - x400	Disable
3000	104	Connection Request - x400-snd	Disable
3000	105	Connection Request - csnet-ns	Disable
3000	109	Connection Request - pop-2	Disable
3000	110	Connection Request - pop3	Disable
3000	111	Connection Request - sunrpc	Disable

continues

Table G-2 *Default Cisco Secure IDS Connection Signatures (Continued)*

Signature ID	Subsignature ID	Signature Name	Recommended Alarm Level
3000	117	Connection Request - uucppath	Disable
3000	119	Connection Request - nntp	Disable
3000	123	Connection Request - ntp	Disable
3000	137	Connection Request - netbios	Disable
3000	138	Connection Request - 138	Disable
3000	139	Connection Request - 139	Disable
3000	143	Connection Request - imap2	Disable
3000	144	Connection Request - NeWS	Disable
3000	177	Connection Request - xdmcp	Disable
3000	178	Connection Request - nextstep	Disable
3000	179	Connection Request - bgp	Disable
3000	194	Connection Request - irc	Disable
3000	220	Connection Request - imap3	Disable
3000	372	Connection Request - ulistserv	Disable
3000	512	Connection Request - exec	Medium
3000	513	Connection Request - login	Medium
3000	514	Connection Request - shell	Medium
3000	515	Connection Request - printer	Disable
3000	530	Connection Request - courier	Disable
3000	540	Connection Request - uucp	Disable
3000	600	Connection Request - pcserver	Disable
3000	750	Connection Request - kerberos-v4	Disable
3000	3128	Connection Request - 3128	Disable
3000	8080	Connection Request - 8080	Disable
4000	7	UDP Traffic - echo	Disable
4000	9	UDP Traffic - discard	Disable
4000	13	UDP Traffic - daytime	Disable
4000	19	UDP Traffic - chargen	Disable
4000	37	UDP Traffic - time	Disable

Table G-2   *Default Cisco Secure IDS Connection Signatures (Continued)*

Signature ID	Subsignature ID	Signature Name	Recommended Alarm Level
4000	53	UDP Traffic - dns	Disable
4000	69	UDP Traffic - tftp	Medium
4000	70	UDP Traffic - gopher	Disable
4000	80	UDP Traffic - www	Disable
4000	88	UDP Traffic - kerberos-v5	Disable
4000	111	UDP Traffic - sunrpc	Disable
4000	123	UDP Traffic - ntp	Disable
4000	177	UDP Traffic - xdmcp	Disable
4000	179	UDP Traffic - bgp	Disable
4000	220	UDP Traffic - imap3	Disable
4000	372	UDP Traffic - ulistserv	Disable
4000	512	UDP Traffic - biff	Disable
4000	513	UDP Traffic - who	Disable
4000	514	UDP Traffic - syslog	Disable
4000	515	UDP Traffic - printer	Disable
4000	517	UDP Traffic - talk	Disable
4000	518	UDP Traffic - ntalk	Disable
4000	520	UDP Traffic - route	Disable
4000	2049	UDP Traffic - nfs	Disable

String Signatures

The Cisco Secure IDS string signatures detect specific textual strings that you consider important. Your sensors examine network traffic using a standard regular expression matching algorithm to trigger your string signatures. The string signatures fall into the 8000 signature series, with the subsignature ID distinguishing the actual string signature that is triggered. You can create custom string signatures based on your operational needs. The default string signatures are listed in Table G-3.

Table G-3   *Default Cisco Secure IDS String Signatures*

Signature ID	Subsignature ID	Signature Name	Recommended Alarm Level
8000	2101	FTP Retrieve Password File	High
8000	2302	Telnet-/etc/shadow Match	High
8000	2303	Telnet-+ +	Low
8000	51301	Rlogin-IFS Match	High
8000	51302	Rlogin-/etc/shadow Match	High
8000	51303	Rlogin-+ +	Low

ACL Signatures

ACL signatures do not exist by default. You must establish these based on ACLs that you have created on your network devices.

Cisco IOS Firewall IDS Signature List

This appendix provides a complete list of Cisco IOS Firewall IDS signatures. It provides the information in two tables:

- Information Signatures
- Attack Signatures

The signatures in each table are listed in numeric order by their signature identification. Each signature entry includes the following fields:

- Signature ID
- Signature Category (attack or info)
- Signature Implementation (atomic or compound)
- Signature Name

NOTE   The signatures in the Cisco IOS Firewall IDS are referred to as either atomic or compound. This is a slight variation from Cisco Secure IDS, whose signatures are either atomic or composite. Compound and composite both refer to signatures that trigger on data from multiple packets.

For more detailed information on the signatures, refer to Chapter 9, "Understanding Cisco Secure IDS Signatures."

The intrusion-detection signatures included in the Cisco IOS Firewall IDS were chosen from a broad cross-section of intrusion-detection signatures as a representative sample of the most common network attacks and information-gathering scans. Because these signatures trigger on traffic that is not commonly seen on your network, the alarms generated indicate activity that should be investigated. Furthermore, the amount of false positives should be minimal.

NOTE	Atomic signatures that are marked with an asterisk (Atomic*) are allocated memory for session states by CBAC. These signatures use more memory on your router and can have a larger performance impact.

Information Signatures

The Cisco IOS Firewall IDS information signatures detect information-gathering activities, such as a port sweep, which attackers use to obtain information about your network. These signatures are listed in Table H-1.

Table H-1   *Cisco IOS Firewall IDS Information Signatures*

Signature ID	Signature Category	Signature Implementation	Signature Name
1000	Info	Atomic	IP options—Bad Option List
1001	Info	Atomic	IP options—Record Packet Route
1002	Info	Atomic	IP options—Timestamp
1003	Info	Atomic	IP options—Provide s, c, h, tcc
1004	Info	Atomic	IP options—Loose Source Route
1005	Info	Atomic	IP options—SATNET ID
1006	Info	Atomic	IP options—Strict Source Route
2000	Info	Atomic	ICMP Echo Reply
2001	Info	Atomic	ICMP Host Unreachable
2002	Info	Atomic	ICMP Source Quench
2003	Info	Atomic	ICMP Redirect
2004	Info	Atomic	ICMP Echo Request
2005	Info	Atomic	ICMP Time Exceeded for a Datagram
2006	Info	Atomic	ICMP Parameter Problem on Datagram
2007	Info	Atomic	ICMP Timestamp Request
2008	Info	Atomic	ICMP Timestamp Reply
2009	Info	Atomic	ICMP Information Request
2010	Info	Atomic	ICMP Information Reply
2011	Info	Atomic	ICMP Address Mask Request
2012	Info	Atomic	ICMP Address Mask Reply

continues

Table H-1   *Cisco IOS Firewall IDS Information Signatures (Continued)*

Signature ID	Signature Category	Signature Implementation	Signature Name
3151	Info	Compound	FTP SYST Command Attempt
6100	Info	Atomic*	RPC Port Registration
6101	Info	Atomic*	RPC Port Unregistration
6102	Info	Atomic*	RPC Dump
6150	Info	Atomic*	ypserv Portmap Request
6151	Info	Atomic*	ypbind Portmap
6152	Info	Atomic*	yppasswdd Portmap Request
6153	Info	Atomic*	ypupdated Portmap Request
6154	Info	Atomic*	ypxfrd Portmap Request
6155	Info	Atomic*	mountd Portmap Request
6175	Info	Atomic*	rexd Portmap Request
6180	Info	Atomic*	rexd Attempt

Attack Signatures

Cisco IOS Firewall IDS attack signatures detect attacks attempted against your protected network, such as denial of service attempts or the execution of illegal commands during an FTP session. These signatures are listed in Table H-2.

Table H-2   *Cisco IOS Firewall IDS Attack Signatures*

Signature ID	Signature Category	Signature Implementation	Signature Name
1100	Attack	Atomic	IP Fragment Attack
1101	Attack	Atomic	Unknown IP Protocol
1102	Attack	Atomic	Impossible IP Packet
2150	Attack	Atomic	Fragmented ICMP Traffic
2151	Attack	Atomic	Large ICMP Traffic
2154	Attack	Atomic	Ping of Death Attack
3040	Attack	Atomic	TCP—No Bits Set in Flags
3041	Attack	Atomic	TCP—SYN and FIN Bits Set
3042	Attack	Atomic	TCP—FIN Bit with No ACK Bit in Flags
3050	Attack	Compound	Half-open SYN Attack/SYN Flood

Table H-2 *Cisco IOS Firewall IDS Attack Signatures (Continued)*

Signature ID	Signature Category	Signature Implementation	Signature Name
3100	Attack	Compound	Smail Attack
3101	Attack	Compound	Sendmail Invalid Recipient
3102	Attack	Compound	Sendmail Invalid Sender
3103	Attack	Compound	Sendmail Reconnaissance
3104	Attack	Compound	Archaic Sendmail Attacks
3105	Attack	Compound	Sendmail Decode Alias
3106	Attack	Compound	Mail Spam
3107	Attack	Compound	Majordomo Execute Attack
3150	Attack	Compound	FTP Remote Command Execution
3152	Attack	Compound	FTP CWD ~root
3153	Attack	Atomic*	FTP Improper Address Specified
3154	Attack	Atomic*	FTP Improper Port Specified
4050	Attack	Atomic	UDP Bomb
4100	Attack	Compound	Tftp Passwd File
6103	Attack	Atomic*	Proxied RPC Request
6190	Attack	Atomic*	statd Buffer Overflow
8000 Subsig ID: 2101	Attack	Atomic	FTP Retrieve Password File

Cisco Secure Communications Deployment Worksheet

When deploying the components of your Cisco Secure IDS, you need to assign PostOffice communication parameters for each device (refer to Chapter 4, "Cisco Secure IDS Overview"). A mismatch between the parameters on your director and your sensor prevents the PostOffice protocol from operating correctly and requires you to spend time trouble-shooting your deployment.

To minimize input errors, it is helpful to lay out the parameters that you need to use for each of your Cisco Secure IDS components before you begin installing them. During installation and after, you need to use the parameters over and over. The worksheet in this appendix provides you with a single location to record all these parameters (see Figure I-1).

The first step in filling out the worksheet involves defining your organization parameters. Your director and sensors use the same organizational parameters. Therefore, you need to define only a single organizational name and ID. This process involves the following steps:

Step 1 Choose your alphanumeric organization name and record it on the worksheet. This name is usually associated with your company or department.

Step 2 Choose your numeric organization ID and record it on the worksheet. Next, you need to decide on the parameters to use for your Director.

Step 3 Choose your Director's alphanumeric host name and record it on the worksheet. You might want to include "director" in this name for easier identification when referencing this name later.

Step 4 Choose your Director's host ID and record it on the worksheet.

Step 5 Identify your Director's IP address and record it on the worksheet.

Finally, you need to determine the parameters for each sensor that you plan to deploy. For each sensor, you need to configure a host name, host ID, and an IP address. Each line in the sensor section of the worksheet represents these parameters for a different sensor. You need to perform the following steps for each sensor that you deploy:

Step 1   Choose an alphanumeric host name for the sensor and record it on the worksheet. You might want to include "sensor" and some reference to the deployment location when creating this name.

Step 2   Choose a host ID for the sensor and record it on the worksheet.

Step 3   Identify the sensor's IP address and record it on the worksheet.

NOTE   The host names must be unique within the same organization. This same restriction applies to the host IDs.

As you install the various components of your Cisco Secure IDS, you can quickly and easily refer to your filled out Cisco Secure Communications Deployment Worksheet when entering the required communications parameters. Furthermore, this worksheet is vital as you expand your Cisco Secure IDS in the future because it can show you the identification parameters for your existing components. If you remember to update your worksheet as you add new components, you can maintain a useful, quick reference for your communications parameters that is handy when debugging problems.

Figure I-1 *Cisco Secure Communications Deployment Worksheet*

Director Communication Parameters

Organization Name		Organization ID

Host Name	Host ID	IP Address

Sensor Communication Parameters

Host Name	Host ID	IP Address

Glossary

A

access control list. See *ACL*.

ACL. An access control list is a filter that you can apply to packets either coming into or leaving a physical interface on a Cisco router.

anomaly detection. An IDS triggering mechanism that uses user profiles as the basis for detecting attacks and policy violations. Anomaly detection is also sometimes referred to as *profile-based detection*. With anomaly detection, you must build profiles for each user group on the system. This profile incorporates a typical user's habits, the services she normally uses, and so on. This profile defines an established baseline for the activities that a normal user routinely does to perform her job.

atomic signature. Signatures that trigger on single packets, which can detect patterns as simple as an attempt to access a specific port on a host and do not require any knowledge of previous packets that have traversed the network.

attack signature. A Cisco IOS Firewall IDS signature that detects attacks attempted into the protected network, such as denial of service attempts or the execution of illegal commands during an FTP session. The Cisco IOS Firewall IDS divides its signatures into two categories: information and attack.

C

Cisco Secure ID Director. See *CSIDD*.

Cisco Secure IDS Director Platform. The Director platform is Cisco Secure IDS's graphical control interface. A single Director can manage and monitor a group of sensors, which enables security personnel to secure a network from a centralized console.

Cisco Secure IDS Sensor. An intrusion detection appliance that analyzes network traffic by using signatures to search for signs of unauthorized activity.

composite signature. Signatures that trigger on a sequence of packets, which can detect complex patterns, such as a sequence of operations distributed across multiple hosts over an arbitrary period of time.

cracker. Someone who breaks into protected resources for profit, for altruistic purposes, or because of the challenge, usually with malicious intent.

CSPM. Cisco Secure Policy Manager is one of the two Director platforms available to manage your Cisco Secure IDS. CSPM runs on Windows NT.

CSIDD. Cisco Secure ID Director is one of the two Director platforms available to manage your Cisco Secure IDS. CSIDD runs on Solaris or HPUX with HP OpenView.

D

DDoS. A distributed denial of service attack is a form of an attack where the attack launched against a victim host or network is launched from multiple attacking hosts.

denial of service attack. See *DoS*.

distributed denial of service. See *DDoS*.

DNS. The Domain Name System is the Internet-wide host name to IP address mapping. DNS enables you to convert human-readable names into the IP addresses needed for network packets.

Domain Name System. See *DNS*.

DoS. A denial of service attack is an attack whose goal is just to disrupt the operation of a specific system or network.

E

event horizon. The maximum amount of time over which an attack signature can be successfully detected (from initial data to complete attack signature).

F

false negative. Occurs when an IDS fails to generate an alarm for actual intrusive traffic that it is designed to detect.

false positive. Occurs when an IDS triggers an alarm on normal user traffic.

firewall. A security device that protects the perimeter of a network.

fragmentation. IP fragmentation involves breaking a single IP packet into multiple segments that are all below the maximum transmission size for the network.

H

hacker. Someone who gains unauthorized accessed to protected resources for personal amusement or gratification, usually without malicious intent.

HTTP. The Hypertext Transfer Protocol is the standard protocol used by Web sites to convey information to Web users. By default, this protocol uses TCP port 80.

Hypertext Transfer Protocol. See *HTTP*.

HTTPS. An extension to the standard HTTP protocol that provides confidentiality by encrypting the traffic from the Web site. By default, this protocol uses TCP port 443.

I

Ident. The Identification (Ident) protocol provides a mechanism to prevent host name and address spoofing, and also identifies false user names (see RFC 1413).

IDSM. Cisco Catalyst 6000 Intrusion Detection System Module is a line card that provides IDS functionality by monitoring traffic directly off your Cisco Catalyst 6000 family switch.

information signature. A Cisco IOS Firewall IDS signature that detects information-gathering activities, such as a port sweep, which attackers use to obtain information about your network. The Cisco IOS Firewall IDS divides its signatures into two categories: information and attack.

intrusion detection. Involves the ongoing monitoring of network traffic for potential misuse or policy violations. It matches network traffic against lists of signatures that look for patterns of misuse.

Intrusion Detection System Module. See *IDSM*.

J

Java Server Pages. See *JSP*.

JSP. Java Server Pages are an extension to the Java servlet technology that was developed by Sun as an alternative to Microsoft's Active Scripting Pages (ASP). Embedded in an HTML page, Java source code (and extensions) add functionality, such as dynamic database queries. Furthermore, JSP is platform-independent.

M

maximum transmission unit. See *MTU*.

misuse detection. Also known as *signature-based detection*; an IDS triggering mechanism that looks for intrusive activity by matching specific signatures.

MTU. The maximum transmission unit represents the maximum packet size that a network segment can handle. If a packet is larger than the MTU, the sending host breaks it into multiple frames and then transmits the multiple frames across the network for reassembly at the destination host.

N

network scanner. Tools that examine hosts on a network to locate security vulnerabilities.

Network Security Database. See *NSDB*.

NrConfigure. The File Configuration Management Utility used to configure your sensors and Directors when you use Cisco Secure ID Director.

NSDB. The Network Security Database is a database of security information that explains the signatures used by your Cisco Secure IDS along with the vulnerabilities on which these signatures are based. The NSDB is included as part of your Cisco Secure IDS.

P

PostOffice protocol. Provides a communication vehicle between your sensors and your Director platform.

R

regular expression. A mechanism by which you can define how to search for a specified sequence of characters in a data stream or file. Many different programs use regular expressions to enable you to create custom string searches. In the UNIX world, the **grep** command is probably the most common program that utilizes regular expressions to search for text.

Remote Procedure Call. See *RPC*.

RPC. Remote Procedure Call is a protocol that enables one program to request a service from another computer on a network. This protocol does not require the requesting computer to understand the layout of the network.

S

SATAN. The Security Analysis Tool for Auditing Networks is one of the original network scanners that was created to enable system administrators to proactively check the security of their networks. This tool has been renamed to Security Administrator Integrated Network Tool (SAINT).

Security Analysis Tool for Auditing Networks. See *SATAN*.

security policy. A set of policies or rules that define allowable practices and services on your network. By minimizing acceptable services and procedures, you can control the security of your overall network by reducing weak links.

signature. A set of rules pertaining to typical intrusive activity, which is compared against the actual network traffic. When network traffic matches a specific set of rules, a unique response is generated for the event. In Cisco Secure IDS, signatures are categorized into two implementation categories: atomic and composite.

signature threshold. A limit that defines a boundary that must be surpassed for the signature to trigger. For example, a port scan might have a signature threshold of 10 ports.

SPAN. Switch Port Analyzer ports enable you to direct traffic from various ports and VLANs on your switch to a specific destination port for analysis by your IDS.

Switch Port Analyzer. See *SPAN*.

U

UNC. The Universal Naming Convention or Uniform Naming Convention is a PC format for specifying the location of resources on a local area network.

Universal Naming Convention. See *UNC*.

V

VACL. VLAN ACL is a security feature that enables access controls for all packets on a Catalyst 6000 switch via a Policy Feature Card (PFC). You can use VACLs to redirect a copy of network traffic from multiple VLANs to your IDSM for analysis.

Virtual Private Network. See *VPN*.

VLAN ACL. See *VACL*.

VPN. A Virtual Private Network provides confidentiality for network traffic between hosts or networks using encryption.

Answers to Review Questions

This appendix contains the answers to each chapter's review questions. Because some of the questions are in short answer format, your answers will vary. The author has given the best possible answer and explanation for each question.

Chapter 1 Answers

1 What are the four types of network security threats?

The four types of network security threats are unstructured threats, structured threats, external threats, and internal threats.

2 What are the three main attack types?

The three main attack types are reconnaissance, access, and denial of service.

3 Why is network security needed?

The global connectivity of the Internet has enabled hackers to attack your network from anywhere in the world.

4 What is a script kiddie?

A script kiddie is an inexperienced attacker who blindly runs scripts against computer networks.

5 What is reconnaissance?

Reconnaissance or information gathering is the unauthorized mapping of systems, services, or vulnerabilities on a network.

6 What is a denial of service (DoS) attack?

A denial of service attack is designed to disrupt the operation of a specific system or network by denying access to that network resource.

7 What are the five security principles that define the security on your network?

The five basic security concepts are authentication, authorization, confidentiality, integrity, and availability.

8 What is the first step in a network attack?

To attack a network, your first step is to define the goals that you want your attack to accomplish. These goals then drive the remaining phases of your attack.

9 Attackers use what attack methodologies?

The attack methodologies used are ad hoc, methodical, surgical strike, and patient (slow).

10 What are common network attack points?

The common network attack points are network resources and network protocols.

Chapter 2 Answers

1 What are the four steps in the Cisco Security Wheel?

The four steps in the Cisco Security Wheel are secure the network, monitor the network, test network security, and improve network security.

2 What two types of monitoring are commonly used to detect violations in your security policy?

The two types of monitoring that are commonly used are active monitoring and passive monitoring.

3 What software tool can you use to test the security of your network?

Network scanners are used to test the security of your network.

4 What are four areas that you need to examine to secure your network?

Four areas that need to be considered when securing your network security are tightening authentication, installing firewalls, establishing VPNs, and vulnerability patching.

5 What is a firewall?

A firewall is a security component that limits traffic flow to a protected network based on a predefined security policy.

6 What two basic security concepts does a VPN provide?

A VPN provides confidentiality and integrity.

7 Where are two places that you can monitor security news on the Web?

Security news can be obtained from security mailing lists and security Web sites.

Chapter 3 Answers

1 What are the two major types of IDS monitoring?

The major types of IDS monitoring are host-based and network-based.

2 What are the two types of IDS triggering?

The two types of IDS triggering are anomaly (profile-based) and misuse detection (signature-based).

3 What is the purpose of an IDS?

An IDS detects attacks against your network.

4 What is anomaly detection?

Anomaly detection is detecting alarms by observing actions that deviate from normal user activity.

5 What is the major drawback to host-based IDS monitoring?

The biggest drawback to host-based IDS monitoring is supporting multiple OSs.

6 What is misuse detection?

Misuse detection is generating alarms by matching data with signatures of known intrusive activity that are stored in a database.

7 What is a major benefit of anomaly detection?

Anomaly detection can detect previously unknown attacks.

8 What are two major limitations of network-based IDSs?

Two major limitations of network-based IDSs are bandwidth and encryption.

9 What is a hybrid IDS?

A hybrid IDS combines multiple IDS technologies into a single IDS to produce enhanced functionality.

10 What are some benefits to signature-based IDSs?

Signature-based IDSs have a signature database based on actual attack data; the attacks detected are well defined; the system is easy to understand; and it detects attacks immediately upon installation.

11 What are the drawbacks to misuse detection?

Misuse detection cannot detect unknown attacks; signature databases need to be updated with new attack signatures; and the system must maintain state information.

12 What are some drawbacks to anomaly detection?

Anomaly detection is complicated and difficult to understand; requires an initial training period; does not protect network during training; and must keep user profiles current. It is difficult to define normal activity and a one-to-one correspondence between alarms and attack type does not exist.

13 What is the difference between a false positive and a false negative?

A false positive is an alarm generated because of normal user traffic, whereas a false negative represents the IDS failing to generate an alarm for a known attack.

Chapter 4 Answers

1 What are the two main components of the Cisco Secure IDS?

The two main components of the Cisco Secure IDS are the Director and the sensor.

2 Is Cisco Secure IDS a network-based IDS?

Yes. Cisco Secure IDS is a network-based IDS.

3 What is intrusion detection?

Intrusion detection is the ability to detect attacks against your network.

4 What are the two Cisco Secure IDS Director Platforms?

The Cisco Secure IDS Director Platforms are the Cisco Secure Policy Manager and the Director for UNIX.

5 What are the features of the PostOffice protocol?

Features provided by the PostOffice protocol are reliability, redundancy, and fault tolerance.

6 What is the IDS triggering mechanism used by Cisco Secure IDS?

Cisco Secure IDS uses a signature database to trigger intrusion alarms, making it a misuse-based IDS, as well as a network-based IDS.

7 How many different types of sensor platforms are supported by Cisco Secure IDS?

Cisco Secure IDS supports two types of sensors: 4200 Series (PC appliances) and the Catalyst 6000 IDS Module (line card).

8 What are the two 4200 Series Sensors?

The two 4200 Series Sensors are IDS-4210 and the IDS-4230.

9 What are the three types of responses that a sensor can perform in reply to an attack?

The three sensor responses to an attack are TCP reset, IP blocking, and IP logging.

10 How do Cisco Secure IDS devices communicate with each other?

Cisco Secure IDS devices communicate with each other by using the proprietary PostOffice protocol.

11 What three identifiers are used to construct a unique addressing scheme for Cisco Secure IDS?

The three identifiers that form a unique address are an organization identifier, a host identifier, and an application identifier.

12 Can multiple systems share the same host ID?

Multiple systems can share the same host ID only if they have different organization IDs.

Chapter 5 Answers

1 What are the common entry points into your network?

The common entry points into your network are your Internet connection(s), extranets, intranets, and remote access connections.

2 When analyzing your network topology to determine sensor deployment, what are the main issues that you need to examine?

The main issues that you need to consider to help determine where to deploy your sensors are the entry points into your network, critical network components, remote networks, size and complexity of your network, and your security policy restrictions.

3 What are some common network boundaries that you can monitor with your Cisco Secure IDS Sensors?

The common network boundaries that you can monitor with your sensors are your network perimeter, connections with your business partners (extranets), intranets, and remote access connections.

4 What are the four common sensor deployment configurations?

The four common sensor deployment configurations are standalone, device management, firewall sandwich, and remote sensor.

5 Where is your perimeter router typically located?

Your perimeter router is typically located between your internal network and your Internet connection.

6 What are intranets?

Intranets are internal divisions within your network.

7   What is IP blocking?

Blocking refers to the process by which your IDS sensor can dynamically update the ACL on a router to block traffic from an attacking host.

8   What are some common servers that are frequently targeted by attackers?

Some common servers frequently targeted by attackers are DNS servers, DHCP servers, HTTP servers, Windows domain controllers, e-mail servers, and NFS servers.

9   What is a firewall?

A firewall is a security device that you use to establish a security barrier that restricts traffic flow between multiple networks.

10   In a firewall sandwich sensor configuration with device management, which features must you enable?

In a firewall sandwich sensor configuration with device management, you must enable Telnet access on your router; you must add the router to the sensor's device management list; and you must permit the Telnet traffic from the sensor to the router.

11   When deploying Cisco Secure IDS Sensors remotely across an untrusted network, what security concepts do you need to employ to protect the traffic from attackers?

When deploying a Cisco Secure IDS Sensor remotely across an untrusted network, you need to ensure confidentiality (via encryption) and integrity of the traffic to protect it from attackers.

12   What is a war-dialer?

A war-dialer is a tool that dials a specified range of phone numbers looking for modem connections.

13   Why is it important to restrict the hosts on the command and control network to only Cisco Secure IDS components and a few infrastructure devices?

To minimize the ability of an attacker to directly attack your IDS components, it is important to minimize the number of hosts on your command and control network.

Chapter 6 Answers

1   Which CSPM installation configurations support Cisco Secure IDS Sensor management?

The Standalone configuration and the Client-Server configuration support Cisco Secure IDS Sensor management.

2 How many permanent license options does CSPM support?

CSPM supports two permanent license options: a Lite License and an Unlimited License.

3 Why do you have to install Cisco Secure PostOffice on your CSPM system?

You need to install Cisco Secure PostOffice on your CSPM system because the Cisco Secure IDS Sensors use this protocol to communicate with the Director Platform.

4 What is the difference between the Lite License and the Unlimited License?

Both licenses provide the same functionality. The only difference is that the Lite License limits the number of managed devices to three.

5 On what operating system does CSPM run?

CSPM runs on Windows NT 4.0, with Service Pack 6a.

6 What is the minimum processor speed recommended for a CSPM host?

The minimum recommended processor speed for a CSPM host is 200 MHZ.

7 What is the minimum amount of RAM recommended on a CSPM client host?

The minimum recommended amount of RAM on a CSPM host is 96 MB.

8 What is the minimum recommended free space for a CSPM server installation?

It is recommended that your system have 8 GB of free space on your hard drive to install CSPM.

9 What formatting must you use for your CSPM disk partition?

Your CSPM disk partition needs to be formatted with NTFS.

10 Why is the TechSmith Screen Capture Codec needed?

The TechSmith decompression software is needed to view the "Getting Started" videos that are supplied with your CSPM software.

11 Can you change the account name used to access CSPM during the installation process?

The account that you initiate the installation process with is the account that you use to access CSPM. You can change this account only by initiating the installation process with another privileged account.

Chapter 7 Answers

1 How many different types of the 4200 Series Sensor exist?

Two models of 4200 Series Sensors exist: IDS-4230 and IDS-4210. The IDS-4230 comes in numerous models based on the network environment in which it will be used.

2   What is the **sysconfig-sensor** script?

The sysconfig-sensor script sets up the basic parameters on the sensor.

3   What are the management options available for accessing your Cisco Secure IDS Sensor?

You can manage your Cisco Secure IDS Sensor through the serial port, the keyboard, Telnet, and through the Director Platform.

4   What account do you need to be logged on to the sensor with to execute the **sysconfig-sensor** script?

You must be logged on as root to execute the sysconfig-sensor script.

5   What are the default accounts on the 4200 Series Sensors?

The default accounts on the 4200 Series Sensors are root and netrangr.

6   Besides setting up the initial parameters on the sensor, for what reason is the root account used?

You use the root account to perform Solaris operating system–level tasks and sometimes to debug the operation of the sensor (such as running snoop to view raw network packets).

7   What are the differences between the IDS-4230 and IDS-4210 Sensors?

The IDS 4230 supports more network types, a dual processor, and more memory, whereas the IDS-4210 has a smaller chassis.

8   What is a policy enforcement point (PEP)?

The policy enforcement points are the devices within your network that actually enforce your security policy. These devices include IDS Sensors, PIX Firewalls, and managed routers.

9   What is a policy distribution point?

The policy distribution point is the host that manages the changes to your security policy. Usually, this is your CSPM host.

10   What are the IP configuration parameters that you must set on your sensor by using **sysconfig-sensor**?

The IP configuration parameters that you need to set with sysconfig-sensor are IP address, IP netmask, IP host name, and default gateway.

11   What are the primary PostOffice parameters that you need to know when installing your sensor?

You need to know the sensor's host ID, the sensor's host name, its IP address, the organization ID, and the organization name.

12 When changing your sensor configuration by using **sysconfig-sensor**, which options require you to reboot your sensor?

If you change options 1–5, you need to reboot your sensor. Furthermore, if you change the time zone through option 7, you need to reboot your sensor.

Chapter 8 Answers

1 What serves as the interface to the alarms in the CSPM database?

The CSPM Event Viewer provides a graphical interface to the alarm data in the CSPM database.

2 What is the NSDB?

The Network Security Database provides the user with a database of information on attack signatures and security vulnerabilities.

3 What is the context buffer?

The context buffer is a buffer (maximum 255 characters) of characters that show the data in a TCP stream around the moment that an attack signature is triggered.

4 What is a subsignature ID?

The subsignature ID is a secondary identification field that some signatures require to provide more information on the attack signature.

5 When you expand more columns on an alarm entry, are those changes present when you open another Event Viewer?

When you expand more columns on an alarm entry, the changes are not persistent. New instances of the Event Viewer will not have these changes.

6 How do you change the default order of columns for new Event Viewers?

You can use Insert/Modify Columns window to alter the columns displayed in new Event Viewers because it is a persistent change. (Note: Just moving the columns using the mouse to click-and-drag columns does not affect a new Event Viewer because the move operation is not persistent.)

7 What are your two options for indicating event severity?

You can choose strict colors or icons.

8 What values can the alarm level assume?

Alarm level is a numeric value that usually ranges between 1 and 5. (The maximum range is 1 to 255.)

9 What values can the alarm severity assume?

The alarm severity can assume the values Low, Medium, and High.

10   Which fields can remove CSPM features if they are deleted from your Event Viewer?

The following fields can remove CSPM features if you remove them from your CSPM Event Viewer: Source Address, Sensor Name, Org Name, App Name.

11   How do you determine the amount of TCP traffic that one of your sensors regularly examines?

Using the Statistics option from the Connection Status pane, you can view the IP statistics for any of your sensors.

12   Which customizations to the Event Viewer are persistent?

Changes to the default column order using the Insert/Modify Columns window, and changes to your Preference settings are both persistent changes.

13   When deleting alarm entries from the Event Viewer, what are your three options?

When deleting alarm entries, you can choose one of three options: From this Grid, From All Grids, and From The Database.

14   What two techniques can you use to enable your CSPM host to resolve host names?

You can manually configure a C:\WINNT\system32\drivers\etc\hosts file defining the host name–IP address pairs that you need to resolve or you can configure your CSPM host to communicate with a DNS server.

15   Is the signature ID equal to the vulnerability ID of the related vulnerability for each signature?

No, the signature ID and the vulnerability ID are not related.

16   If you delete the Source Address field from the Event Viewer, what functions can you no longer perform from the Event Viewer?

By deleting the Source Address field from the Event Viewer, you lose the ability to use the Block and Remove Block functions on the Event Viewer.

17   What menu selection do you need to use to view the running status of the daemons on your sensor?

To view the running status of the daemons on your sensor, you need to use the Service Status menu option.

18   If you delete the App Name field from the Event Viewer, what functions are no longer available?

When you delete the App Name field, you can no longer perform the View Statistics or Reset Statistics commands.

19   If the Blank Right preference option is selected, what will the field to the right of the expansion boundary contain?

If you have the Blank Right preference option selected, the field to the right of the expansion boundary will contain a plus sign (+).

Chapter 9 Answers

1 What are the two signature implementation categories?

The two signature implementation categories are content and context.

2 What are the three severity levels associated with Cisco Secure IDS signatures?

The three severity levels are low, medium, and high.

3 What are the classes of signatures?

The classes of signatures are reconnaissance, informational, access, and denial of service.

4 What does a content signature examine?

A content signature examines the packet payload to look for intrusive activity.

5 Alarms with which severity represent the most significant threat to your network?

High-severity alarms represent the most significant threat to your network.

6 What are the four signature classes that break down signatures based on the goal of the attacker?

The four signature classes based on the goal of the attacker are reconnaissance, informational, access, and denial of service.

7 What is a port scan?

A port scan is detected when an attacker attempts to locate multiple ports/services on a single host.

8 What are the four categories of signatures based on network traffic?

Based on network traffic, signatures fall into four categories: general, connection, string, and ACL signatures.

9 What is a Cisco Secure IDS signature?

A Cisco Secure IDS signature is a set of rules that your sensor uses to detect typical intrusive activity.

10 What are the two structure types for Cisco Secure IDS signatures?

Cisco Secure IDS signatures can either be atomic or composite.

11 What does it mean to say that a signature is composite?

A composite signature needs to examine multiple packets to observe a complete attack signature.

12 What are the major areas of an IP packet that are examined by context signatures?

Context signatures examine port numbers, IP options, IP fragmentation parameters, TCP flags, IP protocol field, checksums (IP, TCP, and UDP), and IP addresses.

Chapter 10 Answers

1   If you notice a 4xxx signature, what do you know immediately (even if you don't know the exact signature that triggered)?

You know that a 4xxx signature involves UDP traffic.

2   If you enable IP fragment reassembly, which fragmentation signatures does Cisco Secure IDS use?

When fragment reassembly is enabled, the 12xx fragment signatures are enabled. Otherwise, the 11xx fragment signatures are used.

3   If your sensor detects a TCP attack, what range does the signature ID fall into?

TCP signatures fall into the 3000 Series signatures.

4   Into which signature series (range of signature IDs) does ICMP fall?

ICMP signatures fall into the 2000 Series of signatures.

5   Which signatures fall into the 1000 series of signatures?

The 1000 Series signatures cover IP signatures.

6   Beside the string to search for, what other parameters do you need to specify for a custom string signature?

For a custom string signature, you must specify port number, traffic direction, and number of occurrences in addition to the actual string.

7   What types of signatures fall into the 6000 Series signatures?

The 6000 Series signatures represent cross-protocol signatures, such as DNS, RPC, and authentication failures.

8   How are string signatures identified?

String signatures all have a Signature ID of 8000. Therefore, you can identify them by their subID.

9   What is a host sweep?

A host sweep is when an attack scans several hosts on a network looking for a specific service.

10   What is fragmentation?

When the size of a packet is too large, it can be broken into several smaller fragments and reassembled by the destination host. This process is known as fragmentation.

Chapter 11 Answers

1   What is IP fragment reassembly?

IP fragment reassembly is the reconstruction of fragmented IP datagrams by the sensor.

2   Which Cisco Secure IDS Sensors support TCP session reassembly?

Currently, TCP session reassembly is available only in the 2.5(X) IDSM software version.

3   What is the Watchdog process?

The Watchdog process monitors the health of the processes running on the local system to verify that they are operational.

4   What are the eight major configuration tabs that you use to configure your sensor parameters?

The eight major configuration tabs are the following: Properties, Sensing, Blocking, Logging, Filtering, Command, Advanced, and Control.

5   Where do you configure the TCP stream reassembly parameters?

The TCP stream reassembly parameters are configured on the Sensing configuration screen.

6   Where do you configure the advanced PostOffice parameters?

The advanced PostOffice parameters are configured using the Advanced configuration screen.

7   Which screen enables you to transfer updated configuration files to your sensor?

The Command screen enables you to update the configuration files on your sensor.

8   What are the advanced PostOffice parameters?

The advanced PostOffice parameters are Watchdog Interval and Timeout, Number of Restarts, Daemon Down and Unstartable Alarm Levels, and the PostOffice Heartbeat Interval.

9   What are the three options for TCP stream reassembly?

The three options for TCP stream reassembly are No Reassembly, Loose Reassembly, and Strict Reassembly.

10   What is the TCP Embryonic Timeout?

The TCP Embryonic Timeout is a TCP stream reassembly parameter that specifies the number of seconds that can transpire before the sensor frees the resources allocated for an initiated, but not fully established, TCP session.

11   What are the main feature differences between the 4200 Series Sensor and the IDSM Sensor?

The IDSM Sensor supports TCP stream reassembly and the 4200 Series Sensor supports blocking.

12   What is the function of the Additional Destinations feature?

The Additional Destinations feature enables you to configure your sensor to send alarm events to multiple sources. These destinations can be services on remote hosts or different services on the local system.

13   What does the Maximum Partial Datagrams field regulate?

The Maximum Partial Datagrams field determines how many separate fragmented packets your sensor can attempt to reconstruct at one time.

14   What is the PostOffice Heartbeat Interval?

The PostOffice Heartbeat Interval is the frequency at which a remote host is checked to verify that PostOffice connectivity is still operational.

Chapter 12 Answers

1   What are the four classes of signatures?

The four classes of signatures are General, Connection, String, and ACL.

2   What are the basic configurable parameters for all signatures in your signature template?

The basic configurable signature parameters are severity, enable/disable, and actions.

3   What three actions can your sensor take when a signature triggers?

The three actions that your sensor can take when a sensor triggers are block, TCP reset, and IP log.

4   Are advanced signature configuration options available on all sensor platforms?

Advanced signature configuration options are not available on all sensor platforms.

5   What advanced signature configuration options does the IDSM Sensor provide?

The IDSM Sensor provides Signature Tuning and Port Mapping.

6   What is the *default* template?

The default template is a template automatically created by CSPM that contains all the Cisco Secure IDS signatures.

7 What options are available for both the source and destination addresses when using advanced filtering?

With advanced filtering, you can specify any IP address, all internal or external IP addresses, a single IP address, a range of IP addresses, or an IP network.

8 What three mechanisms can you use to filter traffic to the CSPM host?

You can filter traffic to the CSPM host by setting the minimum event level to be sent to the management console, through simple filtering and through advanced filtering.

9 What is a SYSLOG data source?

A SYSLOG data source represents a network device on which your sensor is monitoring the SYSLOG messages.

10 What parameters do you need to configure specifically for string signatures?

Besides the basic parameters, you need to configure the following parameters for string signatures: string to find, port, traffic direction, and number of occurrences.

11 What features do advanced filters provide that are not available for simple filters?

With advanced filters, you can specify different exclude options for the source and destination addresses; you have more exclude address options; and you can assign multiple signatures to a single filter.

12 What are the two methods for accessing the Signature Actions pop-up window?

You can access the Signature Actions pop-up window by clicking the Modify button of the Signatures tab, or you can double-click the Actions field of a specific signature.

13 How do you rename a signature template?

To rename a signature template, right-click the signature template name and select Rename from the drop-down menu.

14 Which sensor configuration tab enables you to add simple and advanced filters?

The Filtering Sensor configuration tab enables you to define and modify simple and advanced signature filters.

15 How do you access the Signature Parameter Editor?

You access the Signature Parameter Editor by double-clicking the signature in the Signature Tuning Parameters subtab.

16 Can you use spaces when specifying port numbers for port mapping?

You cannot use spaces when specifying a port list for port mapping. The list must include only port numbers delimited by commas.

17 How do you specify an address for a simple filter?

For a simple filter, you specify an address by entering an address and a network mask.

18 What is the address role in a simple filter?

The address role configures a simple filter's IP address as the destination address, source address, or source or destination address.

19 Can you specify a range of IP addresses for both the source and destination of an advanced filter?

Yes, you can specify a range of addresses for both the source and destination of an advanced filter.

20 Where do you configure the minimum event level?

The minimum event level is located on the Filtering Sensor configuration tab.

21 Through CSPM, what values can you configure for the minimum event level?

The minimum event level can be Low, Medium, or High.

22 What category does the Sensor Signatures section fall under on the main CSPM window?

Sensor Signatures fall under the Tools and Services section.

23 Where do you assign a signature template to a sensor?

You assign a signature template to a sensor through the Active Configuration drop-down menu, which is located on the Sensing tab screen.

24 How do you push updated configuration files to your sensor?

To push updated configuration files to your sensor, click the Approve Now button, which is located on the Command tab screen.

Chapter 13 Answers

1 When a signature is configured to block fires, what does it block?

The automatic blocking for a signature is applied to the source IP address of the host that fired the signature.

2 What is the only way in which to block an entire network?

You can block an entire network only through manual blocking.

3 What is a blocking device?

A blocking device is the Cisco IOS device that enforces the blocking ACL.

4 How does your sensor block attacking traffic?

The sensor telnets into the router and applies an ACL to block traffic.

5 Which two ACL numbers do your sensors use to block traffic by default?

Your sensors use ACL 199 and 198 to implement blocking on your network.

6 What is the default automatic blocking duration?

The default automatic blocking duration is 30 minutes.

7 Where do you view the current IP addresses and networks that are being blocked?

From the Event Viewer, you can view the currently blocked addresses by choosing the View, Block List menu option.

8 Where do you establish manual blocking?

From the Event Viewer, you can block the currently selected alarm entry by choosing either Actions, Block, Host or Actions, Block, or Network.

9 What is the default manual blocking duration?

The default manual blocking duration is 1440 minutes.

10 Where do you change the default manual blocking duration?

Using the Event Viewer, you can change the default manual blocking duration by selecting Edit, Preferences and changing the Time To Block (minutes) in the Actions section.

11 Where do you change the default automatic blocking duration value?

The default automatic blocking duration value is set through the Blocking tab on the sensor view panel.

Chapter 14 Answers

1 What is the active partition on the IDSM?

The active partition on the IDSM is the partition into which the IDSM boots.

2 How many ports does the IDSM line card have?

The IDSM line card has two ports: a monitoring port and a command and control port.

3 What IDSM command enables you to configure the PostOffice communication parameters for the IDSM line card?

The setup command enables you to configure the PostOffice parameters on your IDSM line card.

4 What is the default active partition on the IDSM line card?

The application partition is the default partition.

5 What operating system is required on your Catalyst 6000 family switch to use an IDSM line card?

Catalyst OS 6.1(1) or higher is required to use an IDSM line card on your switch.

6 What hardware is required to use VACLs to capture traffic for your IDSM line card?

To use VACLs to capture traffic, your Catalyst switch must have a Policy Feature Card (PFC).

7 How much traffic can the IDSM line card process?

The IDSM line card can analyze 100 Mbps.

8 What switch command is used to set up a VACL?

The set security, acl ip switch command is used to create a VACL.

9 Which port on the IDSM line card is the command and control interface?

Port 2 on the IDSM line card is the command and control interface.

10 What are the two mechanisms used to capture traffic for the IDSM line card?

You can use SPAN and VACL to capture traffic for the IDSM Sensor.

11 How many VACLs can you have per protocol?

You can have one VACL per protocol.

12 What does an amber status LED indicate on your IDSM line card?

An amber status LED indicates that the IDSM is disabled or running a boot and self-diagnostics sequence.

13 What command do you use to access the console on the IDSM line card?

You use the session switch command to access the console on the IDSM console.

14 What is the default user name/password for console access to the IDSM line card?

The IDSM default console user name is *ciscoids*, and the password is *attack*.

15 What switch command do you use to set up a SPAN association on your switch?

The set span switch command defines a SPAN association on your switch.

16 What are the four types of IDSM software files?

The four types of IDSM software files are application (a), maintenance (m), service packs (sp), and signature (sig).

Chapter 15 Answers

1 How can you determine which Cisco Secure IDS processes are currently running on your CSIDD?

After logging on to the Director with the netrangr account, you can check the Cisco Secure IDS processes that are running by executing the nrstatus command.

2 How do you initially define the basic configuration parameters on your CSIDD?

You use the sysconfig-director script to define the basic configuration parameters for CSIDD.

3 What logon account is created by the CSIDD installation program?

The netrangr logon account is created by the CSIDD installation program.

4 How do you define the basic identification parameters on your sensor?

After logging on to your sensor with the root account, you run the sysconfig-sensor to configure the basic identification/communication parameters for your sensor.

5 What three host types can you add using the Add Host Wizard?

You can configure three host types using the Add Host Wizard: Initialize a newly installed sensor, connect to a previously configured sensor, and forward alarms to a secondary Director.

6 A yellow icon corresponds to what alarm level(s)?

A yellow icon corresponds to an alarm level of 3.

7 Does defining a protected network prevent your Cisco Secure IDS Sensor from detecting intrusive activity from hosts on the protected network?

Defining protected networks defines only which networks are protected by your Cisco Secure IDS. It does not prevent the detection of intrusive activity from systems on these networks.

8 What alarm level(s) does a red icon represent?

A red icon represents an alarm level of 4 or 5.

9 Do you need to reboot your Director after running the **sysconfig-director** script during the installation process?

Yes. You must reboot the Director after running the sysconfig-director during the initial installation process.

10 What is Cisco Secure ID Director (CSIDD)?

CSIDD is one of the two Director Platforms available for Cisco Secure IDS.

11   What software is required to install CSIDD?

CSIDD requires the Solaris or HPUX operating system, as well as HP OpenView Network Node Manager (NNM) to operate.

Chapter 16 Answers

1   What is a transient version?

A transient version is a copy of a configuration that is made when you make configuration changes to an existing configuration version.

2   What is the Configuration Library?

The Configuration Library is a tool that enables you to maintain and manage multiple configurations for your Cisco Secure IDS components.

3   What is the Cisco Secure IDS Configuration File Management Utility or nrConfigure?

The Cisco Secure IDS Configuration File Management Utility (known as nrConfigure) is a central management facility that you use to manage the configuration of your Director, as well as your remote sensors that are distributed across your network when you use the CSIDD.

4   When you delete a sensor through nrConfigure, is its icon on the Cisco Secure IDS Home submap also deleted?

The sensor icon is not deleted when you delete the sensor through nrConfigure.

5   If your only saved configuration versions are 1 and 2, and you modify version 1, what is the version of the transient configuration?

If you have two saved configuration versions (1 and 2) and you modify version 1, the transient version is 1.1.

6   If your only saved configuration versions are 1, 1.1, and 2, and you modify version 1, what is the version of the transient configuration?

If you have three saved configuration versions (1, 1.1, and 2) and you modify version 1, the transient version is 1.0.1.

Chapter 17 Answers

1   Does the Cisco IOS Firewall IDS support as many signatures as the regular sensor appliance? If not, how many does each support?

No. The Cisco IOS Firewall IDS supports only 59 signatures, whereas the sensor appliance supports over 300.

2 What are the three response actions that you can configure?

The three response actions that you can configure for the Cisco IOS Firewall IDS are alarm, TCP reset, and drop packets.

3 What are some deployment issues that must be considered before deploying the Cisco IOS Firewall IDS on your network?

The issues that must be considered before deploying a Cisco IOS Firewall IDS are memory usage and performance impact, signature coverage, and signature updates.

4 What is the command to globally disable an IDS signature on your Cisco IOS Firewall IDS?

The command to globally disable an IDS Signature on the Cisco IOS Firewall IDS is ip audit signature sig-id disable.

5 What command do you use to turn off the IDS functionality on your Cisco IOS Firewall IDS?

The command to turn off the IDS functionality on your Cisco IOS Firewall IDS is clear ip audit configuration.

6 What is the command to set the router's Director PostOffice parameters?

The command to set the router's Director PostOffice parameters is ip audit po remote.

7 What is the command to set the router's local PostOffice parameters?

The command to set the router's local PostOffice parameters is ip audit po local.

8 What command do you use in conjunction with the **ip audit signature** command to exclude a host or network from triggering a specific alarm?

To exclude a host or network from triggering a specific alarm, you use the access-list command in conjunction with the ip audit signature.

9 What command do you use to show your IDS configuration on your router?

To show your IDS configuration on your router, you use the show ip audit configuration command.

10 What destinations can you configure for alarms on your router?

You can configure your router to send alarms to CSIDD, as well as the router's SYSLOG service or console.

INDEX

Symbols & Numerics

A

E

F

S

T

W-Z

CCIE Professional Development

Cisco LAN Switching

Kennedy Clark, CCIE; Kevin Hamilton, CCIE

1-57870-094-9 • AVAILABLE NOW

This volume provides an in-depth analysis of Cisco LAN switching technologies, architectures, and deployments, including unique coverage of Catalyst network design essentials. Network designs and configuration examples are incorporated throughout to demonstrate the principles and enable easy translation of the material into practice in production networks.

Advanced IP Network Design

Alvaro Retana, CCIE; Don Slice, CCIE; and Russ White, CCIE

1-57870-097-3 • AVAILABLE NOW

Network engineers and managers can use these case studies, which highlight various network design goals, to explore issues including protocol choice, network stability, and growth. This book also includes theoretical discussion on advanced design topics.

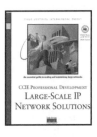

Large-Scale IP Network Solutions

Khalid Raza, CCIE; and Mark Turner

1-57870-084-1 • AVAILABLE NOW

Network engineers can find solutions as their IP networks grow in size and complexity. Examine all the major IP protocols in-depth and learn about scalability, migration planning, network management, and security for large-scale networks.

Routing TCP/IP, Volume I

Jeff Doyle, CCIE

1-57870-041-8 • AVAILABLE NOW

This book takes the reader from a basic understanding of routers and routing protocols through a detailed examination of each of the IP interior routing protocols. Learn techniques for designing networks that maximize the efficiency of the protocol being used. Exercises and review questions provide core study for the CCIE Routing and Switching exam.

Cisco Press

www.ciscopress.com

Cisco Press Solutions

Enhanced IP Services for Cisco Networks
Donald C. Lee, CCIE

1-57870-106-6 • AVAILABLE NOW

This is a guide to improving your network's capabilities by understanding the new enabling and advanced Cisco IOS services that build more scalable, intelligent, and secure networks. Learn the technical details necessary to deploy Quality of Service, VPN technologies, IPsec, the IOS firewall and IOS Intrusion Detection. These services will allow you to extend the network to new frontiers securely, protect your network from attacks, and increase the sophistication of network services.

Developing IP Multicast Networks, Volume I
Beau Williamson, CCIE

1-57870-077-9 • AVAILABLE NOW

This book provides a solid foundation of IP multicast concepts and explains how to design and deploy the networks that will support appplications such as audio and video conferencing, distance-learning, and data replication. Includes an in-depth discussion of the PIM protocol used in Cisco routers and detailed coverage of the rules that control the creation and maintenance of Cisco mroute state entries.

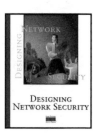

Designing Network Security
Merike Kaeo

1-57870-043-4 • AVAILABLE NOW

Designing Network Security is a practical guide designed to help you understand the fundamentals of securing your corporate infrastructure. This book takes a comprehensive look at underlying security technologies, the process of creating a security policy, and the practical requirements necessary to implement a corporate security policy.

Cisco Press   **www.ciscopress.com**

Cisco Press Solutions

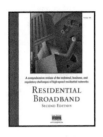

Residential Broadband, Second Edition

George Abe

1-57870-177-5 • AVAILABLE NOW

This book will answer basic questions of residential broadband networks such as: Why do we need high speed networks at home? How will high speed residential services be delivered to the home? How do regulatory or commercial factors affect this technology? Explore such networking topics as xDSL, cable, and wireless.

Internetworking Technologies Handbook, Second Edition

Kevin Downes, CCIE, Merilee Ford, H. Kim Lew, Steve Spanier, Tim Stevenson

1-57870-102-3 • AVAILABLE NOW

This comprehensive reference provides a foundation for understanding and implementing contemporary internetworking technologies, providing you with the necessary information needed to make rational networking decisions. Master terms, concepts, technologies, and devices that are used in the internetworking industry today. You also learn how to incorporate networking technologies into a LAN/WAN environment, as well as how to apply the OSI reference model to categorize protocols, technologies, and devices.

OpenCable Architecture

Michael Adams

1-57870-135-X • AVAILABLE NOW

Whether you're a television, data communications, or telecommunications profes-sional, or simply an interested business person, this book will help you under-stand the technical and business issues surrounding interactive television services. It will also provide you with an inside look at the combined efforts of the cable, data, and consumer electronics industries' efforts to develop those new services.

Performance and Fault Management

Paul Della Maggiora, Christopher Elliott, Robert Pavone, Kent Phelps, James Thompson

1-57870-180-5 • AVAILABLE NOW

This book is a comprehensive guide to designing and implementing effective strategies for monitoring performance levels and correctng problems in Cisco networks. It provides an overview of router and LAN switch operations to help you understand how to manage such devices, as well as guidance on the essen-tial MIBs, traps, syslog messages, and show commands for managing Cisco routers and switches.

Cisco Press   **www.ciscopress.com**

Cisco Press Solutions

EIGRP Network Design Solutions
Ivan Pepelnjak, CCIE

1-57870-165-1 • AVAILABLE NOW

EIGRP Network Design Solutions uses case studies and real-world configuration examples to help you gain an in-depth understanding of the issues involved in designing, deploying, and managing EIGRP-based networks. This book details proper designs that can be used to build large and scalable EIGRP-based networks and documents possible ways each EIGRP feature can be used in network design, implmentation, troubleshooting, and monitoring.

Top-Down Network Design
Priscilla Oppenheimer

1-57870-069-8 • AVAILABLE NOW

Building reliable, secure, and manageable networks is every network professional's goal. This practical guide teaches you a systematic method for network design that can be applied to campus LANs, remote-access networks, WAN links, and large-scale internetworks. Learn how to analyze business and technical requirements, examine traffic flow and Quality of Service requirements, and select protocols and technologies based on performance goals.

Cisco IOS Releases: The Complete Reference
Mack M. Coulibaly

1-57870-179-1 • AVAILABLE NOW

Cisco IOS Releases: The Complete Reference is the first comprehensive guide to the more than three dozen types of Cisco IOS releases being used today on enterprise and service provider networks. It details the release process and its numbering and naming conventions, as well as when, where, and how to use the various releases. A complete map of Cisco IOS software releases and their relationships to one another, in addition to insights into decoding information contained within the software, make this book an indispensable resource for any network professional.

Cisco Press   **www.ciscopress.com**

Cisco Press Fundamentals

IP Routing Primer

Robert Wright, CCIE

1-57870-108-2 • AVAILABLE NOW

Learn how IP routing behaves in a Cisco router environment. In addition to teaching the core fundamentals, this book enhances your ability to troubleshoot IP routing problems yourself, often eliminating the need to call for additional technical support. The information is presented in an approachable, workbook-type format with dozens of detailed illustrations and real-life scenarios integrated throughout.

Cisco Router Configuration

Allan Leinwand, Bruce Pinsky, Mark Culpepper

1-57870-022-1 • AVAILABLE NOW

An example-oriented and chronological approach helps you implement and administer your internetworking devices. Starting with the configuration devices "out of the box;" this book moves to configuring Cisco IOS for the three most popular networking protocols today: TCP/IP, AppleTalk, and Novell Interwork Packet Exchange (IPX). You also learn basic administrative and management configuration, including access control with TACACS+ and RADIUS, network management with SNMP, logging of messages, and time control with NTP.

IP Routing Fundamentals

Mark A. Sportack

1-57870-071-x • AVAILABLE NOW

This comprehensive guide provides essential background information on routing in IP networks for network professionals who are deploying and maintaining LANs and WANs daily. Explore the mechanics of routers, routing protocols, network interfaces, and operating systems.

Cisco Press

www.ciscopress.com

Cisco Press Fundamentals

Internet Routing Architectures, Second Edition
Sam Halabi with Danny McPherson

1-57870-233-x • AVAILABLE NOW

This book explores the ins and outs of interdomain routing network design with emphasis on BGP-4 (Border Gateway Protocol Version 4)--the de facto interdomain routing protocol. You will have all the information you need to make knowledgeable routing decisions for Internet connectivity in your environment.

Voice over IP Fundamentals
Jonathan Davidson and James Peters

1-57870-168-6 • AVAILABLE NOW

Voice over IP (VoIP), which integrates voice and data transmission, is quickly becoming an important factor in network communications. It promises lower operational costs, greater flexibility, and a variety of enhanced applications. This book provides a thorough introduction to this new technology to help experts in both the data and telephone industries plan for the new networks.

For the latest on Cisco Press resources and Certification and

Training guides, or for information on publishing opportunities, visit

www.ciscopress.com

Cisco Career Certifications

Cisco CCNA Exam #640-507 Certification Guide

Wendell Odom, CCIE

0-7357-0971-8 • AVAILABLE NOW

Although it's only the first step in Cisco Career Certification, the Cisco Certified Network Associate (CCNA) exam is a difficult test. Your first attempt at becoming Cisco certified requires a lot of study and confidence in your networking knowledge. When you're ready to test your skills, complete your knowledge of the exam topics, and prepare for exam day, you need the preparation tools found in *Cisco CCNA Exam #640-507 Certification Guide* from Cisco Press.

CCDA Exam Certification Guide

Anthony Bruno, CCIE & Jacqueline Kim

0-7357-0074-5 • AVAILABLE NOW

CCDA Exam Certification Guide is a comprehensive study tool for DCN Exam #640-441. Written by a CCIE and a CCDA, and reviewed by Cisco technical experts, *CCDA Exam Certification Guide* will help you understand and master the exam objectives. In this solid review on the design areas of the DCN exam, you'll learn to design a network that meets a customer's requirements for perfomance, security, capacity, and scalability.

Interconnecting Cisco Network Devices

Edited by Steve McQuerry

1-57870-111-2 • AVAILABLE NOW

Based on the Cisco course taught worldwide, *Interconnecting Cisco Network Devices* teaches you how to configure Cisco switches and routers in multi-protocol internetworks. ICND is the primary course recommended by Cisco Systems for CCNA #640-507 preparation. If you are pursuing CCNA certification, this book is an excellent starting point for your study.

Designing Cisco Networks

Edited by Diane Teare

1-57870-105-8 • AVAILABLE NOW

Based on the Cisco Systems instructor-led and self-study course available worldwide, *Designing Cisco Networks* will help you understand how to analyze and solve existing network problems while building a framework that supports the functionality, performance, and scalability required from any given environment. Self-assessment through exercises and chapter-ending tests starts you down the path for attaining your CCDA certification.

Cisco Press   **www.ciscopress.com**

Cisco Press

Committed to being your long-term learning resource while you grow as a Cisco Networking Professional

Help Cisco Press **stay connected** to the issues and challenges you face on a daily basis by registering your product and filling out our brief survey. Complete and mail this form, or better yet ...

Register online and enter to win a **FREE** book!

Jump to **www.ciscopress.com/register** and register your product online. Each complete entry will be eligible for our monthly drawing to win a FREE book of the winner's choice from the Cisco Press library.

May we contact you via e-mail with information about **new releases, special promotions**, and **customer benefits**?

❐ Yes ❐ No

E-mail address _____

Name _____

Address _____

City _____ State/Province _____

Country _____ Zip/Post code _____

Where did you buy this product?

❐ Bookstore ❐ Computer store/Electronics store ❐ Direct from Cisco Systems
❐ Online retailer ❐ Direct from Cisco Press ❐ Office supply store
❐ Mail order ❐ Class/Seminar ❐ Discount store
❐ Other _____

When did you buy this product? _____ **Month** _____ **Year**

What price did you pay for this product?

❐ Full retail price ❐ Discounted price ❐ Gift

Was this purchase reimbursed as a company expense?

❐ Yes ❐ No

How did you learn about this product?

❐ Friend ❐ Store personnel ❐ In-store ad ❐ cisco.com
❐ Cisco Press catalog ❐ Postcard in the mail ❐ Saw it on the shelf ❐ ciscopress.com
❐ Other catalog ❐ Magazine ad ❐ Article or review
❐ School ❐ Professional organization ❐ Used other products
❐ Other _____

What will this product be used for?

❐ Business use ❐ School/Education
❐ Certification training ❐ Professional development/Career growth
❐ Other _____

How many years have you been employed in a computer-related industry?

❐ less than 2 years ❐ 2–5 years ❐ more than 5 years

Have you purchased a Cisco Press product before?

❐ Yes ❐ No

Cisco Press
201 West 103rd Street
Indianapolis, IN 46290
ciscopress.com

Cisco Press
Customer Registration—CP0500227
P.O. Box #781046
Indianapolis, IN 46278-8046

Cisco Secure Intrusion Detection System (1-58705-034-X)

Thank you for completing this survey and registration. Please fold here, seal, and mail to Cisco Press.

Do you have any additional comments or suggestions?

On what topics would you like to see more coverage?

Are you currently pursuing a certification? (check all that apply)

- ☐ CCNP
- ☐ MCSE
- ☐ CCDP
- ☐ CCNA
- ☐ CCIE
- ☐ CCDA
- ☐ Other

Do you hold any computer certifications? (check all that apply)

- ☐ CCNP
- ☐ MCSE
- ☐ CCDP
- ☐ CCNA
- ☐ CCIE
- ☐ CCDA
- ☐ Other

Which best describes your job function? (check all that apply)

- ☐ Corporate Management
- ☐ Systems Engineering
- ☐ IS Management
- ☐ Cisco Networking
- ☐ Network Design
- ☐ Network Support
- ☐ Webmaster
- ☐ Academy Program
- ☐ Marketing/Sales
- ☐ Consultant
- ☐ Student
- ☐ Instuctor
- ☐ Professor/Teacher
- ☐ Other

How many computer technology books do you own?

- ☐ 1
- ☐ 2–7
- ☐ more than 7

ciscopress.com

Cisco Press

☐ **YES!** I'm requesting a **free** subscription to *Packet*™ magazine.

☐ No. I'm not interested at this time.

☐ Mr.
☐ Ms.

_____   _____
First Name (Please Print)   Last Name

_____
Title/Position (Required)

_____
Company (Required)

_____
Address

_____   _____
City   State/Province

_____   _____
Zip/Postal Code   Country

_____   _____
Telephone (Include country and area codes)   Fax

_____
E-mail

_____   _____
Signature (Required)   Date

☐ I would like to receive additional information on Cisco's services and products by e-mail.

1. Do you or your company:
A ☐ Use Cisco products   C ☐ Both
B ☐ Resell Cisco products   D ☐ Neither

2. Your organization's relationship to Cisco Systems:
A ☐ Customer/End User	E ☐ Integrator	J ☐ Consultant
B ☐ Prospective Customer	F ☐ Non-Authorized Reseller	K ☐ Other (specify):
C ☐ Cisco Reseller	G ☐ Cisco Training Partner	_____
D ☐ Cisco Distributor	I ☐ Cisco OEM	

3. How would you classify your business?
A ☐ Small/Medium-Sized   B ☐ Enterprise   C ☐ Service Provider

4. Your involvement in network equipment purchases:
A ☐ Recommend   B ☐ Approve   C ☐ Neither

5. Your personal involvement in networking:
A ☐ Entire enterprise at all sites   F ☐ Public network
B ☐ Departments or network segments at more than one site   D ☐ No involvement
C ☐ Single department or network segment   E ☐ Other (specify):
_____

6. Your Industry:
A ☐ Aerospace	G ☐ Education (K–12)	K ☐ Health Care
B ☐ Agriculture/Mining/Construction	U ☐ Education (College/Univ.)	L ☐ Telecommunications
C ☐ Banking/Finance	H ☐ Government—Federal	M ☐ Utilities/Transportation
D ☐ Chemical/Pharmaceutical	I ☐ Government—State	N ☐ Other (specify):
E ☐ Consultant	J ☐ Government—Local	_____
F ☐ Computer/Systems/Electronics		

CPRESS

PACKET

Packet magazine serves as the premier publication linking customers to Cisco Systems, Inc. Delivering complete coverage of cutting-edge networking trends and innovations, *Packet* is a magazine for technical, hands-on users. It delivers industry-specific information for enterprise, service provider, and small and midsized business market segments. A toolchest for planners and decision makers, *Packet* contains a vast array of practical information, boasting sample configurations, real-life customer examples, and tips on getting the most from your Cisco Systems' investments. Simply put, *Packet* magazine is straight talk straight from the worldwide leader in networking for the Internet, Cisco Systems, Inc.

We hope you'll take advantage of this useful resource. I look forward to hearing from you!

Cecelia Glover
Packet Circulation Manager
packet@external.cisco.com
www.cisco.com/go/packet

PACKET